Monetary and Fiscal Policy

Monetary and Fiscal Policy

Volume 2: Politics

edited by
Torsten Persson
and
Guido Tabellini

The MIT Press
Cambridge, Massachusetts
London, England

This book was set in Times Roman by Asco Trade Typesetting Ltd., Hong Kong and was printed and bound in the United States of America.

Library of Congress Cataloging-in-Publication Data

Monetary and fiscal policy / edited by Torsten Persson and Guido Tabellini.
p. cm.
Includes bibliographical references and indexes.
Contents: v. 1. Credibility — v. 2. Politics.
ISBN 0-262-16140-0 (v. 1). — ISBN 0-262-66087-3 (v. 1: pbk.). —
ISBN 0-262-16141-9 (v. 2). — ISBN 0-262-66088-1 (v. 2: pbk.)
1. Monetary policy. 2. Fiscal policy. 3. Policy sciences. I. Persson, Torsten.
II. Tabellini, Guido Enrico, 1956– .
HG230.3.M633 1994
332.4′6—dc20 93-35772
CIP

Contents

Introduction

All the chapters in this volume deal with political incentive constraints, that is, with incentives created by or within political institutions. The chapters in volume 1 discuss incentive problems, which stem from a single institutional feature: lack of commitment. Here too, there is a single source for the incentive constraints: the conflict of interest between different voters or between the incumbent policymaker and the voters. The exact nature of the conflict of interest, and thus the exact form of the incentive constraints, varies with the political institution discussed in different chapters. Hence, the themes addressed in this volume are not as linearly ordered in a logical hierarchy, as in volume 1. Research on politics and macroeconomic policy deals with many different issues and does not rely on a common analytical framework. This has made our selection more difficult. We have chosen to highlight four main areas of research: political business cycles, political incentives to accumulate public debt, fiscal redistribution, and structural reform.

Despite their differences, the chapters in this volume have two things in common. First—unlike in many early contributions by the public-choice school—the political equilibrium is explicitly based on voter and incumbent rationality. The chapters treat the political equilibrium and the economic equilibrium symmetrically, in that they both result from the optimization of individuals who act as economic agents and voters. Second, they typically study a dynamic environment. Since we are dealing with macroeconomic policy, decisions are made sequentially over time and the arrival of new information or the accumulation of state variables plays an important role in the analysis. Thus, the political incentive constraints that appear in many chapters of this volume are dynamic incentive constraints. This feature distinguishes these studies from many important contributions in political science.

Finally, compared to volume 1, these chapters add institutional content and thus have sharper empirical implications. For this reason, the interaction between empirical and theoretical research has been more fruitful here than in the literature on credibility.

I Elections and Policy Cycles

Perhaps the most fundamental political institution in a democracy is the appointment of the policymaker through democratic elections. Elections serve several purposes: (1) to control the performance of the elected policymaker: if his performance is disappointing, he will not be reelected; (2) to select the most competent policymaker; and (3) to choose the policymaker whose ideological preferences are closer to those of the majority of the voters. These three purposes create specific incentives for a policymaker motivated by the desire to win the elections and be reappointed. Each of the first three chapters in this section highlights one of these three aspects of elections. The first two chapters focus on the conflict of interest between the voters and the incumbent, while the third focuses on disagreement among different groups of citizens. The fourth chapter describes the evidence and contrasts the predictions of these alternative models.

The theoretical concepts are familiar from volume 1. In these chapters, the voters follow a retrospective voting strategy, reminiscent of the retrospective wage-setting behavior in the reputation models of volume 1. These voting strategies are rational, and create an intertemporal trade-off for the incumbent that induces him to follow short-run suboptimal policies from his point of view. Moreover, the policymaker's incentives are different when elections are imminent. Hence, an electoral policy cycle can occur in equilibrium. However, the properties of these cycles differ in each model, and the evidence can be used to discriminate among them.

I.1 Controlling Moral Hazard

Chapter 1, by John Ferejohn, focuses on the voters' control of the incumbent performance, in the tradition of principal-agent theory. The incumbent is the agent, while the voters are the principals. The incumbent wishes to be reappointed and at the same time wants to minimize his effort. Effort improves performance, which is valued by the voters. The marginal product of effort is a random variable, observed only by the incumbent. The candidates are all alike, so the voters' problem is to control *moral hazard* by the incumbent, and not to elect the most competent candidate. The question is whether the voters can induce the incumbent to provide some effort, by credibly threatening not to reappoint him if observed performance is too low.

The answer is positive, provided that the voters do not disagree among themselves over how to measure performance. In equilibrium, the voters vote according to a retrospective voting strategy: they reappoint the incumbent only if observed performance is above a certain threshold. The voters are rational, and such retrospective voting is credible because, in an infinite horizon setting, it provides the incumbent with the right incentives to exert effort. Moreover, and quite intuitively, the voters' control of the incumbent is more effective the more highly he values holding office.

But if the voters disagree among themselves over how to measure performance, the equilibrium breaks down and the incumbent can get away with no effort. This happens, for instance, if the incumbent chooses both effort as well as how to distribute the payoffs of his performance among the voters. In this case, the incumbent can play one principal against another, and gain the support of a majority of the voters simply by distributing in their favor while exerting no effort. In this case, the only way for the voters to regain control over the incumbent is to vote according to a retrospective rule based on an aggregate measure of performance, rather than on their personal payoffs. Naturally, this may require an unreasonable amount of cooperation among the voters.

Economists are used to thinking of elections as distorting the policymaker's incentives. This paper provides a counterexample. Quite independently of the aggregation of preferences, elections have a welfare-improving role, namely, to control the moral hazard of politicians.[1] The control of politicians, however, requires more than just retrospective voting. It also requires the refusal to vote selfishly.

I.2 Signaling and Policy Cycles

Elections also enable voters to select the most competent politician. Put differently, elections enable them to control *adverse selection* of the incumbent. This role of elections is studied by Kenneth Rogoff in chapter 2. The problem here is how to explain the commonly observed electoral cycles. A body of evidence indicates that just before elections governments tend to stimulate aggregate demand through monetary or fiscal policy. The question is not so much why governments do it—if it helps to win the elections—but why such policies help incumbents to be reelected. The early literature on political business cycles (Nordhaus 1975) sidestepped this question by assuming that voters had adaptive expectations. But why would rational voters compensate a government for engaging in a preelectoral cycle?

The answer suggested by Rogoff is that an electoral cycle is a signal of competence. In the chapter, competence is not observed by the voters, along with some policy choice. All the voters observe is a boom (an expansion in output, or in current government spending).[2] They cannot observe whether this is due to a deliberate policy action, or to having a highly competent incumbent, or both. They do know, however, that a competent incumbent is more likely to engage in a boom than an incompetent one, because an artificial boom is less costly for the competent incumbent. As a result, the boom becomes a signal of competence and it is rewarded by the voters.

In equilibrium the voters realize perfectly well that there is also an artificial (policy-induced) component in the electoral boom. They reward the incumbent nonetheless, because by doing so they will have a better (more competent) government tomorrow. Given this behavior by the voters, it clearly pays a competent incumbent to engage in an electoral boom. Failing to do so would cost him the election, since he would be mistaken for an incompetent government. The chapter thus yields the testable prediction that incumbents who generate a preelection boom stand a better chance to be reelected. Here elections do indeed distort the policymaker's incentives and create an inefficiency. It is not clear, however, how to get rid of the distortion. The reason is that the electoral cycle conveys information to the voters. Trying to suppress it, therefore, may be counterproductive: the voters would choose an incompetent government too often, or alternatively the incumbent could be forced to signal his type in costlier ways.

I.3 Partisan Cycles

The third role of elections is to aggregate conflicting preferences. Because voters are heterogeneous and candidates have ideological (i.e., "partisan") positions, elections enable the majority of voters to select their preferred candidate, that is, the candidate with the closer ideological position. A swing in the preferences or composition of the electorate may result in the election of a different policymaker, with a different partisan position. This gives rise to electoral cycles different from those in chapter 2. Here the cycle takes place *after*, not before, the election. For instance, if a "conservative" (averse to inflation or indifferent to unemployment) policymaker wins the election, a recession takes place after his appointment, while the opposite occurs if a policymaker with different preferences is elected.

This idea was originally suggested by Hibbs (1977). In chapter 3 Alberto Alesina reformulates it, assuming voters, as well as economic agents, have rational expectations. The equilibrium of the model predicts a postelectoral cycle in output and inflation. This cycle is distorting, in the sense that voters would prefer a stable intermediate policy. Can such a stable policy be brought about through a cooperative agreement among the candidates? The answer is provided in this chapter, as well as in Alesina (1988), and it is a positive—though qualified—answer. The incentive to cooperate comes from alternation in office: the elected policymaker moderates his partisan views when he holds office, so as to induce his opponent to do likewise when it is his turn to be elected. Cooperation can or cannot totally eliminate the policy cycles, depending on the assumption about preferences and the frequency of the alternation in office.

I.4 Some Evidence

There is a large empirical literature on political business cycles, which dates back to Nordhaus (1975), McRae (1977), Hibbs (1977) and Tufte (1978). Most of this literature is on postwar U.S. data. Chapter 4 in this volume, by Alesina and Nouriel Roubini, is a comprehensive analysis of panel data in OECD countries. The chapter contrasts the predictions of the partisan model in chapter 3 with those of the "opportunistic" policymaker model in chapter 2.

The implications of the partisan models are clear cut. The appointment of "left-wing" governments is followed by output expansions and inflation, while the opposite occurs if a "right-wing" government is elected. Moreover, in the rational expectations version of the model, expansions and booms are temporary, because they are due to policy (or political) surprises in the face of nominal rigidities in the economy. The implications of the "opportunistic" model are less obvious. Contrary to a commonly held belief, the rational expectations version of the model does *not* predict a boom before every election. Only competent governments signal by creating a boom, while incompetent governments take a passive attitude. Hence, with a competent incumbent the election is preceded by a boom, but with an incompetent incumbent there is a preelectoral recession (because nominal contracts incorporate the expectation of an expansionary policy that does not materialize). Hence, on average, the model predicts no systematic output pattern before elections.

What the model does predict is: (a) the incumbent who generates the boom wins the elections; and (b) on average, elections are preceded by attempts to stimulate demand (as the competent incumbent always tries to do so, while the incompetent type does not manipulate policy either way). The evidence uncovered by Alesina and Roubini is consistent with the rational expectations versions of both the opportunistic and the partisan models. Specifically, contrary to the predictions by Nordhaus (1975), there is no evidence of a systematic preelectoral boom. On the other hand, there is evidence that inflation surges after elections, as predicted by the opportunistic model with rational voters. Finally, in countries where there are identifiable political swings from left to right, there is clear evidence of a partisan cycle, with only temporary output effects.

Alesina and Roubini do not discuss the effect of preelectoral booms on the popularity of the incumbent. Other papers provide mixed evidence, all based on U.S. data. On the one hand, Fair (1978) finds that the president's popularity before the elections is strongly influenced by the growth rate of the economy, as predicted by the opportunistic model. On the other hand, Peltzman (1992) finds that presidents, state governors, and senators are penalized by the voters for their expansionary budgets. Finally, Alesina, Londregan, and Rosenthal (1993), in a model of the U.S. economy that includes both partisan effects and the competency model, confirm Fair's result that economic growth strongly increases the incumbent's popularity, but reject the more specific prediction of the rational expectation model, namely that only the unexpected component of growth should matter.[3]

I.5 Discussion

The existing literature on economic policy and elections has mainly focused on electoral cycles (with the exception of chapter 1 of this volume). Many important normative topics remain to be investigated. First, what is the optimal time between elections? The competence model suggests that there may be a trade-off between giving the voters a more frequent choice and creating more frequent distortions. Taking into account the incumbent-control model or the partisan model further complicates the trade-off. Second, how should a society choose between a proportional versus a majoritarian electoral system? A majoritarian electoral system is likely to produce a single-party majority, while in a proportional system coalition governments are more likely (see also the next section). This suggests another trade-off, between efficiency and representativeness in government decisions. Third, what are the relative merits of political systems in which the citizens directly elect the executive, versus parliamentary systems, where such choice is delegated to an elected assembly? And how do the policymaker's incentives differ in such systems? The answers to these and other fundamental political science questions may have important implications for the analysis of economic policy.

II Public Debt and Political Instability

The partisan model is the stepping stone for a series of papers on public debt. Consider a government or a legislative majority with ideological preferences over some aspect of fiscal policy. The incumbent policymaker knows that with some probability future voters will replace him with another policymaker with different preferences. If there is a state variable under his control, he will then try to use it strategically to influence future policy choices in the desired direction.

This idea is related to the results in volume 1 of Lucas and Stokey (chapter 14) and of Persson, Persson, and Svensson (chapter 15). There, the government manipulates the term structure or the degree of indexation of the outstanding public debt in order to induce future governments to enact the ex ante optimal policy. There, the identity of the government is the same over time, but governments at different dates face different incentive constraints and are thus engaged in a game with each other. Here, there are no incentive constraints due to lacking credibility, but the identity and hence the preferences of the government change over time, which creates incentive constraints that emanate from the equilibrium policy choices of future governments. The government in office today manipulates the public debt, taking into account how this influences the policy choices of a future government with possibly different preferences. Naturally, for this to be possible public debt must be nonneutral. That is, taxes must be distorting, so that changing the time path of public debt has lasting effects on the economy, which cannot be undone by future governments.

II.1 A Conservative Bias for Budget Deficits

In chapter 5 of this volume, Torsten Persson and Lars Svensson apply this idea to a conservative policymaker who knows that he will be replaced by a more liberal successor (i.e., one who wants a larger amount of public spending). By issuing public debt, today's government forces the future government to cut spending. The larger is the debt outstanding, the higher are taxes and hence the larger are the tax distortions. This makes it more costly to finance expenditures.

A conservative government, which knows that future spending will be too high, faces a trade-off. On the one hand, by cutting taxes and issuing public debt today, it bears the cost of a suboptimal distribution of tax distortions: they are too low today and will be too high tomorrow when the debt becomes due. On the other hand, public debt will discourage excessive public spending tomorrow, thus relaxing future incentive constraints.

Persson and Svensson show that when the political incentives are strong enough, the optimal policy is to overissue public debt, bearing the cost of tax distortions in exchange for lower public spending in the future. Moreover, the larger the conflict between the two policymakers, the greater debt issue. This result can explain why a conservative government—such as the Reagan administration in the 1980s—may have a bias in favor of budget deficits. Naturally, a liberal government would have the opposite bias, in favor of excessive budget surpluses.

II.2 Political Instability and Deficit Bias

A similar idea was independently investigated by Guido Tabellini and Alesina in chapter 6 and by Alesina and Tabellini (1990). Here, the alternating governments or majorities disagree over the composition of public spending. Under some assumptions about the concavity of preferences, a deficit bias emerges in equilibrium. The intuitive reason is that a policymaker who borrows faces an asymmetry. When he borrows, he can spend the extra sources of finance in the way he wants. But when the debt is repaid, the spending cuts are not necessarily under his control, since he may be out of office. As a result, he fully internalizes the benefits of the additional spending he can afford, but not the future costs of the spending cuts. Consider for instance a policymaker who wants to spend a lot on defense and little on welfare, and knows he will be replaced by a government with different preferences. He realizes that defense spending will be slashed anyway in the future. He then borrows a lot now, knowing that the marginal cost of repaying the extra dollar of debt will fall on welfare, which he cares little about.

The paper has a testable conclusion. Disagreement among alternating governments or majorities creates a bias in favor of budget deficits. The bias is stronger the more unstable is the political system—i.e., the greater is the likelihood of a government change—and the more polarized are the alternating governments.

II.3 Some Evidence

The empirical evidence is mixed. In the early part of this century, the main episodes of debt accumulation in the bigger industrial countries occurred during wars, as predicted by the tax smoothing model of Barro (1979). After World War II, all industrial countries had stable or declining debt-to-GDP ratios until the late 1960s. The 1970s and 1980s were instead periods of rapid debt accumulation for most industrial countries. In some countries the debt-to-GDP ratio rose but then was stabilized, in others it kept growing until it reached very high levels of 100 percent or more of GDP.

Roubini and Sachs (1989) and chapter 7, written by Vittorio Grilli, Donato Masciandaro, and Tabellini, emphasize a striking stylized fact. Almost all the high-debt industrial countries are governed by a highly proportional electoral system, and vice versa. Eichengreen (1992) argues that a similar correspondence between proportional electoral systems and high public debt is present in the 1920s in several small European countries. A natural question is what explains this correlation, and in particular whether it is consistent with the political theories described above.

Proportional electoral legislations generate very fractionalized party systems. In such systems, governments are often short-lived and sustained by broad parliamentary coalitions. Hence rapid public debt accumulation goes hand in hand with unstable coalition governments. But is it the instability or the coalition attribute that accounts for the deficit bias? According to the theories discussed above, it is the instability that matters. A feature of most coalition governments, however, is that government instability does not really mean political instability. On the contrary, the coalition of parties supporting the government rarely changes. From this point of view, political instability (defined as frequent swings between legislative majorities with very different preferences) is much more pronounced in presidential or majoritarian political systems. The evidence on the industrial countries thus poses more questions than it provides answers. We do not really know whether the difficulties in preventing debt accumulation are due to having unstable or coalition governments, nor do we understand well what forces in a coalition government push for debt accumulation (see, however, chapter 15 below).

The evidence on developing countries is less ambiguous. First, it is easier to identify political instability as a separate and clear-cut phenomenon. Second, several papers have found an association between political instability and various forms of government myopia. Ozler and Tabellini (1990) find political instability to be positively associated with external debt accumulation in the 1970s. Cukierman, Edwards, and Tabellini

(1992) find a positive correlation between political instability and the inefficiency of the tax system. Londregan and Poole (1992) and Alesina, Ozler, Roubini, and Swagel (1991) provide evidence that political instability causes low growth. Many of these results can be rationalized on the basis of the theories outlined in subsection A.2. There is a problem, however. It is difficult to tell what is the chain of causation: whether from political instability to government myopia, or vice versa. (Alesina et al., 1991, indeed show that causality runs in both directions.) This body of empirical evidence thus points toward a new line of research; that is, to try and gain a better understanding of what causes a government change.

II.4 Discussion

The general ideas in this section have a broad range of applications. Alesina and Tabellini (1990) extend the results of chapter 6 to an infinite horizon economy with tax distortions, while Alesina and Tabellini (1989) discuss the debt bias of governments that disagree over the allocation of the tax burden (rather than over the allocation of public spending). Glazer (1989) applies a similar analysis to the choice of public investment. Cukierman, Edwards, and Tabellini (1992) discuss strategic tax reforms in developing countries from this point of view. Finally, Aghion and Bolton (1990) show that governments may manipulate debt policy not only to influence future policy choices, but also to influence the voters and enhance their chances of reelection.

Finally, the finding that political institutions may create a debt bias suggests a possible rationale for external (or constitutional) limits on budget deficits, such as those present in many U.S. states or required by the convergence criteria of the Maastricht treaty for European Monetary Unification. Naturally, these limits are not without costs, in that they may prevent the government from running the optimal debt policy, smoothing tax distortions in the face of recessions or temporary spending increases. In this regard, debt policy presents a trade-off between rules and discretion similar to the trade-off between credibility and flexibility in monetary policy that was discussed in volume 1.

III Redistribution

Redistribution is a key political determinant of fiscal policy. All the chapters in part III of this volume focus on some redistributive aspect of fiscal policy. All of them—except the last one—are also based on the *median voter result*; that is, the political equilibrium, defined as a policy that cannot be beaten under majority rule, is the policy preferred by the median voter. A median voter equilibrium exists only under some restrictions on what the voters choose and/or on their preferences. In these chapters the voters typically choose a linear income or wealth tax accompanied by a lump-sum transfer. This restriction can be motivated by informational constraints on the government. More complicated redistributive rules (such as a nonlinear tax schedules or direct choices of individual allocations) would require much more detailed information about individual conditions to prevent tax arbitrage. Under the constraint that the policy is a linear income tax, voters preferences are generally single peaked or fulfill weaker conditions (Romer 1975; Roberts 1977) such that the median voter result holds.

A median voter equilibrium has two nice properties. It is very easy to compute: all one has to do is solve the policy optimization problem of the median voter. It identifies the fundamental political forces that shape the policy. In a median voter equilibrium, virtually everybody dislikes the equilibrium policy. But half the electorate wants to move the policy in one direction, the other half in the opposite direction. Thus, a median voter equilibrium has a nice attribute. It is directly based on the voters' preferences for the policy, and it balances the opposing tendencies in those preferences. It is as institution-free as a political equilibrium can be. What matters is only who are the eligible voters and what are their preferences. In a sense, a median voter optimum is a bit like a Walrasian equilibrium. We do not really know how this equilibrium is reached. But once the economy is in equilibrium there are fundamental forces that keep it there.

Naturally, the lack of institutional specificity is a mixed blessing. It implies that we cannot analyze the impact of specific political institutions on the equilibrium outcome. For instance, how does a presidential system differ from a parliamentary system? Or in what sense and why is a coalition government less efficient than a government sustained by a single parliamentary majority? To address these and other similar questions, one has to move away from the simple median voter paradigm.

III.1 Inequality and Redistribution

The seminal contribution on the politics of redistribution is chapter 8, by Allan Meltzer and Scott Richard. It is a simple static general equilibrium model, where individuals differ by their productivity and hence by their income. They vote over a linear income tax, the proceeds of which are redistributed to everybody in an equal amount. The tax distorts the labor-leisure choice, and the voters correctly take this into account. It is assumed, realistically, that the distribution of income is skewed to the right. Hence, median income is smaller than average income.

The political equilibrium is the median income holder's optimal tax rate. In determining his preferred tax rate, the median voter trades off redistributive benefits against economic distortions. The more unequal is the distribution of income (that is, the lower is median income relative to average income), the greater is the benefit from redistribution and hence the larger is the equilibrium tax. Meltzer and Richard (1983) provide some favorable empirical evidence.[4]

III.2 Redistribution and Growth

The idea that more inequality breeds higher redistributive taxes has many implications. One of them is that more inequality, leading to higher taxes on savings, may be harmful for growth. Consider an economy with a productive technology that sustains endogenous growth. Suppose further that capital income can be taxed and the proceeds redistributed in the population. An argument similar to that of Meltzer and Richard implies that the political equilibrium tax rate is higher the greater is pre-tax inequality in income and wealth. But a higher capital tax discourages capital accumulation and hence growth. As a result more inequality entails less growth.

A number of recent papers have independently formulated this idea in a general equilibrium endogenous growth model (Persson and Tabellini 1990b; Alesina and Rodrik 1991; Perotti 1990; Bertola 1991). Chapter 9 in this volume, by Persson and Tabellini, surveys this recent literature.

The theoretical argument takes different forms. Persson and Tabellini (1990b) and Perotti (1990) emphasize the size distribution of income between rich and poor, as in Meltzer and Richard. Bertola (1991) and Alesina and Rodrik (1991) emphasize instead the functional distribution of income between fixed and cumulable factors of production. Any tax that redistributes toward the fixed factors (land and labor) and away from the cumulable factors (physical and human capital) is harmful for growth. To the extent that the owners of fixed factors are poorer than the owners of cumulable factors, the political forces that discourage growth are the same as in the Meltzer-Richard and Persson-Tabellini setup.

Chapter 9, as well as some of the above-mentioned papers, finds striking empirical support for the proposition that inequality is harmful for growth. In a broad cross section of developing and developed countries, and after controlling for a number of traditional variables (Barro 1991), income inequality at the start of the period is strongly and negatively associated with growth in the subsequent period. Moreover, the negative correlation between inequality and growth is only present in democratic countries—something that suggests that the link between inequality and growth is political and not purely economic. Persson and Tabellini (1990b) also find similar evidence in a historical panel of nine industrial countries.

There is preliminary evidence that the negative correlation between inequality and growth is due to deliberate redistributive fiscal policies. This evidence is discussed by Persson and Tabellini (1990b) for a small number of OECD countries, and by Easterly and Rebelo (1993) for a much broader group of developing countries. But the question of exactly which redistributive policy instruments are responsible for the negative association of inequality and growth remains to be studied more carefully.

A second important open question concerns the reverse chain of causation, from growth to inequality. In all the papers mentioned above, income distribution is exogenously given. A number of interesting papers study the joint determination of growth and income distribution (Greenwood and Jovanovich (1991), Aghion and Bolton (1992)). But in these papers there is no economic policy. The question of how growth, income distribution and redistributive policy are jointly determined in a political equilibrium remains an open and challenging question for future research. Krusell and Rios-Rull (1992) have recently made some progress on it.

III.3 Risk Sharing and Redistribution

Policies that redistribute income ex post are often designed or justified to share risks ex ante. This is true of many welfare programs, and in particular of unemployment insurance. What political forces shape the design of such risk-sharing programs? Perhaps surprisingly, there are relatively few papers that formally address this important question. One that does so is chapter 10, by Randall Wright.

This chapter considers a dynamic general equilibrium where individuals can either be employed or unemployed. All individuals have the same preferences and the same productivity if employed. They differ by the frequency and duration of unemployment. Individuals vote over an unemployment insurance program that redistributes to the unemployed by taxing the employed. There is no moral hazard, no adverse selection, and no aggregate risk, and taxation is not distorting. Thus, the only consequence of the policy is to redistribute and to share the unemployment risk.

Unemployment insurance is chosen once and for all, and voters choose the policy that maximizes their expected utility in the steady state, given their type and current employment status. The voters preferences are single peaked, so a median voter result holds. The equilibrium policy depends on the frequency and duration of steady-state unemployment of the median voter compared to the average. Thus, if unemployment risk is concentrated in a minority of the population, a risk averse median voter may prefer *not* to have full insurance. The reason is that here the median voter spends less time unemployed than the average. On average, a full insurance system would therefore redistribute away from the median toward the unlucky minority. Conversely, if the median voter spends more time unemployed than the average, he wants a full insurance system even if he is risk neutral (or, equivalently, even if private insurance markets exist). The reason is that in this case the unemployment compensation redistributes ex ante in his favor. Depending on the assumptions, the political equilibrium can deliver more or less insurance than optimal.[5]

Even though this chapter studies a specific example, the forces at work have general validity (see also Persson and Tabellini 1993). Whenever a risk-sharing policy is democratically chosen, the political equilibrium reflects a comparison between the risk parameters of the median voter and the average individual. If the risk of income loss is concentrated in a minority of the population, the median voter is unlikely to benefit from the insurance program, and the equilibrium size of the program is small. Conversely, if the risk is widespread in the population, more voters are likely to be in favor of a large program. This result contrasts with that of Meltzer and Richard, where more concentration of realized income leads to more redistribution.

This suggests a distinction that may be important for empirical tests of these theories. The effect of income inequality on equilibrium redistribution depends critically on when the vote is taken and on how inequality is measured. If voters choose redistributive policies *after* knowing their individual position, we are in the world of Meltzer and Richard, and more *income* equality (defined as a smaller difference between mean and median income) leads to less redistribution. If on the other hand the vote is taken behind a veil of ignorance about one's individual position, a more equal distribution *of risks* brings about a larger redistributive program. Suppose that a more equal distribution of risks also brings about a more equal distribution of realized income—something that is likely, though not necessarily true. Then the observed correlation between the realized distribution of income and the extent of equilibrium redistribution depends critically on when the vote is taken, before or after individual income is known. In empirical work it may be difficult to control for this timing. Such a distinction may potentially explain why countries with a homogenous population and labor force—like the Scandinavian countries—have large social-insurance systems despite an even measured income distribution.

III.4 Intergenerational Redistribution

Many public financial policies, such as social security or debt policies, deliberately or indirectly redistribute across generations. What are the political determinants of these policies? This question has been addressed in a number of papers where individuals vote over a purely intergenerational policy.

Browning (1975) and Boadway and Wildasin (1989) have addressed this question in a median-voter framework with no altruism (see Verbon 1990 for a survey). These papers assume commitment. Once voted upon, the policy remains in effect forever, or for at least one period. Given this assumption, some working individuals not too far from retirement are in favor of a pay-as-you-go pension system. The reason is that they free ride on the young taxpayers: they pay taxes for a few periods, but will receive pensions that correspond to several periods worth of taxes. The old-age individuals are clearly in favor of such a system. Hence, there is generally a majority of voters in favor of a pay-as-you-go system. The equilibrium size of the program depends on the interest rate, the growth rate of the population, and the age profile of earnings, in a predictable way.

In a similar vein, Cukierman and Meltzer (1989) study the political determinants of budget deficits. Here generations are linked by altruism, but to an extent that varies across households. Some households are very altruistic and leave positive bequests. Other households are bequest constrained (that is, would like to leave negative bequests). Currently alive generations vote on the budget deficit. Fully altruistic voters only care about the general equilibrium effects of the policy, since they can undo the direct redistributive effect across generations. Bequest-constrained voters, on the other hand, also value the redistributive effect. A budget deficit enables them to redistribute in their favor and away from future generations. A median-voter result holds. The political equilibrium budget deficit depends on the magnitude of the general equilibrium effect and on how many voters are bequest constrained.

A problem with this approach is that it presupposes a strong form of commitment. The policy redistributes across generations only because future generations do not renege on it later on. In any moment in time, the social security policy redistributes from the majority of the population (the workers) to a minority (the retirees). Hence, an isolated vote on the policy would always generate a majority against. The policy is sustainable only if workers believe that keeping it in place today makes it more likely that future voters will agree to retain it. But is this belief reasonable?[6] A similar problem exists in the paper by Cukierman and Meltzer. Why is the debt not repudiated (or the policy otherwise reversed) by future generations? In general there ought to be a majority always in favor of repudiation. The literature discussed in volume 1 stresses the role of reputation and trigger strategies in sustaining these policies. As we discussed at length in the introduction to that volume, however, that argument is not without problems.

Chapter 10 of this volume, by Tabellini, suggests a different answer to these questions. The idea is that purely intergenerational policies do not exist. A social security program typically redistributes across generations as well as from rich to poor households. Similarly, reneging on the public debt not only harms the old generations: it also harms the rich (who hold more debt) more than the poor. Disentangling these different effects of public financial policies may be impossible, because of informational constraints. Provided there is a moderate amount of intergenerational altruism, a policy that redistributes across generations may therefore be sustained in a political equilibrium by a coalition of voters which includes members of different generations belonging to similar income groups.

Chapter 11 considers public debt policies. It shows that, even without any form of commitment, the old generation succeeds in extracting some income from the future generation by issuing public debt. The debt is not repudiated because the rich members of the young generation vote together with their parents to repay the debt. They do so, even though they receive no bequest, because the loss to their rich parents would be a lot larger than the tax rebate associated with debt repudiation. The young generation here would unanimously prefer that no debt was issued. But it cannot vote before it is born, and so cannot prevent the old generation from issuing debt. When presented with the choice whether to repudiate the debt or not, some young voters side with their parents, and in equilibrium the debt is repaid.

Tabellini (1990) develops a similar argument for social security. The social security system is not rejected because some young voters (here the poor taxpayers) vote with their parents to sustain it. They do so because the benefit for their parents is larger than the cost to them. Again, a coalition of voters belonging to both generations sustains the policy.

Different coalitions support debt and social security, however. The old and the children of the rich support debt repayment. The old and the poor young instead support social security. This difference implies that these two intergenerational policies are not equivalent, even though they would be so in a world with commitment. As in chapters 14 and 15 of volume 1, paying attention to the government incentive constraints breaks a Modigliani-Miller theorem on public financial policies.

III.5 Mobility and Redistribution

In all the chapters on redistribution, so far, the tax base is not mobile. Individuals can escape the tax by working less or saving less. But they cannot relocate. How is the political equilibrium affected by having mobile tax bases and/or mobile voters? This question comes up both in an international context and in local public finance.

Mobility of tax bases is particularly important for capital taxation, and has been extensively studied in international economics. Here it is natural to assume that the voters are immobile, but that they can move their savings to a foreign country. The equilibrium takes the form of a Nash equilibrium among political majorities of different countries, who take into account the effect of their choices on the international allocation of capital. International capital mobility reduces the scope for redistribution, because it makes the capital tax base more elastic to unilateral changes in the tax rate (Wilson 1987). But it also has a political effect. Consider a representative democracy where the policy choice is delegated to an elected representative. The election outcome is determined also by international strategic considerations. The government that wins the elections must be apt at playing the international tax game. Persson and Tabellini (1992) show that the political equilibrium can be moved left or right by higher capital mobility, depending on how a country differs from the rest of the world.

Mobility of voters themselves, is more relevant in local public finance. Here the tax base can be mobile or not. But even if it is not mobile—as in the case of property taxes—voters still have the option of selling their houses (or terminating the rent) and moving elsewhere. When moving, they also exercise their political rights in the new locality. How do these factors affect the political equilibrium and the extent of redistribution?

This question is addressed by Dennis Epple and Thomas Romer in chapter 12. They study an economy with a given number of localities. Each locality chooses a tax on houses by majority rule, the proceeds of which are redistributed lump sum to the local population. Only housing is taxed. All individuals have the same preferences for housing and for a second (numeraire) commodity. They differ by their income. Individuals are free to move at no cost among localities, and vote in the locality where they live. Some houses can be owned by voters of other localities and be rented to domestic voters. An equilibrium is defined by the usual conditions (market clearing, and the policy cannot be beaten under majority rule) plus a new one: that, given the equilibrium policy, nobody wants to move. Voters correctly take into account the effect of policy on house prices and on the migration decisions by other voters.

Epple and Romer show that the equilibrium has the median-voter property. Moreover, under the assumption that housing is a normal good, the voters sort themselves out in stratified localities. The level of taxation and redistribution differs across localities, and is inversely related to household income: the poorest households are located in the communities that provide the highest levels of redistribution. Perhaps surprisingly, Epple and Romer show that mobile voters and small jurisdictions do not necessarily limit redistribution, particularly when renters are a large fraction of voters. The reason is that part of the tax burden is shifted on to property owners who live elsewhere and thus do not have voting rights. Only communities with a large fraction of owner-occupants generate little redistribution.

Stratification of communities by income is predicted by other political models in local public finance. Fernandez and Rogerson (1992) consider a model where individuals are free to move among localities, which provide different amounts of public education by taxing their residents. Again, stratification emerges in political equilibrium, even though rich communities pay more taxes and have better schooling.[7] The paper discusses ways to improve efficiency and reduce inequality.

III.6 Redistribution and Pork Barrel

So far we have only discussed redistributive tax and transfer schemes. But redistribution in kind is also very common. The typical example occurs when the benefits of a project are concentrated among a few voters, while the cost of financing it are widespread. In this case the beneficiaries of the project have a strong incentive to lobby for it, while the taxpayers who only bear a small fraction of the cost do not have similarly strong incentives to oppose it. The result is that too many socially inefficient projects get approved.

This story has many variants and has been extensively studied in the public-choice literature (Mueller 1989). Chapter 13 in this volume, by Barry Weingast, Kenneth Shepsle, and Christopher Johnsen, provides a simple and yet revealing formalization. Suppose that the choice over a number of projects is decentralized to many local constituencies, but that the cost of each project is shared among all constituencies. In a Nash equilibrium each constituency ends up choosing projects that are too large compared to the social optimum. The reason is simple: the local constituency that chooses the projects size fully internalizes its benefits, but only internalizes a fraction of its cost. Thus, decentralization of expenditures plus a tax-sharing rule is a recipe for excessively large governments.

A natural question is why such an inefficient arrangement is ever put into place. The literature does not provide a complete and convincing answer. But it is true, at least in the U.S. Congress, that representatives from different districts represent specific geographic interests, and there is evidence that reciprocity (i.e., the exchange of mutual favors) is a common decision rule in Congress. In practice this means that the choice of projects that benefit a constituency is to some extent decentralized to the representatives of that constituency in Congress. If this is the case, the inefficiency described in chapter 13 applies.

IV Economic Reform and the Status Quo

The last three chapters in the volume all investigate the political determinants of economic reforms. This area of research is still at an early stage, and many interesting questions remain unanswered. The chapters in this part have made some important initial steps forward.

Experience from many developing and industrial countries suggests that efficiency-enhancing reforms often lack political support. This applies to trade reforms, tax reforms, privatizations, and, more recently, to comprehensive transitions from a socialist to a market system. The inefficient status quo is often politically difficult to abandon, even when it is clearly not sustainable in the long run. The chapters in this section all presume that the source of these difficulties is the impossibility or the cost of compensating the losers from the reform. But the exact political mechanisms whereby the losers block the reform are different in each chapter.

IV.1 Uncertainty and Reversibility

Chapter 14, by Raquel Fernandez and Dani Rodrik, considers a trade reform that randomly distributes gains and losses in the population. The reform is efficient, in the sense that the aggregate gains exceed the aggregate losses. Two votes must be taken. One ex ante, to enact the reform, and another ex post, to maintain the reform in place. The default alternative is the status quo in both cases.

Fernandez and Rodrik show that the status quo wins in two distinct cases. The reform may be rejected ex ante, if the expected loss exceeds the expected gain for a majority of the voters. This can happen, even if the benefits will be distributed over a majority of the population while the losses will be born by a minority. As long as individual voters are not certain they will belong to the winning majority, they may vote against the reform. But the reform may also be reversed ex post, if the gains are concentrated in a minority while the majority loses.

Thus, the reform is politically viable only if there is a majority in favor of it *both* ex ante and ex post. Note the asymmetry. A reform not viable ex post has no chance, since it will be reversed. But a reform may be ex post viable and still have no chance, if it is rejected ex ante by a majority of the voters. The reason is that, if the reform is blocked ex ante, the information that would sustain it ex post never gets revealed. Thus, there is a bias in favor of the status quo. The status quo prevails as long as there is a majority in favor of it either ex ante or ex post.

But what prevents the compensation of the losers? This question is not fully addressed in the paper, and remains an open issue for future research.

IV.2 Strategic Delay in Fiscal Stabilization

Political difficulties in changing the status quo are common also when the current policies are clearly not sustainable. A typical example is an unsustainable budget deficit. Even though it would be efficient to close the budget deficit as soon as possible, a political agreement over how to distribute the burden of the stabilization often cannot be found. As a result, the fiscal stabilization is delayed until it becomes very costly for everybody. Why this seemingly irrational delay? In chapter 15 of this volume, Alesina and Allan Drazen suggest that the answer has to do with asymmetric information among key political actors. They study debt stabilization as a war of attrition between two conflicting political groups. As long as the stabilization is delayed, both groups still bear a cost. This cost may differ across the two groups, and it is private information: each party is not fully informed about the cost born by his opponent. The stabilization can only be implemented if both parties agree to it. But the first one to concede bears a larger fraction of the burden. This fraction is exogenously given, and it is common knowledge. Again, the implicit assumption is that the losers from the stabilization are not compensated.

The two parties are thus engaged in a war of attrition. Each has an incentive to postpone concession, in the hope that the opponent will be the first to give in. Thus, in equilibrium the reform is delayed. This strategic delay is a direct consequence of the asymmetric information. Alesina and Drazen show that the delay is longer the more unequal is the division of the burden, once a party concedes (the expected gain from waiting is larger), and the smaller are the costs of living in an unstabilized economy (the cost of waiting is smaller).[8]

Many of the model's qualitative predictions accord with casual evidence. For instance, the model can explain why reforms repeatedly rejected in the past suddenly get implemented, or why a stabilization often coincides with the political victory by one group over another. Moreover, the model agrees with the intuition that reforms are often blocked by conflict over how to distribute the losses. Nevertheless, some of the fundamental assumptions of the model hide important unresolved questions.

For instance, where does the exogenously given share of the stabilization burden come from? Presumably, that share is a direct object of bargaining among the rival groups, and one would like it to be endogenous to the analysis. Moreover, what exactly is the political institution that governs the policy choices, and why is the mutual consent of both parties needed to initiate the reform? And what exactly is the nature of the observed delay? Is it a delay in initiating a reform, as in chapter 15, or is it instead an excessive dose of gradualism in continuing with an already initiated reform? These are difficult questions, still in search of an answer.

IV.3 Structural Reform and Gradualism

Many countries undergoing a transition to a market economy, or countries with an inefficient public sector, face a common problem. To gain efficiency, some sectors of the economy or some large firms have to be made smaller and more productive. The workers in the inefficient sector or firm stand to lose from the reform, and their political opposition has to be overcome. To do so, a benevolent but politically constrained government may have to bribe them—or pay exit fees. This creates a trade-off between budgetary costs and allocative inefficiency. The status quo is inefficient, but changing it imposes budgetary costs on the government. What is the optimal political design of a structural reform, given this trade-off? This is the question addressed by Mathias Dewatripont and Gerard Roland in chapter 16.[9]

The chapter considers an inefficient sector with three types of workers. Some of them have to be laid off. Clearly, it is optimal to retain the workers with a comparative advantage in that sector. In the chapter, those are the workers with the lowest reservation wage, but it could equally well be those with the worst outside productivity. A worker's type is his own private information. Thus, the government faces an adverse selection problem. The rules of the game are as follows. The government is the agenda setter, and can make any proposal. The proposal, however, has to be accepted by the workers in a collective decision. The default is the status quo.

Two main results are derived. First, gradualism may emerge as the equilibrium outcome. That is, the government makes a proposal for period one, that gets accepted and induces some workers to leave. A different proposal is made and accepted in period two, and other workers leave. This gradual reform may be better for the government than trying to get all the workers to leave at once in the first period. The reason is similar to the ratcheting effect in a dynamic adverse-selection problem (Laffont and Tirole 1988). The workers who remain in the sector in the first period reveal information about their type, and this enables the government to complete the initial partial reform having more information.

Second, the lack of commitment may help or hurt depending on whether workers decide by unanimity or by majority rule. When they decide by unanimity, lack of commitment hurts the government. The reason is well known from the contract literature with renegotiation (Hart and Tirole 1988). If the government can make two sequential proposals, it is harder to convince the workers to support the first proposal because they know that initial rejection will force the government to make a second more favorable one. If the workers decide by majority rule, however, two offers with no commitment may leave the government better off (than if it commits to a single offer). This surprising result occurs because, with two offers rather than one, the government can credibly threaten to switch majorities if the first proposal is rejected, which gives it more bargaining power. This result points to an important distinction between unanimity and majority rule in a dynamic context.

It is too early to tell how relevant these results are for the applied problem of designing structural reforms. But they do raise some interesting new issues that could have a broader applicability than to the example being studied. For instance, Roberts (1989) obtains similar insights with regard to voting by trade union members in a paper on hysteresis in unemployment after business cycle shocks.

Notes

1. Persson and Tabellini (1991) discuss a second welfare-improving role of elections. Namely, to appoint politicians with ideological preferences that can overcome incentive constraints such as lack of credibility. See also the chapter by Alesina and Grilli in volume 1.

2. There are different models of electoral cycles in the literature. In the first one to be written, by Rogoff and Sibert (1988), voters observe spending but not taxes. The electoral boom then takes the form of higher spending. In chapter 2 voters do not observe public investment, and the electoral cycle takes the form of both higher spending and lower taxes. In Persson and Tabellini (1990a, chapter 5), the voters observe output but not monetary policy (or inflation), and the boom takes the form of an expansion in output.

3. Alesina, Londregan, and Rosenthal (1993) also provide evidence of "moderating" behavior by the voters in midterm U.S. elections. That is, at midterm elections the voters punish the president's party to moderate its partisan tendencies. This issue is also discussed more theoretically in Alesina and Rosenthal (1993).

4. The large existing literature on how to explain the growth of government redistribution is extensively discussed in Mueller (1989).

5. Optimality here is not trivial to define, since it requires weighing the welfare of different individuals. But the statement holds even when all individuals are ex ante identical, in that they have the same frequency and duration of unemployment. The conflict of interest among voters, in this limiting case, only depends on their employment status.

6. See chapter 7 by Kotlikoff, Persson, and Svensson in volume 1, and our discussion of it in the introduction.

7. Here, unlike in Epple and Romer, voters are myopic and do not take into account that the electorate changes when individuals migrate.

8. Drazen and Grilli (1992) have extended these results to a similar model with an explicit inflation tax.

9. A similar question is addressed by Lewis, Feenstra, and Ware (1990) in a static model of agricultural reform.

References

Aghion, P., and Bolton, P. 1990. Government domestic debt and the risk of default in a political economic model of the strategic role of debt. In R. Dornbusch and M. Draghi, eds., *Public Debt Management: Theory and History*. London: Cambridge University Press.

Aghion, P., and Bolton, P. 1992. Distribution and growth in models with imperfect capital markets. *European Economic Review* 36:603–612.

Alesina, A. 1988. Credibility and policy convergence in a two-party system with rational voters. *American Economic Review* 78:796–806.

Alesina, A., Londregan, J., and Rosenthal, H. 1993. A political economy model of the U.S. *American Political Science Review* 87:1–20.

Alesina, A., Ozler, S., Roubini, N., and Swagel, P. 1991. Political instability and economic growth. Manuscript, Harvard University.

Alesina, A., and Rodrik, D. 1992. Redistributive politics and economic growth. Manuscript, Harvard University.

Alesina, A., and Rosenthal, H. 1993. A theory of divided government. Manuscript, Harvard University.

Alesina, A., and Tabellini, G. 1989. External debt, capital flight and political risk. *Journal of International Economics* 27:199–220.

Alesina, A., and Tabellini, G. 1990. A positive theory of fiscal deficits and government debt. *Review of Economic Studies* 57:403–414.

Barro, R. 1979. On the determination of public debt. *Journal of Political Economy* 87:940–971.

Barro, R. 1991. Economic growth in a cross section of countries, *Quarterly Journal of Economics* 106:407–443.

Bertola, G. 1991. Factor shares, saving propensities and endogenous growth. Manuscript, Princeton University.

Boadway, R., and Wildasin, D. 1989. A median voter model of social security. *International Economic Review* 30:307–328.

Browning, E. K. 1975. Why the social insurance budget is too large in a democratic society. *Economic Inquiry* 13:373–388.

Cukierman, A., Edwards, S., and Tabellini, G. 1992. Seignorage and political instability, *American Economic Review* 82:537–556.

Cukierman, A., and Meltzer, A. 1989. A positive theory of government debt and deficits in a Neo-Ricardian framework. *American Economic Review* 79:713–732.

Drazen, A., and Grilli, V. 1992. The benefit of crisis for economic reform. Manuscript, Birkbeck College, London.

Easterly, W., and Rebelo, S. 1993. Fiscal policy and economic growth: An empirical investigation. Manuscript, The World Bank.

Eichengreen, B. 1992. *Golden fetters: The gold standard and the Great Depression 1919–1939.* New York: Oxford University Press.

Fair, R. C. 1978. The effect of economic events on votes for President, *Review of Economics and Statistics.* 60:159–173.

Fernandez, R., and Rogerson, R. 1992. Income distribution, communities and the quality of public education: A policy analysis. Manuscript, Boston University.

Glazer, A. 1989. Politics and the choice of durability. *American Economic Review* 79:1207–1213.

Greenwood, J., and Jovanovich, B. 1991. Financial development, growth and the distribution of income. *Journal of Political Economy* 98:1076–1107.

Hart, O., and Tirole, J. 1988. Contract renegotiation and Coasian dynamics. *Review of Economic Studies* 55:509–540.

Hibbs, D. 1977. Political parties and macroeconomic policy. *American Political Science Review* 71:1467–1487.

Krusell, P., and Rios-Rull, V. 1992. Vested interests in a positive theory of stagnation and growth. Manuscript, Northwestern University, Evanston, IL.

Laffont, J. J. and Tirole, J. 1988. The dynamics of incentive contracts. *Econometrica* 51:1153–1175.

Laffont, J. J. and Tirole, J. 1993. *A theory of incentives in procurement and regulation.* Cambridge: MIT Press.

Lewis, T., Feenstra, R., and Ware, R. 1990. Eliminating price supports: A political economy perspective. *Journal of Public Economics* 40:150–186.

Londregan, J., and Poole, K. 1992. The seizure of executive power and economic growth: Some additional evidence. In A. Cukierman, Z. Hercowitz, and L. Leiderman, eds., *Political economy, growth, and business cycles.* Cambridge: MIT Press.

McRae, D. 1977. A political model of the business cycle. *Journal of Political Economy* 85: 239–264.

Meltzer, A., and Richard, S. 1983. Tests of a rational theory of the size of government. *Public Choice* 41:403–418.

Mueller, D. 1989. *Public choice II.* Cambridge: Cambridge University Press.

Nordhaus, W. 1975. The political business cycle. *Review of Economic Studies* 42:169–190.

Ozler, S., and Tabellini, G. 1990. External debt and political instability. Manuscript, University of California at Los Angeles.

Peltzman, S. 1992. Voters as fiscal conservatives. *Quarterly Journal of Economics* 107:327–364.

Perotti, R. 1990. Political equilibrium, income distribution and growth. *Review of Economic Studies.* Forthcoming.

Persson, T., and Tabellini, G. 1990a. *Macroeconomic policy, credibility and politics.* London: Harwood Academic Publishers.

Persson, T., and Tabellini, G. 1990b. Is inequality harmful for growth? *American Economic Review*. Forthcoming.

Persson, T., and Tabellini, G. 1991. Representative democracy and capital taxation. *Journal of Public Economics*. Forthcoming.

Persson, T., and Tabellini, G. 1992. The politics of 1992: Fiscal policy and European integration. *Review of Economic Studies* 59:689–703.

Persson, T., and Tabellini, G. 1993. Federal fiscal constitutions: Part I-Risk sharing and moral hazard. Manuscript, Stockholm University.

Roberts, K. 1977. Voting over income tax schedules. *Journal of Public Economics* 8:329–340.

Roberts, K. 1989. The theory of union behavior: Labor hoarding and endogenous hysteresis. Manuscript, London School of Economics.

Rogoff, K., and Sibert, A. 1988. Elections and macroeconomic policy cycles. *Review of Economic Studies* 55:1–16.

Romer, T. 1975. Individual welfare, majority voting, and the properties of a linear income tax. *Journal of Public Economics* 4:163–185.

Roubini, N., and Sachs, J. 1989. Government spending and budget deficits in the industrialized countries. *Economic Policy* 8:700–732.

Tabellini, G. 1990. A positive theory of social security. Manuscript, University of California at Los Angeles.

Tufte, E. 1978. *Political control of the economy*. Princeton, NJ: Princeton University Press.

Verbon, H. 1990. Decision making on old age transfers. Manuscript, University of Amsterdam.

Wilson, J. 1987. Trade, capital mobility and tax competition. *Journal of Political Economy* 95:835–856.

I ELECTIONS AND POLICY CYCLES

1 Incumbent Performance and Electoral Control

John Ferejohn

1 Introduction

In the pure theory of electoral competition, citizens compare the platforms of the candidates and vote for the one whose platform is preferred. Candidate strategies are identified with promises about future performance in office. Models of this sort have been developed in both static (McKelvey 1975) and dynamic (Kramer 1977) settings, and all appear to have the property that if the set of alternatives is "large enough" in some sense, equilibrium platforms rarely exist. But these models have another feature that is quite as disturbing as their instability.

In the static setting discussed by McKelvey, little attention is paid to the possibility that, once in office, the politician's preferences may diverge from those of his constituents and that he may therefore choose policies at variance from his platform. Instead it is simply assumed that promises will be kept whether or not such behavior is congruent with the interest of the officeholder. It is sometimes argued that an "enforcement" mechanism may exist to discipline politicians for failing to keep promises, but without a specification of the mechanism it is not obvious that it would be in the interests of the electorate to carry out threatened punishments.

In Kramer's dynamic model, the incumbent's platform is identified with his current record in office so that, assuming that voters would believe any proposed platform, a challenger will virtually always be able to propose a platform that will defeat the incumbent. But if the incumbent knows that he will lose his reelection bid, he might as well simply pursue his own private interest while in office rather than doing what he promised during the campaign (or doing whatever he did during his previous term); he will be turned out at the next election anyway. Clearly, in this case, the voters have no reason to take challenger platforms as anything other than pure rhetoric; voters would soon learn that rational officeholders would ignore their preferences once in office.

In both of these cases, there is no reason for voters to pay attention to the candidates' choice of platforms. For this reason, there is no cause to

Reprinted from *Public Choice*, 50 (1986) 5–26, by permission of Kluwer Academic Publishers.

believe that there will be any predictable connection between the profile of voter preferences and public policy. If there actually is such a connection, neither of these theories can account for it.

The pure theory of elections pays little attention to the sorts of strategies or decision rules that might be followed by members of the electorate. Instead, it is usually hypothesized that citizens vote for the candidate whose platform they like best, ignoring further strategic considerations. Indeed, in a two-candidate contest, if candidates are assumed to implement their platforms, voting for someone other than the preferred candidate is a dominated strategy. The only interesting question in this case is whether or not to vote.

The purpose of this chapter is to try to construct a coherent model in which voters have an incentive to base their choices on behavior of officeholders and in which officeholders choose their strategies in anticipation of this behavior. Such a model is necessarily dynamic. Voters are assumed to base their evaluations of officeholders on their actual performance in office rather than on hypothetical promises they might make during a campaign. In this model, the key to the voting decision is found not in the earnest pledges of the contenders but, rather, in the infamous remark of a Kansas farmer: "But what have you done for me lately?"

If voters vote on the basis of platforms or "issues," politicians have little incentive to do what they promise. Thus, voters might be well-advised to pay attention to the incumbent's performance in office rather than to the hypothetical promises of competing candidates. By basing their votes on evaluations of performance, voters may be able to motivate officeholders to pay attention to the interests of the electors. That such a strategy may be attractive has been most forcefully argued by V. O. Key (1966). Key argued that if voters reward or punish officeholders on the basis of their performance in office, officeholders will not only be diligent but will also be motivated to use their initiative in the face of new or unexpected events that arise between elections.

There is abundant empirical evidence that the pure theory of elections is, at best, only a partial description of electoral phenomena. Much of recent data suggest that voters do respond to the performance of incumbent candidates in office as well as to the platform promises of competing candidates (Kramer 1971; Fiorina 1981). At both the aggregate and individual level and in virtually all nations that have been studied, the performance of the economy has a major effect on the electoral fate of the incumbent executive. Moreover, there is evidence that officeholders try to anticipate performance-oriented voting in their choice of policies while in office.[1]

Thus, it appears that voters employ decision rules that are based, in part, on the past performance of the government in office. Moreover, the actual evidence for extensive issue voting is fairly weak. If the incumbent administration has been successful in promoting economic growth and avoiding major wars, it will tend to be rewarded at the polls, no matter how attractive the policy positions of the opposition.[2]

This chapter begins an investigation of the structure of electoral behavior that takes account of the motivations of officeholders. We wish to know how voters ought to behave if they wish to get their representatives to pursue the interests of the electors. In order to address this question, we need to develop a formal model within which politicians can be induced to act in the interests of the electors. The natural mechanism to transmit such incentives is the fact that elections take place repeatedly and that officeholders desire to retain office. Under these circumstances, voters can adopt strategies that can affect the incentives of officeholders in various ways. We also insist on separating the actions of the candidates in office from the notion of the performance of a government which is led by an incumbent candidate. With this separation, the situation becomes a variant of the "principal-agent" problem in which the officeholder is an agent of the electors, and voters have the opportunity to structure the incentives facing the officeholder agent to induce him to act to enhance their well-being.

The chapter introduces an alternative theory of elections, as pure in its own way as the classical one exposited by McKelvey and Kramer. In this model voters respond only to the performance of the candidate in office and do not pay any attention whatsoever to the promises of the challenger or, for that matter, to the promises of the incumbent. All that counts for a voter here is how well he fares under a given administration.

In the model, voters assume that a newly elected officeholder will pursue his own interests once in office, no matter what he claimed in the context of the campaign. On this view, promises play no role at all because there is no way for candidates to commit themselves to keep them. As long as politicians are all of the same "type," in the sense that they have the same preferences and abilities, the voter can correctly anticipate how the officeholder will behave in every circumstance that may confront him. No promise to do otherwise would be credible and so none would be heeded.

Given this hypothesis about the behavior of politicians in office, the voters will choose a decision rule that maximizes their well-being subject to the constraint that politicians are pursuing their self-interest. Nevertheless, voters are constrained in their choice of decision rules to recognize that at any future time, prescribed voting behavior must be in the interest of the electors at that time. They are unable to bind or precommit themselves or their offspring to choices in the future that will seem unattractive at that time. Thus, those voting rules based on "incredible" threats are not available because officeholders would recognize that such threats would not be carried out.

2 Previous Research

There has been some investigation of the incentives that certain types of performance-oriented voting rules confer on incumbents (Nordhaus 1975). However, most of this work focuses on a relatively specialized implication of performance-oriented voting: if voters are sufficiently myopic, incumbents have an incentive to behave differently in election years than at other times and therefore to try to create political business cycles. Whether or not incumbents are able to create political business cycles, however, depends on a variety of other factors irrelevant to our present concern with the control of incumbents through the choice of voter-decision rules. Indeed, recent work suggests that if voters are able to take account of economic constraints, politically induced business cycles may not occur (Chappell and Keech 1985). Moreover, the formulation of political business-cycle models does not pay much attention to the choice of *optimal* voter-decision rules, given the opportunities of incumbents.

More relevant to this chapter is Robert Barro's (1973) seminal investigation of the control of politicians. Barro investigates the question of how much the fact of repeated elections may induce officeholders to act on the preferences of the electorate rather than their own objectives. Barro's approach differs from ours in several respects. First, he assumes that officeholders have a finite and commonly known horizon. Thus, in their last term of office their behavior is uncontrollable.[3] In light of this uncontrollability, the electorate would not return an officeholder seeking his last term; the politician would then see this and be uncontrollable in the penultimate term, and the process would unravel. The present model is formulated with an infinite horizon, so that such last-period effects are avoided.

The reader may think of the competitors for office as political parties that last indefinitely and must solve the "last-period" problem for their officeholders through the use of internal incentives.[4]

Second, Barro's model is formulated in a world of perfect information, whereas the present model contains an informational asymmetry: the electorate is not able to observe the actions of politicians directly. With perfect information the voter is able to extract most of the rents in the transaction. In equilibrium, at each period, the electorate demands that the officeholder provide a quantity of effort that leaves him indifferent between leaving and staying in office. Here we allow a natural informational asymmetry in favor of officials, which allows them opportunities to take advantage of their privileged positions. Intuitively, the greater the informational advantage that officials hold, the greater their ability to earn rents from officeholding.

Finally, Barro's model contains only one "representative" voter. In effect, this formulation assumes not only that voter preferences are identical, an assumption that may in some circumstances be justified, but also that there are no distributional issues at stake in political competition, surely a more controversial hypothesis. While we are unable to provide a complete analysis of the general case, we do show that the introduction of distributional issues profoundly changes the nature of the relationship between the electorate and its officials, vastly reducing the level of electoral control.

In the next section we outline a simple dynamic model of electoral competition that allows us to analyze the incentives of officeholders and to see how they would respond to variations in electoral behavior. This model, like Barro's, contains only one voter (or a homogeneous electorate) and two or more candidates. The "space" over which the performance of the officeholder is defined is identified with an interval on the real line. In this context, the restriction to a one-dimensional outcome space is inconsequential, though in other settings it may not be.

When we turn our attention to a model in which there are several voters, the situation changes substantially. In Section 4 we show that the introduction of preference diversity permits the incumbent to escape electoral control unless the voters agree to utilize some sort of aggregate performance index as their criterion for retrospective voting. If voters utilize individualistic or group-based criteria, the incumbent will have the opportunity to exploit voter divisions to his advantage. The nature of such an agreement does not entail any precommitments by the voters, in the sense of requiring anyone to vote against his or her interests at some future point in time, and so such an agreement would be credible. We may interpret this result as saying that electoral control with a nonhomogeneous electorate requires "sociotropic" voting—that is, voting based on an aggregate criterion—rather than individualistic voting (Kiewiet 1983).

3 A Simple Model of Repeated Elections with a Homogeneous Electorate

Many of the activities of officeholders are not directly observable by members of the electorate. Instead, electors are only able to assess the effects of governmental performance on their own well-being. Further, governmental performance is known to depend jointly on the activities of officeholders as well as on a variety of exogenous and essentially probabilistic factors. In other words, the officeholder is an agent of the electorate whose behavior is imperfectly monitored. Officeholders are assumed to desire reelection in order to take advantage of the perquisites of office as well as to pursue their own ideas about policy. It is the desire to retain office together with the possibility of an indirect monitoring by the electorate which drive the incentive effects that we observe in the model.

Before setting out the model, we should emphasize that we have assumed that candidates for office are all essentially the same in the sense that they have the same preferences and abilities, and that this is common knowledge among all the actors. In other words, the voter's problem is to police moral hazard rather than to find and elect the more capable of benevolent officeholders. Rules of the sort we are addressing here may have the property of separating different types of officeholders in an appropriate setting, but we do not address those aspects here.

In this paper we take the liberty of working with explicit functional forms that are relatively easy to analyze. Some of the arguments developed here might be generalized in other settings, but for now we have chosen to try to obtain clear results in the context of a very simple model in order to aid our intuition about the ways in which the behavior of electors might induce officeholders to pay attention to their preferences.

The officeholder observes a random variable, $\theta \in \Omega = [0, m]$, a subset of the nonnegative real numbers, and then takes an action, $a \in [0, \infty)$, conditioned on that observation. We let F denote the distribution function of θ and assume that it is continuously differentiable. The single-period preferences of the officeholder are written as

$$v(a, \theta) = W - \phi(a),$$

where W is the value of holding office for a single term and ϕ is a positive monotone convex function and $\phi(0) = 0$. W may be thought of as the explicit compensation of the officeholder plus any rents he may earn as a result of his tenure and $\phi(a)$ is the cost of action a.

The voter is unable to distinguish the actions of the officeholder from exogenous occurrences. Rather than directly observing "policy," he is restricted to monitoring "performance," which is defined to be a product of policy and exogenous occurrences. Thus, the elector's single-period preferences are represented as

$$u(a, \theta) = a\theta.$$

Lacking an ability to observe the activities of the incumbent, the elector adopts a simple performance-oriented (or retrospective) voting rule: if the utility received at the end of the incumbent's term in office is high enough, he votes to return the incumbent to office; otherwise he removes the incumbent and gives the job to someone else. It is clear that, under certain conditions, such a rule will induce the incumbent to pay attention to the requirements of retaining office. It is also clear that the elector must be careful to set the required utility level appropriately, since if it is set too high the incumbent will not find it worthwhile to try to retain office and will instead choose to take advantage of the opportunities currently available to him as an officeholder. On the other hand, if the level is set too low, the incumbent will find it sufficiently easy to sustain his hold on the office that he will choose too low a level of a.

It will turn out that the incumbent's behavior depends critically on his likelihood of being able to return to office in the future in the event that he is defeated. In the following analysis we consider two polar cases: (1) in the event of a loss of office, the incumbent has no chance of returning; (2) in the event of a loss of office, the incumbent is replaced by another agent and returns to office if and when that other agent loses. We think of the first assumption as corresponding more or less to multiparty competition with small parties, in which a party out of office has a relatively small probability of regaining it at the next election. The loss of office would appear to be quite final from the standpoint of the incumbent party in such a system. This case could also model the candidate's perspective as opposed to the party perspective in a two-party system in which the competitors are party "teams" that alternate in office.

Several remarks about this formulation seem important. First, the model contains an extreme informational asymmetry. The incumbent official is able to resolve all uncertainty before taking his action, while the voter cannot. At the cost of complicating the notation somewhat, we could introduce an additional disturbance representing uncertainty that the candidate is unable to resolve prior to his choice of policy. In this case, the candidate would view his election prospects as uncertain. While this case is perhaps more realistic, it does not permit us to gain any additional insights into either incumbent or voter strategies.

Both officials and voters are assumed to be risk neutral. This assumption simplifies the analysis somewhat and also affects the nature of optimal strategies. If the candidate and voter differ in their risk aversion, issues related to risk sharing would arise. Again, while such cases may be more realistic, they would needlessly complicate the present analysis and so we leave them aside.

Finally, for reasons alluded to in the introduction, the challenger plays no active role in the model. The importance of challengers lies entirely in their availability. It is the existence of willing officeseekers that gives the voter whatever leverage he has on the incumbent. For this reason, it is important that the elective office is valuable enough relative to alternative sources of employment to attract challengers.

Given the one-period preferences outlined above, and assuming that the elector employs a retrospective voting rule, we can utilize standard techniques of dynamic programming to determine optimal candidate behavior. Once the incumbent has observed a value of θ_t, he will choose an action which maximizes his (discounted) utility from that time onward, assuming that the voter employs a retrospective voting rule with cutoff levels, K_t, K_{t+1}, K_{t+2}, $\ldots$, from time t forward. Under the conditions assumed above, this amounts to choosing $a(\theta_t)$ to maximize the present value of utility stream. Obviously, if θ_t is so small that it is not possible to be reelected, then he will choose $a(\theta_t) = 0$. If it is possible to be reelected, then the candidate may choose $a(\theta_t)$ so the reelection constraint is just satisfied: $a(\theta) = K_t/\theta_t$. In no event would he be willing to choose any $a(\theta_t)$ larger than the smallest amount that will ensure his reelection.

In the remainder of this section, we present a characterization of equilibrium voter and incumbent strategies (Propositions 1 through 3). Then, we examine alternative party systems from the standpoint of electoral control (Proposition 4). Finally, in Proposition 5, we present a comparative static result that implies that control of incumbents is greater for more valuable offices.

After each election, the officeholder observes the value θ_t and chooses $a(\theta_t) = K_t/\theta_t$ if and only if

$$W - \phi(K_t/\theta_t) + \delta V^I_{t+1} \geq W + \delta V^0_{t+1}, \tag{1}$$

and, if (1) is not satisfied, he chooses $a(\theta_t) = 0$. In (1), V^I_{t+1} and V^0_{t+1} stand for the expected values of staying in office or leaving office, respectively, given optimal play by voters and candidates from the next election forward, and δ represents the (common) discount factor employed by all agents. It is important to note that V^I_{t+1} and V^0_{t+1} are independent of θ_t and K_t. Re-arranging terms permits us to establish the following characterization of optimal incumbent strategies:

PROPOSITION 1 Given the retrospective voting rule $\{K_t\}^{\infty}_{t=0}$, the optimal incumbent strategy is

$$a(\theta_t) = K_t/\theta_t \text{ iff } \theta_t \geq K_t/\phi^{-1}(\delta(V^I_{t+1} - V^0_{t+1})). \tag{2}$$

Proof (1) implies that $a(\theta_t) = K_t/\theta_t$ if and only if $\theta_t \geq \theta^*_t$, where θ^*_t satisfies $\delta(V^I_{t+1} - V^0_{t+1}) = \phi(K_t/\theta^*_t)$. The inequality then follows from the fact that ϕ is positive monotone, convex, and $\phi(0) = 0$.

In other words, the incumbent will expend effort only if he observes a sufficiently favorable value of θ_t. Notice that this expression implies that if the value of office is relatively small, the incumbent may choose to accept defeat though he could have been reelected.

Remark Given the retrospective voting rule, the incumbent's optimal strategies are optimal at each time t forward. Thus an optimal strategy is credible because the incumbent would actually carry it out for each value of θ_t that he could realize. Or, to put it another way, they are equilibrium strategies in each subgame (e.g., subgame perfect).

In order to characterize an equilibrium, we must determine the optimal retrospective rule. The expected utility of the voter may be expressed as follows:

$$U = \sum_{t=0}^{\infty} \delta^t K_t \Pr\{\theta_t \geq K_t/\phi^{-1}(\delta(V^I_{t+1} - V^0_{t+1}))\} \tag{3}$$

We can give a characterization of optimal retrospective rules by maximizing (3) over all retrospective rules.

PROPOSITION 2 If the θ_t are independent, identically distributed random variables with cumulative distribution function $F(\cdot)$ and density $f(\cdot)$, an optimal retrospective voting rule satisfies the following equality:

$$K_t = \frac{[1 - F(\theta_t^*)]}{f(\theta_t^*)} \phi^{-1}(\delta(V_{t+1}^I - V_{t+1}^0)) \tag{4}$$

Proof This follows directly from the first-order conditions derived from equation (3).

The important thing to notice about equation (4) is that K_t depends positively on $V_{t+1}^I - V_{t+1}^0$. The larger is the value of remaining in office to the incumbent, the more the voter can ask of him. In the special case in which F is uniform and ϕ is the identity function, we obtain a clearer characterization.

Corollary If the θ_t are independent, uniform, random variables on $[0, 1]$, and if $\phi(a) = a$ and $a \in [0, 1]$, an optimal retrospective rule must satisfy the following equation:

$$K_t = \min\{1/2, \delta(V_{t+1}^I - V_{t+1}^0)/2\} \quad \text{for all } t. \tag{4'}$$

Equations (4) and (4′) can be interpreted as follows. In each period, the elector sets K_t to equate the expected value to the incumbent of staying in office to the value of choosing $a(\theta_t) = 0$ and accepting defeat.

PROPOSITION 3 If $[1 - F(x)]/f(x)$ is monotone decreasing function, then θ_t^* is independent of δ, t, and W.

Proof Substitute for K_t using equation (4) in the following expression

$$\theta_t^* = K_t/\phi^{-1}(\delta(V^I - V^0)) \tag{5}$$

yields the equation $\theta_t^* = [1 - F(\theta_t^*)]/f(\theta_t^*)$, which has a unique solution under the assumption of monotonicity.

Remark An optimal retrospective voting rule is subgame perfect in the sense that its restriction to any subgame is an equilibrium strategy in that subgame. Assuming he is restricted to employing some retrospective voting rule, the elector can do no better than employing a rule that satisfies (4). For this reason, incumbents will regard optimal retrospective rules as credible.

Corollary If F is uniform on $[0, 1]$, $\phi(a) = a$ and a is restricted to lie in $[0, 1]$, then $\theta_t^* = 1/2$ and $\Pr(\{\theta_t \geq \theta_t^*\}) = 1/2$.

Remark It follows from the formulation that any solution to (3) must be stationary in the sense that $K_t = K$ for all t. To see this, note that if equation (3) is rewritten as follows,

$$U_0 = K_0 \Pr(\theta_0 \geq \theta_0^*) + \delta U_1 \tag{3'}$$

$U_1 = U_0$ since strategies and payoffs are the same at time 1 as at time 0. Moreover, U_1 does not depend on K_0. Thus, if K_0 maximizes (3′), K_0 must maximize U_1, too, and so on for each t.

In the special case of uniformly distributed disturbances, stationarity implies the following convenient expression for the expected utility of the voter, using an optimal retrospective voting rule, K:

$$U = K/2(1 - \delta) = \min\{1/2, \delta(V^I - V^0)/2\}/2(1 - \delta). \tag{3''}$$

Thus, up to the point where the expected marginal value to the incumbent of continuing in office exceeds 1/2, the voter's expected utility depends on this marginal value. The more attractive the present value of office is to the incumbent, the more satisfaction the voter can anticipate. However, this effect holds only for relatively unattractive offices. Indeed, for very unattractive offices, the voter can expect to receive almost nothing from the officeholder. For more valuable offices, the effects of increasing value do not accrue to the elector in increased control of the incumbent but flow, instead, to the politicians.

Having described optimal strategies, we may now calculate the equilibrium payoffs to the game. Turning first to the incumbent we see that if the voter is playing a stationary retrospective voting strategy with criterion K, we may write the expected value of being an incumbent, before observing θ, as follows:

$$V^I = \int_{\theta^*}^{m} [W - \phi(K/\theta) + \delta V^I] \, \mathrm{dF}(\theta) + \int_0^{\theta^*} [W + \delta V^0] \, \mathrm{dF}(\theta) \tag{6}$$

The discounted expected utility of a candidate out of office may be similarly written.

$$V^0 = \int_0^{\theta^*} [\lambda\delta V^I + (1 - \lambda)\delta V^0] \, \mathrm{dF}(\theta) + \int_{\theta^*}^{m} \delta V^0 \, \mathrm{dF}(\theta) \tag{7}$$

where λ is the probability of obtaining office if the current incumbent is defeated at the next election, which is taken to be exogenously determined. In this interpretation a pure two-party system corresponds to $\lambda = 1$, so that $V^0 = \delta(V^I + V^0)/2$. At the other extreme, a "pure" multicandidate system would have $\lambda = 0$, and therefore, $V^0 = 0$.

Solving (6) and (7) we obtain the following expressions for V^I and V^0,

$$V_\lambda^I = \frac{\left[W - \int_{\theta^*}^{m} \phi(K_\lambda/\theta)\,\mathrm{dF}(\theta)\right][1 - \delta(1 - \lambda p)]}{[1 - \delta(1 - \lambda p)][1 - \delta(1 - p)] - \lambda\delta^2 p^2} \tag{8}$$

$$V_\lambda^0 = \frac{\lambda\delta p\left[W - \int_{\theta^*}^{m} \phi(K_\lambda/\theta)\,\mathrm{dF}(\theta)\right]}{[1 - \delta(1 - \lambda p)][1 - \delta(1 - p)] - \lambda\delta^2 p^2}, \tag{9}$$

where $p = F(\theta^*)$ and where the subscripts indicate the dependence on λ. We can now state our major results.

PROPOSITION 4 An increase in λ lowers the utility of the voter.

Proof By implicitly differentiating $V_\lambda = V_\lambda^I - V_\lambda^0$ with respect to λ and rearranging terms, we see that $\partial V_\lambda/\partial\lambda$ is negative and, from equation (4), this implies that the derivatives of K_λ and U_λ with respect to λ must be negative as well.

Remark As the number of parties is restricted, the welfare of the elector declines. As the proof suggests, this occurs as the number of parties falls (i.e., as λ gets larger) and the incumbent's relative valuation of office declines. He becomes less concerned with losing office and is, therefore, less controllable by the voter.

An alternative interpretation of this result may be given if we let $\lambda = 0$ depict the incentives of candidates rather than parties. In this case we see that the voters can attain higher levels of control by holding candidates rather than parties responsible for poor outcomes. This is accomplished by refusing ever to reelect an officeholder who governed in a period of poor performance.

Finally, essentially the same argument as above yields the following result:

PROPOSITION 5 The utility of the voter is increasing in W.

Proof By implicitly differentiating V_λ with respect to W and solving for $\partial V_\lambda/\partial W$, we see that V_λ is increasing in W. This implies that U increases in W, too.

Most of the conclusions that are drawn from this simple model of repeated elections are in accord with intuition. Like Barro, we find that voters have more control over officeholders when the value of office is relatively high and when the future is less heavily discounted. To the extent that voters can directly affect the value of office, they should choose it optimally. How this should be done is discussed in Barro's paper, and we refer the reader to his discussion. Roughly speaking, an increase in the value of office can be expected not only to cost something but also to increase the level of competition for office among nonincumbents (this is not explicitly modelled either here or in Barro's paper). To the extent that the value of office is determined by the (legal or illegal) behavior of incumbent politicians, that value may tend to be set at a higher level than the voters would wish. In either case, however, we might expect systems to evolve in such a way that politicians desire to hold on to their offices and in which, therefore, the electorate is accorded a modicum of control.

Perhaps more surprising is our conclusion about the comparative merits of party systems. While our depiction of the two systems is simplistic, we believe that the basic conclusion will hold up in more sophisticated models of repeated elections as long as there is no motive for the development of party reputations. As long as the parties do not differ in their capabilities or preferences in some unobserved way, they have no way of distinguishing themselves in the minds of the voters. In such a setting, the restriction of electoral competition to two parties has the effect of decreasing the level of voter control over officeholders. Voters are better off in this model to the extent that they can prevent the system from evolving into two-party competition. In a two-party system the loss of office is not as consequential as it would be in a pure candidate (or, indeed, a multiparty) system and so officeholders are not given a strong incentive to pay attention to the interests of the electors.

4 Electoral Control with a Nonhomogeneous Electorate

The development of the model of electoral control was based on the assumption of homogeneous voter preferences over government performance. While there is some empirical evidence in favor of the hypothesis that voter evaluations of incumbents are correlated, there is still reason to suspect that voters may disagree in their ratings of government performance. Indeed, many of the real differences among parties and candidates may be due to distributional differences in the policies they pursue. How far may the results of our model be extended in a world in which the voters maintain separate evaluative standards for officeholders?

We begin by considering a simple specialization of the model in Section 2 and extending it to the case of N voters, each of whom cares only about the quantity, x_i that he receives. We let the value of office be W, and the incumbent's objective is to maximize $W - a$; but, in this case, the incumbent must also decide how to divide the output, $\theta a(\theta)$, among the voters. Thus, his strategies are represented by an $(N + 1)$-vector (a, x), where $x = (x_1, x_2, x_3, \ldots, x_N)$ and where $\sum x_i = \theta a(\theta)$.

The game proceeds just as before: the voters announce their retrospective voting levels, K_i, and then the incumbent observes θ_t and chooses (a, x). Then each voter observes the output he receives and votes to reelect the incumbent if and only if it is satisfactory in the sense that $x_i \geq K_i$. For the present, we restrict our attention to stationary equilibria in order to economize on notation. This will not entail any essential loss of generality.

The following proposition characterizes the equilibria of this model:

PROPOSITION 6 If $\langle K_1, K_2, K_3, \ldots, K_N, (a, x) \rangle$ is an equilibrium, it is equal to zero in all its components.

Proof Given the voters' choice of K_i, $i = 1, \ldots, N$, the incumbent will choose the majority coalition, $\hat{c}$, to minimize $\sum_c x_i$ subject to the constraint that $x_i \geq K_i$ for all $i \in \hat{c}$. Obviously, this implies that $x_i = K_i$ for $i \in \hat{c}$ and that $\hat{c}$ is a minimal majority. If this minimum is positive, any $j \notin \hat{c}$ would have been better off to offer $K_j < \max\{K_i | i \in \hat{c}\}$, which shows that $K_i = 0$ for all i, and, therefore, that $a = 0$.

In the face of heterogeneous preferences, then, the incumbent has both the opportunity and motivation to play off the voters against one another. The result is that the incumbent is entirely uncontrolled by the electorate. Thus, in the distributive setting, retrospective voting appears to lead to a rather unsatisfactory outcome from the standpoint of the electors. Moreover, from the structure of the argument, it seems clear that similar phenomena will arise in any model in which voter preferences are sufficiently diverse that no majority-rule equilibrium exists.

This phenomenon may be seen as a sort of paradox: seemingly rational individual behavior leads to a collectively undesirable outcome. One might think that the presence of potential competitors for office would prevent the incumbent from exploiting this situation. After all, if the incumbent is entirely uncontrollable, one would expect that the office would be very valuable and that challengers would compete vigorously for the opportunity to become incumbents.

But challengers are unable to make precommitments to the voters and so any nonzero offer by a challenger to a majority would not be credible; once in office, the challenger would be motivated to violate such a promise. Thus, whatever capacity challengers have to discipline incumbent performance lies entirely in their availability and not at all in any strategic offers they might make.

The problem, therefore, is for the voters to choose a voting rule that allows the presence of challengers to discipline incumbent behavior. It is clear that if the voters are able to coordinate their behavior successfully, they might hope to achieve the level of control exhibited in Section 3. The solution to that problem represents the highest attainable level of performance from incumbents.

The potential for exploitation by incumbents may lead the voters to adopt what are sometimes called sociotropic rules: voting rules in which individual electors base their vote on an index of aggregate performance (Kiewiet 1983). Clearly, if voters base candidate evaluations on an aggregate index of performance rather than on their individual shares of aggregate output, the incumbent's ability to exploit divisions among them will be reduced. Indeed, the following simple proposition illustrates this possibility.

PROPOSITION 7 If voters agree to utilize expected aggregate output as the criterion, they will be able to induce the incumbent to provide the same level of service as was exhibited in Section 3.

Proof The voter problem is represented as equation (3) and the incumbent's problem is unchanged.

Of course, the usual collective-action problems arise in the determination of a sociotropic rule. Voters will disagree among themselves as to which is the best one and candidates, for their part, will try to induce voters or groups of voters to "defect" from the sociotropic rule and vote, instead, on a distributional basis. But once a sociotropic rule is agreed upon, though the temptations to defect and vote "selfishly" may be strong, voters will realize that these temptations are not credible.

5 Discussion

We have illustrated the limits of the electoral control of incumbents in a simple setting in which candidates are essentially identical to one another and where the voters' problem is to motivate them to act in a popular fashion. The limits of control are achieved, not surprisingly, in a setting in which the electorate can act in a unitary fashion and in which there is a set of challengers waiting to assume office should the incumbent fail to perform adequately. In that case, popular control of incumbents rests on the structure of the party system and on the rewards of office.

If, however, we take account of the diversity of preferences in the electorate, the degree of popular control becomes problematic. Insofar as the electorate is able to agree on some performance standard, the incumbent may be subject to the same discipline as he is with a homogeneous electorate.

From the standpoint of the electorate, then, we have seen that control of politicians requires more than simple retrospective voting. It seems to require, as well, a refusal to vote selfishly. This result, while perhaps surprising at first encounter, may offer hope of explaining heretofore puzzling empirical findings in the voting behavior literature which suggest the widespread use of sociotropic rules rather than more selfish forms of retrospective voting. Of course, this remark poses the question of how voters might come to agree on a particular sociotropic rule.

Less visible, in our model, is the role of challengers. We have assumed, throughout, that challengers and incumbents are unable to collude—a plausible assumption when there are many challengers—so that it was unnecessary to examine strategies that involved deliberate alternation in office by two collusive competitors and low performance levels. It is evident that, if binding agreements could be arranged among the set of potential officeholders, the solution concept employed here is not adequate. In that case, we would have to examine the cooperative possibilities explicitly and consider the bargaining problem among candidates. Whether such a model is worth developing depends, of course, on the presence of entry restrictions on officeholding. Perhaps we should think of one-party states

—whether in the American South, Eastern Europe, or in various developing countries—as embodying mechanisms that control entry of politicians and, thereby, maintain collusive opportunities for officeholders of the established party. Of course, how these officeholders in the dominant party may prevent competition among themselves remains unresolved.

Notes

John Ferejohn is Senior Research Fellow at the Hoover Institution and Professor of Political Science at Stanford University. Special thanks are due to David Baron, Joseph Greenberg, Tom Palfrey, and Tom Romer for careful reading and criticism of earlier versions of this paper.

1. See the political business-cycle literature, especially Tufte (1978). Recent work on Congress (Mayhew 1974) suggests that similar incentives structure the behavior of congressmen.

2. In spite of the great quantity of statistical investigations of issue voting, the evidence for effects of candidate platforms on the vote is mixed. See Page and Jones (1979).

3. The mechanism suggested to overcome the last-period problem is the one introduced by Becker and Stigler (1974). Becker and Stigler argue that misbehavior can be controlled if officeholders face the loss of a pension (or, equivalently, a posted bond) in the event of malfeasance in their last term. Barro suggests that political parties might offer future appointment to office as an inducement for good last-period performance.

4. See previous note.

References

Barro, R. 1973. The control of politicians: An economic model. *Public Choice* 14:19–42.

Becker, G., and Stigler, G. 1974. Law enforcement, malfeasance, and the compensation of enforcers. *Journal of Legal Studies* 1:1–18.

Chappell, H., and Keech, W. 1985. A new view of political accountability for economic performance. *American Political Science Review* 79:10–27.

Fiorina, M. 1981. *Retrospective voting in American national elections*. New Haven: Yale University Press.

Key, V. 1966. *The responsible electorate*. New York: Vintage.

Kiewiet, D. 1983. *Macroeconomics and micropolitics*. Chicago: University of Chicago Press.

Kramer, G. 1971. Short term fluctuations in U.S. voting behavior, 1896–1964. *The American Political Science Review* 65:131–143.

Kramer, G. 1977. A dynamical model of political equilibrium. *Journal of Economic Theory* 16:310–334.

Mayhew, D. 1974. *Congress: The electoral connection*. New Haven: Yale University Press.

McKelvey, R. 1975. Policy related voting and electoral equilibrium. *Econometrica* 43:815–843.

Nordhaus, W. 1975. The political business cycle. *The Review of Economic Studies* 42:169–190.

Page, B., and Jones, C. 1979. Reciprocal effects of policy references, party loyalties and the vote. *The American Political Science Review* 73:1071–1089.

Tufte, E. 1978. *Political control of the economy*. Princeton, NJ: Princeton University Press.

2 Equilibrium Political Budget Cycles

Kenneth Rogoff

Economists and political scientists have long been intrigued by the coincidence of elections and economic policy cycles.[1] During election years, governments at all levels often engage in a consumption binge, in which taxes are cut, transfers are raised, and government spending is distorted toward projects with high immediate visibility. The proximate cause of the "political budget cycle" does not seem difficult to identify. Any incumbent politician, regardless of his ideological stripes, wants to convince voters that he is doing an efficient job running the government. The deeper question is why rational voters might allow their expectations about postelection performance to be influenced by preelection budget antics.[2]

In this chapter, I offer a dynamic, multidimensional signaling model in which both voters and politicians are rational, utility-maximizing agents. A political budget cycle arises here due to temporary information asymmetries about the incumbent leader's "competence" in administering the public goods production process. The incumbent leader has an incentive to bias preelection fiscal policy toward easily observed consumption expenditures, and away from government investment. In equilibrium, however, voters can deduce the leader's current competency by the degree to which he distorts tax and expenditure policies.[3]

Perhaps the most important reason for trying to develop a fully articulated equilibrium model of political budget cycles is to enable one to analyze the welfare implications of alternative electoral regimes, and of various proposals for tempering election year budget distortions.[4] For example, the popular perception is that political budget cycles are a bad thing. But a central conclusion here is that they may be a socially efficient mechanism for diffusing up-to-date information about the incumbent's administrative competence. Efforts to curtail the cycle can easily reduce welfare, either by impeding the transmission of information or by inducing politicians to select more socially costly ways of signaling.[5]

In Section I, I present the model, including the constitutionally constrained election structure. Section II gives the equilibrium under full information, and Sections III–V characterize the fiscal policy distortions which occur under asymmetric information. There are multiple sequential

Reprinted from *American Economic Review*, 80 (1990) 21–36, by permission of the American Economic Association.

equilibria to the model, but after applying some standard refinements, one obtains a unique equilibrium. In Section VI, I explore some possible approaches to mitigating the cycle, including a constitutional limit on the legislature's ability to undertake new fiscal initiatives directly prior to elections. One interesting alternative electoral structure, common to many countries, gives the incumbent the option of calling for an early election. Finally, I consider whether there are ways for society to channel preelection signaling into dimensions that primarily impact on the incumbent and not on society at large. In the conclusions, the predictions of the equilibrium political budget cycle theory are compared with those of its Keynesian predecessor, the political business cycle theory.

1 The Model

A The Preferences of a Representative Citizen

The economy is composed of a large number of (ex ante) identical citizens, each of whom derives utility both from public goods and from a private consumption good. The representative voter is concerned with the expected value of his utility function, $E_t^P(\Gamma_t)$, where subscripts denote time, E^P denotes expectations based on the general public's information set, and

$$\Gamma_t = \sum_{s=t}^{T} [U(c_s, g_s) + V(k_s) + \eta_s]\beta^{s-t}. \tag{1}$$

In equation (1), c is a representative citizen's consumption of the private good, g is the public "consumption" good (per capita), and k is the public " investment" good (per capita). (Population will be held constant throughout). U and V are both regular strictly concave functions, with U_1, U_2, $V' > 0$. In addition to the usual Inada conditions, I make the further assumption that $\lim_{k \to 0} V(k) = -\infty$ [for example, $V(k) = \log k$]. This condition is sufficient to ensure an interior solution in the asymmetric information case. $\beta < 1$ is the representative citizen's discount rate, and T is his time horizon, which may be infinite. The term η is a random shock, which will later be identified with non-pecuniary leader-specific factors such as the leader's looks.

B Technology

At the beginning of each period, all citizens exogenously receive y units of a non-storable good, which can either be privately consumed or used as an input into the production of public goods. Lump-sum taxes in period t are given by τ_t, so that

$$c_t = y - \tau_t. \tag{2}$$

In addition to taxes, the production of public goods also requires a (single) "leader" whose administrative competency is indexed by ε. A competent administrator (high ε) is able to provide a given level of public goods at a lower level of taxes than an incompetent one can. Specifically, I assume that the public goods production function takes the form[6]

$$g_t + k_{t+1} = \tau_t + \varepsilon_t. \tag{3}$$

Note that whereas the relative cost of producing g and k is unity, the timing of their production differs. To have the public "investment" good k in period $t + 1$, the government must invest in period t.

C Stochastic Structure

All agents are capable of serving as the country's leader. However, at any point in time they differ according to their innate administrative ability. For each agent i, (potential) leadership competency evolves according to the serially correlated stochastic process

$$\varepsilon_t^i = \alpha_t^i + \alpha_{t-1}^i, \tag{4}$$

where each α is an independent drawing from a Bernoulli distribution with $\rho \equiv \text{prob}(\alpha = \alpha^H)$ and $1 - \rho \equiv \text{prob}(\alpha = \alpha^L)$, $\alpha^H > \alpha^L > 0$. The α shocks are independent across agents as well as across time. One reason why competency might realistically be thought to vary across time is that leadership abilities well suited to dealing with the one set of historical circumstances may become outmoded as the problems facing the country change. Also, even if the same leader stays in power, there may be turnover among his key advisors.

In this model, competency is not a choice variable for a leader but an individual characteristic. One may think of competency as administrative IQ.[7] The assumption that competency follows a first-order moving average process simplifies the analysis below considerably, by effectively breaking structural links between elections. However, the main qualitative results here should carry over to more general stochastic processes.

In addition to the competency shock, each agent i experiences a "looks" shock η, which also follows a moving average process:

$$\eta_t^i = q_t^i + q_{t-1}^i, \tag{5}$$

where each q is continuously distributed i.i.d. random variable on $[-\bar{q}, \bar{q}]$, with q_t^i and q_s^j independent for all $s \neq t$, $i \neq j$. The random variable η is intended to capture factors relevant to an agent's leadership ability but uncorrelated with his competence in administering the public goods production function; for example, his "looks." Neither ε^i nor η^i matter for anything when agent i is a private citizen. Throughout, whenever ε, η, α, or q are written without a superscript, they refer to the incumbent.

D The Leader's Utility Function

The country's leaders are drawn from the ranks of ordinary citizens and as such, they derive utility from public and private consumption goods in the same way as other citizens. However, because the position of chief administrator is considered a great honor, the leader receives additional "ego rents" of X per period in office. Thus, for an incumbent leader, expected utility is given by[8]

$$E_t^I(\Gamma_t) + \sum_{s=t}^{T} \beta^{s-t} X \pi_{s,t}, \tag{6}$$

where I denotes the incumbent and Γ is given by (1). E_t^I denotes expectations based on the incumbent's information set at time t, and $\pi_{s,t}$ is the incumbent's time t estimate of his probability of being in office in period s; π will be derived later on. Prospective ego rents (X) do not enter explicitly into the objective function of an ordinary citizen, $E^P(\Gamma)$, only because the population is sufficiently large that the probability of his ever being elected is infinitesimal.

I have motivated the leader's utility function without any appeal to altruism. But it should later be apparent that the analysis would be similar in most respects under a more generous interpretation of the leader's aims. Specifically, one can interpret equation (6) as saying that the leader puts some weight on social welfare, Γ, and some weight on the rents he receives from being in office.

E The Structure of Elections

In order to determine which citizen is awarded the honor of administering the production of public goods, the country's constitution specifies that elections be held every other period. The incumbent leader is allowed to run an indefinite number of times,[9] whereas the opposition candidate is chosen at random from the rest of the population. Note that under the information structure specified below, the fundamental difference between the incumbent leader and his opponent is that the public can infer something about the incumbent's most recent competency shock, but it has no way of inferring anything about the opponent's competency. For voters, the choice is essentially between reelecting the incumbent or selecting an agent from the population at large, all of whom appear identical ex ante.[10]

F The Information Structure and the Timing of Events

Voters observe taxes τ_t and government consumption spending g_t contemporaneously, and employ this information to form *inferences* concerning government investment spending k_{t+1} and the incumbent's competency shock α_t. However, they cannot directly confirm these inferences until the following period. In period $t + 1$, the government's period t investment comes on line and voters also directly observe α_t. Thus the incumbent has a temporary information "advantage" over voters in the sense that he sees his competency shock contemporaneously. I use the word "advantage" in quotation marks because it will turn out that *in equilibrium* voters are always able to deduce the incumbent's private information.

The information structure assumed here is plausible since it is costly for an individual to closely monitor and evaluate a government's performance. Moreover, there is little private incentive for an individual to undertake such monitoring since in equilibrium, he can infer α_t costlessly using his information on g_t and τ_t. Taxes and government consumption spending are variables which individuals need to know and can observe relatively easily. On the other hand, if k represents investment in national defense, there may be national security reasons for not making it public. More broadly, k may be thought of as vesting of public pension funds, off-budget loan guarantees, or any type of government expenditure whose effects are only observed by the representative voter with a lag.

Of course, if some group were able to monitor the government and *credibly* transmit information in a way that would not be too costly for the average citizen to process, then there would be no political budget cycle in the analysis below. Clearly, neither the opposition candidate nor the incumbent can provide this service, since their statements cannot be trusted. The results below should go through in a more general setting in which some voters monitor α_t, as long as there is a sufficient pool of uninformed voters.

The incumbent observes α_t and sets τ_t, g_t, and k_{t+1}.	Voters observe τ_t, g_t, k_t, α_{t-1}, q_t, q_t^O, and then vote.	The winner of the period t election takes office for two periods. The timing of events is as in t except there is no election until $t + 2$
	Election	
period t		period $t + 1$.

Figure 2.1
The timing of events

The public, of course, has no way of inferring α_t^O, where "O" superscripts denote the opponent. All voters know about the opponent is the probability distribution of α. (The incumbent has no way of knowing α_t^O either until he actually tries his hand at running the government.) Prior to voting, voters do observe both q_t and q_t^O, the "looks" shocks.

The incumbent must set g and τ prior to observing the q's. The rationale for this assumption is that it takes time for the government to collect taxes and to make purchases. The q shocks, on the other hand, might capture information revealed in election-eve debates or uncertainty about a last-minute scandal concerning one of the candidates. In a slightly different version of the model in which voters have heterogeneous preferences over looks, q can represent uncertainty about election-day weather, and thus about the composition of voters who come to the polls.[11] Figure 2.1 illustrates the timing of events.

In deciding his vote, the representative voter compares his expected utility under each of the two candidates. If $v = 1$ denotes a vote for the incumbent and $v = 0$ a vote for his opponent, then

$$v_t = \begin{cases} 1 & \text{if } E_t^P(\Gamma_{t+1}) \geq E_t^P(\Gamma_{t+1}^O) \\ 0, & \text{otherwise.} \end{cases} \tag{7}$$

II Equilibrium Under Full Information

Before proceeding, it is useful to analyze the equilibrium which would arise if voters could directly observe α_t prior to voting. In this case, the incumbent's preelection fiscal policy cannot possibly affect voter's expectations about his postelection competency, and thus can have no effect on his chances of remaining in office. With the π terms in (6) exogenous, the incumbent's decision problem becomes equivalent to maximizing the welfare of the representative agent. Given the simple production and storage technology, this problem can be broken down into a sequence of static maximization problems:

$$\max_{\tau_t, c_t, g_t, k_{t+1}} \quad U(c_t, g_t) + \beta V(k_{t+1}), \quad \forall t \geq T \tag{8}$$

subject to (2), (3), and k, c, $g \geq 0$; $k_{T+1} = \bar{k}$.[12]

It is convenient to rewrite the above maximization problem by substituting (2) and (3) into (8):

$$\max_{\tau, g} W(g, \tau, \varepsilon) \equiv U(y - \tau, g) + \beta V(\tau + \varepsilon - g)$$

$$\text{s.t. } g,\ y - \tau,\ \tau + \varepsilon - g \geq 0. \tag{9}$$

(Time subscripts will henceforth be omitted where the meaning is obvious.) The first-order conditions for an interior solution to (9) imply

$$U_1(y - \tau, g) = U_2(y - \tau, g), \tag{10}$$

$$U_1(y - \tau, g) = \beta V'(\tau + \varepsilon - g). \tag{11}$$

One can readily confirm that there is a unique $[g^*(\varepsilon), \tau^*(\varepsilon)]$ which satisfies (10) and (11), and that this point is a global maximum. (Note that U and V are strictly concave and that the constraint set is convex.) Clearly

$$W^*(\varepsilon) = W^*[g^*(\varepsilon), \tau^*(\varepsilon), \varepsilon]$$

is strictly increasing in ε and, if all goods are normal, then $c^*(\varepsilon)$, $g^*(\varepsilon)$, and $k^*(\varepsilon)$ are also increasing. By (2), $\tau^*(\varepsilon)$ must be decreasing in ε.

If t is an election period, then by equations (1), (4), (5), (7), and (9), the incumbent will be reelected ($v = 1$) if

$$E_t^P[W^*(\varepsilon_{t+1})] - E_t^P[W^*(\varepsilon_{t+1}^O)] + q_t - q_t^O \geq 0. \tag{12}$$

Because ε and η follow first-order moving average processes, voters' expected utility is the same under either candidate for periods $t + 2$ and beyond, and thus only expectations over $t + 1$ enter into (12). (Recall from Figure 2.1 that voters observe the q shocks prior to the election.)

If voters directly observe the incumbent's most recent competency shock prior to voting, then the first term in (12) is given by

$$E_t^P[W^*(\varepsilon_{t+1})|\alpha_t = \alpha^i] \equiv \Omega^i = \rho W^*(\alpha^i + \alpha^H) + (1 - \rho) W^*(\alpha^i + \alpha^L);$$
$$i = H, L. \tag{13}$$

Voters have no observations on the opponent's competency; hence

$$E_t^P[W^*(\varepsilon_{t+1}^O)] \equiv \Omega^O = \rho^2 W^*(2\alpha^H) + 2\rho(1 - \rho) W^*(\alpha^H + \alpha^L)$$
$$+ (1 - \rho)^2 W^*(2\alpha^L). \tag{14}$$

Clearly, $\Omega^H > \Omega^O > \Omega^L$.

III Voters' and Leaders' Optimization Problems Under Asymmetric Information

I now return to the asymmetric information structure summarized in Figure 2.1. Although the public cannot observe α_t until period $t + 1$, they can form "beliefs" about α_t given their observations on g_t and τ_t. These beliefs can be parameterized as $\hat{\rho}(g, \tau)$, where $\hat{\rho}$ is the probability weight the public attaches to the possibility that $\alpha_t = \alpha_H$. (Since α_{t-1} is a fixed, known parameter throughout this section, I abbreviate $\hat{\rho}(\alpha_t, \tau_t; \alpha_{t-1})$ as $\hat{\rho}(\alpha, \tau)$).

We will initially focus on the final election period, $t = T - 2$. Since the winner will not be running for reelection, he has no incentive to distort fiscal policy in periods $T - 1$ or T. Thus $E_t^P[W(\varepsilon_{T+1})] = E_t^P[W^*(\varepsilon_{T+1})]$ if the incumbent wins and similarly for his opponent. By equations (12)–(14), if voters have priors $\hat{\rho}(g, \tau)$, the incumbent will be reelected ($v = 1$) if

$$\hat{\rho}\Omega^H + (1 - \hat{\rho})\Omega^L - \Omega^O + q - q^O \geq 0. \tag{15}$$

The incumbent does not know $q - q^0$ when setting his election-year fiscal policy. However, for any choice of (g, τ), he can infer $\hat{\rho}(g, \tau)$ and thus calculate the probability that $q - q^O$ will be high enough for him to win:

$$\pi[\hat{\rho}(g, \tau)] \equiv E^I(v|g, \tau) = 1 - G[\Omega^O - \hat{\rho}\Omega^H - (1 - \hat{\rho})\Omega^L], \tag{16}$$

where G is the probability distribution function of $q - q^O$. The possibility for signaling arises here because there is a limit to how much an incumbent would be willing to distort fiscal policy in order to fool the public about his competency. As a representative agent, he too cares about the mix of consumption and investment; see (6) above.

It is convenient to define $\varepsilon^H = \alpha_{t-1} + \alpha^H$, and $\varepsilon^L = \alpha_{t-1} + \alpha^L$. The incumbent will be described as a "type H" (or "competent type") if $\varepsilon_t = \varepsilon^H$, and a "type L" (or "incompetent type") if $\varepsilon_t = \varepsilon^L$. Using equations (1), (4)–(6), (9), and (16), one can then write an incumbent of type i's maximization problem as

$$\max_{g,\tau} Z[g, \tau, \hat{\rho}(g, \tau), \varepsilon^i] \quad \text{s.t. } g, y - \tau, \tau + \varepsilon^i - g \geq 0; \quad i = H, L, \tag{17}$$

where

$$Z[g, \tau, \hat{\rho}(g, \tau), \varepsilon^i] \equiv \chi^i \pi[\hat{\rho}(g, \tau)] + W(g, \tau, \varepsilon^i)], \tag{18}$$

$$\chi^i \equiv \beta[X(1 + \beta) + \Omega^i - \Omega^o]. \tag{19}$$

The first term on the RHS of (18) is the incumbent's expected chance of winning, π, multiplied by his surplus from winning, χ^i. This surplus is broken down in (19), where the term $X(\beta + \beta^2)$ captures the discounted ego rents for the two postelection periods, and the term $\beta(\Omega^i - \Omega^o)$ is the amount by which the representative citizen's expected utility is higher if the incumbent wins instead of his opponent. I assume $\chi^L > 0$.

Two features distinguish the objective function of a competent type from that of an incompetent type. First, the competent type knows that expected social welfare will be higher if he is reelected than if his unknown opponent wins. The second difference is that for any (g, τ), a type H is investing $\alpha^H - \alpha^L$ more units into k_{t+1} than a type L is, by equation (3). An important implication is that since $V'' < 0$, a type H can cut back on government investment at lower *marginal* cost that can a type L.

IV Sequential Equilibria

The interaction between incumbent politicians and rational voters here can be viewed as a multidimensional signaling problem, with g and τ as signals of the incumbent's (contemporaneously) unobserved competency. As is typically the case in such models, there is a multiplicity of sequential equilibria, including both *separating* and *pooling* equilibria. In a separating equilibrium, the incumbent's choice of fiscal policy perfectly reveals his competency type. In a pooling equilibrium, the incompetent type might mimic the competent type. However, by requiring that voters' beliefs reflect a certain minimal level of sophistication (by excluding "dominated" strategies),[13] it is possible to rule out all but one of the separating equilibria. By further refining the equilibrium concept, using the "intuitive" criterion of In-Koo Cho and David Kreps (1987), one can also rule out pooling equilibria. In the unique equilibrium which survives both refinements, competent types set taxes too low and government spending too high before elections, whereas incompetent types pursue their full information policy. On average, there is a political budget cycle.[14]

In the main text, I will restrict attention to equilibria in pure strategies. For $i = L, H$, let (g^i, τ^i) describe a strategy for the incumbent leader, and let $v[\hat{\rho}(g, \tau), q - q^O]$ describe a strategy for voters. Then the pair $\{(g^i, \tau^i), i = L, H; v[\hat{\rho}(g, \tau), q - q^O]\}$ describes a sequential equilibrium if: (a) Voters set v according to (15); (b) the incumbent chooses (g^i, τ^i) according to (17); and (c) voters' beliefs are *Bayes-consistent*: If $(g^L, \tau^L) \neq (g^H, \tau^H)$, then $\hat{\rho}(g^L, \tau^L) = 0$ and $\hat{\rho}(g^H, \tau^H) = 1$. If $(g^L, \tau^L) = (g^H, \tau^H)$, then $\hat{\rho}(g^L, \tau^L) = \rho$. Henceforth, I will use the term "equilibrium" as an abbreviation for "sequential equilibrium."

A Separating Equilibria

In a separating equilibrium $(g^L, \tau^L) \neq (g^H, \tau^H)$. Note that in any separating equilibrium a type L must be choosing his full-information fiscal policy

$$(g^L, \tau^L) = [g^*(\varepsilon^L), \tau^*(\varepsilon^L)], \tag{20}$$

since otherwise

$$Z\{g^*(\varepsilon^L), \tau^*(\varepsilon^L), \hat{\rho}[g^*(\varepsilon^L), \tau^*(\varepsilon^L)], \varepsilon^L\} - Z(g^L, \tau^L, 0, \varepsilon^L) > 0,$$

which is inconsistent with the requirement that (g^L, τ^L) maximize (17). An incompetent incumbent gains nothing by choosing a level of fiscal policy which is distortionary and yet fails to prevent the public from deducing his type.

I will initially assume that voters' "off-the-equilibrium-path" beliefs are governed simply by $\hat{\rho}(g, \tau) = 0 \ \forall \ (g, \tau) \neq (g^H, \tau^H)$. Given these beliefs, a type L will not benefit by mimicking a type H as long as $(g^H, \tau^H) \in \mathscr{A}$ where

$$\mathscr{A} \equiv \{(g, \tau) | Z(g, \tau, 1, \varepsilon^L) - Z[g^*(\varepsilon^L), \tau^*(\varepsilon^L), 0, \varepsilon^L] \leq 0\}. \tag{21}$$

In Figure 2.2, point I corresponds to $[g^*(\varepsilon^L), \tau^*(\varepsilon^L)]$, and set $\mathscr{A}$ consists of all points on or outside the dashed ellipse. A type L would be willing to choose any point *within* the dashed ellipse over point I if by doing so, he could fool the public into thinking he is a type H. (The assumption that U

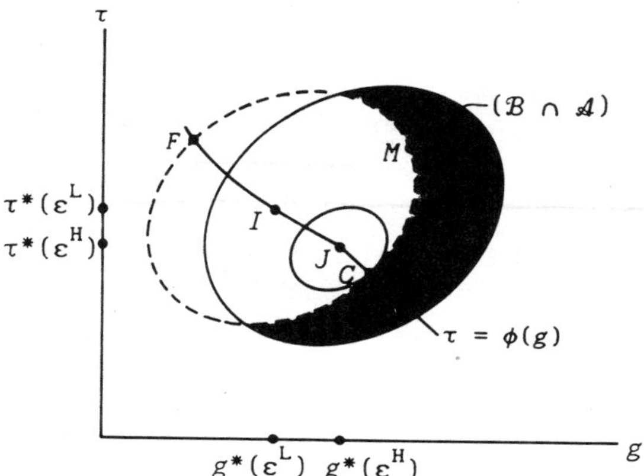

Figure 2.2
Undominated separating equilibrium

and V obey Inada conditions together with the assumption $V(0) = -\infty$ assure that the ellipse is contained within the boundaries $g > 0$, $y - \tau > 0$, and $k^L = \tau + \varepsilon^L - g > 0$. The set of points contained within the ellipse is necessarily convex as drawn, since W is strictly concave in τ and g).

Point J in Figure 2.2 corresponds to $[g^*(\varepsilon^H), \tau^*(\varepsilon^H)]$. Because all goods are normal, J must lie southeast of I. Whether J lies within the dashed ellipse (in which case it cannot be a separating equilibrium strategy for a type H) depends on a number of factors. It is more likely to be interior the larger X (ego rents), the smaller $\varepsilon^H - \varepsilon^L$, and the lower the variance of $q - q^O$. Thus if the high type is sufficiently more competent than the low type, he can choose his first-best fiscal policy and still separate himself.

Another necessary condition for a separating equilibrium is that $(g^H, \tau^H) \in \mathscr{B}$, where

$$\mathscr{B} \equiv \{(g, \tau) | Z(g, \tau, 1, \varepsilon^H) - Z[g^*(\varepsilon^H), \tau^*(\varepsilon^H), 0, \varepsilon^H] \geq 0\}. \tag{22}$$

The large solid ellipse in Figure 2.2 contains the convex set $\mathscr{B}$. The shaded region is $\mathscr{B} \cap \mathscr{A}$; it contains all the possible separating equilibrium strategies for a type H. It is easy to prove that $\mathscr{B} \cap \mathscr{A}$ is nonempty by virtue of the fact $\chi^H > \chi^L$ and $V'' < 0$. Thus

PROPOSITION 1 The set of all separating equilibria is nonempty and is characterized by $(g^L, \tau^L) = [g^*(\varepsilon^L), \tau^*(\varepsilon^L)]$, and $(g^H, \tau^H) \in \mathscr{B} \cap \mathscr{A}$.

B Undominated Separating Equilibria

The range of separating equilibria can be drastically reduced (to a single point) by requiring that $\hat{\rho} = 1$ for all $(g, \tau) \in \mathscr{B} \cap \mathscr{A}$ and not just at (g^H, τ^H). This restriction on voters' beliefs is plausible since there are no circumstances under which a type L might benefit by choosing a point in the shaded region in Figure 2.2. Provided voters' beliefs reflect this minimal level of sophistication, a competent incumbent is essentially free to choose the separating strategy which is most favorable to him, that is, the one which entails the least distortions. In an *undominated* separating equilibrium, (g^H, τ^H) solves[15]

$$\max_{g,\tau} W(g, \tau, \varepsilon^H) \quad \text{s.t. } g, y - \tau, \tau + \varepsilon^H - g \geq 0, \tag{23}$$

and

$$(g, \tau) \in \mathscr{A}.$$

PROPOSITION 2 There exists a unique undominated separating equilibrium, and in this equilibrium $U_1(y - \tau, g) = U_2(y - \tau, g)$.

Note that the condition $U_1 = U_2$ is precisely the same as one of the first-order conditions for a full-information optimum, equation (10). Equation (10) implicitly defines the income expansion path $\tau = \phi(g)$, which passes through points I and J in Figure 2.2; $\phi' < 0$ since both c and g are normal goods. The unique undominated equilibrium is given by point C in Figure 2.2, where $g > g^*(\varepsilon^H)$ and $\tau < \tau^*(\varepsilon^H)$. This equilibrium has the property that signaling is "efficient" in the sense that no reallocation of expenditures between the private and public consumption goods can yield voters higher welfare.

C Pooling Equilibria

Restricting attention to undominated equilibria is not sufficient to rule out all pooling equilibria. For example, if ρ is large enough, then $(g^L, \tau^L) = (g^H, \tau^H) = [g^*(\varepsilon^H), \tau^*(\varepsilon^H)]$; $\hat{\rho}(g^H, \tau^H) = \rho$, can be an equilibrium. To rule out all pooling equilibria (in pure and mixed strategies), it is necessary to further refine the equilibrium concept. Following Cho and Kreps (1987), an equilibrium $\{(g^L, \tau^L), (g^H, \tau^H)\}$ is *unintuitive* if there exists a point $(\bar{g}, \bar{\tau})$ such that[16]

$$Z(\bar{g}, \bar{\tau}, 1, \varepsilon^H) - Z[g^H, \tau^H, \hat{\rho}(g^H, \tau^H), \varepsilon^H] > 0, \tag{24}$$

and

$$Z(\bar{g}, \bar{\tau}, 1, \varepsilon^L) - Z[g^L, \tau^L, \hat{\rho}(g^L, \tau^L), \varepsilon^L] < 0. \tag{25}$$

PROPOSITION 3 All pooling equilibria are unintuitive.

One can easily confirm that the unique undominated separating equilibrium is also an intuitive equilibrium (i.e., not unintuitive). Henceforth, the term "equilibrium" refers to this equilibrium.

V Multiple Elections

The extension to the case of finitely many election periods is straightforward. In off-election years, the incumbent always follows his full-information fiscal policy. Voters are able to monitor the government perfectly with a one-period lag, so there is no incentive to distort in an off-election year. During election years, the signaling problem is the same as above, except that the gain to the incumbent of reelection, χ, becomes larger as the incumbent's expected term in office increases. The prospect of being able to run for reelection again in the future raises the temptation to distort fiscal policy, and thus tends to exacerbate the political budget cycle.

The equilibrium studied here remains an equilibrium when the time horizon is infinite. It is also possible, however, to have "reputational" equilibria in which there is little or no political budget cycle if (a) the leader's rate of time preference is close to one, (b) exogenous uncertainty (here the variance of q) is not too large, and (c) the time between elections is short.[17] In most countries, though, elections are typically spaced many years apart and there is considerable uncertainty over what factors will govern distant elections. Thus incumbents are not likely to place great weight on maintaining a reputation for not engaging in political budget cycles.[18]

VI Alternative Approaches to Mitigating the Political Budget Cycle

If preelection signaling is truly a central cause of the political budget cycle, is there any way for society to mitigate the problem?

A A Constitutional Amendment to Restrain Election-Year Fiscal Policy

One natural alternative is to reform the budget process so that the government cannot alter its fiscal policy rule just prior to an election. Edward

Tufte (1978, p. 152), for example, suggests instituting a change in the timing of the congressional budget cycle. Let us consider a constitutional amendment which forces the government to set fiscal policy on a biennial basis, so that both (g_t, τ_t) and (g_{t-1}, τ_{t-1}) must be set in off-election year $t-1$. (The only relevant source of uncertainty here is the α shock but in interpreting the analysis below, one can think of the government as being allowed to index its fiscal policy rule to any publicly observable shock.) If forced to bind himself in $t-1$ to (g_t, τ_t), the incumbent would solve

$$\max_{g,\tau} E_{t-1}[W(g, \tau, \varepsilon_t)] = \rho W(g, \tau, \alpha_{t-1} + \alpha^H) + (1-\rho) W(g, \tau, \alpha_{t-1} + \alpha^L). \tag{26}$$

Note that the incumbent is prevented from signaling because he does not have any information about his postelection competency type when setting election-year fiscal policy. The budget process reform thus mitigates the political budget cycle, but there are two costs. First, the public no longer has any way of distinguishing between H and L types when voting. If for simplicity we ignore the q shock, the mean cost of this lost information is $\rho\beta(\Omega^H - \Omega^O)$. The other cost is that the leader cannot employ his private information on α_t in setting period t fiscal policy.

The relative costs and benefits of the constitutional amendment are transparent in two extreme cases. If ego rents (X) are small, then the election-year fiscal policy distortions will be minor and the proposed budget process reform makes little sense. At the opposite extreme, as X becomes large, the political budget cycle takes on catastrophic dimensions. Indeed, the public may actually enjoy higher welfare during the election year itself when the incumbent is an incompetent type, since it is the competent type who distorts fiscal policy to signal his type. Nevertheless, a competent type is more likely to win reelection, since citizens vote for the candidate who offers them higher expected future welfare.

The preceding analysis, if anything, overstates the efficacy of trying to legislate away the political budget cycle. In practice, an incumbent has a wide array of fiscal actions with which he can signal, and it is not realistically possible to constrain him in all dimensions. If this is the case, then attempts to block signaling in one set of fiscal policy instruments will tend to exacerbate distortion in others. Indeed, attempts to suppress the political budget cycle may actually reduce the welfare of the representative citizen by inducing competent types to signal inefficiently.

As a simple example, consider a "balanced budget" constraint of the form

$$\tau = \Psi(g), \quad \Psi' > 0. \tag{27}$$

Let us initially assume that $\Psi(g)$ passes through point I in Figure 2.2 and also through point M. Since $\Psi(g)$ passes through $[g^*(\varepsilon^L), \tau^*(\varepsilon^L)]$, this point remains the separating equilibrium choice of a type L. The undominated separating equilibrium strategy for a type H is now found by maximizing (23) subject to the *additional* constraint (27). At the solution point, labeled M in Figure 2.2, the welfare of the representative voter is unambiguously lower than at C, the equilibrium in the absence of the constraint.[19]

Suppose now that $\Psi(g)$ does not pass through point I, so that the constraint (27) also distorts the choice of a type L. Denote a type L's solution to his full-information problem (9), subject to the additional constraint (27), as $[g^{**}(\varepsilon^L), \tau^{**}(\varepsilon^L)]$, and define the set $\mathscr{A}^A$ as

$$\mathscr{A}^A \equiv \{(g, \tau) | Z(g, \tau, 1, \varepsilon^L) - Z[g^{**}(\varepsilon^L), \tau^{**}(\varepsilon^L), 0, \varepsilon^L] \leq 0\}. \tag{28}$$

The separating equilibrium strategy for a type H is again found by maximizing (23) subject to the additional constraint (27), but now with the constraint $(g, \tau) \in \mathscr{A}^A$ in place of $(g, \tau) \in \mathscr{A}$. Note that $\mathscr{A}^A$ is a subset of $\mathscr{A}$; a type L is willing to distort further to convince the public he is a type H when his best alternative is the constitutionally constrained $[g^{**}(\varepsilon^L), \tau^{**}(\varepsilon^L)]$ than when it is the unconstrained $[g^*(\varepsilon^L), \tau^*(\varepsilon^L)]$. Thus the separating strategy for a type H will generally be at some point where voter welfare is even lower than at point M.

To summarize, if a budget process reform forces a pooling equilibrium, voters may or may not be better off, depending on the costs of the lost information versus the benefits of mitigating the political budget cycle. If, however, the incumbent can still find a way to use fiscal policy to signal, the budget process reform is likely to prove counterproductive. One interesting implication of this analysis is that having an independent central bank does not necessarily reduce the *welfare* costs of political budget cycles, even if it insulates monetary policy from election-year pressures.

B Endogenous Elections

Until now, I have treated the timing of elections as immutable. In principle, the framework developed here can be extended to compare social welfare under different electoral structures. For example, in a regime with very short intervals between elections, incompetent leaders can be quickly removed from office. The drawback, of course, is that the political budget cycle will occur at correspondingly high frequencies (though it may be damped since fewer years of ego rents will be at stake in each election).

An especially important alternative class of electoral structures involves giving the incumbent the *option* of calling for an early election. Indeed, many modern industrialized countries, including Canada, the United Kingdom, and Japan, have systems in which the timing of elections is endogenous. In practice, early elections are sometimes forced upon a ruling party after it loses its working majority in parliament. In some instances, however, an incumbent government opportunistically decides to risk its remaining time in office in hopes of winning a fresh new term. For opportunistic early elections, the model suggests that preelection fiscal policy distortions are likely to be less severe than for end-of-term elections. The basic reason is that the call for an early election can serve as an additional (non-distorting) signal.[20]

Recall from Figure 2.2 that the dashed ellipse bounds the fiscal policy distortions a type L would be willing to undertake to fool the public into thinking he is a type H. Of course, this curve is drawn under the assumption that a type L's best alternative is to choose his full information policy (point I), and hope that a very favorable looks shock carries him through the election. If a type L has the superior option of waiting a period before standing for reelection, then the option of calling for an early election and mimicking the fiscal policy of a type H becomes less attractive. By waiting to call an election, a type L not only gets to enjoy a certain extra period of ego rents, but also buys time to wait for a more favorable competency shock. As a result, a competent incumbent does not need to distort fiscal policy as much to separate himself when calling an early election. Indeed, he may not need to distort at all. To assess the overall welfare implications of allowing for early elections, one must trade off the benefits of having smaller distortions with the costs of having more frequent elections.

Most cross-country empirical studies of political business cycles do not systematically distinguish between opportunistic early elections and end-of-term elections, but the above discussion suggests that the distinction may be important.[21]

C Self-Denial as a Signal of Competency

Thus far I have been implicitly restricting the incumbent to signals which adversely affect all citizens and not just the incumbent himself. It is reasonable to ask whether the analysis thereby exaggerates the extent to which the incumbent will use socially destructive fiscal policy distortions to signal his competency.

Suppose, for example, that the incumbent can also signal by publicly destroying σ units of his own personal endowment of the private consumption good.[22] In this case, the incumbent's consumption is given by $c^I = y - \tau - \sigma$, and W in his objective function becomes

$$W^I(g, \tau, \sigma, \varepsilon) = U(y - \tau - \sigma, g) + \beta V(\tau + \varepsilon - g), \tag{29}$$

where $\sigma \geq 0$. Under full information, $\sigma^* = 0$, while g^* and τ^* are governed by (10) and (11) as before. Let $\tilde{Z}(g, \tau, \sigma, \hat{\rho}, \varepsilon^i)$ be the same as Z in equation (18), except with W and $\hat{\rho}(g, \tau)$ replaced by W^I and $\hat{\rho}(g, \tau, \sigma)$.

It is straightforward to show that there exist equilibria in which a competent incumbent, by setting $\sigma^H > 0$, is able to separate himself without distorting fiscal policy as much as in any of the separating equilibria where $\sigma^H = 0$. In the (unique) *undominated* separating equilibrium, however, a type H sets (g^H, τ^H, σ^H) to solve

$$\max_{g, \tau, \sigma} W^I(g, \tau, \sigma, \varepsilon^H) \quad \text{s.t. } g, \sigma, y - \tau - \sigma, \tau + \varepsilon^H - g \geq 0, \tag{30}$$

and

$$(g, \tau, \sigma) \in \tilde{\mathscr{A}},$$

where

$$\tilde{\mathscr{A}} \equiv \{(g, \tau, \sigma) | \tilde{Z}(g, \tau, \sigma, 1, \varepsilon^L) - \tilde{Z}[g^*(\varepsilon^L), \tau^*(\varepsilon^L), 0, 0, \varepsilon^L] \leq 0\}.$$

PROPOSITION 4 In an undominated separating equilibrium, $\sigma^H = 0$, and (g^H, τ^H) solves (23).

A type H incumbent could set $\sigma > 0$ to help signal his type, but by Proposition 4 he will always prefer to do it using fiscal policy alone. It is inefficient for a competent incumbent to signal by dissipating his personal resources, because he has no comparative advantage in that dimension.

Society could *force* the leader to dissipate $\bar{\sigma} > 0$ by requiring any incumbent who wants to run for reelection to pay a fee. It is easily shown that such a scheme can be welfare improving, but not by enough to attain the full-information equilibrium. A fee tends to distort a (selfish) leader's choice of tax policy, because it gives him a different tradeoff between private and public goods expenditure than the representative voter. But the most conspicuous drawback to this approach is that it would be very difficult in practice to find a rule for setting $\bar{\sigma}$, since incumbents differ greatly in wealth and future earning power.

Of course, if there were some way to reduce the leader's rents without causing him to distort fiscal policy, this would lead to the first-best outcome. Unfortunately, massive ego rents seem an inevitable by-product of the public goods production function.

VII Conclusions

The present analysis preserves some of the basic insights of the Keynesian political business cycle model, albeit with significant refinements. Underlying the cycle in the model (for example, William Nordhaus, 1975) is a Keynesian Phillips curve and voter myopia. By increasing money supply growth in the year prior to an election, an incumbent national leader is able to temporarily raise output and employment.[23] Voters respond positively, not recognizing that after the election inflation will rise while output and employment will return to their natural rates. This story has two conspicuous failings. First, elections are perfectly anticipated events, so any systematic accompanying rise in money growth should not have any real effects. Second, preelection macroeconomic policy is a given by the time of the election, and voters' decisions should be governed only by which candidate offers them higher expected postelection welfare.

The Keynesian theory has generated a plethora of empirical studies aimed at testing for electoral cycles in national output, unemployment, and inflation. In light of the theoretical weaknesses of the underlying model, perhaps it should not be too surprising that the results have been mixed.[24] The equilibrium political budget cycle theory suggests that it would be more promising to focus empirical research on testing for electoral cycles in taxes, transfers, and government consumption spending.[25] For these variables, one can also look at data for state and local elections, instead of concentrating solely on the small number of observations available for national elections.

In addition to focusing on different variables, the present model also offers sharper prediction concerning the dynamic structures of the cycle. Here the pre- and postelection values of observable fiscal policy variables tend to be *positively* correlated (when variables are measured in deviations from pre- and postelection means). Competent incumbents, who have greater leeway to cut taxes and raise government consumption spending prior to elections, are more likely to be able to do so after elections as well. The model here also has concrete implications for the nature of political budget cycles under alternative electoral structures. For example, in countries where the incumbent has the option of calling for early elections, the budget distortions which accompany opportunistic early elections tend to be damped compared to those accompanying end-of-term elections.

Does the political budget cycle theory have any bearing on countries such as Mexico and Japan, in which a single party dominates political life? Even in dominant-party systems, the country's leaders still generally care about their party's margin of victory. Its plurality not only affects the leaders' ability to govern the populace, but also their ability to contain internal dissent within the party. (The formal model above is easily extended to the case where plurality matters). The model should also retain some relevance in situations where competing parties share power (for example, if the majority party in the legislature is Democratic and the President is Republican). Although each of the parties may care about increasing its representation in the government, individual legislators have a strong common interest in their own reelection.

Appendix

This Appendix provides the proofs of Propositions 2, 3, and 4.

Proof of Proposition 2 Given the Inada conditions on U and V, any solution to (23) must have $c, g, k > 0$. Thus the Kuhn-Tucker conditions reduce to

$$U_1 - \beta V_H' = \lambda(U_1 - \beta V_L'), \tag{A1}$$

$$U_2 - \beta V_H' = \lambda(U_2 - \beta V_L'), \tag{A2}$$

$$\chi^L \pi(0) + W^*(\varepsilon^L) - \chi^L \pi(1) - U(y - \tau, g) - \beta V(\tau + \varepsilon^L - g) \geq 0,$$

$$(=0 \text{ if } \lambda > 0), \tag{A3}$$

where $V_i' \equiv V'(\tau + \varepsilon^i - g)$. (A1) and (A2) imply that $U_1 = U_2$. This equation governs the downward-sloping income extension path $\tau = \phi(g)$ in Figure 2.2. (A3) is the constraint $(g, \tau) \in \mathscr{A}$, the set of points on or outside the dashed ellipse. Assume that $\lambda > 0$ so that (A3) is binding. Equations (A1)–(A3) are then satisfied at exactly two points. At point C in Figure 2.2, $\beta V_i' > U_1$, $i = H, L$, and $\lambda = (U_1 - \beta V_H')/(U_1 - \beta V_L') < 1$. At point F, $\beta V_i' < U_1$ and $\lambda > 1$. One can show that the second-order conditions hold if

$$(1 - \lambda)[2U_{12} - U_{11} - U_{22}](U_1 - \beta V_L')^2 > 0. \tag{A4}$$

Since all goods are normal, $2U_{12} - U_{11} - U_{22} > 0$. Thus (A4) holds only at point C.

Proof of Proposition 3 Suppose (g^z, τ^z) is any point selected with positive probability by both types. Let

$$R^i(g, \tau) \equiv Z(g, \tau, 1, \varepsilon^i) - Z[g^z, \tau^z, \hat{\rho}(g^z, \tau^z), \varepsilon^i], \quad i = L, H.$$

Select the pair $[\bar{g}, \phi(\bar{g})]$ such that (a) $\phi(\bar{g}) - \bar{g} < \tau^*(\varepsilon^H) - g^*(\varepsilon^H)$, and (b) $R^H[\bar{g}, \phi(\bar{g})] = 0$. Given that $V(0) = -\infty$ and $\pi(1) > \pi(\hat{\rho})$, such a pair exists and is feasible. Note that $\phi(\bar{g}) - \bar{g} < \tau^z - g^z$ since $U[y - \phi(g), g] \geq U(y - \tau^z, g^z)$ if $\phi(g) - g = \tau^z - g^z$. Then since $V'' < 0$, it follows that $R^L[\bar{g}, \phi(\bar{g})] < 0$. Thus by the continuity of R^i, $\exists\ \delta > 0$ such that $R^H[\bar{g} - \delta, \phi(\bar{g} - \delta)] > 0$ and $R^L[\bar{g} - \delta, \phi(\bar{g} - \delta)] < 0$.

The geometric intuition is that there must always exist some point on $\tau = \phi(g)$ sufficiently far southeast of J in Figure 2.2 such that both (24) and (25) hold. (Note in the absence of the q shock, $\pi(1)$ is not necessarily greater than $\pi(\hat{\rho})$, and the intuitive criterion is not generally sufficient to rule out all pooling equilibria).

Proof of Proposition 4 Any solution to (30) satisfies Kuhn-Tucker conditions analogous to (A1)–(A3), plus the additional conditions

$$(\lambda - 1)U_1 + \mu \leq 0 \qquad (=0 \text{ if } \sigma > 0), \tag{A5}$$

$$\sigma \geq 0 \quad (=0 \text{ if } \mu > 0). \tag{A6}$$

Assume in contradiction to the proposition that $\sigma > 0$. Then $\mu = 0$, (A5) must hold with equality and hence $\lambda = 1$. But then (A1) and (A2) require that

$$V'(\tau + \varepsilon^H - g) = V'(\tau + \varepsilon^L - g),$$

which is impossible. Thus $\sigma = 0$ and the solution to (30) is the same as to (23).

Notes

Economics Department, University of California at Berkeley, CA 94720. This research has been supported by the National Science Foundation under grant no. SES-87-20800, and by the Alfred P. Sloan Foundation. Much of the work was conducted while the author was on leave as a National Fellow at the Hoover Institution. I am grateful to Macro Terrones and Maurice Obstfeld for helpful comments on an earlier draft.

1. Important contributions to the modern literature on political business cycles include William D. Norhaus (1975), Assar Lindbeck (1976), and Edward R. Tufte (1978). For a broad survey of the more recent literature on politic and macroeconomic policy, see Alberto Alesina (1988); see also Thomas D. Willet (1989).

2. Kenneth Rogoff and Anne Sibert (1988) show that political budget cycles can be given an equilibrium signaling interpretation. Their model is not sufficiently articulated, however, to address the normative issues raised here.

3. The rationale for political budget cycles here is very different from the one underlying the "partisan" models of Douglas A. Hibbs (1977) and Alesina (1987). In partisan models, two parties with very different preferences over inflation and unemployment compete for office. Consequently, private nominal wage setters have great difficulty predicting postelection monetary policy. For empirical evidence on this approach, see Alesina (1988, 1989), Daniel Cohen (1988) and Steven M. Sheffrin (1988). In principle, it should be possible to generalize the present analysis to incorporate partisan factors.

4. A number of authors have previously addressed normative aspects of political business cycles; see Lindbeck (1976), Henry Chappell and William Keech (1983), Keech and Carl Simon (1985), Alex Cukierman and Allan H. Meltzer (1986), and Willet (1989). None of these analyses, however, are based on fully specified equilibrium models.

5. Tufte (1978, p. 149) also suggests that political business cycles may have socially beneficial aspects. He argues that the government tends to distribute income more equitably prior to elections than at other times.

6. The analysis would be similar in most respects if ε entered the production function multiplicatively, either multiplying $g + k$ or k alone. There would be some differences since a change in ε then has price effects as well as income effects, but the welfare results in Section VI would not be affected.

7. It is tempting to stretch the paradigm here to interpret competency as reflecting the efficacy of a particular political party's general philosophical approach toward managing the government.

8. Implicit in (6) is the assumption that the leader cares just as much about his own "looks" shock as private agents do. The results below would be the same, however, if η did not enter the leader's objective function. Another assumption implicit in (6) is that the leader is not legally allowed to tax himself differently from other individuals; there is no graft.

9. If the incumbent can only run for reelection a finite number of times, then the model predicts that there will be no political budget cycle in the last period. One can also interpret the model along the lines of Rogoff and Sibert (1988), in which electoral competitions match two political parties.

10. The stochastic structure of the model is consistent with Ray C. Fair's (1978) finding that for U.S. presidential elections, voters do not take into account the opposition party's economic performance when last in power; see also Sam Peltzman (1987).

11. The analysis below is quite similar when voters have heterogeneous tastes concerning "looks," except that elections are no longer unanimous.

12. Note that τ is allowed to take on negative values (the government can make net transfers). This assumption is not qualitatively important and the analysis is easily generalized to the case where taxes are constrained to be nonnegative.

13. See Hervé Moulin (1981). The general approach here draws on Paul Milgrom and John Roberts (1986), and Kyle Bagwell and Garey Ramey (1988).

14. The analysis can be generalized to allow for a continuum of types along the lines of Rogoff and Sibert (1988). In their analysis, very competent and very incompetent types distort the least.

15. Formally, a point $(\bar{g}, \bar{\tau})$ is dominated for a type i if $Z[g^*(\varepsilon^l), \tau^*(\varepsilon^l), 0, \varepsilon^i] - Z(\bar{g}, \bar{\tau}, 1, \varepsilon^i) > 0$. Dominated equilibria are ruled out by requiring that $\hat{\rho} = 1$ at points dominated for L but not H. (As a minor technical point. $\mathscr{B} \cap \mathscr{A}$ includes points weakly dominated for L but not dominated for H).

16. Condition (24) states that a type H would prefer to select $(\bar{g}, \bar{\tau})$ over (g^H, τ^H) if, by doing so, he could convince the public of his true type. Condition (25) states that a type L would prefer to select (g^L, τ^L) and elicit voters' equilibrium response $\hat{\rho}(g^L, \tau^L)$, than to choose $(\bar{g}, \bar{\tau})$ even if $\hat{\rho}(\bar{g}, \bar{\tau}) = 1$.

17. Alesina (1987) has analyzed how reputation effects can mitigate partisan political business cycles, and John Ferejohn (1986) has considered how they can provide officeholders with incentives for taking into account the wishes of the electorate; see also Rogoff and Sibert (1988), and Gregory D. Hess (1988).

18. A caveat is that the government's reputation for engaging in political budget cycles may be intertwined with its general reputation for conducting a stable macroeconomic policy; see Rogoff (1989) for a survey of reputational models of macroeconomic policy.

19. For some specifications of $\Psi(g)$ there may not exist any separating equilibrium. Of course, no pure strategy pooling equilibrium can yield higher social welfare than the solution to (26).

20. For an interesting formal development of the case of endogenous elections, see Marco Terrones (1989a) Terrones shows that in the unique undominated equilibrium, the budget distortions accompanying early elections are damped.

21. Two important exceptions are Takatoshi Ito and Jin Hyuk Park (1988), and Terrones (1989b). In their study of Japan, Ito and Park find that the event of an early election does not seem to significantly impact monetary and fiscal policy. Instead, their results suggest that an incumbent government is more likely to call for an early election when recent growth and inflation performance have been strong.

22. Milgrom and Roberts (1986) and Bagwell and Ramey (1988) model advertising by firms in a related fashion. In Bagwell and Ramey's setup, advertising is used in an undominated equilibrium only if it would have a direct positive effect on demand under full information.

23. It may be possible to extend the present model to generate electoral cycles in employment. If taxes distort the labor-leisure decision, then one might expect labor supply to rise during election years when tax rates are low.

24. Bennett T. McCallum (1978), David G. Golden and James Poterba (1980), and Nathaniel Beck (1987), among others, have suggested that there is little empirical evidence of a political business cycle in U.S. inflation and unemployment. Recently, however, Kevin B. Grier (1987), and Stephen E. Haynes and Joe A. Stone (1989) have offered a very different interpretation of the data. They argue that if one does not place arbitrary restrictions on the economy's

dynamic structure, then one finds significant evidence of political business cycles. Haynes and Stone note that their test cannot discriminate between the classical political business cycle theory and the equilibrium political budget cycle theory.

25. Tufte (1978) finds that in the United States, transfers rise significantly prior to presidential elections; see also Alesina (1988) and Eric Ghysels (1988). In their study of U.S. federal taxes for the years 1879–1986. Bizer and Durlouf (1989) conclude that taxes are typically reduced two years prior to successful presidential reelection attempts. Using data from twelve industrialized countries. Alesina (1989) presents evidence that federal government budget deficits tend to rise prior to elections.

References

Alesina, Alberto. 1987. Macroeconomic policy in a two-party system as a repeated game. *Quarterly Journal of Economics* 102:651–678. Reprinted as chapter 3 in the current volume of this work.

Alesina, Alberto. 1988. Macroeconomics and politics. In Stanley Fischer, ed., *NBER Macroeconomics Annual.* Cambridge: MIT Press, 13–61.

Alesina, Alberto. 1989. Politics and business cycles in industrial democracies. *Economic Policy* 8:54–87.

Bagwell, Kyle, and Ramey, Garey. 1988. Advertising and limit pricing. *Rand Journal of Economics* 19:59–71.

Beck, Nathaniel. 1987. Elections and the Fed: Is there a political monetary cycle? *American Journal of Political Science* 31:194–216.

Bizer, David, and Durlauf, Steven. 1989. The behavior of U.S. tax rates: 1879–1986. Manuscript, Stanford University.

Chappell, Henry, and Keech, William. 1983. Welfare consequences of a six-year presidential term evaluated in the context of a model of the U.S. economy. *American Political Science Review* 77:75–91.

Cho, In-Koo, and Kreps, David. 1987. Signaling games and stable equilibria. *Quarterly Journal of Economics* 102:179–221.

Cohen, Daniel. 1988. What caused the rise of conservatism: A French view. *Economic Policy* 6:195–212.

Cukierman, Alex, and Meltzer, Allan. 1986. A positive theory of discretionary policy, the costs of democratic government, and the benefits of a constitution. *Economic Inquiry* 24:367–388.

Fair, Ray C. 1978. The effect of economic events on votes for president. *Review of Economics and Statistics* 60:159–173.

Ferejohn, John. 1986. Incumbent performance and electoral control. *Public Choice* 50:5–25.

Ghysels, Eric. 1988. The political economy of the budget: Some empirical tests. Manuscript, University of Montreal.

Golden, David, and Poterba, James. 1980. The price of popularity: The political business cycle re-examined. *American Journal of Political Science* 24:696–714.

Grier, Kevin. 1987. Presidential elections and Federal Reserve policy: An empirical test. *Southern Economic Journal* 54:475–486.

Haynes, Stephen, and Stone, Joe. 1989. An integrated test for electoral cycles in the U.S. economy. *Review of Economics and Statistics* 71.

Hess, Gregory. 1988. Voting and the issuance of debt in a macro economy. Manuscript, Johns Hopkins University.

Hibbs, Douglas A., Jr. 1977. Political parties and macroeconomic policy. *American Political Science Review* 71:146–187.

Ito, Takatoshi, and Park, Jin Hyuk. 1988. Political business cycles in the parliamentary system. *Economic Letters* 3, 27:233–238.

Keech, William, and Simon, Carl. 1985. Electoral and welfare consequences of political manipulation of the economy. *Journal of Economic Behavior and Organization* 6:177–202.

Lindbeck, Assar. 1976. Stabilization policy in open economies with endogenous politicians. *American Economic Review* 66:1–19.

McCallum, Bennett. 1978. The political business cycle: An empirical test. *Southern Economic Journal* 44:504–515.

Milgrom, Paul, and Roberts, John. 1986. Price and advertising signals of product quality. *Journal of Political Economy* 94:796–821.

Moulin, Hervé. 1981. *Game theory for social sciences.* New York: New York University Press.

Nordhaus, William. 1975. The political business cycle. *Review of Economic Studies* 42:169–190.

Peltzman, Sam. 1987. Economic conditions and gubernatorial elections. *American Economic Review* 77:293–297.

Rogoff, Kenneth. 1989. Reputation, coordination and monetary Policy. In Robert J. Barro, ed., *Handbook of modern business cycle theory.* Cambridge: Harvard University Press.

Rogoff, Kenneth, and Sibert, Anne. 1988. Elections and macroeconomic policy cycles. *Review of Economic Studies* 55:1–16.

Sheffrin, Steven. 1988. Two tests of rational partisan business cycle theory. Manuscript, University of California at Davis.

Terrones, Marco. 1989a. Macroeconomic policy cycles under alternative electoral structures. Manuscript, University of Wisconsin.

Terrones, Marco. 1989b. Economic conditions and the timing of elections. Manuscript, University of Wisconsin.

Tufte, Edward. 1978. *Political control of the economy.* Princeton, NJ: Princeton University Press.

Willet, Thomas, ed. 1989. *Political business cycles: The political economy of money, unemployment and inflation.* Durham, NC: Duke University Press.

3 Macroeconomic Policy in a Two-Party System as a Repeated Game

Alberto Alesina

I Introduction

Two different approaches can be taken in modeling the relationship between the political system and macroeconomic policy. At one extreme it can be assumed, following Downs (1957), that the sole objective of political parties is to remain in office. They do not care about the effects of their policies on the economy except insofar as they influence voters' electoral choices. This assumption produces the result that, for a given voting function and structure of the economy, in a two-party system both parties propose the same platform to the voters and implement the same policies if elected. This result holds even if the parties are uncertain about voters' preferences as long as they share the same information about voters' tastes. The most important macroeconomic application of this approach is probably the "political business cycle" of Nordhaus (1975) and McRae (1977).

The second approach, much less developed in the literature, is to assume that different parties have different preferences concerning the intrinsic properties of their economic policies, for example, because each party represents the interests of a different constituency. In this case, if there is uncertainty about voters' preferences, the two parties propose different platforms even if they share the same information about the distribution of voters' preferences.[1] Thus, different parties are modeled as policymakers with different objective functions. The parties gain access to policymaking via elections with uncertain results.

This chapter adopts the second approach: it is assumed that parties care about the inherent effects of their policies and that parties have different objectives and incentives.[2] Which of the two assumptions about parties' behavior is closer to the truth is an empirical question, the answer to which may vary across countries and time periods. The "political business cycle" approach has received weak support from United States data.[3] On the contrary, a partisan view of macroeconomic policy implying that different parties act differently when in office has received increasing support both for the United States and for other industrialized economies. In

Reprinted from *Quarterly Journal of Economics*, 102 (1987) 651–78, by permission of The MIT Press Journals.

particular, empirical arguments have been made that leftist parties in Europe and the Democratic party in the United States have been relatively more averse to unemployment and less averse to inflation than conservative parties in Europe and the Republican party in the United States.[4]

The existence of two different policymakers that alternate in office raises important questions concerning the credibility and dynamic consistency of policy announcements. This paper analyzes the interaction of two parties with different policy goals and rational forward-looking wage-setters in a game-theoretic model close to that proposed first by Kydland and Prescott (1977) and extended by Barro and Gordon (1983). In that game the private agents (or wage-setters) act first by setting the nominal wage. The policymaker acts second. He has an incentive to announce a policy of low inflation, but then would like to generate unexpected inflation in order to reduce unemployment. Since the wage-setters are rational and informed, they recognize this incentive and set the nominal wage high enough to eliminate any incentive for the policymaker to generate surprise inflation. If binding commitments are unavailable, the result of this game is in general inefficient, even though reputational forces may mitigate the magnitude of the problem, as Barro and Gordon (1983) first pointed out. In equilibrium, employment cannot be affected by the policymaker and inflation is higher than optimal. The model implies complete policy neutrality and an inflationary bias.[5]

The present paper analyzes a similar game in the context of a two-party system. The two parties assign different weights to unemployment and inflation as economic "bads." In particular, the parties differ in two crucial respects: their optimal policies are different, as are their incentives to generate policy surprises. Thus, the two parties want to commit to different policy rules and have different incentives to deviate from their commitments.

The present paper shows that if the two parties are shortsighted, fluctuations in output and inflation connected with the political cycle result in equilibrium. This economic cycle, however, is quite different from the conventional "political business cycle" à la Nordhaus and does not rely on irrational voting behavior, irrational expectations, or misinformation of voters. It is shown that costly economic fluctuations can be avoided if the parties recognize that the adoption of a cooperative common policy rule makes both constituencies better off in the long run. Thus, when a party

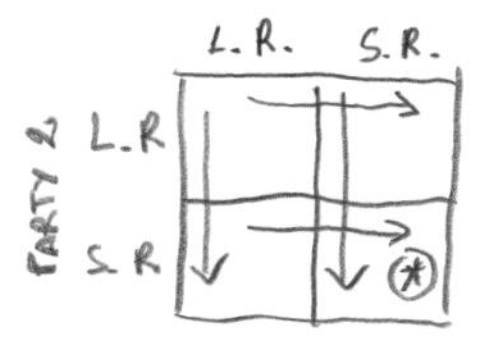

is elected, it faces a choice: it can follow a policy that will maximize short-run benefits for its constituency, or it can follow the cooperative policy that makes both constituencies better off in the long run. If binding commitments are available, the two parties should bind themselves to the cooperative rule. Thus, this paper provides an additional argument in favor of rules rather than discretion.[6]

Even if binding commitments are unavailable, reputational forces arising from the repeated interaction of the two parties can improve upon the discretionary outcome. The first best policy may or may not be sustainable through reputational effects, depending on several characteristics of the economic and political system.

The paper also suggests rather precise empirical implications for the United States; a model based on similar ideas has been successfully tested by Alesina and Sachs (forthcoming).

This paper is organized as follows. Section II presents the model. In Section III the discretionary equilibrium is characterized. In Section IV the efficient frontier of the repeated game is obtained. Sections V and VI address the problem of finding the best subgame perfect policies. Section VII briefly extends the results to multiperiod administrations. The main results of the paper are summarized in the concluding section.

II The Model

The economy is characterized by a standard supply function without capital, expressed for convenience in rate of growth:

$$\dot{y}_t = \gamma(\Pi_t - \dot{w}_t) + \bar{y}; \quad \gamma > 0, \tag{1}$$

where y_t is the rate of growth of output; Π_t is the inflation rate; w_t is the rate of growth of nominal wages; and $\bar{y}$ indicates the rate of growth of output compatible with the natural rate of unemployment and has to be interpreted as the rate of growth prevailing in the absence of policy intervention that changes the real wage.

The private agents may be viewed as uncoordinated wage-setters who set the nominal wage. They attempt to keep the real wage constant at the level compatible with the "natural" rate of growth ($\bar{y}$). Wage contracts last one period and are signed at the end of, say, period $(t-1)$ for period t. These contracts are not contingent on the state of the world; in particular, full indexation is excluded.[7] Therefore, wage-setters set the nominal wage growth equal to expected inflation:

$$w_t = \Pi_t^e = E(\Pi_t | I_{t-1}). \tag{2}$$

The rate of growth of nominal wage is equal to the rational expectation of inflation formed on the basis of the information set available at time $(t-1)$ (i.e., $E(\Pi_t | I_{t-1})$). Thus, the term "expect" can be used interchangeably with the term "set the nominal wage at."

Substituting (2) into (1) yields

$$y_t = \gamma(\Pi_t - \Pi_t^e) + \bar{y}. \tag{3}$$

There are two parties in this economy: party D and party R. They differ in two respects. First, although they agree that inflation above a certain level is a "bad," party D is more sensitive than party R to the cost of unemployment. Therefore, party D has a stronger incentive than party R to generate unexpected inflation to promote growth. The policymakers may judge the rate of unemployment determined by the market to be too high because of distortions in the labor market.[8] Second, apart from considerations about unemployment, the two parties disagree about the level of the optimal inflation rate. Party D believes in higher government spending (for example, to promote welfare programs) and is willing to use money creation as a way of financing it: this implies that the optimal rate of inflation is higher for this party.

The simplest way to characterize the objectives of the two parties is to assume the following cost functions for party D (Z^D) and party R (Z^R):

$$Z^D = \sum_{t=0}^{\infty} q^t z_t^D = \sum_{t=0}^{\infty} q^t \left[\frac{1}{2}(\Pi_t - c)^2 - b' y_t\right],$$

$$c > 0; \quad b' > 0; \quad 0 < q < 1; \tag{4}$$

$$Z^R = \sum_{t=0}^{\infty} q^t z_t^R = \sum_{t=0}^{\infty} q^t \left[\frac{1}{2}\Pi_t^2\right]. \tag{5}$$

In (4) and (5) q is the discount factor, identical for the two parties. In (4) output growth enters linearly and not quadratically. This greatly simplifies the algebra, leaving the results qualitatively unchanged. The positive parameter c represents the optimal inflation rate for party D, regardless of whether or not this inflation is expected. For simplicity and without loss of generality, it is assumed that party R does not attribute any value to unexpected inflation, and that the optimal level of inflation for this party is zero. By substituting (3) into (4), assuming that $\bar{y} = 0$ for simplicity, one gets

$$Z^D = \sum_{t=0}^{\infty} q^t z_t^D = \sum_{t=0}^{\infty} q^t \left[\frac{1}{2} \Pi_t^2 - b(\Pi_t - \Pi_t^3) - c\Pi_t \right], \tag{6}$$

where

$$b \equiv b'\gamma;$$

$$Z^D \equiv {}'Z^D - \tfrac{1}{2} c^2/(1 - q).$$

The cost functions (5) and (6) can also be interpreted as the reduced forms of a different model. Suppose that the economy is characterized not by a Lucas supply function such as (3) but by an exploitable tradeoff between inflation and unemployment so that "expected policy matters." A model with a standard Phillips curve can be reduced to a form identical to (5) and (6) even abstracting from considerations about the inflation tax. The reason is that in such a model the optimal inflation rate for the two parties would be different if they pick different points on the exploitable tradeoff. Consider a simple Phillips curve such as

$$y_t = \Pi_t - \lambda \Pi_t^e, \tag{7}$$

where $0 < \lambda < 1$. Then, even if $c = 0$ in (4), substituting (7) into (4), it follows that

$$Z^D = \sum_{t=0}^{\infty} q^t \left[\frac{1}{2} \Pi_t^2 - b(\Pi_t - \Pi_t^e) - b(1 - \lambda)\Pi_t^e \right]. \tag{8}$$

Equation (8) essentially is equivalent to (6) for the purpose of this paper. The crucial characteristics of the game are in fact the same using either specification: the optimal inflation rates for the two parties are different, and the time-consistent rate of inflation is higher than the optimal rate for party D. The analysis of this paper could also be applied to models with overlapping labor contracts lasting more than one period (Fischer 1977; Taylor 1980) or with sticky prices. These models, however, would be more difficult to analyze in this game-theoretic framework because one would have to consider in period t expectations formed in periods $(t - 1)$, $(t - 2)$, etc.

The model will be solved with (5) and (6), using the first interpretation based on the Lucas supply function (3). It is important to stress that this specification of the model implies complete policy neutrality in a standard one-party system.

It is assumed that the policymaker can control inflation directly. For the purpose of this paper, nothing would be gained by assuming that the party in office can control money creation if the model is then closed by a quantity equation. No distinction is made between the central bank and the government: the assumption is that the party in office has control over monetary policy.[9]

Elections take place at discrete intervals of N periods, with N given exogenously. Elections are held at the beginning of the period. The elected party chooses its policy—the inflation rate—immediately after the election for the same period. The probability distribution of electoral outcomes is taken as exogenous and "common knowledge": party D is elected with probability P; and party R with probability $(1 - P)$. This assumption is adopted for simplicity in order to abstract from issues related to voting. Alesina (1986) shows how this assumption can be relaxed without altering any of the qualitative features of the results presented in this paper as long as voters are rational, forward-looking, and informed about the objectives of the two parties. The crucial assumption is that there is uncertainty about the distribution of voters' preferences. Thus, for given expected policies, the result of the elections is uncertain.

III Discretionary Equilibrium

In a discretionary regime the policymaker minimizes his costs, taking as given the current and future actions of the public and his own future moves. This corresponds to the "one-shot" Nash equilibrium for this game. The timing is as follows. If t is an election year, polls are taken in period $(t - 1)$. They reveal that party D will win with probability P and party R with probability $(1 - P)$. Once the polls are taken, wage contracts are signed for period t. At the beginning of period t, elections are held, and immediately after elections the elected party chooses Π_t.

It is easy to show the following (the superscripts D and R indicate the party):

PROPOSITION 1 The one-shot Nash equilibrium (discretion) is given by

$$\hat{\Pi}_t^D = b + c \quad \forall t;$$

$$\hat{\Pi}_t^R = 0 \quad \forall t;$$

$$w_{t+kN} = \Pi_{t+kN}^e = P(b + c) \quad \text{if } t \text{ is an electoral year; } k\text{: } 0, 1, \ldots;$$

$$w_{t+i+kN} = \Pi_{t+i+kN}^e = b + c \quad i = 1, \ldots, N - 1 \text{ if } D \text{ is elected at time } t + kN;$$

$$w_{t+i+kN} = \Pi_{t+i+kN}^e = 0 \quad i = 1, \ldots, N - 1 \text{ if } R \text{ is elected at time } t + kN.$$

Proof If party D is elected at time t, in every period it solves

$$\min_{\Pi_t} \left[\tfrac{1}{2}\Pi_t^2 - b(\Pi_t - \Pi_t^e) - c\Pi_t\right], \tag{9}$$

taking Π_t^e as given. Solving (9) yields

$$\Pi_t^D = b + c. \tag{10}$$

The analogous problem is solved by party R; the result is $\Pi^R = 0$. If t is an electoral year, the wage-setters set

$$w_t = \Pi_t^e = PE(\Pi_t^D) + (1 - P)E(\Pi_t^R) = P(b + c). \tag{11}$$

In a non-electoral year, wage-setters have perfect foresight, as there are no electoral surprises.

Several empirical implications can be derived from this Proposition.

Q.E.D.

(i) In the first period of a D administration, there is "unexpected inflation" and output growth above the natural level (i.e., zero). In fact, from Proposition 1, using (3), one obtains

$$y_t^D = \gamma(1 - P)(b + c), \quad \text{if } D \text{ is elected at time } t. \tag{12}$$

If party R is elected, there is a recession. In fact, using (3), it follows that

$$y_t^R = -\gamma P(b + c), \quad \text{if } R \text{ is elected at time } t. \tag{13}$$

In the remaining $(N - 1)$ period(s) of both administrations, there cannot be any policy surprises, so output growth is at its natural level.

(ii) The amplitude of these deviations of output growth from zero is positively correlated with the distance between the points of view of the two parties. In fact, the more different are the optimal rates of inflation for the two parties (c and zero) and the more different their incentives to generate policy surprises (b and zero), the bigger are the deviations of output growth from zero (ceteris paribus). Thus, the model implies that the more polarized is the political system, the wider are the economic fluctuations.

(iii) The lower (higher) is P, the higher (lower) is the output growth determined by party D if elected and the smaller (bigger) is the recession determined by party R. In fact, the less expected is the policy implemented by the elected party, the stronger are the real effects of that policy.

(iv) Inflation is always higher during a D administration than during an R administration for two reasons: the optimal inflation rate is higher for party D and this party has a stronger incentive to generate surprises; thus, the time-consistent rate of inflation is higher than the optimal rate for this party.[10]

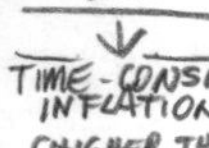

It is worth emphasizing that none of the implications above would change qualitatively had we assumed that $c = 0$; i.e., if we had assumed that the parties have the same optimal policy. For all of the results above to hold, it is necessary and sufficient that the time-consistent policies of the two parties are different. A difference in the time-consistent policies may or may not imply a difference in the optimal policies.

The costs of the discretionary regime as perceived by party D before the elections of time t are, in each period,

$$\hat{z}_t^D = \tfrac{1}{2}P(b^2 - c^2). \tag{14}$$

For party R, the same costs are

$$\hat{z}_t^R = \tfrac{1}{2}P(b + c)^2. \tag{15}$$

The costs for party R are increasing with P, the probability that this party loses the election. The costs for party D are decreasing with P if and only if $b < c$. If b is "too high," the inflationary bias introduced by party D due to its incentive to generate unexpected inflation is so strong that party D itself would prefer to reduce its likelihood of being elected, in order to reduce this inefficiency.

IV The Efficient Frontier

For expositional purposes, let us consider first the case in which $N = 1$; i.e., there are elections every period. In this case every period is exactly alike. The more general case will be discussed in Section VII. The efficient frontier of the game can be found by solving, in each period,

$$\min_{\Pi_t^D, \Pi_t^R} P[\tfrac{1}{2}\Pi_t^{D^2} - b(\Pi_t^D - \Pi_t^e) - c\Pi_t^D] + (1 - P)[\tfrac{1}{2}\Pi_t^{R^2} - b(\Pi_t^R - \Pi_t^e) - c\Pi_t^R] + \theta[P\tfrac{1}{2}\Pi_t^{D^2} + (1 - P)\tfrac{1}{2}\Pi_t^{R^2}]. \tag{16}$$

In (16) θ is the relative weight attributed to party R's cost. Furthermore, we are interested in the portion of the efficient frontier in which both parties are better off than in the one-shot Nash equilibrium. Thus, we want to impose the following constraints of individual rationality:

$$z_t^D \leq \hat{z}_t^D, \tag{17}$$

$$z_t^R \leq \hat{z}_t^R. \tag{18}$$

The solution of this problem yields the following proposition.

PROPOSITION 2 The efficient frontier of the game is given by

$$\Pi_t^D = \Pi_t^R = \Pi_t^e = \frac{c}{1 + \theta} \quad \forall t,$$

where $\theta > 0$ and $\underline{\theta}(P) \leq \theta \leq \bar{\theta}(P)$.

The two bounds of individual rationality ($\underline{\theta}$ and $\bar{\theta}$) can be found by imposing (17) and (18).

The "folk theorem" of repeated games assures that, for q sufficiently close to 1, any individually rational point on the efficient frontier can be sustained as a subgame perfect equilibrium. Therefore, sufficiently farsighted parties can completely avoid macroeconomic fluctuations by choosing a policy intermediate between the two individually most preferred policies. This result is due to the convexity of the cost functions of the two parties: an identical policy rule followed by both parties and thus obtained with certainty, irrespective of the party in office, makes both parties better off than the expected value of the two noncooperative policies weighted by the probability distribution of electoral outcomes.

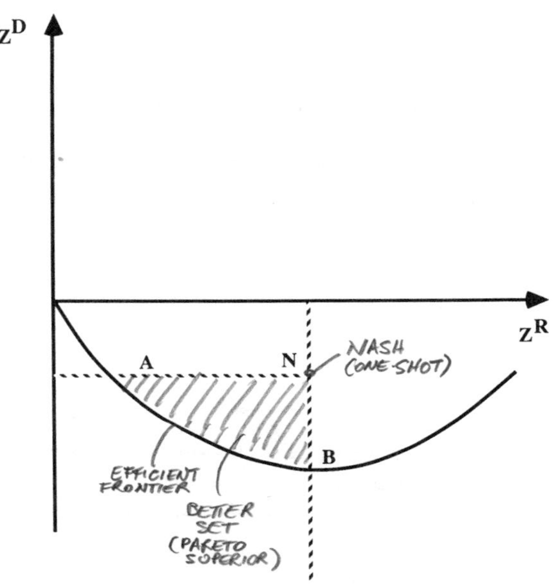

Figure 3.1

By substituting the result of Proposition 2 into the cost functions of the two parties, one obtains the efficient frontier in cost space as

$$z^D = z^R - c\sqrt{2z^R}. \tag{19}$$

This curve is represented in Figure 3.1, where N is the one-shot Nash point and the segment between A and B of the curve is the set of individually rational points on the efficient frontier. Different choices of θ can be identified with different points on the efficient frontier of Figure 3.1. For example, the higher is θ, the closer is the policy chosen to the optimal policy of party R and vice versa.

The choice of θ can be interpreted as a bargaining problem between the two parties. It would be desirable for the resolution of this problem to be related to the relative popularity of the two parties. In other words, the lower is P, the higher should be θ, the relative weight attributed to party R. The Nash bargaining solution has precisely this implication. This solution is based on the assumption that the two parties know that if an agreement is not reached, each party would follow its individually most-preferred policy. These policies characterize the "disagreement point." The following proposition, proved in the Appendix, characterizes this solution.

PROPOSITION 3 If θ^* is the Nash bargaining solution of the game, then the following holds:

(i) θ^* is a function only of P: $\theta^*(P)$;

(ii) $\dfrac{\partial \theta^*}{\partial P} < 0$;

(iii) $\theta^*\left(\frac{1}{2}\right) = 1$;

(iv) $\lim_{P \to 0} \theta^*(P) = \infty; \quad \lim_{P \to 1} \theta^*(P) = 0.$

Thus, even in the case of full cooperation in which both parties adopt the same policy, the chosen policy is dependent upon the popularity level of the two parties. If, for example, P exogenously increases, party D knows that its costs are lower if an agreement is not reached because this party is more likely to be elected at the disagreement point.[11] This increases the bargaining power of party D. As a result, the optimal policy chosen is closer to that party's point of view; i.e., θ is reduced. Therefore, each party benefits from an increase in its own popularity. In fact, it is easy to check that

$$\frac{\partial Z^{D*}}{\partial P} = \frac{\partial Z^{D*}}{\partial \theta}\frac{\partial \theta^*}{\partial P} < 0; \tag{20}$$

and

$$\frac{\partial Z^{R*}}{\partial P} = \frac{\partial Z^{R*}}{\partial \theta}\frac{\partial \theta^*}{\partial P} > 0, \tag{21}$$

where Z^{D*} and Z^{R*} are the costs for the two parties evaluated at the Nash bargaining solution on the efficient frontier. If P tends to either of the extreme values of zero or one, θ^* also tends to its extreme values of zero or infinity, while if the parties are equally likely to be elected, their points of view are weighted equally.

The basic qualitative features of the Nash bargaining solution, namely that the selected point of the efficient frontier is more favorable to the party that is more likely to be elected, would apply also to alternative ways of choosing a point on the efficient frontier. These features derive from the fact that a change in P affects the costs of the two parties at the "disagreement point." Any solution concept used to select a point on the efficient frontier would be sensitive to such a change: in particular, an increase in the welfare of a player at the disagreement point would, ceteris paribus, imply that the selected point on the efficient frontier would be more favorable to that player.[12] In summary, the common sense captured by these results is that the more popular party can impose upon the other an agreement close to its point of view.

V Sustainability of the Efficient Frontier

Not all points on the efficient frontier are sustainable as a subgame perfect equilibrium, i.e., as a time-consistent policy, for any value of P and q unless binding commitments are available. Once elected, each party has an incentive to break the cooperation with the other party and play a policy advantageous to its own constituency in the short run. Suppose that before an election the parties announce that they would follow the optimal cooperative policy; i.e., $\Pi^D - \Pi^R = c/[1 + \theta^*(P)]$. If this announcement is believed by the public, then $\Pi^e = \Pi^D = \Pi^R$. After the election, the victorious party has an incentive to deviate from the announced policy and minimize its short-run costs by playing its one-shot Nash strategy. In particular, party D's incentive arises from two sources: the desire to determine unexpected inflation, therefore "cheating" on the wage-setters' expectations, and the desire to break the implicit agreement with the competing party to cooperate on a "middle policy." Party R faces only the second incentive, since it does not attribute any value to unexpected inflation. Without any form of enforcement, the only possible equilibrium would be the suboptimal one-shot Nash described in Proposition 1. Thus, binding commitment of both parties to the optimal policy would force them to stick to a rule that makes them both better off, even if in the short run both parties would want to follow a different policy more favorable to their own constituencies.

However, even if absolutely binding commitments are unavailable, reputational considerations are taken into account if the players understand that their interaction is repeated over time and thus that today's action influences the actions tomorrow of the other players. The solution concept adopted for the repeated game is that proposed by Friedman (1971): the crucial assumption in this solution concept is that if one player deviates from cooperation, the other players will no longer believe that player's announcements and will play noncooperatively; i.e., they play the "one-shot" Nash strategy.[13] Thus, there is a reversion to the noncooperative outcome if a player cheats. Note that the costs of a deviation from cooperation of, say, party D, arise from two sources: the reversion of party R to the noncooperative policy *and* the reversion of the expectations of the public to the noncooperative equilibrium.

The length of the reversion to the noncooperative outcome, i.e., the "punishment period," is somewhat arbitrary in this type of game. Since the threat of a reversion to Nash is always credible, the "best" equilibrium can be sustained if the length of the punishment period is infinite. This assumption is made here, with no loss of generality. It can be shown easily that the length of the punishment and the value of the discount factor are completely isomorphic. The following result can then be established.

PROPOSITION 4 For any given θ, the conditions that have to be satisfied to make the rules $\Pi^D = \Pi^R = c/(1 + \theta)$ sustainable as a subgame perfect equilibrium are

$$\left(\frac{c}{1+\theta}\right)^2 - \frac{2bc}{1+\theta}(1-q) - \frac{2c^2}{1+\theta} + (b+c)^2(1-q-Pq) + 2Pqc(b+c) \leq 0; \tag{22}$$

$$\left(\frac{c}{1+\theta}\right)^2 - Pq(b+c)^2 \leq 0. \tag{23}$$

Proof Equation (22) is the condition of subgame perfection for party D. It can be obtained as follows. If party D is elected, it faces the temptation (T^D) of playing $\Pi^D = (b + c)$ instead of the cooperative policy $\Pi = c/(1 + \theta)$. Thus,

$$T^D = \frac{1}{2}\left(\frac{c}{1+\theta}\right)^2 - \frac{c^2}{1+\theta} - \frac{1}{2}(b-c)^2 + b\left(b + c - \frac{c}{1+\theta}\right) + c(b+c). \tag{24}$$

If party D plays $(b + c)$, it knows that in the future the one-shot Nash equilibrium will prevail instead of the rule $c/(1 + \theta)$. The enforcement (E^D) is given by the difference between the cost of the Nash equilibrium and the cost of the cooperative rule. Therefore,

$$E^D = \frac{q}{1-q}\left[P\frac{1}{2}(b+c)^2 - Pc(b+c) - \frac{1}{2}\left[\frac{c}{1+\theta}\right]^2 + \frac{c^2}{1+\theta}\right]. \tag{25}$$

Equation (22) follows from a simple manipulation of (24) and (25). Analogous argument applied to party R leads to (23). Note that to obtain these conditions we have considered the private agents acting rationally. They know that if a cheating episode occurred, the outcome of the game would revert to a one-shot Nash forever; therefore, they would expect this outcome forever in the future if they observed a cheating episode. Q.E.D.

Inspection of (22) and (23) confirms that the less the two parties discount the future, the easier it is to sustain the cooperative rule. Furthermore, it is easy to verify that the lower is θ, the more difficult it is to satisfy the sustainability condition for party R, and vice versa. The party whose interests are weighted less would find it less attractive to cooperate because the cooperative rule chosen is farther away from its point of view. Given Proposition 3, one might suspect that it should be easier to sustain full cooperation when P is relatively close to $\frac{1}{2}$. In fact, if P is close to any of its extremes, so is t, and one of the two parties would lose interest in playing cooperatively. Thus, in an unbalanced system in which one party has little chance of ever being elected, cooperation would be harder to sustain because that party has a strong incentive to deviate from cooperation and play its own preferred policy when elected.

In order to quantify these considerations, one would need a closed form for the Nash bargaining solution (θ^*). Lacking this, an approximation can be considered as an example:

$$\theta^* \cong (1-P)/P. \tag{26}$$

It is easy to verify that this expression satisfies all the characteristics described in Proposition 3 for the Nash bargaining solution. This approximation is particularly precise for P close to $\frac{1}{2}$. Furthermore, it can be verified that the qualitative features of the results that follow do not change if different approximations are used. Substituting (26) into (22) and (23) yields the following constraints of subgame perfection:

$$q \geq \frac{Pc^2}{(b+c)^2} \quad \text{(party } R\text{);} \tag{27}$$

$$q \geq \frac{[c(1-P)+b]^2}{b^2(1+P)+(c^2+2bc)(1-P)} \quad \text{(party } D\text{).} \tag{28}$$

These conditions have an intuitive interpretation. Suppose for a moment that $b = 0$. In this case, the game would be symmetric because party D would not face the additional incentive to cheat on private agents' expectations that party R does not have. Conditions (27) and (28) would reduce to

$$q \geq P; \tag{29}$$

$$q \geq 1 - P. \tag{30}$$

In Figure 3.2 the area ABC is the one in which both (29) and (30) are satisfied, and full cooperation is attainable. It is easiest to sustain full cooperation when $P = \frac{1}{2}$; i.e., when two parties are of equal popularity. With $b \neq 0$, the system loses its symmetry because of the additional incentive to deviate from announcements that only party D has. Figure 3.3 shows that because of this additional temptation the area in which full cooperation is sustainable shrinks, and it is easiest to sustain cooperation at $\bar{P} > \frac{1}{2}$. Therefore, in a system in which there is a very weak and a very strong party, there is less incentive for the two parties to cooperate than in a more balanced system. This effect is particularly strong if the weaker party is also the party that benefits more from policy surprises.

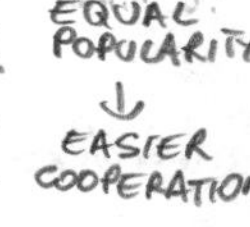

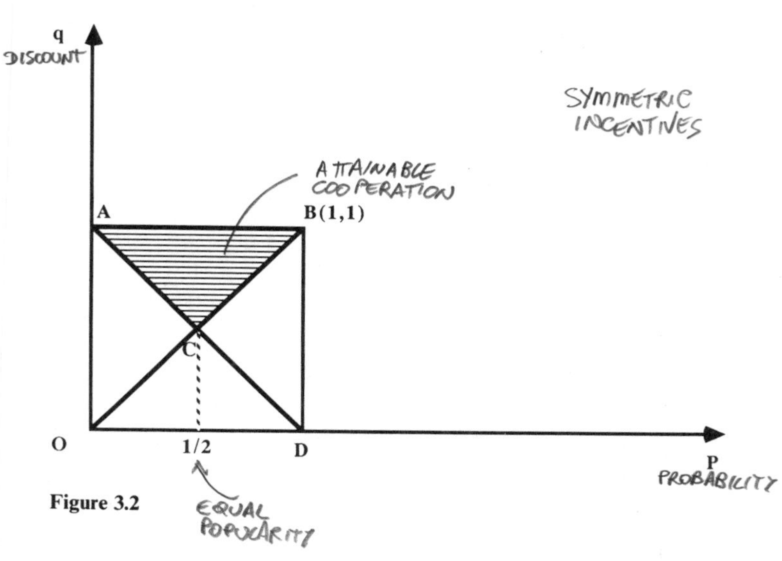

Figure 3.2

VI The Best Credible Policies

Full cooperation may not be sustainable if the parties discount the future heavily. There are several reasons why q may be low. Besides the usual ones, an additional reason stems from the solution concept used for this game and the length of the punishment period chosen. For example, one party may assign a positive probability to the event that the leadership of the opponent party may change in the future and that the new leadership will not carry out the threats of the old. This could be modeled by assigning a positive probability to a finite length of the period in which the system reverts to the one-shot Nash if a cheating episode occurs; in this game this is qualitatively equivalent to assuming a low discount factor.

Let us continue to assume that the parties use the Nash solution to solve the bargaining problem (i.e., to choose θ). The best credible rules can be found by solving problem (16) under the two subgame perfection constraints. These two constraints assure that the policies followed by the two parties are credible, i.e., time-consistent. They can be obtained by imposing that any pair of policies (Π^D, Π^R) has to satisfy the condition that the temptation to deviate from them is not greater than the enforcement associated with this deviation. These constraints can be written following the same steps used in the proof of Proposition 4. The following result characterizes this solution.

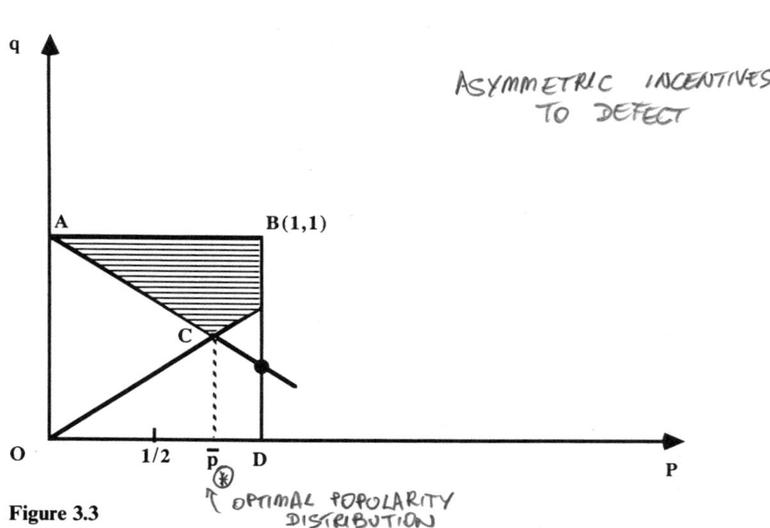

Figure 3.3

PROPOSITION 5 If the Nash bargaining solution on the efficient frontier, $\Pi^D = \Pi^R = \Pi^e = c/[1 + \theta^*(P)]$, cannot be credibly announced by the two parties, then if $q > 0$, the best credible policies $(\overline{\Pi}^D, \overline{\Pi}^R)$ satisfy the following condition:

$$b + c > \overline{\Pi}^D(q, P, b, c) > c/(1 + \theta^*(P)) > \overline{\Pi}^R(q, P, b, c) > 0.$$

If and only if $q = 0$, the best credible policies are

$$\overline{\Pi}^D = b + c; \quad \overline{\Pi}^R = 0.$$

The proof is in the Appendix. In the Appendix it is also shown that under very general conditions the following holds:

$$\frac{\partial \overline{\Pi}^D}{\partial q} > 0, \frac{\partial \overline{\Pi}^R}{\partial q} < 0 \quad \text{for any value of } q. \tag{31}$$

Furthermore, there exists a $\bar{q}$ such that, for $q < \bar{q}$, (31) always holds.

Proposition 5 highlights that if q is low, the parties do not care about the future very much, and they follow policies that tend to minimize their short-run costs. Their announcements become less credible both to the opponent party and the private agents. As a result, the parties' policies tend to diverge toward their respective one-shot Nash policies.

Thus, if full cooperation is not sustainable, the economy exhibits output and inflation fluctuations. In fact, if party D is elected at time t, it follows that

$$y_t = \gamma(1 - P)(\overline{\Pi}^D - \overline{\Pi}^R), \tag{32}$$

and if party R is elected,

$$y_t = -\gamma P(\overline{\Pi}^D - \overline{\Pi}^R).$$

Since $\overline{\Pi}^D > \overline{\Pi}^R$, there is a recession with low inflation with an R administration, and an expansion above the natural rate with a D administration. Furthermore, the variances of output and of inflation are decreasing functions of the discount factor and increasing functions of b and c, i.e., the distance between the two parties' points of view.

In this type of game there is no assurance that the players would indeed pick the "best" of the infinitely many subgame perfect Nash equilibria of the game. The multiplicity of equilibria in this type of game is a well-documented disturbing fact: Rogoff (1987) investigates this issue in the context of monetary policy games. However, the proof of Proposition 5 highlights that if the policies $\Pi^D = \Pi^R = c/(1 + \theta)$ are not sustainable, *all* the subgame perfect equilibria satisfy the condition that $\Pi^D > \Pi^R$. Thus, the positive implications of the paper for the business cycle do not require that the parties pick the best credible policies but only that they pick *any* credible policy when the first best is not sustainable.

VII Extensions

The extension to the case of multiperiod administrations is conceptually quite simple. The one-shot Nash equilibrium for this case has been already characterized in Proposition 1. It is easy to verify that the efficient frontier is the same for a multiperiod administration; i.e., $\Pi^D = \Pi^R = c/(1 + \theta)$ in each period. However, the conditions of sustainability of the efficient frontier as a perfect equilibrium are not the same in different periods of an administration. Consider, for example, party R. Even though its temptation to cheat is the same in every period, the enforcement is a function of the distance in time from the following elections. During the jth year of an R administration, the enforcement (E_j^R) is, in fact,

$$E_j^R = [q^{(N+1-j)}/(1 - q)](\hat{z}^R - z^{R*}). \tag{34}$$

Clearly, the farther away in time is the next election, the farther in the future is the beginning of the "punishment" if a deviation from announcements occurs; therefore, the lower is the enforcement. The same considerations would apply to party D. The only difference for party D is that part of the "punishment" would occur immediately after a cheating episode due to the reversion of expectations of the private agents to the Nash outcome. However, the "punishment" coming from party R's reversion to the one-shot Nash would not occur until the following election. Both parties have then a stronger incentive to deviate from announcements of cooperative agreements at the beginning of the terms of office; thus following Proposition 5, it can be argued that the farther in the future are the following elections the more different are the policies of the two parties. Note, however, that policy surprises creating deviations of output growth from its natural level can occur only in the first period of an administration.

Thus far we have emphasized the strategic interaction of the two parties. This paper can incorporate as a particular case the reputational mechanism involving only the public's expectations, as in Barro and Gordon (1983). Consider, for example, the case in which party R always sets $\Pi^R = 0$ because, for example, it completely discounts the future and cares only about the inflation rate when in office. In this situation party D would not necessarily follow the policy $\Pi^D = b + c$, i.e., the one-shot Nash policy. By engaging in a reputational game with the public, party D can sustain a policy $\tilde{\Pi}^D$ that satisfies the following:

$$c \leq \tilde{\Pi}^D < b + c. \tag{35}$$

Needless to say, party D would never find it in its interest to follow a policy $\Pi^D < c$, since c is the optimal inflation rate for this party and party R is not willing to cooperate to an intermediate policy. A policy such as $\tilde{\Pi}^D$ in (35) could be enforced by means of trigger strategies involving the public's expectations. If party D announces $\tilde{\Pi}^D$ and then deviates, following $\Pi^D = b + c$, the public would expect this party to follow $b + c$ in the future. Thus, some algebra establishes that the enforcement associated with a deviation from the rule $\tilde{\Pi}^D$ in the Jth period of an N period's administration is

$$E^D = \frac{q(1 - q^{N-J})}{1 - q}\left[\frac{1}{2}b^2 - \frac{1}{2}(\tilde{\Pi} - c)^2\right] + \frac{Pq^{N+1-J}}{1 - q}\left[\frac{1}{2}b^2 - \frac{1}{2}(\tilde{\Pi} - c)^2\right]. \tag{36}$$

The first term in (36) represents the costs of the reversion of expectation to $b + c$ during the remaining $(N - J)$ period(s) of the current administration. The second term represents the effect of the reversion of expectations after the end of the current term of office. Using (36), it is easy to verify that the best credible policy for party D satisfies (35). If q is sufficiently close to 1, the policy $\Pi^D = c$ is credible.[14]

VIII Conclusions

This chapter characterizes an economic cycle connected to the political cycle. The predictions of the model are quite different from those of the political business cycle literature which implies that one should observe recessions at the beginning of any type of administration and inflationary expansions toward the end. The prediction of this paper is that in the United States one should instead observe recessions at the beginning of Republican administrations, as compared with output growth above trend and higher inflation at the beginning of Democratic administrations. In the second part of both types of administrations, output growth should be about the same, with higher inflation during a Democratic administration. Alesina and Sachs (forthcoming) find that these empirical implications are not rejected by United States post–World War II data.

The results presented in this chapter do not rely on irrational expectations formation or irrational voting behavior. Although voting is exogenous in this chapter, Alesina (1986) shows that all the results of the present paper can be generalized in a model with rational and perfectly informed voters. The assumption adopted about voting has emphasized the contrast between this chapter and the traditional "political business cycle" literature; Rogoff and Sibert (1985) have shown that a cycle on inflation similar to that of Nordhaus (1975) can be generated in a model with rational but imperfectly informed voters. It should be stressed that the present chapter and the work of Rogoff and Sibert are in many respects complementary, and in principle future research could develop both insights into a unified framework.

The equilibrium with cycles in this model has been shown to be suboptimal. If the parties agree to follow an identical policy, the cycle is avoided. There would be no fluctuations in output and inflation, and both constituencies would be better off. This policy has been characterized formally as the result of a bargaining process between the two parties, in which the more popular party can impose an agreement closer to its point of view. A commitment to the cooperative rule is beneficial because it binds the two parties to a policy that improves welfare for both of them in the long run. Even if binding commitments are not available, reputational forces due to the repeated interaction of the two parties and the public can improve upon the discretionary equilibrium by reducing the magnitude of the fluctuations of inflation and output.

The central ideas of this chapter are quite general and go well beyond the specific example on inflation and output. This chapter has shown how the repeated interaction of political parties may reduce the excess volatility of policies. The reduction of volatility is particularly beneficial in all the cases in which frequent and drastic switches of policies associated with changes in administrations are costly.[15] In all these cases reputational mechanisms such as those described in this chapter create an incentive for the two parties to converge to more similar policies and create less disruption when a change in administration occurs.

Appendix

1. Proof of Proposition 3 The Nash bargaining solution on the efficient frontier is found by solving the following problem (time subscripts are dropped for convenience):

$$\min_{z^D, z^R} (z^D - A^D)(z^R - A^R) \tag{A.1}$$

such that

$$z^D \leq z^R - c\sqrt{2z^R}, \tag{A.2}$$

$$z^D - A^D \leq 0, \tag{A.3}$$

$$z^R - A^R \leq 0. \tag{A.4}$$

where (A^D, A^R) is the disagreement point, i.e., the costs for the two parties if the agreement is not reached. If an agreement is not reached, the two parties would follow their individual most-preferred policies. Therefore, party D would choose $\Pi^D = c$, and party R $\Pi^R = 0$. It follows that

$$A^D = -\tfrac{1}{2}Pc^2; \tag{A.5}$$

$$A^R = \tfrac{1}{2}Pc^2. \tag{A.6}$$

Alternatively, one might choose as the disagreement point the "one-shot" Nash (i.e., $\Pi^D = b + c$, $\Pi^R = 0$). The results would not qualitatively change. Furthermore, it is more reasonable to assume that party D would follow its most preferred policy if an agreement is not reached, rather than a suboptimal policy. (The policy $\Pi^D = c$ is sustainable for party D, if $\Pi^R = 0$, as shown in Section VII if q is sufficiently close to one.) Let us redefine for convenience

$$y \equiv -(z^D - A^D) = -[z^D + \tfrac{1}{2}Pc^2]; \tag{A.7}$$

$$x \equiv -(z^R - A^R) = -[z^R - \tfrac{1}{2}Pc^2]. \tag{A.8}$$

The problem then can be rewritten as follows:

$$\max_{x,y} \Phi = xy, \tag{A.9}$$

such that

$$y = x - Pc^2 + c\sqrt{Pc^2 - 2x}, \tag{A.10}$$

$$y \geq 0, \tag{A.11}$$

$$x \geq 0. \tag{A.12}$$

Equation (A.10) has been rewritten as an equality because the solution must lie on the frontier. Substituting (A.10) into (A.9), the first-order condition of the problem implies that an interior solution satisfies the following:

$$\frac{\partial \Phi}{\partial x} = 2x - Pc^2 + c\sqrt{Pc^2 - 2x} - \frac{cx}{\sqrt{Pc^2 - 2x}} = 0. \tag{A.13}$$

On the frontier the costs for party D in each period are

$$z^D = \frac{1}{2}\frac{c^2}{(1+\theta)^2} - \frac{c^2}{1+\theta}. \tag{A.14}$$

Using (A.5), (A.13), and (A.14), we obtain

$$(Pc^2 - 2x) = c/(1+\theta)^2. \tag{A.15}$$

Substituting into (A.10) and rearranging yields

$$P = (3\theta + 1)/(1+\theta)^3. \tag{A.16}$$

From (A. 16) it is easy to verify that $\theta^*(P)$ is a decreasing function of P for $\theta > 0$. Suppose that $P = 0$. (A.8) and (A.12) imply that

$$c^2/(1+\theta)^2 \leq 0. \tag{A.17}$$

(A.17) can be satisfied only for $\theta \to \infty$. Suppose that $P = 1$. (A.7) and (A.11) imply that

$$\frac{1}{2}\frac{c^2}{(1+\theta)^2} - \frac{c^2}{1+\theta} + \frac{1}{2}c^2 \leq 0. \tag{A.18}$$

(A.18) is satisfied if and only if $\theta = 0$. Finally, it is easy to check that if $P = \frac{1}{2}$ then $\theta^* = 1$, using (A.16). Q.E.D.

2. Proof of Proposition 5 After some algebra, it can be shown that the problem to be solved is the following:

$$\min_{\Pi^D,\Pi^R} \left[P\left[\Pi^D - \frac{c}{1+\theta}\right]^2 + (1-P)\left[\Pi^R - \frac{c}{1+\theta}\right]^2 - \frac{c^2}{(1+\theta)^2}\right], \tag{A.19}$$

such that

$$\Pi^{R^2} + \frac{Pq}{1-q}\Pi^{D^2} - \frac{Pq}{1-Pq}(b+c)^2 \leq 0; \tag{A.20}$$

$$\begin{aligned}(1-q+Pq)&\left(\Pi^D - \frac{(b+c)(1-q)+qPc}{1-q+qP}\right)^2 \\ &+ q(1-P)(\Pi^R - c)^2 - \frac{[(b+c)(1-q)+qPc]^2}{1-q+Pq} \\ &+ (b+c)[(b+c)(1-q-qP)+2Pqc] - q(1-P)c^2 \leq 0.\end{aligned} \tag{A.21}$$

The conditions of individual rationality have also to be satisfied at the solution. The constraint of subgame perfection for party R (A.20) is an ellipse centered on the origin (see Figure 3.4). The intersections with the axes are

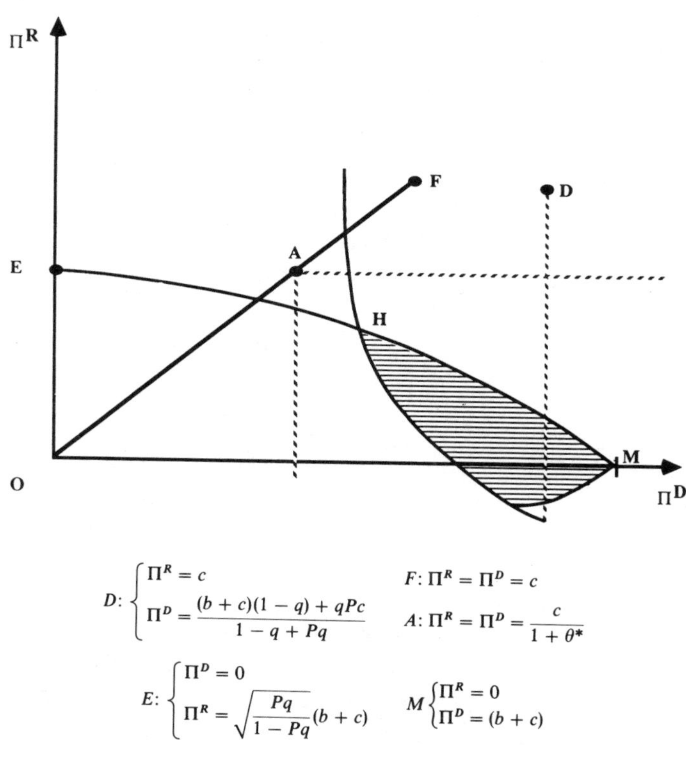

Figure 3.4

$$\Pi^D = \pm(b + c), \tag{A.22}$$

$$\Pi^R = \pm\frac{\sqrt{Pq}}{1 - Pq}(b + c). \tag{A.23}$$

The constraint for party D (A.22) is an ellipse centered at

$$\left[\begin{array}{l} \Pi^R = c, \\ \\ \Pi^D = \dfrac{(b + c)(-q) + qPc}{1 - q + qP}. \end{array}\right. \tag{A.24}$$

Note that

$$c < \frac{(b + c)(1 - q) + qPc}{1 - q + qP} < b + c. \tag{A.25}$$

Suppose that the Nash bargaining solution on the efficient frontier lies outside both feasible sets (point A in Figure 3.4). The solution of the problem is in the dashed area. By construction this proves that, at the solution,

$$\Pi^D > c/(1 + \theta^*) > \Pi^R. \tag{A.26}$$

From (A.19) it follows that a pair of policies $(\tilde{\Pi}^R, \tilde{\Pi}^D)$ with $\tilde{\Pi}^R < 0$ is clearly inferior to the pair $(0, \tilde{\Pi}^D)$ for $\theta > 0$. By construction, if the former pair is sustainable, so is the latter. By construction, a pair of policies $(\tilde{\Pi}^R, \tilde{\Pi}^D)$ with $\tilde{\Pi}^D > b + c$ is not sustainable for party R. Therefore, the first part of the proposition follows. Suppose that $q = 0$. Then the two constraints of subgame perfection, (A.21) and (A.22), become

$$\Pi^{R^2} \leq 0, \tag{A.27}$$

$$[\Pi^D - (b + c)]^2 \leq 0. \tag{A.28}$$

From (A.27) and (A.28) it follows that if $q = 0$, the only subgame perfect equilibrium is the one-shot Nash. It is easy to verify that, as long as $q > 0$, a dashed area such as that of Figure 3.1A exists, and some cooperation is sustainable, i.e., $\Pi^D < b + c$ and $\Pi^R > 0$ at the solution.

Let us now consider a fall in q. The two feasible sets shrink. In fact, any combination of strategies sustainable at a lower q has to be sustainable at a higher q. It is easy to verify algebraically that this is in fact the case. Graphically the shift is described in Figure 3.5, where the two feasible sets at the lower value of q are represented with dashed lines. From (A.24) it follows that the center of party D's ellipses moves to the right along the

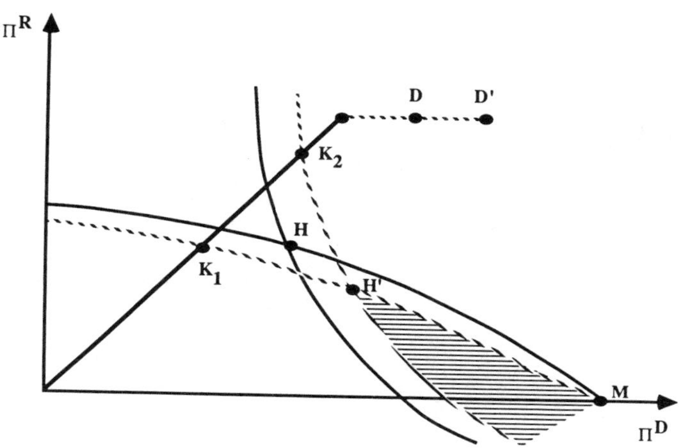

Figure 3.5

horizontal line $\Pi^R = c$, when q falls. Note that if a change in q does not change the value of θ^* at the solution, the following holds (at the solution):

$$\frac{\partial \Pi^D}{\partial q} > 0, \quad \frac{\partial \Pi^R}{\partial q} < 0. \tag{A.29}$$

Conditions (A.29) hold in general if the change in θ at the solution associated with a change in q is not too big. Furthermore, as long as the chosen θ is such that $c/(1 + \theta)$ lies between K_1 and K_2 in Figure 3.5, (A.29) holds. In fact, in this case the solution shifts from H to H^1, thus satisfying (A.29). Thus, by construction, it follows immediately that there exists a value of q, say $\bar{q}$, such that, for $q \leq \bar{q}$, (A.29) always hold. Q.E.D.

Notes

This paper is based on one chapter of my Ph.D. dissertation at Harvard University (May 1986). I am greatly indebted to Jeffrey Sachs for having directed my attention toward these issues and for many helpful conversations and suggestions. I also benefited from conversations with Andrew Abel, Dilip Abreu, Olivier Blanchard, Ramon Caminal, Andrew Caplin, Morris Fiorina, Benjamin Friedman, Herschel Grossman, Maria Herrero, Howard Rosenthal, and Susan Vitka. The comments of a referee greatly improved the paper. Ente "Luigi Einaudi" provided generous financial support. The views expressed in the paper are mine, as is the responsibility for any mistakes.

1. This result is proved in a context similar to that of this paper by Alesina (1986), who extends earlier results by Calvert (1985) and Wittman (1977, 1983).

2. Blanchard (1985) has followed the same approach. In a somewhat different setting, a similar approach is adopted by Minford and Peel (1982).

3. Nordhaus (1975) presents empirical evidence for the United States favorable to his approach. Subsequent papers, for example, McCallum (1978), Golden and Poterba (1980), and several others, have rejected the "political business cycle" theory for the United States.

4. Hibbs (1977) was the first to point out this empirical regularity and recently reinforces his point (forthcoming). Similar findings have been presented by Beck (1982, 1984), Havrilesky (forthcoming), Tabellini and La Via (1986), and Alesina and Sachs (forthcoming). Poole and Rosenthal (1986) have shown that in general there is polarization in American politics concerning economic policy.

5. A rapidly growing body of research has explored in depth this model. Excellent surveys of this literature are Cukierman (1986), Fischer (1986), and Rogoff (1987).

6. The issue of stabilization policy in the presence of unforeseen shocks is not considered in this chapter. Rogoff (1985) explores the relationship between the benefits of binding commitments to policy rules and the need of flexibility for stabilization purposes.

7. None of the qualitative results of this chapter would change if partial indexation were allowed.

8. These distortions may be due to taxes as emphasized, for example, by Barro and Gordon (1983), or monopolistic unions that keep the real wage "too high" to maximize the welfare of union members as emphasized, for example, by Tabellini (1985), and Driffill (1985). Alesina and Tabellini (forthcoming) discuss the connection between these two distortions.

9. The Federal Reserve is certainly not completely independent from the Administration. Havrilesky (1986) has recently stressed this point and surveyed some of the literature on the subject. Weintraub (1978) also raises serious doubts about the independence of the Fed.

10. The rate or inflation generated by party D is constant for the entire term in office. This is due to the fact that output enters linearly in the objective function of this party. Had we assumed a quadratic objective function in output, the inflation in the first period of a D administration would be lower than the inflation in the remaining $(N - 1)$ period(s). More details on this case can be found in Alesina (1985).

11. Alesina (1986) shows that in a model in which the probability of electoral outcome is endogenous, "popularity" of a party has to be interpreted in this context as the likelihood of electing this party, if the noncooperative policies are followed.

12. This would be the case if, for example, the solution proposed by Kalai and Smorodinsky (1975) or an asymmetric Nash-bargaining solution were chosen.

13. Abreu (1983) has shown that harsher punishments than the reversion to the one-shot Nash can be credibly threatened. Rogoff (1987) has applied these more complex strategies to a monetary policy game. Here we restrict our attention to the reversion to the one-shot Nash.

14. It is easy to verify that for $P = 1$, i.e., the case of a single party, (36) is equivalent to the Enforcement of Barro and Gordon (1983); the only difference is that Barro and Gordon consider a punishment of one period, while here the punishment period is infinite. The interaction of the punishment coming from the public and from the opponent party is also explored in a different context by Rogoff and Sibert (1986).

15. A referee has suggested the following example. Suppose that the government has complete freedom of firing civil service employees. Every time the incumbent loses the election, the winner may want to fire everybody and appoint different people. This may create a suboptimally high level of turnover. The repeated interaction of the two parties may lead to an equilibrium in which highly competent party D–affiliated employees are kept in office when party R wins and vice versa.

References

Abreu, Dilip. 1983. Infinitely repeated game with discounting: A general theory and application to oligopoly. Ph.D. thesis, Princeton University.

Alesina, Alberto. 1985. Rules, discretion and reputation in a two-party system. Mimeo.

Alesina, Alberto. 1986. Credibility and policy convergence in a two-party system with rational voters. Mimeo.

Alesina, Alberto, and Sachs, Jeffrey. Forthcoming. Political parties and the business cycle in the United States, 1948–1984. *Journal of Money, Credit and Banking.*

Alesina, Alberto, and Tabellini, Guido. Forthcoming. Rules and discretion with non-coordinated monetary and fiscal policy. *Economic Inquiry.*

Barro, Robert, and Gordon, David. 1983. Rules, discretion and reputation in a model of monetary policy. *Journal of Monetary Economics* 12:101–122. Reprinted as chapter 4 in volume 1 of this work.

Beck, Nathaniel. 1982. Parties, administrations and American macroeconomic outcomes. *American Political Science Review* 26:83–93.

Beck, Nathaniel. 1984. Domestic political sources of American monetary policy: 1955–82. *Journal of Politics* 46:786–815.

Blanchard, Olivier. 1985. Credibility, disinflation and gradualism. *Economics Letters* 17:211–217.

Calvert, Randall. 1985. Robustness of the multidimensional voting model: Candidate motivations, uncertainty and convergence. *American Journal of Political Science* 29:69–95.

Cukierman, Alex. 1986. Central bank behavior and credibility: Some recent theoretical developments. *Federal Reserve Bank of St. Louis Review* 48:5–17.

Downs, Anthony. 1957. *An economic theory of democracy.* New York: Harper.

Driffill, John. 1985. Macroeconomic stabilization policy and trade union behavior as a repeated game. Seminar paper no. 301, Institute for International Economic Studies, Stockholm.

Fischer, Stanley. 1977. Long term contracts, rational expectations and the optimal money supply rule. *Journal of Political Economy* 85:191–206.

Fischer, Stanley. 1986. Time consistent monetary and fiscal policies: A survey. Mimeo.

Friedman, James. 1971. A non-cooperative equilibrium for supergames. *Review of Economic Studies* 38:1–12.

Golden, David, and Poterba, James. 1980. The price of popularity: The political business cycle reexamined. *American Journal of Political Science* 24:696–714.

Havrilesky, Thomas. 1986. Monetary policy signaling from the administration to the Federal Reserve. Mimeo.

Havrilesky, Thomas. Forthcoming. A partisan theory of fiscal and monetary regimes. *Journal of Money, Credit and Banking.*

Hibbs, Douglas. 1977. Political parties and macroeconomic policy. *American Political Science Review* 71:1467–1487.

Hibbs, Douglas. Forthcoming. *The American political economy: Electoral policy and macroeconomics in contemporary America.* Cambridge: Harvard University Press.

Kalai, Ehud, and Smorodinsky, Meir. 1975. Other solutions to Nash's bargaining problem. *Econometrica* 43:513–518.

Kydland, Finn, and Prescott, Edward. 1977. Rules rather than discretion: The inconsistency of optimal plans. *Journal of Political Economy* 85:473–491. Reprinted as chapter 1 in volume 1 of this work.

McCallum, Bennett. 1978. The political business cycle: An empirical test. *Southern Economic Journal* 44:504–515.

McRae, Duncan. 1977. A political model of the business cycle. *Journal of Political Economy* 85:239–264.

Minford, Patrick, and Peel, David. 1982. Political theory of the business cycle. *European Economic Review* 17:253–270.

Nordhaus, William. 1975. The political business cycle. *Review of Economic Studies* 42:169–190.

Poole, Keith, and Rosenthal, Howard. 1986. The dynamics of interest groups: evaluation of congress. GSIA, Carnegie Mellon University working paper no. 3-86-87.

Rogoff, Kenneth. 1985. The optimal degree of commitment to an intermediate monetary target. *Quarterly Journal of Economics* 100:1169–1190. Reprinted as chapter 9 in volume 1 of this work.

Rogoff, Kenneth. 1987. Reputational constraint on monetary policy. Carnegie-Rochester Conference Series on Public Policy, vol. 26, pp. 141–181.

Rogoff, Kenneth, and Sibert, Anne. 1986. Equilibrium political business cycles. National Bureau of Economic Research, working paper no. 1838.

Tabellini, Guido. 1985. Centralized wage setting and monetary policy in a reputational equilibrium. UCLA working paper no. 369.

Tabellini, Guido, and La Via, Vincenzo. 1986. Money, deficit and public debt: An empirical investigation. Mimeo.

Taylor, John. 1980. Aggregate dynamics and staggered contracts. *Journal of Political Economy* 87:1–23.

Weintraub, Robert. 1978. Congressional supervision of monetary policy. *Journal of Monetary Economics* 4:341–362.

Wittman, Donald. 1977. Candidates with policy preferences: A dynamic model. *Journal of Economic Theory* 14:180–189.

Wittman, Donald. 1983. Candidate motivation: A synthesis of alternatives. *American Political Science Review* 76:142–157.

4 Political Cycles in OECD Economies

Alberto Alesina and Nouriel Roubini

1 Introduction

Different models of political cycles emphasize either the "opportunistic" or the "partisan" incentives of policymakers. In "opportunistic" models, the policymakers maximize their popularity or their probability of re-election. In "partisan" models different political parties represent the interests of different constituencies and, when in office, follow policies which are favourable to their supporting groups; specifically, the left-wing parties are more concerned with the problem of unemployment, while the right-wing parties are relatively more willing to bear the costs of unemployment to reduce inflation.

This literature has developed in two clearly distinct phases. The first one, in the mid-seventies, is due to the influential work by Nordhaus (1975), and Lindbeck (1976) on "opportunistic" cycles and by Hibbs (1977) on "partisan" cycles. These papers share a "pre-rational expectaions" model of the economy and are based upon an exploitable "Phillips curve." The "political business cycle" model of Nordhaus predicts pre-electoral high growth and low unemployment, increasing inflation around the election time and a post-electoral recession, regardless of the political orientation of the incumbent government. Hibbs' "partisan" model implies systematic and permanent differences in the inflation/unemployment combination chosen by different political parties.

Macroeconomists soon lost interest in this subject, because at that time the profession was developing (or fighting against) the "rational expectations revolution."[1]

The second phase took off in the mid-eighties as a branch of the game-theoretic approach to the positive theory of policy. Cukierman and Meltzer (1986), Rogoff and Sibert (1988), Rogoff (1990), and Persson and Tabellini (1990) propose rational "opportunistic" models; Alesina (1987) develops a rational partisan approach. These models depart from their predecessors in two important dimensions. First, the assumption of economic agents' rationality makes real economic activity less directly and

Reprinted from *Review of Economic Studies*, 59 (1990) 663–688, by permission of Review of Economic Studies Limited.

predictably influenced by monetary policy. Second, voters' rationality implies that they cannot be systematically "fooled" in equilibrium.

This second generation of models has empirical implications which are quite different from those of the earlier literature: the assumption of rationality reduces the extent and the likelihood of regular political cycles, although it does not eliminate them. For example, in models with rational economic agents and voters, Nordhaus' type cycles are mitigated. Rather than regular multi-year cycles on output and unemployment, one should observe, according for instance to Rogoff and Sibert (1988), short-lived electoral cycles on monetary and fiscal policy instruments, but not necessarily on the level of economic activity. Alesina (1987, 1988b) shows that in a partisan model with nominal wage contracts and rational voters, permanently different inflation rates across parties may result only in temporary, post-election differences in growth and unemployment.

This chapter addresses two questions. First, whether or not the dynamic behaviour of GNP growth, unemployment, and inflation is systematically affected by the timing of elections and of changes of governments. Second, whether or not the second generation of rational models has provided useful insights to interpret the evidence. The paper suggests an affirmative answer to both these questions by examining 18 OECD democracies, in the last three decades.

More specifically our results can be summarized as follows: (a) The "political business cycle" hypothesis, as formulated in Nordhaus on growth and unemployment, is generally rejected by the data. (Some favourable evidence can be found in only two countries); (b) inflation tends to increase immediately after elections, perhaps as a result of pre-electoral expansionary monetary and fiscal policies; this result yields support to the Rogoff and Sibert (1988) and Rogoff (1990) model of "political budget cycles"; (c) we find evidence of temporary partisan differences in output and unemployment and of long-run partisan differences in the inflation rate as implied by the "rational partisan theory" of Alesina (1987). This pattern appears rather unambiguously in countries with a pure two-party system, or with clearly identifiable "right" and "left" coalitions; (d) we find virtually no evidence of permanent partisan differences in output and unemployment. Indirectly, results (c) and (d) yield support to the positive model of inflation developed by Kydland and Prescott (1977) and Barro and Gordon (1983a, 1983b).

The qualitative features of these results are consistent with the finding on the United States by Alesina and Sachs (1988), Alesina (1988a), and Chappell and Keech (1988). The advantage of a multi-country study is that, of course, one has many more degrees of freedom. Elections and changes of governments are relatively infrequent events. Thus, the researcher is left with very few observations and only one country is considered. This is why systematic multi-country studies are particularly useful in this area.

The chapter is organized as follows. In the next section we highlight the empirical implications of several models of political cycles. Since several comprehensive reviews of the literature have recently appeared (Alesina 1988a, Nordhaus 1989, Persson and Tabellini 1990) we sketch the various models very succinctly. In Section 3 we present regressions on a panel data set of all the countries in the sample. Section 4 briefly discusses the results of country-by-country regressions. Section 5 employs Hamilton's (1989) method of timing recessions and expansions. The last section concludes.

2 Models of Politico-Economic Cycles

2.1 The "Political Business Cycle" (Nordhaus 1975)

The assumptions underlying Nordhaus' "political business cycle" (henceforth PBC) can be characterized as follows:

A.1. The economy is described by a Phillips curve:

$$u_t = \bar{u} + \alpha u_{t-1} + \gamma(\pi_t - \pi_t^e) + \varepsilon_t; \quad 0 < \alpha < 1; \gamma < 0. \tag{1}$$

where u is unemployment; $\bar{u}/(1 - \alpha)$ is the steady state "natural" level of unemployment; π is inflation; π^e is expected inflation; ε is a random shock with zero mean; α, γ are parameters. The autoregressive term in (1) captures various sources of persistence. The "natural" level of unemployment is normalized at zero, with no loss of generality. By Okun's law, the same model can be written in terms of output growth, y_t, instead of unemployment. In the empirical work which follows, we will consider both GNP growth and unemployment.

A.2. Inflation expectations are adaptive:

$$\pi_t^e = \pi_{t-1} + \lambda(\pi_{t-1}^e - \pi_{t-1}); \quad 0 < \lambda < 1. \tag{2}$$

A.3. Inflation is directly controlled by the policymakers.[2]

A.4. Politicians are "opportunistic": they only care about holding office, and they do not have "partisan" objectives.

A.5. Voters are "retrospective." They judge the incumbent's performance based upon the state of the economy during the incumbent's term of office, and heavily discount past observations.

A.6. The timing of elections is exogenously fixed.

Under these assumptions, Nordhaus derives the following testable implications: (i) every government follows the same policy; (ii) towards the end of his term of office, the incumbent stimulates the economy to take advantage of the "short run" more favourable Phillips curve; (iii) the rate of inflation increases around the election time as a result of the pre-electoral economic expansion; after the election, inflation is reduced with contractionary policies.[3]

This basic model has recently been developed by investigating the role of rationality.

2.2 Rational Political Business Cycle Models

Persson and Tabellini (1990) propose a simple model which summarizes the basic insights of this approach, due to Rogoff and Sibert (1988). Assumptions A.1, A.3, A.4, and A.6 as in Nordhaus' model are retained. Assumption A.2 is replaced by:

A.2′. $\pi_t^e = E(\pi_t/I_{t-1})$: rational expectations.

A.2″. I_{t-1} includes all the relevant information except the level of "competence" of different policymakers.

Assumption A.5 is substituted by:

A.5′. Voters choose the candidate which is rationally expected to deliver the highest utility, if elected.

A.5″. There are no differences in voters' utility functions.

$E(\cdot)$ is the expectation operator and I_{t-1} is the information set of the voters at time $(t - 1)$ when expectations are formed. A.2″) implies an asymmetry of information between the policymakers and the voters: the former know their own competence, but the latter do not.[4] Policymakers' "competence" is defined as their ability of keeping unemployment low (and GNP growth high) with a relatively low level of inflation.[5]

By taking advantage of this informational asymmetry, and by trying to appear as competent as possible before elections, the politicians behave in a way leading to a Nordhaus' type PBC. However, given voters' rationality and awareness of the politicians' incentives, the latter are limited in their "opportunistic" behaviour. Thus, the resulting cycles are more short-lived and less regular than in Nordhaus' model.

The original proponents of the "competence" model, i.e. Rogoff and Sibert (1988) and Rogoff (1990), consider a budget problem, rather than an inflation/unemployment trade-off, but with identical assumptions about the distribution of information. These papers have empirical implications on opportunistic cycles on monetary and fiscal variables, rather than on unemployment and output. In fact, the model by Rogoff and Sibert (1988) makes predictions on the inflation rate similar to those of the Nordhaus model, but does not imply any correlation between elections and GNP growth or unemployment.

2.3 The "Partisan Theory" (Hibbs 1977, 1987)

A strong version of the "partisan theory" (henceforth PT) based upon a non-rational expectation mechanism, adopts assumptions A.1, A.2, A.3, and A.6. Assumptions A.4 and A.5 are substituted by:

A.4′. Politicians are "partisan," in the sense that different parties maximize different objective functions. Left-wing parties attribute a higher cost to unemployment relative to inflation than right-wing parties.

A.5‴. Each voter is aware of the partisan difference and votes for the party which offers the policy closer to his most preferred outcome.

The assumption of partisanship is justified by the distributional consequences of unemployment. In periods of high unemployment, low growth, and low inflation the relative share of income of the upper middle class increases, and the other way around, as shown by Hibbs (1987).

Thus, this model implies that different parties choose different points on the Phillips curve: output growth and inflation should be permanently higher and unemployment permanently lower when the left is in office than with right-wing governments.[6]

2.4 "Rational Partisan Theory" (Alesina 1987)

Alesina (1987, 1988b) suggests a "rational partisan theory" (henceforth RPT). This model adopts Assumption A.1, A.2′, A.3, A.4′, A.5‴, and A.6. The objective functions of the two parties can be written as:

$$W^i = \sum_{t=0}^{T} \delta^t[-(\pi_t - c^i)^2 - b^i(u_t - K^i)^2], \quad 0 < \delta < 1; \tag{3}$$

where $i = L, R$ identifies the "left" and the "right" parties. The difference between the two parties can be summarized by at least one of these three sets of inequalities:

$$c^L > c^R \geqq 0; \quad b^L > b^R \geqq 0; \quad K^L < K^R \leqq \frac{\bar{u}}{1-\alpha}. \tag{4}$$

The last double inequality implies the time-inconsistency problem in monetary policy pointed out by Kydland and Prescott (1977) and Barro and Gordon (1983a, 1983b). Since at least one of the two parties targets a level of output growth which is above the natural rate (normalized at zero), it introduces an "inflation bias" because of the lack of pre-commitments in monetary policy. Thus, a test of the RPT is indirectly a test for this specification of policymakers' objective functions.

This model generates a political cycle if we assume that uncontingent labour contracts are signed at discrete intervals (which do not coincide with the political terms of office) and that electoral outcomes are uncertain because of shocks to voters' preferences or to voters' participation rates in elections. The basic idea of the model is that, given the sluggishness in wage adjustments, changes in the inflation rate associated with changes in government create temporary deviations of real economic activity from its natural level.

More specifically, the following testable implications can be derived from the model: (i) at the beginning of a right-wing (left-wing) government output growth is below (above) its natural level and unemployment is above (below); (ii) after expectations, prices and wages adjust, output and unemployment return to their natural level; after this adjustment period, the level of economic activity should be independent of the party in office; (iii) the rate of inflation should remain higher throughout the term of a left-wing government; note that this occurs even if $c^L = c^R$ in (3), as long as $K^L < K^R$ or $b^L > b^R$. That is, the time consistent (but sub-optimal) inflation rate remains higher for left-wing parties even after the level of economic activity returns to its natural level.[7]

2.5 Previous Empirical Results

Most of the empirical studies on political cycles use post-war United States data. The evidence in favour of the RPT is relatively strong; evidence of "opportunistic" PBC is found for certain policy instruments (particularly government transfers) for limited sub-samples: for recent surveys of this empirical literature see Alesina (1988a) and Nordhaus (1989).

Multi-country studies are more scarce. Alt (1985) formally tests for partisan patterns in unemployment in twelve OECD democracies and finds evidence quite consistent with this approach. Paldam (1979) finds very weak evidence (if any at all) of Nordhaus' political business cycle on output and unemployment using a sample of seventeen OECD countries. The same author (1989a, 1989b) reports stronger evidence of partisan effects using annual data. Alesina (1989) provides some qualitative tests with annual data using the same sample of countries; his results suggest that the RPT is broadly consistent with the evidence while the same paper does not find clear evidence of PBC on growth and unemployment. Alvarez, Garrett, and Lange (1991) suggest that the degree of success of "partisan policies" may depend upon the characteristics of labour market institutions and of unions' behaviour. On the contrary, Sheffrin (1989) finds inconclusive results for the RPT. However, his definition of "unexpected change" of governments is questionable. Sheffrin disregards the fact that in several countries the same party or coalition was elected repeatedly with no electoral uncertainty. (See Alesina 1990).

The contribution of the present study is that, unlike its predecessors, it considers all the different theories in a unified framework. Furthermore, unlike the recent work by Alesina, Paldam, and Sheffrin, we use quarterly data rather than annual data and make use of different and more robust statistical tests. The use of quarterly data is important since the precise timing of cyclical fluctuations in relation to elections is crucial for the theories.

3 Panel Regressions

3.1 Data

We consider all the OECD countries which have been democracies in the sample period considered, which is 1960 to 1987. The extent of the sample is limited by availability of quarterly data; in fact, for some countries not all the series are available even for this period. The countries included are: Australia, Austria, Belgium, Canada, Denmark, Finland, France, Germany, Japan, Ireland, Italy, the Netherlands, New Zealand, Norway, Sweden, Switzerland, the United Kingdom, and the United States.

The economic data are quarterly observations on inflation, output growth, and unemployment. Inflation is defined as the yearly rate of change of the CPI from IMF, IFS. Output growth is obtained as the rate of change of real GNP (or GDP), also from IMF, IFS. For unemployment, we use the total standardized unemployment rate from OECD. More details on country-specific data issues can be found in Table 4.A1 in the Appendix. The political data are election dates, the dates of changes of governments, and the political orientation of various governments. Dates of regime changes and elections do not always coincide in parliamentary systems in which changes of coalitions take place not only after elections. This information is summarized in Table 4.A2. Sources for these political data are Alt (1985) and Banks (1987). The identification of changes of political orientation of governments is usually unambiguous. Whenever ambiguities occurred in the case of coalition governments, we followed Alt's and Banks' conventions. It should be noted that the countries for which positive results for the partisan theory are found are those in which there are no ambiguities about the classification of government political orientation.

3.2 Specification of Empirical Tests

The most direct way of testing the various theories is to run the following panel regressions of time-series cross-section data, for instance on output growth:

$$y_t = \alpha_0 + \alpha_1 y_{t-1} + \alpha_2 y_{t-2} \cdots \alpha_n y_{t-n} + \alpha_{n+1}\mathrm{PDUM}_t + \varepsilon_t \tag{5}$$

y_t is the stacked vector of time-series data on output growth for the countries in the sample and PDUM is a political dummy which captures the implications of the different theories. The autoregressive specification for the dependent variable is chosen as the "best" using standard techniques. Similar regressions have been performed by McCallum (1978), Hibbs (1987), Alesina and Sachs (1988), and Alesina (1988a) on U.S. data. These tests are based upon the assumption that output growth and unemployment are generated by a covariance-stationary stochastic process that can be expressed in autoregressive form as in (5).

Since the sample includes open economies (most of which are "small"), we must control for the effect of the world economy on domestic economies, for two reasons. First, the "partisan" or opportunistic goals of the politicians are likely to be defined, in small open economies, in relation to the rest of the world. Second, regardless of the governments' goals, international trade and financial linkages make OECD economies highly interdependent.

We have followed three approaches to capture these effects. The first one is to redefine each country's variable as a difference between the actual variable and a proxy for the OECD average of the same variable. The second one is to add as a regressor in equation (5) a proxy for a world or OECD average. The third one is to add time dummies in the regression. Our results concerning the relative performance of various political models are insensitive to the procedure used. As an indicator of an OECD average of each economic variable we consider the average of the seven largest economies in our sample, which are the U.S.A., Japan, Germany, France, the U.K., Italy, and Canada, weighted by each country's share of GNP over the total.[8]

In the remainder of this section we present results of panel regressions on the different political theories of the business cycle. We make use of a fixed-effect model with constant slopes. By doing so we take into account differences in long-term growth rates, unemployment, and inflation across countries but we assume that the other parameters of the model are constant and equal across countries.[9]

3.3 The "Rational Partisan Theory" (RPT)

The political dummy used is:

$$\text{DRPTN} = \begin{cases} +1 & \text{in the } N \text{ quarters starting with that of} \\ & \text{a change of government toward the right} \\ -1 & \text{in the } N \text{ quarters starting with that of} \\ & \text{a change of government toward the left} \\ 0 & \text{otherwise.} \end{cases}$$

tested the cases of $N = 4, 6, 8$. This choice of number of quarters is sistent with a wage contract model in which contracts have an average th of 1 or 2 years.

te that the variable DRPTN assumes values different from zero only ving actual changes of governments, but not after every election if the government is re-appointed. According to the RPT theory, inflation ses and thus output fluctuations may occur even if an incumbent is pinted unexpectedly (Alesina 1987). However, for long periods of many countries in the sample certain parties repeatedly won elecith virtually no political uncertainty. Furthermore, in countries ogenous timing of elections, which are the large majority of the sample (see Table 4.A2), in every period there is at least "some" probability that an election is called and that a change of government may occur. In addition, in parliametary systems sometimes government changes occur in the middle of a term, with no elections. Rather than trying to estimate the degree of political uncertainty in every period, which would be rather difficult, we have chosen to estimate a somewhat weaker form of RPT, testing for temporary effects on real variables after actual *changes* of governments. An additional reason for doing so is that several macroeconomic models in the "neo-Keynesian" tradition imply that not only unexpected, but also expected aggregate demand policy may have some real effects. Thus, according to these approaches, stronger effects should be found after actual changes of governments, with actual changes of policies, relative to the case of reappointment of the same government.

Column (1) of Table 4.1 reports the result of the dynamic panel OLS regressions for the entire sample of countries and the time period fo which data are available.[10] Japan and Switzerland are not included sin they had no political change in the sample.[11] The dependent variable the rate of GNP growth defined as:

$$y = \left[\frac{X_t - X_{t-4}}{X_{t-4}} \cdot 100\right];$$

where X_t = level of real GNP in quarter t. The regressors are self tory: yw_t is the world growth average (described above); the AR fication has been chosen as the "best" using standard tech remaining regressors are country dummies.

The political dummy DRPT 6 has the correct sign and i significant at the 1% confidence level: a change in governme (left) leads to a transitory fall (increase) in output growth. T lag in the political dummy is consistent with a reasonable change of regime (in quarter t) and change of policy (in r regressions with DRPT 4 and DRPT 8 (available u analogous results: the pattern of the coefficients sug effects are observable from about the second to the e after the election. These results are consistent wit States data by Alesina and Sachs (1988) and Alesin

In column (2) of the same table we present the r sion for a subset of countries which have either a or at least more clearly identifiable "left" and "r

Table 4.1
Rational partisan theory (dependent variable: rate of growth of output [Y])

Independent variables	(1) Coefficient (*t*-statistics)	(2) Coefficient (*t*-statistics)	(3) Coefficient (*t*-statistics)	(4) Coefficient (*t*-statistics)
Constant	0.130 (0.55)	−0.180 (−0.81)	0.500 (0.80)	1.282 (3.84)
$Y(-1)$	0.712 (28.1)	0.610 (17.27)	0.689 (25.59)	0.543 (15.04)
$Y(-2)$	−0.062 (−2.55)	−0.01 (−0.28)	−0.065 (−2.46)	−0.009 (−0.24)
YW	0.353 (11.82)	0.305 (9.33)	—	—
DRPT 6(−1)	−0.41 (−3.48)	−0.62 (−4.42)	−0.412 (−3.43)	−0.573 (−4.09)
U.S.A.	−0.45 (−1.49)	0.21 (0.81)	−0.376 (−1.19)	0.250 (1.10)
U.K.	−0.63 (−2.08)	−0.02 (−0.07)	−0.703 (−2.21)	−0.118 (−0.53)
Germany	−0.36 (−1.19)	0.28 (1.09)	−0.400 (−1.25)	0.187 (0.81)
France	−0.14 (−0.45)	0.49 (1.81)	−0.205 (−0.60)	0.440 (1.80)
Canada	0.12 (0.40)	0.80 (3.06)	0.073 (0.23)	0.798 (3.44)
Italy	0.04 (0.15)	— —	0.000 (0.00)	—
Sweden	−0.56 (−1.63)	—	−0.600 (−1.64)	−0.079 (−0.30)
Belgium	−0.42 (−1.40)	—	−0.443 (−1.38)	—
Austria	0.14 (0.48)	—	0.161 (0.51)	—
Norway	−0.03 −(0.10)	—	0.001 (0.00)	—
Finland	0.05 (0.15)	—	0.005 (0.14)	—
Ireland	0.46 (1.13)	—	0.621 (1.40)	—
Australia	0.03 (−0.10)	0.007 (2.67)	0.000 (0.02)	0.658 (3.44)
New Zealand	−0.48 (−1.59)	0.12 (0.48)	−0.512 (−1.60)	—
Denmark	−0.39 (−1.29)	—	−0.399 (−1.24)	—
R^2	0.61	0.60	0.63	0.64
S.E.	2.24	1.61	2.23	1.60

the U.S.A., the U.K., France, Germany, Australia, New Zealand, Sweden, and Canada. The other countries in the sample have more fragmented political systems with governments formed with large coalitions of parties (often centre-left) which sometimes are short-lived and unstable. For obvious reasons, the second group of countries is less likely to exhibit regular partisan cycles. In the second regression, in fact, the coefficients on the political dummy are much larger in absolute value and even more precisely estimated.

The values of the coefficients in the second column of Table 4.1 imply that about eighteen months after a change of regime toward the right (left) the rate of growth of GNP is about 1.3% below (above) "normal." Thus, the difference in the rate of growth between the beginning of a left-wing government and the beginning of a right-wing government reaches a peak of about 2.6%.

Columns (3) and (4) of Table 4.1 report the same regressions in which we added time dummies, instead of the world growth variable. The 27 time dummies, one for each year of our sample, are not reported in the Table. Column (3) includes all the countries; column (4) the same subset of countries of column (2). The coefficient on the DRPT dummy variable is virtually unchanged, relative to columns (1) and (2). Generally, we always found that our results on the political variables are totally unaffected by substituting the "world variable" with time dummies. Therefore, in what follows we report only the result using the world variable. The corresponding results obtained using time dummies are available upon request.

In Table 4.2 the dependent variable is the difference (U_t^{DIF}) between the domestic unemployment rate, U_t, and the "OECD unemployment rate," UW_t, defined analogously to the average GNP growth. In evaluating results on employment one has to be cautious because of problems of hysteresis (see, for instance, Blanchard and Summers 1986). By taking the difference of domestic unemployment from a world weighted average, unit roots problems are somewhat mitigated, but certainly not eliminated. Table 4.2 shows results which are quite consistent with those on GNP growth. The political dummy is significant at the 1% level and the fit improves when the sample is restricted to seven bi-partisan countries (note that New Zealand is missing from these regressions because of lack of quarterly unemployment data). The dummy DRPT 6 is lagged two quarters to capture the slow response of unemployment to policy changes relative to output. In any case, analogous results (available upon request)

Table 4.2
Test of rational partisan theory (dependent variable: U^{DIF})

Variable	(1) Coefficient (t-statistics)	(2) Coefficient (t-statistics)
Constant	0.152 (3.37)	0.101 (2.92)
$U^{DIF}(-1)$	1.284 (42.25)	1.332 (39.35)
$U^{DIF}(-2)$	−0.300 (−11.14)	−0.359 (−10.49)
DRPT 6(−2)	0.063 (3.11)	0.086 (3.20)
Australia	−0.126 (−2.12)	−0.082 (−1.67)
Austria	−0.218 (−3.31)	—
Belgium	−0.030 (−0.54)	—
Canada	−0.128 (−2.30)	−0.051 (−1.18)
Denmark	−0.093 (−1.51)	—
Finland	−0.164 (−2.80)	—
France	−0.110 (−1.83)	−0.06 (−1.25)
Germany	−0.140 (−2.31)	−0.116 (−2.17)
Ireland	0.071 (1.05)	—
Italy	−0.072 (−1.30)	—
Norway	−0.216 (−3.13)	—
Sweden	−0.208 (−3.32)	−0.198 (−3.32)
U.K.	−0.132 (−2.34)	−0.082 (−1.80)
U.S.A.	−0.138 (−2.48)	−0.061 (−1.38)
R^2	0.99	0.98
S.E.	0.35	0.31

are obtained if this variable is lagged only one quarter or when DRPT 4 and DRPT 8 are used. The values of the coefficients in the second column of Table 4.2 imply that about six quarters after a change of regime toward the right (left) the umemployment rate is about 1.5 percentage points above (below) normal.[13]

Let us now turn to inflation. The theory implies that one should observe permanent differences across governments on the inflation rate. Thus, we have defined a political dummy, RADM, as follows:

$$\text{RADM} = \begin{cases} +1 & \text{if a right-wing government is in office, including the quarter of the change of government} \\ -1 & \text{if a left-wing government is in office including the quarter of the change of government.} \end{cases}$$

In Table 4.3 the dependent variable is domestic inflation (π) defined as the rate of change of CPI:

$$\pi_t = \left[\frac{\text{CPI}_t - \text{CPI}_{t-4}}{\text{CPI}_{t-4}} \cdot 100\right].$$

The variable for world inflation (πW) is defined analogously to the world output growth.[14]

In the first regression, which includes the entire sample of countries, the sign of the coefficient on RADM (-1) is correct and it is marginally insignificant at the 10% level ($t = -1.65$). The second regression includes only the eight "bi-partisan" countries: here the coefficient on RADM (-1) is larger and significant at the 5% level.

The value of the coefficients in the second regressions imply a difference in the steady-state inflation rate between the two regimes of about 1.4%. This relatively low value reflects the fact that our sample includes the sixties, with a low and stable inflation, and countries, such as Germany, with a low inflation rate throughout the sample period. We have run the same regressions of Table 4.3 for the post–fixed exchange rates regimes, from 1972 to 1978. In these regressions (available upon request) the coefficient on the RADM dummy is more precisely estimated and implies (in the sample of 8 "bi-partisan" countries) a difference in the inflation rate across political regimes of about 2.5%.

In fact, we have tested whether all the regressions of Table 4.1, 4.2, and 4.3 improve in the post-1971 period, since in the fixed exchange rate

Table 4.3
Rational partisan theory (dependent variable: π)

Variable	(1) Coefficient (t-statistics)	(2) Coefficient (t-statistics)
Constant	−0.075 (−0.63)	0.593 (4.80)
$\pi(-1)$	1.085 (45.54)	1.210 (35.22)
$\pi(-2)$	−0.136 (−3.92)	−0.272 (−5.15)
$\pi(-3)$	−0.097 (−4.34)	−0.074 (−2.30)
πW^*	0.146 (13.15)	0.127 (9.35)
RADM (−1)	−0.05 (−1.65)	−0.084 (−2.17)
Australia	0.329 (2.15)	−0.307 (−2.27)
Austria	−0.064 (−0.42)	—
Belgium	0.027 (0.18)	—
Canada	0.070 (0.45)	−0.580 (−3.97)
Denmark	0.352 (2.27)	—
Finland	0.41 (2.65)	—
France	0.333 (2.18)	−0.293 −(2.19)
Germany	−0.255 (−1.66)	−0.853 (−5.68)
Ireland	0.66 (4.22)	—
Italy	0.665 (4.13)	—
New Zealand	0.66 (4.27)	—
Norway	0.299 (1.94)	—
Sweden	0.264 (1.69)	−0.405 (−2.83)
U.K.	0.516 (3.34)	−0.14 (−1.07)
U.S.A.	−0.041 (−0.27)	−0.65 (−4.55)
R^2	0.94	0.95
S.E.	1.13	0.98

period (1960–1971 in our sample) the macroeconomic policies of each country were more constrained and integrated. All the t-statistics on the political dummies improve and the value of the coefficients increase in absolute value in the post-1971 regressions. However, the problem in pursuing this comparison, pre- and post-1971, is that there are very few changes of regimes in the pre-1971 period (see Table 4.A1); in many countries there are *no* changes of regimes in the sixties. Thus, the political dummies in the pre-1971 regression are very imprecisely estimated and hard to compare with the post-1971 sample.[15]

Finally, it is worth noting that in the inflation regression several of the coefficients on the country dummies are statistically significant, indicating, as it is well known, that different countries have had substantially different average inflation rates in the sample period considered here. An often cited explanation for these country differences is the degree of Central Bank independence (Alesina 1989; Grilli, Masciandaro, and Tabellini 1991; Alesina and Summers 1992). More independent Central Banks appear to have been associated with lower average inflation rates.[16]

In summary, these results are quite favourable to the RPT. The implication of this hypothesis is not rejected on both the level of economic activity (growth and unemployment) and inflation, particularly for a subset of countries with more clearly identifiable government changes from left to right and vice versa.[17]

3.4 "Partisan Theory" with Permanent Effects

Hibbs' PT implies permanent differences in output and unemployment in addition to permanent differences in inflation across governments. Thus, one way of comparing the Hibbs' PT with the RPT is to run the same regressions of Tables 4.1 and 4.2 using the "permanent" partisan dummy RADM rather than the "transitory" political dummy DRPTN. The results are shown in Tables 4.4 and 4.5: all the coefficients on the political dummy are insignificant, even though with the right sign. In these tables the fixed-effects coefficients are not reported since they are very similar to those of Tables 4.1 and 4.2. Additional regressions with alternative lag structures (for instance lagging RADM more than one quarter) yield no support for the theory.

An additional test confirmed our results. We defined a new dummy variable DPRTNX, which is the "complement" of the DRTPN variable; that is, it takes the value of 1 during right-wing governments *after* the first

Table 4.4
Partisan theory (Hibbs) (dependent variable: Y)

Variable*	(1) Coefficient (t-statistics)	(2) Coefficient (t-statistics)
Constant	0.12 (0.51)	−0.17 (−0.79)
$Y(-1)$	0.720 (28.47)	0.629 (17.76)
$Y(-2)$	−0.061 (−2.53)	−0.01 (−0.26)
YW	0.349 (11.62)	0.289 (8.77)
RADM (−1)	−0.03 (−0.54)	−0.02 (−0.35)
R^2	0.61	0.59
S.E.	2.25	1.61

*The estimated regression includes country fixed effects that are not reported in the table.

Table 4.5
Partisan theory (Hibbs) (dependent variable: U^{DIF})

Variable	(1) Coefficient (t-statistics)	(2) Coefficient (t-statistics)
Constant	0.14 (3.41)	0.016 (0.62)
$U^{DIF}(-1)$	1.29 (49.0)	1.43 (41.1)
$U^{DIF}(-1)$	−0.20 (−11.3)	−0.45 (−12.7)
RADM (−1)	0.009 (1.00)	0.0009 (−0.09)
R^2	0.98	0.98
S.E.	0.33	0.24

*The estimated regression includes country fixed effects that are not reported in the table.

N quarters, and -1 *after* the first N quarters of left-wing governments. We added this new variable in our panel regressions of Tables 4.1 and 4.2. The coefficient on this variable has the opposite sign to the DRPTN dummies and is statistically insignificant. The coefficients on the DRPTN dummies, instead, remain statistically highly significant. This test confirms that the effects of changes of governments on growth and unemployment are transitory.

The results on the RPT and PT viewed together, indirectly provide some empirical support to the inflation-bias model of Kydland and Prescott (1977) and Barro and Gordon (1983a, 1983b). In fact, our regressions show that a permanent difference in inflation rate is associated with temporary deviations of output and unemployment from trend. Thus, the governments that are more concerned about growth and unemployment relative to inflation, after a temporary initial expansion, are caught in the sub-optimal equilibrium with an inflation bias. In fact, inflation remains high even though the level of economic activity returns to its "natural" value. This is precisely the feature of the sub-optimal time-consistent equilibrium.

3.5 The "Political Business Cycle"

Nordhaus' (1975) PBC model can be tested on growth and unemployment by constructing a political dummy of the following form:

$$\text{NRDN} = \begin{cases} 1 & \text{in the } (N-1) \text{ quarters preceding an election} \\ & \text{and in the election quarter} \\ 0 & \text{otherwise.} \end{cases}$$

We have chosen $N = 4$, 6, and 8. A relatively short pre-electoral output expansion is consistent with this theory, which views the electorate as short-sighted (Nordhaus 1975, 1989). Furthermore, since in many countries in the sample several elections occur in less than four year intervals, a longer specification of the pre-electoral period seems unreasonable.

Tables 4.6 and 4.7 report the results on output and unemployment for the 18 countries in the sample, using NRD 6. (The fixed-effect coefficients are not reported.) In both tables the coefficients of NRD 6 are insignificant; in the growth regression the coefficients has the opposite sign from the theory prediction. Several alternative specifications with NRD 4 and NRD 8, using the difference of domestic growth from the world as the

Table 4.6
Test for political business cycle theory (dependent variable: Y)

Variable*	(1) Coefficient (t-statistics)	(2) Coefficient (t-statistics)
Constant	0.12	−0.19
	(0.49)	(−0.81)
$Y(-1)$	0.732	0.631
	(29.49)	(17.27)
$Y(-2)$	−0.059	−0.015
	(−2.48)	(−0.43)
YW	0.344	0.280
	(12.02)	(8.47)
NRD 6	−0.09	0.06
	(−0.78)	(0.49)
R^2	0.65	0.60
S.E.	2.25	1.73

* The estimated regression includes country fixed effects that are not reported in the table.

Table 4.7
Political business cycle theory (dependent variable: U^{DIF})

Variable*	(1) Coefficient (t-statistics)	(2) Coefficient (t-statistics)
Constant	0.166	0.020
	(3.75)	(0.68)
$U^{DIF}(-1)$	1.323	1.433
	(51.02)	(39.67)
$U^{DIF}(-2)$	−0.336	−0.446
	(−12.81)	(−12.08)
NRD 6	−0.011	−0.001
	(−0.64)	(−0.63)
R^2	0.99	0.98
S.E.	0.32	0.24

* The estimated regression includes country fixed effects that are not reported in the table.

dependent variable and alternative lag structures, yield no support for the theory. In fact, the coefficient on the political dummy has the "wrong" sign in the majority of the regressions.

We also tested whether the NRD dummy approaches statistical significance when partisan effects are held constant. Regressions including both the DRPT and the NRD dummies were run, with no support for the PBC, while the DRPT dummy remained statistically significant (results are available).[18]

The PBC not only as formulated in Nordhaus (1975) but also, with caveats discussed above, in the "rational" models by Rogoff and Sibert (1988) and Persson and Tabellini (1990) implies an increase of the inflation rate around elections. Furthermore, governments may prefer to raise prices under their direct control after rather than before elections, thus directly contributing to a post-electoral upward jump in inflation. We have tested this implication in Table 4.8, where the dummy ELE is defined as follows:

$$\text{ELE} = \begin{cases} 1 & \text{in the 4 quarters following an election, and in the election quarter.} \\ 0 & \text{otherwise.} \end{cases}$$

Table 4.8
Political business cycle (dependent variable: π)

Variable	Coefficient (t-statistics)
Constant	−0.131 (−1.08)
$\pi(-1)$	1.078 (46.90)
$\pi(-2)$	−0.113 (−3.36)
$\pi(-3)$	−0.113 (−5.23)
πW	0.141 (13.09)
ELE	0.263 (4.61)
R^2	0.93
S.E.	1.14

* The estimated regression includes country fixed effects that are not reported in the table.

The dummy ELE is significant at the 1% level. Additional regressions (available upon request) confirm that the upward jump in inflation does not occur before the election, but only in the election quarter, and lasts three to five quarters.[19] If confirmed by direct findings on policy instruments, this result suggests that around elections monetary and fiscal policy instruments may be manipulated, even though these policies do not seem to affect real economic activity, as implied by Rogoff and Sibert (1988) and Rogoff (1990). Alesina, Cohen, and Roubini (1992) present evidence on monetary and fiscal policy instruments which is consistent with this hypothesis.

Up to this point, the different theories have been tested separately, that is, by including only one political dummy variable in each regression. Our results were also confirmed when we ran a general nesting model. Specifically, we estimated repressions on growth and unemployment in which all three dummy variables, DRPT, RADM, and NRD, were included. Only the DRPT variable was significant. We also calculated an F-test comparing the unrestricted model with all the three political variables and the restricted model with only the DRPT: for both samples of countries we could not reject the restricted model, at very high levels of significance.

As far as inflation is concerned, we tested whether the two dummies RADM and ELE remain jointly significant when used as regressors in the same equation. For the smaller group of eight countries we reject the hypotheses that either one or both variables are zero. F-tests reject models in which either one or both variables are excluded. For the complete sample of countries, our F-tests continue to reject the hypothesis that the coefficient on ELE is zero, but we cannot reject, at standard levels of confidence, the hypothesis that the coefficient on RADM is zero. These different results on the two samples of countries are consistent with the evidence presented in Tables 4.3 and 4.8 above.[20]

4 Country Results

In this section we summarize the results obtained by performing country-by-country regressions with the same specification of the panel regressions. These results are presented more extensively in the working paper version of this chapter (NBER working paper no. 3478).

We begin with the RPT. Growth and unemployment regressions were run for each country using six dummies DRPTN $(-J)$ with $N = 4, 6, 8$

and $J = 1, 2$. Countries may differ with regard to the time delay in implementing a new policy after a regime change or with regard to how persistent the transitory increase in output will be after the policy change. This is why the most appropriate specification for the DRPTN dummy may vary across countries. For inflation we run regressions using the dummy RADM $(-J)$ $J = 1, \ldots, 5$. Longer lags for inflation, relative to the growth regression, can be easily explained by the lag between output and inflation movements following changes in macroeconomic policies. Our results can be summarized in three points:[21]

(1) In seven countries, Australia, Denmark, Germany, France, New Zealand, the U.S., and the U.K., all the regressions on growth, inflation, and unemployment show evidence favourable to the RPT, although not all the coefficients on the political variables are significant at the usual confidence levels (5 or 10%) in every regression. The results on the U.K. are greatly strengthened if the sample is restricted to the post–fixed rates period.[22]

(2) In seven other countries, Austria, Belgium, Finland, Ireland, the Netherlands, Norway, and Sweden, the coefficients on the political dummies exhibit the sign predicted by the theory sometimes approaching statistical significance, in either the growth and/or the unemployment regressions. No significant results were found in the inflation regressions. For example, Sweden has a very strongly significant coefficient on DRPT 6 in the growth equation.

(3) Canada and Italy show no significant coefficients in any regressions. The case of Canada, however, is explained by the almost perfect correlation between the U.S. and Canadian business cycles. In fact the U.S. political dummies are statistically quite significant (5% confidence level) in the Canadian equations! Thus, it is not clear whether for the purpose of this chapter Canada really provides an independent observation.

In summary, six of the eight countries with more clearly identifiable left-right governments (that is the U.S., Germany, France, the U.K., Australia, and New Zealand) plus Denmark exhibit evidence of RPT effects.[23] All the parliamentary systems with large coalition governments show little sign of RPT, particularly on inflation.[24]

We find that the implications for growth and unemployment of the PT with permanent effects are rejected in every country except for Germany and for the borderline case of Sweden. All the other countries clearly reject the theory; in several cases the sign of the coefficient on the political dummy is opposite to the theory prediction.

In order to test the implication of the PBC model, we run the unemployment and growth regressions trying both the NRD 4 and NRD 6 dummies. In four countries, Germany, Japan, the U.K., and New Zealand, the coefficient on at least one of the NRD's is significant. In Australia and France the coefficients have the sign inconsistent with the theory and are statistically significant. In all the other countries the coefficients are insignificant.

Finally, we performed the PBC regressions on inflation, using the dummy ELE as for the panel regressions of Table 4.8. Several countries, such as Denmark, France, Germany, Italy, and New Zealand, show significant (10% or better) post-electoral upward jumps in the inflation rate. In several other countries (e.g., Japan, Norway, and the U.K.) the sign is correct but the *t*-statistic does not reach a significant level, although it is above 1.

In summary, in only two countries, Germany and New Zealand, both the level of economic activity and the inflation rate follow the predictions of Nordhaus' PBC model. The results for New Zealand are not too unexpected, given that, until recently, this country had one of the least independent Central Banks. On the contrary, the case of Germany, with a Central Bank with a strong reputation for independence, appears somewhat surprising.[25]

5 Tests of the RPT Model Using Hamilton's Model

One of the strongest and most interesting results which we have highlighted thus far is that downturns and upsurges in growth tend to follow changes of governments, as predicted by the RPT. In this section we pursue this observation further by deriving direct measures of the dating of the business cycle in different countries and study their relation to the dates of government changes. From a conceptual point of view, the recent literature on the unit roots and GNP has offered a number of alternative approaches to the problem of distinguishing between trend and cyclical components of output. Most of the literature[26] is based on the assumption that GNP growth is characterized by a linear stationary process.

Hamilton (1989) studies the implications of specifying the first differences of log GNP as a non-linear stationary process. His idea is to view the economy as characterized by two states, a high-growth (expansion) state and a low-growth (recession) state and model the switch between these two states as being governed by a Markov process. One of the by-products of the estimation of the model is a non-linear filter that delivers optimal estimates of the dating of the business cycle based on past observations on output. In particular, for each quarter the filter provides an estimate of the probability that the economy is in a recession (or a boom) given the information available in the data. Given Hamilton's success in characterizing the U.S. business cycles, using his filter, we used the same statistical approach to derive estimates of the dating of the business cycle for other OECD countries in our sample. After having done that, we tested the relation between these estimates of the business cycle and the changes of governments.

Given the positive evidence in favour of the RPT model for countries with a political system close to a two-party structure, we have considered only these countries.[27] To control for the effects of the world business cycle on the growth rate of the various economies, in our maximum likelihood estimates of Hamilton's model we use y^{DIF} (defined as the difference between country *i* growth rate and the average growth rate of the major OECD countries) as the two-state variable to be explained.

Once we have obtained an estimate of the dating of the business cycle, we perform a regression of the estimated probability (PROBS) of being in a low-growth state (relative to the OECD average) on a constant, the dummy for the RPT model (DRPTN), and the first lag of the dependent variable. The latter is introduced to capture the observed persistence of the probability of being in a particular state of the world. The basic regressions is:

$$\text{PROBS}_t = \alpha_0 + \alpha_1 \,\text{PROBS}_{t-1} + \alpha_2 \,\text{DRPTN}_{t-1} + \varepsilon_t. \tag{6}$$

Table 4.9 reports the results of fixed-effects panel regressions of equation (6) above for seven countries with a political structure close enough to a two-party system, as discussed above.[28] The political variable (DRPT 6), used to capture the effects of the RPT model, has the correct sign and is statistically significant at the 1% confidence level.

The Table 4.10 we report the results of separate time series regressions for each of the seven countries considered. The coefficient on the RPT dummy (DRPT) is significant at the 10% confidence level or better in five of the seven countries: the United States, Germany, France, Australia, and Sweden. The DRPT coefficient for the United Kingdom is significant (at

Table 4.9
Test of the RPT model using Hamilton's filter for the business cycle. Dependent variable: probability of being in a low (relative to average OECD) growth state. Panel regressions on seven bi-partisan countries.

Variable	Estimated coefficient	(t-statistics)
Constant	0.09	4.74
PROBS ($t-1$)	0.82	38.43
DRPT 6	0.046	3.10
United States	−0.08	−3.26
Germany	0.05	2.33
France	0.002	0.01
Australia	−0.024	−1.05
Canada	−0.020	−0.891
Sweden	−0.029	−1.14
$R^2 = 0.80$		
S.E. = 0.167		

Table 4.10
Test of the RPT model using Hamilton's filter for the business cycle. Dependent variable: probability of being in a low (relative to average OECD) growth state. Time series regressions on seven bi-partisan countries.

Country	Constant	Lagged dep. variable	DRPTN	*R2*	*D.W.*
Uunited States	0.02 (1.55)	0.73 (12.0)	0.08[a] (3.07)	0.67	2.08
Germany	0.14 (3.31)	0.83 (16.9)	0.06[a] (1.59)	0.80	1.60
France	0.04 (1.65)	0.92 (23.9)	0.09[b] (2.10)	0.88	1.83
Australia	0.11 (3.04)	0.71 (10.4)	0.10[c] (1.83)	0.53	1.98
Canada	0.05 (2.01)	0.85 (16.7)	0.04[b] (0.71)	0.73	1.93
Sweden	0.13 (3.80)	0.62 (6.66)	0.05[c] (2.04)	0.51	1.96
United Kingdom	0.20 (4.68)	0.61 (7.73)	0.02[b] (0.81)	0.37	1.95
United Kingdom	0.21 (4.52)	0.56 (6.19)	0.06[a] (1.87)	0.41	1.93

a. DRPT 6.
b. DRPT 4.
c. DRPT 8.
d. 1967–1987 Sample.

the 10% level) only if we start the sample in 1970 (as discussed in Section 4). The seventh country, Canada, does not show statistical significance for the RPT variable, as discussed in the previous section.

6 Conclusions

The most interesting result of this study is that the more recent models of political cycles significantly outperform their predecessors. The rational partisan model by Alesina (1987) and the rational "opportunistic" model by Rogoff and Sibert (1988) are consistent with the overall pattern of results for several countries.

The main findings of this chapter can be summarized as follows:

(1) With the exception of two countries (Germany and New Zealand), we found no evidence of a systematic opportunistic cycle of the Nordhaus type either for output or unemployment.[29]

(2) The data show an electoral cycle on the inflation rate, consistent with the models of budget cycles of Rogoff and Sibert (1988).

(3) The implications of the "rational partisan theory" are consistent with the empirical evidence particularly for a subset of countries with a bi-partisan system or with clearly identifiable movements from left to right and vice versa. This theory is less applicable, and in fact tends to fail, in countries with large coalition governments with frequent goverment collapses.

(4) The "partisan theory" with permanent effects on output and unemployment is generally rejected.

Thus, a political cycle which seems to appear fairly consistently in several countries in the following: left-wing governments expand the economy when elected; for a while (about 2 years) they succeed, then inflation expectations adjust and the economy returns to its natural rate of growth. At this point, left-wing governments are trapped into the time-consistent equilibrium with an inflation bias à la Barro and Gordon (1983b). Note that, when left-wing governments approach the new election in this high inflation, they may try to reduce the latter, particularly if inflation is preceived as the main economic problem of the time (Lindbeck 1976). When right-wing governments are elected they fight inflation, causing a recession or a growth slowdown. Later in their term, the economy goes back to its natural rate of growth and inflation remains low.

Two explanations can account for the relatively little evidence of a Nordhaus-type opportunistic cycle on growth and unemployment: first, a "rational" electorate imposes a limit on this behaviour; an excessive attempt to pursue opportunistic policies may be perceived as counter-productive by policymakers. Second, it may be quite difficult to create expansions precisely timed before elections.

However, the results on post-electoral inflation increase may signal the occurrence of pre-electoral opportunistic budget policies. In fact, Alesina (1989) and Alesina, Cohen, and Roubini (1992) show that budget deficits and money growth tend to increase in election years in several OECD democracies. Similar evidence on budget cycles in the U.S. is also discussed in Tufte (1978), Alesina (1988a), and Nordhaus (1989). Pre-electoral fiscal "favours" to key constituencies may be electorally very useful and easy to implement, relative to an attempt to increase the rate of growth of GNP. These opportunistic monetary and fiscal policies can very well co-exist with the partisan cycles found in the data. Even "partisan" politicians prefer to be in office, rather than out; by being in office they can implement their desired goals. Thus, they may engage in short term pre-electoral opportunistic policies if the latter enhance their chances for re-election.

Appendix

Table 4.A1
Description of data

Inflation: Inflation is obtained as: $\pi_1 = [(P_t - P_{t-4})/P_{t-4}]^{\times 100}$ where P_t is the Consumer Price Index in quarter t. For all countries the sample is 1960:1, 1987:4, and CPI is taken from line 64 of IMF-IFS.

Output and Unemployment: Country-by-country sample and sources.

Note: Countries which use other measures of GDP do so because real quarterly GDP is not available.

Australia	GDP-real quarterly GDP from OECDMEI (1960:1–1987:4). Unemployment-unemployment rate-adjusted-OECDMEI (1965:1–1987:4).
Austria	GDP-real quarterly GDP from IMF-IFS (1960:1–1987:4). Unemployment-unemployment rate-total-adjusted-OECDMEI (1969:1–1986:4).

Table 4.A1 (continued)

Belgium	GDP-quarterly Industrial Production from OECDMEI (1960:1–1987:4). Unemployment-unemployment rate-total insured-adjusted-OECDMEI (1960:1–1987:4).
Canada	GDP-real quarterly GDP from IMF-IFS (1960:1–1987:4). Unemployment-unemployment rate-total-adjusted-OECDMEI (1960:1–1987:4).
Denmark	GDP-real ANNUAL GDP from IMF-IFS (1960:1–1987:4) (coverted into quarterly data by assuming that quarter-to-quarter annual change corresponds to year-to-year change). Unemployment-unemployment rate-registered unemployed-adjusted-OECDMEI (1970:1–1987:4).
Finland	GDP-real quarterly GDP from IMF-IFS (1970:1–1987:4). Unemployment-unemployment rate-total-adjusted-OECDMEI (1960:1–1987:4).
France	GDP-real quarterly GDP from IMF-IFS (1965:1–1987:4). Unemployment-unemployment rate-total-adjusted-OECDMEI (1967:1–1987:4).
Germany	GDP-real quarterly GDP from IMF-IFS (1960:1–1987:4). Unemployment-unemployment rate-adjusted-OECDMEI (1965:1–1987:4).
Ireland	GDP-quarterly Industrial Production from OECDMEI (1975:1–1986:4). Unemployment-unemployment rate-adjusted-OECDMEI (1975:1–1987:4).
Italy	GDP-real quarterly GDP from IMF-IFS (1960:1–1987:4). Unemployment-unemployment rate-adjusted-OECDMEI (1960:1–1987:4).
Japan	GDP-real quarterly GDP from IMF-IFS (1960:1–1987:4). Unemployment-unemployment rate-adjusted-OECDMEI (1965:1–1987:4).
Netherlands	GDP-quarterly Industrial Production from OECDMEI (1960:1–1987:4). Unemployment-unemployment rate-registered unemployed-OECDMEI (1971:1–1987:4), no adjusted available.
New Zealand	GDP-real ANNUAL GDP from IMF-IFS (1960:1–1987:4) (converted into quarterly data by assuming that quarter-to-quarter annual change corresponds to year-to-year change). Unemployment-not available.
Norway	GDP-real ANNUAL GDP from IMF-IFS (1960:1–1987:4) (converted into quarterly data by assuming that quarter-to-quarter annual change corresponds to year-to-year change). Unemployment-unemployment rate-adjusted-OECDMEI (1972:1–1987:4).
Sweden	GDP-real quarterly GDP from IMF-IFS (1969:1–1987:4). Unemployment-unemployment rate-total insured-adjusted-OECDMEI (1969:1–1983:4).
Switzerland	GDP-real quarterly GDP from IMF-IFS (1967:1–1986:4). Unemployment-ratio of total unemployment to labor force-adjusted-OECDMEI (1974:4–1987:3).

Table 4.A1 (continued)

U.K.	GDP-real quarterly GDP form IMF-IFS (1960:1–1987:4). Unemployment-unemployment rate-registered-civilian-adjusted-OECDMEI (1960:1–1987:4).
U.S.A.	GDP-real quarterly GDP from IMF-IFS (1960:1–1987:4). Unemployment-unemployment rate-total-adjusted-OECDMEI (1960:1–1987:4).

Table 4.A2
Election and regime change
E = Election; CH L = Change Left; Ch R = Change Right

AUSTRALIA: Endogenous timing, 3 yrs			
1961:4	E	RIGHT	a
1963:4	E		
1966:4	E		
1969:4	E		
1972:4	E	CH L	
1974:2	E		(∗)b
1975:4	E	CH R	
1977:4	E		
1980:4	E		
1983:1	E	CH L	
1984:4	E		(∗)
1987:3	E		

AUSTRIA: Endogenous timing, 4 yrs			
1959:2	E	RIGHT	c
1962:4	E	E	
1966:1	E	CH R	
1970:1	E	CH L	
1971:4	E		(∗)
1975:4	E		
1979:2	E		
1983:2	E	CH R	c
1986:4	E	CH R	

BELGIUM: Endogenous timing, 4 yrs			
1961:1	E	RIGHT	
1965:2	E		
1968:1	E	CH L	
1971:4	E		
1973:1		CH R	
1974:1	E		
1977:2	E	CH L	
1978:4	E		(∗)
1981:4	E	CH R	
1985:4	E	CH L	
1987:4	E		

CANADA: Endogenous timing, 5 yrs			
1962:2	E	RIGHT	
1963:2	E	CH L	(∗)
1965:4	E		
1968:2	E		
1972:4	E		
1974:3	E		(∗)
1979:2	E	CH R	
1980:1	E	CH L	(∗)
1984:3	E	CH R	

DENMARK: Endogenous timing, 4 yrs			
1960:4	E	LEFT	
1964:3	E		
1966:4	E		
1968:1	E	CH R	(∗)
1971:3	E	CH L	
1973:4	E	CH R	
1975:1	E	CH L	(∗)
1977:1	E		
1979:4	E		
1981:4	E		
1982:3		CH R	
1984:1	E		
1987:3	E		

FINLAND: Endogenous timing, 4 yrs		
1962:1	E	LEFT
1963:4		CH R
1966:1	E	CH L
1970:1	E	
1972:1	E	
1975:3	E	CH R
1977:2		CH L
1979:1	E	
1983:1	E	CH R
1987:1	E	CH R

Table 4.A2 (continued)

FRANCE: Endogenous timing, 5 yrs			
1962:4	E	RIGHT	
1967:1	E		
1968:2	E		(*)
1973:1	E		
1978:1	E		
1981:2	E	CH L	
1984:3		CH R	
1986:1	E	CH R	

GERMANY: Endogenous timing, 4 yrs			
1961:3	E	RIGHT	
1965:3	E		
1966:4		CH L	c
1969:3	E	CH L	
1972:4	E	CH R	
1976:4	E		
1980:4	E		
1982:4		CH R	
1983:1	E		
1987:1	E		

IRELAND: Endogenous timing, 5 yrs			
1961:4	E	RIGHT	
1965:2	E		
1969:2	E		
1973:1	E	CH L	
1977:2	E	CH R	
1981:2	E	CH L	
1982:1	E	CH R	(*)
1982:4	E	CH L	(*)
1987:1	E		

ITALY: Endogenous timing, 5 yrs			
		RIGHT	
1962:4		CH L	
1963:2	E		
1968:2	E		
1972:2	E		
1974:4		CH R	
1976:2	E	CH L	
1979:2	E		
1983:2	E		
1987:2	E		

JAPAN: Endogenous timing, 4 yrs			
1960:4	E	RIGHT	
1963:4	E		
1967:1	E		
1969:4	E		
1972:4	E		
1976:4	E		
1979:4	E		
1980:2	E		(*)
1983:4	E		
1986:3	E		

NETHERLANDS: Endogenous timing, 4 yrs			
1959:1	E	RIGHT	
1963:2	E		
1965:2		CH L	
1967:1	E	CH R	
1971:1	E		
1972:4	E		(*)
1973:2		CH L	
1977:2	E		
1977:4		CH R	
1981:2	E	CH L	
1982:3	E	CH R	(*)
1986:2	E		

NEW ZEALAND: Exogenous timing, 3 yrs			
1960:4	E	RIGHT	
1963:4	E		
1966:4	E		
1969:4	E		
1972:4	E	CH L	
1975:4	E	CH R	
1978:4	E		
1981:4	E		
1984:3	E	CH L	
1987:3	E		

NORWAY: Endogenous timing, 4 yrs			
1961:3	E	LEFT	
1965:3	E	CH R	
1969:3	E		
1971:4		CH L	
1972:4		CH R	
1973:3	E	CH L	
1977:3	E		
1981:3	E	CH R	
1985:3	E		
1986:2		CH L	

Table 4.A2 (continued)

SWEDEN: Endogenous timing, 3 yrs since late '60s, constitutional reform

1960:3	E	LEFT	
1964:3	E		
1968:3	E		
1970:3	E		
1973:3	E		
1976:3	E	CH R	
1979:3	E		
1982:3	E	CH L	
1985:3	E		

SWITZERLAND: Exogenous timing, 4 yrs

1959:4	E	RIGHT	
1963:4	E		
1967:4	E		
1971:4	E		
1975:4	E		
1979:4	E		
1983:4	E		
1987:4	E		

U.K.: Endogenous timing, 5 yrs

1959:4	E	RIGHT	
1964:4	E	CH L	
1966:1	E		(*)
1970:2	E	CH R	
1974:1	E		
1974:3	E	CH L	(*)
1979:2	E	CH R	
1983:2	E		
1987:2	E		

U.S.A.: Exogenous timing, 4 yrs

		RIGHT	
1960:4	E	CH L	
1964:4	E		
1968:4	E	CH R	
1972:4	E		
1976:4	E	CH L	
1980:4	E	CH R	
1984:4	E		

a. RIGHT or LEFT indicates the type of government in power at the beginning of the sample which is 1959:1. We also indicate for each country whether elections dates are endogenous or exogenous and the official number of years between two elections.
b. Elections denoted with an asterisk "*" are not included in tests of the political business cycle theory because they are too close (less than two years) to previous elections. They are however included in tests of the opportunistic endogenous election model.
c. Both Germany and Austria had grand coalitions of Left and Right parties. Thus, a finer administration variable was used in the the RPT inflation and partisan (Hibbs) regressions. This also explains the occurrence of a rightward shift from an already central Right leaning party.
Source: Election dates are obtained from Banks (1989); dates of changes of government and their classification of "Right" and "Left" are obtained from Alt (1985) and Banks (1987).

Notes

Prepared for the conference on Economic Policy in Political Equilibrium, Stockholm, June 14–16, 1990. We are especially grateful to our discussant Assar Lindbeck and to many other conference participants for very useful comments. James Hamilton generously shared his computer programs. Mathias Dewatripont, Benjamin Friedman, Sule Ozler, Torsten Persson, Dani Rodrik, James Stock, Philippe Weil, three anonymous referees, and participants of seminars at Carnegie-Mellon, Chicago, Harvard, MIT, NBER, North Carolina, Trade Union Institute in Stockholm, and NBER Summer Institute provided very helpful comments on earlier drafts. Gerald Cohen was our excellent research assistant. The first draft of this paper was written while Alesina was an Olin Fellow at the NBER; he gratefully acknowledges financial support from the Olin and Sloan Foundations.

1. Furthermore, Nordhaus' "political business cycle" model did not receive much empirical support. Soon after the publication of Nordhaus' paper McCallum (1978) and Paldam (1979)

presented negative empirical results for the U.S. and OECD economies respectively. More favourable results are shown by Tufte (1978), but only on a sample including a few American elections.

2. To be precise, Nordhaus (1975) assumes the policymakers control aggregate demand and, indirectly, inflation. This difference is inessential.

3. Nordhaus' (1975) model predicts that inflation should increase *before* the election. However, given time lags between the effect of aggregate demand policies on output and inflation, one can build a model in which inflation increases after rather than before the election. (See Lindbeck 1976).

4. In Cukierman and Meltzer (1986) the asymmetry of information is related to the knowledge of the realization of a random shock to the economy.

5. Formally, the degree of competence is modelled by adding a term in equation (1) which changes over time and is known by the policymaker but becomes known to the voters with a lag. For an explicit test of this model on U.S. data see Alesina, Londregan, and Rosenthal (1990).

6. Nordhaus' PBC and Hibbs' PT can co-exist. If one assumes that politicians are both opportunistic and partisan and voters are retrospective as implied by A.5, one obtains a "weaker" form of PT which incorporates elements of pre-electoral opportunistic behaviour. See Frey and Schneider (1978) and Nordhaus (1989).

7. With the exception of Lindbeck (1976), very little attempt has been devoted to build political business cycle models (opportunistic and/or partisan) for small open economies. For such economies the exchange rate regime would greatly influence the options available to the politicians.

8. In the regressions for the seven countries included in the creation of the proxy for the OECD averages, we have used different proxies which exclude the country in the left-hand side of the regression.

9. A priori, the correct dynamic specification of the model could differ across countries but in country-by-country regressions we found that the same AR specification is the best for almost all the countries in the sample. However, even if the same AR specification applies to each country, the estimates of the coefficients on the dynamic part of the model could differ across countries and suggest the use of a variable-slopes *and* variable-intercepts model. Given the loss of degrees of freedom involved, this procedure was not adopted. Country-specific results are discussed in Section 4, and more extensively in the working paper version of this chapter.

10. It is known that in dynamic fixed-effects panel models the correlation between the error term and the lagged dependent variables might lead to biased and inconsistent estimates of the parameters (Hsiao 1986). The problem is serious in panel sets where the number of agents (N) considered is large but the number of times series observations (T) is small. In that case, the maximum likelihood estimator of the dynamic model is inconsistent even if the number of agents becomes very large (Anderson and Hsiao 1982 and Nickell 1981). The solution to this problem is to use instrumental-variable methods such as those suggested by Bhargava and Sargan (1983) and Pakes and Griliches (1984). Our panel data set, however, does not suffer of the above problem because of the use of a long time series (usually 112 data points). In the case where the time period T is large, the parameter estimates of the standard fixed-effects dynamic model are consistent (Hsiao 1986).

11. Our results are unaffected by the inclusion of these two countries.

12. Analogous results on the political dummy available are obtained by using as a dependent variable the difference between domestic and world growth.

13. The variable U_t^{DIF} shows a high level of persistence. Thus, even a "temporary" policy shock has rather persistent effects.

14. One could add oil prices to the equation but the inclusion of the world inflation variable already proxies for this role of world-wide oil shocks.

15. We also tested whether the dynamic process of inflation has changed moving from the fixed to the flexible rate system. The regressions of Table 4.3 were computed allowing the coefficients on the lagged dependent variable to be different before and after 1972. The results (available upon request) confirm that inflation is significantly more persistent in the post-1972 period with flexible rates. However, our results concerning the statistical significance of the variable RADM remain unchanged, even when we allow for a structural break in 1972. These results are available.

16. We thought about adding as a regressor in the inflation equation one of the indices of Central Bank independence; (see for instance Alesina and Summers 1992). However, such indices assign numerical values to different countries and these numbers do not vary over time. Therefore, the country dummies which are already included in the regression capture the same effect.

17. The significance of the coefficients of the political dummies in Tables 4.1, 4.2, and 4.3 is not due to the predominant influence of any single country. If one drops any of the 16 countries and retains the other 15, the coefficients on the political dummies remain significant.

18. An even more extreme version of this model of voters' myopia would imply that they ignore the influence of the world economy on their countries' performance and thus politicians simply attempt to expand their economies, regardless of the world economy. This hypothesis can be tested running the same regressions of Tables 4.6 and 4.7. without correcting for the effect of the world economy. The results (available upon request) show no support for the PBC.

19. The statistical significance of the coefficient on ELE is unaffected by allowing for a structural break of the inflation process in 1972. See also note 15.

20. All the results of these *F*-tests are available from the authors. Also, there is no difference in the results of these tests regardless of whether we use time dummies or "world variables."

21. All the regressions from which the following results are derived are displayed in the NBER Working Paper version of this chapter.

22. The significant difference between the pre- and post-1971 results for the U.K. is explained primarily by the observation of the Labour government elected in October 1964. This government, constrained by a commitment not to devalue the pound, could not pursue expansionary policies.

23. Our results regarding the RPT theory on output growth and unemployment are confirmed by another set of regressions in which we used a distributed lag of the variable representing the changes in partisan regime, instead of the DRPT variable. For the countries with a significant DRPT effect we find that an *F*-test on the distributed lag variable rejects the null hypothesis that the sum of all coefficients is equal to zero.

24. A referee has noted that in this group of eight countries we have several "large" economies, while many of the countries with coalition governments are small and have very open economies, and has suggested that it may be the size and the degree of openness of the economy which affect the government's ability to implement partisan macroeconomic policies.

25. It is interesting to note that in his original paper, Nordhaus (1975) had found support for his theory precisely on these two countries!

26. See Nelson and Plosser (1982); Campbell and Mankiw (1987); Watson (1986); Clark (1987); King, Plosser, Stock, and Watson (1987).

27. Given our country results, Hamilton's tests on the other countries are not likely to support the theory.

28. New Zealand is excluded because of lack of quarterly data.

29. Following Ito (1990), in the Working Paper version of this chapter, we also tested for an opportunistic model with "endogenous timing of elections." We checked whether the probability that early elections are called is affected by the state of the economy. We confirmed Ito's results on Japan, but we did not find supporting evidence for this hypothesis in any other country in our sample.

References

Alesina, A. 1987. Macroeconomic policy in a two-party system as a repeated game. *Quarterly Journal of Economics* 102:651–678.

Alesina, A. 1988a. Macroeconomics and politics. *NBER Macroeconomics Annual.* Cambridge: MIT Press. 13–52.

Alesina, A. 1988b. Credibility and policy convergence in a two-party system with rational voters. *American Economic Review* 78:796–806.

Alesina, A. 1989. Politics and business cycles in industrial democracies. *Economic Policy* 8:55–87.

Alesina, A. 1990. Evaluating rational partisan business cycle theory: A response. *Economics and Politics* 3: 63–72.

Alesina, A., Cohen, G., and Roubini, N. 1992. Macroeconomic policy and elections in OECD democracies. *Economics and Politics* 5:1–30.

Alesina, A., Londregan, J., and Rosenthal, H. 1990. A political-economy model of the United States. Manuscript.

Alesina, A., and Sachs, J. 1988. Political parties and the business cycle in the United States, 1948–1984. *Journal of Money, Credit and Banking* 20:63–82.

Alesina, A., and Summers, L. 1992. Central Bank independence and macroeconomic performance: Some comparative evidence. *Journal of Money, Credit and Banking.* Forthcoming.

Alt, J. 1985. Political parties, world demand, and unemployment: Domestic and international sources of economic activity. *American Political Science Review* 79:1016–1040.

Alvarez, M., Garrett, G., and Lange, P. 1989. Government partisanship, labor organizations and macroeconomic performance. *American Political Science Review* 85:539–556.

Anderson, T., and Hsiao, C. 1982. Formulation and estimation of dynamic models using panel data. *Journal of Econometrics* 18:47–82.

Banks, A. 1987. *Political handbook of the world.*

Barro, R., and Gordon, D. 1983a. Rules, discretion, and reputation in a model of monetary policy. *Journal of Monetary Economics* 12:101–122. Reprinted as chapter 4 in volume 1 of this work.

Barro, R., and Gordon, D. 1983b. A positive theory of monetary policy in a natural rate model. *Journal of Political Economy* 31:589–610.

Bhargava, A., and Sargan, J. 1983. Estimating dynamic random effects models from panel data covering short time periods. *Econometrica* 51:1635–1659.

Blanchard, O., and Summers, L. 1986. Hysteresis and the European unemployment problem. *NBER macroeconomics annual 1986.*

Campbell, J., and Mankiw, N. 1987. Permanent and transitory components in macroeconomic fluctuations. *American Economic Review* (*Papers and Proceedings*) 77:111–117.

Clark, P. 1987. The cyclical component of U.S. economic activity. *Quarterly Journal of Economics* 102:797–814.

Cukierman, A., and Meltzer, A. 1986. A theory of ambiguity, credibility, and inflation under discretion and asymmetric information. *Econometrica* 53:1099–1128.

Frey, B., and Schneider, F. 1978. An empirical study of politico-economic interaction in the United States. *The Review of Economics and Statistics* 60:174–183.

Grilli, V., Masciandaro, D., and Tabellini, G. 1991. Political and monetary institutions and public financial policies in the industrial countries. *Economic Policy* 13:341–392. Reprinted as chapter 7 in the current volume of this work.

Hamilton, J. 1989. A new approach to the economic analysis of non-stationary time series and the business cycle. *Econometrica* 57:357–384.

Hibbs, D. 1977. Political parties and macroeconomic policy. *The American Political Science Review* 7:1467–1487.

Hibbs, D. 1987. *The American political economy*. Cambridge: Harvard University Press.

Hsiao, C. 1986. *Analysis of panel data*. Cambridge: Cambridge University Press.

Ito, T. 1990. The timing of elections and political business cycles in Japan. *Journal of Asian Economics* 1:135–146.

King, R., Plosser, C., Stock, J., and Watson, M. 1987. Stochastic trends and economic fluctuations. NBER working paper no. 2229.

Kydland, F., and Prescott, E. 1977. Rules rather than discretion: The inconsistency of optimal plans. *Journal of Political Economy* 85:473–490. Reprinted as chapter 1 in volume 1 of this work.

Lindbeck, A. 1976. Stabilization policies in open economies with endogenous politicians. *American Economic Review (Papers and Proceedings)* 66:1–19.

McCallum, B. 1978. The political business cycle: An empirical test. *Southern Economic Journal* 44:504–515.

Nelson, C., and Plosser, C. 1982. Trends and random walks in macroeconomic time series: Some evidence and implications. *Journal of Monetary Economics* 10:139–162.

Nickell, S. 1981. Biases in dynamic models with fixed effects. *Econometrica* 49:1399–1416.

Nordhaus, W. 1975. The political business cycle. *Review of Economic Studies* 42:169–190.

Nordhaus, W. 1989. Alternative models to political business cycles. *Brookings Papers on Economic Activity*, No. 2.

Pakes, A., and Griliches, Z. 1984. Estimating distributed lags in short panels with an application to the specification of depreciation patterns and capital stock constructs. *Review of Economic Studies* 51:243–262.

Paldam, M. 1979. Is there an electoral cycle? *Scandinavian Journal of Economics* 81:323–342.

Paldam, M. 1989a. Politics matter after all: Testing Alesina's theory of RE partisan cycles. Aarhus University working paper.

Paldam, M. 1989b. Politics matter after all: Testing Hibbs' theory of partisan cycles. Aarhus University working paper.

Persson, T., and Tabellini, G. 1990. *Macroeconomic policy, credibility and politics*. London: Harwood Academic Publishers.

Rogoff, K. 1990. Equilibrium political budget cycles. *American Economic Review* 80:21–36. Reprinted as chapter 2 in the current volume of this work.

Rogoff, K., and Sibert, A. 1988. Equilibrium political business cycles. *Review of Economic Studies* 55:1–16.

Sheffrin, S. 1989. Evaluating rational partisan business cycle theory. *Economics and Politics* 1:239–259.

Terrones, M. 1987. Macroeconomic policy cycles under alternative electoral structures: A signalling approach. Manuscript.

Tufte, E. 1978. *Political control of the economy*. Princeton, NJ: Princeton University Press.

Watson, M. 1986. Unvariate detrending methods with stochastic trends. *Journal of Monetary Economics* 18:49–75.

II PUBLIC DEBT AND POLITICAL INSTABILITY

5 Why a Stubborn Conservative Would Run a Deficit: Policy with Time-Inconsistent Preferences

Torsten Persson and Lars E. O. Svensson

I Introduction

Suppose that the current government knows that it will be replaced in the future by a new government with different objectives, for instance, a government that is in favor of a larger public sector. How does that affect the current government's behavior? More specifically, what are the implications for the current government's choices between distortionary taxes and borrowing? In particular, will the current government run fiscal deficits when it knows that its successor's choice of public spending will be influenced by the level of public debt that the successor inherits? These are the questions that we attempt to answer in this chapter.[1]

We can think of the described situation as one where the two governments have time-inconsistent *preferences*. As is well known, time-consistency problems also arise if governments have time-inconsistent *constraints*, for instance, because demand or supply functions for some tax base differ ex ante and ex post. In order to isolate the problem of time-inconsistent preferences, we shall make assumptions such that constraints are time consistent.

Our work in this chapter is related to the small but growing literature on political models of fiscal policy; see Alesina and Tabellini (1988) for a recent survey. Our work is, of course, also related to the rapidly growing literature on time consistency of government policy; see Rogoff (1987) and Persson (1988) for recent surveys. In particular, it is closely related to the papers by Lucas and Stokey (1983), Persson and Svensson (1984), and Persson, Persson, and Svensson (1987). These papers show that the second-best optimal fiscal and monetary policy under commitment can be enforced under discretionary policy-making, if each government leaves its successor with a particular maturity structure of the public debt. This specific result suggests a more general principle: as long as the current government can affect some state variable that enters (in an essential way) in its successor's decision problem, it can affect the policy carried out by the successor.

Reprinted from *Quarterly Journal of Economics*, 104 (1989) 325–345, by permission of The MIT Press Journals.

In this chapter the (level of the) public debt is the state variable that gives the current government an instrument to control the future government. We show that a conservative government may borrow more when it knows that it will be succeeded by a more expansionary government than when it knows that it will remain in power in the future. Since borrowing more creates a distorted tax profile over time, such a policy is optimal only if the government is "stubborn" (in a sense to be specified), however. We believe our analysis may shed some new light on the U.S. fiscal deficits that have been caused by the Reagan administration. But we also believe that the general principle has wider applications, as further discussed in the concluding section.[2]

The paper has six sections. Section II presents the model and derives the equilibrium for time-consistent preferences; that is, for the situation when the same government remains in power both in the current period and in the future. Section III derives and discusses the equilibrium with time-inconsistent preferences; that is, when a new government with more expansionary prefereces is in power in the future. Section IV discusses an alternative interpretation, with capital controls. Section V discusses some empirical material. Section VI concludes and mentions possible extensions. Some of the mathematical details are collected in the Appendix.

II Taxation with Time-Consistent Preferences

We assume a small open economy. There are two periods, 1 and 2. There is one good. The economy can borrow and lend at a given world rate of interest equal to zero. (A model of a closed economy, where the technology was linear in capital, would produce similar results.) Therefore, present-value prices of the good in the two periods are equal to unity, $p_1 = p_2 = 1$. Goods output in the two periods, y_1 and y_2, are produced with labor input, l_1 and l_2, according to a linear technology, $y_1 = l_1$, and $y_2 = l_2$. It follows that the competitive before-tax wage rate is unity in both periods.

The representative consumer has a labor endowment of one unit in each period. Preferences over private consumption of goods, c_1 and c_2, and labor supply, l_1 and l_2, in the two periods are described by an additively separable concave utility function, increasing in consumption and decreasing in labor supply,

$$u(c_1, l_1, c_2, 1_1) = f(c_1) + h_1(1 - l_1) + c_2 + h_2(1 - l_2). \tag{1}$$

Maximizing (1) subject to the intertemporal budget constraint that the present value of consumption equals the present value of after-tax wage income gives rise to an indirect utility function $U(w_1, w_2)$ of after-tax wage rates w_1 and w_2, and to labor supply functions $L_1(w_1)$ and $L_2(w_2)$ in the two periods.

The additive separability and the linearity in period 2 consumption of the utility function (1) make labor supply in each period depend only on the after-tax wage rate in the same period. This makes sure that ex ante and ex post labor supply in period 2 coincide, which is necessary for the governments' constraints to be time consistent. The indirect utility function $U(w_1, w_2)$ and the labor supply functions $L_1(w_1)$ and $L_2(w_2)$ summarize consumer behavior. Next we look at government behavior.

Consumers' preferences for *government* (public) consumption may enter in an additively separable way in the above utility function. The different governments considered below can then be viewed as representing different parts of the population with different preferences for government consumption (but with the same preferences over private consumption of goods and leisure). Alternatively, we can think of consumers as being indifferent to the level of government consumption, with the governments having their own preferences over public consumption, independent of consumers' preferences.

There is government consumption in period 2 only. Government consumption in period 1 can easily be introduced, and below we shall also report results on that case. The government in power in period 1 is called government 1. For future reference we first look at the case when government 1 is in power in both periods 1 and 2. Government consumption in period 2, g, enters government 1's overall preferences:

$$U(w_1, w_2) + v^1(g), \tag{2}$$

the sum of private (indirect) utility and a concave utility function $v^1(g)$ of government consumption.

We assume that government consumption can be financed only by wage taxes. Lump sum taxes are excluded, since otherwise the problem would be trivial. Capital taxes are excluded to avoid more than one source of time-consistency problems. Tax revenues in the two periods are functions of the after-tax wage rates, $(1 - w_1)L_1(w_1)$ and $(1 - w_2)L_2(w_2)$, respectively. (Since the before-tax wage rate is unity, the wage taxes in period 1 and 2 are equal to $1 - w_1$ and $1 - w_2$.) The intertemporal budget constraint can be split up into a budget constraint for each period,

$$(1 - w_1)L_1(w_1) = -b \quad \text{and} \quad (1 - w_2)L_2(w_2) = b + g, \tag{3}$$

where b is net government borrowing in period 1 (absent government consumption in period 1 net borrowing will be negative). It is assumed—although not explained—that the government in period 2 always honors the debt that it inherits.

Government 1 would like to choose w_1, w_2, b, and g, so as to maximize (2) subject to (3). It is convenient to treat this decision problem in several steps. *First*, the after-tax wage rates can be solved as functions of borrowing and government consumption from the budget constraints (3), $w_1(b)$ and $w_2(b + g)$.[3] If we substitute these wage functions into the indirect utility function $U(w_1, w_2)$, we get a new indirect utility function that expresses private utility (of private consumption) as a function of borrowing and government consumption:

$$V(b, g) \equiv U(w_1(b), w_2(b + g)). \tag{4}$$

Second, by choosing the level of borrowing so as to maximize $V(b, g)$ for given government consumption, government 1 determines its preferred borrowing policy. We describe the preferred policy by the *preferred-debt function* $b(g)$; a function of government consumption defined by the first-order condition,

$$V_b(b(g), g) \equiv 0. \tag{5}$$

(If the labor supply functions in the two periods are symmetric, the preferred debt function is simply $b(g) = -g/2$. That is, half of government consumption is financed by period 1 taxes, and half by period 2 taxes.) *Third*, if we substitute the preferred-debt function into the indirect utility function $V(b, g)$, we get yet another indirect utility function that expresses private utility as a function of government consumption only, $\bar{V}(g) \equiv V(b(g), g)$. *Finally*, government 1 chooses government consumption so as to maximize

$$\bar{V}(g) + v^1(g). \tag{6}$$

We define the ex ante marginal cost of government consumption as $\bar{\lambda}(g) \equiv \bar{V}_g(g)$, and we denote the marginal utility of government consumption for government 1 by $\mu^1(g) \equiv v_g^1(g)$. Then the first-order condition for the maximum of (6) can be written as

$$\bar{\lambda}(g) = \mu^1(g). \tag{7}$$

An illustration is provided in the upper half of Figure 5.1. The preferred government consumption for government 1, $\bar{g}^1$, is given by the intersection between the marginal cost curve $\bar{\lambda}(g)$ and the marginal utility curve $\mu^1(g)$ at point A. As is usual in optimum taxation problems, the second-order conditions are not necessarily fulfilled. The second-order condition here is that the slope of the ex ante marginal cost curve is larger than the slope of the marginal utility curve, $\bar{\lambda}_g > \mu_g^1$. The marginal utility curve is downward-sloping by the concavity assumption. We assume that the ex ante marginal cost curve is upward-sloping, as in Figure 5.1, $\bar{\lambda}_g > 0$.

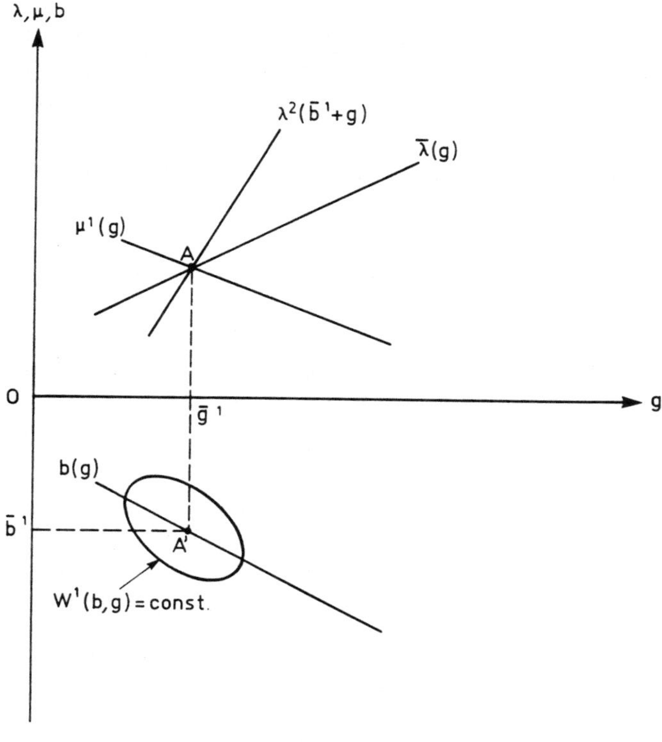

Figure 5.1

An alternative illustration in (b, g) space is provided in the lower half of Figure 5.1. (Since there is no government consumption in period 1, $b(g)$ is negative for positive g unless private preferences are very asymmetric.) An indifference curve for the function $W^1(b, g) \equiv V(b, g) + v^1(g)$ is shown, as well as the preferred-debt function $b(g)$. The function (6) is given by the value of $W^1(b, g)$ along $b(g)$. The maximum occurs for $g = \bar{g}^1$ and the corresponding preferred debt level is $\bar{b}^1 = b(\bar{g}^1)$.

Let us also describe the behavior of government 1 ex post, if it remains in power in period 2. Ex post, government 1 has to use period 2 tax revenues to finance total government expenditure in period 2, namely of the sum of government consumption g and repayment of predetermined debt $\bar{b}^1$. Default on the debt is ruled out. (For the case without period 1 government consumption, the debt level is negative so there is no incentive to default.) The after-tax period 2 wage rate consistent with expenditure $\bar{b}^1 + g$ will be given by the function $w^2(\bar{b}^1 + g)$ derived above. As in the ex ante problem, one can define an ex post marginal cost of government consumption, $\lambda^2(\bar{b}^1 + g)$.[4] Ex post, then, government 1 chooses government consumption to equate the ex post marginal cost and marginal utility of government consumption.

This is also illustrated in Figure 5.1. The ex post marginal cost curve is steeper than the ex ante marginal cost curve. The reason is that when government consumption is raised ex post, only the period 2 tax rate is raised, since the period 1 tax rate is predetermined. This is more distortionary than when both periods' tax rates are raised as in the ex ante problem underlying the ex ante marginal cost curve. The ex post marginal cost curve intersects the marginal utility curve at point A, for the same level of government consumption as the ex ante marginal cost curve. This illustrates that the constraints of government 1 are time consistent: ex post it has incentive to pursue the same policy as it had ex ante. As further discussed in Persson and Svensson (1987), with a different private utility function the ex post marginal cost curve will intersect the marginal utility curve at a different level than the ex ante marginal cost curve, giving rise to a time-consistency problem even with time-consistent preferences.

III Taxation with Time-Inconsistent Preferences

Now instead let a new government, called government 2, be in power in period 2. It differs from government 1 in having a different utility function for government consumption, $v^2(g)$. As illustrated in Figure 5.2, the marginal utility of government consumption for government 2, $\mu^2(g) \equiv v_g^2(g)$, exceeds that of government 1 for all levels of g, $\mu^2(g) > \mu^1(g)$. Government 2 faces the same ex post optimum taxation problem as the one discussed for government 1 above, and hence the same ex post marginal cost curve for government consumption. Given the level of debt it inherits from government 1, it equates the ex post marginal cost of government consumption with its own marginal utility of government consumption. If government 2 inherits the government 1 preferred debt level $\bar{b}^1$, it would choose the level of government consumption corresponding to point B, the intersection between the ex post marginal cost curve for $\bar{b}^1$ and the marginal utility curve. If government 2 were in power in both periods, it would choose its preferred level of government consumption, $\bar{g}^2$, given by the

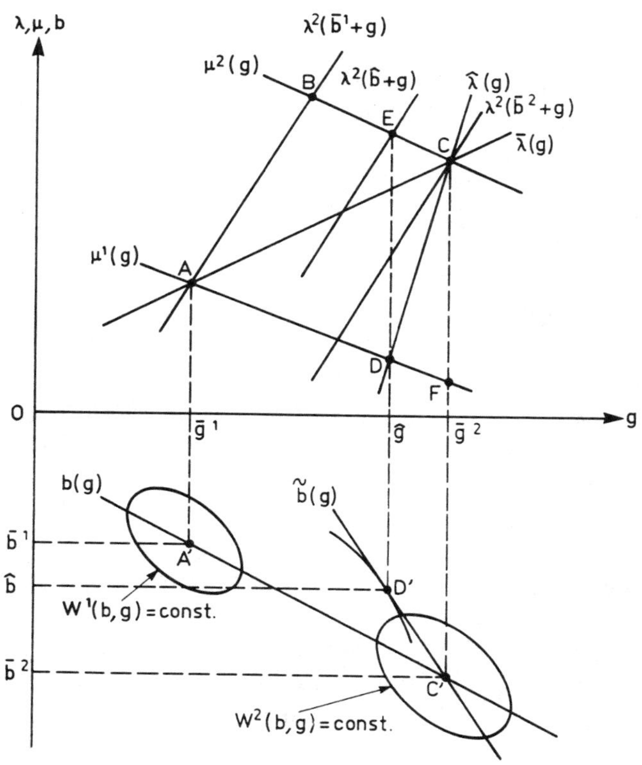

Figure 5.2

intersection of the ex ante marginal cost curve and its marginal utility curve at point C. The corresponding preferred level of debt, $\bar{b}^2$, makes the ex post marginal cost curve also intersect the marginal utility curve at point C.

The situation for government 2 is also illustrated in (b, g) space in Figure 5.2. An indifference curve for its ex ante objective function, $W^2(b,g) \equiv V(b,g) + v^2(g)$, is shown, as well as its preferred level of government consumption, $\bar{g}^2$ and debt $\bar{b}^2$ at point C'. The preferred-debt function $b(g)$ is common for the two governments, since by (5) it depends only on the indirect utility function $V(b,g)$ and not on the governments' preferences for government consumption, $v^1(g)$ and $v^2(g)$.

For an arbitrary level of debt b, government 2 will hence choose government consumption, $g^2(b)$, such that its ex post marginal cost curve intersects the marginal utility curve,

$$\lambda^2(b + g) = \mu^2(g). \tag{8}$$

It follows that government consumption is a decreasing function of inherited debt. The inverse of that function, also a decreasing function, is denoted $\tilde{b}(g)$ and called the *required-debt function*.This function gives the debt level required to induce government 2 to choose a particular level of government consumption. The required-debt function has a slope steeper than -1,[5] and is hence steeper than the preferred-debt function $b(g)$. It is also shown in Figure 5.2.[6]

Let us now return to the behavior of government 1, when it anticipates that it will be replaced by government 2 in period 2. The required-debt function enters as an incentive-compatibility constraint in the decision problem of government 1. Government 1 then simply maximizes $W^1(b,g)$ subject to $b = \tilde{b}(g)$, which results in the time-consistent level of borrowing $\hat{b} = \tilde{b}(\hat{g})$. This is illustrated in Figure 5.2, where an indifference curve for the function $W^1(b,g)$ is tangent to the curve describing the required debt function at point D', for $(\hat{b}, \hat{g})$.

The time-consistent equilibrium can also be illustrated in another way. In order to see this, first, when the level of borrowing is given by the required-debt function, we define the indirect utility function $\hat{V}(g) \equiv V(\tilde{b}(g), g)$, and the time-consistent marginal cost of government consumption $\hat{\lambda}(g) = -\hat{V}_g(g)$. Then the first-order consumption for a maximum of $\hat{V}(g) + v^1(g)$ can be written as

$$\hat{\lambda}(g) = \mu^1(g); \tag{9}$$

the time-consistent marginal cost of government consumption should equal the marginal utility of government consumption for government 1. This first-order condition again defines the time-consistent level of government consumption $\hat{g}$. In Figure 5.2 the time-consistent marginal cost curve $\hat{\lambda}(g)$ intersects the marginal utility curve of government 2 for the level of government consumption $\bar{g}^2$, at point C. The time-consistent curve $\hat{\lambda}(g)$ is at least as steep as the ex post marginal cost curve $\lambda^2(\bar{b}^2 + g)$ (see the derivation of inequality (A.20) in the Appendix). It intersects the marginal utility curve of government 1 at point D, at the time-consistent level of government consumption $\hat{g}$.

It follows from Figure 5.2 that the time-consistent level of government consumption $\hat{g}$ corresponding to point D is a compromise between the two governments' preferred levels,

$$\bar{g}^1 < \hat{g} < \bar{g}^2. \tag{10}$$

It also follows from Figure 5.2 that government 1 induces government 2 to choose a lower level of government consumption by leaving government 2 with a higher level of debt than government 2 prefers. That is,

$$\hat{b} > \bar{b}^2. \tag{11}$$

This is obvious since any tangency of indifference curves from $W^1(b, g)$ must be to the left of $\bar{g}^2$, when the required debt curve has a negative slope.

But, is the time-consistent level of borrowing $\hat{b}$ larger or smaller than the level of borrowing $\bar{b}^1$ that government 1 would choose if it were in power in both periods? This depends on whether the point E vertically above D is to the left or right of point B in the upper half of Figure 5.2, or whether point D' is above or below point A' in the lower half of Figure 5.2. If to the left and above, time-consistent borrowing is larger; if to the right and below, time-consistent borrowing is smaller. Numerical examples demonstrate that both cases can occur, and we cannot expect to find general global results, since the curves in Figure 5.2 may have a variety of shapes.

We have, however, been able to derive a local result (for technical details, see the Appendix). Suppose that points A and C (and A' and C') in Figure 5.2 are close. Then we can show that the time-consistent level of borrowing is larger or smaller depending upon whether the marginal utility curve for government 1 is steeper or flatter than the marginal utility curve for government 2. That is,

$$\hat{b} \gtrless \bar{b}^1 \text{ if and only if } -\mu_g^1 \gtrless -\mu_g^2. \tag{12}$$

Let us extend on the intuition for that result. Government 1 is trading off two different distortions. One is to have too much government consumption, what we call the volume distortion. The other is to have, for a given level of government consumption, a time profile of taxes that differs from the ex ante optimum taxation solution, what we call the intertemporal distortion. Consider again Figure 5.2. Suppose that government 1 would leave to government 2 the debt level $\bar{b}^2$ preferred by government 2. Then government 2 would choose its preferred level of government consumption, $\bar{g}^2$, corresponding to point C. The equilibrium would be the one government 2 would have chosen if it were in power in both periods, and there would be no intertemporal distortion. From the point of view of government 1, however, there would be a considerable volume distortion. The marginal cost of government consumption would be given by the distance between the horizontal axis and point C, but the marginal utility would be much less, given by the distance between the horizontal axis and point F. It is better for government 1 to decrease the volume distortion by increasing the debt level, shifting the ex post marginal utility curve to the left, and forcing government 2 to cut back on government consumption. This causes period 1 tax rates to be too low relative to period 2 tax rates, and hence creates an intertemporal distortion. If government 1 has a relatively steep marginal utility curve for government consumption, it puts relatively large weight on the volume distortion, and is therefore prepared to create a considerable intertemporal distortion. In this case, we say that government 1 is "stubborn." Hence, our result (12) can be interpreted as saying that if government 1 is relatively stubborn, it increases the level of borrowing so much that the ex post marginal cost curve actually shifts to the left of the marginal utility curve for $\bar{b}^1$. Then it borrows more than it would if it had remained in power in both periods.[7]

Let us finally comment on the situation when there is government consumption also in period 1. Think of government 1 as having preferences over government consumption g_1 and g_2 in periods 1 and 2 described by the additively separable utility function $v_1^1(g_1) + v_2^1(g_2)$. If government 1 were in power in both periods, it would choose optimum levels of government consumption, $\bar{g}_1^1$ and $\bar{g}_2^1$, say, and an optimum level of borrowing $\bar{b}^1$. In the time-consistent equilibrium when government 1 is replaced by government 2 in period 2, would the time-consistent level of government consumption in period 1, $\hat{g}_1$, fall short of or exceed $\bar{g}_1^1$? The answer is that as long as the above utility function is additively separable, the time-consistent level of government consumption in period 1 is larger or smaller depending upon whether the time-consistent level of borrowing is larger or smaller than the level when government 1 is in power in both periods:

$$\hat{g}_1 \gtrless \bar{g}_1^1 \text{ if and only if } \hat{b} \gtrless \bar{b}^1. \tag{13}$$

The reason is that if borrowing is larger, for a constant level of period 1 government consumption, the period 1 tax rate on labor is smaller, and the distortion in period 1 is lower. This makes the marginal cost of period 1 government consumption lower, and allows an expansion of period 1 government consumption. (With intertemporal distortion of relative taxes, the marginal cost of government consumption in the two periods differs.)

IV Capital Controls

We shall now show an alternative setup that leads to the same formal analysis.[8] Consider a two-period small open exchange economy with one good. Governments have access to a world credit market, but due to capital controls consumers lack access to a credit market. Lump sum taxes are feasible. The only distortion is hence consumers' lack of access to the world credit market. A conservative government with preferences for a low government consumption is in power in period 1, and a more expansionary government is in power in period 2.

More precisely, let the private utility function be

$$u(c_1) + u(c_2). \tag{14}$$

With lump sum taxes T_1 and T_2 and no private borrowing, the private budget constraints are

$$c_1 = y_1 - T_1 \quad \text{and} \quad c_2 = y_2 - T_2, \tag{15}$$

where y_1 and y_2 are given private endowments of the one good.

The budget constraint of government 1 is

$$b + T_1 = 0 \quad \text{and} \quad g + b = T_2, \tag{16}$$

where b is international borrowing by the government (the world real interest rate is set to zero).

Substitution of (15) and (16) into (14) makes it possible to define the indirect utility function,

$$V(b, g) \equiv U(y_1 + b, y_2 - (b + g)), \tag{17}$$

which is analogous to the indirect utility function defined in (4). The analysis can then proceed almost exactly as in Sections II and III.

V Examples

We have shown how one may construct a theory where elements of political strategy influence the design of fiscal policy. Obviously, our model rests on many drastic simplifications in order to make our point as clearly as possible. But even if some assumptions were relaxed—along the lines suggested in the next section—the political considerations would only be one out of several determinants of fiscal policy. Finding clear empirical evidence in support of this theory will therefore not be easy.

Our argument rests on two basic premises: (a) when taking decisions on fiscal policy, governments look forward with a strategic motive, to influence prospective opposition governments; and (b) the inherited public debt influences a newly elected government's decision on taxation and spending.

Premise (a) is probably the harder one to verify. One of our motivations when writing the chapter, was the allegations about discussions in the (first) Reagan administration that the only way to lower government spending in the future was to lower current taxes in order to affect future congresses and administrations. The decrease in (total) U.S. government tax revenue less transfers in the 1980s and the deterioration in the budget position is clear from Figure 5.3a.[9] Unfortunately, we cannot yet check how the massive buildup of public debt during the Reagan administration affects the next presidential administration along the lines of premise (b).

Premise (b) is, of course, not unique to our theory. It also underlies more conventional analyses of dynamic fiscal policy where the government is viewed as a Pigovian agent interested in the welfare of the representative consumer (as in the references cited in Section I). Recent developments in countries other than the United States suggest that public debt inherited from previous governments do affect tax and spending policies. The Swedish experience in the last 10–15 years is a case in point. After a long period

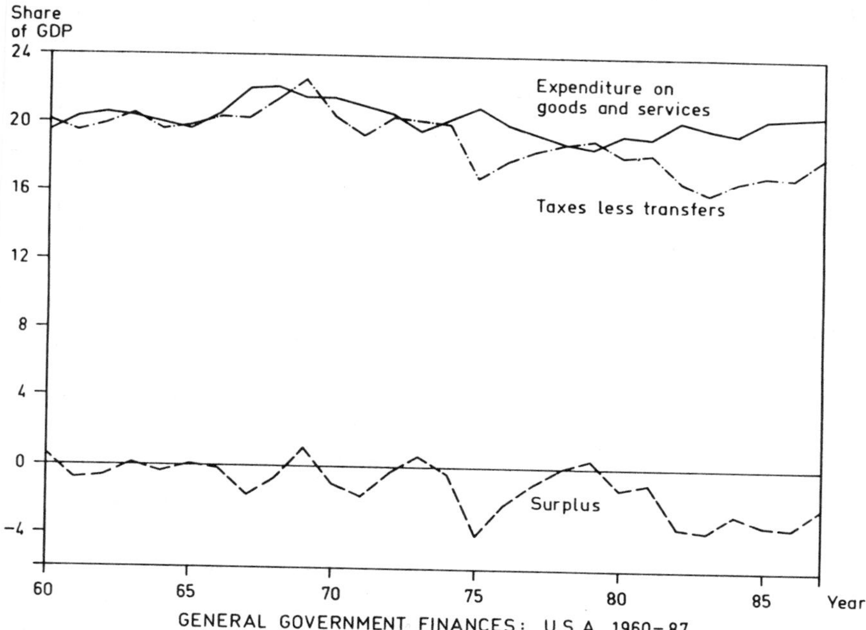

Figure 5.3a
General government finances: U.S.A. 1960–87

of Social Democratic rule, a nonsocialist government took office in 1976. As can be seen from Figure 5.3b, the previous growth in government expenditures continued in the six years of nonsocialist rule, whereas net taxes were lowered a bit.[10] This led to an even greater increase in the government (net) deficit (as a share of GDP) than for the United States during the 1980s. After 1982 when the Social Democrats were reelected, government spending has been virtually flat, however, while taxes have increased again to close the deficit and even create a surplus. The "bad public finances" and the accumulating government debt was indeed one of the main official motivations for the crunch in growth of public spending after 1982 and for the increase in net taxes. This is documented, for instance, in *The Swedish Budgets* (1983, especially pp. 21–23, and 36–37; 1984, especially pp. 30–31 and 41–43). It remains to be seen whether Figure 5.3a, when redrawn in the mid-1990s, will show a similar change in U.S. fiscal policy from 1989 and onward.

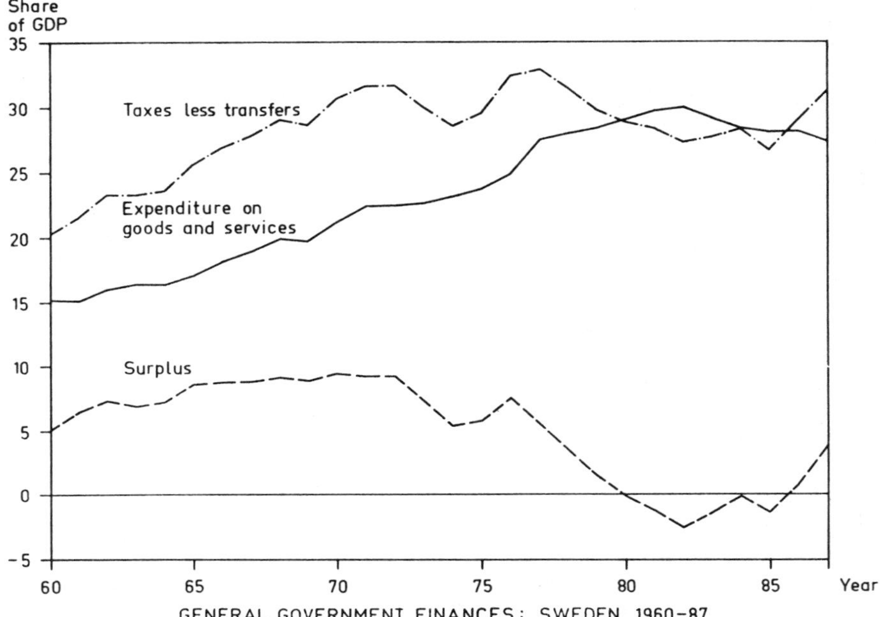

Figure 5.3b
General government finances: Sweden 1960–1987

What we have cited in this section is at best circumstantial evidence. Clearly, much more substantial empirical work is necessary to test the political theory of fiscal policy.

VI Conclusions and Possible Extensions

We have shown how a government can exert some influence over the future level of government consumption when preferences over government consumption are time inconsistent. A government, which is conservative in the sense of being less expansionary than its (liberal) successor, will collect less taxes and leave more public debt than the successor would prefer. This makes the time-consistent level of government consumption somewhere in between what each of the two governments would prefer if they would rule on their own. Especially, if the conservative government is relatively stubborn, it may end up borrowing more when it knows that it will be succeeded by the liberal government, compared with when it knows that it will remain in power. Stubbornness here refers to the weight the government attaches to reaching its preferred level of government consumption relative to the welfare cost of a distorted tax profile over time. Of course, the argument is completely symmetric, so a "stubborn" liberal government would choose to borrow less if it knew it would be succeeded by a more conservative government. Stretching our model slightly, it suggests that politically motivated deficits would be run by stubborn conservatives and "pragmatic" liberals.

Technically, the problem we have dealt with is a principal-agent problem, with government 1 being the principal and government 2 being the agent. The behavior of government 2 enters as an incentive-compatibility constraint in the decision problem of government 1.

There are several extensions of our analysis that may be worth pursuing. We have simplified the problem to a two-period perfect-foresight framework, where the current government knows with certainty that it will be succeeded by a more expansionary government. This framework may still be rather realistic when it refers to a president in his second term, with the constitution prohibiting reelection.[11] Nevertheless, it is clearly desirable to extend the analysis to one with several periods, and to one where there is uncertainty about the nature of succeeding governments, because of electoral uncertainty.

Such an analysis has independently been provided in a very interesting paper by Alesina and Tabellini (1986). They consider a situation with two governments that prefer different *kinds* of public goods, rather than different *levels* of the same public good as in our model. There is uncertainty in each period about whether the current government will remain in power or will be succeeded by the other government.[12] Since each current government knows that with some probability it will be succeeded in the next period by a government that will spend taxes on a kind of public good that the current government does not like, it perceives a low expected marginal utility of next period's public consumption. This provides an incentive to restrict next period's public consumption by borrowing more in the current period, compared with a situation when the current government would remain in power next period with certainty. Both governments perceive the same incentive to borrow more, hence there will be a bias toward larger public debt levels, whichever government is in power.

As mentioned, our analysis allows for the distinction between more and less expansionary (liberal and conservative) governments. The analysis ought to be extended to a situation with uncertainty and many periods, but we conjecture that uncertainty about whether the current government is succeeded or remains in power would not fundamentally change the behavior we have derived under perfect foresight.

Another very interesting expansion, although as far as we can see a very complicated one, would be to make the probability of being reelected depend upon the policy pursued. Additional extensions include the consideration of other state variables than public debt. For instance, if public goods can be produced only after previous investment in a public capital stock, the level and perhaps the composition of that public capital stock becomes an obvious state variable through which a government can affect its successor.

As already mentioned, the idea that a government can influence its successor by affecting the constraints of the successor is a very general one, and extends far beyond fiscal policy. Recent examples include the privatization policy of the Thatcher government in Britain, or the settlements policy of previous Likud governments in Israel, both of which policies will change (or have already changed) the constraints for succeeding governments with possibly very different preferences. In our view, this general view of "creating facts" for your successor sets an exciting agenda for future research.

Appendix: Derivation of (12)

Consider the following parameterization of government 2. Let the parameter γ in the utility function $v^2(g, \gamma)$ denote how expansionary government 2 is, in the sense that an increase in γ shifts up the marginal utility curve $\mu^2(g, \gamma)$. We call γ the expansion index. It follows that the level of government consumption if government 2 is in power in both periods will be an increasing function $\bar{g}^2(\gamma)$ of the expansion index. The time-consistent level of government consumption will also be an increasing function $\hat{g}(\gamma)$ of the expansion index. Choose the parameterization such that $\hat{g}(0) = \bar{g}^2(0) = \bar{g}^1$. That is, when the expansion index is zero, the two governments would prefer the same level of government consumption, which then of course coincides with the time-consistent level of government consumption. The time-consistent level of borrowing is also a function $\hat{b}(\gamma)$ of the expansion index. When the expansion index is zero, the time-consistent level of borrowing will coincide with the preferred level of borrowing of government 1 and government 2 (the level of borrowing each of them would choose if each were in power in both periods), $\hat{b}(0) = \bar{b}^1 = \bar{b}^2(0)$.

Now consider a small increase (from 0) in the expansion index. Whether the time-consistent borrowing increases above, or decreases below the level of borrowing $\bar{b}^1$, is determined by the sign of the derivative $\hat{b}_\gamma(\gamma)$ for $\gamma = 0$. More precisely, let $\hat{b}(\gamma) \equiv \tilde{b}(\hat{g}(\gamma, \gamma)$, where

$$\lambda^2(\tilde{b}(g, \gamma) + g) = \mu^2(g, \gamma), \tag{A.1}$$

$$\begin{aligned}\hat{\lambda}(g, \gamma) \equiv\ & -L_1[w_1(\tilde{b}(g, \gamma)]w_{1b}(\tilde{b}(g, \gamma))\tilde{b}_g(g, \gamma),\\ & -L_2[w_2(\tilde{b}(g, \gamma) + g)]w_{2G}(\tilde{b}(g, \gamma) + g)(\tilde{b}_g(g, \gamma) + 1)\end{aligned} \tag{A.2}$$

and

$$\hat{\lambda}(\hat{g}(\gamma), \gamma) = \mu^1(\hat{g}(\gamma)). \tag{A.3}$$

The expression for $\hat{\lambda}(g, \gamma)$ in (A.2) follows since $\hat{\lambda} = -\hat{V}_g$ and

$$d\hat{V} = dV = l_1\, dw_1 + l_2 dw_2. \tag{A.4}$$

Similarly,

$$\lambda^2(b + g) = -L_2[w_2(b + g)]w_{2G}(b + g), \tag{A.5}$$

since

$$dV^2 = l_2\, dw_2. \tag{A.6}$$

For $\gamma = 0$ we have

$$\hat{g}(0) = \bar{g}^1 \quad \text{and} \quad \hat{b}(0) = \bar{b}^1. \tag{A.7}$$

We assume that $L_1(w_1)$ and $L_2(w_2)$ are identical, that is, that the utility function (1) is symmetric in x_1 and x_2. Let $\bar{w}_1 = w_1(\bar{b}^1)$ and $\bar{w}_2 = w_2\bar{b}^1 + \bar{g}^1$. Then

$$\bar{w}_1 = \bar{w}_2 = \bar{w}, \tag{A.8}$$

and for $w_1 = w_2 = \bar{w}$ we have

$$l_1 = l_2, \quad L_{11} = L_{22}, \quad w_{1b} = -w_{2G}, \quad \text{and} \quad w_{1bb} = w_{2GG}. \tag{A.9}$$

Differentiation of (A.2) with respect to g for $\gamma = 0$ and use of (A.9) yields

$$\hat{\lambda}_g(\bar{g}^1, 0) = [-L_{22}(w_{2G})^2 - l_2 w_{2GG}][(\tilde{b}_g)^2 + (\tilde{b}_g + 1)^2]. \tag{A.10}$$

Differentiation of (A.5) gives

$$\lambda_G^2(\bar{b}^1 + \bar{g}^1) = -L_{22}(w_{2G})^2 - l_2 w_{2GG}. \tag{A.11}$$

Together (A.10) and (A.11) imply that for $\gamma = 0$

$$\hat{\lambda}_g = \gamma_G^2[(\tilde{b}_g)^2 + (\tilde{b}_g + 1)^2]. \tag{A.12}$$

Similarly, differentiating (A.2) with respect to γ at $\gamma = 0$, we obtain

$$\hat{\lambda}_\gamma = \lambda_G^2(2\tilde{b}_g + 1)\tilde{b}_\gamma. \tag{A.13}$$

From (A.1) we get

$$\tilde{b}_g = -(\lambda_G^2 - \mu_g^2)/\lambda_G^2 \leq -1 \tag{A.14}$$

and

$$\tilde{b}_\gamma = \mu_\gamma^2/\lambda_G^2 > 0, \tag{A.15}$$

and from (A.3)

$$\hat{g}_\gamma = -\hat{\lambda}_\gamma/(\hat{\lambda}_g - \mu_g^1). \tag{A.16}$$

Finally, from (A.1) we have

$$\hat{b}_\gamma = \tilde{b}_g \hat{g}_\gamma + \tilde{b}_\gamma. \tag{A.17}$$

We can use the results in (A.12)–(A.14) and (A.16) to evaluate $\hat{b}_\gamma$ as expressed in (A.17). We carry out the substitutions and manipulate the resulting expression to get

$$\hat{b}_\gamma = \tilde{b}_\gamma(\mu_g^2 - \mu_g^1)/[(\tilde{b}_g)^2 + (\tilde{b}_g + 1)^2 - \mu_g^1/\lambda_G^2]. \tag{A.18}$$

The denominator is positive, and by (A.15) $\tilde{b}_\gamma > 0$.

It follows that

$$\text{sign}\, \hat{b}_\gamma = \text{sign}[-\mu_g^1 - (-\mu_g^2)]. \tag{A.19}$$

Note that (A.12) and (A.14) imply that

$$\hat{\lambda}_g \geq \lambda_G^2. \tag{A.20}$$

Notes

This is an extended and revised version of Persson and Svensson (1987), which was presented at the Sapir Conference on Economic Effects of the Government Budget in Tel-Aviv, December 22–24, 1986. Support from NSF Grant No. SES-8605871 is gratefully acknowledged. We have benefited from comments by participants in seminars at the University of Rochester, University of Pennsylvania, Columbia University, Harvard University, Stanford University, University of California, Los Angeles, Federal Reserve Bank in Minneapolis, by participants in the Conference, in particular Maurice Obstfeld, and by an anonymous referee.

1. Alesina and Tabellini (1986) have independently pursued a very interesting analysis of public debt in the complementary case when different governments have preferences for different kinds of public goods, rather than as in our case preferences for different volumes of the same public good. A comparison with their analysis and results is given in the concluding section.

2. Phelps and Pollak (1968) provide an early analysis of equilibrium savings ratios in a model with time-inconsistent preferences. In their analysis there are nonoverlapping generations, such that each generation lives for only one period, but has preferences over consumption of future generations. Each generation discounts the utility from future generations' consumption in a way that makes generations' preferences time inconsistent. There is no state variable through which a generation can affect future generations' behavior. Hence the issue of how to affect your successor in an optimal way does not arise.

3. The solutions to (3) need not be unique. If two or more wage rates are solutions to (3), the wage functions correspond to the largest of these wage rates, which are the wage rates that minimize welfare loss. It is only these wage rates that solve an optimum taxation problem. (This reasoning is equivalent to being on the relevant side of the Laffer curve.)

4. The ex post indirect utility of private consumption can be written as a function of predetermined period 1 consumption and labor supply, savings from period 1, and the wage rate in period 2. With additive separability the indirect utility function can eventually be written as $U^2(w_2; l_1, w_1)$ (see Svensson and Persson 1987 for details). Define the ex post indirect utility function, $V^2(b+g; l_1, w_1) \equiv U^2(w_2(b+g); l_1, w_1)$, and define the ex post marginal cost of government consumption as

$$\lambda^2(b+g) \equiv -V_G^2(b+g).$$

(Since the period 2 indirect utility function $V^2(b+g; l, w_1)$ will be additively separable in $b+g$, the ex post marginal cost will be independent of period 1 labor supply and after-tax wage rate. Total government expenditure in period 2, $b+g$, is denoted by G.)

5. We have $\tilde{b}_g = -(\lambda_G^2 - \mu_g^2)/\lambda_G^2 \leq -1$.

6. Note that the required debt function is the locus of points for which the indifference curves of the function $V^2(b+g; l_1, w_1) + v^2(g)$ (not shown in the figure) are horizontal, *not* the locus where indifference curves of the function $W^2(b,g) = V(b,g) + v^2(g)$ (shown in the figure) are horizontal.

7. In terms of the lower half of the figure, a flatter marginal utility curve for government 2 makes the required debt curve flatter, which tends to move the tangency point D' up.

8. We owe the idea for this alternative interpretation to Maurice Obstfeld.

9. The U.S. data are from the *Economic Report of the President 1988*.

10. The Swedish data are from the *National Accounts: Annual Reports* (various issues).

11. Another interpretation is that there is uncertainty about the preferences of the successor, that the probability distribution over preferences is one-dimensional (conservative-liberal) and has a finite support, and that the current government is extreme in the sense of being at the conservative (liberal) end of the support. Then any succeeding government, and the expected succeeding government, is more liberal (conservative) than the current one.

12. Exogenous uncertainty about the composition of the electorate creates uncertainty about election outcomes, when voters vote for the government whose preferences are most similar to the voters' own preferences.

References

Alesina, A., and Tabellini, G. 1986. A Positive theory of fiscal deficits and government debt in a democracy. Mimeo.

Alesina, A., and Tabellini, G. 1988. Credibility and politics. *European Economic Review* 32:542–550

Lucas, R. E., Jr., and Stokey, N. L. 1983. Optimal fiscal and monetary policy in an economy without capital. *Journal of Monetary Economics* 12:55–93. Reprinted as chapter 14 in volume 1 of this work.

Persson, M., Persson, T., and Svensson, L. 1987. Time consistency of fiscal and monetary policy. *Econometrica* 6:1419–1431. Reprinted as chapter 15 in volume 1 of this work.

Persson, T. 1988. Credibility of macroeconomic policy: An introduction and a broad survey. *European Economic Review* 32:519–532.

Persson, T., and Svensson, L. 1984. Time-consistent fiscal policy and government cash-flow. *Journal of Monetary Economics* 14:365–374.

Persson, T., and Svensson, L. 1987. Checks and balances on the government budget. IIES Seminar paper no. 380.

Phelps, E. S., and Pollak, R. A. 1968. On second-best national saving and game-equilibrium growth. *Review of Economic Studies* 35:185–199.

Rogoff, K. 1987. Reputational constraints on monetary policy. *Carnegie-Rochester Conference Series on Public Policy* 26:141–181.

The Swedish Budget 1983/84: A summary published by the Ministry of Finance. Stockholm: Minab/Gotab, 1983.

The Swedish Budget 1984/85: A summary published by the Ministry of Finance. Stockholm: Minab/Gotab, 1984.

6 Voting on the Budget Deficit

Guido Tabellini and Alberto Alesina

Opinion polls show that American voters disapprove of the federal budget deficit. However, it is politically difficult to reach an agreement on how to balance the budget: several polls show that even though voters dislike deficits, they are not in favor of any specific measure to reduce them.[1]

Two explanations for this apparent inconsistency of opinions are commonly proposed. One is that voters do not understand the concept of budget constraint, and suffer from "fiscal illusion." However, this notion is difficult to reconcile with standard assumptions of rationality.[2] The other is that disagreement generates cycling and prevents the existence of a stable majority in favor of balancing the budget. As a result, individual preferences about intertemporal fiscal policy cannot be aggregated, and no action can be taken to balance the budget. However, this argument is consistent with any outcome (deficit, surplus, balance) since the political equilibrium is indeterminate.

This chapter provides an alternative explanation of budget deficits, that is based upon the inability of current voters to bind the choices of future voters. This lack of commitment, coupled with disagreement between current and future majorities, introduces a time inconsistency in the dynamic social choice problem that determines the size of budget deficits or surpluses. The policies desired by the current majority would not be carried out if future majorities exhibit different preferences. This induces the current majority to choose a debt policy that is not ex ante optimal for society as a whole. The deviation from optimality can be in the direction of excessive surpluses or deficits. The chapter shows that a large class of individual utility functions leads to a social choice of budget *deficits*. This explains why it is hard to agree on how to eliminate deficits, even if there is a consensus that they may be socially suboptimal.

Our results have a simple economic intuition. Consider a rational voter who is presented with a number of options on how much to spend in the current period, and over what items. He votes not only on the intertemporal profile of spending, but also on how to allocate the resources acquired by issuing debt (or lost through a surplus). Suppose that there is uncertainty about the future composition of public spending, because the

Reprinted from *American Economic Review*, 80 (1990) 37–49, by permission of the American Economic Association.

identity of future majorities is still unknown. Then, whereas the majority who runs a budget deficit also chooses how to allocate the debt proceeds, the allocation of the burden of repaying the debt is not under its control. Under appropriate conditions this asymmetry prevents the current majority from fully internalizing the costs of budget deficits, the more so the greater is the difference between its preferences and the expected preferences of the future majority.

The chapter also shows that if this asymmetry is removed, and the vote on the deficit is taken behind a "veil of ignorance" on how the debt proceeds are spent, then the voters unanimously choose a balanced budget. That is, in this model a balanced budget is ex ante efficient. This implies that current voters would like to precommit future governments to a balanced budget rule, but no majority wants to be bound by the rule. Thus, a balanced-budget rule is enforceable only if a qualified majority is required to abrogate it.

Our results are related to those of other papers on intertemporal politico-economic models of fiscal policy. In particular, Alberto Alesina and Guido Tabellini (1987, 1989) and Guido Tabellini (1989) analyze a general equilibrium model in which two ideologically motivated parties randomly alternate in office and disagree on the optimal composition of public spending, or on the level of taxation of different constituencies. Torsten Persson and Lars Svensson (1989) consider a government that knows that its successor will want to increase public spending. In these papers as in ours, public debt is a strategic variable that affects the actions of future policymakers.

In this earlier literature, however, either the political equilibrium is exogenously given (as in Torsten Persson and Lars Svensson, 1989), or voters have to choose between two ideological candidates with fixed positions (as in Alberto Alesina and Guido Tabellini, 1987, 1989, and Guido Tabellini, 1989). In the latter case, in equilibrium both parties choose the same deficit, even though they choose a different composition of government spending. Thus, in effect, voters in these papers do not have a choice on the deficit. In particular, the question remains of whether the deficit would disappear if a centrist party, promising to balance the budget, enters the political arena. In this chapter there are no constraints on the policy options available to the voters. Any proposal can be voted upon in a pairwise comparison, and the voters directly vote on the size of the deficit.

The idea that state variables can be used to influence future voting outcomes is applicable to other public choice problems, besides those concerning budget deficits. For example, Ami Glazer (1987) exploits this insight to investigate the choice of durability in public capital projects. He shows that uncertainty about future voting outcomes generates a bias toward overinvesting in long-run projects. Other possible applications are to privatization decisions and defense policy.

Finally, our argument is completely different from the idea that deficits occur because the current generation does not internalize the costs of taxing future generations: in our model everybody has the same time horizon. In an overlapping generations model with no altruism, on the other hand, current voters would be unanimously in favor of the largest possible budget deficit, so as to redistribute the income of future generations toward themselves. In such a model, the equilibrium would always be a corner solution and the size of budget deficits would be determined exclusively by the borrowing capacity of the government.[3]

The rest of the chapter is organized as follows. Section I describes the model. The political equilibrium is computed in Section II. Section III discusses normative and positive implications for the issue of balanced budget amendments. The last section suggests some extensions.

I The Model

A group of heterogeneous individuals decides by majority rule on the consumption of two public goods, g and f. The group is endowed with one unit of output in each period, and it can borrow from or lend to the rest of the world at a given real interest rate, with no loss of generality, assumed to be 0. The world lasts two periods, and all the outstanding debt has to be repaid in full at the end of the second period. Thus, the group faces the intertemporal constraint:

$$g_1 + f_1 - b \leq 1 \tag{1a}$$

$$f_2 + g_2 + b \leq 1, \tag{1b}$$

where subscripts denote time periods and b denotes debt. In addition, the nonnegativity constraints hold: $g_i, f_i \geq 0, i = 1, 2$. Hence, (1b) immediately implies $-1 \leq b \leq 1$. Throughout the chapter we assume that in equilibrium $-1 < b < 1$. The extension to the case $b = 1$ is straightforward, and just involves some changes in notation. At the beginning of each period, the group votes on how much to consume of each public good in that period. Thus, in period 1 the group cannot precommit to consume a specific quantity of g_2 and f_2 in the following period.

The preferences of the ith member of the group are:

$$W^i \equiv E\left\{\sum_{t=1}^{2} [\alpha^i u(g_t) + (1 - \alpha^i)u(f_t)]\right\} \tag{2}$$

where $u(\cdot)$ is concave, strictly increasing, twice continuously differentiable, and satisfies the Inada condition: $u'(0) \rightarrow \infty$. $E(\cdot)$ denotes the expectation operator. With no loss of generality, we assume that voters do not discount the future; thus the rate of time preference is equal the world real interest rate. This eliminates any incentive to borrow or lend other than those which are the explicit focus of this chapter.

The parameter α^i which identifies voter i is distributed over the $[0, 1]$ interval. With only a minor change in notation, all the results can be extended to allow for values of α^i greater than 1 or negative.

This specification of individual preferences allows for disagreement about which proportion of the two public goods to consume. However, it implies that all individual preferences belong to the class of "intermediate preferences" defined by Jean Michel Grandmont (1978).[4] This class has the following useful property: individual preferences are indexed by the parameter α^i and the distribution of preferences within the group is fully summarized by the distribution of α^i. As shown by Grandmont (1978), since α^i is a scalar, preferences are single peaked and the median voter result applies: provided that all policy options are compared pairwise, the group decisions under majority rule coincide with the most preferred policy of the individual corresponding to the median value of α, denoted α^m. Thus, the political equilibrium can be computed by solving the problem of maximizing (2) subject to (1), with $\alpha^i = \alpha^m$ in (2).

A crucial feature of the model is that even though individual preferences remain stable over time, the identity of the median voter need not be the same in periods 1 and 2 (this is the reason for having the expectations operator in equation 2). Changes in the identity of the median voter over time may be due to: (i) random shocks to the costs of voting that affect the participation rate (see John Ledyard, 1984, for a formalization of this idea); or (ii) changes in the eligibility of the voting population (for instance, because of minimum age requirements, or because of geographical movements of the population). As discussed in subsection II.D below, the extent to which these events change the median voter's preferences, in turn, depends on the underlying distribution of individual preferences.

This simple setup can be interpreted as a stylized version of several richer models. The most direct interpretation is that of a "club" with a fixed endowment to be allocated to different uses. With minor changes, the club can be interpreted as a country in which taxes are fixed and economic agents have access to a linear storage technology or to international capital markets. In an interior equilibrium, the real rate of interest on public debt equals the technologically given rate of return on storage or the world rate of interest. The extension to a model with endogenous distortionary taxation significantly increases the complexity of the analysis, without qualitatively changing the basic message of this chapter. Alberto Alesina and Guido Tabellini (1987) illustrate this point in a model with a much simpler political structure.

II Political Equilibrium

A The Last Period

Consider the last period, and let α_2^m denote the value of α^i corresponding to the median voter in period 2. Two cases are possible, depending on the value of α_2^m.

If $1 > \alpha_2^m > 0$, then the median voter is at an interior optimum. In this case, his choices satisfy the following first-order condition:

$$\alpha_2^m u'(g_2) - (1 - \alpha_2^m)u'(1 - b - g_2) = 0. \tag{3}$$

Equations (3) and (1b) implicitly define the equilibrium values g_2^* and f_2^* as a function of α_2^m and b. Let us indicate these functions as $g_2^* = G(\alpha_2^m, b)$ and $f_2^* = 1 - b - g_2^* \equiv F(\alpha_2^m, b)$. The implicit function theorem applied to (3) and (1b), shows that, for $1 > \alpha_2^m > 0$, $G_\alpha = -F_\alpha > 0$, $-1 < G_b < 0$, and $-1 < F_b < 0$, where G_α, G_b, F_α and F_b denote the partial derivative of $G(\cdot)$ and $F(\cdot)$ with respect to a_2^m and b, respectively.

If, instead, $\alpha_2^m = 1$ or $\alpha_2^m = 0$, then the median voter of period 2 is at a corner. If $\alpha_2^m = 1$, he sets $g_2^* = 1 - b$ and $f_2^* = 0$; thus $G_b = -1$ and $F_b = 0$. Symmetric results hold if $\alpha_2^m = 0$.

B The First Period: Preliminary Results

In period 1 there is uncertainty about the identity of the median voter of period 2. Hence, from the point of view of the voters in period 1, the parameter α_2^m in (3) is a random variable. The policy most preferred by the median voter of period 1 (whose preferences are denoted by α_1^m) can be found by solving the following optimization problem:

$$\max_{g_1, b} \{\alpha_1^m u(g_1) + (1 - \alpha_1^m) u(1 - g_1 + b) + E[\alpha_1^m u(G(\alpha_2^m, b)) + (1 - \alpha_1^m) u(F(\alpha_2^m, b))]\}. \tag{4}$$

The current median voter maximizes an expected utility function, since in the second period g_2 and f_2 may be chosen by a different majority. The expectation operator is taken with respect to α_2^m. Thus, today's voters choose the value of the state variable b taking into account how this choice influences the policies chosen by future majorities.[5]

If $1 > \alpha_1^m > 0$, the first-order condition relative to g_1 is:

$$\alpha_1^m u'(g_1) - (1 - \alpha_1^m) u'(1 + b - g_1) = 0. \tag{5}$$

Equation (5) implicitly defines the optimal values g_1^* and f_1^*, as a function of α_1^m and b: $g_1^* = g(\alpha_1^m, b), f_1^* = f(\alpha_1^m, b)$. Using the same notation as before, it can be shown that, for $1 > \alpha_1^m > 0$, $1 > g_b > 0$, and $f_b = 1 - g_b$. If instead $\alpha_1^m = 1$ (or $\alpha_1^m = 0$), then the median voter in period 1 is at a corner and chooses respectively $f_1^* = 0$ and $g_1^* = 1 + b$ (or $g_1^* = 0$ and $f_1^* = 1 + b$).

The intertemporal choice is described by the first-order condition of problem (4) relative to b, which for $b < 1$ is:

$$\alpha_1^m u'(g(\alpha_1^m, b)) + E[\alpha_1^m u'(G(\alpha_2^m, b)) G_b + (1 - \alpha_1^m) \times u'(F(\alpha_2^m, b)) F_b] = 0, \tag{6}$$

where G_b and F_b are functions of α_2^m and b. Despite the concavity of $u(\cdot)$, the second-order conditions are not satisfied unless an additional mild condition is imposed. We assume throughout the paper that this condition is satisfied for any value of α_2^m and α_1^m.[6]

The first term on the left-hand side of (6) is the marginal gain of issuing one more unit of debt; at the optimum, this must coincide with the marginal utility of spending one extra unit on either of the two public goods (good g in equation 6). The second term of (6) is the expected marginal disutility of repaying the debt, by cutting public spending tomorrow. This term takes into account that the future composition of public spending depends on α_2^m. The solution to equation (6) determines the equilibrium value of debt, b^*, chosen by majority rule in period 1.

In order to sign b^* in the next subsection we consider equation (6) at the point $b = 0$. If at this point equation (6) is satisfied, then $b^* = 0$. If instead at $b = 0$ the left-hand side of (6) is positive (negative), then by the second-order condition $b^* > 0$ ($b^* < 0$).

C The Equilibrium Level of Debt

Consider first the case in which the median voter at time 1 is certain that he will also be the median voter in period 2 (i.e., $\alpha_1^m = \alpha_2^m$ with certainty). The second term in (6) reduces to $\alpha_1^m u'(G(\alpha_1^m, b))$, so that $b^* = 0$ is the only solution to (6) for any value of α_1^m. Intuitively, since the discount rate coincides with the real interest rate (they are both zero), in the absence of political instability the median voter chooses to spend an equal aggregate amount in both periods. It is easy to show that $b^* = 0$ is also the policy that would be chosen by a social planner maximizing a weighted sum of individual utilities, for any choice of weights in the planner's objectives. Thus, with no disagreement between current and future majorities, the political equilibrium lies on the Pareto frontier.

The remainder of this section investigates the case in which $\alpha_2^m \neq \alpha_1^m$ with positive probability. It is convenient to divide the second term on the left-hand side of (6) into the weighted average of two conditional expectations: the expectation conditional on the event that $1 > \alpha_2^m > 0$; and the expectation conditional on the event that $\alpha_2^m = 1$ or $\alpha_2^m = 0$.

Although special, the second case provides the simplest illustration of why political instability creates incentives to issue public debt. In this case future median voters are expected to be at a corner, so that they spend in only one kind of public good: g_2 if $\alpha_2^m = 1$, and f_2 if $\alpha_2^m = 0$. If $\alpha_2^m \neq \alpha_1^m$ with positive probability, we have:

PROPOSITION 1 (i) If either $\alpha_2^m = 0$ or $\alpha_2^m = 1$, then b* > 0. (ii) b* is greater the larger is the difference between α_1^m and the expected value of α_2^m.

Proof (i) Let $\alpha_2^m = 1$ with probability π and $\alpha_2^m = 0$ with probability $1 - \pi$, $1 > \pi > 0$. Then, using (5), equation (6) can be rewritten as:

$$\alpha_1^m u'(g_1^*) - \tilde{\alpha} u'(1 - b) = (1 - \alpha_1^m) u'(f_1^*) - \tilde{\alpha} u'(1 - b) = 0, \tag{7}$$

where $\tilde{\alpha} = \alpha_1^m \pi + (1 - \pi)(1 - \alpha_1^m)$. Clearly, $\tilde{\alpha} \leq \text{Max}(\alpha_1^m, (1 - \alpha_1^m))$, with strict inequality if $\alpha_1^m \neq 1/2$. Moreover, at the point $b = 0$, $u'(1 - b) \leq u'(g(\alpha_1^m, b))$ and $u'(1 - b) \leq u'(f(\alpha_1^m, b))$, with strict inequality if $1 > \alpha_1^m > 0$. Hence, at the point $b = 0$ the two terms in the left-hand sides of (7) are always strictly positive. By the second-order conditions this implies $b^* > 0$. (ii) The expected value of α_2^m is π. Fix α_1^m, and consider b^* as a function of π. We have:

$$\frac{db^*}{d\pi} = \frac{db^*}{d\tilde{\alpha}}\frac{d\tilde{\alpha}}{d\pi} = \frac{db^*}{d\tilde{\alpha}}(2\alpha_1^m - 1). \tag{8}$$

Applying the implicit function theorem to (7), we obtain that $db^*/d\tilde{\alpha} < 0$. Hence,

$$\frac{db^*}{d\pi} \lesseqgtr 0 \quad \text{as} \quad \alpha_1^m \gtreqless \frac{1}{2}. \tag{9}$$

Thus, if $\alpha_1^m > 1/2$, a lower value of π increases b^*. And conversely, if $\alpha_1^m < 1/2$, a higher value of π increases b^*. Hence, b^* increases with the difference between α_1^m and the expected value of α_2^m. □

The intuition is that an increase in debt today implies a reduction of aggregate spending tomorrow. But tomorrow only one kind of public good will be consumed. Hence, with positive probability (and with probability 1 if $1 > \alpha_1^m > 0$), this reduction of spending will affect only the good with a low marginal utility from the point of view of today's median voter. Thus, the median voter of period 1 does not fully internalize the cost of issuing debt: he finds it optimal to spend in excess of the current aggregate endowment. Moreover, the incentive to borrow is stronger the lower is the marginal utility of the future public good. This is more likely to happen if the future median voter has very different tastes from the current median voter.

We now show that, under appropriate conditions, this basic intuition extends to the more general case in which α_2^m lies in the open interval (0,1). With no loss of generality, suppose that over this interval α_2^m is distributed according to a continuous probability function $H(\cdot)$, where $H(\alpha) \equiv \text{prob}(\alpha_2^m \leq \alpha)$. Then (6) can be rewritten as:

$$\int_0^1 [\alpha_1^m u'(g_1^*) - v(\alpha_2^m)]\, dH(\alpha_2^m) = 0, \tag{10}$$

where $u(\alpha_2^m)$ is the marginal cost of repaying the debt, given that in period 2 the median voter tastes parameter is α_2^m. After some transformations obtain:

$$v(\alpha_2^m) = \frac{u'(g_2^*)u'(f_2^*)[\alpha_1^m\lambda(f_2^*) + (1 - \alpha_1^m)\lambda(g_2^*)]}{u'(g_2^*)\lambda(g_2^*) + u'(f_2^*)\lambda(f_2^*)}, \tag{11}$$

where $g_2^* = G(\alpha_2^m, b)$, $f_2^* = F(\alpha_2^m, b)$, and where $\lambda(\cdot) \equiv -u''(\cdot)/[u'(\cdot)]^2$ is the "concavity index" of $u(\cdot)$ as in Gerard Debreu and Tjalling C. Koopmans (1982).

We now assume that $u(\cdot)$ has the following property.[7]

(c) The concavity index of $u(x)$, $\lambda(x)$, is decreasing in x, for $1 > x > 0$.

That is, we assume that $u(\cdot)$ becomes less concave in the sense of the index of Gerard Debreu and Tjalling C. Koopmans (1982) as consumption increases. This hypothesis is more restrictive than decreasing absolute risk aversion: it implies that the coefficient of absolute risk aversion falls more rapidly than marginal utility as consumption increases. This hypothesis is satisfied for several commonly used utility functions, such as any CES function $u(x) = x^\gamma/\gamma$ with $1 > \gamma > 0$.

The Appendix proves that, at the point $b = 0$, $\alpha_1^m u'(f_1) - u(\alpha_2^m) > 0$ for any $\alpha_2^m \neq \alpha_1^m$ if $u(\cdot)$ satisfies condition (c). Hence, under this condition, at the point $b = 0$ the marginal gain of issuing debt exceeds the corresponding expected marginal cost (i.e., the left-hand side of (10) is strictly positive at the point $b = 0$). Thus:

PROPOSITION 2 Given that $\alpha_2^m \in (0, 1)$, $b^* > 0$ if (c) holds.

Next, let us define the probability distribution $H(\alpha_2^m)$ as "more polarized relative to α_1^m" than the distribution $K(\alpha_2^m)$ if, for any continuous increasing function $f(\cdot)$, the following condition is satisfied:

$$\int_0^1 f(|\alpha_2^m - \alpha_1^m|)\, dH(\alpha_2^m) > \int_0^1 f(|\alpha_2^m - \alpha_1^m|)\, dK(\alpha_2^m). \tag{12}$$

That is, a more polarized probability distribution assigns more weight to values of α_2^m that are further apart from α_1^m. The Appendix also proves that, if condition (c) holds, then for any $b > 0$ the expression $[\alpha_1^m u'(g_1^*) - v(\alpha_2^m)]$ is an increasing function of $|\alpha_2^m - \alpha_1^m|$ (strictly increasing if $|\alpha_2^m - \alpha_1^m| > 0$). Then, using (10) and appealing to the second-order conditions, we also have:[8]

PROPOSITION 3 Under the same condition of Proposition 2, b^* is larger the more polarized is the probability distribution of α_2^m relative to α_1^m over the interval (0, 1).

If the concavity index $\lambda(x)$ is everywhere increasing (constant) for $1 > x > 0$, then Propositions 2 and 3 hold in reverse: $b^* < 0$ ($b^* = 0$), and b^* is more negative if $H(\alpha_2^m)$ is more polarized. If $\lambda(x)$ is not monotonic over $1 > x > 0$, then the sign of b^* is ambiguous.

The role played by condition (c) is highlighted in Figure 6.1. The downward sloping line denotes the opportunity set faced by the median voters in both periods if $b = 0$. A positive value of b shifts this line to the right in period 1, and to the left in period 2. A and B denote the points chosen in periods 1 and 2 by the median voters of type α_1^m and α_2^m respectively, again for $b = 0$. For concreteness, it has been assumed that $\alpha_1^m > 1/2 > \alpha_2^m$. The indifference curves for the median voter of type α_1^m in periods 1 and 2 are labeled I and II, respectively. Finally, the upward sloping lines EP_1 and EP_2 denote the income expansion paths of types α_1^m and α_2^m. With a decreasing concavity index, the voters' indifference curves become flatter at higher levels of income; that is, the two public goods become closer substitutes. As a result, the divergence between the choices of the two types of

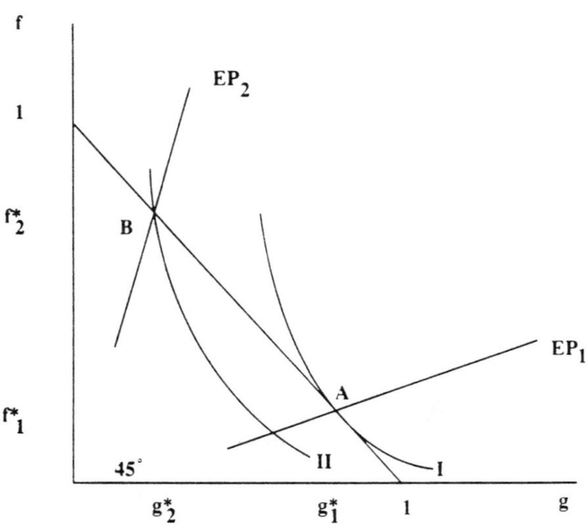

Figure 6.1

median voter increases with income, and their income expansion paths diverge.[9] To put it differently, with a decreasing concavity index for $u(\cdot)$, disagreement concerning the optimal composition of g and f is a luxury good: it grows with the overall size of public spending.

The ambiguity of the sign of b^* for $1 > \alpha_2^m > 0$ is due to the opposite influence of two countervailing forces. By running a surplus ($b < 0$), the median voter in period 1 moves A to the left along EP_1 and B to the right along EP_2; this has the effect of reducing the distance between the indifference curves labeled I and II. Hence, a surplus "buys insurance" for the median voter of period 1, since it tends to equalize the median voter's utility in the two periods. This is the force that works in the direction of making a surplus today more desirable.

On the other hand by running a deficit ($b > 0$), the median voter of period 1 moves B to the left along EP_2. This takes the future composition of public spending toward the point that is preferred by today's median voter. This is the force that provides the incentive to issue public debt today. Debt is used strategically, to influence the future spending decision in the direction preferred by the current majority.

Condition (c) guarantees that the second effect dominates the first. This condition is more likely to be satisfied if the slopes of EP_1 and EP_2 are very divergent from each other (that is, if the substitutability of g and f increases very rapidly with income); or if the indifference curves are very flat (that is, if the utility function is not very concave), because in this case the indifference curves labeled I and II are close to each other.

Summarizing, Propositions 1–3 imply that an equilibrium with debt occurs if: (i) the future median voter has extreme preferences and is at a corner (i.e., $\alpha_2^m \notin (0, 1)$); or (ii) the concavity index of $u(\cdot)$ is decreasing. Moreover, in both cases, the size of debt is larger the greater is the likelihood of values of α_2^m very different from α_1^m; that is, using the previous terminology, the more polarized are the current and future majorities.

In a more general model, the future median voter could be at a corner even if $1 > \alpha_2^m > 0$. For instance, if the utility function $u(\cdot)$ did not satisfy the Inada conditions, so that the indifference curve of Figure 6.1 would intersect either the horizontal or the vertical axis. Alternatively, if the public goods g and f had to be provided in some minimum amounts (for instance, because of survival reasons), the future decision maker could be at a corner even for $1 > \alpha_2^m > 0$. In both cases, the income expansion paths of future majorities would be either vertical or horizontal, so that issuing debt would always take the composition of public spending in the desired direction.[10]

D Positive Implications

Propositions 1–3 relate the size of budget deficits to the instability of the median voters' preferences over time. This type of instability, in turn, depends upon the distribution of individual preferences within society. We now argue that the more "homogeneous" the preferences of different individuals, ceteris paribus, the more stable the median voter preferences over time.

Consider a family of density functions indexed by ε: let $\gamma(\alpha, \varepsilon)$ be the frequency distribution of α over the $[0, 1]$ interval, where α is the parameter that summarizes individual preferences in equation (2). Thus, ε represents a perturbation of the distribution of the voters' preferences, associated with random shocks to the voting participation or to the eligibility of the voting population.

The median voter's preferences, $\alpha^{\mathrm{m}}(\varepsilon)$, are then defined implicitly by:

$$\int_0^{\alpha^m} \gamma(\alpha, \varepsilon)\, d\alpha - \frac{1}{2} = 0. \tag{13}$$

The relationship between α^m and ε depends on the properties of the density function $\gamma(\alpha, \varepsilon)$: by applying the implicit function theorem to (13) one obtains:

$$\frac{d\alpha^m}{d\varepsilon} = -\frac{\displaystyle\int_0^{\alpha^m} \gamma_\varepsilon(\alpha, \varepsilon)\, d\alpha}{\gamma(\alpha^m, \varepsilon)}, \tag{14}$$

where $\gamma_\varepsilon(\alpha, \varepsilon) \equiv \partial\gamma(\cdot)/\partial\varepsilon$. The numerator of (14) is the area underneath the density function that is shifted from one side to the other of α^m as ε varies. According to (14), for a given value of the numerator, the term $d\alpha^m/d\varepsilon$ is larger in absolute value the smaller is $\gamma(\alpha^m, \varepsilon)$. That is, if there are relatively few individuals in the population that share the median voter's preferences (i.e., if $\gamma(\alpha^m, \varepsilon)$ is small for all ε), then α^m varies a lot as the distribution is perturbed. Conversely, if the median voter preferences are representative of a large part of the population (i.e., if $\gamma(\alpha^m, \varepsilon)$ is large), then α^m is stable even in the face of large perturbations.

This result is illustrated in Figure 6.2. Consider the top distribution first. When ε changes from ε_1 to ε_2, a fraction of individuals corresponding to the area A is moved from the right to the left of $\alpha_1^m = \alpha^m(\varepsilon_1)$, to the area $A^1 = A$. This area is the numerator of (14). The new median voter, $\alpha_2^m = \alpha^m(\varepsilon_2)$, is found by equating the area between α_1^m and α_2^m, B, to the area A. Repeat the same perturbation to the distribution in the bottom of Figure 6.2. Clearly, the same area B corresponds to a larger horizontal distance between α_1^m and α_2^m: since the frequency of the population around α^m is relatively small, the median voter's preferences shift more than in the case of the upper distribution. This is the sense in which a more polarized distribution of voters' preferences is associated with more instability in the induced probability distribution of the median voter's preferences.

These considerations are suggestive of a testable implication that can explain the observed cross-country differences in debt policies. In more unstable and polarized political systems, there is a higher probability that future majorities will allocate government revenues to uses that are not

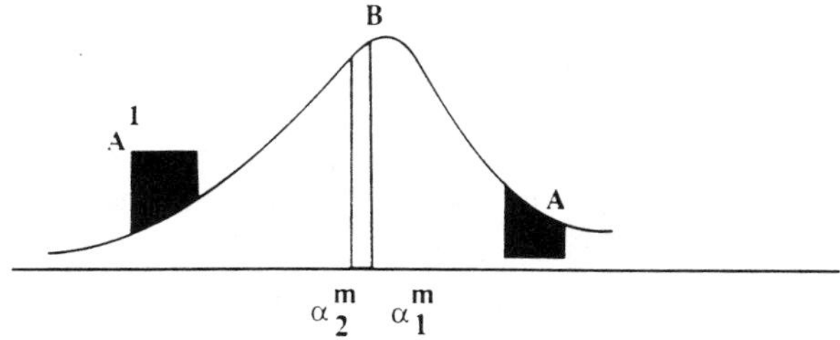

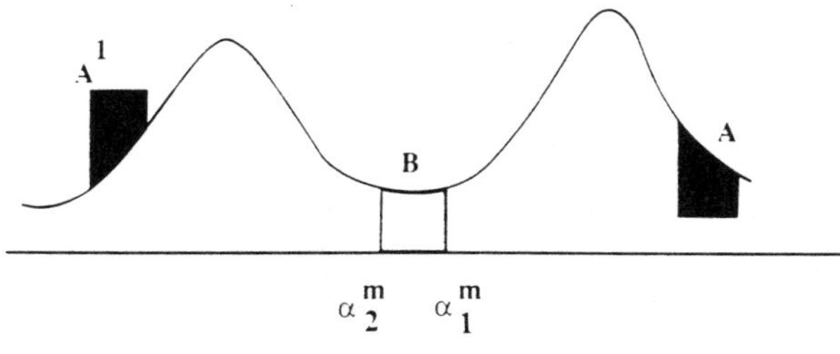

Figure 6.2

valued by the current majority. Hence, according to our results, more polarized and politically unstable societies should exhibit larger deviations from budget balance, and if condition (c) is satisfied, these deviations should be in the direction of budget deficits.

III Constitutional Constraints on the Budget Deficit

Section II.C show that a social planner with stable preferences always chooses $b^* = 0$, for any weighting of individual utilities. That is, a balanced budget is always a component of the first best policy. On this ground, it is tempting to conclude that a budget deficit is inefficient in this model. However, this argument should be qualified. By assumption, a social planner chooses the composition of public goods for both periods 1 and 2, according to a stable social welfare function. This assumption is violated in the political equilibrium of the model and in any real-world political regime: the current majority cannot precommit the spending choices of future majorities. Hence, the solution to the social planner's optimum is not necessarily the optimal social contract for a group of individuals who cannot precommit the spending choices of future governments.

In order to characterize such an optimal social contract, we need to ask what is the optimal level of debt when there is uncertainty about the median voter preferences in both period 2 *and* period 1. Suppose that b is chosen under a "veil of ignorance," before knowing the composition of public spending in period 1. Following John Rawls (1971) and James Buchanan and Gordon Tullock (1962), we can think of a constitutional amendment on budget deficits as being chosen in this way. The optimal level of b for agent i is then determined as the solution to the following problem:

$$\underset{b}{\text{Max}}\; E\{\alpha^i[u(g(\alpha_1^m, b) + u(G(\alpha_2^m, b))] + (1 - \alpha^i)[u(f(\alpha_1^m, b)) + u(F(\alpha_2^m, b))]\}, \tag{15}$$

where E is the expectations operator with respect to the random variables α_1^m and α_2^m; and where $g(\cdot)$, $f(\cdot)$, $G(\cdot)$, and $F(\cdot)$ are defined implicitly by (5) and (3) of the previous section. If α_1^m and α_2^m are drawn from the same prior distribution, then it is easy to show that the only solution to (15) is $b = 0$, for any value of α^i. Using the terminology of Bengt Holmstrom and

Robert Myerson (1983), we conclude that a balanced budget rule is "ex ante efficient": before knowing the identity of the current majority, the group unanimously favors a balanced budget.[11]

If however the value of α_1^m is known when choosing b, then we are back in the equilibrium examined in the previous section, where a majority might support a deficit. These results may explain why the majority of voters seems to generally favor an abstract notion of balanced budgets, even though when choosing specific policies the same majority votes in favor of budget deficits (see the literature quoted in note 1). Balanced budgets are ex ante efficient; therefore, voters asked in a poll would approve of a balanced budget constitutional amendment. However, the same voters may favor a budget deficit in the current period, if uncertain about the preferences of future majorities.

More generally, each current majority does not want to be bound by the rule, even though it wants the rule for all future majorities. However, a budget rule taking effect at some prespecified future date would be irrelevant: if the rule can be abrogated by a simple majority, then any future majority would follow the policy described in Section II and would abrogate the rule. Using again the terminology of Bengt Holmström and Robert Myerson (1983), we conclude that in our model a balanced budget rule, though ex ante efficient, is not "durable" under a simple majority.

This problem could be overcome by requiring a qualified majority to abrogate the rule. But this requirement would greatly reduce the flexibility with which to respond to unexpected events. A budget rule could contain escape clauses, such as for cyclical fluctuations of tax revenues or wars. However, since it is very difficult or even impossible to list all relevant contingencies, requiring a very large majority to abandon (even temporarily) the budget balance constraint may be counterproductive. Presumably, in a model with uncertainty and constraints on the degree of "complexity" of the rule, there would be an "optimal qualified majority" corresponding to the optimal point on the tradeoff between commitment and flexibility.

Summarizing, there is a role for institutions that enable society to separate its intertemporal choices from decisions concerning the allocation of resources within any given period. Without this separation, the conflict over the allocation of resources within each period distorts society's intertemporal choices. However, there is also an inescapable conflict between preserving sufficient flexibility to meet unexpected contingencies, and the enforcement of this separation. Thus, as in many other problems of macroecomomic policy, such as monetary policy, society has to choose between simple rules and discretion.[12]

IV Summary and Extensions

Disagreement between current and future voters about the composition of public expenditure generates a suboptimal path of public debt. Public debt is the legacy left by today's majority to the future, and under specific conditions it tends to increase with the likelihood of disagreement between current and future voters. The results of this paper are in principle testable. On time-series data for a single country, we should observe sustained budget deficits whenever a government with extreme preferences relative to the historical average wins the temporary support of a majority of the voters. On cross-countries data, more polarized and politically unstable countries should have a larger stock of debt outstanding than more homogeneous and stable societies. Nouriel Roubini and Jeffrey Sachs (1989a, 1989b) present encouraging evidence along these lines.

Some possible generalizations of the basic framework of this chapter are suggested in Section I. Another feasible extension would be to have an infinite horizon, by applying the dynamic programming solution procedure discussed in Alberto Alesina and Guido Tabellini (1987). With an infinite horizon, cooperation between current and future majorities could be sustained by trigger strategy equilibria. In these equilibria the path of public debt would approach the socially efficient value. However, this would require cooperation between successive majorities: cooperation among different voters within the same time period would not solve the intertemporal distortions that are the focus of this chapter. Hence, this form of cooperation necessitates substantial coordination among voters. In addition, with discounting of the future, the qualitative implications of reputational equilibria are similar to those of the equilibrium studied in the present chapter, as argued in a different context by Alberto Alesina (1987, 1988a).

Finally, a natural and yet difficult extension of the basic model would be to allow the voters to choose whether or not to repudiate the debt. In fact, the results of this chapter are driven by an asymmetry in the possibility of commitments: even though voters cannot bind the future allocation of spending, they can force future majorities to fully service the debt. This assumption is realistic if applied to industrialized economies during recent decades. But still the puzzle remains of what is the source of this asymmetry. Some recent literature has emphasized that reputation creates incentives to honor the debt of previous governments.[13] A second answer closer to the spirit of this chapter is that defaulting on the government debt brings about political and redistributional costs.[14] Further investigation of this point is the task of future research.

Appendix

For a given value of b, $v(\alpha_2^m)$ is continuous in $1 > \alpha_2^m > 0$ (since $u(\cdot)$ is assumed to be twice continuously differentiable). After some algebra, $v'(\alpha_2^m)$ simplifies to:

$$v'(\alpha_2^m) = \frac{u'(g_2^*)\Delta\left(\frac{1-\alpha_1^m}{\alpha_1^m} - \frac{1-\alpha_2^m}{\alpha_2^m}\right)}{[R(g_2^*) + R(f_2^*)]^2} \frac{dg_2^*}{d\alpha_2^m},$$

where

$$\frac{dg_2^*}{d\alpha_2^m} > 0 \tag{A1}$$

and

$$\Delta = R(g_2^*)[R(f_2^*)^2 + R'(f_2^*)] + [R(g_2^*)^2 + R'(g_2^*)].$$

If $\lambda(x) \equiv -u''/[u'(x)]^2 \equiv R(x)/u'(x)$ is decreasing in x for $1 > x > 0$, then $\Delta < 0$. Hence for any b:

$$v'(\alpha_2^m) \gtreqless 0 \quad \text{as} \quad \alpha_2^m \lesseqgtr \alpha_1^m, \tag{A2}$$

if (c) holds. These properties imply that, under (c), $v(\alpha_2^m)$ reaches a maximum at the point $\alpha_2^m = \alpha_1^m$, and is strictly decreasing in $|\alpha_2^m - \alpha_1^m|$ if $\alpha_2^m \neq \alpha_1^m$. Hence, for given α_1^m and given b, the expression $[\alpha_1^m u'(g_1) - v(\alpha_2^m)]$ reaches a minimum at $\alpha_2^m = \alpha_1^m$ and is strictly increasing in $|\alpha_2^m - \alpha_1^m|$ if $\alpha_2^m \neq \alpha_1^m$.

Consider now this expression at the point $b = 0$. The discussion on p. 165 of the text implies that, at $b = 0$, $\alpha_1^m u'(g^1) - v(\alpha_1^m) = 0$. Since as shown above, under (c) α_1^m – argmax $v(\alpha_2^m)$, we have that, if $b = 0$:

$$\alpha_1^m u'(g_1) - v(\alpha_2^m) \geq 0$$

with strict inequality if $\alpha_2^m \neq \alpha_1^m$.

Notes

University of California, Los Angeles, Center for Economic Policy Research and National Bureau of Economic Research, Harvard University, Center for Economic Policy Research and National Bureau of Economic Research, respectively. We would like to thank three anonymous referees, Alex Cukierman, Patrick Kehoe, Thomas Romer, Jorgen Weibull, and participants in workshops at the Bank of Italy, Brandeis, CalTech, UC Davis, Harvard, the Hoover Institution, the Institute for International Economic Studies (Stockholm), the Bank of Israel, Tel Aviv University, University of Pittsburgh, Princeton, and UC Santa Barbara for several helpful comments.

1. Both recent polls (*New York Times*, November 1987) and polls taken in the early 1980s (Allan Blinder and Douglas Holtz-Eakin, 1983) show that a large majority of Americans is in favor of balanced budget amendments. A much lower fraction of voters is in favor of any specific measure to reduce budget deficits.

2. For recent arguments explaining the deficit as the result of "fiscal illusion," see James Buchanan, Charles Rowley, and Robert Tollison (1987) and the references quoted therein. Kenneth Rogoff and Anne Sibert (1988) show that suboptimal budget deficits may be observed if voters are rational but imperfectly informed, but only before elections and not over long time periods.

3. Alex Cukierman and Allan Meltzer (1989) analyze an overlapping generations model in which individuals have a bequest motive of various intensities. The equilibrium budget deficit in that model reflects the preferences for intergenerational redistribution of current voters. Our approach and that of Cukierman and Meltzer are by no means contradictory, although very different.

4. Any expected utility function that is linear in a vector of parameters belongs to this class. Linearity is not essential in Grandmont (1978), but it is here, since we consider an *expected* utility function. The essential property of intermediate preferences is that supporters of distinct proposals are divided by a hyperplane in the space of most preferred points. See also Andrew Caplin and Barry Nalebuff (1988).

5. This setting is reminiscent of that analyzed in Robert Strotz (1956) and Bezalel Peleg and Menahem Yaari (1973), where a consumer with time-inconsistent preferences solves a dynamic optimization problem. In those papers, as here, the time-consistent solution is the noncooperative equilibrium of a game played by successive decision makers.

6. This second-order sufficient condition can be stated as follows:

$$R(f_2)^3R(g_2) + R(g_2)^2R(f_2)^2 + (1-\gamma)R'(g_2)R(f_2)^2 + \gamma R(g_2)^3R(f_2) + \gamma R(g_2)^2R(f_2)^2 + (\gamma - 1)R'(f_2)R(g_2)^2 > 0, \tag{F.1}$$

where

$$\gamma = \frac{1-\alpha_1^m}{\alpha_1^m}\frac{1-\alpha_2^m}{\alpha_2^m}$$

and where

$$R(\cdot) = -u''(\cdot)/u'(\cdot).$$

is the coefficient of absolute risk aversion of $u(\cdot)$. In turn, a sufficient (but not necessary) condition for (F.1) to hold is that $R(f_2)R(g_2) + R(g_2)^2 + R'(g_2) > 0$ and $R(f_2)R(g_2) + R(f_2)^2 + R'(f_2) > 0$.

7. This condition can also be stated as:

$$u'''(x) > 2[u''(x)]^2/u'(x), \quad 1 > x > 0.$$

8. The same results would go through if other measures of distance between α_2^m and α_1^m were used in (12), such as euclidean norm or $(\alpha_1^m - \alpha_2^m)^2$.

9. The income expansion paths are not necessarily linear: Their slopes can be shown to equal $R(g_2^*)/R(f_2^*)$ and $R(f_2^*)/R(g_2^*)$ for EP_2 and EP_1, respectively, where $R(\cdot) \equiv -u''(\cdot)/u'(\cdot)$ is the coefficient of absolute risk aversion of $u(\cdot)$. Note that the income expansion paths would be divergent even if points A and B were both below the 45° line, that is, if either $\alpha_1^m, \alpha_2^m > 1/2$, or $\alpha_1^m, \alpha_2^m < 1/2$.

10. Note however that the probability that the future decision maker is at a corner would be endogenous in this case, and in particular it would depend on the size of the debt. This adds another dimension to the problem.

11. If α_1^m and α_2^m have the same probability distribution, say $H(\cdot)$, then the first-order condition of (15) with respect to b can be written as:

$$\alpha^i \int_0^1 [u'(g(\alpha, b))g_b(\alpha, b) + u'(G(\alpha, b))G_b(\alpha, b)]\, dH(\alpha)$$

$$+ (1 - \alpha^i) \int_0^1 [u'(f(\alpha, b)f_b(\alpha, b) + u'(F(\alpha, b))F_b(\alpha, b)]\, dH(\alpha) = 0$$

If $b = 0$, the terms inside each integral sum to zero. Hence, by the second-order conditions, $b = 0$ is the solution to (15). Unanimity would be lost if the distributions of α_1^m and α_2^m in (15) were different.

12. Interestingly, in the case of budget deficits in the United States this conflict has been resolved in different ways at the federal and state government levels. Whereas the federal government and legislature have retained full discretion in their borrowing policies, the constitution of most states in the United States forbids the issue of state or local government debt to finance current expenditures. These state restrictions on public borrowing probably reflect the 19th-century history of defaults of local and state debts (see B. V. Ratchford, 1941, and William A. Scott, 1893). But the asymmetry between the federal and state restrictions on public borrowing may also be due to the value of discretion being higher at the federal than at the state level: expenditures and revenues of state governments are generally easier to predict than those of the federal government.

13. See in particular Herschel Grossman and John Van Huyck (1987). A larger literature has investigated the problem of external debt repudiation, for instance, Jeffrey Sachs (1984), Jeremy Bulow and Kenneth Rogoff (1989), Herschel Grossman and John Van Huyck (1988).

14. Recent accounts of historical episodes of debt repayments in Europe during the interwar period lend support to this second view (see, for instance Alberto Alesina 1988b, and Barry Eichengreen 1989). Guido Tabellini (1989) analyzes a model in which in equilibrium a majority of the voters is in favor of repaying the public debt outstanding, so as to avoid wealth redistributions.

References

Alesina, Alberto. 1987. Macroeconomic policy in a two-party system as a repeated game. *Quarterly Journal of Economics* 102:651–678. Reprinted as chapter 3 in the current volume of this work.

Alesina, Alberto. 1988a. Credibility and policy convergence in a two-party system with rational voters. *American Economic Review* 78:796–805.

Alesina, Alberto. 1988b. The end of large public debts. In F. Giavazzi and L. Spaventa, eds., *High public debt: The Italian experience*. Cambridge: Cambridge University Press and CEPR.

Alesina, Alberto, and Tabellini, Guido. 1987. A positive theory of fiscal deficits and government debt in a democracy. NBER working paper no. 2308.

Alesina, Alberto, and Tabellini, Guido. 1989. External debt, capital flights and political risk. *Journal of International Economics.*

Barro, Robert. 1979. On the determination of public debt. *Journal of Political Economy.* 87:940–947.

Blinder, Allan, and Holtz-Eakin, Douglas. 1983. Public opinion and the balanced budget. NBER working paper no. 1234.

Buchanan, James, Rowley, Charles, and Tollison, Robert. 1987. *Deficits.* Oxford: Blackwell.

Buchanan, James, and Tullock, Gordon. 1962. *The calculus of consent.* Ann Arbor: University of Michigan Press.

Bulow, Jeremy, and Rogoff, Kenneth. 1989. A recontracting model of external debt. *Journal of Political Economy* 79:155–178.

Caplin, Andrew, and Nalebuff, Barry. 1988. On 64% majority rule. *Econometrica* 56: 787–814.

Cukierman, Alex, and Meltzer, Allan. 1989. A political theory of government debt and deficits in a neo-Ricardian framework. *American Economic Review* 79:713–731.

Debreu, Gerard, and Koopmans, Tjalling C. 1982. Additively decomposed quasi-convex functions. *Mathematical Programming.* 24:1–38.

Eichengreen, Barry. 1989. The capital levy in theory and practice. In R. Dornbusch and M. Draghi, eds., *Public debt management: Theory and history.* Cambridge: Cambridge University Press.

Ferejohn, John. 1986. Incumbent performance and electoral control. *Public Choice* 50: 5–26. Reprinted as chapter 1 in the current volume of this work.

Glazer, Ami. 1987. politics and the choice of durability. Mimeo. University of California at Irvine.

Grandmont, Jean Michel. 1978. Intermediate preferences and the majority rule. *Econometrica* 46:317–330.

Grossman, Herschel, and Van Huyck, John. 1987. Nominally denominated sovereign debt, risk shifting and reputation. NBER working paper no. 2259.

Grossman, Herschel, and Van Huyck, John. 1988. Sovereign debt as a contingent claim: Excusable default, repudiation, and reputation. *American Economic Review* 78:1088–1097.

Holmstrom, Bengt, and Myerson, Robert. 1983. Efficient and durable decision rules with incomplete information. *Econometrica* 51:1799–1819.

Ledyard, John. 1984. The pure theory of large two-candidate elections. *Public Choice* 44:7–41.

Lucas, Robert, and Stokey, Nancy. 1983. Optimal monetary and fiscal policy in an economy without capital. *Journal of Monetary Economics* 12:55–93. Reprinted as chapter 14 in volume 1 of this work.

Peleg, Bezalel, and Yaari, Menahem. 1973. On the existence of a consistent course of action when tastes are changing. *Review of Economic Studies* 40:391–401.

Persson, Torsten, and Svensson, Lars. 1989. Why a stubborn conservative would run a deficit: Policy with inconsistent preferences. *Quarterly Journal of Economics* 104:325–346. Reprinted as chapter 5 in the current volume of this work.

Ratchford, B. V. 1941. *American state debts.* Durham, NC: Duke University Press.

Rawls, John. 1971. *A theory of justice.* Cambridge: Harvard University Press.

Rogoff, Kenneth, and Sibert, Anne. 1988. Equilibrium political business cycles. *Review of Economic Studies* 55:1–16.

Roubini, Nouriel, and Sachs, Jeffrey. 1989a. Political and economic determinants of budget deficits in industrialized democracies. *European Economic review.*

Roubini, Nouriel, and Sachs, Jeffrey. 1989b. Government spending and budget deficits in the industrial countries. *Economic Policy* 8.

Sachs, Jeffrey. 1984. Theoretical issues in international borrowing. *Princeton Studies in International Economics* 54.

Scott, William A. 1893. *The repudiation of state debts.* Boston: T. Crowell.

Strotz, Robert. 1956. Myopia and inconsistency in dynamic utility maximization. *Review of Economic Studies* 23:165–180.

Tabellini, Guido. 1989. Domestic politics and the international coordination of fiscal policies. *Journal of International Economics.*

Tabellini, Guido. 1989. The politics of intergenerational redistribution. NBER working paper no. 3058. Updated and reprinted as chapter 11 in the current volume of this work.

7 Political and Monetary Institutions and Public Financial Policies in the Industrial Countries

Vittorio Grilli, Donato Masciandaro, and Guido Tabellini

1 Introduction

The post-war experience of industrialized countries features striking differences in public debt policies. Table 7.1 reports data on the accumulation of net public debt in 18 OECD countries. At the end of the 1980s, the debt to GNP ratio in these countries ranged from about 10% in Switzerland to over 100% in Belgium and Ireland.

What are the reasons for these differences? Normative macroeconomic theory stresses the "shock absorber" and "distortion smoothing" role of budget deficits and prescribes that government debt should be adjusted over time to respond to exogenous shocks. According to this view, public debts differ because the various national economies have undergone different shocks. This is quite unconvincing for the OECD countries that are quite similar and highly interconnected. In addition, the positive trend displayed by government debt in many countries after World War II is difficult to reconcile with the view that budget deficits were only smoothing the effects of temporary shocks. This is why we focus instead on those political and institutional aspects which may affect the process of policy formation, and ask whether constitutional differences among the various democratic regimes have any bearing on debt policy decisions. For example, does the level of government debt depend on electoral and representational systems?

Public debt is not the only dimension along which countries differ. In Table 7.2 we observe that, in the 1980s, average inflation was 3% in Japan and 21% in Greece. In the current debate over the European monetary union, an important issue is whether such divergences in inflation are related to the differences in fiscal policies described above. Are large deficits associated with inflation? Is there any connection between the political system and inflation? If this were the case the creation of a monetary union among countries with dissimilar fiscal policies could be problematic.

To explain international differences in monetary stability, we extend the institutional analysis beyond the general characteristics of political

Reprinted from *Economic Policy*, October (1991) 342–392, by permission of Economic Policy, and published by Cambridge University Press.

Table 7.1
Government net debt (% of GNP)

	1960	1970	1980	1989
Australia	na	40.1	24.9	16.5
Austria	na	19.4	37.2	57.8
Belgium	82.3	52.6	69.3	122.4
Canada	27.5	11.6	13.0	38.0
Denmark	na	−2.8	4.3	23.1
France	na	9.7	14.3	25.4
Germany	na	−8.1	14.3	21.9
Greece	9.2	21.3	27.8	79.0
Ireland	na	35.7	78.0	122.6
Italy	25.2	36.8	54.0	94.3
Japan	−4.4	−6.5	17.3	14.1
Netherlands	na	29.9	24.9	57.2
New Zealand	na	na	na	74.7
Portugal (a)	23.0	24.0	40.0	71.8
Spain	na	na	7.9	29.3
Switzerland	na	na	na	10.4
U.K.	123.2	79.2	47.3	30.3
U.S.	45.0	27.8	18.8	29.2

Source: *OECD Economic Outlook* and Bank of Portugal.
Note: (a) Only data for gross debt are available.

systems to include regulations which are specific to the activity of national central banks such as their degree of independence. In the current debate over monetary and political union in Europe one of the crucial issues is whether a complete convergence in monetary and fiscal policy should be achieved before the monetary union. If it can be established that the institutional and political systems have a significant and independent effect on the choice of economic policy, then waiting for further convergence would be inappropriate. Complete convergence, in fact, could only be achieved by a political and monetary union.

Our investigation is also motivated by the recent positive theories of economic policy. This literature studies the incentives brought on policymakers by political and monetary institutions. So far, though, there exist very few empirical studies which attempt to explore the implications and hypotheses of these recent theories. An important forerunner of this chapter is the work of Roubini and Sachs (1988, 1989) who also relate observed fiscal policies to political institutions in the industrial countries. Some of our results confirm their previous findings, but this chapter is based on a more detailed description of the institutional environment, and bears a

Table 7.2
Inflation rate (%)

	1950–59	1960–69	1970–79	1980–89
U.S.	1.8	2.3	7.1	5.6
U.K.	3.5	3.6	12.6	7.4
Austria	6.8	3.3	6.1	4.0
Belgium	1.9	2.7	7.1	5.1
Denmark	3.8	5.3	9.3	7.1
France	6.2	3.8	8.9	7.8
Germany	1.1	2.4	4.9	2.9
Italy	2.9	3.4	12.5	11.8
Netherlands	3.8	4.2	7.1	3.1
Switzerland	1.1	3.1	5.0	3.3
Canada	2.4	2.5	7.4	6.7
Japan	3.1	5.4	9.1	2.5
Greece	6.5	2.0	12.3	20.1
Ireland	3.9	4.0	12.7	9.9
Portugal	0.7	4.0	17.1	18.2
Spain	6.2	5.8	14.1	10.6
Australia	6.5	2.5	9.8	7.6
New Zealand	5.0	3.2	11.4	12.5
Mean	3.7	3.5	9.7	8.1
Standard deviation	1.99	1.08	3.28	5.04

Source: International Monetary Fund, *International Financial Statistics.*
Note: Inflation is based on the GNP deflator.

closer tie to the theoretical debate. In addition, we study monetary policy and monetary institutions, which were absent from their research.[1] The recent literature, pioneered by Rogoff (1985), showed that the design of the monetary regime can be a fundamental determinant of public financial policies and more generally of macroeconomic performance. Our chapter investigates the empirical validity of this approach, providing an accurate definition of central bank independence.

A preliminary caveat is in order. When trying to establish a link between institutional structure and economic policy decisions, one has to keep in mind that the terms of the contract establishing a central bank and even the constitutional structure of a country evolve and change over time. Institutional arrangements are possibly affected by economic performance. These types of feedback, however, occur over long periods of time, and thus we take institutional arrangements as given over the relatively short horizon which is the focus of our analysis. When we take into account institutional changes we ignore the possibility that they may have been induced by current economic performance.

The chapter's outline is as follows. In Section 2 we analyse the determinants of debt policies and ask whether observed fiscal decisions are consistent with "shock absorber" behaviour, as predicted by the theory of optimal taxation. For many countries they are definitely not. In fact, in a number of countries, public debt is on an explosive path: this will require major changes in future spending and tax policies. In Section 3, we ask whether the political system has any effect on public deficits. A comparison of political systems of the 18 OECD countries shows that, in almost all instances, explosive debts are found in countries governed by highly proportional electoral systems, with short-lived coalition or minority governments. In Sections 4 and 5 we turn to monetary policies. The recent literature on seigniorage (e.g., Mankiw 1987) stresses that inflation is a source of revenue and should be considered a part of the global budgetary policy. There is little evidence that this is a fruitful way of looking at monetary policies. Moreover, contrary to popular opinion, we find no evidence that budget deficits lead to lax monetary policies. If for some countries seigniorage is indeed an important source of government revenue, for most countries seigniorage has actually declined in the 1980s when the budget deficits were largest. Next, in Section 5, we compare the monetary regimes of the 18 countries. While lower and less variable inflation is associated with central bank independence, there is no indication that the monetary regime matters for real economic performance (growth or unemployment) or for budgetary choices. Thus, fiscal discipline and monetary discipline seem to be unrelated, being determined by respectively the political and the monetary institutions. Section 6 concludes and summarizes the main findings.

2 The Evolution of Public Debt

2.1 Sustainable Paths for Public Debt

Governments, like private economic agents, face budget constraints. However, unlike private agents, governments do not always bear the burden of servicing the debt that they have issued; the burden can be pushed onto future governments or future generations of tax payers. What determines whether governments pay attention to their budget constraints? In particular, what determines the division between taxes and deficits? According to the theory of optimal taxation, public deficits should be designed to minimize the distortionary effects (the so-called excess burden) of taxation, given a politically desired path of public spending. The government should equate the marginal distortions associated with the last dollar of revenue collected on all tax bases at all points in time. The role of public debt should be to "smooth" tax distortions over time. Temporary expenditures or temporary shortfalls in revenue should thus be financed by issuing debt, whereas tax rates should be changed right away in the face of permanent shocks. In particular, government debt should not be used to postpone unavoidable tax increases, since doing so would simply result in larger tax distortions when the debt eventually has to be serviced.[2]

Without knowing the exact nature of the economic shocks, this normative theory is difficult to test. There are, however, certain minimal conditions that an efficient debt policy should satisfy, irrespective of the particular shocks which affect the economy. In particular, the government should not allow the debt to become unsustainable. More precisely government debt (as a percentage of GNP) cannot forever grow faster than the excess of its rate of return over the growth rate of the economy.[3] Only then is the stock of debt outstanding at any point in time equal to the present discounted value of all future surpluses.

2.2 The Evidence

Several pieces of evidence suggest that, in many countries, the debt path is unsustainable. Table 7.3 presents 10-year averages of primary (i.e. exclusive of interest payments) and total surpluses in the post-war period (both measures disregard seigniorage revenues). The pattern of the two variables is similar. We observe an increase over time in both the size and the cross-country dispersion of deficits. In the 1960s and especially in the 1950s surpluses were as common as deficits. A number of countries—Austria, Belgium, Italy, Greece, Ireland (and possibly Portugal and Spain for which we lack data)—have kept running primary deficits throughout the period. The consecutive build-up of debt and debt service explains why their total budget deficits far exceed those of the remaining countries. These five, possibly seven, countries are thus the most likely to have an unsustainable debt path. These conclusions are confirmed by the examination of Figure 7.1 where we present the evolution of net debt to GNP ratios in the OECD area. The countries can be divided into two groups. In

Table 7.3
Government surplus (% of GNP)

	Primary				Total			
	1950–59	1960–69	1970–79	1980–89	1950–59	1960–69	1970–79	1980–89
U.S.	1.3	0.9	−0.3	−1.5	−0.2	−0.6	−2.1	−3.9
U.K.	2.6	2.2	−0.5	0.0	−1.1	−0.9	−3.7	−3.7
Austria	−2.1	−1.2	−2.0	−2.2	−2.4	−1.8	−2.5	−4.7
Belgium	−2.0	−0.1	−1.6	na	−4.1	−2.6	−4.5	−11.3
Denmark	1.8	1.5	1.5	−0.7	−0.1	1.0	0.8	−4.9
France	−2.7	−0.2	0.1	−1.0	−4.4	−1.0	−0.6	−2.4
Germany	−0.6	−0.1	−0.5	−0.6	−0.8	−0.5	−0.9	−1.6
Italy	−1.5	−1.4	−6.9	−5.0	−3.2	−2.7	−9.8	−13.5
Netherlands	1.2	0.0	−0.5	−3.1	1.2	−1.3	−1.9	−5.3
Switzerland	1.3	0.7	−0.3	0.2	0.4	0.2	−0.7	−0.03
Canada	2.2	0.8	−1.1	−4.5	0.4	−1.0	−2.7	−4.4
Japan	na	na	na	na	na	na	na	na
Greece	−1.1	−1.1	−1.6	−2.9	−1.2	−1.6	−3.0	−9.4
Ireland	−0.5	−2.3	−5.2	−5.8	−4.8	−5.4	−9.6	−12.5
Portugal	na	na	na	na	na	na	−5.8	−10.8
Spain	na	na	na	na	na	−1.5	−1.5	−6.2
Australia	na	na	na	na	1.5	−1.8	−1.9	−2.0
New Zealand	na	na	na	na	−2.7	−3.0	−4.9	−6.1
Mean	−0.01	−0.02	−1.45	−2.53	−1.43	−1.53	−3.25	−6.04
Standard deviation	1.74	1.21	2.16	2.46	1.98	1.42	2.86	4.04

Source: International Monetary Fund, *International Financial Statistics*.

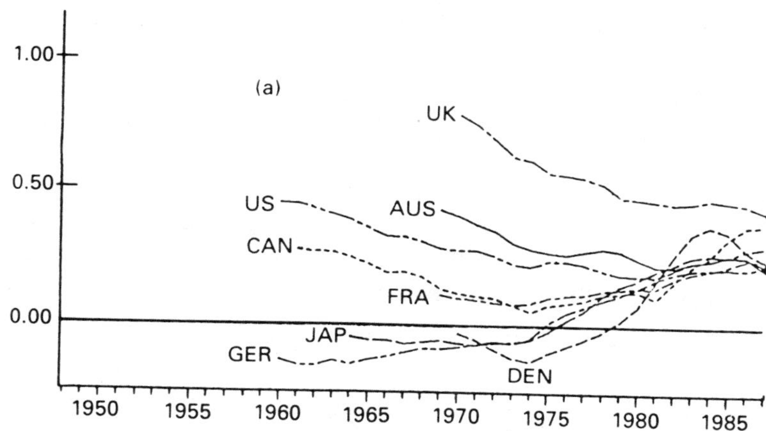

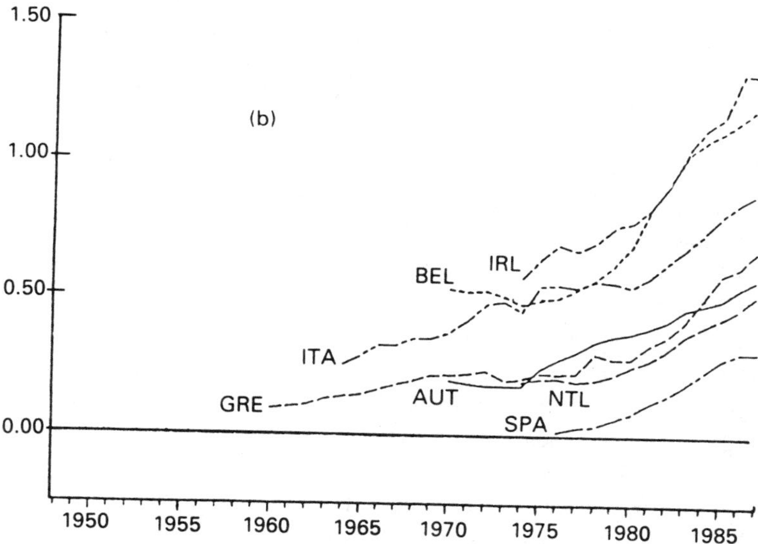

Figure 7.1
Net debt to GNP ratios
Source: *OECD Economic Outlook.*

the first group (Panel a) the debt to GNP ratio is stable or converges toward moderate levels of about 35%. In the second group (Panel b) the debt to GNP ratio has a clearly explosive pattern. In this group we find Austria, Belgium, Italy, Greece, Ireland, Portugal, Spain, as before, and the Netherlands.

A more formal approach is presented in Appendix A and provides indications of debt unsustainability for the same seven countries: Austria, Belgium, Italy, Greece, Ireland, Portugal and Spain. The consistency in the results makes it difficult to accept the view that public debt accumulation in those countries was the optimal response to temporary economic shocks.

3 Political Institutions and Fiscal Policy

3.1 Political Theories of Government Debt

Can international differences in debt accumulation be due to differences in the political incentives faced by the governments? We attempt to answer this question by comparing the domestic political institutions of the OECD countries. The recent literature on the theory of economic policy pays considerable attention to how political institutions shape the policy-makers' incentives. (For a survey, see Persson and Tabellini 1990). A first approach (pioneered by Alesina and Tabellini 1990, Persson and Svensson 1989, and Tabellini and Alesina 1990) investigates how the political system affects over time the behaviour of governments with different ideological preferences which alternate in office. The central result concerns how policy-makers weigh the future (their rate of time discount). Two features of the political system matter: instability (i.e. how likely it is that the current government or legislative majority will be thrown out of office) and polarization (i.e. how strong is the disagreement between the alternating policy-makers). More unstable and polarized political systems behave more myopically, i.e. they discount the future more. This approach yields the sharp empirical prediction that public debts should be larger in more unstable and polarized societies.

The second theoretical approach also focuses on disagreement between different political actors and on the role of different decision-makers (such as cabinet ministers or levels of government). The greater is the conflict between these different decision-makers, the more difficult it is to change the status quo or to enact controversial policies. (This idea has been applied to: the coordination of monetary and fiscal policies by Tabellini, 1986; the choice of stabilization programmes by Alesina and Drazen, 1989; the inflation tax by Aizenman, 1989, and Drazen and Grilli, 1990; and budget decficits by Sanguinetti, 1990). Disagreement results in the postponement of unpopular policies. Thus, here too, collective decisions are short-sighted and political conflict is associated with the accumulation of public debt, and the more so, the more difficult is the resolution of the political conflict.

There is an important conceptual difference between the first and the second explanation of why political institutions can induce collective myopia. The second approach stresses *government weakness* so that the postponement of unpopular decisions is not a deliberate policy choice. Rather, it reflects a sequence of disparate and unrelated spending and taxing decisions, accompanied by the inability to change the status quo. The first approach, on the other hand, emphasizes *political stability* to explain how the electorate ends up favouring budget deficits because their future costs are not fully recognized. This distinction is important, because it leads to different policy implications. According to the second approach, what matters is the support that governments enjoy in the legislature and among the voters at large. According to the first line of thought, instead, collective myopia is not caused by the weakness of the executive, but rather by its instability. In the empirical analysis, we attempt to discriminate between these two alternative hypotheses.

3.2 The Political Institutions

The countries that we study were democracies throughout the post-war period, except for Greece, Portugal and Spain, and all of them have been democracies since the second half of the 1970s. We describe three main features of these democracies: (a) their broad constitutional rules; (b) their party systems; and (c) the attributes of their governments. Except for France and for the countries that became democracies, the constitutions did not significantly change during the post-war period, at least along the dimensions considered in this section. Hence the features described under (a) are independent of economic policies in general, and of the evolution of public debts in particular. While the political indicators examined below can in principle be influenced by economic events and by previous economic policy decisions, these indicators are quite stable over time. In fact, they can be classified quite precisely according to the constitutional rules and the properties of the party system. This suggests that, even for the features described under (c), the main direction of causation runs from the political system to economic policies, and not vice versa.

3.2.1 The Political Constitution

The first distinction (column 1 in Table 7.4) is between presidential and parliamentary democracies. In the former, the president is voted directly into office and has significant independent authority. In the latter, the prime minister is accountable to the legislature. Even though there are some mixed arrangements (Switzerland can almost be considered a multiperson presidential system, and since 1958 France combines elements of both systems), most countries are parliamentary democracies. Parliamentary systems in turn differ by the degree of proportionality of the electroral laws. We follow Bingham Powell (1982) in identifying the degree of proportionality with the number of representatives per district (column 2 of Table 7.4). Systems with less than five representatives per district are classified as majoritarian, with five or more as representational. Naturally, electoral laws differ in several other dimensions, which can reinforce or weaken the degree of proportionality of a political system.[4]

All the countries that seem to have an unsustainable debt, except Ireland and Portugal, are governed by representational systems. Conversely, all representational democracies except Denmark have unsustainable fiscal policies. This finding is strikingly illustrated in Figure 7.2 which displays for three country groupings the average net debt in 1989 and the average primary deficit between 1950 and 1989, both as a percentage of GNP. Group 1 consists of all representational democracies, Group 2 is made up of majoritarian parliamentary systems and Group 3 of presidential democracies (except Portugal, for which data are missing).[5] Clearly, net debts and primary deficits are much larger in the representational democracies.

This strong association between representational political systems and lack of fiscal discipline is also evident from particular episodes of constitutional reform. In 1958, France reformed its electoral law and enacted a number of constitutional changes. The constitutional role of the president was strengthened relative to the parliament and the government, while the government in turn was strengthened relative to the parliament. The electoral law was changed from proportional to majoritarian. As can be seen

Table 7.4
Political fractionalization

Country	Democracy (a)	Representatives (b)	Fractionalization (c)		
			1960–64	1965–76	1980–90
Australia	Pa-M	1	0.63	0.61	0.59
Austria	Pa-R	6	0.54	0.54	0.59
Belgium	Pa-R	7	0.63	0.76	0.86
Canada	Pa-M	1	0.62	0.63	0.52
Denmark	Pa-R	10	0.72	0.79	0.81
France	Pr	1	0.69	0.71	0.68
Germany	Pa-M	2	0.58	0.57	0.66
Greece	Pa-R	6	0.59	0.68	0.55
Ireland	Pa-M	4	0.62	0.61	0.64
Italy	Pa-R	19	0.73	0.73	0.75
Japan	Pa-M	4	0.54	0.60	0.63
Netherlands	Pa-R	150	0.77	0.84	0.73
New Zealand	Pa-M	1	0.51	0.49	0.49
Portugal	Pr	14 (d)	na	0.68 (d)	0.66
Spain	Pa-R	7 (d)	na	0.76 (d)	0.62
Switzerland	Pa-M	na	0.79	0.81	0.82
U.K.	Pa-M	1	0.50	0.48	0.53
U.S.	Pr	1	0.44	0.61	0.48

Sources: Bingham Powell (1982), Banks (1987) and various other years, Keasing archives, various years.

Notes: (a) Pr = Presidential Democracy, Pa-M = Majoritarian parliamentary democracy, Pa-R = Representational parliamentary democracy; (b) Representatives per district, defined as the number of legislators in the popular house of the legislature, divided by the number of electoral districts. The numbers refer to the late 1960s. In 1971 Austria decreased the number of districts, increasing the number of representatives per district to nearly 20; (c) Fractionalization index, defined as the probability that two legislators chosen at random belong to different parties. The second column is computed from elections in the 1966–1976 period, and refers to the average votes taken by each party. The other two columns refer instead to the average number of seats in the lower house taken by each party in elections held during the specified periods; (d) Years 1975 and 1976 only (dictatorship prior to then).

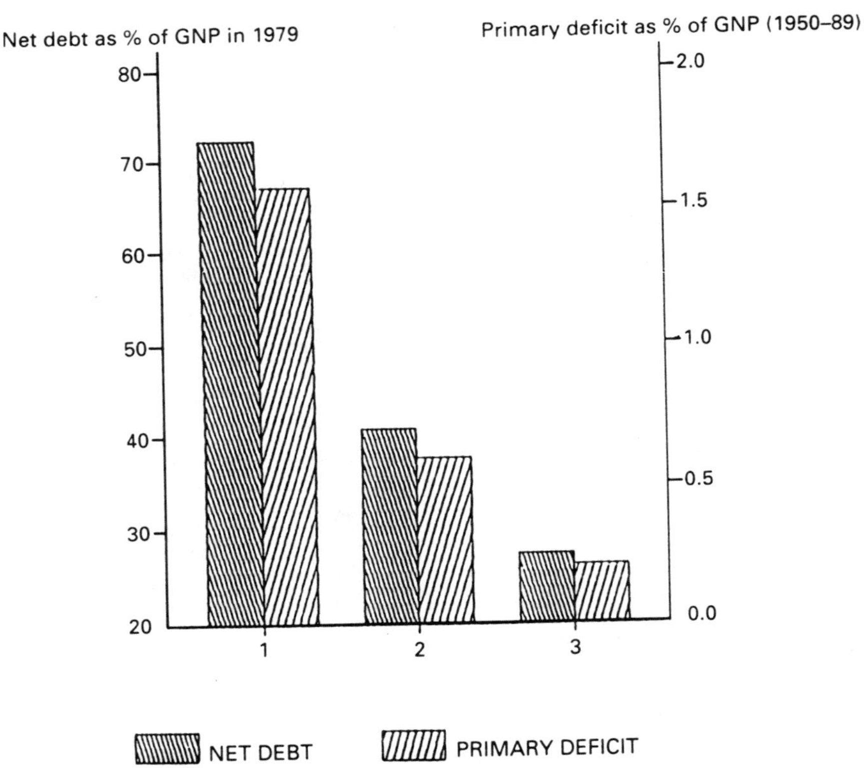

Figure 7.2
Net debt and primary deficits
Notes: Group 1: Representational parliametary democracies (Austria, Belgium, Denmark, Greece, Italy, the Netherlands, Spain); Group 2: Majoritarian parliamentary democracies (Australia, Canada, Germany, Ireland, Japan, New Zealand, Switzerland, U.K.); Group 3: Presidental democracies (France, U.S.). France 1950–1958 is included in Group 1. Only the years of democratic regime for Greece and Spain are included. Data for Portugal are missing.

from Table 7.3, the size of fiscal deficits changed dramatically. While in the 1950s France had an average primary deficit of 2.7% of GNP (the largest of all countries in the sample), its average primary deficit from 1960 to 1989 was 0.4% of GNP, one of the smallest in the sample.

3.2.2 The Party System

The electoral laws, and in particular their degree of proportionality, influence two central features of a party system: the number of parties, and the extent to which minority interests are represented in the legislature. With a high degree of proportionality, several parties are likely to coexist; moreover, extremist parties that represent the interests of minorities are more likely to survive. These two features determine the kind of government (coalition, majority government or minority government) that is likely to be formed, as well as its durability, thereby indirectly shaping the policy-making process.

The last three columns of Table 7.4 present an indicator of fractionalization of the party system over three sub-periods. We follow the literature in defining fractionalization as the probability that two legislators chosen at random belong to different parties.[6] This index ranges between 0 and 1. A value of 0.5 is associated with a perfectly balanced two-party system. A value larger than 0.5 is generally associated with more than two parties. The larger the index, the greater is the number of parties in the legislature. The lowest values of this index are found in two-party systems, such as the U.S., the U.K. and New Zealand. Countries with several parties, such as Italy, Denmark, Switzerland or the Netherlands, have the highest values. The fractionalization index is quite stable over time, and it is highly positively correlated with the index of proportionality of the electoral system. This confirms that proportionality of the electoral laws leads to fractionalization.

The relative importance of extremist parties (measured by their percentage of votes in the elections) is reported in Table 7.5. These parties promise radical changes of the status quo and represent either stable constituencies or temporary dissatisfaction with the existing political apparatus. The classification is due to Bingham Powell (1982). He defines a party as extremist if it is associated with any of the following characteristics: (a) a well developed non-democratic ideology; (b) a proposal to change the boundaries of the nation; (c) diffuse alienation and distrust of the existing political system. The communist parties in France and Italy, or the linguistic

Table 7.5
Political extremism

Country	1960–64	1965–75	1980–90
Australia	0	0	2
Austria	0	1	2
Belgium	6	21	15
Canada	0	0	0
Denmark	10	18	20
France	22	25	12
Germany	0	3	4
Greece	7	11	5
Ireland	2	0	0
Italy	32	37	38
Japan	4	16	14
Netherlands	5	13	4
New Zealand	0	1	0
Portugal	na	20	15
Spain	na	7	12
Switzerland	2	8	5
U.K.	0	3	3
U.S.	0	0	0

Sources: Bingham Powell (1982) and *Europe World Yearbook* Various years.
Notes: The first and last columns refer to the average number of seats in the Lower House taken by extremist parties, whereas the second column refers to their average votes.

parties in Belgium are examples of extremist parties. Like fractionalization, extremism is stable over time and is more prevalent under highly proportional electoral systems. Naturally, historical events beside electoral laws are important determinants of the size of extremist parties.

Tables 7.4 and 7.5 show that unsustainable fiscal policies are prevalent in countries with fractionalized party systems and where there are large extremist parties. To further understand this finding, we now turn to a description of the types of government that are generally formed in each country.

3.2.3 The Government

The political theories of public debt summarized in Subsection 3.1 have different predictions regarding which government attributes create the incentives to borrow. Government weakness means that public debt is a residual source of finance which simply reflects government inability to cut expenditures or raise taxes. The political stability interpretation instead views public debt as a legacy deliberately left by a government to its successors. The borrowing government does not expect to inherit tomorrow the debt issued today, because it does not expect to be reappointed in office. The less likely is the reappointment, the higher is the amount borrowed. This second approach thus predicts that public debt is larger in countries with more frequent government changes from one party or leading group to another, i.e. in more politically unstable environments.

Government weakness is a rather vague concept which is difficult to quantify. A first possibility is to consider government support in the legislature. We distinguish between three kinds of government: majority, coalition and minority governments. A majority government is supported by a single party that has a majority in the legislature. A coalition government is supported by a coalition of parties that together reach a legislative majority. A minority government is supported by a single party or by a coalition without a legislative majority. Clearly, decision-making capacity is greatest in majority governments and lowest in minority governments. The first three columns of Table 7.6 describe the fraction of time between 1950 and 1990 for which the government was of each of these three types. A second measure of government weakness is average durability, defined as the average number of years between one government change and the next. A short-lived government is also likely to be weak, and frequent government crises are a symptom of a divided executive with weak support in the legislature. Average government durability between 1950 and 1989 is displayed in the fourth column of Table 7.6.

A change in government does not result in a significant change in political leadership if the new government is still supported by the same political parties and/or it is made up by the same group of individuals as the previous one. Thus it would be wrong to use government durability as an index of political stability. To construct an index of political stability, we compute the average number of years between significant government changes, those which result in a transfer of power from one leading group or party to another. We define a government change to be significant if the following conditions are met: for a majoritarian parliamentary system, there is a change in the party of the prime minister; for a representational parliamentary system, there is a change in both the prime minster party *and* the coalition of parties supporting the government; and for a presidential system, there is a change in the party of either the prime minister or the president (except for the U.S., where the president is also prime minister). Naturally, any change from a democracy to a dictatorship or vice

Table 7.6
Government attributes

Country	Government type (a)			Government durability (b)	Political stability (c)
	Maj.	Coa.	Min.		
Australia	26.8	73.3	0.0	4.44	10
Austria	39.0	58.5	2.4	2.67	40
Belgium	9.8	90.2	0.0	1.43	10
Canada	80.5	0.0	19.5	4.00	8
Denmark	0.0	34.1	65.9	2.11	5.7
France	41.5	39.0	19.5	1.29	2.5
Germany	9.6	90.0	0.0	2.00	20
Greece (d)	91.2	5.9	2.9	0.97	4
Ireland	65.9	24.4	9.8	1.90	5
Italy	0.0	95.1	4.9	0.95	10
Japan	80.5	12.2	7.3	1.67	40
Netherlands	0.0	100.0	0.0	3.33	6.7
New Zealand	100.0	0.0	0.0	4.44	8
Portugal (e)	26.7	53.3	20.0	1.48	5
Spain (f)	50.0	35.7	14.3	2.00	20
Switzerland	0.0	100.0	0.0	1.60	20
U.K.	92.7	0.0	7.3	4.00	8
U.S.	41.5	0.0	58.5	5.00	8

Sources: Banks (1987) various volumes, Taylor and Jodice (1983), Keasing Archives, various years.
Notes: (a) Maj. = single party majority, Coa. = coalition majority, Min. = Minority (coalition or single party). The number in each column refers to the percentage of years in which the government was of each of the three types, out of the years of democratic regime between 1950 and 1990. The type is defined with reference to the popular chamber; (b) Durability of the executive between 1950 and 1990 (average number of years); (c) Average number of years between "significant" government changes in the period 1950–89. See the text for more details; (d) Dictatorship between 1967 and 1973; (e) Dictatorship until 1973. New democratic constitution in 1976; (f) Dictatorship until 1974. First democratic election in 1977.

versa is recorded as a significant change. The resulting political stability variable is shown in the last column of Table 7.6 for the period 1950–1989.

Table 7.6 shows that representational democracies tend to have shorter-lived governments and more coalition or minority governments than the other two political regimes. Average government durability is 1.9 years in representational democracies, three years in majoritarian democracies and 3.2 years in presidential democracies. The percentage of governments supported by a single party majority is 23.3%, 57.0% and 49.1% in representational, majoritarian and parliamentary democracies, respectively.[7] These government attributes reflect the greater fractionalization and strength of extremist parties in representational democracies. On the other hand, there is no significant difference in the political stability index across the three kinds of constitutional regimes. Note that the three government attributes measured in Table 7.6 are not correlated with each other in our sample of 18 countries. The correlation coefficients are: 0.02 between political stability and single party majority; 0.12 between political stability and government durability; and 0.31 between durability and single party majority.

3.3 Government Attributes and Public Debt

How do these three government attributes relate to the accumulation of public debt? Table 7.7, which performs cross-country comparisons, provides a very clear answer. The first part of the table reports correlations between the change in net debt (as percentage of GNP) from 1970 to 1989 (*DEBT*) and the following variables, also measured in the period 1970–1989 in a sample of 15 countries:[8] the percentage of governments supported by a single party majority (*MAJORITY*), average government durability (*DURABILITY*) and the political stability index (*STABILITY*). Debt accumulation is strongly negatively correlated to average government durability, while it is not correlated with either of the other two variables. The same results are obtained when we regress debt accumulation on all three variables (plus an intercept). The results are displayed in the second part of Table 7.7: only durability has a negative and significant coefficient. The overall fit of the regression is remarkably good

Table 7.7
Debt accumulation and government attributes

	Correlation matrix		
	MAJORITY	*DURABILITY*	*STABILITY*
DEBT	−0.298	−0.713	−0.061
MAJORITY		0.332	−0.044
DURABILITY			0.295

Regression

$$\underset{(0.904)}{DEBT = 3.732^{**}} - \underset{(0.011)}{0.002}\, MAJORITY - \underset{(0.304)}{0.981^{**}}\, DURABILITY + \underset{(0.066)}{0.048}\, STABILITY$$

$\overline{R}^2 = \underset{(0.066)}{0.408}$ $SE = 1.409$ Number of observations = 15

Note: Debt is the change in net debt to GNP ratio between 1970 and 1989. The remaining variables are as defined in Table 7.6, and also refer to 1970–1989. Standard errors are in parenthesis. A* (**) denotes significance at the 5% (1%) level.

(government attributes explain over 50% of the variance in public debts), and the impact of durability is also quantitatively significant.

More information can be obtained from cross-country differences by separating the whole period 1950–1989 into four decades. Since in 1950 many countries had large stocks of debt inherited from the war, it is preferable to consider primary deficits (as percentage of GNP), dropping the years of non-democratic regime in Spain and Portugal. To avoid truncation problems at the start and end of each decade, we replaced the variables *DURABILITY* and *STABILITY* with the frequency of government changes (*FREQUENCY*) and of significant government changes (*SIGNIFICANT*) within each decade (the data used to construct these indices are shown in Appendix B). The regression results in Table 7.8 confirm the previous findings.[9] The frequency of government changes always leads to higher deficits and the effect is significant in three out of four decades. The estimated coefficients for the other two variables are generally of the wrong sign and are never significantly different from zero.

These findings are partly consistent with the view that budget deficits are a residual source of finance, used by a weak government that does not have any politically viable alternative. However, it is surprising that budget deficits are not systematically related to the extent of government support in the legislature. On the other hand the results are inconsistent with the view that political instability is a cause of budget deficits. Budget deficits are related to the frequency of *any* government change, not only

Table 7.8
Primary budget deficits and government attributes (Dependent variable: primary budget deficit/GNP)

Explanatory variables	1950–59	1960–69	1970–79	1980–89
FREQUENCY	2.868*	1.902*	4.925**	4.460
	(0.944)	(0.765)	(1.256)	(2.604)
SIGNIFICANT	−1.361	−2.205	−4.123	1.566
	(1.721)	(2.148)	(2.657)	(6.110)
MAJORITY	−0.008	0.006	0.007	0.011
	(0.007)	(0.007)	(0.008)	(0.011)
$\bar{R}^2$	0.242	−0.066	0.386	0.458
SE	1.578	1.298	1.763	1.893
Number of observations	13	13	13	12

Notes: Intercept not reported. Standard errors in parenthesis. A* (**) denotes significance at the 5% (1%) level. The system is estimated by seemingly unrelated regressions.

to changes which transfer power from one leading group to another, as the theory predicts. Could it be that the results are sensitive to the definition of what represents a "significant" change in government? To explore this possibility, the definition is weakened by considering that more changes in government are "significant." This provides mixed results. First, the effects of any government change in general (i.e. the variables *DURABILITY* and *FREQUENCY*), reported in Tables 7.7 and 7.8, are confirmed. Second, the variables *STABILITY* and *SIGNIFICANT* that only refer to significant government changes now are correlated with budget deficits, *but only if the other measures of government change are excluded*. Thus the modified variable *STABILITY* has a high and negative simple correlation coefficient with the change in net debt between 1970 and 1989. Similarly the variable *SIGNIFICANT* has a significant and positive effect on the budget deficit if the variable *FREQUENCY* is omitted from the specification, but otherwise it is generally insignificant and of the wrong sign.

These findings strongly indicate that high government turnover plays a crucial role in explaining public borrowing. Yet they do not convincingly discriminate between the two competing views: that short government durability is a symptom of a weak executive, or that it is an indication of political instability. Moreover, other plausible indicators of government weakness (such as government support in the legislature) are not systematically related to government borrowing. Naturally, there may be other explanations, beside these two, of why short government durability creates incentives to borrow.

Summarizing, our analysis of political institutions in the OECD countries suggests the following "stylized facts." First, lack of fiscal discipline is almost exclusively found in countries governed by representational democracies and, conversely, there are very few examples of representational democracies that do not have a high public debt problem. Second, the one feature of representational democracies that seems responsible for the lack of fiscal discipline is short government durability. Exactly why that is so remains an issue open for further research.

4 Evidence on Inflation and Seigniorage

Turning to the analysis of cross-country differences in monetary policies and inflation, the first question is whether there exists a relationship

Table 7.9
Government fiscal aggregates (% of GNP)

	1950–59			1960–69			1970–79			1980–87		
	Public spending	Tax revenue	Seign.	Public spending	Tax revenue	Seign.	Public spending	Tax revenue	Seign.	Public spending	Tax revenue	Seign.
U.S.	18	18	0.2	18	18	0.3	20	18	0.5	24	20	0.4
U.K.	27	29	0.5	28	31	0.4	35	34	0.8	40	37	0.1
Austria	21	18	1.6	21	20	1.1	33	31	1.0	39	35	0.4
Belgium	23	18	0.8	24	21	0.9	43	38	0.9	54	45	0.2
Denmark	14	16	0.3	21	23	0.6	34	34	0.2	43	40	0.3
France	na	20	1.5	na	22	1.1	35	32	0.7	43	41	0.5
Germany	15	14	1.1	14	13	0.6	27	26	1.0	31	29	0.3
Italy	17	16	1.9	17	16	1.6	26	19	3.2	37	27	1.8
Netherlands	24	25	0.7	25	25	0.7	42	41	0.5	57	51	0.4
Switzerland	9	9	0.9	8	8	1.9	9	8	1.5	9	9	0.3
Canada	16	17	0.3	16	16	0.4	20	20	0.7	24	20	0.2
Japan	14	14	0.7	13	12	1.2	12	9	1.3	na	na	0.6
Greece	17	16	1.7	18	17	1.8	22	19	2.6	32	23	3.7
Ireland	26	21	0.6	29	24	1.7	40	31	2.2	55	41	0.9
Portugal	na	na	1.4	na	na	1.7	25	21	4.1	44	35	3.3
Spain	na	na	1.4	12	12	1.5	21	21	2.2	31	26	3.2
Australia	23	25	0.1	23	21	0.4	22	23	0.7	28	26	0.6
New Zealand	32	29	0.3	28	27	−0.1	32	31	0.7	42	38	0.2
Mean	19.7	19.1	0.9	19.7	19.2	1.0	27.7	25.3	1.4	37.2	31.9	1.0
Standard deviation	0.06	0.05	0.006	0.06	0.06	0.006	0.09	0.09	0.010	0.12	0.10	0.012

Source: International Monetary Fund, *International Financial Statistics* and *Government Finance Statistics.*

between fiscal and monetary policies and, in particular, whether budget deficits affect the rate of inflation. The potential existence of a link between fiscal policy and inflation is stressed by the public finance approach to monetary policy. This approach considers inflation as just one form of taxation, and as such, it is viewed a source of distortion like any other tax. The principle of optimal taxation asserts that taxes should be set in such a way that the last amount collected with each tax be equally distortionary. Hence, if taxes need to be changed, all of them should be changed in the same direction. In particular, the rate of inflation should be positively correlated with all other tax rates.[10]

4.1 The Cross-Country Evidence

In Table 7.9, government revenues are broken down in two broad categories: (i) tax revenues, which include all forms of "explicit" taxation, like income taxes, sales taxes, VAT, etc., and (ii) seigniorage, i.e. revenues from monetization (defined as the change in base money). For all countries tax revenues reached their *highest* post-war levels in the 1980s, while in the majority of countries (10 out of 18) this was the decade where seigniorage was *lowest*, and in only two countries (Greece and Spain) was seigniorage higher in the 1980s than in the 1970s. The 1980s was also the period of largest budget deficits. This fact alone should cast serious doubts on the popular opinion that budget deficits are a cause of inflation.

On the other hand, seigniorage is on average higher in the countries that have an unsustainable debt path. This is particularly true for Spain, Greece, Portugal and Italy. In the 1980s the average level of seigniorage for these four countries was 3% of GNP, against less than 0.4% elsewhere. The other three countries on an unsustainable debt path (Austria, Belgium and Ireland) do not have seigniorage levels significantly higher than the rest of the sample. Thus across countries there is some evidence of a link between budget deficits and seigniorage, but not so over time.

4.2 The Time Series Evidence

To check whether the inflation tax is correlated over time with other distorting tax rates, as predicted by the theory of optimal taxation, we approximate the tax rate on seigniorage by the inflation rate.[11] The non-inflation tax rate is measured as the ratio of tax revenue to GNP. For each country, we regress the change in the rate of inflation on the change in the tax rate. The results, reported in Table 7.10 show that there is no systematic relationship between tax rates and inflation. For all countries but three (Australia, Canada and France), the link is insignificantly different from zero, and sometimes it has the wrong (negative) sign. Table 7.11 further shows that in most countries the change in government spending is strongly positively correlated with the change in the tax rate (the estimated coefficient on the tax rate is always positive and generally highly significant), while there is no evidence of a positive correlation between changes in spending and inflation.[12] Thus while the tax rate seems to respond to spending changes, inflation does not and this is the reason for the lack of complementarity between taxes and inflation.

It might be that the monetary authorities disregard in the short run the budgetary consequences of their actions. Could the principle of optimal taxation be relevant only in the long run? A way to test this hypothesis is to look for a positive long-run relationship between the average tax rate and the rate of inflation (technically we conduct cointegration tests, not reported).[13] There is no evidence of such a long-term relationship (except

Table 7.10
Inflation and taxes (partial correlation)

Australia	0.882* (0.377)	Italy	−0.059** (0.019)
Austria	1.278 (0.721)	Japan	0.937 (0.797)
Belgium	0.573 (0.472)	Netherlands	−0.806 (0.537)
Canada	1.075** (0.366)	New Zealand	0.268 (0.296)
Denmark	0.325 (0.460)	Portugal	−0.324 (1.334)
France	1.034 (0.472)	Spain	1.133 (1.174)
Germany	0.518 (0.408)	Switzerland	−0.923* (0.373)
Greece	0.381 (0.420)	U.K.	−0.330 (0.361)
Ireland	0.500 (0.321)	U.K.	0.330 (0.361)

Notes: Partial coefficient of correlation from regressions of inflation on taxes in first differences. The estimation period is 1950–1987 or a fraction of it, according to the availability of data. Standard errors in parenthesis. A* (**) denotes significance at the 5% (1%) level. The system is estimated by OLS.

Table 7.11
Inflation, taxes and government expenditure (partial correlation)

	Inflation and government expenditure	Taxes and government expenditure
Australia	0.295 (0.455)	0.755** (0.149)
Austria	1.152 (0.519)	0.436** (0.100)
Belgium	−0.074 (0.236)	0.210 (0.087)
Canada	0.475 (0.377)	0.225 (0.156)
Denmark	0.288 (0.315)	0.122 (0.116)
France	0.514 (0.390)	0.339* (0.146)
Germany	−0.235 (0.147)	0.087** (0.064)
Greece	−0.589 (0.369)	0.684** (0.101)
Ireland	0.520** (0.190)	0.458** (0.072)
Italy	−0.025** (0.009)	0.329** (0.056)
Japan	−0.821 (0.888)	0.259 (0.233)
Netherlands	0.614 (0.328)	0.383** (0.085)
New Zealand	−0.23 (0.319)	0.490** (0.175)
Portugal	−0.956 (0.763)	0.169 (0.168)
Spain	0.078 (0.875)	0.459** (0.129)
Switzerland	−0.045 (0.435)	0.522** (0.157)
U.K.	0.607 (0.380)	0.570** (0.154)
U.S.	−0.313 (0.348)	0.208 (0.158)

Notes: Coefficients from regressions of inflation or taxes on government, expenditures in first differences. The estimation period is 1950–87 or fraction of it, according to the availability of data. Standard errors in parenthesis. A* (**) denotes significance at the 5% (1%) level. The system is estimated by OLS.

for Switzerland where anyway the correlation is negative in contradiction to the theoretical prediction). This accords with the earlier observation that, in the 1980s, tax rates were increasing while seigniorage revenues were declining in most countries.

These results could still be reconciled with the principle of optimal taxation if the velocity of circulation of money is continuously increasing over time. Then the general tax base (income) grows relatively to the base of the inflation tax (money), and it becomes optimal to rely increasingly more on general taxation than on inflation. In this case, Poterba and Rotemberg (1989) and Trehan and Walsh (1989) show that we should expect a long-run relationship between three variables: the tax rate, inflation and velocity. When this is tested (and not reported here) evidence of a positive comovement between inflation and other taxes is found only for the U.S. and U.K. but not for the remaining 16 countries.

4.3 Summary

First, we have found that the countries that rely most on seigniorage typically have unsustainable debt paths, but the converse is not true: some countries with unsustainable debt paths have managed to maintain low inflation. Second, for most countries regular taxes and inflation are not "complementary" sources of revenues: these rates do not vary together as predicted by the theory of optimal taxation. Third, inflation does not vary systematically with expenditures, either in the short or in the long run, and not even across countries. The conclusion is that for most OECD countries fiscal policy has not been a major determinant of monetary stability in the post-war period. Rather, the evidence suggests that the often observed combination of large seigniorage and high public debt may reflect some other fundamental determinant, possibly linked to monetary institutions.

5 Monetary Institutions, Credibility, and Economic Policy

The principle of optimal taxation completely overlooks the fact that policy-makers face political constraints and incentives. In the case of monetary policy, credibility has long been known to be of fundamental importance. The reason is that the monetary authorities have an incentive to collect the inflation tax by surprising the private sector with unexpected monetary expansions. Indeed, unexpected inflation acts as a non-distortionary tax precisely because, being unanticipated, it does not affect private behaviour, at least ex ante. However, once this is understood, private agents are likely to raise their inflation expectations accordingly. If they cannot convince the private sector that they do not intend to engineer such surprises, the monetary authorities may be forced to accommodate these expectations, with the consequence that inflation will be higher than desired. Lack of credibility, therefore, results in an excessive reliance on seigniorage revenues.

This credibility problem can be overcome by delegating monetary policy to an independent central bank, committed to the goal of low inflation. Having a credible monetary policy may matter not only for the price and wage decisions of the private sector, but also for the budgetary decisions of the public sector. In particular a credible commitment not to inflate away the debt and not to provide monetary financing of the fiscal deficit may strengthen the government incentive to balance its budget. Hence low inflation as well as a more disciplined fiscal policy are more likely to be observed in countries with a more independent central bank.[14] Naturally, having an independent central bank committed to low inflation has its cost too: monetary policy is less likely to respond optimally to unexpected shocks and may tolerate excessive output fluctuations. Similarly, an independent central bank may pay too little attention to the budgetary consequences of its actions. This is why the design of the monetary regime should be an important determinant of public financial policies and, more generally, of macroeconomic performance. In particular, we expect central bank independence to be associated with low inflation and smaller budget deficits, but also with larger output fluctuation and greater deviations from the predictions of the theory of optimal taxation.

5.1 The Monetary Institutions

To compare the monetary regimes we focus exclusively on institutional features, disregarding behavioural indicators such as the average rate of growth of the money supply or the level and variability of interest rates. There is no doubt that such behavioural indicators shape expectations and thus contribute to identify a monetary regime. The independence of the Bundesbank is due to specific central bank laws but also of its reputation and its tradition of monetary discipline. Hence, by neglecting behavioural indicators we miss an important dimension of monetary regimes. Our stance can be justified on the following grounds. First, to assess the effect of institutional design on policy performance we need to keep institutions and behaviour as distinct as possible. Second, behavioural indicators have often varied over time (e.g. with the personalities in charge of monetary policy) whereas monetary institutions have generally been more invariant and, to the extent that there have been institutional reforms they are more clearly identifiable.

Monetary institutions can be characterized by the political and economic independence of the central bank. Political independence is the capacity to choose the *final goal* of monetary policy, such as inflation or the level of economic activity. Economic independence is the capacity to choose the *instruments* with which to pursue these goals. The few studies which compare monetary regimes in a large number of countries are not consistently linked to the theoretical debate and their classifications are based on somewhat arbitrary criteria. The most comprehensive studies of the political dimension of central bank independence are Fair (1978) and Bade and Parkin (1982). The economic dimension has recently been stressed by Masciandaro and Tabellini (1988), who compare the central banks of the U.S., Canada, Australia, New Zealand and Japan; by Tabellini (1987b) in a study of Italy; and by Masciandaro (1990).

5.1.1 Political Independence of the Central Bank

The capacity of the monetary authorities to choose the final goals of policy is primarily determined by three aspects of a monetary regime. (i) the procedure for appointing the members of the central bank governing bodies; (ii) the relationship between these bodies and the government; and (iii) the formal responsibilities of the central bank. In principle, independence to choose the final goals can be defined without reference to the contents of such goals. In practice, however, the main virtue of having an independent central bank is that it can provide credibility. This is why we identify independence with autonomy to pursue the goal of low inflation. Any institutional feature that enhances the central bank capacity to pursue this goal will, on our definition, increase central bank independence.

Table 7.12 contrasts these three aspects of the monetary regimes in the 18 countries. Each column refers to a different attribute. A star indicates that the country in question possesses that attribute. Appendix C provides more information on each column. The first four columns describe the rules for appointing the governor and the board of the central bank. The

Table 7.12
Political independence of central banks

	Appointments				Relationship with government		Constitution		Index of political independence
Countries	(1)	(2)	(3)	(4)	(5)	(6)	(7)	(8)	(9)
Australia		*					*	*	3
Austria						*	*	*	3
Belgium				*					1
Canada	*	*					*	*	4
Denmark		*				*	*		3
France		*		*					2
Germany		*		*	*	*	*	*	6
Greece			*					*	2
Ireland		*				*	*		3
Italy	*	*	*		*				4
Japan							*		1
Netherlands		*		*	*	*	*	*	6
New Zealand									0
Portugal					*				1
Spain				*	*				2
Switzerland		*			*	*	*	*	5
U.K.					*				1
U.S.				*	*	*	*	*	5

Sources: See Appendix C.
Notes: (1) Governor *not* appointed by government; (2) Governor appointed for >5 years; (3) *All* the Board *not* appointed by government; (4) Board appointed for >5 years; (5) No mandatory participation of government representative in the Board; (6) No government approval of monetary policy formulation is required; (7) Statutory requirements that central bank pursues monetary stability amongst its goals; (8) Legal provisions that strengthen the central bank's position in conflicts with the government are present; (9) Overall index of political independence, constructed as the sum of the asterisks in each row. See Appendix C for more details.

political independence of the central bank is clearly higher if the appointments are not under the control of the government (but are determined by representatives of the bank, like in Italy or in Canada), and if they are for a long and predetermined period of time. Columns 5 and 6 summarize the relationship between the central bank governing bodies and the government. The political independence of the central bank is greater if there is no mandatory participation of a government representative in the board and if prior government approval of monetary policy is not legally required.[15] Finally (columns 7 and 8) the central bank's constitutional position is clearly strengthened if its role in preserving monetary stability is explicitly stated in the constitution, and if there are explicit legal directives that, in case of conflict between the bank and the government, describe a transparent procedure for how the conflict is to be resolved. In other words, both attributes enhance the "gate keeping" power of the monetary regime: they make it less likely that, in case of conflict, the bank's position will be overruled by the government.

The overall degree of central bank political independence is determined by a combination of these attributes. Combining them is unavoidably arbitrary so we adopt the simplest procedure of adding them up. The result, shown in the last column of Table 7.12, is our synthetic indicator of the political independence of the central bank. Switzerland, West Germany and the U.S., but also the Netherlands, Canada and Italy, enjoy the highest degree of political independence. At the other end are Austria, New Zealand, the U.K., Belgium and Portugal, and not far above, Greece, Spain and France.[16]

5.1.2 Economic Independence of the Central Bank

The autonomy of a central bank in choosing the instruments of monetary policy is described by: (i) the influence of the government in determining how much to borrow from the central bank; and (ii) the nature of the monetary instruments under the control of the central bank. If the government can influence the quantity and the conditions on which it borrows from the central bank, it also influences the creation of monetary base and lessens the economic independence of the central bank. The first five columns of Table 7.13 summarize the government's ease of access to central bank credit. This can be done in two ways: through direct credit facilities (columns 1–4), and by purchasing government securities in the primary market (column 5: a star indicates that the central bank does not participate as a buyer in this market and is more free from implicit or explicit pressures to lend to the government). Economic independence of the central bank is greater if direct credit to the government is: non-automatic (column 1), at a market interest rate (column 2), explicitly stated as temporary (column 3), and in a limited amount (column 4).

The second aspect, the nature of the monetary instruments under the control of the central bank, is described in the next two columns of Table 7.13. If the central bank does not have control of the discount rate, its ability to determine the general level of interest rates is severely impaired. Column 6 reveals that most, but not all, central banks are responsible for setting the discount rate. Column 7 is concerned with banking supervi-

Table 7.13
Economic independence of central banks

	Monetary financing of budget deficit					Monetary instruments		Index of economic independence
Countries	(1)	(2)	(3)	(4)	(5)	(6)	(7)	(8)
Australia	*	*	*	*	*	*		6
Austria			*	*	*	*	**	6
Belgium		*		*	*	*	**	6
Canada	*	*	*	*		*	**	7
Denmark		*			*	*	**	5
France				*	*	*	**	5
Germany	*	*	*	*	*	*	*	7
Greece				*		*		2
Ireland		*	*	*		*		4
Italy				*				1
Japan	*		*		*	*	*	5
Netherlands			*	*	*	*		4
New Zealand			*	*		*		3
Portugal				*		*		2
Spain			*	*			*	3
Switzerland		*	*	*	*	*	**	7
U.K.	*	*	*	*		*		5
U.S.	*	*	*	*	*	*	*	7

Sources: See Appendix C.
Notes: (1) Direct credit facility: not automatic; (2) Direct credit facility: market interest rate; (3) Direct credit facility; temporary; (4) Direct credit facility: limited amount; (5) Central bank does not participate in primary market for public debt; (6) Discount rate set by central bank; (7) Banking supervision *not* entrusted to the central bank (**) or not entrusted to the central bank alone (*); (8) Overall index of economic independence (being the sum of the asterisks is columns 1–7). See Appendic C for more detailed information.

sion and in particular with administrative instruments such as portfolio constraints on bank intermediaries or ceilings to private bank loans. Such instruments facilitate the financing of government borrowing by administratively increasing the private demand for government securities. They can weaken central bank independence by partially removing monetary control from the market. In column 7 we classify as most independent (denoted with two stars) a bank that has no responsibility for bank supervision, as relatively independent (denoted with one star) a bank that is sharing responsibility for bank supervision with some other institution, and as least independent (no asterisk) a bank which is the only institution in charge of bank supervision.

As before, to determine the overall degree of economic independence of the central bank, we add up the attributes. The resulting indicator appears in the last column of Table 7.13. Economic independence of the central bank is high in West Germany, Switzerland, the U.S., but also in Austria and Belgium. Conversely, central banks in Italy, New Zealand, Portugal, Greece and Spain have very little economic independence. Interestingly, political and economic independence are not always positively correlated. Thus a ranking that pays attention to only one of the two dimensions can give rise to very misleading international comparisons.

5.1.3 Central Bank Independence and Seigniorage

Figure 7.3 summarizes Tables 7.12 and 7.13 showing the overall degree of economic and political independence of the 18 countries under consideration. Four groups of countries are identifiable. Those in the upper-right portion of the diagram have the most independent central banks, those which enjoy both political and economic independence. The countries on the lower-left portion have the least independent central banks, both economically and politically. The remaining two groups of countries are in between, with monetary institutions independent in only one of the two dimensions.

It is instructive to compare Figure 7.3 with Figure 7.1 and Table 7.9. Of the four countries with highly dependent central banks (Greece, New Zealand, Portugal and Spain), three (Greece, Portugal and Spain) also have highly unstable political systems and unsustainable debt paths. These are the three countries with the highest level of seigniorage. Other politically unstable countries also have unsustainable debt policies (Austria, Belgium, Ireland, Italy and the Netherlands), but they have relatively independent central banks, at least on one dimension. These other countries (with the exception of Italy and possibly Ireland) collect much smaller seigniorage revenues. These facts suggest that central bank independence may bring about monetary stability and low inflation even if there are political incentives towards lax budgetary policies. It also means that a European monetary union among countries with very different debt policies is feasible provided that the monetary authorities face adequate incentives and independence.

5.2 Central Bank Independence and Economic Performance

To find out whether inflation is related to central bank independence, we divide the period 1950–1989 into four decades and measure the effect of the indicators presented in the previous section on cross-country differences

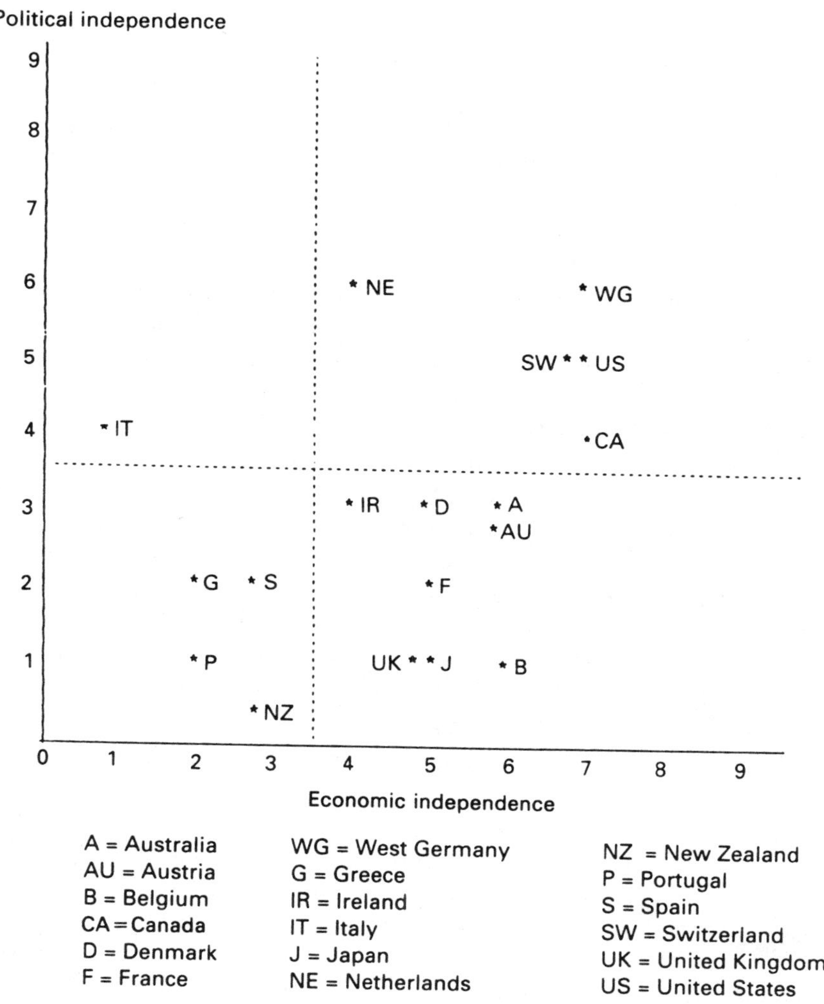

Figure 7.3
Political and economic independence of central banks.
Source: As Tables 7.12 and 7.13.

in inflation rates (using seemingly unrelated regressions). An interesting question is the role played by the EMS. For high inflation countries like Italy, participation in the EMS may have strengthened the independence of the central bank vis-à-vis the national government because it has increased its commitment to price stability. This argument does not necessarily hold for low inflation countries, like West Germany, since the EMS has transformed a technical issue (exchange rate management) into a major political issue (whether or not to realign the EMS parities) on which the government may have more to say than the central bank. For this reason, we treat EMS participation as a separate dimension of the regime, not included in the ranking of central bank independence. This is done by including a dummy variable that takes a value of 1 for the EMS countries and O otherwise in the regressions for the 1980s.

Table 7.14 reports the estimated effects on inflation of the indicators of economic and political central bank independence plus the EMS dummy for the last decade. The indicators of central bank independence always have the expected (negative) sign. The indicator of economic independence is significant in the periods of high inflation, while the indicator of political independence is significant only in the 1970s. On the other hand, the estimated coefficient of the EMS dummy is not significantly different from zero. The results also hold for the average inflation rate throughout the whole period 1950–1989, as shown in the last column. So monetary institutions matter, indirectly, through their effects on credibility, and directly,

Table 7.14
Inflation and central bank independence (dependent variable: inflation)

Explanatory variables	1950–59	1960–69	1970–79	1980–89	1950–89
Intercept	5.288**	4.457**	17.183**	18.670**	11.637**
	(1.252)	(0.679)	(1.108)	(1.934)	(0.148)
Economic independence	−0.167	−0.135	−1.211**	−1.913**	−0.897**
	(0.261)	(0.142)	(0.231)	(0.402)	(0.148)
Political independence	−0.266	−0.101	−0.611*	−0.429	−0.0277
	(0.275)	(0.149)	(0.243)	(0.431)	(0.0163)
EMS	—	—	—	−0.685	−0.854
	—	—	—	(0.927)	(0.541)
$\bar{R}^2$	0.109	0.111	0.745	0.658	0.782
SE	2.061	1.118	1.825	3.249	1.039

Notes: Standard errors in parenthesis. A* (**) denotes significance at the 5% (1%) level. The system is estimated by seemingly unrelated regression, except for the last column, which is estimated by OLS.

by shaping the central bank incentives. Our results also confirm previous findings obtained by other authors for a different sample of countries and a slightly different ranking of independence (see Bade and Parkin 1982; and Alesina 1989).

Central bank independence might conceivably be related to the broad political characteristics used in the analysis of budget deficits. To check whether this is the case, we have included the variables *FREQUENCY*, *SIGNIFICANT* and *MAJORITY* as additional regressors. To save on degrees of freedom, we sum together the two measures of central bank independence to obtain a single indicator.[17] The results which appear in Table 7.15, show that central bank independence always has a negative estimated effect on inflation, and that is is significant half of the time. The political variables also play a role, but their coefficient is often not of the expected sign. Estimates over the whole period (last column) confirms the greater importance of central bank independence as compared to political variables.

One of the alleged benefits of an independent central bank is that it is more credible in its resolve not to engage in public financing. This may affect the Treasury's behaviour, reducing the likelihood of unsustainable

Table 7.15
Inflation, political instability and central bank independence (dependent variable: inflation)

Explanatory variables	1950–69	1960–69	1970–79	1980–89	1950–89
Intercept	8.419** (1.716)	4.329** (1.040)	6.76* (3.186)	16.653** (2.941)	10.343** (1.454)
FREQUENCY	1.661 (0.103)	−0.363 (0.705)	5.944** (1.838)	6.008* (0.678)	0.076 (1.295)
SIGNIFICANT	4.037 (2.185)	−0.084 (2.222)	6.785* (2.895)	24.592** (4.714)	7.423 (3.471)
MAJORITY	−0.018 (0.009)	−0.002 (0.006)	0.020 (0.013)	−0.012 (0.019)	−0.008 (0.009)
Independence	−0.453** (0.146)	−0.087 (0.088)	−0.327 (0.208)	−1.093** (0.226)	−0.559** (0.108)
EMS	—	—	—	−1.112 (1.204)	−1.126 (0.675)
$\bar{R}^2$	0.206	−0.186	0.796	0.760	0.748
SE	1.720	1.101	1.533	2.473	1.117

Notes: Standard errors in parenthesis. A* (**) denotes significance at the 5% (1%) level. Columns (1)–(4) are estimated by seemingly unrelated regressions. Column 5 is estimated by ordinary least squares.

debt policies (see, for instance, Tabellini 1987a). This hypothesis receives no support from the data. In a regression of the primary deficit on the political variables *FREQUENCY, SIGNIFICANT* and *MAJORITY,* and the overall indicator of central bank independence, INDEP, the latter variable is always insignificant (though generally with a negative estimated coefficient). The coefficient of the political variables, on the other hand, are not very different from those reported in the previous section. Similar results are obtained if the primary deficit is replaced by net debt accumulation.

Finally, does central bank independence come with a cost in overall macroeconomic performance? For the whole period, we find no systematic effect of the two indicators of central bank independence on the real growth rate of real output. In Table 7.16, even though central bank independence seems to be associated with lower output growth, the estimated effect is generally insignificant. The same results are obtained if the regressions are estimated by averaging the data over the four decades, if the political variables are added as regressors, or if we replace the growth rate with the rate of unemployment (in this last case, the EMS dummy has a positive and significant estimated coefficient).[18] Hence, it does not seem that there is a sharp tradeoff in the design of monetary institutions. A more independent central bank brings about low inflation, but not necessarily worse real macroeconomic performance.

Table 7.16
Central bank independence and real macroeconomic performance

Dependent variables/ explanatory variables	Output growth	Standard error of output growth
Intercept	0.042**	0.071*
	(0.008)	(0.025)
Economic independence	−0.0009	−0.005
	(0.001)	(0.005)
Political independence	0.002	−0.001
	(0.001)	(0.005)
EMS	−0.007	0.013
	(0.006)	(0.018)
$\bar{R}^2$	−0.070	−0.013
SE	0.012	0.035

Notes: Standard errors in parenthesis. A* (**) denotes significance at the 5% (1%) level. Each equation is separately estimated by OLS. Each observation is the average over the 1950–1987 period.

6 Summary and Conclusions

The striking differences in the public financial policies of the industrialized countries throughout the post-war period cannot be explained as the optimal government response to different shocks or to different initial conditions. A more convicing explanation is that the governments of these countries were subject to different political or economic incentives, and as a result they enacted different policies. Four main results emerge.

First, the accumulation of large public debts is concentrated among countries characterized by (i) representational democracies (as opposed to majoritarian parliamentary democracies and presidential democracies); and (ii) fractionalized party systems. These institutional features induce budget deficits because they lead to short-lived governments.

Second, while countries that extensively rely an seigniorage also have high public debt, the converse is not true. In some high debt countries seigniorage is a trivial source of revenue. These countries share the characteristic of having an independent central bank. In general, central bank independence leads to low inflation, irrespective of political institutions and budgetary problems. At the same time, monetary independence does not discourage budget deficits. Monetary and fiscal discipline thus seem to be orthogonal to each other: a country can have either, both or neither of them, depending on its monetary and political institutions.

Third, if central bank independence is on average associated with lower inflation, there is no systematic impact on real output growth, nor on its variability. Thus having an independent central bank is almost like having a free lunch; there are benefits but no apparent costs in terms of macroeconomic performance.

Fourth, there is very little evidence that over time the inflation tax is caused by lax budgetary policies or that it is used efficiently. Few countries use seigniorage and regular taxes as complementary sources of revenues. And in most countries changes in government spending are absorbed by changes in regular taxes rather than by changes in the inflation tax.

These findings have some important implications for the ongoing debate over the feasibility and appropriate sequencing of the European monetary integration. On the one hand, they suggest that there is no need to subordinate monetary integration to having first achieved fiscal convergence. The future European Central Bank has been designed to be very independent from the national governments and from the European

Commission. On our criteria, it would be one of the most—if not the most—independent of all OECD central banks. Our results suggest that this should be sufficient to insulate the common European monetary policy from the accommodating pressure coming from the budget deficits of some countries.

On the other hand, there is a case for accompanying monetary integration with some budgetary rules binding on the national governments. Such rules may be in the interest of the high debt countries. Because debt accumulation in the representational democracies is probably due to some domestic political distortion, binding external rules—such as a balanced budget on current expenditures and revenues—may act as an offsetting force and hence be welfare improving. As for monetary policy, one of the advantages of joining an international agreement may consist in "tying one's hands," in this case, the hands of the fiscal authorities.

There is one additional, historical, argument in favour of fiscal rules in a new European monetary constitution. Our finding that the lack of fiscal discipline does not necessarily lead to monetary instability only relates to the post-war period. This period, however, may be too short and, as recently argued by Giovannini and Spaventa (1991), the real challenges for the European monetary union are more likely to come from the management of the high stocks of public debt. Furthermore, the pre-war experience indicates that fiscal crises and public debt runs did occur, and were often accompanied by monetary instability. For this reason, the credibility of a unified European monetary system would be enhanced by fiscal rules that guaranteed the long-run solvency of the high debt countries.

Appendix A Tests of Debt Sustainability

There is a large literature on how to test Equation (3) in note 3. The literature originates with Hamilton and Flavin (1986) with more recent contributions from Wilcox (1989), Trehan and Walsh (1988) and Grilli (1989). A problem with all of this literature, which is present also in the present chapter, is the failure to distinguish between current and capital public expenditure, for lack of consistent data. This distinction matters because capital expenditures are presumably self-financing, since they generate future revenues. Hence treating all expenditures as current amounts to underestimating future revenues. On the other hand, the probability of a war—and high military spending—is positive even during peacetime, so there is a risk that future expenditures are likely to exceed actually observed expenditures. These two effects tend to offset each other.

The idea is to check for the stationarity of the (appropriately discounted) debt or of the total (i.e. inclusive of interest payments) deficit. One critical problem of this approach is that the appropriate discount factor, q, is not observable. Bohn (1990) shows that the discount factor varies across states of nature and time, depending on the stochastic properties of output and government spending, and does not necessarily bear any relationship to the expected or realized rate of return on government debt. These tests, therefore, are really joint tests of the stationarity hypothesis and of the assumption made about q. Here we present results obtained using the technique suggested by Trehan and Walsh (1988). Their method tests Equation (3) under the assumption that q, even if not observable, is approximately constant over time.[19] Trehan and Walsh (1988) show that, under this assumption, and if the underlying expenditure and revenue series are stationary in first differences, a necessary and sufficient condition for (3) to hold is that the deficit inclusive of interest (as a percentage of GNP) is a stationary variable with zero drift.[20] To test the null hypothesis that the deficit is non-stationary, we proceed as follows (see also Perron, 1988). First we test the existence of a unit root against the more general alternative of a stationary autoregressive model with drift and time trend. This is the $Z(\tau\tau)$ test. If rejection of the unit root is not possible, we test the existence of the unit root against more restrictive alternatives, i.e. a stationary autoregression model with drift ($Z(\tau\mu)$) and a pure autoregressive model ($Z(\tau)$). However, in order to be able to apply these two tests, we first check for the existence of drift, which is done by testing the joint hypothesis of unit root and no drift ($Z(\Phi_2)$). If the hypothesis of no drift is rejected, in fact, the more specialized tests cannot be used. The results are shown in Table 7.A1. Note that for the U.K. the evidence of non-stationarity is clearly due to the implosive path of the debt to GNP ratio, and hence it cannot be taken as evidence of unsustainability.

Appendix B Indicators of Government Attributes

The political event data used to construct the variables *FREQUENCY* and *SIGNIFICANT* of Table 7.8 are reported in Table 7.B1.

Table 7.A1
Unit root tests (total deficit/GNP)

	$Z(\tau\tau)$	$Z(\Phi_2)$	$Z(\tau\mu)$	$Z(\tau)$
U.S.	99%			
U.K.	—	—	—	—
Austria	—	—	—	—
Belgium	—	—	—	—
Denmark	—	—	—	97.5%
France	—	—	—	95%
Germany	99%			
Italy	—	—	—	—
Netherlands	90%			
Switzerland	99%			
Canada	99%			
Japan	na	na	na	na
Greece	—	—	—	—
Ireland	—	—	—	—
Portugal	—	—	—	—
Spain	—	—	—	—
Australia	—	—	—	90%
New Zealand	95%			

Notes: $Z(\tau\tau)$-H1: autoregressive model with drift and time trend; $Z(\Phi_2)$-joint hypothesis of unit root and no drift; $Z(\tau\mu)$-H1: autoregressive model with drift; $Z(\tau)$-H1: pure autoregressive model; $x\%$ = confidence level for rejection of unit root; — = rejection of unit root is not possible at conventional confidence levels.

Table 7.B1
Government instability and political instability

	Frequency				Significant			
Country	1950–59	1960–69	1970–79	1980–89	1950–59	1960–69	1970–79	1980–89
Australia	0	3	5	1	1	0	2	1
Austria	5	5	3	2	0	0	1	0
Belgium	8	4	8	8	2	0	2	0
Canada	1	3	3	3	1	1	1	2
Denmark	4	5	6	4	2	1	3	1
France	15	5	5	6	9	3	1	3
Germany	5	9	3	3	0	1	0	1
Greece	15	16	7	3	3	4	1	2
Ireland	5	2	8	6	3	0	2	3
Italy	8	10	11	13	0	0	0	4
Japan	8	4	5	7	1	0	0	0
Netherlands	2	4	3	3	1	2	3	0
New Zealand	2	1	5	1	1	1	2	1
Portugal	3	1	15	8	0	0	4	4
Spain	0	2	12	6	0	0	1	1
Switzerland	10	8	6	1	2	0	0	0
U.K.	4	2	4	0	1	1	3	0
U.S.	1	3	2	2	1	2	1	1

Sources: Jodice and Taylor (1982), Banks (1987), Keasing Archives, various years.
Notes: Frequency = Number of government changes for the decade; Significant = Number of "significant" government changes for the decade.

Appendix C Indicators of Central Bank Independence

The institutional information used to construct our indicators of central bank independence is summarized in Tables 7.C1–7.C4.

Table 7.C1
Central bank governor

Country	Governor appointed by	Term (years)	Reappointability
Belgium	Sovereign (i.e. government)	Five	Yes
Denmark	Sovereign	Indefinite	—
France	President	Indefinite	—
Germany	President proposal of the government	Eight	—
Greece	Government proposal of the bank	Four	Yes
Ireland	President proposal of the government	Seven	Yes
Italy	Bank Board approval of the government	Indefinite	—
Netherlands	Sovereign (i.e. government) proposal of the bank	Seven	Yes
Portugal	Government	Five	Yes
U.K.	Sovereign proposal of the government	Five	Yes
Spain	Sovereign proposal of the government	Four	Yes
Switzerland	Government	Six	Yes
Australia	Government	Seven	Yes
Canada	Board	Seven	Yes
Japan	Government	Five	Yes
New Zealand	Government	Five	Yes
U.S.	President	Four	Yes
Austria	President	Five	Yes

Sources: Aufricht (1967) and national legislation.

Table 7.C2
Central bank board

Country	Board appointed by	Members (*)	Term (years)	Reappointment	Government inst. representatives
Belgium	Sovereign (i.e. government)	3–6	Six	Yes	Yes Government Commissioner (advisory/suspensive rights)
Denmark	Parliament (8); Trade Min. (2); Bank Board (15)	25	Five	Yes	Yes Minister of Trade (supervisory right)
France	Minister of Finance (9) Bank (1)	10	Six	Yes	Yes Director Minister of Finance (advisory/suspensive right)
Germany	President proposal Government	8	Eight	—	No
Greece	Shareholders General Meeting	9	Three	Yes	Yes Government Commissioner (suspensive right)
Ireland	Government	3–8	Five	—	Yes Permanent Secretary Minister of Finance ?
Italy	Shareholders Regional Meetings	13	Three	Yes	No
Netherlands	Sovereign (i.e. government)	3–5	Seven	Yes	No (yes in the Bank Council: Royal Commissioner)
Portugal	Government	7–9	Five	Yes	No (yes in the General Council)
U.K.	Sovereign (i.e. government)	16	Four	—	No

Spain	Government (6); Min. Fin. (2) Governor (1–4); Bank (1)	10–14	Two	—	No
Switzerland	Government (25) Bank (15)	40	Four	Yes	No
Australia	Government	7	Five	Yes	Yes Secretary of Treasury (voting right)
Canada	Government	12	Three	Yes	Yes Deputy Minister of Finance (advisory right)
Japan	Government (4); Econ. Ag. & Min. Fin. (2)	6	Four	Yes	Yes Representatives Min. of Finance Min. Ec. Planning (advisory right)
New Zealand	Government	5	Five	Yes	Yes Secretary of the Treasury (casting vote)
U.S.	President	5	Fourteen	No	No
Austria	Government (5) Sh. Gen. Meeting (6)	11	Five	Yes	Yes Government Commissioner (advisory and suspensive right)

Source: Aufricht (1967) and national legislation.
Note: (*) except Governor and Vice-Governor(s), government representative(s).

Table 7.C3
Government financing accommodation: monetary and regulatory framework

	Monetary framework		Regulatory framework		
Country	Direct cred. (characters)	Primary issue	Central bank	Other institutions	Government
Belgium	OVERDRAFT *limited *automatic *disc. rate *no terms	No	—	Banking Commission	—
Denmark	OVERDRAFT *unlimited *automatic *disc. rate *no terms	No	—	Supervisor of Comm. Banks & Savings Bank	—
France	OVERDRAFT *limited *automatic *no rate *no terms	No	—	Banking commission	—
Germany	ADVANCES *limited *discretion *disc. rate *terms (3 m)	No	Yes	Federal Banking Supervisory Office	—
Greece	ADVANCES *limited *automatic *symbolic rate *terms	Yes	Yes	—	—
Ireland	OVERDRAFT *limited *automatic *terms (m) *market rate	Yes	Yes	—	—
Italy	OVERDRAFT *limited *automatic *symbolic rate *no terms	Yes	Yes	—	—
Netherlands	OVERDRAFT *limited *automatic *no rate *terms	No	Yes	—	—
Portugal	OVERDRAFT *limited *automatic *no rate *terms (1 y)	Yes	Yes	—	—

Table 7.C3 (continued)

Country	Monetary framework: Direct cred. (characters)	Monetary framework: Primary issue	Regulatory framework: Central bank	Regulatory framework: Other institutions	Regulatory framework: Government
U.K.	No	Yes	Yes	—	—
Spain	OVERDRAFT *limited *automatic *no rate *terms (1 y)	Yes	Yes	—	Ministry of Finance
Switzerland	OVERDRAFT *limited *automatic *market rate *terms (m)	No	—	Federal Banking Commission	—
Austria	OVERDRAFT *limited *discretion *m. rate *terms	No	Yes	—	—
Canada	ADVANCES *limited *discretion *bank rate *terms	Yes	—	General Inspector of Banks	—
Japan	ADVANCES *limited *discretion *no m. rate *terms	No	Yes	—	Ministry of Finance
U.S.	No	No	Yes	Comptroller of the Currency FDIC FHLB	
Austria	Advances *limited *discretion *no m. rate *terms (d)	No	—	—	Ministry of Finance

Sources: Aufricht (1967) and national legislation.

Table 7.C4
Central bank, government, and accountability

Country	Relation with government	Relation with parliament	Monetary stability objective	Provisions in case of disagreement central bank-gov't
Belgium	Approval	Through government	No	Yes Government directives
Denmark	Consulation	Annual report	Yes	No
France	Approval	Through government	No	No
Germany	Consulation	Not accountable	Yes	Yes Temporary post-position
Greece	Consulation		No	Yes Arbitration commission
Ireland	Consulation	Annual report	Yes	No
Italy	Approval	On call	No	Yes Government directives
Netherlands	Consulation	Through government	Yes	Yes Government directives
Portugal	Approval	Through government	No	Yes Government directives
U.K.	Approval	Through government annual report	No	No
Spain	Approval	Through government	Yes	No
Switzerland	Consulation	Annual report	Yes	No (independence guarantee)
Australia	Approval	Annual report	Yes	Yes Government directives informing Parliament
Canada	Approval	On call	Yes	Yes Government directives informing Parliament
Japan	Approval	Approval	Yes	No
New Zealand	Approval	Annual report	No	No
U.S.	Consulation	Approval	Yes	Yes Parliament directives
Austria	Consulation	Not accountable	Yes	Yes Arbitration tribunal

Source: Aufricht (1967) and national legislation.

Notes

We wish to thank, without implicating, Charlie Bean, Jeff Frieden, David Gowland, Edmond Malinvaud, Marco Pagano, Luigi Spaventa, Charles Wyplosz and the participants in the *Economic Policy* panel, as well as in workshops at the Bank of Italy, the Bank of Portugal and the Universities of Cagliari, Campbasso and Milan for several helpful comments on an earlier draft. Charles Wyplosz deserves particular gratitude. His comments and help throughout the editorial process were essential for us. We also thank G. Albrecht, A. Grimes, H. Jepsen, J. Larsen, I. L. Macfarlane, K. Rohl and G. Spencer for providing us with information about the monetary institutions of various countries, and Cindy Miller for editorial assistance. Vincenzo Galasso provided excellent research assistance. Guido Tabellini gratefully acknowledges financial support from the NSF grant SES-8909 and from the UC Center for Pacific Rim Studies.

1. Empirical evidence similar to that of Roubini and Sachs (1988) and to the evidence of this chapter is presented, for developing countries, in Edwards and Tabellini (1990,1991).

2. The "tax smoothing" principle of debt policy was first applied by Barro (1979, 1986) to explain the debt policies of the U.S. and the U.K.

3. Consider the government budget constraint (all variables are expressed as a percentage of GNP):

$$b_t \geq R_t b_{t-1} + d_t \tag{1}$$

where b is public debt, R is one plus the rate of return divided by one plus the growth rate of real GNP, and d is the primary deficit. By recursive forward substitution, Equation (11) can be rewritten as:

$$b_{t-1} \leq \sum_{t=0}^{N-1} q_{t+i} d_{t+i} + q_{t+N} b_{t+N} \tag{2}$$

where:

$$q_{t+i} = \prod_{k=0}^{i} R_{t+k}$$

Since the market will not allow public debt to grow in excess of the government capacity to service it,

$$\lim_{N \to \infty} q_{t+N} b_{t+N} = 0 \tag{3}$$

4. In particular, Germany, Ireland and Japan also have less representational features in their electoral laws.

5. France is included in the second group, but its primary deficit is only averaged between 1960 and 1989, since before 1959 it was a representative democracy. The primary deficit of France in 1950–1959 is instead included in Group 1.

6. This definition is based on Rae (1967); it is $(1 - \sum_{i=1}^{N} T_i^2)$, where N is the number of parties and T is the ith party's decimal share of the vote in the legislature. See also Bingham Powell (1982, p. 233).

7. In computing these numbers, France was considered a representational democracy in 1950–1958, and a presidential democracy in 1959–1989. Only the years of democratic regime in Spain, Greece and Portugal were included.

8. Net debt data are missing for Spain, Switzerland and New Zealand. For Portugal the data refer to gross public debt.

9. Regressions performed using the method of seemingly unrelated regressions.

10. The fiscal approach to inflation has been developed by Phelps (1973; see also Mankiw 1987). Faig (1988) and Kimbrough (1986) show that since money performs the role of an intermediate input, it should not be taxed. However, as shown by Aizenman (1987), this conclusion does not apply in the presence of tax evasion or tax collection costs.

11. This is standard practice in the literature. Using the rate of money growth instead leads to the same results, while data on the nominal interest rate are not available for all countries over long enough periods of time.

12. The same results are obtained if the inflation regressions are estimated with instrumental variables, with lagged variables as instruments.

13. Two non-stationary (i.e. with no stable mean) series are said to be cointegrated if there exists a linear combination of them which is stationary. Cointegration tests are common in the empirical literature on optimal taxation—see Grilli (1989), Trehan and Walsh (1989), among others, However, they raise a problem. The prediction that "optimal" tax rates are non-stationary is derived from models which neglect the constraint that the rates are bounded between O and 1. Proper microfoundations, such as in Lucas and Stokey (1983), imply that the optimal tax rate is stationary, in which case the notion of cointegration does not apply. We reject non-stationarity of the tax rate for the U.S. the U.K., Austria, Denmark, Switzerland, Greece and Ireland. For the inflation rate, non-stationarity is rejected in Austria, Belgium, Denmark, France, Germany, the Netherlands, Switzerland and Japan. Hence, the cointegration tests reported in the text should be taken with a grain of salt.

14. This point is shown in Rogoff (1985). Tabellini (1987a, 1987b) analyses the connection between central bank independence and budget deficits.

15. In some countries—e.g. Italy—the requirement that monetary policy be approved by the government is a mere formality that has never resulted in the approval being denied or even threatened with denial. Nevertheless, we classify these countries as requiring government approval for two reasons. First, as stated in the text, we want to be consistent in classifying institutions rather than behaviour. Second, just observing that approval is never denied is no proof that the formal requirement is not binding: a rational and fully informed central bank would never pursue a policy that would not be approved by the government, even in the case of a strong disagreement.

16. Towards the late 1980s New Zealand reformed its monetary system and now has perhaps the most independent central bank of all OECD countries. Its new central bank law even contains an explicit clause stating that the governor can be dismissed if the inflation target is exceeded. Our rankings are based on the older law.

17. The same results are obtained if we use instead a ranking of 1 to 4, corresponding to the four quadrants of Figure 7.3, or if we use the two indicators separately, again with economic independence being more important than political independence. Finally, similar results are obtained if some of the political variables are omitted.

18. Alesina and Summers (1990) independently obtained similar results based on a different sample of countries and a central bank ranking analogous to our political independence index.

19. We also tried other tests of (3), along the lines of Wilcox (1989). But they were unable to discriminate across countries; we could not reject the hypothesis that all countries were on an unsustainable path. This test presupposes that the correct rate of return with which to discount the budget constraint coincides with the realized real rate on government debt. As noted by Bohn (1990), however, this presumption is very likely to be incorrect.

20. Since we did not subtract seigniorage from the deficit, we are not consolidating the balance sheets of the Treasury and the central bank together. Thus our test of the transversality condition (3) applies to the sum of the debt held by the private sector and by the central bank.

References

Aizenman, J. 1987. Inflation, tariffs and tax enforcement costs. *Journal of International Economic Integration.*

Aizenman, J. 1989. Competitive externalities and the optimal seigniorage. NBER working paper no. 2937.

Alesina, A. 1989. Inflation, unemployment and politics in industrial democracies. *Economic Policy.*

Alesina, A., and Drazen, A. 1989. Why are stabilizations delayed? Mimeo, Harvard University. Updated and reprinted as chapter 15 in the current volume of this work.

Alesina, A., and Summers, L. 1990. Central bank independence and macroeconomic performance: Some comparative evidence. Mimeo, Harvard University.

Alesina, A., and Tabellini, G. 1990. A political theory of fiscal deficits and government debt in a democracy. *The Review of Economic Studies.*

Aufricht, H. 1967. *Central banking legislation.* International Monetary Fund Monograph Series, Washington, DC

Bade, R., and Parkin, M. 1982. Central bank laws and inflation: A comparative analysis. Mimeo, University of Western Ontario.

Banks, A. 1987. *The political handbook of the world.*

Barro, R. 1979. On the determination of public debt. *Journal of Political Economy.*

Barro, R. 1986. The behavior of U.S. deficits. In R. Gordon, ed., *The American Business Cycle.* Chicago: University of Chicago Press.

Bingham Powell, A. 1982. *Contemporary Democracies: Participation, Stability and Violence.* Cambridge: Harvard University Press.

Bohn, H. 1990. The sustainability of budget deficits in a stochastic economy. Mimeo, The Wharton School.

Drazen, A., and Grilli, V. 1990. The benefit of crisis for economic reform. Mimeo, Birbeck College, London.

Edwards, S., and Tabellini, G. 1990. Explaining fiscal policies and inflation in developing countries. NBER working paper no. 3493.

Edwards, S., and Tabellini, G. 1991. Political instability, political weakness and inflation: An empirical analysis. Mimeo, University of California at Los Angeles.

Faig, M. 1988. Characterization of the optimal tax on money when it functions as a medium of exchange. *Journal of Monetary Economics.*

Fair, D. 1978. Relationships between central banks and governments in the determination of monetary policy. SUERF working paper.

Giovannini, A., and Spaventa, L. 1991. Fiscal rules in the European Monetary Union: A no-entry clause. CEPR discussion paper no. 516.

Grilli, V. 1989. Seigniorage in Europe. In M. De Cecco and A. Giovannini, eds., *A European Central Bank?* Cambridge: Cambridge University Press.

Hamilton, J., and Flavin, M. 1986. On the limitations of government borrowing: A framework for empirical testing. *American Economic Review.*

Kimbrough, K. 1986. The optimal quantity of money rule in the theory of public finance. *Journal of Monetary Economics.*

Lucas, R., and Stokey, N. 1983. Optimal fiscal and monetary policies in an economy without capital. *Journal of Monetary Economics.* Reprinted as chapter 14 in volume 1 of this work.

Mankiw, G. 1987. The optimal collection of Seigniorage: Theory and evidence. *Journal of Monetary Economics.*

Masciandaro, D. 1990. Central bank independence, macroeconomic models and monetary regimes. Mimeo, Centre for Monetary and Financial Economics, Bocconi University.

Masciandaro, D., and Tabellini, G. 1988., Monetary regimes and fiscal deficits: A comparative analysis. In H. S. Cheng, ed., *Monetary policy in Pacific Basin countries.* Dordrecht: Kluwer.

Perron, P. 1988. Trend and random walks in macroeconomic time series. *Journal of Economic Dynamics and Control.*

Persson, T., and Svensson, L. 1989. Why a stubborn conservative would run a deficit: policy with time inconsistent preferences. *Quarterly Journal of Economics.* Reprinted as chapter 5 in the current volume of this work.

Persson, T., and Tabellini, G. 1990. *Macroeconomic policy credibility and politics.* London: Harwood Academic Publishers.

Phelps, E. 1973. Inflation in the theory of public finance. *Swedish Journal of Economics.*

Poterba, J., and Rotemberg, J. 1989. Inflation and taxation with optimizing governments. *Journal of Money, Credit and Banking.*

Rae, D. 1967. *The political consequences of electoral laws.* New Haven: Yale University Press.

Rogoff, K. 1985. The optimal degree of commitment to an intermediate monetary target. *Quarterly Journal of Economics.* Reprinted as chapter 9 in volume 1 of this work.

Roubini, N., and Sachs, J. 1988. Political and economic determinants of budget deficits in the industrial democracies. *European Economic Review.*

Roubini, N., and Sachs, J. 1989. Government spending and budget deficits in the industrialized countries. *Economic Policy.*

Sanguinetti, P. 1990. Fiscal deficits and federal government. Mimeo, University of California at Los Angeles.

Tabellini, G. 1986. Money, debt and deficits in a dynamic game. *Journal of Economic Dynamics and Control.*

Tabellini, G. 1987a. Central bank reputation and the monetization of budget deficits. *Economic Inquiry.*

Tabellini, G. 1987b. Monetary and fiscal policy coordination with a high public debt. In F. Giavazzi and L. Spaventa, eds., *Surviving with a high public debt: Lessons from the Italian experience.* Cambridge: Cambridge University Press.

Tabellini, G., and Alesina, A. 1990. Voting on the budget deficit. *American Economic Review.* Reprinted as chapter 6 in the current volume of this work.

Taylor, C., and Jodice, D. 1983. *World handbook of political and social indicators.* 3d edition. New Haven: Yale University Press.

Trehan, B., and Walsh, C. 1988. Common trends, the government budget constraint and revenue smoothing. *Journal of Economic Dynamics and Control*

Trehan, B., and Walsh, C. 1989. Seigniorage and tax smoothing in the United States: 1914–1986. Mimeo, University of California at Santa Cruz.

Wilcox, D. 1989. The sustainability of government deficits: Implications of the government borrowing constraint. *Journal of Money, Credit and Banking.*

III REDISTRIBUTION

8 A Rational Theory of the Size of Government

Allan H. Meltzer and Scott F. Richard

I Introduction

The share of income allocated by government differs from country to country, but the share has increased in all countries of western Europe and North America during the past 25 years (Nutter 1978). In the United States, in Britain, and perhaps elsehwere, the rise in tax payments relative to income has persisted for more than a century (Peacock and Wiseman 1961; Meltzer and Richard 1978). There is, as yet, no generally accepted explanation of the increase and no single accepted measure of the size of government.

In this chapter, the budget is balanced.[1] We use the share of income redistributed by government, in cash and in services, as our measure of the relative size of government and develop a theory in which the government's share is set by the rational choices of utility-maximizing individuals who are fully informed about the state of the economy and the consequences of taxation and income redistribution.[2]

The issues we address have a long intellectual history. Wicksell (1958) joined the theory of taxation to the theory of individual choice. His conclusion, that individual maximization requires government spending and taxes to be set by unanimous consent, reflects the absence of a mechanism for grouping individual choices to reach a collective decision. Following Downs (1957), economists turned their attention to the determination of an equilibrium choice of public goods, redistribution, and other outcomes under voting rules that do not require unanimity.

Several recent surveys of the voluminous literature on the size or growth of government are now available (see Brunner 1978; Peacock 1979; Aranson and Ordeshook 1980; and Larkey, Stolp, and Winer 1980).[3] Many of the hypotheses advanced in this literature emphasize the incentives for bureaucrats, politicians, and interest groups to increase their incomes and power by increasing spending and the control of resources or rely on specific institutional details of the budget, taxing, and legislative

Reprinted from *Journal of Political Economy*, by permission of The University of Chicago Press. *Journal of Political Economy*, 1981, vol. 89, no. 5.

processes. Although such studies contribute to an understanding of the processes by which particular programs are chosen, they often neglect general equilibrium aspects. Of particular importance is the frequent failure to close many of the models by balancing the budget in real terms and considering the effect on voters of the taxes that pay for spending and redistribution (see, e.g., Olson 1965; Niskanen 1971; and Hayek 1979). A recent empirical study by Cameron (1978) suggests that decisions about the size of the budget are not the result of "fiscal illusion," so the neglect of budget balance cannot be dismissed readily.

We differ from much of the recent literature in three main ways.

Wagner's law, relating taxation to income, has generated a large literature and has been tested in various ways. Our analysis shows that Wagner's law should be amended to include the effect of relative income in addition to absolute income.

Kuznets (1955) observed that economic growth raises the incomes of skilled individuals relative to the incomes of the unskilled. In this way, economic growth can lead to rising inequality and, if our hypothesis is correct, to votes for redistribution. The rising relative size of government slows when the relative changes come to an end and reverses if the relative changes reverse in a mature stationary economy.

The distinctive feature of our analysis is not the voting rule but the relation between individual and collective choice. Each person chooses consumption and leisure by maximizing in the usual way. Anyone who works receives a wage equal to his marginal product. Taxes on labor income provide revenues for redistribution, however, so everyone benefits from decisions to work and incurs a cost when leisure increases.

The analysis explains why the size of government and the tax rate can remain constant yet be criticized by an overwhelming majority of citizens. The reason is that at the voting equilibrium nearly everyone prefers a different outcome. If unconstrained by the voting rule, everyone but the decisive voter would choose a different outcome. But only the decisive voter can assure a majority.

An extension of our argument may suggest why real government debt per capita, as measured in the budget, has increased more than 20-fold in this century. The decisive voter has as much incentive to tax the future rich as the current rich. An optimal distribution of the cost of redistribution would not tax only the current generation because, with economic growth, the future generation will be richer than the current generation. By shifting the burden of taxation toward the future, income is redistributed intertemporally.

To pursue these questions more fully and to analyze any effect of defense and public goods, it seems necessary to embed the analysis in a model with saving, capital accumulation, and public goods and to explore the effect of permitting relative shares to change as income changes. From an analysis of a growing economy, we can expect to develop a rational theory of the growth of government to complement our analysis of the government's size.

First, voters do not suffer from "fiscal illusion" and are not myopic. They know that the government must extract resources to pay for redistribution. Second, we concentrate on the demand for redistribution and neglect any "public goods" provided by government (see also Peltzman 1979). Third, we return to the earlier tradition of de Tocqueville ([1835] 1965) who associated the size of government, measured by taxes and spending, with two factors: the spread of the franchise and the distribution of wealth (property).[4]

Our hypothesis implies that the size of government depends on the relation of mean income to the income of the decisive voter. With universal suffrage and majority rule, the median voter is the decisive voter as shown by Roberts (1977) in an extension of the well-known work of Hotelling (1929) and Downs (1957). Studies of the distribution of income show that the distribution is skewed to the right, so the mean income lies above the median income. Any voting rule that concentrates votes below the mean provides an incentive for redistribution of income financed by (net) taxes on incomes that are (relatively) high. Extensions of the franchise to include more voters below mean income increase votes for redistribution and, thus, increase this measure of the size of government.

The problem with this version of the de Tocqueville hypothesis is that it explains too much. Nothing limits the amount of redistribution or prevents the decisive voter from equalizing incomes or, at a minimum, eliminating any difference between his disposable income and the disposable income of those who earn higher incomes. Incentives have been ignored. Higher taxes and redistribution reduce the incentive to work and thereby lower earned income. Once we take account of incentives, there is a limit to the size of government. To bring together the effect of incentives, the desire for redistribution, and the absence of fiscal illusion or myopia, we develop a general equilibrium model.

Section II sets out a static model. Individuals who differ in productivity, and therefore in earned income, choose their preferred combination of consumption and leisure. Not all individuals work, but those who do pay a portion of their income in taxes. The choice between labor and leisure, and the amount of earned income and taxes, depend on the tax rate and on the size of transfer payments.

The tax rate and the amount of income redistributed depend on the voting rule and the distribution of income. Section III shows how income redistribution, taxes, and the size of the government budget change with the voting rule and the distribution of productivity. A conclusion summarizes the findings and main implications.

II The Economic Environment

The economy we consider has relatively standard features. There are a large number of individuals. Each treats prices, wages, and tax rates as givens, determined in the markets for goods and labor and by the political process, respectively. Differences in the choice of labor, leisure, and consumption and differences in wages arise solely because of differences in endowments which reflect differences in productivity. In this section, we extend this standard model to capture the salient features of the process by which individuals choose to work or subsist on welfare payments and show the conditions under which these choices are uniquely determined by the tax rate.

The utility function is assumed to be a strictly concave function, $u(c, l)$, for consumption, c, and leisure, l. Consumption and leisure are normal goods, and their marginal utility is infinite when the level of consumption or leisure is zero, respectively. There is no capital and no uncertainty.

The individual's endowment consists of ability to produce, or productivity, and a unit of time that he allocates to labor, n, or leisure, $l = 1 - n$. Individual incomes reflect the differences in individual productivity and the use of a common, constant-returns-to-scale technology to produce consumption goods. An individual with productivity x earns pretax income, y:

$$y(x) = xn(x). \tag{1}$$

Income is measured in units of consumption.

Tax revenues finance lump-sum redistribution of r units of consumption per capita. Individual productivity cannot be observed directly, so taxes are levied against earned income. The tax rate, t, is a constant fraction of earned income but a declining fraction of disposable income. The fraction of income paid in taxes net of transfers, however, rises with income.[5] There is no saving; consumption equals disposable income as shown in (2):

$$c(x) = (1 - t)nx + r, \quad c \geq 0. \tag{2}$$

If there are individuals without any ability to produce, $x = 0$, their consumption is $r \geq 0$.

Each individual is a price taker in the labor market, takes t and r as givens, and chooses n to maximize utility. The maximization problem is:

$$\max_{n \in [0,1]} u(c, l) = \max_{n \in [0,1]} u[r + nx(1 - t), 1 - n]. \tag{3}$$

The first-order condition,

$$0 = \frac{\partial u}{\partial n} = u_c[r + nx(1 - t), 1 - n]x(1 - t) - u_l[r + nx(1 - t), 1 - n], \tag{4}$$

determines the optimal labor choice, $n[r, x(1 - t)]$, for those who choose to work. The choice depends only on the size of the welfare payment, r, and the after-tax wage, $x(1 - t)$.[6]

Some people subsist on welfare payments. From (4) we know that the productivity level at which $n = 0$ is the optimal choice is

$$x_0 = \frac{u_l(r, 1)}{u_c(r, 1)(1 - t)}. \tag{5}$$

Individuals with productivity below x_0 subsist on welfare payments and choose not to work; $n = 0$ for $x \leq x_0$.

Increases in redistribution increase consumption. For those who subsist on welfare, $c = r$, so $\partial c/\partial r = 1$. Those who work must consider not only the direct effect on consumption but also the effect of redistribution on their labor-leisure choice. The assumption that consumption is a normal good means that $\partial c/\partial r > 0$. Differentiating (4) and using the second-order condition, $D < 0$, in note 6 restricts u_{cl}:

$$\frac{\partial c}{\partial r} = \frac{u_{cl}x(1-t) - u_{ll}}{-D} > 0. \tag{6}$$

Consumption increases with r for both workers and nonworkers provided consumption is a normal good.

The positive response of c to r takes one step toward establishing conditions under which we find a unique value of r that determines the amount of earned income and the amount of redistribution for each tax rate. The next step is to show that normality of consumption is sufficient to establish that earned income (income before taxes) increases with productivity.

Pretax income is

$$y(r,t,x) = xn[r, x(1-t)]. \tag{7}$$

People who do not work, $x \leq x_0$, have $y = 0$ and $\partial y/\partial x = 0$. For all others,

$$\frac{\partial y}{\partial x} = n + x\frac{\partial n}{\partial x}. \tag{8}$$

The first-order condition (eq. 4) yields

$$\frac{\partial n}{\partial x} = \frac{u_c(1-t) + u_{cc}nx(1-t)^2 - u_{cl}n(1-t)}{-D}. \tag{9}$$

The sign of $\partial n/\partial x$ is indeterminate; as productivity increases, the supply of labor can be backward bending. Pretax income, $y = nx$, does not decline, however, even if n falls. Substituting (9) into (8) and rearranging terms shows that the bracketed term in (10) is the numerator of $\partial c/\partial r$ in (6). Hence, $\partial y/\partial x$ is positive for all $x > x_0$ provided that consumption is a normal good:

$$\frac{\partial y}{\partial x} = \frac{u_c(1-t)x + n[u_{cl}x(1-t) - u_{ll}]}{-D} > 0. \tag{10}$$

The final step in establishing that there is a unique equilibrium solution for any tax rate uses our assumption that leisure is a normal good. The government budget is balanced and all government spending is for redistribution of income. If per capita income is $\bar{y}$, then

$$t\bar{y} = r. \tag{11}$$

Let $F(\cdot)$ denote the distribution function for individual productivity, so that $F(x)$ is the fraction of the population with productivity less than x. Per capita income is obtained by integrating:

$$\bar{y} = \int_{x_0}^{\infty} xn[r,(1-t)x]\,dF(x). \tag{12}$$

Equation (12) shows that per capita income, and therefore total earned income, is determined once we know x_0, t, and r. From (5), we know that x_0 depends only on t and r, and from (11) we know that, for any tax rate, there is at least one value of r that balances the budget.[7] If leisure is a normal good, the value of r that satisfies (11) for each t is unique.[8]

Once r or t is chosen, the other is determined. The individual's choices of consumption and the distribution of his time between labor and leisure are determined also. The choice of r or t uniquely determines each individual's welfare and sets the size of government.

III The Size of Government

The political process determines the share of national income taxed and redistributed. The many ways to make this choice range from dictatorship to unanimous consent, and each produces a different outcome. We call each political process that determines the tax rate a voting rule.

In this section, we consider any voting rule that allows a decisive individual to choose the tax rate. Two examples are dictatorship and universal suffrage with majority rule. A dictator is concerned about the effect of his decisions on the population's decisions to work and consume, but he alone makes the decision about the tax rate. Under majority rule, the voter with median income is decisive as we show below. We then show that changes in voting rules and productivity alter the tax rate and the size of government.

The decisive voter chooses the tax rate that maximizes his utility. In making his choice, he is aware that his choice affects everyone's decision to work and consume. Increases in the tax rate have two effects. Each dollar of earned income raises more revenue but earned income declines; everyone chooses more leisure, and more people choose to subsist on redistribution. "High" and "low" tax rates have opposite effects on the choice of labor or leisure and, therefore, on earned income.

Formally, the individual is constrained to find a tax rate that balances the government budget, equation (11), and maximizes utility subject to his own budget constraint, equation (3). The first-order condition for the decisive voter is solved to find his preferred tax rate:

$$\bar{y} + t\frac{d\bar{y}}{dt} - y_d = 0, \tag{13}$$

where y_d is the income of the decisive voter.

Roberts (1977) showed that if the ordering of individual incomes is independent of the choice of r and t, individual choice of the tax rate is inversely ordered by income. This implies that with universal suffrage the voter with median income is decisive, and the higher one's income, the lower the preferred tax rate. By making the additional assumption that consumption is a normal good, we have shown that incomes are ordered by productivity for all r and t. Combining Roberts's lemma 1 (1977, p. 334) with our results, we can order the choice of tax rate by the productivity of the decisive voter.[9] The higher an individual's productivity, the lower is his preferred tax rate.

Figure 8.1 illustrates the proposition and shows the effect on the tax rate of changing the voting rule. The negatively sloped line is the relation between individual productivity, x, and the individual's preferred tax rate. This line need not be linear.

The maximum tax rate, $t_{\max}$, is chosen if the decisive voter does not work. An example is $x = x_{d1}$. In this case, $x \leq x_0$; the decisive voter consumes only r, so he chooses the tax rate ($t_{\max}$) that maximizes r. Any higher tax rate reduces aggregate earned income, tax collections, and the amount available for redistribution. From equation (5), we see that the maximum tax rate must be less than $t = 1$.

As productivity rises from x_0 to $\bar{x}$, the tax rate declines from $t_{\max}$ to 0. At $x_d = \bar{x}$, the decisive voter is endowed with average productivity and cannot gain from lump-sum redistribution, so he votes for no redistribution by choosing $t = 0$.[10] From equation (5) and $u_c(0, \cdot) = \infty$, we see that everyone works when $r = 0$. If the decisive voter's productivity exceeds $\bar{x}$, t and r remain at zero and aggregate earned income remains at society's maximum.

Changes in the voting rule, which spread the franchise up or down the productivity distribution, change the decisive voter and raise or lower the tax rate. Our hypothesis implies that changing the position of the decisive

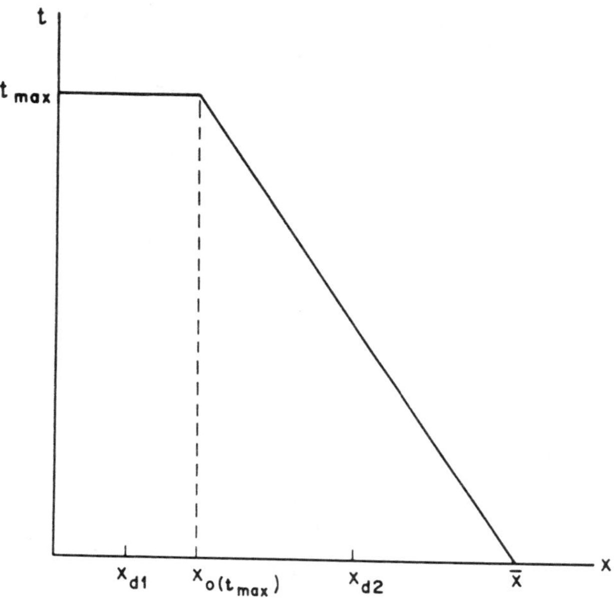

Figure 8.1

voter in the distribution of productivity changes the size of government provided $x_0 < x_d < \bar{x}$. Major changes in x_d have occurred in two ways. Wealth and income requirements for voting were reduced or eliminated, gradually broadening the franchise and lowering the income of the decisive voter. Social security retirement systems grew in most countries after the franchise was extended. By increasing the number of retired persons, social security systems increase the number of voters who favor increased redistribution financed by taxes on wages. Some of the retired who favor redistribution also favor low taxes on capital, property, and the income from capital.

The size of government changes also if there are changes in relative income, as shown by equation (13), or relative productivity. Conclusions about the precise effect of changes of this kind are difficult to draw. We cannot observe productivity directly and can only infer changes in the distribution of productivity, $F(\cdot)$, by observing changes in relative income. Recent literature makes clear that these effects are disputed (see Sahota 1978; King 1980; and others). Further, we cannot deduce the effect of changes in productivity on t directly from equation (13). The reason is that

$\bar{y}$ depends on t, so finding the effect of changes in relative productivity requires the solution to a nonlinear equation in t. Instead, we rewrite (13) in a form which involves the (partial) elasticities of per capita income ($\bar{y}$) with respect to redistribution (r) and the wage rate ($x[1 - t]$).

Let $\tau = 1 - t$ be the fraction of earned income retained. From (12), $\bar{y}$ depends on r and τ only. The total derivative

$$\frac{d\bar{y}}{dt} = \frac{\bar{y}_r\bar{y} - \bar{y}_\tau}{1 - t\bar{y}_r}, \tag{14}$$

where $\bar{y}_r$ and $\bar{y}_\tau$ are the two partial derivatives. Substituting (14) into (13), we solve for t:

$$t = \frac{m - 1 + \eta(\bar{y}, r)}{m - 1 + \eta(\bar{y}, r) + m\eta(\bar{y}, \tau)}, \tag{15}$$

where m is the ratio of mean income to the income of the decisive voter, $\bar{y}/y_d$, and the η's are partial elasticities. Using the common economic assumption that the elasticities are constant, the tax rate rises as mean income rises relative to the income of the decisive voter, and taxes fall as m falls:

$$\frac{dt}{dm} = \frac{\eta(\bar{y}, \tau)[1 - \eta(\bar{y}, r)]}{[m - 1 + \eta(\bar{y}, r) + m\eta(\bar{y}, \tau)]^2} > 0. \tag{16}$$

Relaxing the assumption of constant elasticities weakens the conclusion, but we expect the sign of (16) to remain positive provided the change in the elasticities is small.

One of the oldest and most frequently tested explanations of the growth of government is known as Wagner's law. This law has been interpreted in two ways. The traditional interpretation is that government is a luxury good so that there is a positive relation between the relative size of government and the level of real income. Recently Alt (1980) has questioned this interpretation of Wagner's idea. Alt (1980, p. 4) notes that Wagner argued that there is "a proportion between public expenditure and national income which may not be permanently overstepped." This suggests an equilibrium relative size of government rather than an ever-growing government sector.

The traditional statement of Wagner's law—that government grows more rapidly than income—has been tested many times, but with mixed results. Peacock and Wiseman (1961), Cameron (1978), and Larkey, Stolp, and Winer (1980) discuss these tests. Our hypothesis suggests that the results are ambiguous because Wagner's law is incomplete. The effect of absolute income on the size of government is conditional on relative income. Average or absolute income affects the elasticities in equation (15), and the relative income effect is given by m.

To make our hypothesis testable, we must identify the decisive voter. The applicable voting rule in the United States is universal franchise and majority rule. Under this rule, the voter with median income is decisive in single-issue elections, as we argued above. Hence the median voter is decisive in elections to choose the tax rate, so m is the ratio of mean to median income.[11]

IV Conclusion

Government spending and taxes have grown, relative to output, in most countries with elected governments for the past 30 years or longer. Increased relative size of government appears to be independent of budget and tax systems, federal or national governments, the size of the bureaucracy, and other frequently mentioned institutional arrangements, although the relative rates of change in different countries may depend on these arrangements.

Our explanation of the size of government emphasizes voter demand for redistribution. Using a parsimonious, general equilibrium model in which the only government activities are redistribution and taxation, the real budget is balanced, and voters are fully informed, we show that the size of government is determined by the welfare-maximizing choice of a decisive individual. The decisive individual may be a dictator, absolute monarch, or marginal member of a junta.

With majority rule the voter with median income among the enfranchised citizens is decisive. Voters with income below the income of the decisive voter choose candidates who favor higher taxes and more redistribution; voters with income above the decisive voter desire lower taxes and less redistribution. The decisive voter chooses the tax share. When the mean income rises relative to the income of the decisive voter, taxes rise, and vice versa. The spread of the franchise in the nineteenth and twentieth centuries increased the number of voters with relatively low income. The position of the decisive voter shifted down the distribution of income, so tax rates rose. In recent years, the proportion of voters receiving social security has increased, raising the number of voters favoring taxes on wage and salary income to finance redistribution. A rational social security recipient with large property income supports taxes on labor income to finance redistribution but opposes taxes on income from property. In our analysis, there is neither capital nor taxes on property, so the increase in social security recipients has an effect similar to an extension of the franchise.

Our assumption that voters are fully informed about the size of government differs from much recent literature. There, taxpayers are portrayed as the prey sought by many predators who conspire to raise taxes relative to income by diffusing costs and concentrating benefits, or in other ways (Buchanan and Tullock 1962; Olson 1965; Niskanen 1971; Hayek 1979). We acknowledge that voters are ill informed about the costs of particular projects when, as is often the case, it is rational to avoid learning details. Knowledge of detail is not required to learn that the size of government has increased and that taxes have increased relative to output or income. Long ago it became rational for voters to anticipate this outcome of the political process.

Notes

We are indebted to Karl Brunner, Dennis Epple, Peter Ordeshook, and Tom Romer for many helpful discussions and to the participants in the Carnegie-Mellon Public Economics Workshop, and anonymous referee, the editor, and the Interlaken Seminar for constructive comments on an earlier version.

1. All variables are real. There is no inflation. Budget balance means that redistribution uses real resources. Public goods are neglected.

2. Ideally the size of government would be measured by the net burden imposed (or removed) by government programs.

3. Larkey, Stolp, and Winer (1980) include a survey of previous surveys. Recent surveys by Mueller (1976) and Sahota (1978) summarize recent contributions by Downs (1957), Musgrave (1959), Olson (1965), Niskanen (1971), Buchanan and Tullock (1972), Riker and Ordeshook (1973), and others to such related topics as the determination of equilibrium collective decisions and the effects of government policies on the distribution of income.

4. We are indebted to Larkey, Stolp, and Winer (1980) for pointing out the similarity between de Tocqueville and the conclusion we reached in an earlier version and in Meltzer and Richard (1978). De Tocqueville's distribution of property finds an echo in the concerns about "mob rule" by the writers of the U.S. Constitution.

5. Reliance on a linear tax follows a well-established tradition. Romer (1975) analyzed problems of unimodality using a linear tax and predetermined government spending. Roberts (1977), using a linear tax and a predetermined budget, showed that the median voter dominates the solution if incomes are ordered by productivity. Linear tax functions are used also when the social welfare function is used to determine the optimal tax (see Sheshinski 1972). The degree to which actual taxes differ from linear taxes has generated a large literature.

Pechman and Okner (1974) find that the tax rate is approximately constant. King (1980) writes that most redistribution in the United States and the United Kingdom comes from the transfer system, not from the tax system. Browning and Johnson (1979) show that conclusions about proportionality of the tax rate depend heavily on assumptions used to allocate the burden of indirect business taxes.

6. By assumption, u is strictly concave, so the second-order condition is negative and (4) defines a maximum. The second-order condition is $\partial^2 u/\partial n^2 = D = u_{cc}x^2(1-t)^2 - 2u_{cl}x(1-t) + u_{ll} < 0$.

7. The left side of (11) is nonnegative and is a continuous function of r that is bounded by $t\bar{x}$, where $\bar{x}$ is the average of x.

8. The normality of leisure means that $\partial l/\partial r > 0$ and, therefore, $\partial n/\partial r = -\partial l/\partial r < 0$. Since

$$\frac{\partial \bar{y}}{\partial r} = \int_{x_0}^{\infty} x \frac{\partial n}{\partial r} dF(x) < 0,$$

the left side of (11) is a strictly decreasing, continuous function of r. The right side of (11) strictly increases with r. This implies that there is a unique value of r that satisfies (11).

9. The formal statement of the result is: Consider any two pairs (r_1, t_1) and (r_2, t_2). If $t_2 > t_1$, then for all x: x is indifferent between (r_1, t_1) and (r_2, t_2) implies that x' weakly prefers (r_2, t_2) to (r_1, t_1) for all $x' < x$ and x'' weakly prefers (r_1, t_1) to (r_2, t_2) for all $x'' > x$; x strictly prefers (r_1, t_1) to (r_2, t_2) implies that x'' strictly prefers (r_1, t_1) to (r_2, t_2) for all $x'' > x$; x strictly prefers (r_2, t_2) to (r_1, t_1) implies that x' strictly prefers (r_2, t_2) to (r_1, t_1) for all $x' < x$. Note that this result does not require unimodality of voter preferences for tax rates.

10. We have omitted public goods. In an earlier version we showed that under carefully specified conditions, public goods can be included without changing the result for redistribution.

11. The many tests of the median-voter hypothesis using regression analyses are inconclusive. One reason is that many of the tests do not discriminate between the median and any other fractile of the income distribution (see Romer and Rosenthal 1979). Cooter and Helpman (1974) use income before and after taxes net of transfers to estimate the shape of the social welfare function implicit in U.S. data. They conclude that "the assumption that ability is distributed as wages per hour ... —perhaps the best assumption on distribution of ability—vindicates the median voter rule."

References

Alt, James. 1980. Democracy and public expenditure Multilithed, Washington University, St. Louis.

Aranson, Peter, and Ordeshook, Peter. 1980. Alternative theories of the growth of government and their implications for constitutional tax and spending limits. Multilithed, Carnegie Mellon University, Pittsburgh.

Browning, Edgar K., and Johnson, William R. 1979. *The distribution of the tax burden.* Washington: American Enterprise Institute.

Brunner, Karl. 1978. Reflections on the political economy of government: The persistent growth of government. *Schweizerische Zeitschrift Volkwirrtschaft und Statis* 114:649–680.

Buchanan, James M., and Tullock, Gordon. 1962. *The calculus of consent: Logical foundations of constitutional democracy.* Ann Arbor: University of Michigan Press.

Cameron, David. 1978. The expansion of the public economy: A comparative analysis. *American Political Science Review* 72:1243–1261.

Cooter, Robert, and Helpman, Elhanan. 1974. Optimal income taxation for transfer payments under different social welfare criteria. *Quarterly Journal of Economics* 88:656–670.

Downs, Anthony. 1957. *An economic theory of democracy.* New York: Harper & Row.

Hayek, Friedrich A. 1979. Law, legislation and liberty. Vol. 3: *The political order of a free people.* Chicago: University of Chicago Press.

Hotelling, Harold. 1929. Stability in competition. *Economic Journal* 39:41–57.

King, Mervyn A. 1980. How effective have fiscal policies been in changing the distribution of income and wealth? *American Economic Review Papers and Proceedings* 70:72–76.

Kuznets, Simon. 1955. Economic growth and income inequality. *American Economic Review* 45:1–28.

Larkey, P. D., Stolp, C., and Winer, M. 1980. Theorizing about the growth and decline of government: A research assessment. Multilithed, Carnegie Mellon University.

Meltzer, Allan H., and Richard, Scott F. 1978. Why government grows (and grows) in a democracy. *Public Interest* 52:111–118.

Mueller, Dennis C. 1976. Public choice: A survey. *Journal of Economic Literature.* 14:395–433.

Musgrave, Richard A. 1959. *The theory of public finance: Study in public economy.* New York: McGraw-Hill.

Niskanen, William A. 1971. *Bureaucracy and representative government.* Chicago: Aldine-Atherton.

Nutter, G. W. 1978. Growth of government in the West. Washington: American Enterprise Institute.

Olson, Mancur, Jr. 1965. *The logic of collective action: Public goods and the theory of groups.* Cambridge: Harvard University Press.

Peacock, Alan T. 1979. *Economic analysis of government and related theories.* New York: St. Martin's.

Peacock, Alan T., and Wiseman, Jack. 1961. *The growth of public expenditure in the United Kingdom.* Princeton, NJ: Princeton University Press.

Pechman, Joseph A., and Okner, Benjamin A. 1974. *Who bears the tax burden*? Washington: Brookings Institution.

Peltzman, Sam. 1979. The growth of government. Multilithed. University of Chicago.

Riker, William H., and Ordeshook, Peter C. 1973. *An introduction to positive political theory.* Englewood Cliffs, NJ: Prentice-Hall.

Roberts, Kevin W. 1977. Voting over income tax schedules. *Journal of Public Economy* 8: 329–340.

Romer, Thomas. 1975. Individual welfare, majority voting, and the properties of a linear income tax. *Journal of Public Economy* 4:163–185.

Romer, Thomas, and Rosenthal, Howard. 1979. The elusive median voter. *Journal of Public Economy* 12:143–170.

Sahota, Gian Singh. 1978. Theories of personal income distribution: A survey. *Journal of Economic Literature.* 16:1–55.

Sheshinski, Eytan. 1972. The optimal linear income tax. *Review of Economic Studies.* 39:297–302.

Tocqueville, Alexis de. 1835. *Democracy in America.* Reprint ed. Oxford: Oxford University Press, 1965.

Wicksell, Knut. 1958. A new principle of just taxation. Reprinted in Richard A. Musgrave and Alan T. Peacock, eds., *Classics in the theory of public finance.* New York: St. Martin's.

9 Growth, Distribution, and Politics

Torsten Persson and Guido Tabellini

A glaring fact of economic development is the diffeence in the growth rate across countries. Table 9.1 displays the average growth rate of real GDP per capita between 1960 and 1985— as well as other statistical indicators of growth—in about eighty developing countries, grouped by continent. Asian countries have, on average, grown twice as fast as Latin American countries and three times as fast as African countries, and the differences within each continent are much larger. Explaining this fact is still one of the most challenging questions in economics. In this chapter we review some recent attempts at an answer that have focused on the interaction of economics and politics.

Consider the stylized aggregate production function: $Y = AF(K, N)$, where Y is GDP, A is a measure of technology, K is "capital," and N is population. Any theory of economic growth must then ultimately explain the variables appearing on the right-hand side of the following equation:

$$g^{y} = g^{A} + RI - \alpha g^{N}. \tag{1}$$

In equation (1) g^{y} is the rate of growth of per capita GDP, g^{A} and g^{N} are the rates of exogenous technical progress and of population growth, R is the marginal product of capital, I is the investment rate (expressed as a percentage of GDP), and α is the income share of capital.

The early growth accounting literature ascribed a large share of growth to g^{A}. But the recent literature on endogenous growth has basically widened the definition of capital to include not only physical capital but also other cumulative factors such as human capital and productive knowledge. Under this view, I includes all such productive accumulation, while residual exogenous technical progress, g^{A}, becomes a negligible number. Suppose further that the population growth rate is primarily determined by noneconomic factors, and the capital share of income (broadly defined) is fairly constant across countries.[1] We are then left with only two reasons for why countries grow at different rates: either their investment rates differ or their marginal products differ. We now want to argue that economic policy, and in particular bad economic policy, plays a central role in explaining both differences.

Reprinted from *The Political Economy of Business Cycles and Growth.* A. Cukierman, C. Hercowitz, and L. Leiderman, (eds.), 1992, by permission of MIT Press, Cambridge.

Table 9.1
Average growth rates

	Number of countries	Growth 1960–1985	GDP 1960	S.E. growth	Range growth
Asia	23	3.08	1,434	2.28	−0.39, 7.44
Latin America	19	1.55	1,835	1.54	−1.61, 4.79
Africa	41	0.96	585	0.94	−2.83, 5.40

Source: Summers and Heston (1988). The country groupings are based on the IMF classification. GDP 1960 is average per capita income in 1960.

Consider first the marginal product of capital, broadly defined. It is difficult to argue that in the slow-growth African and Latin American countries the *potential* marginal product is lower than in the rest of the world. These are the countries where cumulative factors are scarce. Any reasonable economic model would then suggest that investment would be very productive—if anything, more productive than elsewhere. So if marginal products are low, it must be because *realized* marginal products are low. This could happen for a variety of reasons, but most of them have to do with policy. First, investment could go to the wrong sector or firm or be the wrong kind of investment. Second, there may be indivisibilities that prevent investment on a sufficiently large scale. Third, high marginal product investment may be something like infrastructure, with a considerable public-goods component. And so on. But in all these cases, economic policy could either correct the distortions or else it is directly responsible for them. It seems plausible that a "benevolent dictator" in a poor African country would not face a lower physical marginal product of capital than elsewhere in the world. So if slow growth is due to a low marginal product, we must ask why economic policy preserves a gap between the potential and the realized marginal product of capital in some countries but not in others.

Consider next the investment rate. One reason why countries may invest little is that they cannot afford to save. Rebelo (1992) and Atkeson and Ogaki (1990) have recently shown how plausible forms of preferences lead to low savings rates at low levels of income. Taken literally, this argument says that poor countries *prefer* to grow slowly. More generally, it says that there may be a role for policy in attracting foreign direct investment.[2] A second reason why the investment rate differs across countries is more directly related to policy. The marginal product of capital, R in equation (1), need not coincide with the rate of return that can be privately appropriated by investors. Any externality or any explicit or implicit tax on investment income would create a wedge between them. Two countries with the same marginal product will have different investment rates if investors face different appropriable returns. Therefore, policies that define the property rights of investors become a major determinant of growth.

The new research program on endogenous growth, in fact, stresses how economic policy can play a major role in explaining growth. Indeed, one reason why this research program is generating so much excitement is that it is making progress on analyzing the growth consequences of alternative economic policies with the powerful tools of modern economic theory.[3] However, the research on endogenous growth typically views cross-country differences in economic policy as exogenous to the analysis. Policy plays the role of a free parameter in a theoretical model or is an exogenous variable in cross-country regressions, as for instance in Fischer (1991) or in Easterly (1991). In a sense, the early development literature—with its emphasis on planning and government intervention—had a similar mechanistic view of policy: an exogenous set of instruments that could freely be set to achieve desired results.

But this view of policy is hard to swallow. Economic policy is not a random variable that varies freely across countries. Rather, policy is the result of deliberate and purposeful choices by individuals and groups, who have specific incentives and constraints, just like private economic agents. If we maintain that it is policy differences that explain growth differences, what we ultimately have to explain is why these deliberate and purposeful choices differ systematically across countries. To us, the most promising avenue toward such an explanation is to be found in the study of political incentives and political institutions. This is indeed the view of many modern development economists. For instance Kreuger (1990), in a recent paper on the state of development economics, sketches an ambitious research agenda entailing theoretical and empirical work on "the interaction between political and economic forces" and "the functioning of alternative institutions."

We very much agree with the agenda, and we believe that the right way to make progress is to borrow the insights from modern development economics and the tools from neoclassical economics. Operationally, this means that the theory of endogenous growth must be married with the theory of endogenous policy.[4] The next section describes a recent body of research—the first offspring of this marriage.

1 Property Rights and Economic Growth

This recent literature starts from the argument that the enforcement of property rights determines the incentive to invest in cumulative factors. To explain differences in growth rates, it attempts to explain why property rights are enforced differently across countries.

Benhabib and Rustichini (1991) address the question in a model without an explicit institutional structure or political mechanism. In their model, two groups of agents consume and invest. Property rights are not well defined, so at any point in time the two groups may also try to redistribute consumption toward themselves from the resources available in the economy. The paper shows how the quest for redistribution may impose binding incentive constraints on the two groups, which manifest themselves in low accumulation and growth. It also shows how the incentives to redistribute may reduce growth at low, as well as high, levels of income. An advantage of this framework is its generality. Because the analysis is highly abstract, the results do not depend on the specific assumptions about the policy instruments or the political environment. But the generality is not without costs. In particular, it becomes difficult to obtain precise testable implications.

Other papers on the topic are more explicit about the political mechanism and the policy formation process. A first group of papers studies conflict over the *size* distribution of income in a democratic society. The model of redistribution borrows from Meltzer and Richard (1981), where rational voters choose a linear income tax and the revenue is distributed lump sum. The outcome depends primarily on the degree of inequality among voters: with more inequality more voters favor redistribution, and the equilibrium tax rate is higher. Persson and Tabellini (1991a) embed such a political mechanism in an overlapping-generations model, where redistribution is harmful for growth, and obtain the testable prediction that more inequality brings about slower growth. Perotti (1990) obtains a similar result in a model that focuses on educational investment, with the qualification that in a poor society, where educational investment is indivisible, more inequality may lead to higher growth. Similarly, Saint-Paul and Verdier (1991) show that more inequality may lead to higher growth if it leads to more redistribution in the form of public education.[5]

A second group of papers focuses instead on conflict over the *functional* distribution of income. In Alesina and Rodrik (1991) and Bertola (1991) there are two kinds of factors: “capital,” which is cumulative, and “labor,” which is fixed. Different individuals own these factors in different proportions. The government taxes factor income directly, and a tax on the cumulative factor is bad for growth. Under democratic government, the equilibrium policy depends on how factor ownership is distributed among the voters. If wealthy voters have relatively more capital, these models again predict that income inequality is bad for growth because it leads to more capital taxation.

However, the same observable input typically contains a combination of both fixed and cumulative factors, and there is no way to tax them separately. For example, income from labor reflects a combination of human capital and a fixed input. And income from land reflects a combination of improvements to the quality and fertility of the soil and a fixed input. It is only to the extent that different observable variables contain different combinations of income from fixed and cumulative factors that economic policy can redistribute across factors. Persson and Tabellini (1991b) analyze a model of sectoral policy, where different sectors rely on different factors in different proportions. The government observes only the output produced in different sectors. A policy that redistributes away from the capital intensive sector is bad for growth. But conflict over the functional distribution of income still drives the results, since individuals differ in their factor ownership. The model predicts that growth is slower if the owners of the fixed factor have a strong influence over sectoral policy. A good example would be a country where land owners have the balance of power and manage to induce a policy that favors agriculture at the expense of manufacturing.

The next section illustrates some of these ideas in a common analytical framework.

2 A Simple Model

In this section we formulate a simple model that illustrates some of the results derived in the previously mentioned literature. The model branches out into two special cases, each one of which illustrates a different aspect of the interaction between growth and income distribution.

In the basic model all individuals live for two periods and have the following identical preferences:

$$U(c^i) + d^i + f^i. \tag{2}$$

A variable with an i superscript is specific to the ith consumer and a variable without such a superscript denotes an average. In equation (2) c denotes first-period consumption, while d and f denote second-period consumption of two goods, which are produced in different sectors. In period 1 there is no production, but individuals derive income from given initial endowments. In period 2 good d is produced only with a cumulative factor, k, which we call capital, according to the linear technology: $d = k^d$. Good f is produced with capital and a fixed input l, which we call land, according to the concave constant-returns technology: $f = F(k^f, l)$. Since the two goods are perfect substitutes in consumption, their relative consumption price is fixed at unity. Consumers may differ in two dimensions. They may have different first-period income, and they may own different amounts of land. For simplicity, we assume that land cannot be traded, so land holdings only enter the consumer budget constraint in the second period. Finally, there is one-period-ahead commitment: policy is chosen in the first period but takes effect in the second period.

Income Taxes

Consider first a tax on all second-period income, used to finance a lump-sum transfer payment. Here sectoral differences are only of secondary importance, so we assume that all individuals own the same amount of land. Let e^i denote the first-period income of the ith individual, and let θ denote the income tax. Then the consumer budget constraints are

$$e^i \geq k^{id} + k^{if} + c^i \tag{3a}$$

$$(1 - \theta)(k^{id} + k^{if} + F_l l) + g \geq d^i + f^i, \tag{3b}$$

where k^{ix} is individual i's holdings of capital in sector x, and where F_l is the partial of $F(k^f, l)$ with respect to l. We have also used the fact that equilibrium returns to capital in the two sectors are equalized: $(1 - \theta) = (1 - \theta)F_k(k^f, l)$. The government budget constraint is $g = \theta(k + F_l l)$, where $k = k^d + k^f$ is average capital.

Solving the consumer problem we find that individuals accumulate capital in direct proportion to their first-period income:

$$k^i \equiv k^{id} + k^{if} = e^i - U_c^{-1}(1 - \theta) \equiv e^i - C(\theta). \tag{4}$$

Using equations (3), (4), and the government budget constraint to substitute into the ith consumer's utility function, we can then write the consumer's indirect utility, v^i, as a function of Policy θ.

$$v^i = v(\theta) + (1 - \theta)(e^i - e). \tag{5}$$

In equation (5), $v(\theta) \equiv U(C(\theta)) + e - C(\theta) + F_l l$ is the indirect utility of an individual with average first-period income e.[6] Since the tax distorts the savings decision and is purely redistributive, this average individual has nothing to gain from the tax. Hence, $v(\theta)$ is strictly decreasing in θ. Clearly then, individuals richer than the average are harmed by the tax, while individuals poorer than the average may gain from it since the tax redistributes in their favor.

Suppose now that tax policy is chosen democratically, under majority rule. It is easy to show that the voters' preferences are single peaked under a mild restriction on the form of $U(c)$. Then, the equilibrium tax is that preferred by the median voter, the voter with first-period income given by e^m. From equations (4) and (5), the voter's optimum value of θ must satisfy the first-order condition

$$(E - e^m) - \theta C_\theta(\theta) = 0. \tag{6}$$

The lower is median income relative to average income, the more the median gains from redistributing, and the higher is the equilibrium tax. Since a higher tax discourages investment—that is, $C_\theta(\theta)$ is positive—we obtain the testable prediction that investment is lower in more unequal democracies.

Persson and Tabellini (1991a) use a similar framework embedded in an overlapping-generations model, which permits endogenous growth because of an intertemporal (and intergenerational) externality. In such a model, predictions for investment translate into predictions for growth: the equilibrium growth rate thus becomes a decreasing function of income inequality.

Sectoral Taxes

We now slightly modify the model to allow for a sector-specific tax. Let the tax, τ, be a tax on the capital intensive sector, d. Again, the tax is chosen in period 1, enacted in period 2, and the proceeds are distributed lump sum to all individuals. Since aggregate income no longer plays a central role, let us assume that all individuals have the same first-period income, e. Given the preferences in equation (2), every consumer will then save the same amount, k. The second-period budget constraint can now be written as

$$(1 - \tau)k^d + F_k k^f + F_l l^i + g \geq d^i + j^i. \tag{7}$$

Consumers allocate capital optimally across time and across sectors, such that

$$F_k(k^f, l) = (1 - \tau) = U_c(e - k). \tag{8}$$

Because $F_{kk}(\cdot)$ and $U_{cc}(\cdot)$ are both negative, these conditions make k a decreasing function of τ and k^f an increasing function of τ. Hence, k^d becomes a decreasing function of τ. Since $F_{lk} > 0$, the returns to land are increasing in the tax rate: $Q(\tau) = F_l(k^f, l)$, with $Q_\tau > 0$. Intuitively, a tax on the capital intensive sector drives down the marginal return to capital, reducing aggregate investment. And since capital flows to the land-using sector, the return on land rises.

Imposing the government budget constraint, $g = \tau k^d$, we can again write the indirect utility of the ith individual as a function of the policy and of his relative endowment. But here it is the relative endowment of land, not relative first-period income, that matters

$$v^i = v(\tau) + Q(\tau)(l^i - l). \tag{9}$$

The indirect utility of the average landowner $v(\tau)$ is decreasing in τ for two reasons, both revealed by equation (8): the tax distorts both the savings and the capital allocation decisions. Since $Q_\tau > 0$, we now obtain the result that individuals with less than average land are harmed by the tax, while individuals with more than average land may benefit from it, the more so the larger is their relative land endowment.

It is not very plausible to view a sector-specific policy as chosen under majority rule, even in a democracy. Unlike a general policy like a broad income tax, the benefits of a sectoral policy are highly concentrated among a possibly small subset of individuals, while its costs are broadly distributed among the population at large. It is more plausible to follow the tradition in the trade policy literature and view equilibrium policy as the outcome of lobbying or bargaining between different organized groups in society.[7] With this view, we should expect the individuals who have the most to gain from the policy to have the strongest incentives to organize themselves and take costly political action. These individuals will thus acquire the most power over the policy process.

In the context of our model, it is evident from equation (9) that the individuals with the most "intense" policy preferences are those with a large concentration of land. We thus predict that τ is higher and aggregate investment lower the more concentrated is the ownership of land. Persson and Tabellini (1991b) embed a similar framework in a dynamic model with altruistic overlapping generations and obtain the prediction that land concentration is harmful for growth.[8]

Discussion

To summarize, we have described a stylized model where equilibrium policy depends on conflicting interests over the distribution of income. The *size* distribution of income matters for the choice of a general income tax. The *functional* distribution of income—and particularly the distribution of the fixed factor—matters for the choice of a sectoral tax.

However, the way income distribution shapes policy depends critically on political institutions, because it is political institutions that aggregate conflicting interests into public policy. We argued that in a democracy a general income tax is likely to reflect the preferences of the majority of the population. For this reason, we expect the tax to be higher in more unequal democracies. But this prediction does not apply to nondemocracies, where there may not be any mapping at all from the income distribution of the population at large to the redistributive policy preferred by the decisive individual or group. We also argued that a sectoral tax is more likely to reflect the intensity of preferences of those who gain, rather than the number of gainers and losers in the population. So we expect policies that redistribute in favor of the sectors where factor ownership is more concentrated and organized. Moreover, since the political pressure is likely to operate through other forms of political participation than voting, there are strong reasons to believe that organized lobbies and pressure groups should be able to shape sectoral policies both in democracies and in dictatorial regimes.

We would also like to add that the tax policies in our simple model need not be taken literally. Taxation can be either explicit or implicit, and many other policies are similar, in that they affect the incentives for productive accumulation and entail a redistributive component. Most important among general policies—that is, policies that affect different sectors symmetrically—are probably some aspects of the regulatory system: patent legislation and enforcement of intellectual and general property rights. Most important among sectoral policies—that is, policies that affect different sectors asymmetrically—are probably trade, industrial, and regional policies, and sectoral regulation. Other policies of this type can be analyzed in a similar way and with similar conclusions.

The discussion in this section leaves us with a number of testable hypotheses regarding the effect of income distribution on economic growth. First, growth should be higher in more equal democracies, but it should not be related to the size distribution of income in nondemocratic countries. Second, growth should be lower in countries where land ownership is highly concentrated, irrespective of the form of government. The next section asks if the available evidence is consistent with these hypotheses.

3 Some Evidence

As in our other work (Persson and Tabellini 1991a and 1991b), we estimate regressions of growth on income distribution and on other explanatory variables. Income distribution is measured at the start of the period over which we measure growth, so as to avoid reverse causation. Our sample includes both developing and industrial countries. The list of countries and the available data are shown in table 9.2. The dependent variable is the average growth rate of per capita real GDP between 1960 and 1985, drawn from the Summers and Heston (1988) data set.

The sample size is constrained by the availability of data on income distribution and land ownership. Paukert (1973) provides data on the pretax income distribution of households around 1960 in about fifty countries. Our measure of income *equality* is the fraction of income received by the third quintile of the distribution: MIDDLE. The third quintile includes median income, so MIDDLE measures the distance between median and mean income. We expect MIDDLE to have a positive effect on growth. Taylor and Hudson (1972) and Taylor and Jodice (1983) provide data on the concentration of land ownership in about seventy countries. Our measure of land concentration is the Gini coefficient for the distribution of land ownership: GINILA. We expect this variable to have a negative effect on growth. Combining these two sources, we are left with a sample of about forty countries for which we have both measures of distribution.[9]

The other variables in the regressions are the same as in Persson and Tabellini (1991a and 1991b) and control for other features of the economy that contribute to explain growth differentials. They are: the percentage of the relevant age group enrolled in primary school, PSCHOOL, as a measure of human capital;[10] the initial level of real GDP per capita in 1960,

Table 9.2
List of variables

Country	Growth	GDP	PSCHOOL	AGRIL	MIDDLE	GINILA
United States	2.12	7380	118	7	17.6	71.0
United Kingdom	2.22	4970	92	4	16.6	72.3
Austria	3.31	3908	105	24	.	70.7
Denmark	2.74	5490	103	18	18.8	45.8
France	3.19	4473	144	22	14.0	52.5
Germany	2.88	5217	133	14	13.7	66.8
Italy	3.32	3233	111	31	14.6	73.2
Netherlands	2.65	4690	105	11	16.0	57.9
Norway	3.70	5001	100	20	18.5	67.6
Sweden	2.62	5149	96	14	17.4	50.6
Switzerland	1.77	6834	118	11	.	49.4
Canada	2.79	6069	107	13	.	55.8
Japan	5.76	2239	103	33	15.8	47.0
Finland	3.27	4073	97	36	15.4	35.1
Greece	4.43	1474	102	56	13.3	48.8
Ireland	2.86	2545	110	36	.	59.4
Australia	2.14	5182	103	11	17.8	88.2
New Zealand	1.45	5571	108	15	.	73.4
South Africa	1.57	2627	89	32	10.2	70.0
Argentina	0.48	3091	98	20	13.2	86.7
Bolivia	0.84	882	64	61	12.0	.
Brazil	4.79	991	95	52	10.2	84.5
Chile	0.69	2932	109	30	12.0	.
Colombia	2.64	1344	77	51	9.0	86.4
Costa Rica	1.86	1663	96	51	11.2	78.2
Ecuador	2.95	1143	83	57	16.1	86.4
El Salvador	0.48	1062	80	62	8.8	82.7
Guatemala	0.95	1268	45	67	.	86.0
Honduras	0.79	748	67	70	.	75.7
Mexico	2.45	2157	80	55	11.1	69.4
Nicaragua	0.90	1588	66	62	.	80.1
Panama	3.37	1255	96	51	13.8	73.5
Paraguay	2.80	991	98	56	.	.
Peru	0.82	1721	83	53	8.3	93.3
Venezuela	−1.61	5308	100	35	16.0	90.9
Jamaica	0.63	1472	92	39	10.8	77.0
Trinidad, Tobago	1.36	4904	88	22	14.6	69.1
Iran	3.03	1839	41	54	.	62.5
Iraq	0.43	2527	65	53	8.0	88.2
Israel	3.17	2838	98	14	18.6	.
Jordan	2.52	1124	77	44	.	.
Egypt	3.49	496	66	58	.	.
Bangladesh	1.51	444	47	87	.	.
Sri Lanka	1.83	974	95	56	13.8	.
Hong Kong	6.62	1737	87	8	.	.

Table 9.2 (continued)

Country	Growth	GDP	PSCHOOL	AGRIL	MIDDLE	GINILA
India	1.37	533	61	74	16.0	64.0
Korea	5.95	690	94	66	18.0	38.7
Malaysia	4.52	1103	96	63	15.7	47.3
Nepal	0.38	478	10	95	.	.
Pakistan	2.90	558	30	61	15.5	51.8
Philippines	1.77	874	95	61	12.0	53.4
Singapore	7.45	1528	111	8	.	.
Thailand	4.06	688	83	84	.	46.0
Burundi	−0.71	412	18	90	.	.
Cameroon	3.08	507	65	87	.	44.5
Central Africa	−0.44	485	32	94	.	37.2
Chad	−2.83	515	17	95	15.4	37.7
Congo, P.R.	3.46	563	78	52	.	28.9
Benin	−0.46	595	27	55	.	.
Ethiopia	0.34	285	7	88	.	.
Ghana	−1.70	534	38	64	.	.
Cote d'Ivoire	0.85	743	46	89	12.0	42.2
Kenya	0.96	470	47	86	.	69.2
Madagascar	−1.13	659	52	93	11.3	.
Mauritania	1.14	414	8	91	.	.
Morocco	3.25	542	47	62	7.7	.
Niger	1.65	284	5	95	15.6	.
Nigeria	0.20	552	36	71	9.0	.
Zimbabwe	1.73	615	96	69	.	.
Rwanda	1.34	244	49	95	.	.
Senegal	−0.01	756	27	84	10.0	.
Sierra Leone	1.82	281	23	78	9.1	45.8
Somalia	−1.31	483	9	88	.	.
Sudan	−0.84	667	25	86	14.3	.
Tanzania	2.14	208	25	89	11.0	.
Togo	0.66	415	44	80	.	.
Tunisia	3.51	852	66	56	10.0	.
Uganda	0.30	322	49	89	.	.
Zambia	−0.95	740	42	79	11.1	75.7
Papua, New Guinea	1.24	1008	32	89	.	.

Note: Total number of countries: 80.

Table 9.3
Growth, investment, and distribution

	Growth				
Dependent variable	1	2	3	4	5
# OBS	36	35	36	48	50
CONSTANT	5.093 (1.673)	4.575 (1.698)	7.315 (1.985)	4.189 (1.691)	5.600 (2.546)
GDP	−0.11E-2 (−4.112)	−0.91E-3 (−3.885)	−0.12E−2 (−4.199)	−0.99E-3 (−4.102)	−0.79E-3 (−3.902)
PSCHOOL	0.038 (3.187)	0.029 (2.727)	0.034 (2.081)	0.024 (1.862)	0.029 (2.494)
AGRIL	−0.061 (−2.572)	−0.045 (−2.109)	−0.063 (−2.690)	−0.040 (−1.895)	−0.048 (−2.526)
MIDDLE	0.135 (1.466)	0.171 (2.076)	−0.067 (−0.475)	−0.042 (−0.343)	
GINILA	−0.039 (−2.595)	−0.042 (−3.191)	−0.028 (−1.076)		−0.028 (−1.794)
MIDDLEDM			0.352 (1.814)	0.406 (2.484)	
GINILADM			−0.009 (−0.269)		−0.027 (−1.193)
DEMOCRACY			−3.631 (−0.848)	−4.750 (−2.298)	2.014 (1.204)
$\bar{R}^2$	0.540	0.556	0.563	0.427	0.481
SEE	1.258	1.111	1.225	1.376	1.232

Note: Method of estimation: OLS.

GDP, as a measure of initial development; and the percentage of the labor force in the agricultural sector, AGRIL, as a measure of the structure of production as well as an additional measure of the relative political strength of the agricultural sector. All these variables are sampled at the start of the period.[11]

The results of the OLS estimation are shown in table 9.3. In column 1 we report the basic regression, where all the variables have been included. The fit of the regression is very good for a cross section, all the estimated coefficients have the expected sign, and many of them are significantly different from zero. In particular, the coefficients on the two distributional measures have the right sign; GINILA is clearly significant, MIDDLE is not, strictly speaking, but still has a marginal significance level (p-value) of 0.145. Checking the residuals reveals that there is one outlier: Chad, with an average growth rate of −2.8 percent. Column 2 displays the same regression, once we drop Chad from the sample. The fit of the regression improves and all variables are now statistically significant. In the remaining regressions, we leave this outlier in the sample, even though the results continue to improve if we exclude it.

As we argued at the end of the previous section, the theory has more detailed predictions for the link between growth and income distribution in countries governed by different political systems. Specifically, we expect growth to be positively related to income equality in democracies but not in dictatorships. And we expect concentration of land ownership to have a negative effect on growth irrespective of the political regime. To test this more specific prediction, we add to the regressions a dummy variable, DEMOCRACY, taking a value of 1 for democratic countries and 0 otherwise. This variable is entered in the regressions by itself (to control for an independent effect of the political system on growth), and interactively with the two distributional variables: a DM suffix at the end of a variable indicates that it is interacted with DEMOCRACY. We expect to find MIDDLE to have a significant impact on growth only when interacted with DEMOCRACY, and we expect the opposite result for GINILA. The results, shown in column 3, are weakly supportive of the theory. The estimated coefficients are of the sign predicted by the theory, and MIDDLE has a much stronger effect on growth when interacted with DEMOCRACY, while the opposite is true for GINILA, also as predicted by the theory. But the coefficients on the distributional variables are not statistically significant (even though MIDDLEDM has a t-statistic of 1.814, p-value 0.083).

The problem is probably that there are too few observations. Most of the countries in the sample with both distributional variables are democracies (we only have data for ten nondemocratic countries), so there is not enough variability in the political regime. To gain observations, we then run two separate regressions—one where only income equality is included and the other where only land concentration is included. Again, the income distribution variable is interacted with DEMOCRACY. The results, shown in columns 4 and 5, are now exactly as predicted by the theory. Equality of income is the right sign and significant only when interacted with DEMOCRACY, and land concentration has the same negative effect on growth in democracies and nondemocracies.[12]

As a further check on the robustness of our results, in table 9.4 we report the results of some sensitivity analysis. The first two columns add a second

Table 9.4
Some sensitivity analysis

Dependent variable	Growth				Investment
	1	2	3	4	5
# OBS	46	49	48	50	31
CONSTANT	2.780 (1.129)	5.394 (2.533)	2.550 (1.009)	6.926 (3.058)	4.886 (0.318)
GDP	−0.99E-3 (−4.325)	−0.73E-3 (−3.808)	−0.88E-3 (−4.577)	−0.719E-3 (−4.386)	−0.12E-2 (−0.973)
PSCHOOL	0.024 (2.025)	0.024 (2.156)	0.032 (2.671)	0.0159 (1.494)	0.123 (2.306)
SSCHOOL	0.033 (1.789)	0.016 (1.148)			
AGRIL	−0.023 (−1.095)	−0.034 (−1.825)	−0.278 (−1.532)	−0.049 (−2.969)	−0.078 (−0.661)
MIDDLE	0.039 (−0.310)		−0.066 (−0.418)		0.747 (1.743)
GINILA		−0.034 (−2.301)		−0.037 (−1.750)	0.038 (0.505)
MIDDLEDM	0.325 (1.960)		0.396 (2.065)		
GINILADM		−0.016 (−0.762)		−0.013 (−0.525)	
DEMOCRACY	−4.174 (−2.065)	1.111 (0.683)	−4.074 (−1.697)	1.500 (0.785)	
$\bar{R}^2$	0.443	0.475	0.399	0.480	0.365
SEE	1.339	1.136	57.096	51.520	5.544

Note: Method of estimation: Columns 1, 2, 5: OLS. Columns 3, 4: weighted least squares, with GDP as weight.

measure of human capital, the percentage of individuals enrolled in secondary school (SSCHOOL), to columns 4 and 5 of table 9.3. The new variable is almost significant and of the right sign in one of the two regressions, but the results of table 9.3 are otherwise confirmed. In particular, MIDDLEDM and GINILA are both significant and of the predicted sign. We also tried adding to the regression the percentage of the population living in urban areas, but it was generally insignificant and it did not change the other estimated coefficients.

The estimated residuals reveal a systematic pattern. They tend to be larger for the poor countries in the sample. As a possible correction for this heteroskedasticity, we reestimated the model by weighting observations with GDP. The results are shown in columns 3 and 4 of table 9.4.

Again, they remain very similar to those of table 9.3. We obtained similar results for other specifications, not reported in the table.

Next, we ask if our results are robust to the possibility of measurement error and apply the techniques of Klepper and Leamer (1984). Following their approach, we estimate column 1 of table 9.3 minimizing in the direction of all the independent variables potentially measured with error. Klepper and Leamer (1984) show that if all the estimated coefficients thus obtained retain their signs from table 9.3, then the results are robust to measurement error. Furthermore, the two maximum likelihood coefficients lie in a known and bounded interval. In our case, the variables most likely to be measured with error are GDP, AGRIL, and the two measures of distribution, MIDDLE and GINILA. Hence we ran four "reverse regressions," in each of which we replaced the dependent variable by one of the incorrectly measured regressors. The estimated coefficients retain their sign only in three out of the four regressions. In particular, if we assume that one of the two distributional variables (it does not matter which one) is measured correctly, then we can compute consistent bounds for the coefficients of the remaining three variables. But if both MIDDLE and GINILA are measured with error, then we can argue that the results are robust (in the sense of retaining their sign) only if we are willing to assign specific priors to the percent size of measurement error in the regressors relative to the true R^2. We conclude that our results are somewhat sensitive to the possibility of measurement error in the variables MIDDLE or GINILA, but not in the remaining variables.

As a further check on our measures of income distribution, we replaced the variable MIDDLE with other measures of income inequality, such as the percentage of income received by the top 5 percent of the population or the Gini coefficient obtained from the distribution of pretax income (the source is always Paukert 1973). The results, not reported in the table, were essentially unchanged.

From these results taken together, we conclude that they are supportive of the theory: a more unequal size distribution of income is bad for growth in democracies, while more land concentration is bad for growth everywhere. These effects of distribution on growth are also quantitatively significant: a one-standard-deviation change in MIDDLE and in GINILA both affect average annual growth by at least half a percentage point (according to the point estimates in table 9.2).

Finally, the theory also has predictions for investment in cumulative factors. As explained in the previous section, distributional variables are important for growth because they affect the investment rate of different countries. In the last column of table 9.4 we change the dependent variable, replacing the average growth rate with the average physical investment rate between 1960 and 1985 (the source is still Summers and Heston 1988).[13] The results are now less supportive of the theory. The size distribution of income enters with the correct sign and is almost significant. But land ownership is not significantly different from zero and has the wrong sign. In a sense this is not too surprising, since the measure of investment does not correspond with the implications of the theory. First, our measure of investment is the sum of public and private investment, while the theory only refers to private investment. Second, accumulation of human capital and of productive knowledge is not included in the measure of investment, while it should be according to the theory.

4 Conclusions

The main predictions of the simple theory outlined in the chapter seem to be largely supported by the data. Income inequality and land concentration are bad for growth. In principle, these facts are consistent with other, nonpolitical reasons for why income distribution and the distribution of land ownership influence growth.[14] Our theory, however, also predicts that the distributional variables interact in a specific way with the form of government. This additional prediction is also consistent with the data and thus discriminates in favor of a political explanation of why distribution matters for growth.

The theory has predictions about the link between income distribution and policy and about the link between policy and growth. Future empirical research should try to identify both these links, rather than estimating reduced forms, as we have done in this chapter. We think this is going to be pretty hard work, though. As we argued in section 2, "taxes" in the model can be interpreted in a variety of ways. These various general and sectoral policies are going to be hard to measure in a satisfactory way across countries.

The literature surveyed here has studied the link between income distribution at a point in time and policies affecting growth. But the evidence collected by development economists and economic historians suggests that the relationship between growth and income goes both ways: the literature on the Kuznets curve argues that income distribution is systematically related to the income level.[15] Future theoretical research should try to study the joint dynamics of growth, income distribution, and policy formation. A natural, but difficult, way to do this would be to extend earlier work on human capital and income distribution to incorporate endogenous policy formation.[16] Another challenging task involves building a bridge to the literature, surveyed by Aghion and Bolton (1991), on growth and income distribution under incomplete capital markets.

Notes

Much of the work on this chapter was done when we were visiting the Research Department of the International Monetary Fund. We gratefully acknowledge financial support from the Fund, from the Swedish Social Science Research Council, from the Mattei Foundation, and from the NSF, grant S.E.S-8909263. We thank Giuseppe Bertola, John Londregan, Ariel Rubinstein, and the editors for helpful comments, and we thank Kerstin Blomqvist for secretarial assistance.

1. However, there is a literature that studies optimizing fertility choice and thus makes population growth the object of economic analysis (see, for instance, the recent paper by Barro and Becker, 1990).

2. The contribution of foreign direct investment to GDP growth may be particularly important if there are indivisibilities or other nonconvexities that keep the marginal product of capital low when capital is scarce. The relationship between foreign direct investment, domestic policy, and growth has been recently studied by Cohen and Michel (1991).

3. See for instance Barro and Sala-i-Martin (1992) and Rebelo (1991).

4. The theory of endogenous economic policy has developed in two somewhat different traditions. One development—surveyed by Persson and Tabellini (1990)—is oriented toward macroeconomic policy and public finance. The other development—surveyed by Hillman (1989) and Magee, Brock, and Young (1989)—is oriented toward trade policy.

5. Glomm and Ravikumar (1991) study an overlapping-generations model with heterogenous agents where income taxes finance public education. They obtain the conclusion that more inequality produces less growth. But their assumptions are such that all agents prefer the same tax rate, so there is no distributional conflict in their model.

6. F_l, the return to land in the expression for v, is pinned down by the requirement that $F_k(k^f, l) = 1$ and thus does not depend on the tax.

7. See Hillman (1989) and Magee, Brock, and Young (1989).

8. A tax on the capital intensive sector here is bad for growth for two reasons. First, there is the disincentive to save, which was also present in the other model. Second, capital is driven out of the capital intensive sector, which is typically the sector driving growth. This sectoral distortion further reduces the growth rate (on this point see also Easterly 1991).

9. For six countries, GINILA is observed in the early 1970s, but for all other countries it is observed in the early 1960s.

10. This is a flow measure of human capital. A stock measure, such as the literacy rate, would be more closely tied to the model, but it is measured with much bigger error than school enrollment.

11. The source for GDP is Summers and Heston (1988). The source for AGRIL and PSCHOOL is the World Development Report, 1988.

12. The correlation coefficient between MIDDLE and GINILA is −0.28. This is not very high, but under the null hypothesis that both variables should be included in the regression, excluding one of them may bias the estimates.

13. We leave the other independent variables in the equation. PSCHOOL may not seem to belong there, but it does—according to some versions of endogenous growth theory—since human capital may increase the return to physical investment (see Romer 1990).

14. For example, Murphy, Shleifer, and Vishny (1989), building on earlier work in development economics, have suggested another, purely economic, reason why more equality may be good for growth: you may need a sufficiently large middle class to generate demand for manufacturing products that is sufficient for a growth takeoff.

15. Regarding the evidence on the Kuznets curve, see Williamson (1989) and Lindert and Williamson (1985) for an overview of the historical evidence, and Fields (1980) for an overview of the postwar evidence across developing countries.

16. The papers mentioned in section 1, by Perotti (1990), Saint-Paul and Verdier (1991), and Glomm and Ravikumar (1991), all take some steps in this direction but are forced to make simplifying assumptions that rule out an interesting part of the problem.

References

Aghion, P., and Bolton, P. 1991. Distribution and growth in models with imperfect capital markets. Forthcoming in *European Economic Review.*

Alesina, A., and Rodrik, D. 1991. Redistributive politics and economic growth. Manuscript.

Atkeson, A., and Ogaki, M. 1990. Engel's law and savings. Manuscript.

Barro, R., and Becker, G. 1990. Fertility choice in a model of economic growth. *Econometrica* 57:481–501.

Barro, R., and Sala-i-Martin, X. 1992. Public finance in models of economic growth. *Review of Economic Studies.* Forthcoming.

Benhabib, J., and Rustichini, A. 1991. Social conflict, growth and income distribution. Manuscript.

Bertola, G. 1991. Market structure and income distribution in endogenous growth models. Manuscript.

Cohen, D., and Michel, P. 1991. Property rights on foreign capital and long-run growth. Manuscript.

Easterly, W. 1991. Distortions and growth in developing countries. Manuscript.

Fields, G. 1980. *Poverty, inequality and development.* Cambridge: Cambridge University Press.

Fischer, S. 1991. Growth, macroeconomics and development. *NBER Macroeconomics Annual* 1991:329–363.

Glomm, G., and Ravikumar, B. 1991. Public vs private investment in human capital: Endogenous growth and income inequality. Manuscript.

Hillman, A. 1989. *The political economy of protection.* London: Harwood.

Klepper, S., and Leamer, E. 1984. Consistent sets of estimates for regressions with errors in all variables. *Econometrica* 52:163–183.

Krueger, A. 1990. Government failures in development. *Journal of Economic Perspectives* 4:9–23.

Lindert, P., and Williamson, J. 1985. Growth, equality and history. *Explorations in Economic History* 22:341–377.

Magee, S., Brock, W., and Young, L. 1989. *Black hole tariffs and endogenous policy theory*. Cambridge: Cambridge University Press.

Meltzer, A., and Richard, S. 1981. A rational theory of the size of government. *Journal of Political Economy* 52:914–927. Reprinted as chapter 8 in the current volume of this work.

Murphy, K., Shleifer, A., and Vishny, R. 1989. Income distribution, market size and industrialization. *Quarterly Journal of Economics* 104:537–564.

Paukert, F. 1973. Income distribution at different levels of development: A survey of the evidence. *International Labor Review* 108:97–125.

Perotti, R. 1990. Political equilibrium, income distribution and growth. Manuscript.

Persson, T., and Tabellini, G. 1990. *Macroeconomic policy, credibility and politics*. London: Harwood.

Persson, T., and Tabellini, G. 1991a. Is inequality harmful for growth? Theory and evidence. Manuscript.

Persson, T., and Tabellini, G. 1991b. Factor ownership, distribution and growth. In preparation.

Rebelo, S. 1991. Long-run policy analysis and Long-run growth. *Journal of Political Economy* 99:500–521.

Rebelo, S. 1992. Growth in open economies. *Carnegie-Rochester Conference Series*. Forthcoming.

Romer, P. 1990. Human capital and growth: Theory and evidence. *Carnegie-Rochester Conference Series*, vol. 32, pp. 251–283.

Saint-Paul G., and Verdier, T. 1991. Education, growth and democracy. Manuscript.

Summers, R., and Heston, A. 1988. A new set of international comparisons of real product and price levels: Estimates for 130 countries. *The Review of Income and Wealth* 34:1–25.

Taylor, C., and Hudson, M. 1972. *World handbook of political and social indicators*. 2nd ed. New Haven: Yale University Press.

Taylor, C., and Jodice, D. 1983. *World handbook of political and Social indicators*. 3rd ed. New Haven: Yale University Press.

Williamson, J. 1989. Inequality and modern economic growth: What does history tell us? Discussion paper 1448, Harvard University.

World Bank. 1988. *World Development Report*. Washington, DC: The World Bank.

10 The Politics of Intergenerational Redistribution

Guido Tabellini

I Introduction

This paper studies government debt as an instrument of intergenerational redistribution. Two features distinguish debt from other redistributive instruments. First, issuing debt involves the promise of future transfers from yet-unborn generations. Second, the promise is made without the consent of the future generations that will bear the burden of the redistribution. Two natural questions arise: Under what circumstances are these promises kept, and why? And can older generations take advantage of the fact that future generations do not participate in the decision to borrow? Both questions are addressed in this chapter.

The recent interesting literature on intergenerational redistribution does not provide a satisfactory answer to these questions. Most of the literature assumes that issuing debt commits future generations to repay it.[1] But this assumption has no counterpart in any real-world political institutions. An exception is Kotlikoff, Persson, and Svensson (1988), who study an implicit reputation mechanism. However, their equilibrium is not renegotiation-proof and the equilibrium intergenerational distribution is indeterminate.[2]

In this chapter, reputation does not play a role and commitment is ruled out. The policy is chosen in each period by a majority of the voters currently alive. Yet in equilibrium, debt is repaid and the old take advantage of the fact that the young do not participate in the decision to borrow. The intuitive reason is that issuing debt creates a constituency in favor of repaying it. Once debt is issued, the decision whether or not to repay it concerns both the intergenerational and the intragenerational distribution of resources: debt repudiation harms the old, but it harms the wealthy more than the poor. The desire to avoid an intragenerational redistribution may induce some young taxpayers (the children of the wealthiest debt holders) to oppose repudiating the debt. Hence debt repayment is favored by a coalition that includes both old and young voters. If debt is not too

Reprinted from *Journal of Political Economy*, by permission of The University of Chicago Press. *Journal of Political Economy*, 1991, vol. 99, no. 3.

large and at the same time is sufficiently widely held, this coalition is the winning coalition.[3]

There is a precise sense in which the old take advantage of the fact that debt is issued without the consent of the young. The young who favor repaying the debt do so only ex post, once the debt is issued. If they could precommit ex ante not to repay the debt, before the debt was issued, they would all wish to do so. The reason is that ex ante the policy has only intergenerational, but no intragenerationl, effects. Hence if the young could vote on the decision to issue debt, they would all oppose it.

Thus the lack of commitment cuts both ways. On the one hand, the inability to commit to repay the debt prevents the old generation from achieving all the desired intergenerational redistribution. But the impossibility to commit *not* to repay the debt, on the other hand, induces some of the young to vote in favor of an intergenerational transfer that ex ante they would have opposed! For this reason, issuing government debt "creates facts" that can alter future collective decisions, even without commitment.

This emphasis on the incentives to honor preexisting obligations also points to an important difference between debt and social security. If there was commitment, debt and social security would be equivalent instruments of intergenerational redistribution. But with no commitment, this equivalence disappears. The reason is that the ex post incentives to honor debt and social security are different. Debt repayment is supported by a coalition of old voters and the young children of the wealthy. This coalition is different from the one that would support a social security system. In the model of this chapter, for instance, a social security system would never be viable, even if debt repayment is an equilibrium. In a related paper (Tabellini 1990), I show that social security is supported by a coalition of old voters and the poorest fraction of the young voters. These considerations may contribute to explain why debt and social security coexist in the same society at the same time. More generally, this distinction between debt and social security is reminiscent of the Lucas and Stokey (1983) result, that the maturity structure of government debt matters. There, as here, a Modigliani-Miller theorem on the equivalence of alternative public financial instruments fails to hold because of some ex post government incentive constraints.

The chapter is organized as follows. Section II sets up the model of a two-period closed economy with overlapping generations. The first generation is born in period 1 and lives two periods. The second generation is born in period 2 and lives only one period. Both generations are linked by bidirectional altruism. This altruism is sufficiently weak that no private transfers occur in equilibrium; altruism matters only for how agents vote. The first generation is heterogeneous, and different individuals hold different amounts of public debt. The economic equilibrium is briefly described in Section III. Section IV analyzes the vote that takes place in the last period over how much debt to repay. Young voters trade off the benefit of debt repayment for their parents against the taxes that they have to pay. If their parents hold a very large amount of debt, young voters may favor repayment. Old voters face a similar, but opposite, trade-off. Debt repayment is a political equilibrium if debt is not too large and it is sufficiently widely held. The decision to issue debt and the determinants of the equilibrium intergenerational redistribution are studied in Section V. Finally, Section VI contains some concluding remarks.

II The Model

Consider a two-period closed economy. In period 1 only one generation—called "parents"—is alive. In period 2 another generation—called "kids"—is born. Each parent has $1 + n$ kids. Thus $n \gtreqless 0$ is the rate of population growth. Parents live two periods and kids live one period. Both generations are altruistic. Thus the ith parent maximizes

$$W^i = U(c^i) + d^i + \delta(1 + n)V(x^i), \quad 1 > \delta > 0, \tag{1}$$

where c^i and d^i denote the parent's consumption in periods 1 and 2, respectively, and x^i denotes the kid's consumption in period 2. The ith kid maximizes

$$J^i = \frac{\gamma}{1 + n} d^i + V(x^i), \quad 1 > \gamma > 0. \tag{2}$$

The functions $U(\cdot)$ and $V(\cdot)$ are twice continuously differentiable, concave utility functions, and the coefficients δ and γ measure the altruism of parents and kids. Altruism is weighted by the rate of growth of the population. Thus as the family size increases (as n grows), parents give less weight to their own welfare relative to their kids' welfare; the opposite is true about the kids' altruism. This specification of preferences is plausible and simplifies the algebra but is not crucial for results.

I consider the following government policy. In period 1, each parent receives a nonnegative lump-sum transfer, g. The transfer is financed by issuing government debt. In period 2, the debt is repaid by a combination of taxes on the kids' income and on the outstanding debt. Clearly, if the kids pay a positive tax, this policy redistributes in favor of the parents' generation.

Different families have the same preferences but different endowments. At the beginning of life, the ith parent receives $1 + e^i$ units of nonstorable output. The individual-specific variable e^i is observed only by the ith parent. It can be either positive or negative and is distributed in the population according to a known distribution $G(\cdot)$, with zero mean, nonpositive median, and bounded support $[\underline{e}, \bar{e}]$ inside the interval $[-1, 1]$. Let s^i denote parent i's savings. Then write the ith parent's budget constraint for period 1 as

$$c^i + s^i \leq 1 + e^i + g. \tag{3}$$

The only store of value is government debt, b, that before taxes earns a gross rate of return q and is taxed (or repudiated) at the rate $1 \geq \theta \geq 0$. Hence, savings are constrained to be nonnegative: $s^i \geq 0$ for all i.

In period 2, parents cash in on their savings (if any) and receive a second endowment, a.[4] Parents can leave nonnegative bequests to their kids and kids can give nonnegative transfers (gifts) to their parents. Kids of different families are all alike. At birth they receive w units of output, which is taxed at the rate $1 \geq \tau \geq 0$. Hence, the budget constraints of parents and kids in period 2 can be written, respectively, as

$$\begin{aligned} &c^i + t^i \leq q(1 - \theta)s^i + f^i(1 + n) + a, \\ &x^i + f^i \leq w(1 - \tau) + \frac{t^i}{1 + n}, \end{aligned} \tag{4}$$

where $f^i \geq 0$ and $t^i \geq 0$ denote gifts and bequests, respectively.

There is no government consumption. Hence, if we denote average variables by omitting the i superscript, the government budget constraints are

$$g \leq b, \quad q(1 - \theta)b \leq (1 + n)\tau w. \tag{5}$$

Finally, period 1 equilibrium in the asset market requires that average savings equal average government debt:

$$\int_0^\infty s^i \, dH(s^i) = b, \tag{6}$$

where $H(\cdot)$ is the endogenous distribution of savings in the parents' population. By Walras's law, equations (3)–(6) imply that the good markets are also in equilibrium.

Tax policy is chosen by majority rule at the beginning of each period and before any private economic decision is made. In period 1, parents vote on how much debt to issue. In period 2, both parents and kids vote on the tax rate on debt, θ. The government budget constraints determine the lump-sum transfer g and the tax rate on kids, τ, residually.

A political-economic equilibrium must satisfy three conditions: (i) Economic equilibrium: for any given policy, economic decisions are optimal for private agents and markets clear. (ii) Political equilibrium: in every period, the policy implemented is (weakly) preferred to any other policy by a majority of the voters currently alive. (iii) Rationality: the expectations of individuals in their roles as economic agents and voters are fulfilled.

There are three features of the model that deserve special attention. First, whereas parents have heterogeneous endowments, all kids have the same income. This assumption captures the well-known fact that wealth inequality is much more pronounced than income inequality. This extreme asymmetry of the model can be relaxed, at the price of some complications, provided that the parents' wealth and the kids' income are not perfectly positively correlated. Second, since the parents' endowments are not publicly observed, individual savings are also private information. This in turn implies that nonlinear taxation of savings is not feasible. Parents can be taxed only by repudiating the debt, in proportion to how much debt they hold. Together, these two features imply that debt repudiation redistributes wealth from rich to poor families as well as across generations. Finally, since the parents' preferences are linear in their own period 2 consumption, private intergenerational transfers are the same for all families, irrespective of the parents' initial endowments. This third feature considerably simplifies the description of the political equilibrium because it implies that the voters' preferences are single-peaked. It could be replaced by a more general utility function provided that single-peakedness is satisfied.

III The Economic Equilibrium

In this section individuals are considered in their roles as economic agents, who take the current and expected future policy as given. It is straightforward to verify that optimality for all families in period 2 implies

$$1 \geq \delta V_x(x^i) \geq \delta\gamma, \quad \text{all } i, \tag{7}$$

where a subscript on a function denotes a derivative. If the first (second) inequality is strict, the nonnegativity constraint on bequests (gifts) is binding.[5] As noted above, by (7) all households are in the same position with respect to the gift and bequest constraints: If one household is constrained, so are all the others. As a consequence, the kids' consumption is the same for all families, and from now on the superscript is dropped from x. I assume throughout that

$$1 > \delta V_x(w) > \delta\gamma. \tag{8}$$

Thus in the absence of any government intervention, both parents and kids would like to leave negative transfers to each other. This assumption guarantees that there is a conflict of interest between the two generations and hence that there is a potential role for public policy.

The amount saved by each parent in period 1 is determined by the first-order condition

$$U_c(1 + e^i + b - s^i) \geq q(1 - \theta^e) \equiv r^e, \tag{9}$$

with equality if $s^i > 0$, where θ^e denotes the expectation of θ and r^e is the expected net-of-tax rate of return on public debt. Thus the savings of parent i can be written as

$$s^i \equiv \max(0, z + e^i), \tag{10}$$

where z is implicitly defined by

$$U_c(1 + b - z) - r^e = 0. \tag{11}$$

All parents with $e^i \leq -z$ save a zero amount. All other parents save an amount $s^i = z + e^i$.

Recalling that e^i is distributed in the population according to the cumulative function $G(\cdot)$, with support $[\underline{e}, \bar{e}]$, $\bar{e} > 0 > \underline{e}$, we can express the equilibrium condition in the market for government debt, (6), as

$$b - z[1 - G(-z)] - \int_{-z}^{\bar{e}} e^i \, dG(e^i) = 0. \tag{12}$$

Equations (11) and (12) jointly define the equilibrium values of z and r^e as functions of government debt: $z^* = Z(b)$ and $r^{*e} = R(b)$. Section A of the Appendix proves that $Z_b > 0$ and that $R(b)$ can be drawn as in figure 10.1: the equilibrium interest rate is increasing for $b \leq -\underline{e}$ and is constant for $b > -\underline{e} > 0$. To the right of point A (for $b > -\underline{e}$), every parent saves a positive amount; here, the constant interest rate simply reflects the constant marginal utility of period 2 consumption. To the left of point A (for $b \leq -\underline{e}$), the no-borrowing constraint is binding for some of the poorer parents. In this region, issuing debt raises the interest rate since some of the constrained parents must be induced to forgo current consumption and buy public debt.

I now examine the political equilibrium.

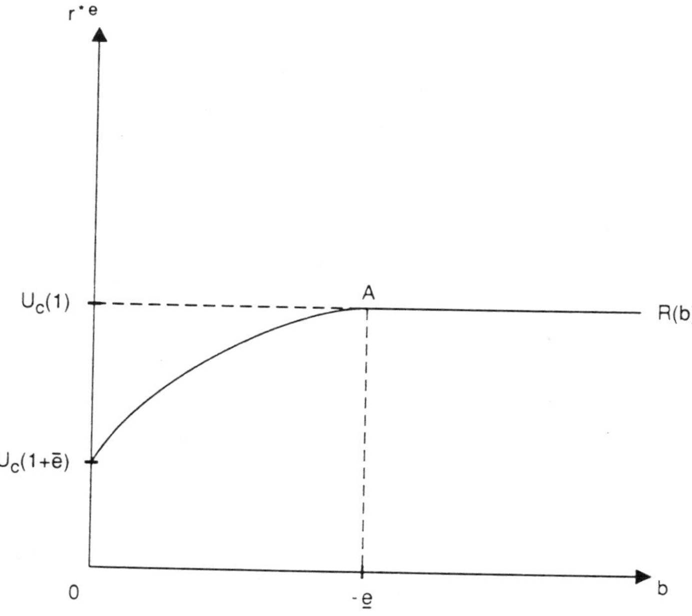

Figure 10.1

IV Voting on Debt Repudiation

Before turning to the issue of debt repayment, consider the following policy. Suppose that in period 2 both parents and kids were to vote on a social security system that collects a tax from every kid and distributes the proceeds as a lump sum to every parent. By (8), all parents would be in favor of such a system and all kids would oppose it. Hence, with population growth (if $n > 0$), in this model a social security system would not be politically viable under majority rule. The central result of this section is that debt repayment instead is politically viable: even though the kids outnumber the parents and even though both are eligible to vote, repudiating the debt in period 2 may be opposed by a majority of the voters.

A The Voters' Preferences

In period 2, the voters take the debt outstanding and the interest rate q as given. Hence, voting for a repudiation rate θ is equivalent to choosing an actual net-of-tax rate of return on public debt, $r \equiv q(1 - \theta)$. Since θ is constrained to be in the interval $[0, 1]$, r must lie in the interval $[0, q]$.[6] Let us write the private budget constraints in terms of this ex post rate r. Inserting the government budget constraint, (5), in the private budget constraints, (4), and imposing the nonnegativity constraints on private transfers, we obtain

$$d^i + (1 + n)x \leq w(1 + n) + r(s^i - b) + a, \tag{13a}$$

$$d^i \leq rs^i + f^i(1 + n) + a, \tag{13b}$$

$$(1 + n)x \leq w(1 + n) - rb + t^i. \tag{13c}$$

Equation (13a) is the family budget constraint, and (13b) and (13c) are implied by the nonnegativity constraints on bequests and gifts, respectively.

Consider now the welfare effect of changing r on the ith parent, W_r^i. Applying the envelope theorem to (1) and (13) and after some transformations, we find[7]

$$W_r^i = b\left(\frac{s^i}{b} - \delta V_x\right). \tag{14}$$

By (14), each dollar of debt repaid affects the ith parent's welfare in two ways. On the one hand, it increases his wealth (and hence his utility) by

s^i/b. On the other hand, it increases the tax burden on his kids by the fraction $1/(1+n)$ of one dollar; this gives the parent a disutility of δV_x. This second effect is the same for all parents. The net welfare effect depends on the relative wealth of the ith parent and is more likely to be positive the wealthier the parent is.

The effect of changing r on the ith kid's welfare, J_r^i, depends on whether or not the bequest constraint (13b) is binding. When the constraint is not binding (i.e., if $\delta V_x = 1$), changing r affects the welfare of every kid in the same direction as that of his parent. Intuitively, changing the rate of return on debt here has the only effect of redistributing wealth across families and not across generations. On the other hand, if the bequest constraint (13b) binds, so that $t^i = 0$ and $\delta V_x < 1$, then J_r^i can be computed as illustrated above for W_r^i to obtain

$$J_r^i = \frac{b}{1+n}\left(\gamma\frac{s^i}{b} - V_x\right), \tag{15}$$

which can be interpreted along the same lines as (14).

I now show that the following lemma is true.

LEMMA 1 In equilibrium, the nonnegativity constraint on bequests, (13b), is always binding.

Proof By assumption, the median e^i does not exceed the average e^i. Hence, by (10) and (12), the savings of the median parent do not exceed average savings, b.[8] Thus when parents leave positive bequests, so that $\delta V_x = 1$, by (14) at least 50 percent of the parents favor a lower rate of return on debt. Next, consider the kid of a parent with average wealth, such that $s^i = b$. For him, changing r redistributes only between him and his parents and not between his family and all other families. Since he discounts the welfare of his parents, this average kid prefers a rate of return r so low that the bequest constraint is binding. All the kids of poorer parents (at least 50 percent of the kids) prefer even lower rates of return on debt, since for them reducing r also redistributes from other families to their own family. Hence, a value of r such that parents leave positive bequests cannot be supported as a political equilibrium under majority rule. Q.E.D.

This result is important for two reasons. First, it underscores that the absence of commitment matters: there is an upper bound to the amount of intergenerational redistribution that is politically viable in equilibrium. Second, this result implies that we can restrict our attention to the case in which the bequest constraint binds. In this case, the kids' preferences for the ex post rate r are given by (15).

In summary, there are two groups of voters, parents and kids. By (14) and (15), in both groups the voters' preferences can be ranked in terms of the parents' relative wealth: wealthier voters prefer higher rates of return on public debt. But parents and kids in the same family have different preferences: since δ, $\gamma < 1$, the parents prefer higher rates of return than their own kids. Finally, it can be shown that individual preferences are single-peaked. As a consequence, the equilibrium policy is that preferred by the median voter of period 2.

As will be shown in the next subsection, the median voters are a pair: a parent and a kid (not his own kid) who vote in the same way and have the same desired rate of return on public debt. Let s^m/b be the relative wealth of the median voter parent in period 2. By (14) and (13c), and the fact that $q \geq r \geq 0$, the rate of return preferred by the median voter parent is defined by

$$r = q \quad \text{if} \frac{s^m}{b} > \delta V_x\left(w - \frac{qb}{1+n}\right), \tag{16a}$$

$$r = 0 \quad \text{if} \frac{s^m}{b} < \delta V_x(w). \tag{16b}$$

Otherwise $r \in [q, 0]$ is defined by

$$\frac{s^m}{b} - \delta V_x\left(w - \frac{rb}{1+n}\right) = 0. \tag{16c}$$

But under rational expectations, $r = r^{*e}$ (or, equivalently, $\theta = \theta^e$), where $r^{*e} = R(b)$ is the rate that clears the market for public debt in period 1. As shown in figure 10.1, $R(b) > 0$ if $b > 0$. Hence by (16), in a political-economic equilibrium, government debt can be issued only in amounts that satisfy

$$\frac{s^m}{b} - \delta V_x\left(w - \frac{R(b)b}{1+n}\right) \geq 0. \tag{17}$$

This condition defines a *politically viable* set of values of public debt. Any amount of debt in this set is fully repaid in equilibrium, and any amount not in this set cannot be sold in equilibrium. I now turn to a more careful investigation of (17).[9]

B The Median Voter

To characterize the politically viable set, we have to identify the median voter. That requires combining the two groups of voters, parents and kids. Consider a parent with period 2 relative wealth equal to s^i/b. By (14) and (15), the optimal rate of return for this parent is the same as that for the kid of a parent whose relative wealth s^k/b is defined by [10]

$$\frac{s^k}{b} = \frac{1}{\delta\gamma}\frac{s^i}{b} > \frac{s^i}{b}. \tag{18}$$

Equation (18) enables us to match each kid with a parent (not his own parent, but a poorer one) that votes exactly like him. Let $H(\cdot)$ be the cumulative distribution of the parents' relative wealth at the beginning of period 2. Then the median voters in period 2 are the parent with relative wealth s^m/b and the kid of the parent with relative wealth $s^m/\gamma\delta b$, where s^m/b is defined by

$$H\left(\frac{s^m}{b}\right) + (1+n)H\left(\frac{s^m}{\delta\gamma b}\right) = \left[1 - H\left(\frac{s^m}{b}\right)\right] + (1+n)\left[1 - H\left(\frac{s^m}{\delta\gamma b}\right)\right]. \tag{19}$$

The left- (right-) hand side of (19) represents all the parents and kids who prefer a rate of return on debt smaller (greater) than or equal to that preferred by the parent s^m/b. They are the poorest (richest) parents and kids. For s^m/b and $s^m/\delta\gamma b$ to be the median voter parent and kid, there must be an equal number of voters on both sides of them. This condition is illustrated in figure 10.2 for the case in which $s^i > 0$ for all i. The solid curve in the upper panel represents a hypothetical distribution of the parents' relative savings, $H(\cdot)$. By (18), this distribution can be mapped into the kids' distribution by matching each kid with a parent who votes like him. The solid curve in the lower panel depicts such a transformation. Since $\delta\gamma < 1$, the kids' distribution is shifted to the left and has a different shape compared to the parents' distribution; intuitively, each kid votes like a poorer parent. By construction, a parent and a kid on the same vertical line vote alike. The relative wealth of the median voter parent, s^m/b, is found by equating the sum of the two shaded areas (the one on the

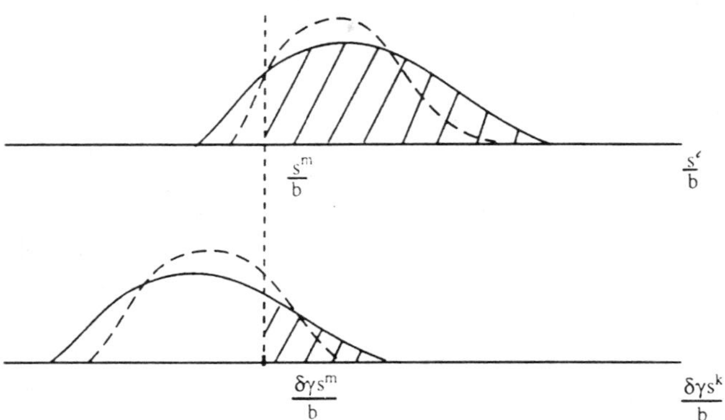

Figure 10.2

lower panel weighted by $1 + n$) to the (weighted) sum of the nonshaded areas.

Equation (19) simplifies to

$$H\left(\frac{s^m}{b}\right) + (1 + n)H\left(\frac{s^m}{\gamma\delta b}\right) = 1 + \frac{n}{2}, \tag{20}$$

which uniquely defines the relative wealth of the median voter parent, s^m/b, in terms of the (endogenous) cumulative distribution of relative wealth, $H(\cdot)$. Since $\delta\gamma < 1$, (20) implies that s^m/b is to the left of the median value of s^i/b (and hence also that $s^m/b < 1$), and $s^m/\gamma\delta b$ is to the right of it (see note 11 below). Hence, as illustrated in figure 10.2, the coalition to the right of the median voters pair (the right-hand side of equation 19) consists of a majority of the parents and a minority of the kids.

To complete the discussion of how s^m/b is determined in equilibrium, we need to derive the distribution of relative wealth, $H(\cdot)$, from the primitive distribution of initial endowments, $G(\cdot)$. Doing that results in the following lemma.

LEMMA 2 In period 2 the median voter parent has relative wealth $s^m/b = S(b)$, where $S(\cdot)$ is a continuous function such that

$$S(b) = 0 \qquad \text{if } b \leq \tilde{b} > 0,$$

$$S(b) > 0 \qquad \text{if } b > \tilde{b},$$

$$S_b(\tilde{b}) > 0, S_b(b) \gtrless 0 \quad \text{if } b > \tilde{b}.$$

Proof By (10), s^m/b can be expressed as a function of government debt and of the median voter's initial endowment, e_2^m:

$$\frac{s^m}{b} = \max\left(0, \frac{z^* + e_2^m}{b}\right), \tag{21}$$

where $z^* = Z(b)$ is defined implicitly by (6) and (11), as discussed in Section III above. To determine e_2^m, consider the random variable $(z^* + e^i)/b$, which is a known transformation of the random variable e^i. For any $y \geq 0$, $\text{prob}[(z^* + e^i)/b \leq y] = G(by - z^*)$. Hence, by (21) and after some simplifications, we can rewrite (20) as

$$G(e_2^m) + (1 + n)G\left[\frac{e_2^m + (1 - \delta\gamma)z^*}{\delta\gamma}\right] - 1 - \frac{n}{2} = 0. \tag{22}$$

Equation (22) implicitly defines the initial endowment of the median voter parent as a function of government debt: $e_2^m = E(b)$. By the implicit function theorem, $E(b)$ is continuous and $E_b(b) < 0$.[11] Hence

$$\frac{s^m}{b} = \max\left[0, \frac{Z(b) + E(b)}{b}\right] \equiv S(b).$$

Differentiating this function with respect to b completes the proof. Q.E.D.

An example of the function $S(b)$ is illustrated in figure 10.3. Its properties as well as the threshold value $\tilde{b}$ depend on the form of the utility function, $U(\cdot)$, and on the distribution of initial endowments, $G(\cdot)$. Figure 10.3 has been drawn under the assumption that $U(\cdot)$ is logarithmic and $G(\cdot)$ is uniform.

The ambiguity in the slope of $S(b)$ for $b > \tilde{b}$ reflects two opposite effects of issuing government debt. Since the debt proceeds are distributed as a lump sum to every parent, issuing debt reduces the inequality of period 2 wealth. More equal wealth affects the political equilibrium in two opposite ways. On the one hand, it increases the size of the parents' coalition to the right of the median voter parent: since the median voter parent is poorer than the average ($s^m/b < 1$), more equal wealth means that there are fewer parents to the left of s^m/b and more to its right.[12] This fact tends to push s^m/b to the right and hence to increase the equilibrium rate of return on debt. Intuitively, as debt is more widely held, there are more parents who benefit from higher rates of return on debt. Thus issuing debt creates a constituency in favor of repaying it. On the other hand, more equal wealth

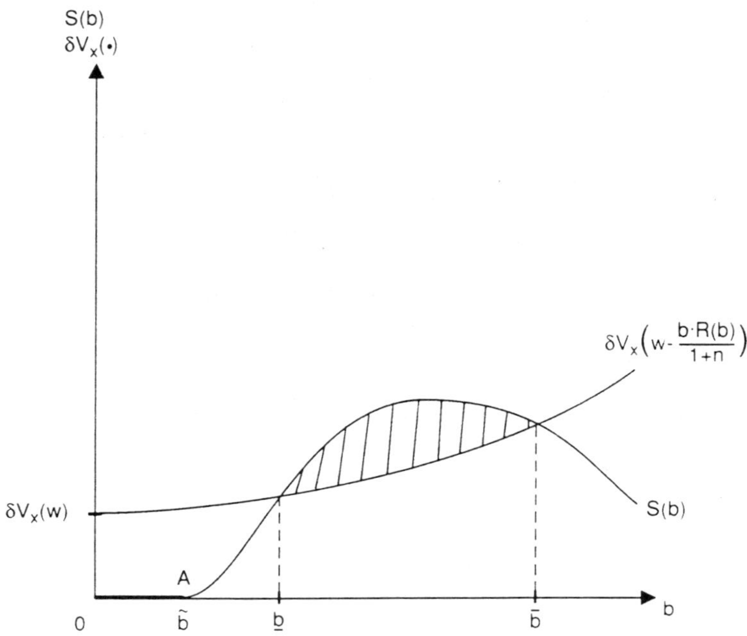

Figure 10.3

reduces the size of the kids' coalition supporting more debt repayment. The reason is that the kids in this coalition are the wealthiest kids; as wealth becomes more equal, there are fewer such kids. This fact tends to push s^m/b to the left and, hence, to decrease the equilibrium rate of return on debt.

These two effects of issuing government debt when $s^m/b > 0$ are illustrated in figure 10.2. As debt rises, the parents' and the kids' distributions change as indicated by the dashed curves. The shaded area in the upper panel increases, and that in the lower panel shrinks. Depending on which of these two effects prevails, s^m/b can either increase or decrease. If the first effect prevails, $S_b > 0$, and as debt rises, there are more voters in favor of repaying it. Otherwise the opposite is true. This finding, that issuing government debt changes the political equilibrium in period 2, is important. It implies that, even in the absence of commitments, debt can be used strategically to influence future policy decisions. This implication is analyzed more thoroughly throughout the remainder of the chapter.

C The Politically Viable Set

I now turn to a discussion of the repudiation rate chosen in the political equilibrium and of how this constrains the redistributive policies that can be implemented in period 1.

Lemma 2 and condition (17) together imply the following proposition.

PROPOSITION 1 The politically viable set of values for public debt is defined by the inequality

$$S(b) - \delta V_x\left(w - \frac{R(b)b}{1+n}\right) \geq 0. \tag{23}$$

This set is illustrated in figure 10.3 by the interval $[\underline{b}, \bar{b}]$. The second term in (23), $\delta V_x(\cdot)$, is drawn as the upward-sloping curve. This term always has a positive slope since the function $V(\cdot)$ is concave. The first term, $S(b)$, is drawn as the curve that first increases and then decreases. As already remarked, by lemma 2 the slope of $S(b)$ is unambiguously positive only at point A in the diagram. Hence, the politically viable set could be nonconvex, or it could even be empty. The Appendix provides an example of a nonempty and convex politically viable set, similar to that of figure 10.3, for the case of a uniform distribution $G(\cdot)$ and logarithmic utility function $U(\cdot)$.

We already know from lemma 1 that the politically viable set is bounded from above. It turns out that it is also bounded away from zero, from below. This can be seen by noting that for any $b \leq \tilde{b}$, $S(b) = 0$, whereas $\delta V_x > 0$, so that (23) is violated. Thus under majority rule, society will choose not to repudiate only if government debt is large enough. This result may seem surprising, but it has a simple explanation. If debt is too small, it is held by a minority of the parents. Hence there will always be a majority of the voters in favor of debt repudiation. But once enough debt is issued and hence debt is sufficiently widely held, the constituency of debt holders may be large enough that repudiation is no longer viable.

If the politically viable set is nonempty, some intergenerational redistribution can take place in equilibrium, even in the absence of any commitment. This finding is particularly striking in light of the previous observation that a social security system is not viable in this economy. Why does issuing government debt succeed where a simple social security system fails? The answer is that, by issuing government debt, the parents tie together the intergenerational and the intragenerational effects of reneging on the policy. The tax on a kid to repay the debt can be much smaller than the amount reimbursed to his wealthy parent. Hence, by issuing debt, the parents gain the support of the wealthier kids for a policy that transfers income to the parents.

V Equilibrium Intergenerational Redistribution

I now turn to a description of the political equilibrium of period 1, in which the parents vote on how much debt to issue. Two main results are derived in this section. First, I show that the parents benefit from being able to issue debt without the kids' consent. Hence, even if commitments are not feasible, the parents have a "first-mover advantage" with respect to the yet-unborn generation. Second, I characterize the determinants of the equilibrium intergenerational redistribution. Throughout the section I assume that the politically viable set is nonempty, for otherwise no debt could be issued.

Since there is no uncertainty, the voters in period 1 realize that issuing an amount b of debt in the politically viable set results in a lump-sum transfer to every parent that, in terms of period 2 consumption goods, is worth $R(b)b$ (naturally, different parents consume the transfer in different periods). The transfer is financed by a tax $\tau w = R(b)b/(1 + n)$ on the kids. No amount outside the politically viable set can be sold since nobody would buy it. Consider the welfare effect on the ith parent of marginally raising b. Repeating the procedure illustrated in Section IV.A, we find

$$W_b^i = U_c^i - r^{*e}\delta V_x + bR_b\left(\frac{s^i}{b} - \delta V_x\right). \tag{24}$$

The first two terms on the right-hand side of (24) summarize the net direct effect of issuing debt: namely, to increase the parents' income by one unit (which yields a marginal utility of $U_c^i = U_c(c^i)$ to voter i) and to decrease the kids' income by r^{*e} units (which costs a disutility of $-r^{*e}\delta V_x$). Since $U_c^i \geq r^{*e}$ and $1 - \delta V_x \geq 0$, this direct effect is always nonnegative and strictly positive if the parent is bequest-constrained (i.e., if $1 - \delta V_x > 0$). The third term on the right-hand side of (24) summarizes the indirect general equilibrium effect of issuing debt, operating through the change in the interest rate. This indirect effect is evaluated differently by different consumers. Issuing debt can raise the interest rate, and this redistributes income from poor to wealthy households. Hence this third term is nonnegative for households wealthier than the average, but it can be negative for poor households.

To simplify the analysis, I assume that for all parents the direct effect always dominates the indirect effect. As shown in section B of the Appendix, this happens if

$$[1 - G(-z^*)](1 - \delta V_x)r^{*e} + G(-z^*)\delta V_x U_{cc} b > 0 \tag{25}$$

for all $b \leq -\underline{e}$, where U_{cc} is evaluated at the point $1 + b - z^*$, V_x is evaluated at the point $w - [(r^{*e}b)/(1 + n)]$, and the equilibrium conditions (9) and (12) hold. Intuitively, this condition says that for poor parents the nonnegativity constraint on bequests binds more than the nonnegativity constraint on savings. The Appendix provides an example in which $U(\cdot)$ is logarithmic and $G(\cdot)$ is uniform, in which condition (25) is satisfied for an appropriate $V(\cdot)$ function. The Appendix also proves that under (25) the parents' preferences are single-peaked and that they all would like to issue debt up to the point at which the nonnegativity constraint on bequests is not binding (i.e., up to the point at which $\delta V_x = 1$). But by lemma 1, this point is outside the politically viable set. The political equilibrium of period 1 is then very simple, as shown in proposition 2.

PROPOSITION 2 Under condition (25), with unanimity the equilibrium level of debt coincides with the upper bound of the politically viable set (point $\bar{b}$ in fig. 10.3).[13]

This result underscores that incomplete political participation matters. As explained in the previous section, the equilibrium intergenerational redistribution is supported by the wealthier fraction of the kids because it is tied to the intragenerational effects of the policy. But ex ante, this tie is much weaker than ex post. Ex post, once the debt is issued and expectations have been formed, repudiating the debt redistributes wealth from rich to poor families. Ex ante, on the other hand, the intragenerational consequences of issuing debt are due only to the general equilibrium effect of issuing debt. By (25), this effect is not very large, and it disappears altogether for $b \geq -\underline{e}$. Hence, there is a difference between the ex ante and ex post attitude of the kids toward intergenerational transfers through public debt. Incomplete political participation matters because it enables the parents to exploit this difference. If the kids could also vote in period 1, they would anticipate their ex post preferences toward repaying the debt, and they would generally oppose issuing it.[14]

Hence, even in the absence of commitments, issuing government debt can "create facts" that are not reversible. To reverse the initial policy, the government would have to tax each parent in a lump-sum fashion (and to undo the general equilibrium effects of issuing debt that operate through the change in interest rate). But the government does not have the information to do this: once debt is issued, the government loses track of who holds it and in what proportion. Even though it knows the aggregate distribution of the parents' savings, the government cannot observe the amounts held by a specific individual. Hence, each parent can be taxed only in proportion to his savings and not in a lump-sum fashion. This irreversibility of the original policy is what gives rise to the difference between the ex ante and the ex post preferences of the kids. It is for this reason that the parents have a first-mover advantage with respect to the yet-unborn generations.

I now discuss how the equilibrium intergenerational redistribution is affected by changes in the underlying parameters. Throughout I assume that condition (25) holds, so that proposition 2 applies. Consider first an increase in the kids' per capita income, w. Referring to figure 10.3, we see that increasing w leaves the $S(b)$ curve unaffected and shifts the δV_x curve downward. Hence, a higher value of w increases the upper bound of the sustainable region and leads to more intergenerational redistribution. The intuition is simple: when the kids' income increases, the altruistic motive of kids becomes stronger and that of the parents becomes weaker. Hence, in period 2 all voters prefer a higher rate of return on government debt, which in turn enables the parents to issue a larger amount of debt in period 1. This finding is similar to that derived by Cukierman and Meltzer (1989) under the commitment assumption.

Next, consider an increase in the rate of growth of the population, n. The curve δV_x in figure 10.3 shifts down since the burden of repaying the debt is now shared among a larger population of kids. It can be shown that the curve $S(b)$ is also shifted downward.[15] Intuitively, as n increases, the proportion of voters in favor of less debt repayment (the kids) rises, so that the political equilibrium of period 2 supports a smaller amount of intergenerational redistribution. Thus the net effect is ambiguous: a higher rate of population growth can lead to either more or less intergenerational redistribution, depending on the specific properties of the kids' utility function and of the initial wealth distribution.

Finally, the size of the politically viable set depends on the distribution of initial endowments, $G(\cdot)$. As discussed in Section IV.B and illustrated in figure 10.2, the relationship between this set and the initial distribution of wealth is ambiguous. On the one hand, the more concentrated the initial wealth is, the smaller is the coalition of parents who support debt repayment. In the limit, if this coalition is too small, the politically viable region is empty, in which case no domestic government debt can be issued. On the other hand, if the initial wealth distribution is too equal, then the kids' coalition supporting debt repayment may be too small. In the limit, if every parent has the same wealth, then debt repudiation is equivalent to a lump-sum tax on the parents. In this case, no kid would favor repaying the debt and the viable set would also be empty. Hence, too much inequality and too little inequality both limit the politically viable intergenerational redistribution.

VI Concluding Remarks

There is a widespread opinion that domestic government debt is honored because of reputation incentives.[16] Recently Bulow and Rogoff (1989) have cast doubt on this idea by showing that reputation incentives work only if a repudiating government is shut out from world capital markets also as a lender and not just as a borrower. It is hard to believe that domestic debt repudiation would have such dismal consequences.

This chapter has explored an alternative line of thought, which emphasizes the redistributive consequences of debt repudiation. The main insight of the paper is that issuing debt creates a constituency in support of repaying it. Thus issuing debt "creates facts" even in the absence of commitments. The reason is that once debt is issued, repudiation has redistributive consequences. Opposition to such a redistribution can give rise to a majority in favor of repaying the debt.

This idea has been applied in the paper to explain why a generation can extract resources from future, yet-unborn, generations. By issuing government debt, the intergenerational redistribution is tied to the intragenerational consequences of choosing how much debt to repay. Young voters motivated by the desire to avoid intragenerational redistributions may accept transferring resources to the older generation, even though they would have opposed such a transfer if it was voted on in isolation. This may explain why alternative methods of intergenerational redistribution, such as social security and government debt, coexist at the same time in the same society. These methods may be equivalent from an economic point of view. But they differ in their political viability since they tie the intergenerational aspect to other redistributive issues in a different way.

This same idea can be analyzed in alternative frameworks, unrelated to the intergenerational issue. Aghion and Bolton (1989) have independently applied it to an economy in which there is no intergenerational conflict but individuals differ in their preferences for private versus public consumption. It can be applied to more general forms of wealth taxation besides debt repudiation and to privatization decisions.

Appendix

A Economic Equilibrium

Applying the implicit function theorem to (11) and (12), we see that $R(b)$ and $Z(b)$ are continuous functions with slope

$$R_b = -\frac{G(-z^*)U_{cc}}{1 - G(-z^*)} \geq 0,$$
$$Z_b = \frac{1}{1 - G(-z^*)} > 0. \tag{A1}$$

Consider the poorest parent, for which $e^i = \underline{e}$. By (9)–(11), the no-borrowing constraint is just binding for this parent when $b = -\underline{e}$. Hence, if $b > -\underline{e}$, all parents save a positive amount. By (12), then, if $b \geq -\underline{e}$, we have $z^* = b$ and $G(-z^*) = 0$. This, together with (9), implies $r^e = U_c(1)$ for any $b \geq -\underline{e}$. Conversely, if $b < -\underline{e}$, then the savings of at least some parents are zero. Hence, $G(-z^*) > 0$, so that by (A1) $R_b > 0$. By continuity of $R(b)$, equations (11) and (12) imply that $R(0) = U_c(1 + \bar{e})$. Hence, $R(b)$ can be drawn as in figure 10.1.

B Proof of Proposition 2

i) Consider the case $b \leq -\underline{e}$. Using (11), we can rewrite equation (24) as

$$W_b^i = U_c^i - r^{*e}\delta V_x - \frac{G}{1 - G} U_{cc} b \left(\frac{s^i}{b} - \delta V_x\right), \tag{A2}$$

where $G(\cdot)$ is evaluated at the point $-z^*$ and $U_{cc}(\cdot)$ is evaluated at the point $1 + b - z^*$. Consider parent j, for whom $e^j = -z^*$. This parent is just borrowing constrained. Hence, for him, $s^j = 0$ and (8) holds as an equality. Thus, for this parent, (A2) yields

$$W_b^j = r^{*e}(1 - \delta V_x) + \frac{G}{1-G} U_{cc} b \delta V_x, \tag{A3}$$

which is positive by (25).

All parents with $e^i < e^j$ also have $s^i = 0$. But since they are borrowing constrained, by (8) they also have $U_c^i > r^{*e}$. Hence, by (A2) and (A3), for all these parents, $W_b^i > W_b^j > 0$. Finally, all parents with $e^i > e^j$ save a positive amount. Hence, for them, $U_c^i = r^{*e}$ and (A2) becomes

$$W_b^i = r^{*e}(1 - \delta V_x) + \frac{G}{1-G} U_{cc} \delta b V_x - \frac{G}{1-G} U_{cc} s^i. \tag{A4}$$

Thus, again, $W_b^i > W_b^j > 0$. Thus under (25), $W_b^i > 0$ for all voters when b is in the range $[0, -\underline{e}]$.

ii) Next, consider the case $b > -\underline{e}$. As in the results of Section II, if $b \geq -\underline{e}$, then $s^i > 0$ for all i; in this case, $U_c^i = U_c(1) = r^{*e}$ for any $b \geq -\underline{e}$ and all i, and only the direct effects of issuing debt matter. Hence, for $b \geq -\underline{e}$, equation (24) reduces to

$$W_b^i = U_c(1)\left[1 - \delta V_x\left(w - \frac{U_c(1)b}{1+n}\right)\right] \geq 0 \tag{24'}$$

with strict inequality if $1 - \delta V_x > 0$.

Combining cases i and ii, we then conclude that, for all voters, $W_b^i > 0$ for any value of b smaller than that for which the bequest constraint binds (i.e., for which $1 - \delta V_x > 0$). The parents then are unanimous: they all want to issue debt until $1 - \delta V_x = 0$. Q.E.D.

C Example

Suppose that the distribution of initial endowments is uniform, with support $[-e, e]$, where $1 > e > 0$. Thus

$$G(e^i) = \frac{e^i + e}{2e}, \quad g(e^i) = \frac{1}{2e}. \tag{A5}$$

Suppose further that $U(c) = \ln c$. By (12), after some transformations, we obtain

$$z^* = -e + 2\sqrt{eb} \quad \text{for } b \leq e,$$
$$z^* = b \qquad\qquad\quad \text{for } b > e. \tag{A6}$$

Combining (A5) and (A6), we get

$$1 - G(-z^*) = \frac{\sqrt{eb}}{e}. \tag{A7}$$

Moreover, by (11) and (A6),

$$r^{*e} = \frac{1}{1 + b - z^*} = \frac{1}{1 + b + e - 2\sqrt{eb}} \tag{A8}$$

and

$$U_{cc}(1 + b - z^*) = -\left(\frac{1}{1 + b - z^*}\right)^2 = -(r^{*e})^2. \tag{A9}$$

Combining all this information, we can rewrite (25) as

$$\frac{\sqrt{eb}}{e}(1 - \delta V_x) - \left(1 - \frac{\sqrt{eb}}{e}\right)\delta V_x b r^{*e} > 0. \tag{A10}$$

With (A8) this expression simplifies to

$$\frac{1 + b + e - 2\sqrt{eb}}{1 + e - \sqrt{eb}} > \delta V_x\left(w - \frac{r^{*e}b}{1 + n}\right), \tag{A11}$$

which is satisfied for appropriate specifications of the function $V(\cdot)$.

Retaining the same specifications for $G(\cdot)$ and $U(\cdot)$, consider now equation (22) in lemma 2. It can be rewritten as

$$\frac{e_2^m + e}{2e} + (1 + n)\frac{[e_2^m + (1 - \delta\gamma)z^*]\dfrac{1}{\delta\gamma} + e}{2e} - 1 - \frac{n}{2} = 0. \tag{A12}$$

Making use of (A6) and simplifying yields

$$e_2^m = \frac{(1 + n)(1 - \gamma\delta)(e - 2\sqrt{eb})}{1 + n + \gamma\delta}. \tag{A13}$$

Moreover, by (21) and (A6),

$$s^m = \max\left[0, 2\sqrt{eb} - e + \frac{(1 + n)(1 - \gamma\delta)(e - 2\sqrt{eb})}{1 + n + \gamma\delta}\right], \tag{A14}$$

which in turn yields

$$S(b) = \frac{s^m}{b} = \max\left(0, \frac{2\sqrt{eb} - e}{b}\phi\right), \tag{A15}$$

where $\phi = \gamma\delta(2 + n)/(1 + n + \gamma\delta)$. Thus $S(b) = 0$ for $b \leq e/4$ and $S(b) > 0$ for $b > e/4$. Moreover, for $b \geq e/4$, we have

$$S_b(b) = \frac{\phi e}{b^2\sqrt{eb}}(\sqrt{eb} - b) \tag{A16}$$

and

$$S_{bb}(b) = -\frac{\phi}{b}\left(\frac{e}{b^2} - \sqrt{eb}\right). \tag{A17}$$

By (A16), $S(b)$ reaches a maximum at the point $b = e$. Incidentally, this is the smallest value of b for which even the poorest parent is not borrowing constrained. To the left of this point, $S_b > 0$. To the right, $S_b < 0$. At the point $b = e$, we have

$$S(e) = \phi = \frac{\gamma\delta(2 + n)}{1 + n + \gamma\delta}. \tag{A18}$$

Thus S_b can be drawn as in figure 10.3. By (23) a sufficient condition for the sustainable set to be nonempty is

$$V_x\left(w - \frac{e}{1 + n}\right) < \frac{\gamma(2 + n)}{1 + n + \gamma\delta}. \tag{A19}$$

For if (A19) holds, then by (A8) and (17), $\delta V_x < S(b)$ at the point $b = e$.

Notes

I wish to thank Dan Peled, Torsten Persson, two anonymous referees, and the participants in workshops at the Institute for International Economic Studies, the National Bureau of Economic Research Summer Institute, University of California at Berkeley and Los Angeles, University of Southern California at Claremont, and at the Carnegie Mellon Political Economy Conference for many extremely helpful comments and discussions.

1. This assumption is made explicitly in Cukierman and Meltzer (1989) and implicitly in Hansson and Stuart (1989). The latter assume that a policy can be changed only if there is unanimity. Since in their model the old are always opposed to changing the policy, the unanimity requirement is equivalent to a commitment technology.

2. A second exception is Rotemberg (1989), who studies a bargaining model between the two generations currently alive. But it is difficult to interpret this bargaining equilibrium with reference to a political institution.

3. The idea that redistributive considerations may provide incentives not to create policy surprises has also been studied in Rogers (1986) and with respect to capital taxation in Persson and Tabellini (1989, 1990). None of these works, however, focuses on intergenerational redistribution.

4. The nonnegativity constraint on savings can be relaxed, and the algebra would actually be simpler, if we assume that negative savings are subsidized at the same rate θ at which positive savings are taxed. Moreover, the only role of the second-period endowment is to ensure that in equilibrium $d^i > 0$ for all i. All the results go through identically if $a = 0$, but the proofs would be more complicated.

5. In deriving (7), I relied on the fact that $d^i > 0$ for all i and, hence, that $a > 0$ and is sufficiently large.

6. As noted above, the constraint $\theta \leq 1$ follows from the assumption that the endowment e^i is private information. On the other hand, the constraint $\theta \geq 0$ cannot be derived from any primitive informational assumption. In equilibrium, however, this nonnegativity constraint is never binding, as implied by proposition 2 in Section V.

7. Equation (14) has been derived as follows. Let λ^i and μ^i be the Lagrange multipliers associated with (13b) and (13c). Then the envelope theorem implies

$$W_r^i = \lambda^i(s^i - b) + \mu^i s^i - \mu^i(1 + n)\frac{df^i}{dr}.$$

By the parents' first-order conditions, $\mu^i = 1 - \delta V_x$ and $\lambda^i = \delta V_x$. Moreover, by (8), the kids are always gift constrained for any $b \geq 0$. Hence, $df^i/dr = 0$. Using these facts in the equation above yields (14).

8. This can be seen by noting that eq. (9) and fig. 10.1 imply $b \geq z$, with strict inequality if $b < -\underline{e}$. Hence, $s^i = \max(0, z + e^i) \leq \max(0, b + e^i)$. The average e^i is zero and the median e^i is negative. Hence, for at least 50 percent of the parents, $s^i \leq \max(0, b)$.

9. When (17) is satisfied with equality, the equilibrium value of θ is unique given q. However, the model does not pin down a unique equilibrium combination of q and θ. This occurs because, since debt is the only asset, a fully anticipated wealth tax is of no consequence whatsoever. This would not be true if there were other taxable forms of wealth with returns technologically fixed, such as land or capital. A previous version of this chapter considered this extension and derived analogous but much more complicated results.

10. Equation (18) has been obtained by setting (14) and (15) equal to zero and by noting that only δV_x in (14) and (15) depends on r. Thus (18) matches the votes, but not necessarily the preferences, of parents and kids (since for some voters the optimal rate of return could be outside the interval $[0, q]$). As stated earlier, the voters' preferences are single-peaked. Hence, the characterization of the political equilibrium in (18) and in lemma 2 below applies irrespective of whether or not any voter is at the corners 0 and q.

11. Applying the implicit function theorem to (22), we get

$$\frac{de_2^m}{db} = \frac{-G\{[e_2^m + (1 - \delta\gamma)z^*]/\delta\gamma\}}{[1 - G(-z^*)](g(e_2^m)\delta\gamma + g\{[e_2^m + (1 - \delta\gamma)z^*]/\delta\gamma\})} < 0,$$

where $g(\cdot) = G_e(\cdot)$. Hence, issuing debt changes the identity of the median voter parent: as debt rises, the median voter parent corresponds to a parent with a smaller initial endowment. Note that, since $\delta\gamma < 1$, eq. (22) implies that $e_2^m < e^m$, where e^m is the median e^i. Thus as claimed above, the median voter parent is poorer than the median.

12. By (10) and (11) and if $s^i > 0$, then $\text{sign}[(\partial s^i/b)/\partial b] = \text{sign}(\{b - [1 - G(-z)]s^i\})$. Thus $(\partial s^i/b)/\partial b > 0$ for any parent poorer than the average.

13. If condition (25) does not hold, then the general equilibrium effects of the fiscal deficit may induce a majority of the parents to oppose issuing debt up to the upper bound of the politically viable set. In this case, the absence of commitment would not impose a binding constraint on the period 1 voters. This case is analogous to that studied by Cukierman and Meltzer (1989). Naturally, the results of proposition 1 concerning the politically viable set itself do not depend on condition (25). Finally, if (25) is violated, the parents' preferences are not necessarily single-peaked.

14. All the kids would always oppose issuing a debt larger than $-\underline{e}$. Some of the wealthy kids may vote in favor of issuing a debt smaller than $-\underline{e}$.

15. Using (22) (and since e_2^m is smaller than the median of e^i), we can show that e_2^m is a decreasing function of n. That is, increasing n leads to a poorer median voter parent. By (21), this then implies that s^m/b is decreasing in n.

16. The literature on reputation and wealth taxation is surveyed in Persson and Tabellini (1989). Grossman and Van Huyck (1988) and Chari and Kehoe (1989) study reputation incentives with reference to debt repudiation.

References

Aghion, Philippe, and Bolton, Patrick. 1989. Government domestic debt and the risk of default: A political-economic model of the strategic role of debt. Manuscript, Massachusetts Institute of Technology.

Bulow, Jeremy, and Rogoff, Kenneth. 1989. Sovereign debt: Is to forgive to forget? *American Economic Review* 79:43–50. Reprinted as chapter 8 in volume 1 of this work.

Chari, V. V., and Kehoe, Patrick J. 1989. Sustainable plans and debt. Manuscript, University of Minnesota.

Cukierman, Alex, and Meltzer, Allan H. 1989. A political theory of government debt and deficits in a neo-ricardian framework. *American Economic Review* 79:713–732.

Grossman, Herschel I., and Van Huyck, John B. 1988. Sovereign debt as a contingent claim: Excusable default, repudiation, and reputation. *American Economic Review* 78:1088–1097.

Hansson, Ingemar, and Stuart, Charles. 1989. Social security as trade among living generations. *American Economic Review* 79:1182–1195.

Kotlikoff, Laurence J., Persson, Torsten, and Svensson, Lars E. O. 1988. Social contracts as assets: A possible solution to the time-consistency problem. *American Economic Review* 78: 662–677. Reprinted as chapter 7 in volume 1 of this work.

Lucas, Robert E., Jr., and Stokey, Nancy L. 1983. Optimal fiscal and monetary policy in an economy without capital. *Journal of Monetary Economics* 12:55–93. Reprinted as chapter 14 in volume 1 of this work.

Persson, Torsten, and Tabellini, Guido. 1989. Representative Democracy and Capital Taxation. Manuscript, University of California at Los Angeles.

Persson, Torsten, and Tabellini, Guido. 1990. *Macroeconomic policy, credibility and politics.* London: Harwood.

Rogers, Carol Ann. 1986. The effect of distributive goals on the time inconsistency of optimal taxes. *Journal of Monetary Economics* 17:251–269.

Rotemberg, Julio. 1989. Constituencies with finite lives and the valuation of government bonds. Manuscript, Massachusetts Institute of Technology.

Tabellini, Guido. 1990. A positive theory of social security. NBER working paper no. 3272.

11 The Redistributive Roles of Unemployment Insurance and the Dynamics of Voting

Randall Wright

1 Introduction

In an economy where unemployment occurs with positive probability and re-employment takes time, one would think that risk averse workers will generally desire some form of unemployment insurance (UI). Typically such insurance is provided by a public UI system—that is, one in which benefits are paid by the government and financed by taxation.[1] However (as is the case with many publicly provided goods), when agents are heterogeneous, public UI can also play a redistributive role. In his comprehensive study of the American UI system, Hamermesh (1977) concludes that "determining the level of benefits a typical recipient *should* receive is inherently a value judgement, at least if we are concerned with income replacement alone and ignore any possible incentive effects" (p. 91). The only "tenable argument" for a given benefit level or benefit/wage ratio "is thus the subjective one that society has agreed to guarantee its citizens (at least those qualifying for UI benefits) that their incomes will not fall by more than some fixed fraction" (p. 92).

The purpose of this paper is to present a model in which it is legitimate to ignore incentive effects, and concentrate exclusively on this "value judgement" by analyzing the parameters of the public UI system that are preferred by different individuals.[2] There are two ways in which individuals can be different: they can differ intrinsically, which we model here in terms of heterogeneous stochastic employment opportunities, or they can differ in the way the "luck of the draw" influences their current conditions. Since different agents do not generally prefer the same UI system the question naturally arises: how were the actual policy parameters determined in the economy? Hamermesh suggests that "society *through the electoral process* has expressed its tastes for an income distribution with certain characteristics" (p. 92, emphasis added). This leads us to analyze the majority voting equilibria in our model.

One result of this analysis is that, even in a simple version of the model in which agents are intrinsically identical, the democratically determined

Reprinted from *Journal of Public Economics*, by permission of Elsevier Science Publishers BV. *Journal of Public Economics* 31 (1986) 377–99. © North-Holland.

policy can differ from some policies that have been described as "optimal" in the UI literature, by Mortensen (1983), Shavell and Weiss (1979), Flemming (1978), Baily (1977b, 1978), and Easley, Kiefer and Possen (1985). This is due to the impact on voting of the inescapable heterogeneity induced by the dynamics. A second reason for studying the majority voting equilibrium is that we are able to analyze explicitly the feedback from the frequency or duration of unemployment to UI compensation and tax variables. These results should be of interest to researchers who have in the past concentrated exclusively on feedback in the other direction. In a well-known empirical study, Ehrenberg and Oaxaca (1976) recognize the argument that "since state benefit levels may be correlated with historical differentials in state unemployment rates, causing high benefit levels rather than vice-versa, findings based upon cross-section estimates could be biased" (note 16); but no one seems to have handled this problem explicitly. When we do endogenize the policy choice, it turns out that economies with more frequent or more lengthy average unemployment spells will have *lower* benefit levels (counter to Ehrenberg and Oaxaca's intuition). This can be understood by recognizing that economies with a higher unemployment rate cannot afford to be as generous.

In the next section the model is described in detail, and we determine different individuals' preferences over feasible UI tax and benefit levels. Three factors are relevant: future employment opportunities, current employment conditions, and risk aversion. Then in section 3, the majority voting equilibrium is characterized. Among other things, we show that even in an economy with complete private markets the provision of unemployment insurance may be socialized via the electoral process. In section 4 we analyze the effects of exogenous changes in the frequency and duration of unemployment spells, as well as the rate of time preference, on the equilibrium tax-compensation parameters. In section 5 we generalize the policy decision to that of choosing a tax rate and a function that determines benefits based on the duration of unemployment. We show that in equilibrium the benefit schedule declines with duration (and compensation eligibility can expire in finite time), we contrast these results to those of Shavell and Weiss (1979), and we characterize the effects of exogenous changes in the underlying parameters. The concluding section summarizes the results, considers the relevance of the implications, and describes some potential directions for future research.

2 The Economy

Time is indexed by the positive integers, $k = 1, 2, \ldots$. All agents in the economy are endowed with one unit of labor at every date. There is one non-storable consumption good, and at date k each agent has (the same) preferences over consumption sequences described by the utility function

$$\Phi(x_k, x_{k+1}, \ldots) = \sum_{j=k}^{\infty} \beta^{j-k} u(x_j),$$

where $u\colon \boldsymbol{R}_+ \to \boldsymbol{R}$ is twice differentiable with $u' > 0$ and $u'' < 0$, while $\beta \in (0, 1)$ is the discount factor. The assumption $u'' < 0$ means that agents are strictly risk averse. While all employed workers earn the same pre-tax real wage, which we normalize to 1, stochastic transitions into and out of employment are individual specific. Thus, index worker types by the parameters (λ, θ), where $\lambda \in (0, 1)$ is the probability that an employed worker becomes unemployed (is laid off), while $\theta \in (0, 1)$ is the probability that an unemployed worker remains unemployed (is not recalled) at each date. Let $F(\lambda, \theta)$ be the distribution function of types, so that $F(\lambda_0, \theta_0)$ is the proportion of the population for whom $\lambda \leqq \lambda_0$ and $\theta \leqq \theta_0$, and assume for convenience that there is a continuum of workers of each type. All agents know their own type and the economy-wide distribution of other types.

Layoffs and recalls are independent across agents and across time, so there is no aggregate risk and no business cycle. For an unemployed agent, the mean time until re-employment can be computed to be $1/(1 - \theta)$, which is increasing in θ.[3] Hence one can think of λ as measuring the frequency of unemployment and θ as measuring the duration of unemployment. Let w_k denote the state of an agent in period k: $w_k = 1$ if employed, $w_k = 0$ otherwise; then an individual employment history is a two state Markov chain with transition probabilities $\text{prob}(w_{k+1} = 0 | w_k = 0) = \theta$ and $\text{prob}(w_{k+1} = 0 | w_k = 1) = \lambda$.[4] The steady state unemployment rate for agents of type (λ, θ), which can be interpreted either as the percentage of this type that will be unemployed in steady state or as the proportion of time an agent of this type will spend unemployed over a long horizon, is given by

$$U^*(\lambda, \theta) = \frac{\lambda}{1 - \theta + \lambda}. \tag{1}$$

The aggregate (average) steady state unemployment rate is given by

$$U^* = \int U^*(\lambda,\theta)\,\mathrm{d}F(\lambda,\theta). \tag{2}$$

In this section we assume that all unemployed agents collect a constant UI benefit of c, and all employed agents pay a tax of t. For now these policy variables are taken parametrically. Assuming there are no private credit markets (an assumption that is relaxed below), employed agents simply consume $1 - t$ and unemployed agents consume c at each date. We impose the restriction $1 - t \geqq c$ to make employment "incentive compatible." We also require that the UI system be self financing in steady state: $cU^* = t(1 - U^*)$.[5] This generates a "government budget constraint" of the form

$$c = zt, \tag{3}$$

where $z \equiv (1 - U^*)/U^*$ does not depend on c or t. Using (3), the incentive compatibility restriction can be written $t \leqq 1 - zt$, which can be rearranged as $t \leqq T \equiv 1/(1 + z) = U^*$. The feasible set of tax rates is therefore $[0, T]$, and the feasible set of benefits is $[0, C]$, where $C \equiv zT = 1 - U^*$. The policy $t = T$ and $c = C$ implies complete insurance, since under this policy the net replacement ratio is unity and consumption is independent of employment status: $C = 1 - T$.

Let $V_w(\lambda,\theta)$ denote the expected lifetime utility of a type (λ,θ) agent when he is currently in state w. Then $V_0(\lambda,\theta)$ is his expected lifetime utility when currently unemployed and $V_1(\lambda,\theta)$ is his expected lifetime utility when currently employed. Observe that

$$u(c)/(1 - \beta) \leqq V_0(\lambda,\theta) \leqq V_1(\lambda,\theta) \leqq u(1 - t)/(1 - \beta),$$

so lifetime expected utility is always finite. It is also obvious that expected utility depends only on the state (and not on the date), and we can write

$$V_0(\lambda,\theta) = u(c) + \beta[\theta V_0(\lambda,\theta) + (1 - \theta)V_1(\lambda,\theta)],$$

$$V_1(\lambda,\theta) = u(1 - t) + \beta[\lambda V_0(\lambda,\theta) + (1 - \lambda)V_1(\lambda,\theta)].$$

Solving this system of equations, we find

$$(1 - \beta)(1 + \lambda\beta - \theta\beta)V_0(\lambda,\theta) = (1 - \theta)\beta u(1 - t) + (1 - \beta + \lambda\beta)u(c), \tag{4}$$

$$(1 - \beta)(1 + \lambda\beta - \theta\beta)V_1(\lambda,\theta) = (1 - \theta\beta)u(1 - t) + \lambda\beta u(c). \tag{5}$$

Steady state utility for an individual of type (λ, θ), which can be interpreted as the expected utility of a randomly selected such agent in steady state, or as the expected utility of such an agent not conditioned on his current employment status (that is, behind the proverbial Rawlsian veil of ignorance) is given by

$$V^*(\lambda, \theta) = U^*(\lambda, \theta) V_0(\lambda, \theta) + [1 - U^*(\lambda, \theta)] V_1(\lambda, \theta).$$

Using (1), this can be rearranged to yield[6]

$$(1 - \beta)(1 - \theta + \lambda) V^*(\lambda, \theta) = \lambda u(c) + (1 - \theta) u(1 - t). \quad (6)$$

Substituting the government budget constraint into the right-hand sides of (4), (5) and (6), we can define three (indirect utility) functions of the tax rate:

$$f_0(t; \lambda, \theta) = (1 - \theta)\beta u(1 - t) + (1 - \beta + \lambda\beta) u(zt),$$

$$f_1(t; \lambda, \theta) = (1 - \theta\beta) u(1 - t) + \lambda\beta u(zt),$$

$$f_*(t; \lambda, \theta) = (1 - \theta) u(1 - t) + \lambda u(zt).$$

Each f_j constitutes a potential "welfare function" over taxes. Given a type (λ, θ) agent, f_0 measures his welfare as a function of t when he is currently unemployed, f_1 measures his welfare when he is currently employed, and f_* measures his steady state welfare. Notice that as β approaches 1, both f_0 and f_1 approach f_*. Since each f_j is continuous and strictly concave while the set of feasible tax rates is compact, each f_j has a unique maximizer on $[0, T]$, call it $t_j(\lambda, \theta)$, and an associated benefit level, $c_j(\lambda, \theta) = zt_j(\lambda, \theta)$. The tax-benefit pair $[t_j(\lambda, \theta), c_j(\lambda, \theta)]$ is thus the "optimal" self financing policy, according to the criterion $f_j(t; \lambda, \theta)$.

3 Majority Voting Equilibrium

It is obvious that for any $t \in [0, T]$, $t_j(\lambda, \theta) \leqq t$ if and only if $f_j'(t; \lambda, \theta) \leqq 0$ (welfare is decreasing in the tax at t). Let

$$G_j(t) = \text{prob}[f_j'(t; \lambda, \theta) \leqq 0]$$

denote the proportion of the population in state j who prefer a tax rate no greater than t. If the economy is at its steady state unemployment rate, then the proportion of the entire population who prefer a tax rate no greater than t will be given by

$$G(t) = U^*G_0(t) + (1 - U^*)G_1(t).$$

Suppose the citizens in this economy held an election on tax rates. Since preferences are single peaked (each f_j is strictly concave), there are no strategic voting considerations and each agent votes for a marginal tax increase just in case the current rate is below the one that maximizes his welfare. In this situation the median voter will be decisive, and the majority voting equilibrium will be the tax rate that solves $G(t) = 1/2$.[7]

In characterizing this equilibrium there are several effects to sort out, including the effect of intrinsic heterogeneity (different values of λ and θ), the effect of current conditions (whether the agent is currently employed or unemployed), and the effect of risk aversion. To begin, we will abstract from the impact of current conditions by considering the limiting case in which approaches 1, which implies that both f_0 and f_1 approach f_*. Differentiating f_*,[8]

$$f_*'(t;\lambda,\theta) = -(1-\theta)u'(1-t) + z\lambda u'(zt). \tag{7}$$

Recall that complete insurance is provided when $t_*(\lambda,\theta) = T$, since $1 - T = z$. Thus, full insurance will be preferred by (λ,θ) if and only if $f_*'(T;\lambda,\theta) \geqq 0$, which holds if and only if

$$z = \frac{1-U^*}{U^*} \geqq \frac{1-\theta}{\lambda} = \frac{1-U^*(\lambda,\theta)}{U^*(\lambda,\theta)}. \tag{8}$$

Condition (8) holds if and only if $U^*(\lambda,\theta) \geqq U^*$. We conclude that with no discounting there will be full insurance in majority voting equilibrium if and only if the median voter spends more time unemployed than the average worker. In spite of their aversion to risk, agents with below average unemployment rates will prefer to forgo some insurance, since the system transfers resources from them to high unemployment types.[9]

Notice that $t_*(\lambda,\theta) > 0$ if and only if $f_*'(0;\lambda,\theta) > 0$, which holds if and only if

$$\frac{u'(0)}{u'(1)} > \frac{1-\theta}{z\lambda} = \frac{1-U^*(\lambda,\theta)}{U^*(\lambda,\theta)} \cdot \frac{U^*}{1-U^*}. \tag{9}$$

If agents were risk neutral u' would be constant, so the left-hand side would equal unity and (9) would hold if and only if $U^*(\lambda,\theta) > U^*$. Thus, with discounting and risk neutrality the majority voting equilibrium entails $t > 0$ if and only if the median voter spends more time unemployed than the average. Risk aversion implies the left-hand side of (9) exceeds unity, so $U^*(\lambda, \theta) > U^*$ is not necessary for $t > 0$. Hence, the equilibrium tax-benefit policy could be positive even if the median voter spends less time unemployed than average, since he is willing to pay something to reduce employment-consumption risk.[10] We now re-introduce the impact of current conditions (that is, whether an individual is currently employed or on layoff) on voter preferences and thus on equilibrium.

Current conditions matter when $\beta < 1$, which means that f_0 and f_1 are not equal. Differentiating these functions, we have

$$f_0'(t; \lambda, \theta) = -(1-\theta)\beta u'(1-t) + z(1-\beta+\lambda\beta)u'(zt), \tag{10}$$

$$f_1'(t; \lambda, \theta) = -(1-\theta\beta)u'(1-t) + z\lambda\beta u'(zt). \tag{11}$$

Now $t_j(\lambda, \theta) = T$ if and only if $f_j'(T; \lambda, \theta) \geqq 0$. With a little algebra, this can be seen to hold if and only if

$$U^*(\lambda, \theta) \geqq U^* + \gamma_j(\lambda, \theta)U^*,$$

where

$$\gamma_0(\lambda, \theta) \equiv -\frac{(1-\beta)(1-\theta)}{\lambda(1-\beta+\lambda\beta)} < 0, \quad \gamma_1(\lambda, \theta) \equiv \frac{(1-\beta)}{\lambda\beta} > 0.$$

Hence, $U^*(\lambda, \theta) \geqq U^*$ is not sufficient for a currently employed worker to prefer full insurance, while $U^*(\lambda, \theta) \geqq U^*$ is not necessary for a currently unemployed worker to prefer complete insurance. For interior solutions—that is, for $0 < t_j(\lambda, \theta) < T$—implicit differentiation of (10) and (11) can be shown to imply $\partial t_j/\partial\lambda > 0$ and $\partial t_j/\partial\theta > 0$, $j = 0, 1$. Since $c_j = zt_j$, this further implies $\partial c_j/\partial\lambda > 0$ and $\partial c_j/\partial\theta > 0$. We conclude that *within a population distribution* (so that z is constant), agents with higher λ or θ prefer both higher taxes and more benefits.

With risk neutrality, (10) and (11) would imply $t_j(\lambda, \theta) = T$ if $U^*(\lambda, \theta) > U^* + \gamma_j(\lambda, \theta)U^*$ and $t_j(\lambda, \theta) = 0$ if $U^*(\lambda, \theta) < U^* + \gamma_j(\lambda, \theta)U^*$, so workers either want complete insurance or no insurance, depending on both their individual type, and their current employment status (as reflected in their discount factor). Interestingly, then, majority voting can yield an equilibrium with a public UI program that provides full insurance even if workers are risk neutral, simply due to the redistributive aspects of the system.

Since workers are effectively neutral to employment risk when there are complete contingent markets that they can use to smooth their consumption, this suggests a reason why socialized insurance might come into existence in an economy with complete markets, and hence in an economy where agents could insure themselves privately.

To briefly consider this idea, suppose a complete set of contingent claims markets exists. Let $y_j(\lambda, \theta)$ denote the present market value of expected lifetime earnings for a type (λ, θ) agent who is currently in state j. If the interest rate is given by $1/(1 + R) = \beta$, we have

$$y_0(\lambda, \theta) = 0 + \beta[\theta y_0(\lambda, \theta) + (1 - \theta) y_1(\lambda, \theta)],$$

$$y_1(\lambda, \theta) = 1 + \beta[\lambda y_0(\lambda, \theta) + (1 - \lambda) y_1(\lambda, \theta)],$$

which can be solved to yield:

$$y_0(\lambda, \theta) = (1 - \theta)\beta(1 - \beta)^{-1}(1 - \theta\beta + \lambda\beta)^{-1}.$$

$$y_1(\lambda, \theta) = (1 - \theta\beta)(1 - \beta)^{-1}(1 - \theta\beta + \lambda\beta)^{-1}.$$

Without working through the details, since there is no aggregate uncertainty in our model it is apparent that in competitive market equilibrium agents can, and therefore will, completely smooth consumption. Worker consumption x at each date equals *permanent income* given his status j when markets first open: $x_j(\lambda, \theta) = (1 - \beta) y_j(\lambda, \theta)$.

Now reconsider the public UI system. For the sake of example suppose that the median voter is currently employed, and that he prefers full insurance, $t_1 = T = U^*$. His lifetime utility under the market system and under the public UI system are, respectively,

$$\Phi_M = u[x_1(\lambda, \theta)]/(1 - \beta)$$

$$\Phi_P = u(1 - U^*)/(1 - \beta).$$

Hence, he does better under public UI if and only if

$$1 - U^* > x_1(\lambda, \theta) = (1 - \theta\beta)/(1 - \theta\beta + \lambda\beta).$$

This is certainly a possibility; for instance, as $\beta \to 1$ (which does indeed imply $t = T$), the right-hand side approaches $1 - U^*(\lambda, \theta)$, and the median voter is in favor of public UI if and only if he is unemployed more than the average. Hence, a democratic majority can elect (a candidate who proposes) a socialized UI system even if private insurance is available. Since in this example there is complete insurance under the public program, no agent will privately purchase supplementary coverage, but one can imagine equilibria where this is not the case. Of course, for our argument to be valid, we require that it is not possible to "opt out" of the public system.[11]

Having said this, from now on we ignore private insurance. Under a public system, if types are perfectly observable ex ante then in principle taxes could be fully "experience rated" so that there would be no transfers from low to high unemployment agents. This effectively institutes a separate system for each type, each with its own tax and benefit levels, $t(\lambda, \theta)$ and $c(\lambda, \theta)$, and budget constraint, $U^*(\lambda, \theta)c(\lambda, \theta) = [1 - U^*(\lambda, \theta)]t(\lambda, \theta)$. Under such a regime, it is as though there was no intrinsic heterogeneity. However, there would remain the inescapable dynamic heterogeneity resulting from current employment conditions. To isolate these dynamic effects, unless stated otherwise we will assume that (λ, θ) is the same across all agents for the remainder of the analysis. In an economy with no intrinsic heterogeneity we have $U^* \equiv U^*(\lambda, \theta) = \lambda/(1 - \theta + \lambda)$, and we will also write $f_j(t; \lambda, \theta) = f_j(t)$.

It turns out that in an intrinsically homogeneous economy, as long as the discount factor is less than 1, currently unemployed (employed) agents always prefer complete (incomplete) insurance. To see this, first notice that $z = (1 - \theta)/\lambda$, and therefore

$$f_0'(t) = -(1 - \theta)\beta u'(1 - t) + \lambda^{-1}(1 - \beta + \lambda\beta)(1 - \theta)u'(t(1 - \theta)/\lambda)),$$

$$f_1'(t) = -(1 - \theta\beta)u'(1 - t) + \beta(1 - \theta)u'(t(1 - \theta)/\lambda)).$$

Evaluating at $t = T$ and simplifying, we have

$$f_0'(T) = \lambda^{-1}(1 - \theta)(1 - \beta)u'(1 - T) > 0,$$

$$f_1'(T) = -(1 - \beta)u'(1 - T) < 0.$$

Let us make the reasonable assumption that $U^* < 1/2$. This means that the median voter is currently employed, and the majority voting equilibrium tax is $t = t_1 < T$, while the equilibrium benefit level is $c = t_1 z = t_1(1 - \theta)/\lambda < C$. Hence, in equilibrium we have $c < 1 - t$, and insurance is incomplete.

Note that there is an element of time inconsistency to voting behavior here.[12] Employed workers who vote for $t < T$ at date k will regret that insurance is incomplete when they get laid off at some future k', and if the vote was recast at k' they would change their ballots. Unemployed workers always prefer higher benefits, but as soon as they are recalled they change their minds, and their votes. This apparent inconsistency is *not* the result of irrationality or misperceptions about the true probabilities in our model. It is simply that for workers who are currently employed, the gain from full insurance is outweighed by the cost of financing benefits for the current unemployed out of their wages, and so they prefer $t < T$. In steady state, no matter when the vote is taken a dynamic majority—that is, a majority comprised of different individuals at different dates—always prefers $t < T$. Hence, complete insurance will never be democratically achieved.[13]

With no intrinsic heterogeneity, the steady state welfare function f_* (or V^*) is easily seen to be maximized by complete insurance, $t = T$. Therefore the majority voting equilibrium does not maximize steady state welfare which, we recall, can be interpreted as the expected utility of a randomly selected individual in steady state, or as the expected utility (not conditional on initial conditions) of an agent over his infinite horizon. Hence, even with non-distorting taxation, and no moral hazard problems or other market failures, there is a sense in which the economy in equilibrium is "worse off on average" than it feasibly could be. Steady state welfare is the criterion used by Mortensen (1983) in his analysis of optimal UI, and therefore he calls full insurance the first best solution. Whether or not f_* is the "right" welfare function is a tricky question; the point here is that the electoral process will not achieve Mortensen's first best outcome even in a first best world.[14]

To close this section, we point out that although we *allow* agents to recast their ballots at each date, they need not actually do so. As long as the economy is stationary, the policy preferred by the median voter will not change (although the median voter changes) over time; so once this policy is instituted there is no sense in calling another election. Voters rationally expect the policy that wins to be maintained indefinitely. We also note that in actual practice elections are typically over candidates taking positions on a wide range of issues, and a majority in favor of one policy does not necessarily imply that this policy will be implemented. In this economy, however, the only issue is the UI system, and representative democracy is equivalent to a direct vote on policy. Finally (in response to a referee's comment), we concede that individuals in this model vote exclusively in their own self interest; any "altruism" on the part of workers with favorable future employment prospects or current employment conditions towards their less fortunate fellow critizens would mitigate some of the results.

4 Effects of Changes in the Parameters

In this section we analyze the impact on the majority voting equilibrium of changes in the underlying parameters. We wish to answer the following questions: How does the incidence or duration of unemployment affect equilibrium tax and compensation policy?[15] This reverses the questions typically addressed in the literature, where the emphasis has been on the impact of taxes or benefits on incidence or duration. Of course, people are not unaware of the fact that, as Hamermesh (1977, p. 47) puts it, "the impact of a more liberal UI system on unemployment is difficult to disentangle from the effects of perpetually higher unemployment on the political decision to increase the generosity of the state's system." Here we will concentrate exclusively on the latter effect, and we will show that the effect of perpetually higher unemployment is to *decrease* the generosity of the public UI system. This is obvious for the full insurance policy, $(t, c) = (T, C) = (U^*, 1 - U^*)$: anything that increases U^* (which in our model means an increase in either λ or θ) obviously increases T while lowering C, keeping the net replacement ratio at $C/(1 - T) = 1$.

Now consider the impact of parameter changes on the majority voting equilibrium (when $U^* < 1/2$), $(t, c) = (t_1, c_1)$. We know $t_1 < T$, and we can guarantee $t_1 > 0$ by the condition $u'(x) \to \infty$ as $x \to 0$. Therefore we concentrate on interior solutions, $0 < t_1 < T$, for which

$$f_1'(t) = -(1 - \theta\beta)u'(1 - t) + (1 - \theta)\beta u'(t(1 - \theta)/\lambda) = 0 \tag{12}$$

is a necessary and sufficient condition. Implicitly differentiating (12), after some simplification we find that

$$\partial t/\partial\beta = \Delta[\theta u'(1 - t) + (1 - \theta)u'(c)] > 0,$$

$$\partial t/\partial\lambda = -\Delta\lambda^{-1}(1 - \theta)\beta c u''(c) > 0,$$

$$\partial t/\partial\theta = \Delta\beta[u'(1 - t) - u'(c) - cu''(c)]?$$

where $\Delta \equiv -[(1 - \theta\beta)u''(1 - t) + (1 - \theta)\beta\lambda^{-1}u''(c)] > 0$. Since $c = t(1 - \theta)/\lambda$, we also find

$$\partial c/\partial\beta = \Delta\lambda^{-1}(1-\theta)[\theta u'(1-t)+(1-\theta)u'(c)] > 0,$$

$$\partial c/\partial\lambda = \Delta\lambda^{-1}(1-\theta\beta)cu''(1-t) < 0,$$

$$\partial c/\partial\theta = \Delta\lambda^{-1}\{(1-\theta\beta)tu'(1-t)+(1-\theta)\beta[u'(1-t)-u'(c)]\} < 0.$$

That a larger value of β implies larger values of t and c should not be surprising, since a higher discount factor means that the long-term benefits of insurance will be given more weight relative to the short-term cost of taxation. However, some of the other results go against the intuition of Hamermesh (as quoted above) and Ehrenberg and Oaxaca (as quoted in the introduction). An increase in the frequency of layoffs, λ, increases t but lowers c, while an increase in the probability of no recall, θ (equivalently, an increase in the average duration of unemployment), has an ambiguous effect on t but also lowers c.[16] Since U^* is increasing in λ and θ, other things being equal, economies with more unemployment will have *lower* benefit levels. This must be due to the fact that economies with more unemployment, even though they have a greater need for insurance, simply cannot afford to be so generous.

To pursue this in more detail, recall that the government budget equation is given by $c = zt$, where $z = (1 - U^*)/U^*$. The variable z represents the cost of insurance, in the sense that each tax dollar provides z dollars of UI benefits. Considering first the impact of layoffs on the tax rate, notice that we can always decompose $\partial t/\partial\lambda$ as

$$\frac{\partial t}{\partial\lambda} = \left.\frac{\partial t}{\partial\lambda}\right|_{\mathrm{d}z=0} + \frac{\partial t}{\partial z}\frac{\partial z}{\partial\lambda}. \tag{13}$$

The first term on the right-hand side is the "insurance effect" of a change in the probability of layoff holding the government budget equation fixed, while the second term is the "budget effect" of a change in z resulting from a change in the economy-wide probability of layoff. Implicit differentiation with respect to λ of the first order condition (11) in the previous section, holding z constant, implies

$$\left.\frac{\partial t}{\partial\lambda}\right|_{\mathrm{d}z=0} = \Delta\beta z u'(c) > 0,$$

and so the insurance effect is always positive. Differentiating (11) with respect to z,

$$\frac{\partial t}{\partial z} = \Delta\lambda\beta[u'(c) + cu''(c)],$$

so the budget effect is of ambiguous sign. Interestingly, observe that the sign of this budget effect depends on whether the coefficient of relative risk aversion, defined by $-cu''(c)/u'(c)$, is greater than or less than unity.

We can decompose our other derivatives similarly:

$$\partial t/\partial\theta = \Delta\beta u'(1-t) + \Delta\lambda\beta[u'(c) + cu''(c)]\partial z/\partial\theta,$$

$$\partial c/\partial\lambda = \Delta z(1-\theta)\beta u'(c) + \Delta[(1-\theta)\beta u'(c) - (1-\theta\beta)tu''(1-t)]\partial z/\partial\lambda,$$

$$\partial c/\partial\theta = \Delta z\beta u'(1-t) + \Delta[(1-\theta)\beta u'(c) - (1-\theta\beta)tu''(1-t)]\partial z/\partial\theta.$$

In each case the first term represents the insurance effect, which is always positive, while the second term is the budget effect and cannot generally be signed (the analogy to the Slutsky equation is apparent). Note that if we substitute $\partial z/\partial\lambda$ and $\partial z/\partial\theta$ into these expressions we can simplify to recover the expressions for the derivatives obtained earlier, some of which we were able to sign. This is due to the fact that, in our model, sometimes one effect unambiguously dominates another; but the decomposition is nevertheless useful in general as a method for isolating and interpreting the impact of exogenous changes. The message we wish to emphasize is the following: the suggestion that economies with more unemployment ought to have higher UI benefits is not robust. Although the exact nature of the feedback from unemployment to policy will obviously depend on the particular model being studied, this suggestion is generally valid only if higher unemployment does not imply that higher taxes are required to finance a given level of per capita benefits.

5 Compensation as a Function of Duration

One feature of many actual unemployment insurance programs is that benefits are not constant over time.[17] In this section, we investigate the predictions of our model concerning this phenomenon (where to simplify the presentation we assume no intrinsic heterogeneity). Generalize the policy options to a tax and, instead of a level of compensation, a *function* relating benefits to the length of time unemployed—that is, a non-negative sequence $\{c_n\}$, where c_n is compensation paid to an agent in his nth period of unemployment. It makes sense to restrict the choice of $\{c_n\}$ by imposing the incentive constraints $c_n \leqq 1 - t$ for all n, but it will be seen that these are not binding in equilibrium. To describe the state of an agent we now specify his employment status, plus, if he is unemployed, his current duration. Let V_1 denote the expected lifetime utility of a worker who is currently employed, and now let $V_0(n)$ denote the expected lifetime utility of an agent who is currently in his nth consecutive period of unemployment. Then

$$V_1 = u(1 - t) + \beta\lambda V_0(1) + \beta(1 - \lambda)V_1, \tag{14}$$

$$V_0(n) = u(c_n) + \beta\theta V_0(n + 1) + \beta(1 - \theta)V_1, \quad n = 1, 2, \ldots. \tag{15}$$

Define the forward shift operator S as follows: $S\phi(n) = \phi(n + 1)$, for any function ϕ defined on the integers.[18] Then (15) can be written $V_0(n) = u(c_n) + \beta\theta S V_0(n) + (1 - \theta)\beta V_1$, or

$$[1 - \beta\theta S]V_0(n) = u(c_n) + (1 - \theta)\beta V_1.$$

Since $|\beta\theta| < 1$, we can invert the operator $[1 - \beta\theta S]$ to yield

$$\begin{aligned} V_0(n) &= [1 - \beta\theta S]^{-1}[u(c_n) + (1 - \theta)\beta V_1] \\ &= \sum_{j=0}^{\infty} (\theta\beta)^j u(c_{n+j}) + (1 - \theta\beta)^{-1}(1 - \theta)\beta V_1 \end{aligned} \tag{16}$$

as the solution to (15).[19] In particular, setting $n = 1$ and substituting (16) into (14), we find

$$\begin{aligned} V_1 = u(1 - t) &+ \lambda\beta \sum_{j=0}^{\infty} (\theta\beta)^j u(c_{1+j}) \\ &+ \lambda(1 - \theta\beta)^{-1}(1 - \theta)\beta^2 V_1 + (1 - \lambda)\beta V_1, \end{aligned}$$

which can be simplified to

$$(1 - \theta\beta)^{-1}(1 - \theta\beta + \lambda\beta)(1 - \beta)V_1 = u(1 - t) + \lambda\beta \sum_{n=1}^{\infty} (\theta\beta)^{n-1} u(c_n). \tag{17}$$

This represents the expected lifetime utility of the current employed as a function of the tax rate t and benefit schedule $\{c_n\}$.[20] The utility of the unemployed, of any vintage n, can now be found by substituting (17) back into (16).

Continue to let U^* be the aggregate steady state unemployment rate, and now let $U^*(n)$ denote the steady state proportion of agents who are currently in their nth period of unemployment. Then we have

$$U^*(1) = \lambda(1 - U^*) = \lambda(1 - \theta)/(1 - \theta + \lambda), \tag{18}$$

while for any $n > 1$, we have $U^*(n) = \theta U^*(n - 1)$, which implies

$$U^*(n) = \frac{\lambda(1 - \theta)\theta^{n-1}}{1 - \theta + \lambda}. \tag{19}$$

The government budget constraint still requires that total payments to all of the unemployed equal tax receipts,

$$\sum_{n=1}^{\infty} U^*(n)c_n = (1 - U^*)t,$$

which simplifies if we use (18) and (19) to

$$t = \lambda \sum_{n=1}^{\infty} \theta^{n-1}c_n. \tag{20}$$

Substituting (20) into the right-hand side of (17) gives us the welfare of the current employed as a function of the benefit schedule,

$$f(c_1, c_2, \ldots) = u\left(1 - \lambda \sum_{n=1}^{\infty} \theta^{n-1}c_n\right) + \lambda\beta \sum_{n=1}^{\infty} (\theta\beta)^{n-1}u(c_n).$$

Since f is (proportional to) the expected utility of a currently employed agent, the compensation sequence that maximizes f will be the one preferred by the median voter and therefore the majority voting equilibrium (as long as $U^* < 1/2$). This sequence is characterized by the conditions

$$\partial f/\partial c_n = -\lambda\theta^{n-1}u'(1 - t) + \lambda\theta^{n-1}\beta^n u'(c_n) \leqq 0, = \text{if } c_n > 0,$$

which can be written

$$u'(c_n) \leqq \beta^{-n}u'(1 - t), = \text{if } c_n > 0 \tag{21}$$

for all n.[21] Marginal utility increases, and therefore benefits decrease, with the duration of unemployment: $c_{n+1} \leqq c_n$, with strict inequality if $c_n > 0$. Since $\partial f/\partial c_1$ evaluated at $c_1 = 1 - t$ is negative, we conclude $c_1 < 1 - t$, and therefore $c_n < 1 - t$ for all n; thus insurance is incomplete in equilibrium, no matter how risk averse workers are. The interpretation is similar to that in the earlier model: the benefits of insurance accrue to an employed worker only in the future, while the cost of financing the current unemployed out of his wages must be paid immediately. As long as $u'(0) < \infty$, (21) also implies that there is some $N < \infty$ such that $c_n = 0$ for all $n > N$; that is, benefit eligibility runs out in finite time.

It is interesting to compare the voting equilibrium with the policy that maximizes steady state utility,

$$W = (1 - U^*)u(1 - t) + \sum_{n=1}^{\infty} U^*(n)u(c_n).$$

Using (18), (19) and (20), we find

$$(1 - \theta)^{-1}(1 - \theta + \lambda)W = u\left(1 - \lambda \sum_{n=1}^{\infty} \theta^{n-1}c_n\right) + \lambda \sum_{n=1}^{\infty} \theta^{n-1}u(c_n).$$

It is not difficult to see that W is maximized by complete insurance: $t = T$ and $c_n = 1 - T$ for all n, so once again the majority voting equilibrium does not maximize steady state utility. It is instructive to also contrast our results with Shavell and Weiss (1979). They choose as their welfare criterion the expected utility of an unemployed individual and fix $\lambda = 0$, but these differences are immaterial at present. The critical difference is that they posit a government budget constraint of the form

$$\sum_{n=1}^{\infty} \theta^n(1 + R)^{-n}c_n = B, \tag{22}$$

where R is the real interest rate and $B > 0$ is exogenous.

This constraint indicates that the expected present value of payments to a newly unemployed agent must equal some constant—but taxes are not required to raise the revenue. The policy that maximizes V_1 subject to (22) obviously sets $t = 0$, and sets c_n to satisfy

$$\lambda\beta^n u'(c_n) = \mu(1 + R)^{-n},$$

where μ is the Lagrange multiplier for their budget constraint. Since they consider only the case where $\beta = (1 + R)^{-1}$, this implies constant benefits: $c_n = c$ for all n. From the budget equation we can solve for the constant benefit level, $c = B(1 + R - \theta)/\theta$. The difference in our model is therefore the fact that we are assuming that the government must raise the revenue to pay for UI benefits by taxation. In deciding among feasible policy options, our electorate takes account of the fact that more generous benefit levels for the unemployed must be accompanied by higher taxes on the employed.[22]

We now analyze the effects of changes in the underlying parameters. First, observe that for any $c_n > 0$, equation (21) can be written $c_n = g(\beta^{-n}u'(1 - t))$, where the function g is defined by $g^{-1}(\cdot) = u'(\cdot)$, which implies $g' < 0$. From the budget equation (20) we define the implicit function

$$H(t, \beta, \lambda, \theta) = t - \lambda \sum_{n=1}^{N} \theta^{n-1} g(\beta^{-n} u'(1 - t)) = 0$$

where the upper limit in the summation, N, is the last n for which c_n is positive. Differentiating,

$$H_t = 1 + \lambda \sum [\theta^{n-1} g'(\cdot) \beta^{-n} u''(\cdot)] > 0,$$

$$H_\beta = \lambda \sum [\theta^{n-1} g'(\cdot) u'(\cdot) n \beta^{-n-1}] < 0,$$

$$H_\lambda = -\sum \theta^{n-1} g(\cdot) < 0,$$

$$H_\theta = -\lambda \sum (n - 1) \theta^{n-2} g(\cdot) < 0,$$

and so by the implicit function theorem we conclude

$$\partial t / \partial \beta = -H_\beta / H_t > 0,$$

$$\partial t / \partial \lambda = -H_\lambda / H_t > 0,$$

$$\partial t / \partial \theta = -H_\theta / H_t > 0.$$

When benefits are positive, $c_n = g(\beta^{-n} u'(1 - t))$, we can also determine the following effects:[23]

$$\partial c_n / \partial \beta = -g'(\cdot)[n \beta^{-n-1} u'(\cdot) + \beta^{-n} u''(\cdot) \partial t / \partial \beta]?$$

$$\partial c_n / \partial \lambda = -g'(\cdot) \beta^{-n} u''(\cdot) \partial t / \partial \lambda < 0,$$

$$\partial c_n / \partial \theta = -g'(\cdot) \beta^{-n} u''(\cdot) \partial t / \partial \theta < 0.$$

Finally we work out a simple example. Suppose $u(x) = \ln(x)$; then $u'(x) \to \infty$ as $x \to 0$, so we know $c_n > 0$ for all n. Thus (21) holds with equality and can be rearranged to yield $c_n = \beta^n(1 - t)$, a special case of the general result $c_n = g(\beta^{-n} u'(1 - t))$. Substituting c_n into the budget equation and simplifying we have

$$t = \frac{\lambda \beta}{1 - \theta \beta + \lambda \beta}.$$

Therefore the equilibrium compensation function is given by

$$c_n = \frac{(1 - \theta \beta) \beta^n}{1 - \theta \beta + \lambda \beta}.$$

If we restrict ourselves to constant compensation as in previous sections for comparison, $c_n = c$ for all n, the equilibrium can be determined to have the same tax rate and a benefit level of

$$c = \frac{(1 - \theta)\beta}{1 - \theta\beta + \lambda\beta}.$$

Notice $c_n > c$ for low n, but since $c_n \to 0$ as $n \to \infty$, we see that $c_n < c$ for large n. Hence, when we allow benefits to depend on duration they become concentrated at the beginning of unemployment spells.

6 Summary and Conclusions

We have constructed a dynamic economic model in which there are no aggregate risk, adverse selection, moral hazard, or monitoring problems. In this model we have shown how different individuals prefer different UI benefit levels, or duration-benefit schedules, and taxes. This led us to characterize the majority voting equilibrium for our economy, selecting the feasible policy preferred by the median voter and reflecting his intrinsic future employment opportunities as well as his current employment status. An explanation for the public (vis-à-vis private) provision of UI, based exclusively on its redistributive roles, was suggested. Even in the special case where agents are intrinsically identical there is an inescapable heterogeneity due to changing individual conditions over time, implying that a dynamic majority will maintain incomplete insurance perpetually and steady state welfare will not be maximized. Finally, we analyzed the effects on the endogenously determined policy of changes in the underlying parameters of the model.

At this point one might well ask if, since the equilibrium policy reflects democratic choice, the status quo is to be approved of. Should we be in favor of a democratic or some other solution, perhaps the steady state welfare maximizing solution? It is difficult to answer such questions objectively; to recall the words of Hamermesh in the opening paragraph, these seem to be issues that inherently involve value judgements. We have attempted to make explicit the nature of these value judgements, without having definitive answers. But from a different perspective, perhaps one of the contributions of the analysis is to provide a positive rather than normative discussion of the endogenous determination of UI policy, based here on voting. This allows us to make predictions about the policy that *will* occur in equilibrium without taking a stand on what *should* occur. Of course, one still has to ask if the model is reasonable. One critic of an earlier version (the version contained in Wright 1985) argued along the following line: "A first impression is that the voting, which is crucial to the model, does not correspond to anything taking place in reality."

While obviously citizens do not literally vote for tax or benefit schedules in actual elections, it is clear that UI policy (and economic policy more generally) is ultimately shaped by political forces reflecting their preferences. It is also pretty clear that agents with different intrinsic employment possibilities will have different stakes in the UI system, and political opinion must reflect the distribution of opportunities. But the following phenomenon has also been observed. Two friends, Ken and Vince, work in the same town and have virtually the identical education, abilities, and as far as anyone can tell, preferences. Apparently due to nothing more than bad luck, last year Vince was laid off while Ken and the majority of others in town were not. Vince lamented that he was having trouble surviving on the reduced income provided by his UI benefits, while Ken was fond of pointing out the generosity of compensation and the fact that his taxes were already sufficiently high. Ken has since been laid off, and is now of the revised opinion that both tax and benefit levels ought to be increased, but Vince has since been recalled and is now unable to help Ken campaign for UI reform.

So at least among my friends, there seems to be something to this dynamic heterogeneity—as well as the more obvious intrinsic heterogeneity—captured in the present model. Hence, it can be argued that the formalization does provide reasonable insights into the dynamic political views shaping policymaking. Several extensions suggest themselves. It would be relatively easy to allow different workers to have different wages while employed. More difficult but potentially more interesting, one might incorporate some non-trivial search behavior or a genuine leisure–labor tradeoff in order to study the interaction between the incentive and redistributive effects of UI, or one might attempt to analyze a model with aggregate disturbances (a business cycle). Other generalizations can be imagined. This project has intentionally avoided these complications in order to focus clearly on the redistributive roles of unemployment insurance, to study the various factors that determine individual attitudes, and to analyze the implications of these factors for democratically determined policy in a reasonably simple model.

Notes

Many of the ideas in this chapter were suggested in discussions with Gary Wright. I would also like to thank the following people for comments and suggestions: Dan Hamermesh, George Jakubson, Nick Kiefer, Lars Muus, Uri Possen, Bob Hutchens, Dan Usher, and participants in seminars at Cornell, George Washington, Toronto, the Federal Reserve Bank of Minneapolis, and at the 1986 Canadian Economics Association meetings in Winnipeg. Two anonymous referees also provided some very helpful input. As usual, of course, responsibility for any errors rests exclusively with the author.

1. The model developed here actually applies to any type of public insurance program where a "loss" involves a spell in a bad state (like unemployment, sickness, or disability), and not simply an instantaneous event (like a fire). The reason for *public* insurance, as opposed to private market insurance, is not always made explicit in the literature: often complete insurance markets are simply ruled out, with a vague appeal to moral hazard or monitoring problems. We will argue below that a public UI system with non-trivial implications for welfare can arise even if there are complete markets in the economy.

2. This is not to argue that the incentive effects of UI are unimportant. These have been analyzed extensively elsewhere in the literature. A representative sample of theoretical work includes Feldstein (1976), Baily (1977a), Mortensen (1977, 1983), Grossman (1980), Burdett and Hool (1979, 1983), and Burdett and Wright (1986). Ehrenberg and Oaxaca (1976), Feldstein (1978), Topel and Welch (1980), Topel (1983), Solon (1985), and some of the work of the Katz (1977) volume provide examples of empirical work. Wright and Loberg (1985) have looked at how UI influences the distribution of income in the sense of affecting employment and wages differently for high and low wage workers. Boadway and Oswald (1983) have looked at UI as a tool for redistributing income in the absence of lump sum taxation. The analysis here, which will emphasize voting, is closer to Meltzer and Richard's (1981) model of the size of government (see Atkinson and Stiglitz 1980, section 13–2 also), but here risk aversion and not incentive effects will play a critical part. The "socialization of commodities" literature, due to Usher (1977), Wilson and Katz (1983), and others, is also quite relevant, as we will discuss further below.

3. For an individual who has just been laid off, the probability of being unemployed for a duration of n periods is given by $\text{prob}(D = n) = (1 - \theta)\theta^{n-1}$. Hence,

$$ED = (1 - \theta) \sum_{n=1}^{\infty} n\theta^{n-1} = 1/(1 - \theta).$$

4. One can interpret this as a dynamic "reduced form" version of Feldstein's (1976) temporary layoff model, or as a special case of the job search model described in Sargent (forthcoming) or in Wright (1986), in which agent (λ, θ) has layoff rate λ and the trivial offer distribution

$$w = (0, 1) \quad \text{with probability } (\theta, 1 - \theta).$$

Mortensen (1983) explores this fundamental connection between the temporary layoff and search paradigms in more detail.

5. As long as $c \leqq 1 - t$ the UI system causes no distortions, so there are no incentive effects to worry about. Note that the typical UI system operating in actual economies is financed by a payroll tax on employers, and not a tax on workers. One can think of this as a payroll tax that is fully shifted, either backward via lower wages or forward via higher prices, so that the net result will be an equilibrium real wage of $1 - t$. Also, it does not matter that benefits are not taxed here (as it does in some models); imposing a tax on c and then raising c to keep the net consumption of the unemployed the same is neutral.

6. Each V_j can be thought of as an indirect utility function of the parameters t and c. It is not difficult to show that each V_j can be written

$$V_j(\lambda, \theta) = \pi_j(\lambda, \theta)\frac{u(c)}{1-\beta} + [1 - \pi_j(\lambda, \theta)]\frac{u(1-t)}{1-\beta},$$

where $0 < \pi_1(\lambda, \theta) < \pi_*(\lambda, \theta) < \pi_0(\lambda, \theta) < 1$. Therefore, each V_j is a weighted average of the utility of being unemployed forever and the utility of being employed forever.

7. As Meltzer and Richard (1981) point out, "the analysis explains why the size of government [here, the level of benefits] and the tax rate can remain constant yet be criticized by an overwhelming majority of citizens. The reason is that at the voting equilibrium nearly everyone [except the median voter] prefers a different outcome" (p. 925).

8. Note that $t_*(\lambda, \theta)$ is actually a function only of $U^*(\lambda, \theta)$, and not λ and θ individually.

9. This is clearly related to Arrow's (1971) theorem that says risk averse agents will always take a positive (but potentially small) part of a favorable bet.

10. The condition $u'(x) \to \infty$ as $x \to 0$ always guarantees $t_*(\lambda, \theta) > 0$.

11. The idea that public UI might be voted in by the median voter even if private insurance is available is similar to the analysis of the "socialization of commodities" by Usher (1977). He defines a commodity as being socialized when the "government appropriates the whole supply by purchase or by production in the public sector and reallocates the supply among consumers equally or according to some other nonpecuniary criterion" (p. 151). With progressive taxation people with income below the mean pay less than their proportional shares of the cost and hence tend to favor socialization, although heterogeneous preferences can complicate this. See also Wilson and Katz (1983) and the references contained therein.

12. Kydland and Prescott (1977) discuss in detail, and provide some classic examples of, time inconsistency. Similar issues of time heterogeneity come up in overlapping generations models, which is what makes the notion of optimality so intriguing in (especially stochastic version of) those models, and which also has potentially important consequences for voting behavior; see Loewy (1986), and on a related point, see Townley (1981).

13. One way out of this dilemma would *seem* to be a stipulation that agents are not eligible for benefits until after they have worked for some number of periods. This would mean that when UI is first introduced the current unemployed receive no benefits, and hence are not subsidized by the current employed. The problem is that in each future period the current employed would vote in favor of a proposal to re-initialize the system and declare the current unemployed ineligible, with a promise (that cannot be kept) that it will not happen again. This is a serious time inconsistency problem, quite similar to those discussed by Kydland and Prescott. To avoid the quagmire introduced by these strategic considerations, here we have restricted attention to tax-benefit policies that are constant across agents and over time. In section 5 we generalize the model somewhat by allowing benefits to vary according to the length of time an agent has been unemployed.

14. Flemming's (1978) analysis of optimal unemployment insurance, when applied to an economy of homogeneous agents, also uses V^* as the social welfare function (consider his eq. 30 in his "uniform case"). Baily's (1977b) and (1978) model uses the expected utility of an employed individual, which makes good sense since he only considers two-period economies where everyone is employed in the first period. His first best solution implies complete insurance because his agents do not discount. Shavell and Weiss (1979), whose work is discussed further in section 5, use the expected utility of an unemployed individual as their welfare function. This makes sense in their model because they assume the expected discounted value of benefits is exogenous (and *not* related to taxes on workers) and jobs, once found, are never lost; hence, the employed have no stake in their UI system. Their first best solution (with no borrowing) also implies full insurance in the relevant sense.

15. Note that in this section we are mainly concerned with the impact of an increase in λ or θ for *all* agents in the economy. This is to be contrasted with the derivatives examined in the previous section, which described the effect of drawing a higher λ or θ from a fixed population.

16. The ambiguity in the sign of $\partial t/\partial\theta$ is not just apparent; simple (quadratic) examples can be constructed in which it is positive and in which it is negative. However, using algebra similar to that in the next two paragraphs in the text, it is not difficult to verify that a straightforward sufficient condition for $\partial t/\partial\theta > 0$ is that the coefficient of relative risk aversion, defined by $-cu''(c)/u'(c)$, be greater than unity.

17. For instance, although the rules differ from state to state, in the U.S. basic coverage typically runs out after 26 weeks, beyond which extended benefits may be available depending on economic conditions. Often there is also a waiting period after a layoff before compensation begins.

18. The forward shift operator S is the inverse of the lag operator L discussed at length in Sargent's (1979) textbook (among many other places).

19. This is the stationary solution to (15); non-stationary solutions can be ruled out here since we know V_1 is bounded. Formally, the inverse of $[1 - \beta\theta S]$ has been expanded in a Neuman series; see Naylor and Sell (1982), Section 5.8.

20. Notice that we could write V_1 as a weighted average of the utilities of being in each state for all time, as was the case for each of the V_j in note 6.

21. The simplicity of condition (21) is an implication of rational expectations: the subjective probabilities used in calculating expected utility cancel with the objective probabilities that enter the budget constraint through the steady state unemployment rates.

22. Shavell and Weiss also study the case where the agent has some control (which cannot be monitored) over the probability of moving from unemployment to employment, and find that compensation ought to decline with duration to encourage a quick escape. In another case where unemployed agents have no control over the probability but start with some initial wealth and have access to credit markets, they conclude that compensation should increase with duration. The point here is not to suggest that the declining benefit schedule derived in the text will arise in all dynamic models; rather, we simply wish to point out that the democratically chosen policy can differ from what has been described as optimal in this more general framework, as well as in the simpler model of section 3.

23. It is perhaps surprising that $\partial c_n/\partial\beta$ cannot be signed. It may be shown that $\partial c_n/\partial\beta > 0 \Rightarrow \partial c_k/\partial\beta > 0$ if $k > n$. Also, since a higher β increases taxes, c_n must increase for some n. Hence, a higher β can reduce c_n for at most the first M values of n, where M is some finite number (possibly zero). Examples exist in which $\partial c_n/\partial\beta < 0$ for the first few n.

References

Arrow, Kenneth. 1971. *Essays in the theory of risk bearing.* Chicago: Markham.

Atkinson, Anthony, and Stiglitz, Joseph. 1980. *Lectures on public economics.* New York: McGraw-Hill.

Bailey, Martin. 1977a. On the theory of layoffs and unemployment. *Econometrica* 45:1043–1063.

Baily, Martin. 1977b. Unemployment insurance as insurance for workers. *Industrial and Labor Relations Review* 30:495–504.

Baily, Martin. 1978. Some aspects of optimal unemployment insurance. *Journal of Public Economics* 10:379–402.

Boadway, Robin, and Oswald, Andrew. 1983. Unemployment insurance and redistributive taxation. *Journal of Public Economics*. 20:193–210.

Burdett, Kenneth, and Hool, Bryce. 1979. Temporary layoffs and the unemployment insurance system. SSRI working paper 7904, University of Wisconsin, Madison.

Burdett, Kenneth, and Hool, Bryce. 1983. Layoffs, wages and unemployment insurance. *Journal of Public Economics* 21:325–357.

Burdett, Kenneth, and Wright, Randall. 1986. The effects of unemployment insurance on layoffs, hours per worker, and wages. Cornell University Department of Economics working paper no. 363.

Easley, D., Kiefer, N., and Possen, Uri. 1985. An equilibrium analysis of optimal unemployment insurance and taxation. *Quarterly Journal of Economics* 100, Supplement, 989–1010.

Ehrenberg, Ronald, and Oaxaca, Ronald. 1976. Unemployment insurance, duration of unemployment, and subsequent wage gain. *American Economic Review* 66:754–766.

Feldstein, Martin. 1976. Temporary layoffs in the theory of unemployment. *Journal of Political Economy* 84:937–957.

Feldstein, Martin. 1978. The effect of unemployment insurance on temporary layoff unemployment. *American Economic Review* 68: 834–846.

Flemming, John. 1978. Aspects of optimal unemployment insurance: Search, leisure, savings and capital market imperfections. *Journal of Public Economics* 10:403–425.

Grossman, Herschel. 1980. Risk shifting, unemployment insurance and layoffs. In Zmira Hornstein, Joseph Grice, and Alfred Webb, eds., *The economics of the labour market*. London: HMSO. 259–277.

Hamermesh, Daniel. 1977. *Jobless pay and the economy*. Baltimore: Johns Hopkins University Press.

Katz, Arnold, ed. 1977. The economics of unemployment insurance: A symposium. *Industrial and Labor Relations Review* 30.

Kydland, Finn, and Prescott, Edward. 1977. Rules rather than discretion: The inconsistency of optimal plans. *Journal of Political Economy* 85:473–491. Reprinted as chapter 1 in volume 1 of this work.

Loewy, Michael. 1986. An overlapping generations model with voting. Manuscript, George Washington University.

Meltzer, Alan, and Richard, Scott. 1981. A rational theory of the size of government. *Journal of Political Economy* 89:914–927. Reprinted as chapter 8 in the current volume of this work.

Mortensen, Dale. 1977. Unemployment insurance and job search decisions. *Industrial and Labor Relations Review* 30:507–517.

Mortensen, Dale. 1983. A welfare analysis of unemployment insurance: Variations on second best themes. *Carnegie-Rochester Series on Public Policy* 19:67–98.

Naylor, Arch, and Sell, George. 1982. *Linear operator theory in engineering and science*. New York: Springer-Verlag.

Sargent, Thomas. 1979. *Macroeconomic theory*. New York: Academic Press.

Sargent, Thomas. Forthcoming. *Dynamic macroeconomic analysis*. New York: Academic Press.

Shavell, Steven, and Weiss, Laurence. 1979. The optimal payment of unemployment insurance benefits over time. *Journal of Political Economy* 87:1347–1362.

Solon, Gary. 1985. Work incentive effects of taxing unemployment benefits. *Econometrica* 53: 295–306.

Topel, Robert. 1983. On layoffs and unemployment insurance. *American Economic Review* 73:541–559.

Topel, Robert, and Welch, Finis. 1980. Unemployment insurance: Survey and extensions. *Economica* 47:351–379.

Townley, Peter. 1981. Public choice and the social insurance paradox: A note. *Canadian Journal of Economics* 14:712–717.

Usher, Dan. 1977. The welfare economics of the socialization of commodities. *Journal of Public Economics* 8:151–168.

Wilson, L., and Katz, Michael. 1983. The socialization of commodities. *Journal of Public Economics* 20: 347–356.

Wright, Randall. 1985. Unemployment insurance and the dynamics of voting. Cornell University Department of Economics working paper no. 340.

Wright, Randall. 1986. Job search and cyclical unemployment. *Journal of Political Economy* 94:38–55.

Wright, Randall, and Loberg, Janine. 1985. Unemployment insurance taxes and unemployment. Cornell University Department of Economics working paper no. 348. Forthcoming in *Canadian Journal of Economics.*

12 Mobility and Redistribution

Dennis Epple and Thomas Romer

I Introduction

The ability of people to move from one jurisdiction to another is generally seen as a constraint on the amount of redistribution that each jurisdiction within a system of governments can undertake. In this chapter, we look at this proposition by developing a positive analysis of income redistribution by local governments in a federal system. We ask how much redistribution occurs when only local governments can have tax/transfer instruments, people can move freely among jurisdictions, and voters in each jurisdiction are fully aware of the migration effects of redistributive policies.

A model must have several features to make it a useful vehicle for studying redistribution by local governments: (1) Clearly, it must have more than one locality, and households must be able to move among localities. (2) For the study of income redistribution to be interesting, the population must be heterogeneous. Thus the assumption of identical individuals used as a convenient simplification in many investigations of local governments (Courant and Rubinfeld 1978; Epple and Zelenitz 1981; Wilson 1987a; Wildasin 1988) is untenable in studies of local redistribution. (3) Redistributive decisions of localities must be endogenous. In a positive model, it is desirable that decisions of localities emerge from a collective choice process such as majority rule. In existing models of multicommunity equilibrium with voting (Westhoff 1977; Epple, Filimon, and Romer 1984), voters treat the community tax base and population as fixed when voting on the community tax-expenditure policy. This is unsatisfactory in a model focusing on the limits that mobility imposes on redistribution since one would not want results driven by the assumption of voter myopia.[1] A model of local redistribution must endow voters with greater sophistication than models to date have done, and this proves to require a different approach to analyzing voting. (4) The potential importance of differences in incentives faced by homeowners and renters has been emphasized in discussions of local governments (Oates 1986), but previous research has not provided a way of modeling the differing preferences of owners and renters.[2]

Reprinted from *Journal of Political Economy*, by permission of The University of Chicago Press. *Journal of Political Economy*, 1991, vol. 99, no. 4.

These observations lead us to develop a model of multicommunity equilibrium in which the population of each community is endogenously determined. Tax rates and levels of redistribution are chosen by majority vote of residents of each local jurisdiction. Voters anticipate changes in housing prices and the in- or out-migration that will occur in response to changes in the local tax rate and level of redistribution. We distinguish between renters and owners and show this distinction to have a central role in determining preferences for local redistribution. By bringing these features together in a single model, we not only provide a framework for studying the substantive problem of local redistribution but also broaden the set of phenomena that can be encompassed in models of equilibrium among local jurisdictions.

To provide further insight into the limits of redistribution by local governments, we use functional forms and parameters that are consistent with American data to compute equilibria. These computations illuminate the relationships among redistribution, relative community sizes, and patterns of property ownership. They also illustrate the potential usefulness of the analytical framework for further study of questions that arise in the political economy of systems of governments.

This paper draws on several previous lines of research. Important early discussions of the subject of redistribution in a federal system may be found in Stigler (1957) and Oates (1972). They emphasize that mobility of households is likely to undermine attempts by local governments to redistribute income. More recent contributions by Oates (1977) and Ladd and Doolittle (1982) point to migration as the central issue in the normative evaluation of which level of government should undertake redistribution.[3] A positive analysis of redistribution by local governments under direct democracy is offered by Brown and Oates (1987). Following Orr (1976), they emphasize concern by the wealthy for the poor as the factor giving rise to income redistribution policies. The alternative approach, adopted here, treats income redistribution as an outcome of majority rule with self-interested voters. In following this approach, the chapter builds on the work of Romer (1975) and Meltzer and Richard (1981). Altruism may be important in practice. In this chapter, however, we are concerned with identifying the prospects for redistribution even when altruism is absent. Rather, the motives for redistribution, if any, emerge from the majoritarian nature of the political process. The political side of the model abstracts from explicit consideration of the role of bureaucrats or politicians in determining levels of redistribution. Again, such influences may be important in practice, but valuable insights can be obtained without the complications introduced by attempting to model these influences. As to the analysis of equilibrium among local jurisdictions, this chapter extends the work of B. Ellickson (1971), Westhoff (1977), Rose-Ackerman (1979), and Epple, Filimon, and Romer (1984).[4]

In Sections II and III, we present the model, define equilibrium, and establish some of its properties. We develop a computational model in Section IV and present results based on it. We make some concluding observations in Section V.

II The Model

Our framework is a two-good, many-community model with a continuum of households. The local government in each community imposes a tax proportional to the value of property and divides the proceeds equally among the residents of the community. The tax rate of each jurisdiction is endogenously determined, as well as the population and tax base of each community. The two goods in the model are housing and a composite good. Thus communities do not supply a distinct local public good; the good they distribute is a perfect substitute for the composite commodity.

The model is sufficiently general to allow a locality to be thought of simply as one of a system of jurisdictions among which households are free to migrate. One natural interpretation is that the locality is one of several municipalities in a metropolitan area. For convenience we shall refer to the collection of localities as a metropolitan area, but it should be understood that the model is not limited to this interpretation. For example, one may think of subunits of a nation among which households are free to locate.

More specifically, consider a metropolitan area inhabited by a continuum of households. There are two goods: housing, h, and a numeraire bundle, b. All households have the same strictly quasi-concave, twice continuously differentiable utility function, $U(h, b)$. We assume that both commodities are normal goods. Households differ only in their endowed income y. The distribution of income over all communities is characterized by a continuous density function $f(y)$, with support $[0, M]$.

A look at U.S. data reveals that once boundaries dividing the land area of a region among a set of local jurisdictions are drawn, they are rarely redrawn (Epple and Romer 1989b). Hence, we assume that the homogeneous land in the metropolitan area is divided among J jurisdictions, each of which has fixed boundaries.

Jurisdictions may differ in the amount of land contained within their boundaries. Each jurisdiction may impose a proportional tax, t, on the value of housing and use the proceeds to pay a lump sum, g, to each resident. Hence, the budget constraint faced by a household with income y located in community j is

$$y + g^j = p^j h + b,$$

where p^j is the gross-of-tax price in community j. From now on, the household with income y will be named y.

From a household's viewpoint, a community is characterized by the grant/housing price pair (g, p). For given g and p, the utility of a household is given by the indirect utility function V:

$$V(p, g, y) = U(h(p, y + g), y + g - ph(p, y + g)). \tag{1}$$

On the right-hand side of (1), $h(p, y + g)$ is y's demand function for housing, capturing the way consumption of housing services responds to changes in the gross-of-tax price of housing and gross-of-grant income. With the assumption that housing is a normal good, y's indifference curves in the (g, p) plane are upward sloping:

$$\left.\frac{dp}{dg}\right|_{V=\bar{V}} = -\frac{\partial V/\partial g}{\partial V/\partial p} = \frac{1}{h(p, y + g)} > 0. \tag{2}$$

The slope of an indifference curve through a point (g, p) decreases with y:

$$\frac{\partial(dp/dg|_{V=\bar{V}})}{\partial y} = -\frac{1}{[h(p, y + g)]^2} h_2 < 0, \tag{3}$$

where h_2 is the derivative of $h(\cdot)$ with respect to its second argument. (Since housing is a normal good, h_2 is positive.)

We define *equilibrium* in the system of communities as an allocation such that

1. all communities are in internal equilibrium; that is, within each community
a) the housing market clears,
b) the community budget is in balance, and
c) there is a majority rule voting equilibrium, and
2. no one wants to move.

We begin by developing the implications of part 2 of this definition. The requirement that no one wishes to move is natural in any static model of residential location. With costless mobility, a household's locational choice must maximize $V(p^j, g^j, y)$ over $j = 1, \ldots, J$.

Consider two points (g^i, p^i) and (g^j, p^j) such that $g^j > g^i$. Then (2) and (3) imply that

$$V(p^i, g^i, y) \geq V(p^j, g^j, y) \Rightarrow V(p^i, g^i, y') > V(p^j, g^j, y') \quad \text{for } y' > y \tag{4a}$$

and

$$V(p^i, g^i, y) \leq V(p^j, g^j, y) \Rightarrow V(p^i, g^i, y') < V(p^j, g^j, y') \quad \text{for } y' < y. \tag{4b}$$

This ordering of preferences by income means that locational equilibrium generates considerable structure on community characteristics.[5] These are summarized in the following proposition. (The proposition follows readily from the properties of $V(\cdot)$. For more details, see Epple, Filimon, and Romer 1984).

PROPOSITION 1 Consider an allocation in which no two communities have the same housing price. Necessary conditions for such an allocation to be one in which no one wishes to move to another community follow:

a) Stratification Each community is formed of households with incomes in a single interval. If y and y' live in the same community, with $y' > y$, then $y'' \in [y, y']$ also lives in that community.

b) Boundary indifference Communities can be ordered from lowest to highest income levels. When they are ordered this way, there is a "boundary" income between two successive communities. The "border" household (i.e., one with the boundary income) between any two adjacent communities is indifferent between the communities.

c) Decreasing bundles If y^i is the highest income in community i and y^j is the highest income in community j, then, in equilibrium, $p^i < p^j$ and $g^i < g^j$ if $y^i > y^j$.

Proposition 1 focuses on allocations in which no two communities have the same housing price. Next, we consider allocations in which this is not so, that is, allocations in which at least one pair of communities has the same housing price. For such an allocation to be an equilibrium, it must be the case that any two communities with the same housing price also have the same grant, g. Otherwise, all households would prefer the member of the pair with the higher g. Hence, in equilibrium, households will be indifferent between two communities with the same housing price. Thus to generalize proposition 1 to the case in which more than one community has the same price, assign all communities with the same price to a group. Proposition 1 then applies, with "community group" replacing "community" in the statement of the proposition. The population will be stratified across community groups, but there is no necessary stratification within community groups. There is no loss of generality, however, for the analysis that follows in assuming that households are stratified within community groups as well. For convenience, we shall adopt this convention.

Part *a* of proposition 1 implies that redistributive taxation will induce sorting by income groups. Part *c* predicts that redistributive expenditure per household will be inversely related to household income in a comparison across communities. These are precisely the outcomes hypothesized by Oates (1977, p. 5): "An aggressive policy to redistribute income from the rich to the poor in a particular locality may, in the end, simply chase the relatively wealthy to other jurisdictions and attract those with low incomes."

By condition *a* of proposition 1, in any equilibrium the total population must be partitioned into a set of single-interval communities. We shall therefore restrict our attention to such communities. Henceforth, let y^j denote the income of the household at the border between communities j and $j+1$, with $y^j < y^{j+1}$, and let $y^0 = 0$ and $y^J = M$. From part *b* of the proposition it must be the case that

$$V(p^j, g^j, y^j) = V(p^{j+1}, g^{j+1}, y^j), \quad j = 1, 2, \ldots, J-1. \tag{5}$$

Next, we turn to *internal equilibrium*, that is, equilibrium within a community (pt. 1 of the definition of equilibrium). We begin with the housing market. Aggregate demand in each community is determined by integrating the household demand function over the income interval of households in the community, so for community j we have

$$H_d(p^j, g^j, y^j, y^{j-1}) = \int_{y^{j-1}}^{y^j} h(p^j, y + g^j) f(y)\, dy. \tag{6}$$

We assume that the housing supply function, $H_s^j(p_h^j)$, for a community with fixed land area is continuous and strictly increasing for $p_h \geq 0$, for all $j = 1, \ldots, J$. The gross-of-tax price of housing is determined by the identity

$$p^j = p_h^j(1 + t^j). \tag{7}$$

In equilibrium the housing market must clear:

$$H_d(p^j, g^j, y^j, y^{j-1}) = H_s^j(p_h^j). \tag{8}$$

It is also necessary that the community's budget balance:

$$g^j \int_{y^{j-1}}^{y^j} f(y)\,dy = t^j p_h^j H_s^j(p_h^j). \tag{9}$$

Voting on Local Grants

Finally, we need to characterize the way that public-sector choices are determined in each community. We assume that the (t, g) pair in each community is chosen by majority rule. In each community, voters assume that the (t, g) pairs in all other communities are fixed. Since we are interested in the limits to redistribution in the face of mobility among jurisdictions, we assume that voters are sophisticated about the impact of taxes and grants in their community. They recognize two types of effects of changing (t, g) in their own community. First, changing taxes and transfers affect housing prices and, hence, housing consumption of current inhabitants. Second, a change in the (t, g) pair in the community (given policies in other jurisdictions) will induce migration into or out of the community.

Let $t^{-k} = (t^1, \ldots, t^{k-1}, t^{k+1}, \ldots, t^J)$ and $g^{-k} = (g^1, \ldots, g^{k-1}, g^{k+1}, \ldots, g^J)$. The alternatives facing voters in community k when other communities' tax-transfer policies are (t^{-k}, g^{-k}) are defined as follows: (i) equations (5)–(8) hold for all communities, and (ii) community k's budget is in balance; that is, equation (9) holds for community k. Together, parts i and ii determine a relationship between the gross-of-tax housing price p^k and the feasible levels of the grant g^k perceived by the voters in community k, given (t^{-k}, g^{-k}). We shall call this relationship the *redistribution possibility frontier* (RPF).

For a given community, a point (g^*, p^*) is a majority voting equilibrium if and only if it is on the community's RPF and there is no point on the RPF strictly preferred to (g^*, p^*) by a majority of the community's residents. In general, neither voter indifference curves in the (g, p) plane nor the RPF will be concave or convex. Consequently, voters' preferences over points on the RPF (and, effectively, over tax-transfer policies) will not be single-peaked. In the absence of single-peakedness, it is usually the case that majority voting equilibrium fails to exist: voting cycles occur. An attractive feature of this model, however, is that we can show the existence of voting equilibrium even without single-peaked preferences.[6]

PROPOSITION 2 A point on the community RPF that maximizes the utility of the median-income voter in the community is a majority voting equilibrium.

To prove the proposition, consider an arbitrary community. Suppose that the point (g^*, p^*) in figure 12.1 is a point on the community RPF that maximizes the utility of the median-income voter in the community. Let $\bar{V}^*$ be the indifference curve of the median-income voter through this point. There are no points on the community RPF anywhere in region A of figure 12.1. The existence of such a point would contradict the assumption that (g^*, p^*) is a point on the community RPF that maximizes the utility of the median-income voter. Thus points on the community RPF must fall in regions B and C or on their boundaries.

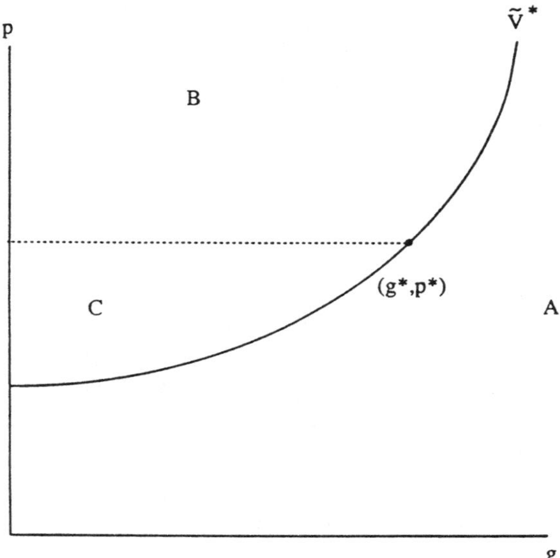

Figure 12.1

We can apply (4a) and (4b) to comparisons of points within a single community. By (4a), all voters with incomes greater than the median, $\bar{y}$, strictly prefer (g^*, p^*) to any other point within region B or on its boundary.[7] Since the median-income voter will also vote for (g^*, p^*) over any other point within or on the boundary of region B, a majority will vote for (g^*, p^*) over any other point within or on the boundary of region B. Similarly, by (4b), all voters with incomes less than $\bar{y}$ strictly prefer (g^*, p^*) to any other point within or on the boundary of region C. Thus a majority will vote for (g^*, p^*) over any other point within or on the boundary of region C. Thus no point on the community RPF is preferred to (g^*, p^*) by a majority, and so (g^*, p^*) is a majority voting equilibrium.[8] Q.E.D.

The analysis thus far has established sufficient conditions for a proposed allocation to satisfy our definition of equilibrium. With the results in propositions 1 and 2 combined, an allocation is an equilibrium if it satisfies stratification, boundary indifference, decreasing bundles, and, within each community, the allocation yields a (g, p) pair that is a point on the community RPF that maximizes the utility of the median-income voter in the community. These results thus embody the implications of our definition of equilibrium in the context of the model we are studying.

An Aside on Voter Myopia

We have taken voters to be quite sophisticated in their assumption about how others adjust. Had we assumed myopic voters, the analysis of voting in a pure redistribution context would not be particularly illuminating. Suppose that voters take no account of adjustments in aggregate housing demand, from either current residents or possible migrants. This means that, when voting, they take p_h as fixed and assume that the aggregate housing stock stays constant at H and community population at N. The perceived community budget constraint then is $tp_hH = Ng$, so that the perceived RPF is given by

$$p = p_h + \frac{Ng}{H} = p_h + \frac{g}{\bar{h}},$$

where $\bar{h}$ is average perceived housing consumption. The perceived RPF is linear with slope $1/\bar{h}$. As an illustration of voting outcomes, consider the case in which $U(h, b)$ is homothetic, so that the income elasticity of demand for housing equals one. Then for income distributions skewed the usual way, the housing consumption of the median-income voter, $\bar{h}$, is less than the average housing consumption, $\bar{h}$. For any pair (g, p), the slope of the decisive voter's indifference curve $(1/h)$ is greater than the slope of the perceived RPF at that (g, p), which is $1/\bar{h}$. This implies that any value of g would be defeated by a higher value: no voting equilibrium would exist. Or if there were an arbitrary limit set on the magnitude of g, the voting equilibrium would occur at that limit. With more general preferences, nonextreme values of g could be equilibria only in the unlikely case in which $\tilde{h} \geq \bar{h}$.

One might foresee other formulations with voter myopia. For example, voters might be assumed to take community population as fixed when making their assessments of the effects of changing the community tax rate. Any such characterization of voter myopia is inherently arbitrary. To guard against the possibility that some such arbitrary assumption about myopia might drive our results, we have opted for a formulation in which voters correctly anticipate the consequences of changes in their community's tax-grant package.

A Two-Community Illustration of Equilibrium

A two-community example will serve to clarify equilibrium in the model. The opportunities facing voters in community 1 may be determined as follows. Community 1 takes the tax rate and grant (t^2, g^2) in community 2 as given. For given (t^2, g^2), the choice of a tax rate in community 1 determines prices in both communities, the population in both communities, and the grant in community 1. To see this, recall that equation (5) must be satisfied, that (7) and (8) must be satisfied in each community, and that community 1's budget must be in balance: equation (9) must hold for $j = 1$. Thus, given (t^2, g^2) and a choice of t^1, all remaining variables are determined by the equations above. By varying t^1 over the set of feasible (i.e., nonnegative) values, we can trace out the opportunities perceived by voters in community 1. Notice from the indirect utility function (1) that voters' utility depends on p and g but not on t. Voters care about t only as it affects the values of p and g that emerge.

The top half of figure 12.2 illustrates the (g^1, p^1) pairs traced out as community 1 (assumed to be the poor community) varies its tax rate over the set of feasible values. This is community 1's RPF, given (t^2, g^2). The lowest point at which the RPF intersects the vertical axis corresponds to

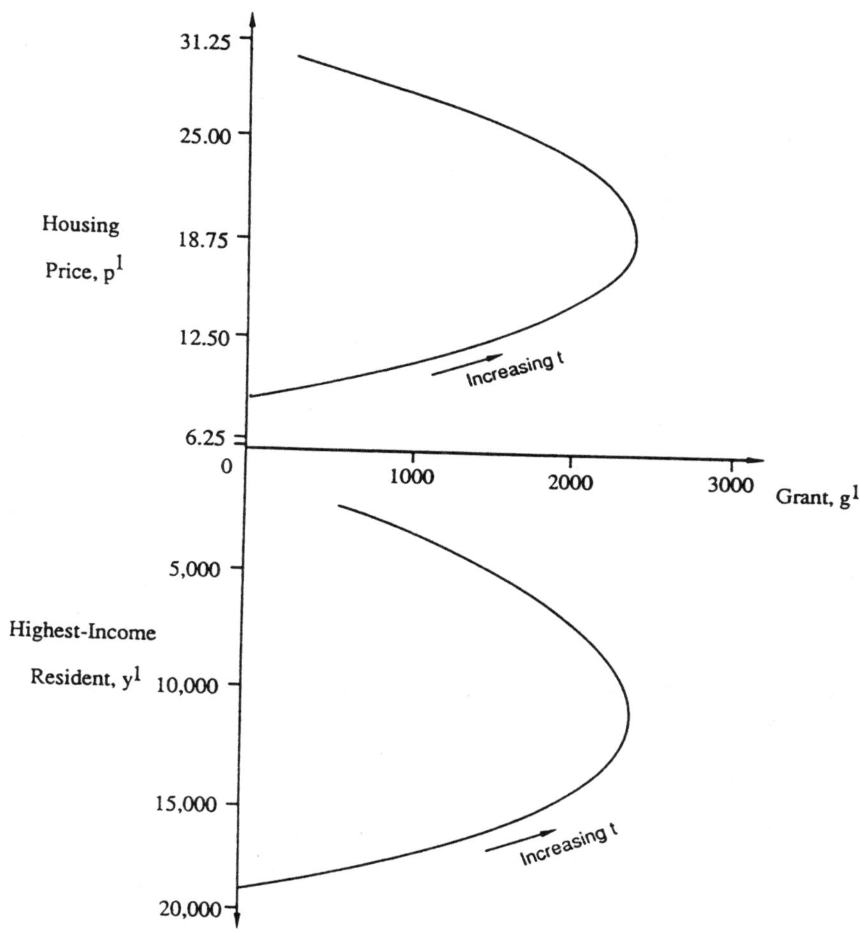

Figure 12.2
Effects of redistributive taxation in community 1 on housing prices, grant level, and migration

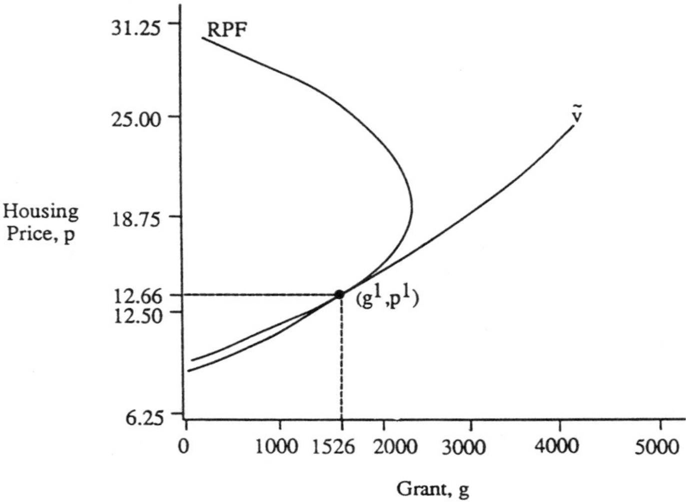

Figure 12.3
Voting equilibrium at (g^1, p^1)

$t^1 = 0$. Clearly, when $t^1 = 0$, $g^1 = 0$. As t^1 is increased, g^1 rises, and the gross-of-tax price p^1 rises. Eventually, a point is reached at which the increase in revenue from further tax increases does not offset the loss in tax base due to out-migration. At that point, the RPF in figure 12.2 begins to bend back. In general, the RPF need not be as "well behaved" as we have drawn it here and may be neither concave nor convex.

The community's housing market clears and the community's budget is in balance for all points on the community RPF. Hence, a point on the community RPF that is a majority voting equilibrium will be an internal equilibrium in the community. An example of such an equilibrium with an interior solution is shown in figure 12.3 as a point at which the indifference curve of the decisive voter in community 1, labeled $\tilde{V}$, is tangent to the RPF of community 1. (The equilibrium may, in some cases, involve a corner solution, with $g = 0$.) By proposition 2, the income of the decisive voter, $\tilde{y}^1$, is the median income in community 1.

In general, the RPF in community 1 will differ for different (t^2, g^2) pairs in community 2, and the decisive voter in community 1 will differ as well. Figure 12.4 shows a two-community equilibrium. The utility of the deci-

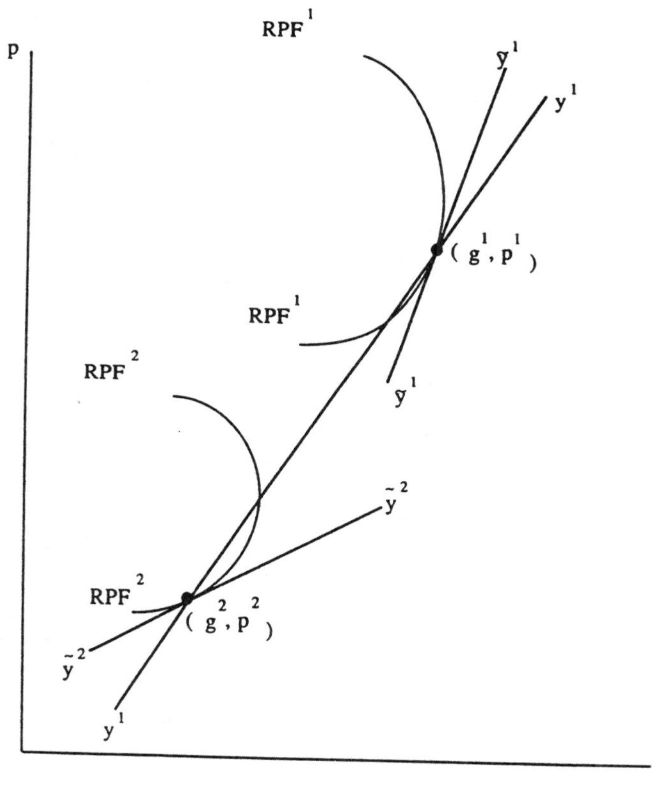

Figure 12.4
Equilibrium with two communities

sive voter $\tilde{y}^i$ is maximized over points on RPF^i. The RPF in community 1 is drawn with the (t^2, g^2) pair corresponding to (g^2, p^2) taken as given, and the RPF in community 2 is drawn with the (t^1, g^1) pair that corresponds to (g^1, p^1) taken as given. The border household is indifferent between the two communities. For this to be a two-community equilibrium, proposition 1 requires that all residents in community 1 have incomes less than y^1 and all residents in community 2 have incomes greater than or equal to y^1. If this is the case, the stratification and "decreasing bundles" conditions will be satisfied. These conditions, the "boundary indifference" condition, and internal equilibrium within each community are sufficient for the existence of a two-community equilibrium.

With more than two communities, equilibrium is determined in a similar fashion. The RPF of community j is the (g^j, p^j) frontier traced out as community j varies t^j over the set of feasible values (the nonnegative real line). Tax rates and spending levels in other communities (t^{-j}, g^{-j}) are held fixed while t^j is varied. Housing markets in all communities clear, and the budget constraint in community j is balanced for each t^j. As in the two-community case, a point on the community RPF that is a majority voting equilibrium is an internal equilibrium. An allocation that satisfies proposition 1 in which all communities are in internal equilibrium is a J-community equilibrium.

Effects of Changing Relative Land Areas

One would expect the community's RPF to expand if the community's share of metropolitan land area were increased. Expansion of the community's share of land will tend to increase its share of total population. Since community 1 in our two-community example is occupied by the low-income portion of the income distribution, expansion of its population will increase the income of the border household, y^1. It follows that the average income level of the community will rise. Ceteris paribus, this will increase the tax base per capita. In addition, an increase in the share of metropolitan land occupied by the community will increase the community's "market power," in that land outside the community becomes scarcer and housing relatively more expensive. The increase in market power provides greater latitude for the community to engage in redistributive policies.

The net effect of an increase in the share of land area depends not only on the expansion of the RPF but also on how the income of the pivotal voter changes. These effects may be offsetting. With two communities, for example, the RPF of the poor community may well expand as the community's share of land increases, making higher grants per household feasible. But, for any given (g^1, p^1, g^2, p^2), a higher fraction of the total population occupies the low-income community when that community's share of total land area increases. Thus, for any given (g^1, p^1, g^2, p^2), the income of the decisive voter increases as the community's share of total land area increases. Ceteris paribus, higher-income voters prefer lower g. As a result, although higher grants are *feasible*, the political process may limit the increase in transfers.

III The Contrasting Preferences of Owners and Renters

The discussion so far has treated all residents of local jurisdictions as renters. Rents are paid to absentee landlords who do not vote in any of the communities.[9] Suppose, by contrast, that all residents of local jurisdictions are owner-occupants. They locate in a jurisdiction and purchase housing there before participating in the voting process that determines the level of redistributive taxation. There are no transactions costs in the purchase and sale of housing. Households can adjust their level of housing consumption (i.e., sell their current house and purchase another dwelling) in response to price changes without incurring transaction costs. As in the preceding model with rental housing, households correctly anticipate how their housing consumption will change in response to a change in the price of housing induced by a change in redistributive taxation. Households also anticipate the capital gain or loss that they will incur as a result of a change in the net-of-tax price of housing induced by a change in the level of redistributive taxation.

Let h_0 be the amount of housing purchased at price $p_{h,0}$ by a household with endowed income y. When making decisions about whether to change their consumption bundle, homeowners face the budget constraint

$$y + g + (p_h - p_{h,0})h_0 = ph + b,$$

with h_0 and $p_{h,0}$ fixed. The third term on the left-hand side is the capital gain from selling the household's existing dwelling.[10] The demand function for housing for such a household is of the form

$$h = h(p, y + g + (p_h - p_{h,0})h_0).$$

Substituting this demand function into the budget constraint and substituting both into the utility function yields the indirect utility function $V(p, g, y + (p_h - p_{h,0})h_0)$. The slope of the indifference curve through a point (g, p) is

$$\left.\frac{dp}{dg}\right|_{V=\bar{V}} = \frac{1}{h} + \frac{h_0}{h}\left.\frac{dp_h}{dg}\right|_{\text{RPF}}. \tag{10}$$

In contrast to the renter case, dp/dg for a homeowner depends on the net-of-tax price of housing as well as its gross-of-tax price, because capital grains depend on p_h. In characterizing voting equilibrium when all voters are owner-occupants, we assume that dp/dg given in (10) is decreasing in y for all $p \geq 0$ and g such that p_h and dp_h/dg are defined along the RPF. It can be shown that a point on the RPF that maximizes the utility of an owner-occupant with median endowed income is a majority voting equilibrium among points such that this assumption holds (Epple and Romer 1989a, app. 1).

As is standard in static models, we assume that all transactions occur in equilibrium.[11] Evaluating (10) for $h_0 = h$ and $p_{h,0} = p_h$ yields

$$\left.\frac{dp}{dg}\right|_{V=\bar{V}} = \frac{1}{h} + \left.\frac{dp_n}{dg}\right|_{\text{RPF}}. \tag{11}$$

Since all transactions occur in equilibrium, the results in proposition 1 continue to hold as in the renter case. Thus when the assumption in the previous paragraph holds, sufficient conditions for equilibrium in this owner-occupancy model are the same as in the renter model: stratification, boundary indifference, decreasing bundles, and maximization (given the RPF constraint) of the utility of the median-income voter in each community.

An increase in the grant (and the associated tax rate) will typically lead to a reduction in the net-of-tax price of housing. Hence, the second term on the right-hand side of (11) will normally be negative. Thus a homeowner with a given level of income will normally have a flatter indifference curve through the point (g, p) where (11) holds than a renter with the same level of income (for whom $dp/dg = 1/h$). Hence, for a given RPF, *an owner with a given endowed income will prefer a lower level of redistributive taxation than a renter with the same income.*

In summary, the theoretical analysis thus far gives insight into the general structure of equilibrium in our model. Comparative-static analysis yields ambiguous results, as often happens with equilibrium models. Development of more specific implications about the features of equilibrium requires more specific information about preferences, technology, the distributions of income and housing tenure, the number of communities, and the land area of each. We therefore turn to numerical computations based on the structure we have presented. To do this we have chosen functional forms and parameter values that are broadly consistent with empirical evidence on housing supply and demand functions and the distribution of income in the United States.

IV Computed Equilibria

Households have the Cobb-Douglas utility function $U(h, b) = h^{\alpha}b^{1-\alpha}$. The unitary price and income elasticities implied by this utility function are well within the range of values found in empirical studies (Polinsky 1977; Harmon 1988). This utility function implies the following indirect utility function for a household with income y in a community with housing price p and grant g:

$$V(p, g, y) = \alpha^{\alpha}(1 - \alpha)^{1-\alpha}p^{-\alpha}(y + g).$$

Net-of-tax expenditure shares on housing of 25–30 percent coupled with property tax rates (as a percentage of annual implicit rent) of 20–30 percent suggest a gross-of-tax expenditure share for housing on the order of one-third. Hence, we chose a value of $\alpha = .33$.

We assume the following constant-elasticity housing supply function: $H_s^j(p_h^j) = L^j(p_h^j)^{\theta}$. This supply function is implied by a constant returns to scale Cobb-Douglas production function, with θ being the ratio of the value of nonland to land inputs in production. On the basis of a land share of roughly 25 percent (Mills 1972), we set $\theta = 3$.

A lognormal distribution is generally considered to be a reasonably good characterization of the U.S. income distribution (except possibly for the upper tail). The parameters of a lognormal distribution can be calculated using data on the mean and median from the population (Lindgren 1962, p. 89). With 1979 mean ($21,418) and median ($17,880) income for households in U.S. standard metropolitan statistical areas (SMSAs) (U.S. Bureau of the Census 1980a, table 107), the implied mean for the distribution of the logarithm of income is 9.8 and the variance is 0.36. Hence, in our computations, incomes are assumed lognormally distributed with $\ln(y) \sim N(9.8, 0.36)$.

The computations assume three communities: a poor community, a middle-income community, and a wealthy community. We assume throughout that one community does not redistribute income (i.e., for this community $t = g = 0$). We know from the descending bundles condition of proposition 1 that in any equilibrium this community will be the one in which the highest-income people live. Land areas of the three communities are varied in the computations to illustrate the effects of changing relative community sizes. We chose units of land so that the combined amount of land in all three communities sums to one unit.

The structure of our three-community examples should not be interpreted literally as meaning that all the wealthy households live in a single community, although for computational reasons it makes sense to do so. The spirit of these examples is better captured by thinking of the wealthy as living in many small communities that do not redistribute and that in the aggregate occupy a given fraction of the available land area. These nonredistributing communities provide the opportunity for anyone who wishes to migrate to a jurisdiction in which no redistribution occurs. (In equilibrium, by proposition 1, this must be the one in which those with highest income locate.) Since we are interested in how much redistribution occurs even when it is possible to escape taxation altogether, we have allowed in our examples for half the land area to be occupied by the jurisdictions that are constrained to have zero taxes.

All-Renter Communities

We look first at the case in which all residents are renters. To compute equilibria, we rely on the results of propositions 1 and 2.[12] To provide an intuitive feel for the behavior of the model, we first present results for the case in which at most one community engages in redistribution. (By proposition 1, this will be the low-income community.) The top half of figure 12.2 shows the RPF of community 1 when $L^1 = .25$ and $L^2 + L^3 = .75$. The bottom part depicts the out-migration (decline in y^1) that occurs as community 1's tax rate increases.

Figure 12.5 shows the RPFs obtained with four different values for community 1's share of metropolitan land area: $L^1 = .1, .25, .5,$ and $.75$. In addition to having the anticipated shape, the RPF does indeed expand as community size increases.

Voting equilibrium in community 1 when $L^1 = .25$ is shown in figure 12.3. This is the point on the RPF most preferred by a voter with income $y = \$10{,}542$, the median in community 1. Since, by assumption, the other communities do not undertake redistribution, the outcome in figure 12.3 is an equilibrium. In this equilibrium, $g^1 = \$1{,}526$ and 37 percent of the metropolitan area population lives in community 1. The gross-of-tax price of housing in community 1 is \$12.66, and in the other communities it is \$9.41.

An investigation of equilibrium with various values of L^1 reveals that the outward shift of the RPF slightly outweighs the effect of increasing the income of the pivotal voter as the population of community 1 rises. The

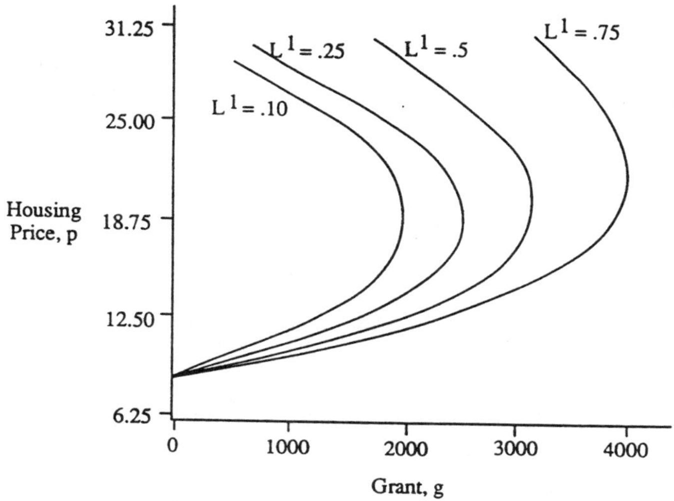

Figure 12.5
Redistribution possibility frontiers for four different community 1 shares of metropolitan land area

equilibrium level of grants per household rises as the land area of the poor community rises. For example, increasing the land area of the poor community from .25 to .45 results in an increase in the equilibrium grant per household from $1,526 to $1,744.

Results for the case in which both communities 1 and 2 may redistribute income are presented in table 12.1. For these results, the land area of the community constrained to have $g = 0$ is fixed at $L^3 = .5$, and the relative land areas of the low- and middle-income communities are varied. In this and other tables, the tax rates should be interpreted as rates *per dollar of rental price.* To obtain the more familiar tax rates per dollar of *property value*, the rental value of housing must be capitalized at some discount rate. With a 10 percent discount rate, this would imply property tax rates of *one-tenth* the rates listed in the tables.

The most striking finding of the model with only renters is that relatively high levels of redistribution are chosen by the middle-income community when that community has a comparatively small land area.[13] This is illustrated in columns 1–3 of table 12.1, where we present equilibria for cases in which community 2 has 5 percent, 1 percent, and 0.001 percent of

Table 12.1
Effects of varying the relative amounts of land occupied by the low- and middle-income communities for two alternative tenure arrangements

	All households rent			All households are owner-occupants		
	(1)	(2)	(3)	(4)	(5)	(6)
p^1	12.40	12.39	12.39	9.28	9.35	9.37
p^2	12.28	12.21	12.18	9.21	9.22	9.22
p^3	9.72	9.70	9.70	9.20	9.22	9.22
g^1	1,780	1,799	1,804	68	120	133
g^2	1,711	1,684	1,676	5	0	0
t^1	.62	.58	.57	.014	.025	.028
t^2	.31	.29	.28	.0006	0	0
N^1	.54	.60	.61	.68	.71	.72
N^2	.07	.01	.000013	.04	.009	8×10^{-6}
y^1	19,145	20,980	21,459	23,844	25,222	25,574
y^2	21,213	21,436	21,460	27,725	25,609	25,575
L^1	.45	.49	.49999	.45	.49	.49999
L^2	.05	.01	.00001	.05	.01	.00001

Note: $L^3 = .50$ in all cases. N^j is community j's share of the total population ($j = 1, 2, 3$). $N^3 = 1 - N^1 - N^2$.

the metropolitan land area. Another striking observation about these results is that the levels of local redistributive expenditures are quite high compared to levels observed in U.S. municipalities.[14]

Consider column 3 of table 12.1. The land area of the middle-income community is a small fraction (.00001) of total land in the metropolitan area. In equilibrium, the population is a comparably small fraction (.000013) of the metropolitan area population. The residents of the community are essentially homogeneous; the range of incomes between the wealthiest and poorest households in the community is less than \$1.00. Household income in the community (\$21,560) is well above the median (\$17,880) and mean (\$21,418) income for the metropolitan area. Roughly 39 percent of the households in the metropolitan area live in communities that do not tax or redistribute income. Nonetheless, households in the middle-income community vote to impose a 28 percent tax on the value of housing services and use the proceeds to finance grants per household of \$1,676. (This would correspond to a 2.8 percent tax on property value if one uses a 10 percent rate for discounting.) They do this recognizing that it will induce migration out of the community and increase the equilibrium housing price to \$12.18—26 percent higher than the no-tax equilibrium price of \$9.70.

These results contradict the widely held belief that small communities cannot opt for high levels of transfers. The results show that they can, and that the decisive voter may well prefer a high level of grants. Moreover, the RPFs reveal that the politically chosen grants are significantly lower than the highest feasible grant. In other words, were the communities interested in maximizing the level of grants per household, they could choose higher g than those shown in the table, even given all the mobility considerations.

Why do residents of small and relatively high-income jurisdictions opt for such high grants in this model? Taxation for redistribution increases the gross-of-tax price of housing and decreases the net-of-tax price of housing relative to the no-tax level. The reduction in the net-of-tax housing price implies that a portion of the cost of redistribution is borne by property owners. Since land is immobile and jurisdictional boundaries are fixed, landowners cannot move their land to avoid paying a portion of the redistributive tax. Again, consider column 3 of table 12.1. The net-of-tax price of housing in the middle-income community is \$9.51. This compares to a no-tax price of \$9.70. Thus owners of land in the community receive a lower net-of-tax price than that obtained by those who own land outside the community. Landowners pay \$0.19 (=\$9.70 − \$9.51) of the \$2.67 difference (\$12.18 − \$9.51) between the gross- and net-of-tax price of housing in community 2. The incidence of the tax is such that landowners pay roughly 7 percent of the tax, and this is sufficient to induce residents of the community to adopt a relatively high redistributive tax.[15] Thus even in small, relatively high-income jurisdictions, residents find comparatively high levels of redistributive taxation to be attractive. These results echo the finding by Epple and Zelenitz (1981) that governments in small local jurisdictions can follow discretionary policies that expropriate a portion of land rent.

A key message of the computations in this section is that "smallness" of local jurisdictions need not prevent relatively high transfers. We should stress that the results are not due to voter myopia; voters correctly perceive how taxation for redistribution will affect migration and housing prices. The functional forms and parameter values in these computations are realistic enough that the results are not likely to be an artifact of the specification. The argument presented above suggests that these results arise because residents are renters who shift a portion of the burden of redistribution to property owners.

Owners-Only Communities

We used the functional forms and parameter values of the renter model to solve the owner-occupancy model.[16] The results, shown in columns 4–6 of table 12.1, change dramatically. *In this table, for all values of relative community size for the poor and middle-income communities, the equilibrium level of redistributive taxation is quite modest.* The change in results from those in columns 1–3 is due entirely to the change in voter preferences induced by home ownership. With owner-occupancy, any reduction in the net-of-tax price of housing caused by an increase in redistributive taxation leads to a capital loss for the owner-occupant. This capital loss is sufficient to offset almost completely the benefits of redistribution for median voters in communities of the sizes shown in table 12.1.

Investigation of the preferences of nonmedian voters in the case in which $L^1 = L^2 = .25$ reveals that there is a large majority of voters (roughly 47.5 percent) in the low-income community who prefer positive levels of redistribution. Since the observed proportion of owners in the United States is lower at low incomes than at high ones, this suggests that a model with both owner-occupants and renters might yield results quite different from those with only renters or owners. We discuss this next.

Equilibrium with Both Renters and Owner-Occupants

In order to consider communities with a mix of renters and owners, let $\rho(y)$ be the proportion of residents with income y who are renters. Since transactions occur only in equilibrium, the choice of community depends only on income, not on whether the household will own or rent. Proposition 1 holds for a model with both owners and renters.

For owners, assume that dp/dg is given in (10) is decreasing in y. Then it can be shown (Epple and Romer 1989a, app. 1) that the preferences of owners as a subgroup vary systematically with income, as do the preferences of renters. It is therefore possible to determine the identity of pivotal voters in each community in equilibrium even when there are both owners and renters, and both are free to move among jurisdictions.

Since there are two types of voters, we shall be looking for voting equilibrium in each community, such that it is a point on the community RPF that maximizes the utility of renter-voter $\tilde{y}_r$ and owner-voter $\tilde{y}_o$, where $\tilde{y}_r$ and $\tilde{y}_o$ satisfy

$$\int_{\underline{y}}^{\tilde{y}_r} \rho(y)f(y)\,dy + \int_{\underline{y}}^{\tilde{y}_o} [1 - \rho(y)]f(y)\,dy = \frac{1}{2}\int_{\underline{y}}^{\bar{y}} f(y)\,dy, \tag{12}$$

and $\underline{y}$ and $\bar{y}$ are, respectively, the lowest and highest endowed incomes of residents of the community.

Equation (12) indicates that a majority voting equilibrium will be an allocation in which an owner ($\tilde{y}_o$) with income below the community median income and a renter ($\tilde{y}_r$) with income above the community median are both pivotal voters. They are pivotal since one-half of the voters in the community prefer a lower point on the community RPF and one-half prefer a higher point on the community RPF than $\tilde{y}_0$ and $\tilde{y}_r$ do.

To investigate the model with both owners and renters, we need to specify the function $\rho(y)$ parametrically. We adopted the specification

$$\rho(y) = \begin{cases} \gamma y^{-\delta} & \text{for } y > \gamma^{1/\delta} \\ 1 & \text{for } y \leq \gamma^{1/\delta}. \end{cases}$$

We chose this function for analytic convenience, but it provides a good fit to the available data. We estimated the parameters γ and δ as follows. The U.S. Bureau of the Census (1980b, tables B-3, B-4) presents the number of renter- and owner-occupied housing units in the U.S. SMSAs for nine household income classes. We computed average income, $\bar{Y}$, in each income class, using the lognormal distribution of household income presented in Section III. Regressing the log of the proportion of households that are renters, $\bar{\rho}$, against the log of $\bar{Y}$ gives estimates of γ and δ. The resulting regression, with t-statistics in parentheses, is

$$\ln \bar{\rho} = \underset{(6.43)}{5.98} - \underset{(7.69)}{.729} \ln \bar{Y}, \quad R^2 = .89.$$

This regression confirms that the proportion of households that are renters declines as income rises ($\gamma = \exp[5.98] = 395$, $\delta = .729$).[17]

As in the all-renter and all-owner cases, increasing the relative size of the lowest-income community will tend to cause the community's RPF to expand. As before, this effect tends to favor an increase in the level of redistribution. An opposing effect, also present in the renter model, is that more high-income voters occupy the community when the community expands. Those voters oppose high levels of redistribution. A second opposing effect, which is not present in the renter model, is that the proportion of residents who are homeowners increases as the share of land occupied by the low-income community rises and, ceteris paribus, homeowners prefer less redistribution than renters.

Table 12.2
Effects of varying the relative amounts of land occupied by the low- and middle-income communities in the model with both renters and owner-occupants

	(1)	(2)	(3)	(4)	(5)	(6)	(7)
p^1	12.09	11.31	10.87	10.71	10.65	10.64	10.64
p^2	10.22	10.01	9.78	9.62	9.49	9.45	9.44
p^3	9.42	9.38	9.36	9.36	9.40	9.43	9.44
g^1	1,213	1,030	920	904	933	954	960
g^2	647	528	359	215	74	15	0
t^1	.80	.48	.32	.26	.24	.23	.23
t^2	.13	.10	.06	.03	.01	.002	0
N^1	.13	.24	.40	.53	.63	.67	.68
N^2	.55	.45	.29	.16	.05	.01	.00001
y^1	9,284	11,756	15,473	18,796	22,072	23,405	23,741.0
y^2	23,868	24,210	24,423	24,350	24,019	23,804	23,741.4
$\bar{y}_o^1$	4,250	6,454	8,777	10,377	11,642	12,082	12,187
$\bar{y}_r^1$	8,322	10,515	13,264	15,273	16,876	17,432	17,564
$\bar{y}_o^2$	14,189	15,859	18,538	20,843	22,856	23,572	23,741.2
$\bar{y}_r^2$	18,914	19,976	21,504	22,647	23,464	23,694	23,741.3
PR^1	.64	.56	.49	.45	.42	.41	.41
PR^2	.35	.33	.30	.28	.26	.25	.25
L^1	.10	.15	.25	.35	.45	.49	.49999
L^2	.40	.35	.25	.15	.05	.01	.00001

Note: $L^3 = .50$ in all cases. PR^j is the proportion of community j's population that are renters. N^j is community j's share of the total population $(j = 1, 2, 3)$. $N^3 = 1 - N^1 - N^2$.

Results of our computations for the mixed-tenure cases are shown in table 12.2.[18] Comparing these results to those in table 12.1 reveals that the equilibrium grant levels are lower in the model with both owners and renters than in the model with only renters. It is interesting to note that increasing the size of the low-income community results in a decrease rather than an increase in the equilibrium level of redistribution. The changes in community 1's composition as its share of land area increases are sufficient to offset the effect of the expansion of the community RPF, with the result that the equilibrium level of grants falls as the size of the community increases. (In the low-income community, the proportion of renters falls from 64 percent in table 12.2 to 41 percent as community size increases. The community's median income rises.)

Looking across the columns of table 12.2, one sees that the amount of redistribution in community 2 falls as the size of community 1 increases relative to community 2. This result is due in part to the declining size of community 2. However, the major factor causing the decline in redistribution in community 2 is the increase in household income and owner-occupancy in community 2 as the size of community 1 rises relative to community 2. This is evident in the increase in income of the poorest resident in community 2 (y^1) as the share of metropolitan land area occupied by community 1 rises. These results are in sharp contrast to those in columns 1–3 of table 12.1.

Finally, we varied the parameter δ that determines the proportion of renters at each income level.[19] The results are graphed in figure 12.6, for $L^1 = .45$ and $L^2 = .05$. In the figure, PR^1, PR^2, and PR^T are the proportions of renters in community 1, community 2, and the total population, respectively. As δ increases, the proportion of households at each income level that are owners increases. (The dashed line in fig. 12.6 indicates the case corresponding to col. 5 of table 12.2.) The all-renters and all-owners equilibria emerge at extreme values of δ. Parametrically varying δ illustrates the decline in the level of the grant in each community as the fraction of households that are owners increases.

The striking differences in equilibrium grant levels among the all-renters, all-owners, and mixed-tenure settings make a compelling case that housing tenure plays a central role in local redistribution. The effects of tenure arise not by changing what is feasible but by changing what voters prefer. The computational results thus highlight the interplay between individual incentives and collective actions that is a central focus of our model.

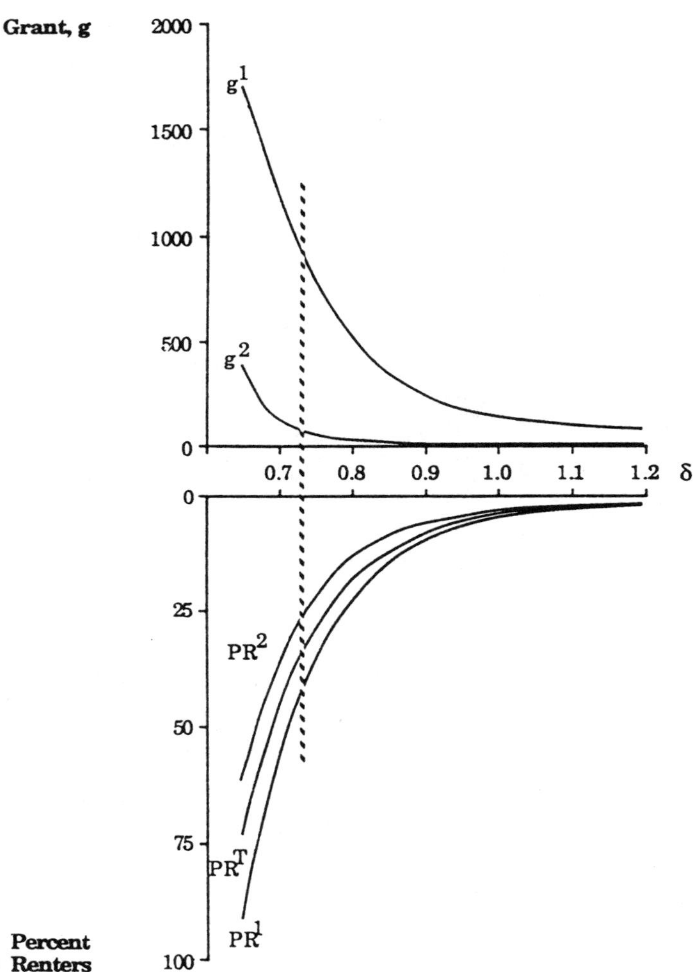

Figure 12.6
Effects of varying δ; $L^1 = .45$, $L^2 = .05$, $L^3 = .50$

V Conclusions

Some results of the analysis in this chapter accord very well with prior expectations. Local redistribution leads to a sorting of the population, with the poorest households located in the communities that provide the highest levels of redistribution (proposition 1). Larger communities within a system of jurisdictions have greater scope for redistribution than smaller ones do.

Some results of the analysis are unexpected. Even though mobility is costless in this model, high levels of transfers can emerge in equilibrium in computations with reasonable parameter values. Indeed, as shown in Section IV, even small, relatively high-income communities opt for high grant levels if all voters are renters. Results with owner-occupancy contrast sharply with those with only renters. Owner-occupants prefer less redistribution than renters. It therefore appears that it is not the threat of out-migration that leads to observed low levels of local redistribution in most municipalities in U.S. metropolitan areas. Costless mobility does not shrink the feasible set of grants sufficiently to prevent local redistribution. Instead, our results suggest that the preference for low levels of redistribution is a political one, and it is closely linked to the relatively high proportion of owner-occupants in most municipalities. The results in the model with both owners and renters suggest that the proportion of residents who are renters is a major factor affecting the local choice of level of redistribution. It would be worthwhile to explore this implication of our model more directly with data on U.S. municipalities.

A central assumption of our model is that moving is costless. Empirical evidence suggests that households do migrate in response to differentials in welfare payments (Gramlich and Laren 1984; Peterson and Rom 1989). However, the evidence also suggests that the response is not instantaneous, and it is clear that perfect stratification does not emerge in practice. Hence, it would be desirable to extend the model in this chapter by introducing factors that lead households to be attached to particular locations. Perhaps the most straightforward way to do this would be to endow households with preferences for some locations relative to others. Another approach is to have the system of jurisdictions vary in location relative to a central area, so that communities would differ in some important respect, such as the amount of time required to commute to the center. As we show in Cassidy, Epple, and Romer (1989), our framework is quite amenable to incorporating a spatial dimension to the analysis.

The debate about local redistribution has focused on whether mobility makes local redistribution infeasible. In our model, local redistribution proves to be feasible. The amount of redistribution turns out to be relatively modest in the empirically most relevant cases because anticipated capital losses by homeowners deter them from voting for high grant levels per household. It is likely that local redistribution would be limited further by demands for other services from local governments. A useful direction to develop the model would be to introduce a local public good in addition to local redistribution. This would permit investigation of the allocation of public expenditures between redistribution and the provision of services. This extension poses a substantial challenge since the voting problem becomes more complex.

Our model focuses on the implications of one resident, one vote and ignores the possibility that absentee owners may attempt to influence the political process within the jurisdiction through means other than by casting a vote directly. The introduction of these more indirect channels of political influence in the context of a model of mobile households is an intriguing problem for future work.

Our existing model or its straightforward modifications can readily be applied to a variety of policy issues. The level of redistribution that would be chosen with a single central government can be compared to the case in which only local governments redistribute. When both central and local governments redistribute, one can investigate how changes in redistribution by the central government affect the amount of redistribution done locally. The effect of intergovernmental grants on the level of local redistribution can be studied. The model can be used to determine how consolidation of local governments affects the amount of local redistribution. Our framework, in sum, provides a useful way of combining the essential features we enumerated in Section I. The computed equilibria provide insight into the way these features interact and suggest the value of addressing other issues in fiscal federalism using extensions of this structure.

Notes

This research is supported by grants from the National Science Foundation. Romer thanks the Hoover Institution, Stanford University, for its hospitality during the 1988–89 academic year. We have benefited from the comments of participants at workshops and conferences at which we presented earlier versions of this work. These took place at Carnegie Mellon, California at Santa Barbara and at Berkeley, Michigan, North Carolina at Greensboro,

Washington University, Columbia, Chicago, Harvard, Caltech, Pennsylvania, Miami University, National Bureau of Economic Research, Stanford, Princeton, Maryland, Texas A&M, Yale, and the 1988 meetings of the Public Choice Society. We thank Glenn Cassidy for his assistance with some of the computations.

1. As a technical matter, we show in this paper that no equilibrium exists when voters behave in this myopic fashion.

2. In a model with only owner-occupants, Yinger (1982) introduces a distinction between "movers" and "stayers." This device serves to contrast choices facing households selecting a community with those facing households residing in a community. The stayers do not plan to change houses, and hence they ignore capital gains and losses when voting.

3. Empirical studies of migration in response to differentials in local redistribution have been made by Gramlich and Laren (1984), Rosenzweig and Wolpin (1988), Peterson and Rom (1989), and others. A review of some of the empirical evidence is presented in Brown and Oates (1987).

4. Bucovetsky (1982) recognizes the importance of mobility-related effects in analyzing the response of systems of local jurisdictions to changes in public-sector policies. He focuses on exogenous policy changes and is not concerned with community collective choice. In two recent papers, Wilson (1987a, 1987b) has explored the role and patterns of trade in private goods in an economy with mobile factors and multiple jurisdictions. In both papers, he focuses on the efficiency properties of local taxation and public goods provision. For the most part, the analyses deal with a setting in which individuals are identical, so political processes or redistributive issues play no role. Goodspeed (1988) uses a simulation model to investigate the welfare losses and extent of redistribution in decentralized provision of a "congestable" local public good. Steen (1987a, 1987b) looks at multicommunity equilibrium in a spatial setting, with the level of public services in each community set exogenously.

5. Conditions (2) and (3) imply that the indifference curve of a given household crosses the indifference curve of any other household at most once and that the indifference curve of the poorer of any two households cuts the indifference curve of the wealthier of the two from below. Models in which indifference curves are assumed to have these monotonicity and single-crossing properties have been studied in a variety of contexts. B. Ellickson (1971), Westhoff (1977), and Epple, Filimon, and Romer (1984), among others, use such an assumption to study equilibrium in models of local jurisdictions. Matthews and Moore (1987) provide an illuminating review and discussion of the use of analogous marginal rate of substitution assumptions in screening models. In these models, the marginal rate of substitution property is employed to demonstrate that certain self-selection constraints are satisfied. In our model, the marginal rate of substitution condition plays this role (proposition 1), and it also plays a key role in characterizing the outcome of the voting problem (proposition 2). In the context of voting, Roberts (1977) named this condition "hierarchical adherence" and relied on it to prove the existence of a voting equilibrium. An attractive feature of the model we study in this chapter is that the marginal rate of substitution condition relevant to our analysis, condition (3), emerges naturally from the economics of the problem.

6. Proposition 2 is based on a result of Roberts (1977).

7. All voters strictly prefer (g^*, p^*) to points in B such that $g < g^*$ and $p > p^*$. By (4a) we can compare (g^*, p^*) to other points in region B, for voters with $y > \tilde{y}$.

8. There may be more than one point on the community RPF that yields global maximum utility for the median-income voter. Let E be the set of such points. Any point in E will defeat all points not in E, so E is the set of majority voting equilibria. (In our computations, E was always a singleton.)

9. This treatment of absentee landlords is consistent with a strict interpretation of current legal doctrine. R. Ellickson (1982) has noted that cities generally have one-resident, one-vote rule. Challenges by nonresident landowners to this voting rule have typically met with failure, at least since Avery v. Midland County, 390 U.S. 474 (1968).

10. Suppose that housing does not depreciate and that the real rate of interest is r. Then the capital gain from sale of the house is the present value of the change in annual implicit rentals on the house: $(p_h - p_{h,0})h_0/r$. This increase in wealth will pay an annuity of $(p_h - p_{h,0})h_0$. This annuity is added to the household's annual endowed income y and grant g to obtain its total annual income.

11. While the actual process of achieving equilibrium is not typically captured in static models, a heuristic "story" about how equilibrium might emerge may be useful. In our models with only renters, this requires no elaboration. In the model with owners, perhaps the easiest process to visualize is the one in which all land is initially owned by price-taking absentee owners. When they locate in a community, households in the model buy from these absentee owners. Since there is no uncertainty, transactions occur at equilibrium prices.

The key difference between owners and renters in the model is that owners would suffer any capital gains or losses that would arise from a change in the tax rate or grant level in the community in which they choose to locate. As voters, they take account of such potential gains and losses when choosing among feasible tax rates and spending levels. Since they choose not to vote for departures from the equilibrium tax rate and grant in the community in which they live, such capital gains and losses do not arise in equilibrium.

12. Details of our computational procedure appear in Epple and Romer (1989a, app. 2).

13. There may be multiple intercommunity equilibria (Epple and Romer 1989a, app. 2). Since (along with much of the literature) we expected that mobility considerations would rule out equilibria with g much greater than zero, it is instructive that such equilibria are possible.

14. Data on local redistributive taxation and expenditure are difficult to obtain for two reasons. First, redistribution often takes the form of goods and services rather than money, and the selection of the set of expenditures to classify as redistribution is not entirely straightforward. Second, local expenditures for redistribution may be financed by contributions from several levels of government so that the local revenue contribution is often hard to isolate. Taking an expansive definition of local government redistributive expenditures—including all items classified by the census as public welfare, health, and hospitals—and counting all local government expenditures in these categories regardless of source of funds, one can obtain an upper-bound estimate of local redistributive expenditures. The per capita average of these expenditures across all municipalities in the United States in fiscal year 1985 was \$84. The average in municipalities with a population greater than 1 million was \$389, while in municipalities with a population under 50,000 it was \$26. For all local governments in 75 major SMSAs, the fiscal year 1983 figure was \$192 per capita. For amounts per household, the per capita numbers should be multiplied by approximately three. There is great variability across states and municipalities, but these numbers suggest the order of magnitude (see Tax Foundation 1988, tables F2, F9).

15. Thus a portion of the tax is exported to nonresidents (absentee landlords). Johnson (1988) discusses tax exporting as a possible source of redistributive motives in a federal system.

16. In our computations, we verified that dp/dg as given by (10) is decreasing in y and that proposition 2 can be applied over all the points on the RPF. For details, see Epple and Romer (1989a, appl. 1).

17. Using time-series data, Rosen, Rosen, and Holtz-Eakin (1984) obtain an estimate of .707 for the elasticity of home ownership with respect to permanent income. This is remarkably close to our estimate of δ.

18. An interesting feature of our computations is that in both the all-owners model and the all-renters model, for values of L^1 on the order of .34 or less, our computations find allocations satisfying stratification, boundary indifference, and internal equilibrium. However, these allocations do not satisfy decreasing bundles, and, hence, they are not equilibria. By contrast, in the more realistic mixed-tenure case, our computations yield equilibrium allocations for the full range of values of L^1 that we investigate, as illustrated in table 12.2.

19. We thank an anonymous referee for suggesting these computations.

References

Brown, Charles, and Oates, Wallace. 1987. Assistance to the poor in a federal system. *Journal of Public Economics* 32:307–330.

Bucovetsky, Sam. 1982. Inequality in the local public sector. *Journal of Public Economics* 90:128–145.

Cassidy, Glenn, Epple, Dennis, and Romer, Thomas. 1989. Redistribution by local governments in a monocentric urban area. *Regional Science and Urban Economics* 19:421–454.

Courant, Paul, and Rubinfeld, Daniel. 1978. On the measurement of benefits in an urban context: Some general equilibrium issues. *Journal of Urban Economics* 5:346–356.

Ellickson, Bryan. 1971. Jurisdictional fragmentation and residential choice. *American Economic Review Papers and Proceedings* 61:334–339.

Ellickson, Robert. 1982. Cities and homeowners associations. *University of Pennsylvania Law Review*. 130:1519–1580.

Epple, Dennis, Filimon, Radu, and Romer, Thomas. 1984. Equilibrium among local jurisdictions: Toward an integrated treatment of voting and residential choice. *Journal of Public Economics* 24:281–308.

Epple, Dennis, and Romer, Thomas. 1989a. Mobility and redistribution. Working paper no. E-89-26, Hoover Institution, Stanford University.

Epple, Dennis, and Romer, Thomas. 1989b. On the flexibility of municipal boundaries. *Journal of Urban Economics* 26:307–319.

Epple, Dennis, and Zelenitz, Allan. 1981. The implications of competition among jurisdictions: Does Tiebout need politics? *Journal of Political Economy* 89:1197–1217.

Goodspeed, Timothy. 1988. A reexamination of the use of ability-to-pay taxes by local governments. Working paper, U.S. Treasury Department, Washington, DC.

Gramlich, Edward, and Laren, Deborah. 1984. Migration and income redistribution responsibilities. *Journal of Human Resources* 19:489–511.

Harmon, Oskar. 1988. The income elasticity of demand for single-family owner-occupied housing: An empirical reconciliation. *Journal of Urban Economics* 24:173–185.

Johnson, William. 1988. Income redistribution in a federal system. *American Economic Review* 78:570–573.

Ladd, Helen, and Doolittle, Fred. 1982. Which level of government should assist the poor? *National Tax Journal*. 35:323–336.

Lindgren, Bernard. 1962. *Statistical theory*. New York: Macmillan.

Matthews, Steven, and Moore, John. 1987. Monopoly provision of quality and warranties: An exploration in the theory of multidimensional screening. *Econometrica* 55:441–467.

Meltzer, Allan, and Richard, Scott. 1981. A rational theory of the size of government. *Journal of Political Economy* 89:914–927. Reprinted as chapter 8 in the current volume of this work.

Mills, Edwin. 1972. *Urban economics*. Glenview, IL: Scott, Foresman.

Mills, Edwin, and Oates, Wallace, eds. 1975. *Fiscal zoning and land use controls: The economic issues*. Lexington, MA: Heath.

Oates, Wallace. 1972. *Fiscal federalism*. New York: Harcourt Brace Jovanovich.

Oates, Wallace. 1977. An economist's perspective on fiscal federalism. In Wallace Oates, ed., *The political economy of fiscal federalism*. Lexington, MA: Heath.

Oates, Wallace. 1986. The estimation of demand functions for local public goods: Issues in specification and interpretation. Working paper, University of Maryland, College Park.

Orr, Larry. 1976. Income transfers as a public good: An application to AFDC. *American Economic Review* 66:359–371.

Peterson, Paul, and Rom, Mark. 1989. American federalism, welfare policy, and residential choices. *American Political Science Review* 83:711–728.

Polinsky, A. Mitchell. 1977. The demand for housing: A study in specification and grouping. *Econometrica* 45:447–461.

Roberts, Kevin. 1977. Voting over income tax schedules. *Journal of Public Economics* 8:329–340.

Romer, Thomas. 1975. Individual welfare, majority voting, and the properties of a linear income tax. *Journal of Public Economics* 4:163–185.

Rose-Ackerman, Susan. 1979. Market models of local government: Exit, voting and the land market. *Journal of Urban Economics* 6:319–337.

Rosen, Harvey, Rosen, Kenneth, and Holtz-Eakin, Douglas. 1984. Housing tenure, uncertainty, and taxation. *Review of Economics and Statistics* 66:405–416.

Rosenzweig, Mark, and Wolpin, Kenneth. 1988. Migration selectivity and the effects of public programs. *Journal of Public Economics* 37:265–289.

Steen, Robert. 1987a. Effects of governmental structure in urban areas. *Journal of Urban Economics* 21:166–179.

Steen, Robert. 1987b. Effects of the property tax in urban areas. *Journal of Urban Economics* 21:146–165.

Stigler, George. 1957. The tenable range of functions of local government. In Joint Economic Committee, *Federal expenditure policy for economic growth and stability*. Washington: Government Printing Office.

Tax Foundation. 1988. *Facts and figures on government finance*. 24th ed. Baltimore: Johns Hopkins University Press.

U.S. Bureau of the Census. 1980a. *Census of population: Characteristics of the population: General, social and economic characteristics, U.S. summary*. Washington: Government Printing Office.

U.S. Bureau of the Census. 1980b. *Census of housing: Metropolitan housing characteristics, U.S. summary*. Vol. 2. Washington: Government Printing Office.

Westhoff, Frank. 1977. Existence of equilibria in economies with a local public good. *Journal of Economic Theory* 14:84–112.

Wildasin, David. 1988. Nash equilibria in models of fiscal competition. *Journal of Public Economics* 35:229–240.

Wilson, John. 1987a. Trade, capital mobility, and tax competition. *Journal of Political Economy* 95:835–856.

Wilson, John. 1987b. Trade in a Tiebout economy. *American Economic Review* 77:431–441.

Yinger, John. 1982. Capitalization and the theory of local public finance. *Journal of Political Economy* 90:917–943.

13 The Political Economy of Benefits and Costs: A Neoclassical Approach to Distributive Politics

Barry R. Weingast, Kenneth A. Shepsle, and Christopher Johnsen

The inefficiency of public decision making has long been a concern for students of public policy. Models of bureaucratic behavior, legislative institutions, interest-group influence, vote-maximizing politicians, and fiscal illusion all point toward sources of bias in these nonmarket contexts.[1] Yet none has established why a cooperative legislature would stand for policies which are Pareto dominated. Specifically, if the bias works to the benefit of some identifiable group, then why do political actors not insist on efficiency in combination with a compensation scheme? This would leave the identified group at least as well off, all others at least as well off, and then leave the efficiency gain at the political discretion of representatives, thereby enhancing their role. From the anomaly of sustained political inefficiency, it appears that there is a divergence between normative economic principles, on the one hand, and the preferences of political actors on the other. Prominence is given in the following analysis to the political mechanisms that create and maintain this divergence.

In this chapter, we develop a model of the public choice mechanisms comprising a representative legislature in order to show the political sources that systematically bias public decisions toward larger than efficient projects in the area of distributive policymaking. By distributive policies we mean those projects, programs, and grants that concentrate the benefits in geographically specific constituencies, while spreading their costs across all constituencies through generalized taxation.[2] This collection of public decisions includes the traditional pork barrel of public works and rivers and harbors projects as well as the more recent examples of highway construction, categorical grants-in-aid, urban renewal, mass transit, and sewage treatment plants. The model identifies the political sources of efficiency bias—and there are several—by unpacking the democratic institutions into their components, thereby focusing on the influence of each. This takes the form of a progression of models beginning with an efficiency benchmark. Then, one by one, political features are added until the final form models a representative legislature divided into n districts. The approach shows how political institutions transform the

Reprinted from *Journal of Political Economy*, by permission of The University of Chicago Press. *Journal of Political Economy*, 1981, vol. 89, no. 5.

economic basis of costs and benefits into political costs and benefits. The latter, and not their economic counterparts, define rational decisions for political actors.

The model reveals three important sources of bias. The first is a consequence of the political definition of benefits and costs and its divergence, in important respects, from the economic definition. The second source stems from the districting mechanism which divides the economy into *n* disjoint political units called districts. The method of project financing through generalized taxation constitutes the third source of bias. Moreover, we show that the mechanism of popular election of legislative representatives complements these sources of bias so that these three sources, in conjunction with the reelection mechanism, explain the inefficiency of political choice.

The General Approach

Our model is one of policymaking in the realm of distributive policy, so we begin by clarifying that concept. A distributive policy is a political decision that concentrates benefits in a specific geographic constituency and finances expenditures through generalized taxation. These policies—sewage treatment plants, land reclamation, the rivers and harbors omnibus, urban renewal projects—authorize collections of projects, each targeted to a geographic location and each generating benefits in that geographic location unrelated to projects in other locations. This latter characteristic is crucial since the omnibus-like quality of distributive programs allows decisions to be made on a project-by-project, locality-by-locality basis. Each project of the omnibus may be fashioned independently of others in the omnibus.

While it is clear that all policies have a geographic incidence of benefits and costs, what distinguishes a distributive policy is that benefits are geographically targeted. In contrast, a nondistributive program, say an entitlement program, though having geographic incidences, is fashioned with nongeographic constituencies in mind, for example, socioeconomic groups. Subsidies to beekeepers, for example, generate a distribution of benefits that depends on the geographic distribution of beekeppers. No geographic area has a claim on program benefits except as it contains residents in the entitled category. Thus, by our definition, programs targeted to the malnourished (food stamps), the unhealthy (Medicare), the poor (welfare), the retired (social security), the injured worker (workers' compensation), or the automobile driver (automotive product safety) are not distributive policies because any citizen may obtain program benefits if he falls in the specific category. Thus, an entitlement program confers benefits on all individuals in the designated category, benefits which may not be varied without similarly varying them for others in the category. Although the motivation to create nondistributive programs may have a geographic basis (as when a politician is moved to support a policy because many of his constituents fall into the beneficiary group), the fact remains that the beneficiary group is not geographically defined or determined. In contrast, geography is the hallmark of distributive politics: Programs and projects are geographically targeted, geographically fashioned, and may be independently varied. Importantly, geography is also the basis for political organization and representation.

A distributive policy for the jth district, $P_j(x)$, is a project located in that district, where x is a decision parameter. Although x may be treated as a vector of project characteristics, we assume that x simply describes the scale or size of the project. Associated with the project $P_j(x)$ are both benefits and costs. Let $b(x)$ represent the present value of the economic benefits which flow from the project to the particular political constituency. This includes consumption benefits, say cleaner water from a sewage treatment plant, and potential pecuniary gains to producers, for example, increased profits to project input owners from price rises in factor markets.[3]

ASSUMPTION 1 $b'(x) > 0, b''(x) < 0$.

Let $c(x)$ represent the total resource cost involved in producing the project. It decomposes into three components, $c(x) = c_1(x) + c_2(x) + c_3(x)$. The first component, $c_1(x)$, is the real resource expenditures for project inputs spent in the constituency in which the project is located; $c_2(x)$ is the real resource expenditures for project inputs spent outside the district; $c_3(x)$ is nonexpenditure real resource costs imposed on the district (e.g., nonpecuniary externalities, such as the destruction of the natural environment, and pecuniary externalities in the form of price rises to consumers in factor markets).[4]

ASSUMPTION 2 $c_i'(x) > 0, c_i''(x) \geq 0, i = 1, 2, 3$.

The expenditures are financed through taxes so that the tax bill for $P_j(x)$ is

$$T(x) = c_1(x) + c_2(x). \tag{1}$$

We assume a tax system that covers all expenditures, assigning nonnegative tax share t_i to the ith district, where $\sum_{i=1}^{n} t_i = 1$ and n is the number of districts. The tax bill for the ith district for the project $P_j(x)$, therefore, is $t_i[c_1(x) + c_2(x)]$.

As the above development suggests, there are several mechanisms at work in the realm of distributive policy which our model captures. First, economic benefits are geographically concentrated in a politically relevant way. Second, production costs may be unpacked, again in a politically relevant way. Some costs are extracted from the economy and returned as geographically earmarked expenditures—$c_1(x)$ and $c_2(x)$; other costs are nonexpenditure in nature, imposed on the local economy in which the project is located—$c_3(x)$. Third, the tax bill, $T(x)$, is paid for by each political subdivision according to the tax shares t_i, $i = 1, \ldots, n$. The relevant mechanisms which we examine below are (1) the political cost-accounting mechanism, (2) the districting mechanism, and (3) the taxation mechanism. After examining these mechanisms and their effects on the characteristics of distributive policy, we explore the complementarity of legislators' reelection objective. First, however, we develop the familiar efficiency criterion.

Model E Maximizing Economic Efficiency

The benchmark for the entire set of political institutions developed below is the efficiency criterion. This requires the maximization of economic net benefits. This is given simply by

$$\max_x E(x) = b(x) - c(x). \tag{2}$$

The familiar first- and second-order conditions are

$$b' - c' = 0,$$

and \hfill (3)

$$b'' - c'' < 0.$$

The second-order condition follows directly from assumption 1 and assumption 2 so that the solution to (2), x^E in figure 13.1, is a unique global maximum.

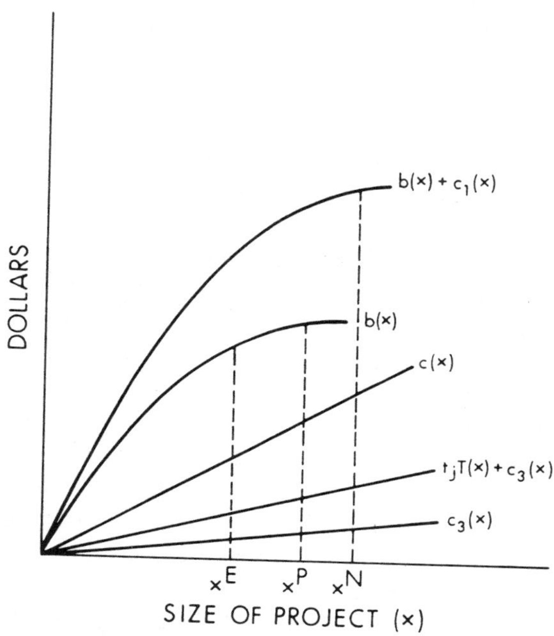

Figure 13.1

The Politicization of Expenditures

The first transformation of the standard approach is the politicization of economic costs. This transformation rests on a crucial political property. Project costs, paid from general revenues, become geographically earmarked expenditures. The political process distributes those expenditures in the form of c_1-type and c_2-type costs. Thus, for $P_j(x)$ in district j, production inputs are purchased from firms and individuals in the district (c_1) and from their counterparts outside the district (c_2). More important is the political evaluation of the distribution of geographically earmarked expenditures. While these expenditures are not lump-sum transfers of wealth to factor owners, they do entail pecuniary gains since they represent increases in demand for project input factors, thereby driving up their prices.[5] Not only does the public project entail new business for input owners; it allows them to receive a higher price for the sale of inframarginal units as well.[6] As this discussion suggests, geographic expenditures are important because they distribute pecuniary effects. Consequently, the distributional effects of local expenditures combine with consumption benefits in the district's valuation of a project. Put simply, a dollar's valuation of a project may come in either of two forms: a pecuniary gain to a factor owner or a benefit to a project consumer. Partly as a consequence of these distributional effects, and partly for additional reasons enumerated below, the political evaluation of pecuniary effects diverges from their economic treatment.

We may distinguish several classes of agents who are differentially advantaged or harmed (in addition to their tax obligations) by the provision of $P_j(x)$: (1) *in-district consumers*, who receive benefits through consumption of the public project but are unaffected by pecuniary effects; (2) *in-district factor owners*, who obtain pecuniary gains in production of, as well as benefits in consumption from, $P_j(x)$; (3) *out-of-district factor owners*, who obtain pecuniary gains in production (but no consumption benefits since they do not reside in the local constituency); (4) *in-district consumers who make factor market purchases*, who obtain consumption benefits from the project but suffer pecuniary losses in the form of higher prices for factors; and (5) *out-of-district purchasers of factors*, who suffer pecuniary losses through higher prices in factor markets (and who, moreover, obtain no consumption benefits since they do not reside in the district). Public good theorists like Samuelson, Bator, and Head, in their market-failure models of public good provision, typically focus only on type 1 agents and the nonappropriable product of public projects. Cost-benefit studies and welfare analyses (Prest and Turvey 1965; Mishan 1976) also focus on type 1 agents, limiting the role played by the other four types. These studies compute costs and benefits in consumption followed by an appropriate adjustment for pecuniary effects. But these studies may have missed the point. As Aranson and Ordeshook (1978) have emphasized generally, and Stigler (1971) and Peltzman (1976) for the case of regulation, it may well be the appropriable pecuniary gains and losses of factor owners and competing factor users, respectively, that drive the political production process. In this latter view, the consumption benefits of the public project—clean water, mass transit, or whatever—are a by-product of factor owners and factor users seeking pecuniary gains and the avoidance of pecuniary losses, respectively.

How these pecuniary effects are distributed geographically, and whether they are gains or losses, have different kinds of political impacts. Since political representation is geographic, legislators care about who gains and who loses in proportion to their geographic locations. We assume that local gains and losses are politically more significant to the legislator's objectives (reelection and constituency service) than nonlocal effects. Hence representatives use whatever legislative influence they can exercise on behalf of those affected locally by pecuniary effects.

Additionally, there are several reasons to believe that pecuniary gains are exaggerated and pecuniary losses diminished in the representative's political calculus. They relate to the concentration of pecuniary gains and the dispersion of pecuniary losses. First, in what might be termed the "Robert Moses effect" (named after that famous New Yorker who appreciated and exploited it so effectively), is the observation that pecuniary gains in the form of increased jobs, profits, and local tax revenues go to named individuals, firms, and localities from whom the legislator may claim credit and exact tribute. Pecuniary gains may be targeted to constituents; pecuniary losses, on the other hand, are often more widely dispersed, falling on constituents and nonconstituents alike. Second, pecuniary losses, principally through higher prices in factor markets, are not always fully linked to the effects of increased factor demand from the project in question. Indeed, the illustion may be such that pecuniary losers are unable to distinguish the source of their losses from general price inflation. Hence there is a perceptual asymmetry between pecuniary gains and losses. Accompanying this asymmetry in perception is an asymmetry in capacity to convert perceptions of gains and losses into political influence. Third, then, as Peltzman (1976) has noted in another context, gainers typically are smaller in number, more cohesive in political interest, and, consequently, better organized politically. They are capable of rewarding the local legislator for delivering the bacon in a fashion in which pecuniary losers are unable to punish. The combined impact of the Moses, the illusion, and the Peltzman effects is an exaggerated political importance accorded to local pecuniary gainers. The local legislator, then, is strongly encouraged to generate projects with large c_1-type components (vs. c_2-type) and tends to be less concerned with associated pecuniary losses (vs. pecuniary gains).

Since, on the arguments above, there is political value in securing local expenditures for their own sake, the representative, in assessing the project $P_j(x)$, incorporates, on the benefit side of his political calculus, both the consumption benefits his constituents obtain, $b(x)$, and the politically distorted pecuniary effects. Since the latter depend on local expenditures

($c_1[x]$), we write it as $f[c_1(x)]$. For the propositions below, we stipulate $f[c_1(x)] = c_1(x)$ to enable the clear presentation of results unencumbered by mathematical detail; our results are qualitatively unaffected so long as f and f' are positive.[7] Thus, the representative of the single political constituency j seeks a project scale that maximizes his political maximand which, in turn, depends on his constituency's benefits minus its share of the costs: $[b(x) + c_1(x)] - [t_j T(x) + c_3(x)]$.

Model P A Single Political Constituency

Consider the case of a single national constituency. Then $t_j = 1$ and expenditures earmarked for the constituency now consist of all expenditures, that is, $c_1(x) + c_2(x)$. With these assumptions and the identity in (1), the political objective function reduces to

$$\max_x P(x) = [b(x) + c_1(x) + c_2(x)] - [c_1(x) + c_2(x) + c_3(x)]$$

$$= b(x) - c_3(x). \tag{4}$$

The first-order condition is

$$b' - c_3' = 0, \tag{5}$$

and the second-order condition requires that

$$b'' - c_3'' < 0.$$

The solution to equation (5) yields point x^P on figure 13.1. The following theorem shows that $x^P > x^E$.

THEOREM 1 $x^P > x^E$.

Proof From assumptions 1 and 2, x^E is the unique global maximum of $E(x) = b(x) - c_1(x) - c_2(x) - c_3(x)$. Consequently, $b'(x^E) - c_1'(x^E) - c_2'(x^E) - c_3'(x^E) = 0$. From assumption 2, $c_1'(x^E) + c_2'(x^E) > 0$; therefore, $P'(x^E) = b'(x^E) - c_3'(x^E) > 0$. But this violates the first-order condition for a maximum of $P(x)$. Indeed, from the properties of strictly concave functions, since $P'(x^E) > 0$, then either (i) $P'(x) = 0$ for $x = x^P > x^E$, or (ii) $P'(x) = 0$ for no finite x. In the first case, x^P is a global interior maximum which exceeds x^E. In the second case, there is no interior maximum since $P(x)$ increases without bound. A fortiori, a project scale larger than x^E is preferred. Q.E.D.

Model N Non Est *e* Pluribus Unum, or Every District for Itself

The next stage in our examination of political mechanisms is to partition the single national constituency into multiple, disjoint political units called "districts" with representation in a legislature. Each district, through its representative, is presumed to maximize its net (private) benefits without regard to the costs imposed on other districts. Publicly supported projects are funded through taxes which fall primarily on other districts. Hence, the benefits are concentrated while the costs are diffused.

Any political choice institution consisting of representatives of multiple, disjoint constituencies is characterized by a principle of aggregation—that is, a voting or decision rule—and by the substantive choices made under that decision rule. There are several literatures which address these issues.[8] The theoretical thrust of these literatures is twofold: (1) Why is one institutional decision rule employed rather than another? and (2) What are the policy consequences of a given decision rule? Regarding the first, with special emphasis on majority rule, theorists have focused on the instability of decisive coalitions, the ex ante uncertainty surrounding the composition of winning coalitions, and the cost of organizing and monitoring coalition partners. Their express purpose is to address how institutional actors seek, through suitably arranged institutional practices, to improve their circumstances by evolving coping strategies, formal rules, and other mechanisms (called norms in the sociological literature, rules or binding commitments in the game theory literature, and contracts in the property rights literature). The second question takes institutional practices as fixed and examines the policy decisions implied by those practices. The historical origins of and rationales for institutional rules are of little concern in these latter analyses.

Our chief concern is the second question in which we assess the project choices of a legislature in the distributive policy area. In those policy areas characterized by a project-by-project orientation, the geographic concentration of benefits, and the diffusion of costs, there is abundant evidence that universalism and reciprocity are prevailing decision rules in the U.S. Congress. The former practice assures any interested district a project; the latter, in recognition of the fact that district differences translate into different policy priorities, facilitates a process of mutual support and logrolling. These two practices combine to permit packages of distinct projects earmarked for interested districts to obtain the support even of those without a stake in the package in exchange for reciprocal treatment. Empirical studies, moreover, repeatedly observe the operation of universalistic criteria. Examples include the pork barrel of rivers and harbors (Maass 1951; Ferejohn 1974); model cities and urban renewal (Plott 1968); tax loopholes (Manley 1970); the traditional tariff (Schattschneider 1935); private member bills (Froman 1967); military procurement (Rundquist 1973); and categorical grants-in-aid (Mayhew 1974). Indeed, some scholars observe a tendency to infuse controversial policies with distributive elements in order to build a more inclusive coalition.[9]

Elsewhere (Fiorina 1978; Weingast 1979; Shepsle and Weingast 1981) the conditions under which institutional actors prefer universalistic criteria to pure majority rule are derived. These results, together with the preponderance of empirical evidence cited above, provide the basis for our focus on universalism and its policy consequences. First we explore the consequences of universalism in the extreme in which each legislator independently determines whether to propose a project and, if so, at what scale. The following section then examines the conditions under which there are incentives for legislators to coordinate project selection. Consider legislator j's maximand regarding his district's project:[10]

$$N_j(x) = b(x) + c_1(x) - t_j T(x) - c_3(x). \tag{6}$$

The legislator is presumed to maximize the district's private benefits, $b(x) + c_1(x)$, minus its share of the taxes, $t_j T(x) = t_j[c_1(x) + c_2(x)]$, minus the externalities of the project which fall on the district, $c_3(x)$. This simply reflects the proposition that legislators are reelection oriented and that their prospects are positively associated with the net benefits they deliver to their constituents. According to this reelection mechanism, voter decisions correspond to a "what have you done for me lately?" evaluation.[11]

Maximization of (6) yields the first-order condition

$$b' + c_1' - t_j T' - c_3' = 0,$$

or

$$b' + c_1' = t_j(c_1' + c_2') + c_3'. \tag{7}$$

The second-order condition requires

$$b'' + c_1'' - t_j(c_1'' + c_2'') - c_3'' < 0.$$

Equation (7) has a solution yielding a maximum point x^N for (6) depicted in figure 13.1. The next theorem establishes that, in a wide set of circumstances, x^N exceeds x^P.

THEOREM 2 If $c_1' > t_j(c_1' + c_2')$, then $x^N > x^P$.

Proof Note that $N(x)$ defined in (6) may be recast as

$$N(x) = P(x) + c_1(x) - t_j[c_1(x) + c_2(x)],$$

where $P(x) = b(x) - c_3(x)$. At the maximum of $P(x)$, $x = x^P$,

$$P'(x^P) = b'(x^P) - c_3'(x^P) = 0.$$

This implies that at $x = x^P$

$$\begin{aligned} N'(x^P) &= P'(x^P) + c_1'(x^P) - t_j[c_1'(x^P) + c_2'(x^P)] \\ &= c_1'(x^P) - t_j[c_1'(x^P) + c_2'(x^P)]. \end{aligned}$$

Therefore, the premise of the theorem implies that $N'(x) > 0$ for all $x \leq x^P$. Consequently, if $N(x)$ possesses a maximum—call it x^N—then $x^N > x^P$. Moreover, if $N(x)$ does not possess a maximum, then our theorem obtains a fortiori since $N(x)$ then increases without bound. Q.E.D.

The condition in the premise of theorem 2, $c_1' > t_j(c_1' + c_2')$, can be presumed to hold in most circumstances. This condition requires that, in district-initiated projects, locally earmarked expenditures grow more rapidly with project scale than local taxes. Since t_j is ordinarily quite small, only a modicum of imagination by legislators is required to find projects with this local expenditure characteristic. For example, if taxes are shared evenly by districts, then $t_j = 1/n$, where n is the number of districts, and the condition becomes

$$c_1' > \frac{1}{n}(c_1' + c_2').$$

That is, so long as district-targeted expenditures grow with project scale at a rate at least $1/n$th as fast as total expenditures, the premise (and hence the conclusion) of theorem 2 holds; in even moderate-sized legislatures this is a fairly weak condition.

More generally, suppose $t_j = t_j(z)$ where z might be any characteristic (examples of which are given below). Then the following comparative statics result may be established.

THEOREM 3 Let x^N be the optimum for (6). Then $dx^N/dz > 0$ if and only if $t_j' < 0$.

Proof Rewriting (6), we have

$$N(x) = b(x) + [1 - t_j(z)]c_1(x) - t_j(z)c_2(x) - c_3(x),$$

and first-order condition

$$N'(x) = b'(x) + [1 - t_j(z)]c_1'(x) - t_j(z)c_2'(x) - c_3'(x) = 0.$$

The second-order requirement is

$$N''(x) = b''(x) + [1 - t_j(z)]c_1''(x) - t_j(z)c_2''(x) - c_3''(x) < 0.$$

Totally differentiating the first-order condition yields

$$\{b''(x) + [1 - t_j(z)]c_1''(x) - t_j(z)c_2''(x) - c_3''(x)\}\, dx$$
$$= [c_1'(x) + c_2'(x)]t_j'(z)\, dz.$$

Thus,

$$\frac{dx}{dz} = \frac{[c_1'(x) + c_2'(x)]}{\{b''(x) + [1 - t_j(z)]c_1''(x) - t_j(z)c_2''(x) - c_3''(x)\}}\, t_j'(z).$$

The numerator of the coefficient on the right-hand side is positive (from assumption 2) and the denominator is negative (from the second-order condition). The coefficient, therefore, is negative, establishing that the sign of dx/dz is opposite that of $t_j'(z)$:

$$t_j'(z) < 0 \rightarrow \frac{dx}{dz} > 0,$$

$$t_j'(z) > 0 \rightarrow \frac{dx}{dz} < 0.$$

Q.E.D.

COROLLARY (The Law of $1/n$): If district tax share is a declining function of the number of districts (n), then the degree of inefficiency in project scale $(x^N - x^E)$ is an increasing function of the number of districts.

Proof Let $t_j = t_j(n)$ with $t_j'(n) < 0$. Then, from theorem 3, $dx^N/dn > 0$. Q.E.D.

The corollary indicates that when taxes are apportioned as a decreasing function of the number of political units—for example, $t_j(n) = 1/n$ for all j—then the optimum project scale for any district grows as the polity is more finely partitioned into districts.[12] Theorem 3, however, is more general, for it applies to tax mechanisms that may be the function of any politically relevant characteristic. If a district's tax share is a decreasing function of certain of its legislator's institutional characteristics (membership or influence on tax-writing committee), political characteristics of its representative (is he a committee chairman? is he associated with the majority party?), or economic or demographic characteristics of the district (proportion of families below poverty level, proportion of population above age 65), then we can associate increasingly inefficient projects with particular kinds of districts as defined by these tax-relevant characteristics. In all these cases, theorem 3 indicates that the equilibrium scale of a district's project (and, given the assumptions, its degree of inefficiency) changes with respect to some tax criterion in precisely the opposite way the tax share changes with respect to that criterion.

Institutional Incentives to Restrict Project Size

We have just shown that decentralized choice by a representative legislature characterized by a universalism mechanism, a tax-sharing rule, and a political objective function yields a vector of projects $x^N = (x_1^N, \ldots, x_n^N)$. Theorems 1 and 2 provide the conditions in which $x_i^N > x_i^E$, $i = 1, \ldots, n$. However, x_i^N, the project scale for district i that maximizes its legislator's political objective function (6), is computed in isolation of computations by other legislators; therefore, it does not take the expenditure and tax externalities (positive and negative) generated by those other projects into account.

In this section, we seek to determine whether or not there is an institutional basis for restraining unbridled universalism.[13] In particular, we turn to an examination of packages of projects and seek to discover whether there exists a package of constitutionally restricted projects, $x^C = (x_1^C, \ldots, x_n^C)$, with the property that $x^C \succ_i x^N$ (where $\succ_i$ is the preference order of district i over packages of projects). To accomplish this, consider the complete political maximand of legislator j, $B^j(x_1, \ldots, x_n)$, which rewrites (6) to incorporate the effects of projects in other districts. The net benefits to district j consist of b-type benefits from its own project, $b(x_j)$; c_1-type expenditures from its own project, $c_1(x_j)$; c_2-type expenditures spent in district j from other projects, $\sum_{i \neq j} c_{2j}(x_i)$; nonexpenditure costs from its own project $c_3(x_j)$; and its tax share of the total expenditures, $t_j \sum_{i=1}^{n} [c_1(x_i) + c_2(x_i)]$. Thus

$$B^j(x_1, \ldots, x_n) = \left[b(x_j) + c_1(x_j) + \sum_{i \neq j} c_{2j}(x_i) \right] - \left\{ c_3(x_j) + t_j \sum_{i=1}^{n} [c_1(x_i) + c_2(x_i)] \right\}. \tag{8}$$

Before considering the possibility of restrictions on project size, we first characterize choice under the complete political maximand, $B^j(x_1, \ldots, x_n)$. Calling x_j^B legislator j's solution to the maximization of (8), we have:

THEOREM 4 $x_j^B = x_j^N$.

Proof Equation (8) may be rewritten

$$B^j = \{b(x_j) + c_1(x_j) - c_3(x_j) - t_j[c_1(x_j) + c_2(x_j)]\} + \left\{ \sum_{i \neq j} c_{2j}(x_i) - t_j \sum_{i \neq j} [c_1(x_i) + c_2(x_i)] \right\}, \tag{9}$$

which, from (6), becomes

$$B^j = N_j(x_j) + \left\{ \sum_{i \neq j} c_{2j}(x_i) - t_j \sum_{i \neq j} [c_1(x_i) + c_2(x_i)] \right\}. \tag{10}$$

Since the terms in braces are not functions of x_j, the first- and second-order conditions for B^j are the same as those for $N_j(x_j)$; thus, their respective maxima are the same. Q.E.D.

Theorem 4 establishes that our initial focus on N_j (instead of B^j) involved no loss of generality for questions about decentralized project choice. Moreover, theorem 4 establishes that x_j^N is a Nash strategy for legislator j and that the project vector, x^N, is a Nash equilibrium.[14]

Turning to the role of cooperatively imposed restrictions on project size, we state a characterization theorem that establishes the circumstances under which districts (or their representatives) prefer a restricted collection of projects, x^C, to the collection under unrestrained universalism, x^N. For the vector of projects $x^K = (x_1^K, \ldots, x_n^K)$, let $E_j(x^K)$ represent the tax and expenditure effects of other projects on district j. Specifically,

$$E_j(x^K) = \sum_{i \neq j} \{t_j[c_1(x_i^K) + c_2(x_i^K)] - c_{2j}(x_i^K)\}.$$

In effect, $E_j(x^K)$ is the tax bill for district j for all other projects net of local expenditures to district j from these other projects—that is, net negative external costs.

THEOREM 5 $x^C \succ_j x^N$ if and only if $N_j(x^N) - N_j(x^C) < E_j(x^N) - E_j(x^C)$.

Theorem 5 conveys the following idea: Legislator j has an interest in substituting a collection of projects $x^C = (x_1^C, \ldots, x_n^C)$ for $x^N = (x_1^N, \ldots, x_n^N)$ if and only if his district's reduction in political benefits from the reduced scale of its own project is compensated for by a concomitant reduction in its burden of net negative external costs. There are several ways in which this may fail to hold for a given district j. For example, (i) district j has a sufficiently small tax share, t_j; (ii) district j is, disproportionately, a source of project inputs for other districts, in which case the $c_{2j}(x_i)$ terms are large; and (iii) the political benefits for district j with project scale x_j^N, $b(x_j^N) + c_1(x_j^N)$, are inordinately large. In each of these cases, the condition may fail, implying the absence of a unanimous preference for x^C over x^N. Moreover, there do not appear to be any interesting properties associated with the family of functions $b(x)$, $c(x)$, and $t(x)$ that satisfy the condition in theorem 5; nor is there any ex ante basis for supposing that the condition in theorem 5 will be encountered in empirical settings.

Despite the lack of unanimous preference for restriction under all circumstances, legislators have something to gain by properly accounting for the pecuniary externalities of project scale selection. The next theorem provides some insight into the optimal set of projects which internalizes these effects.

THEOREM 6 x^P maximizes $\sum_{j=1}^n B^j(x)$, given in (8).

Proof

$$L = \sum_{j=1}^n B^j(x) = \sum_{j=1}^n \left\{ b(x_j) + c_1(x_j) + \sum_{i \neq j} c_{2j}(x_i) - c_3(x_j) \right.$$
$$\left. - t_j \sum_{i=1}^n [c_1(x_i) + c_2(x_i)] \right\}$$

$$= \sum_{j=1}^{n} [b(x_j) + c_1(x_j) + c_2(x_j) - c_3(x_j) - c_1(x_j) - c_2(x_j)]$$

$$= \sum_{j=1}^{n} [b(x_j) - c_3(x_j)].$$

The first-order conditions are

$$\frac{\partial L}{\partial x_j} = b'(x_j) - c_3'(x_j) = 0, \quad j = 1, \ldots, n.$$

Noting that $(\partial^2 L)/(\partial x_i \partial x_j) = 0$ for $i \neq j$, the second-order conditions are

$$\frac{\partial^2 L}{\partial x_j^2} = b''(x_j) - c_3''(x_j) < 0, \quad j = 1, \ldots, n.$$

These equations and inequalities are the same as (5), which identifies the vector x^P in figure 13.1. Q.E.D.

Theorem 6 shows that total political net benefits are maximized with the vector $x^P = (x_1^P, \ldots, x_n^P)$. Potential gains may be captured if the system of universalistic project selection is amended so that, while each district is assured a project, the project scale is determined as if there were but a single district (as in model P above). Notice that theorem 6 does not assert that $x^P \succ_j x^N$, $j = 1, \ldots, n$ (substituting x^P for x^C, theorem 5 shows the restricted circumstances in which this will hold). What theorem 6 does assert is that a compensation scheme which redistributes net benefits is feasible so that x^P together with this compensation is preferred by all districts not only to x^N but to any other omnibus of projects.

It is occasionally asserted that the distributive politics game is a prisoner's dilemma in the economic sense—that unrestrained universalism produces a project package that is an economically inefficient Nash equilibrium, on the one hand, and is unanimously regarded as less preferable than x^E ($x^E \succ_j x^N$, $j = 1, \ldots, n$) on the other. Theorems 1, 2, and 4 establish the first part of this assertion. However, retaining the political conceptualization of net benefits given in (8), theorem 5 shows that the second part of the assertion does not always follow. The collection x^E is not always unanimously regarded as preferable to x^N. More importantly, theorem 6 shows that even when all representatives favor restrictions, the *politically* optimal set of projects is x^P, not x^E.

This discussion underscores the basic point of the chapter. The efficient collection, x^E, though normatively attractive in welfare analysis, is not always behaviorally relevant. The implication of the political maximand (8) and theorems 1, 2, 5, and 6 is that legislators hold no brief for efficiency, per se, either with regard to their own project selection or a package of such projects.

Extensions and Discussion

The model developed in the previous sections roots the inefficiency of distributive politics in democratic mechanisms and especially in the geographic basis of political constituencies. This latter feature produces two independent sources of bias. First, locally targeted expenditures are counted by the local constituency as benefits. Second, the districting mechanism in conjunction with the taxation system provides incentives to increase project size beyond the efficient point by attenuating the relationship between beneficiaries and revenue sources. A cooperative legislature has no incentive to remove entirely these sources of inefficiency (beyond that described in the discussion following theorem 6).

In this section, we examine several related themes and applications. Each of these is either an extension of our model to domains beyond that of traditional distributive policy or a specialization of our model to substantively relevant cases of distributive policy.

Congressional Limitation on Project Size

A well-known behavioral mechanism has operated in Congress since the 1880s that restrains the attempts of legislators to fund their pet projects. At the authorization stage, a universalism mechanism is at work—the annual omnibus public works bill, for example, typically contains authorizations for projects in most congressional districts. Following the passage of authorizing legislation comes the separate stage of actually appropriating monies. Here, the Committee on Appropriations systematically scales down each project (for a description of this process, see Fenno 1966 and Ferejohn 1974).

Our model sheds some light on this well-established congressional practice. First, suppose the premise of theorem 5 holds, where $x^P = x^C$. Hence, $x^P \succ_j x^N$, $j = 1, \ldots, n$. Second, assume legislator j and only legislator j

knows x_j^P and x_j^N. Theorem 5 implies that legislators unanimously favor a mechanism reducing project sizes from the uncoordinated choice, x^N. But there does not appear to be a straightforward "demand-revealing" mechanism inducing legislators to announce anything other than their maximizing Nash strategy, x_j^N. Thus, in the face of imperfect information, the simpler mechanism of scaling down all projects—the current practice of the appropriations committee—may yield a vector of project sizes less than x^N and preferred by all legislators.[15]

Examination of Interesting Subclasses

We mention briefly, as an indication of the utility of this approach, some interesting special cases of the political maximand (6):

$$N(x_j) = b(x_j) + c_1(x_j) - c_3(x_j) - t_j[c_1(x_j) + c_2(x_j)].$$

The details may be provided by the reader.

1 Benefit Tax This tax scheme requires the district to pay the entire cost of a strictly local public project ($t_j = 1$). The maximand becomes

$$N_j(x_j) = b(x_j) - c_2(x_j) - c_3(x_j),$$

and assumptions 1 and 2 imply a project scale x_j^* with the property $x_j^E \leq x_j^* \leq x_j^P < x_j^N$. Note that if $c_2(x_j) = 0$, then $x_j^* = x_j^P$ whereas, if $c_1(x_j) = 0$, then $x_j^* = x_j^E$. This last fact suggests that a benefit tax in conjunction with no local expenditures is a sufficient condition for public sector efficiency.

2 Free-Ride Tax In this case, $t_j = 0$ and the maximand is

$$N(x_j) = b(x_j) + c_1(x_j) - c_3(x_j),$$

which implies a scale $x_j^* > x_j^N$. This case approximates local public goods, financed by user fees, where the local residents rarely number among the users. For example, if Yellowstone National Park were financed by user fees assessed states in proportion to their respective share of the population using the park, then Wyoming residents receive a cheap, if not free, ride on taxes.

3 Foreign Aid versus Military Assistance We can interpret the political popularity of the latter and unpopularity of the former via the following calculation. Let x^F and x^M describe levels of the two forms of aid; assume $b(x_j^F) = b(x_j^M)$, ceteris paribus, for any political constituency (assumed, in any event, to be small unless the constituency contains partisans of or emigrants from the benefiting country); for some constituencies (producers of military hardware), $c_1(x_j^M) > 0$; for all constituencies, on the other hand, $c_1(x_j^F) = 0$; for all constituencies, $c_3(x_j^M) = c_3(x_j^F) = 0$. Thus,

$$N(x_j^M) = b(x_j^M) + (1 - t_j)c_1(x_j^M) - t_j c_2(x_j^M),$$

$$N(x_j^F) = b(x_j^F) - t_j c_2(x_j^F).$$

Assumptions 1 and 2 imply $(x_j^M)^* > (x_j^F)^*$, an observation consistent with their respective popularities. It also makes sense of the recent policy innovation of attaching strings to foreign aid requiring recipients to make purchases in the United States (c_1-type expenditures).

4 Rube Goldberg Machines and Military Bases Suppose $b(x_j) = 0$ for a project in a given constituency, j. Then

$$N(x_j) = (1 - t_j)c_1(x_j) - t_j c_2(x_j) - c_3(x_j).$$

Even though $b(x_j) = 0$, the (politically) optimal project scale may be greater than zero. Specifically,

$$x_j^N > 0 \quad \text{if } N'(0) > 0, \quad \text{or} \quad (1 - t_j)c_1'(0) - t_j c_2'(0) - c_3'(0) > 0.$$

Consider the case of many military bases (and other Rube Goldberg machines) which, by the Department of Defense's own admission, provide virtually no contribution to defense ($b[x] = 0$). These nevertheless remain attractive to local constituencies (hence $x_j^N > 0$) because of the overriding importance of these projects to the local economy in the form of c_1-type benefits. Throughout this chapter, we have emphasized the political inappropriateness of economic net benefits as a relevant decision criterion. In this special case, it appears that even the absence of economic benefits altogether is not a disqualifying characteristic in political choice.

Generalization to Non–Pork Barrel Policies[16]

One of the central features of our models is the unpacking of costs in politically relevant ways in which we distinguish project costs returned to the district as expenditures, costs returned to other districts, and non-expenditure costs borne within the district. We focused, however, on distributive or pork barrel projects, defined as projects whose benefits are geographically concentrated and whose costs are spread through general taxation. Two extensions offer further insight into nondistributive policies.

The first distinguishes an additional cost, $c_4(x)$, or external, nonexpenditure costs borne by other districts. The second defines another source of economic benefits, $b_2(x)$, that accrues to other constituencies as a consequence of a project in a particular district.

1 Additional External Costs If additional external costs of the jth project spill over into other districts, it can easily be shown that the degree of inefficiency increases when governed by decentralized project choice under the political maximand, $N(x)$. Since the model now divides externalities into their politically relevant components, $c_3(x)$ and $c_4(x)$, we can make further observations about the degree to which the political system can be relied upon to internalize externalities associated with public activities. If the externalities are not too large (in the sense that they are local and do not extend into neighboring districts), the public sector action governed by a representative legislature internalizes them. However, if they are large, public sector action may not.

The politically relevant (though economically arbitrary) distinction implied by district boundaries suggests that the public sector can only provide certain categories of public goods which are not available through private market arrangements. Hence, jurisdictional questions become of paramount importance when producing a local public good like flood walls along a river which divides two political jurisdictions. Some of the most infamous cases of pork barrel politics illustrate this point: The flood walls along the lower part of the Mississippi River, which divides Louisiana from Mississippi, are 3 feet higher on the Mississippi side (see Ferejohn 1974, pp. 56–58). Similarly, the levees on the Indiana side of the Wabash River are higher than those on the Illinois side. Thus, a universalistic representative legislature is biased toward projects with low c_3-type costs while failing to consider c_4-type costs.

2 Additional External Benefits Let $b(x_j) = b_1(x_j) + b_2(x_j)$ where $b_1(x_j)$ are the benefits of the jth project concentrated in district j and $b_2(x_j)$ are the benefits consumed by residents of other districts (presumed zero throughout the body of the chapter). That is, $b_2(x_j)$ is the positive consumption externalities (as compared with $c_2[x_j]$, which are the positve production externalities).

Because the benefits outside the district are not readily internalized under a distributive policy mechanism, large multidistrict (multistate) projects are likely to be rare relative to projects with concentrated local benefits. Consequently, multidistrict public goods (in the economic sense) are not only likely to be underproduced by a market mechanism but by a representative legislature as well (see Aranson and Ordeshook 1978). A universalistic representative legislature is biased toward projects with high b_1-type benefits, while failing to internalize b_2-type benefits. Thus, both positive and negative externalities adversely affect public as well as private provision.

Conclusion

Throughout this chapter we have focused on the sources of inefficiency in public decision making. Our model demonstrates that democratic institutions play an important role. Three mechanisms were shown to influence the politically optimal project choice: the political cost-accounting mechanism, the districting mechanism, and the taxation mechanism. These features of the political economy systematically tranform the economic benefits and costs into political counterparts. Since it is the latter that determine the maximands for political actors and not their economic counterparts, these govern political choice.

While our modeling of the districting and taxation mechanisms is straightforward and uncontroversial, there are circumstances in which our treatment of the incidence of gains and losses from local expenditures is implausible. We have presumed that pecuniary gainers figure more prominently than pecuniary losers in a legislator's reelection constituency. However, under some circumstances this may not be true. A legislator's reelection constituency, for example, may be dominated not by factor owners of a public project but by those who would bear the brunt of the pecuniary losses and the nonpecuniary external costs of the project. We would not, therefore, expect the legislator to seek such projects. Indeed, since the menu of distributive programs is sufficiently diverse, there normally is something available for everyone. Thus we tend to find reclamation projects in the West, locks and dams in river districts with an active construction industry, and wildlife refuges in Sierra Club districts. Because of this diversity in policy preferences and program categories, the logic supporting the political distortion of pecuniary incidences continues to hold.

Our principal conclusion is that since political institutions fundamentally alter the perceptions and incidence of benefits and costs, they systematically bias project choices away from the efficient outcomes. In the context of distributive politics, this was shown to imply larger projects and programs than are economically warranted.

Notes

Mr. Weingast is assistant professor of Economics and research associate at the Center for the Study of American Business. Mr. Shepsle is professor of Political Science and research associate of the Center for the Study of American Business. Mr. Johnsen is a doctoral candidate in the Department of Political Science. The authors thank Roger Noll of the California Institute of Technology for a timely conversation. They are also grateful for the constructive comments of Morris Fiorina, George Stigler, and an anonymous referee.

1. Consult Downs 1957, 1967; Niskanen 1971; Riker and Brams 1973; Breton 1974; Ferejohn and Fiorina 1975; Wagner 1976; Aranson and Ordeshook 1978; and Fiorina and Noll 1978.

2. See Lowi (1964) for a discussion of different kinds of policies based on the characteristics of beneficiaries as well as the mechanisms of financing.

3. Some students of cost-benefit analysis, e.g., McKean (1958, chap. 8), argue against including pecuniary external effects in the calculations, claiming instead that these constitute distributional effects that are not germane for efficiency determinations. The treatment of pecuniary external effects remains controversial in cost-benefit analysis. Our results reported in this chapter do not depend on how this controversy is resolved.

4. There is a fourth component of costs, namely, nonexpenditure real resource costs that spill over into other political constituencies. Since $P_j(x)$ is a concentrated project, we ignore this for the present. We return to this point in the concluding section. For analysis of other kinds of policies not possessing the particular properties of distributive projects, see Shepsle and Weingast (1980).

5. This statement presumes that factors of production are geographically fixed in the short run. This does not preclude the bidding away of pecuniary gains as the long-run supply of factors adjusts to this change in demand. For some projects, which are one shot and nonrepetitive in nature, the short-run analysis holds since the long-run adjustment process is attenuated. For other programs, in which a permanent increase in demand has occurred (e.g., the continuing flow of military procurement projects to a district), long-run market forces adjust with the concomitant bidding away of pecuniary gains. Nevertheless, the political effect is the same, though now manifested in an aversion to pecuniary losses suffered if demand were to contract (i.e., the flow of projects cease).

6. There are pecuniary losers as well—namely, other users of project factors who experience rising prices.

7. A straightforward comparative statics analysis, which we do not pursue here, would examine how alternative specifications of f affect optimal choices. Such an analysis would confirm that as long as f is positive, the qualitative nature of our results stands. As noted, it is not too misleading to equate $f[c_1(x)]$ with $c_1(x)$ or some linear function thereof, namely, $f[c_1(x)] = \beta c_1(x)$, in the relevant range. But only up to a point! If expenditures yield not only consumption benefits but β dollars per dollar expended of additional "benefit," then, subject only to external costs ($c_3[x]$), legislators would be motivated to expend the entire GNP, clearly an absurdity. The function $f[c_1(x)]$ is meant to represent the political (read: electoral) advantage secured by the legislator who delivers $c_1(x)$ dollars of public expenditure to his district. Ultimately this advantage must tail off so that, in a general mathematical analysis, $f[c_1(x)]$ eventually exhibits diminishing returns.

8. These include research on logrolling, constitutional choice, and distributive policymaking. There is a large literature on each of these topics, but Buchanan and Tullock (1962) remains the best introduction and overview.

9. See Stockman (1975) and Fiorina (1978) for illustrations.

10. Eq. (6) does not contain district j's total benefits and costs, only those falling within its control. Theorem 4 below establishes the innocuousness of this omission.

11. This model of voting is known as retrospective voting in contrast to the prospective voting model, initially popularized by Downs (1957), in which voters respond to promises for future policy.

12. This analysis presumes that the only change in $N(x)$ following a change in the number of districts is the tax rate, t_j. If, however, $c_1(x)$, $c_2(x)$, and $c_3(x)$ depend on the configuration of districts, then two countervailing tendencies may be observed. Increasing the number of districts (1) transforms some portion of $c_1(x)$ into $c_2(x)$ and (2) decreases the tax share of the district. Since the first effect reduces and the second increases the optimal project scale, the net effect is ambiguous without further specification.

13. In Shepsle and Weingast (1981), we describe results that demonstrate the ex ante superiority of universalism to pure majority rule in the eyes of each legislator. Here we ask whether a restricted form of universalism, in turn, is superior to pure universalism.

14. This view interprets our model of unrestricted universalism as a game. The choice set for player j is the size of his project, x_j, when project choice is governed by a universalism mechanism. The Nash equilibrium follows from the separability of the positive and negative externalities of other projects in (10). As a result, each district makes its own decisions without attending to the externalities it produces or consumes.

15. A complete analysis must resolve two issues. First, as a consequence of the scaling down practice by the Appropriations Committee, will the legislator strategically seek a project scale in excess of x_j^N so that, when it is scaled down, it will eventually reach size x_j^N? Alternatively, are there sanctions discouraging artificial inflation of project scale at the authorizing stage? Second, are there sanctions available to be applied against the Appropriations Committee to ensure it does not scale down too much? See Fenno (1966) for some empirical details. These issues concerning demand revelation mechanisms are theoretically intriguing but take us too far afield to be dealt with here.

16. These themes are developed in more detail in Shepsle and Weingast (1980).

References

Aranson, Peter, and Ordeshook, Peter. 1978. The political bases of public sector growth in a representative democracy. Paper presented at the Conference on the Causes and Consequences of Public Sector Growth, Dorado Beach, Puerto Rico.

Breton, Albert. 1974. *The economic theory of representative government*. Chicago: Aldine.

Buchanan, James, and Tullock, Gordon. 1962. *The calculus of consent: Logical foundations of constitutional democracy*. Ann Arbor: University of Michigan Press.

Downs, Anthony. 1957. *An economic theory of democracy*. New York: Harper & Row.

Downs, Anthony. 1967. *Inside bureaucracy*. Boston: Little, Brown.

Fenno, Richard, Jr. 1966. *The power of the purse: Appropriations politics in Congress*. Boston: Little, Brown.

Ferejohn, John. 1974. *Pork barrel politics: Rivers and harbors legislation, 1947–68*. Stanford, CA: Stanford University Press.

Ferejohn, John, and Fiorina, Morris. 1975. Purposive models of legislative behavior. *American Economic Review Papers and Proceedings* 65:407–414.

Fiorina, Morris. 1978. Legislative facilitation of government growth: Universalism and reciprocity practices in majority rule institutions. Paper presented at the Conference on the Causes and Consequences of Public Sector Growth, Dorado Beach, Puerto Rico.

Fiorina, Morris, and Noll, Roger. Voters, bureaucrats and legislators: A rational choice perspective on the growth of bureaucracy. *Journal of Public Economics* 9:239–254.

Froman, Lewis, Jr. 1967. *The congressional process: Strategies, rules, and procedures.* Boston: Little, Brown.

Lowi, Theodore. 1964. American business, public policy, case-studies, and political theory. *World politics* 16:677–715.

Lowi, Theodore. 1979. *The end of liberalism: The second republic of the United States.* 2d. ed. New York: Norton.

Maass, Arthur. 1951. *Muddy waters: The Army Engineers and the nation's rivers.* Cambridge, MA: Harvard University Press.

McKean, Roland. 1958. *Efficiency in government through systems analysis, with emphasis on water resources development.* New York: Wiley.

Manley, John. 1970. *The politics of finance: The House Committee on Ways and Means,* Boston: Little, Brown.

Mayhew, David. 1974. *Congress: The electoral connection.* New Haven: Yale University Press.

Mishan, E. J. 1976. *Cost-benefit analysis.* 2d. ed. New York: Praeger.

Niskanen, William. 1971. *Bureaucracy and representative government.* Chicago: Aldine-Atherton.

Peltzman, Sam. 1976. Toward a more general theory of regulation. *Journal of Law and Economy* 19: 211–240.

Plott, Charles. 1968. Some organizational influences on urban renewal decision. *American Economic Review Papers and Proceedings* 58:306–321.

Prest, Alan, and Turvey, Ralph. 1965. Cost-benefit analysis: A survey. *Economic Journal* 75:683–735.

Riker, William, and Brams, Steven. 1973. The paradox of vote trading. *American Political Science Review.* 67:1235–1247.

Rundquist, Barry. 1973. Congressional influences on the distribution of prime military contracts. Ph.D. dissertation, Stanford University.

Schattschneider, Elmer. 1935. *Politics, pressures and the tariff.* Englewood Cliffs, NJ: Prentice-Hall.

Shepsle, Kenneth, and Weingast, Barry. 1980. Political solutions to market problems: The political incidence of economic benefits and costs. Paper presented at the annual meeting of the Public Choice Society, San Francisco.

Shepsle, Kenneth, and Weingast, Barry. 1981. Political preferences for the pork barrel: A generalization. *American Journal of Political Science* 25:96–111.

Stigler, George. 1971. The theory of economic regulation. *Bell Journal of Economics and Management Science* 2:3–21.

Stockman, David. 1975. The social pork barrel. *Public Interest* 39:3–30.

Wagner, Richard. 1976. Revenue structure, fiscal illusion, and budgetary choice. *Public Choice* 25:45–61.

Weingast, Barry. 1979. A rational choice perspective on congressional norms. *American Journal of Political Science* 23:245–263.

IV ECONOMIC REFORM AND THE STATUS QUO

14 Resistance to Reform: Status Quo Bias in the Presence of Individual-Specific Uncertainty

Raquel Fernandez and Dani Rodrik

Why do governments so often fail to adopt policies that economists consider to be efficiency-enhancing? This is one of the fundamental questions of political economy. The answer usually relies on what may be called a "nonneutrality" in the way that the gains and losses from the reform are distributed within society: the gainers from the status quo are taken to be politically "strong" and the losers to be politically "weak," thereby preventing the adoption of reform. (Nondistorting transfers would of course short-circuit this problem, but they are usually ruled out as unavailable.) In pressure-group models, this nonneutrality typically expresses itself in the form of differential organizational ability: for example, the gains from the status quo may be concentrated on a small number of individuals while the losses are diffuse, such that free riding hampers the lobbying efforts of the second group to a much greater extent.[1] In voting models, the nonneutrality operates through distributional consequences across individuals, so that the median voter may prefer the status quo to a reform that would increase aggregate real income.[2]

We propose a different source of nonneutrality in this chapter, one that relies on *uncertainty* regarding the distribution of gains and losses from reform. What we will show, specifically, is that there is a bias toward the status quo (and hence against efficiency-enhancing reforms) whenever (some of) the individual gainers and losers from reform cannot be identified beforehand.[3] There are reforms which, once adopted, will receive adequate political support but would have failed to carry the day ex ante. Significantly, the result holds even if individuals are risk-neutral, forward-looking, and rational and in the absence of *aggregate* uncertainty regarding the consequences of reform. Moreover, the conclusion does not rely on hysteresis due to sunk costs.

While the logic is general, we will use trade liberalization as an example to motivate our approach and the specific model. Trade reform is a particularly interesting example because there is possibly no area in which there is greater consensus among economists.[4] Despite the well-known gains from trade, however, trade liberalization is politically one of the most contentious actions that a government can take. Historically, significant

Reprinted from *American Economic Review*, 81, (1991) 1146–1155, by permission of The American Economic Association.

liberalizations have almost always been associated with changes in political regime or else have been undertaken at a point of economic crisis. There is by now a large literature on the political economy of trade policy.[5]

A striking paradox, particularly in developing countries, is that while trade reform typically turns out to be a boon to large segments of the private sector, these same groups are rarely enthusiastic about reform early on. This is a pattern observed in Taiwan and South Korea (early 1960s), Chile (1970s), and Turkey (1980s), the leading cases of trade liberalization in the developing world. In all three cases, reform was imposed by authoritarian regimes and against the wishes of business, even though business emerged as the staunchest defender of outward orientation once the policies were in place.[6] Existing models of trade reform cannot account for such apparently inconsistent behavior. However, the anomaly is consistent with the results of our model. In each of these cases, there existed considerable uncertainty regarding the identity of the eventual beneficiaries (and losers) from the reform. As with any large-scale price reform, it was difficult to predict ex ante precisely which sectors and which entrepreneurs would be the winners. In such a setting, the nonneutrality identified in this chapter comes into play in full force: when individuals do not know how they will fare under a reform, aggregate support for reform can be lower than what it would have been under complete information, even when individuals are risk-neutral and there is no aggregate uncertainty. Moreover, the role of uncertainty in determining the outcomes is not symmetric, since reforms that are initially rejected will continue to be so in the future while reforms that are initially accepted may find themselves reversed over time.

In Section I, we provide a simple, diagrammatic exposition which shows the logic of the argument in as transparent a manner as possible. In Sections II and III, we develop a model which embeds the results within standard trade theory and demonstrates that the results can obtain within a general-equilibrium framework. We conclude the chapter in Section IV.

I The Argument

The maintained assumption in this chapter is that a policy reform is more likely to be adopted the larger is the number of individuals in favor of it.

For concreteness, it is convenient to use the language of majority voting (although our argument will also hold for some other social-choice mechanisms).

Figure 14.1A shows schematically an economy in which individuals are aligned uniformly on a continuum between 0 and 1, as represented by the horizontal axis. The midpoint of the axis is indicated by "*M*." We assume that the economy has two productive sectors, sectors W (for winners) and L (for losers). D represents the demarcation point between the status quo allocation of individuals in the two sectors: individuals in sector L are located to the left of D, and individuals in sector W are to the right of D. As drawn, a majority of the individuals are in the L sector prior to reform.

Now consider a reform that, if adopted, would increase the return to W-sector individuals, lower the return to L-sector individuals, and draw individuals from the second sector to the first. The top panel of Figure 14.1A shows the distributional outcome, with the two boxes representing the gains and losses accruing to individuals on different segments of the continuum. The magnitudes of gains and losses are indicated by the numbers corresponding to each box. All individuals already in the W sector naturally gain, but there are also some gainers among individuals who were previously employed in the other sector. Since the reform is taken to enhance efficiency, the gainers' box is larger in area than the losers' box (the net gain is 0.04). Notice that, as the figure is drawn, gainers constitute a majority. In the presence of complete certainty, the reform in question would therefore be adopted: the potential winners in the L sector would join W-sector individuals to pass the reform.

Now suppose that the individuals in the L sector do not know who among them will be winners and who will be losers and that ex ante they consider it equally likely that any single one of them will be a winner. All that they know is the aggregate number (or the proportion) of winners. Will there still be a majority in favor of reform? Note that uncertainty renders all L-sector individuals identical ex ante. To know which way to vote, they will compute the expected benefit from reform. The expected benefit equals the weighted average of the gains and losses, with the weights equaling the probability of each outcome occurring. The lower panel of Figure 14.1A shows that the expected benefit is negative (-0.067 per L-sector individual). Since the L sector represents a majority of the economy at the outset, the proposed reform would not be adopted. The losses to the many are pulling down the gains to the few, leaving an

A. Majority is better off with reform ex post:

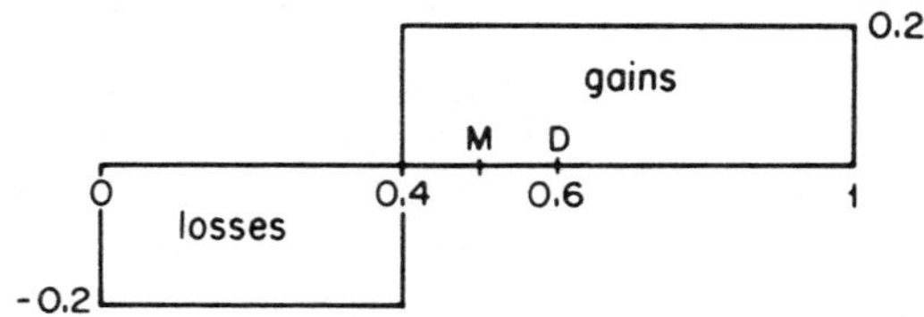

But majority votes against reform ex ante:

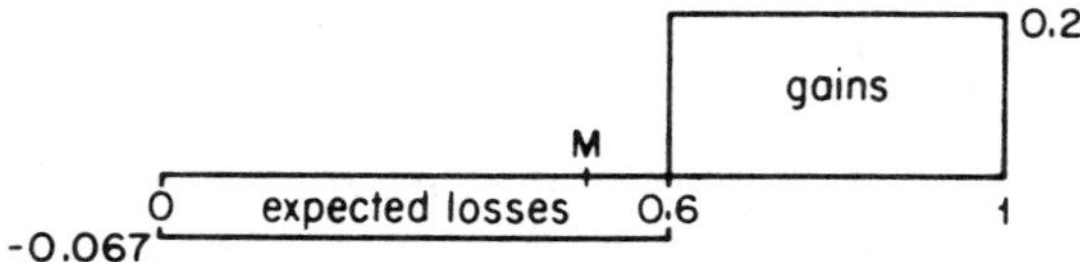

B. Majority is worse-off with reform ex post:

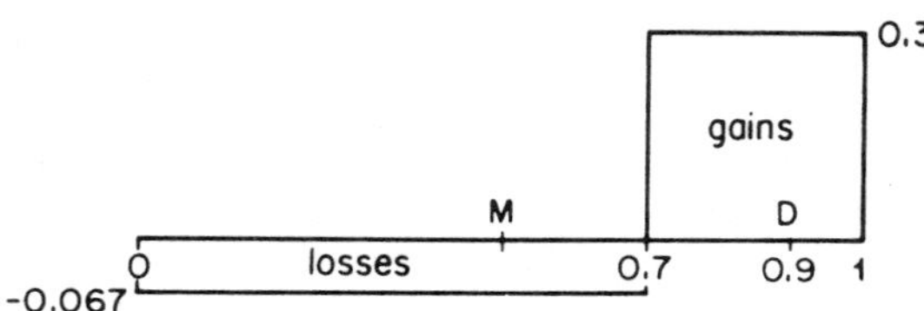

But majority votes for reform ex ante:

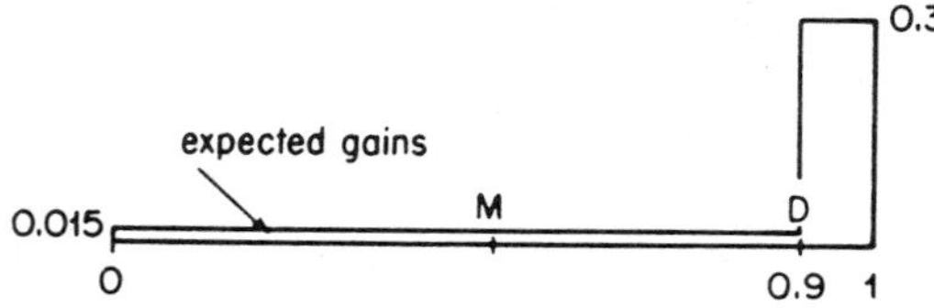

Figure 14.1
Gains and losses from reform

expected loss for all but the individuals already in the W sector. Note that the reform is not adopted even though (i) individuals are risk-neutral, (ii) a majority would vote for the reform ex post, and (iii) both (i) and (ii) are common knowledge.

This example establishes that the presence of individual-specific uncertainty can distort aggregate preferences. However, it does not establish that there will necessarily be a bias against reform. One can also construct examples in which this type of uncertainty leads to the adoption of a reform that turns out to be unpopular ex post.[7] Figure 14.1B shows such an example. The top panel once again displays the actual outcomes under reform, with only a minority benefiting this time. Under certainty, therefore, this reform would not command majority support. However, when L-sector individuals are all equally uncertain about how they will fare under reform, the outcome could be different. When there is uncertainty, the expected benefit could be positive for all. This is shown in the lower panel of Figure 14.1B. The expected gain per L-sector individual can be calculated to be 0.015 in this case: $[(0.3 \times 0.2) + (-0.067 \times 0.7)] \times (0.9)^{-1}$.

There is an important asymmetry between the two cases, however. In the second case (in which a reform is passed and turns out to be unpopular), information is revealed as to how individuals actually fare under the reform. Therefore, if there is ever a second vote or a chance to reconsider, the reform may be repealed. In the other case (in which reform is not passed), no new information is revealed, since the status quo is maintained. This asymmetry between the two cases leads to a status quo bias.

This may appear to be a contrived example with many loose threads. For example, what keeps returns in the two sectors from being equalized in equilibrium, and is that necessary to the argument? What is the source of uncertainty regarding the identities of gainers and losers? As we will show in the next section, it is possible to generalize the example and to place it in the context of a simple general-equilibrium model.

II The Model

Consider a two-sector perfectly competitive economy in which each sector produces a distinct good, X or Y, using one factor of production, labor (L), and with constant-returns-to-scale technology. There is no harm in thinking of X and Y as aggregates made up of individual commodities. Workers (or individuals) in each sector can by the same logic be interpreted as producing different products. Thus,

$$X = L_x/a_x$$

$$Y = L_y/a_y$$

and

$$L_x + L_y = \bar{L}$$

where $a_j > 0$, $j = x, y$.

Labor cannot relocate between sectors costlessly. The cost to an individual's relocation is modeled as having two components: θ, a known general investment cost incurred prior to switching sectors, and c_i, an individual-specific cost element incurred only upon actually switching sectors. The value of the second component, however, is unknown to the individual and is revealed only if the general investment cost is incurred. Only the distribution of c_i, $f(c)$, is known.[8] The interpretation behind this formulation is that workers have different abilities and productivities and, therefore, that their "net" wages in another sector will differ. Workers cannot know what their true abilities are before sinking the cost θ, which can also be thought of as investment in sector-specific human capital.[9] Alternatively, entrepreneurs may not have the information necessary to be able to determine precisely what their firm's cost structure would be in the new industry. Only after obtaining this information at cost θ is their cost structure revealed. This is a plausible way of capturing the uncertainty that is likely to surround each individual's prospects under reform.

Workers must therefore make two decisions: (i) whether to undertake the general investment cost and, if the first is decided affirmatively, then (ii) whether to switch sectors and thereby incur the cost c_i. To find the optimal choice, we start with the second decision. A worker who has invested θ will choose to switch from industry y to industry x if the difference between wages in the two industries is larger than her c_i. Thus, for any wage difference, there exists a level of c, $\tilde{c}$, such that all workers with $c_i \leq \tilde{c}$ will switch to industry x. Therefore, let

$$\tilde{c} = \tilde{w}_x - \tilde{w}_y \tag{1}$$

where $\tilde{w}_j$ is the equilibrium wage in sector j that results from the reform.

Ex ante, workers are identical and atomistic. Consequently, a worker in sector Y will decide to incur the general investment cost if her expected net benefit from doing so is nonnegative, that is, if

$$F(\tilde{c})\left[\tilde{w}_x - \int_{\underline{c}}^{\tilde{c}} f(c)c\,dc[F(\tilde{c})]^{-1}\right] + [1 - F(\tilde{c})]\tilde{w}_y - \theta \geq \tilde{w}_y \tag{2}$$

where $\underline{c} \geq 0$ is the infimum over the values taken by c_i and $F(c)$ is the cumulative distribution function. The left-hand side represents expected income when θ is incurred, while the right-hand side is the (certain) level of income in the absence of the investment. Rearranging terms, we obtain

$$[\tilde{w}_x - \tilde{w}_y]F(\tilde{c}) - \int_{\underline{c}}^{\tilde{c}} f(c)c\,dc - \theta \geq 0. \tag{3}$$

In order to illustrate our argument most clearly, we consider a country that is small in world markets, so relative prices within each aggregate are fixed by world price ratios. Let this country initially have a tariff of a magnitude such that

$$P^0 = a_x/a_y$$

where $P = p_x/p_y$ is the (tariff-inclusive) relative price of good X in terms of good Y. We normalize the domestic price of the imported good, good Y, to equal 1. Thus, decreases in the value of the tariff have the effect of increasing the relative price of good X. Labor's initial distribution between sectors, L_y^0 and L_x^0, is given by history. Perfect competition in the labor market ensures that

$$w_j = p_j/a_j \quad j = x, y. \tag{4}$$

Therefore, given the initial tariff level, $w_x^0 = w_y^0$. Note that w_y is invariant with respect to P and equal to $1/a_y$.

Let us analyze the behavior of this economy with respect to changes in the tariff rate commencing at P^0. As the tariff rate falls, $\tilde{w}_x - \tilde{w}_y$ increases, but initially no individual will choose to undertake the general investment cost. Simultaneously, the value of $\tilde{c}$ increases, as $d\tilde{c}/dP = d\tilde{w}_x/dP = 1/a_x$. Note that the left-hand side (LHS) of (3) is increasing with P (i.e., $d(\text{LHS})/dP = F(\tilde{c})/a_x > 0$). Therefore, at a sufficiently high relative price, P^*, all y-sector individuals are indifferent between incurring the investment cost and not. Those individuals who choose to undertake the general

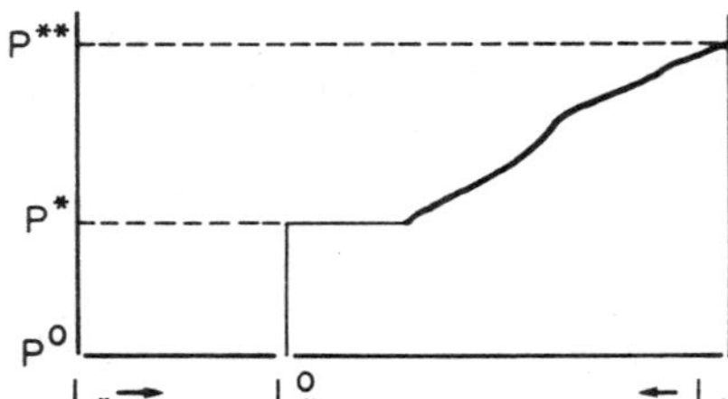

Figure 14.2
Allocation of labor between sectors as a function of relative prices

investment cost and have a $c_i \leq c^*$ will move to sector x (where c^* is the $\tilde{c}$ associated with P^*).[10] Any further increases in the relative price have all y-sector individuals strictly preferring to incur the general investment cost and, as $\tilde{c}$ and the relative wage of sector x increase monotonically with P, further labor reallocation (see Fig. 14.2).

We wish to show that there exist circumstances in which trade reform (in the manner of a tariff decrease) would be voted in under complete certainty as to the ex post identity of individuals but would be rejected under uncertainty, despite the fact that individuals are risk-neutral. Consider, therefore, an initiative to change prices in this economy from P^0 to P^* by reducing the tariff level accordingly. Since P^* is the price ratio at which all individuals are exactly indifferent between undertaking the investment cost and not, c^* is exactly that level of $\tilde{c}$ such that

$$\tilde{c}F(\tilde{c}) - \int_{\underline{c}}^{\tilde{c}} f(c)c\,dc - \theta = 0.$$

If asked to vote on whether to undertake this reform, all individuals in sector y would vote against this proposal. To see this, note that the purchasing power of the wage earned by an individual who remains in sector y is unchanged in terms of good Y and is strictly lower in terms of good X. Given that at P^* y-sector individuals are indifferent between undertaking the investment cost (under the assumption that the reform will go through) and not investing and reamaining in sector y under the new price system, these individuals' expected real income from the reform must be lower than that resulting from remaining with the status quo. Therefore, if $L_y^0 \geq L_x^0$, this measure would be rejected by majority vote.

If, on the other hand, individuals knew ex ante what their identities would be under the new regime (i.e., if each individual knew her c_i) and were then asked if they would be willing to pay $\theta + c_i$ in order to switch sectors, there may now be some y-sector individuals who would be willing to do so and, accordingly, willing to vote in favor of the reform.[11] That is, it is easy to show that, in general, there exist c_i such that

$$v(P^*, w_x^* - \theta - c_i) > v(P^0, w_y^0)$$

where $v(\cdot)$ is the individual's indirect utility function.[12]

In order to provide a clear example, we further specify some characteristics of this economy: we assume that individuals' preferences are identical, risk-neutral, and given by

$$V(P, I) = v(P)I = \frac{I}{P^\gamma}$$

where I is the individual's income level and $1 \geq \gamma > 0$. The function $f(c)$ is assumed to be distributed uniformly on the interval $[0, \bar{c}]$, so $f(c) = 1/\bar{c}$, and thus, $\tilde{c} = (2\theta\bar{c})^{0.5}$.

Note first that $w_x^* = P^*/a_x = w_y^* + \tilde{c} = w_y^0 + \tilde{c} = (1/a_y) + \tilde{c}$ and, therefore, $P^* = P^0 + \tilde{c}a_x$. Thus, we must show that there exist c_i such that

$$v(P^*)[w_y^0 + \tilde{c} - \theta - c_i] > v(P^0)w_y^0.$$

That is, we must show

$$(P^*)^{-\gamma}[w_y^0 + \tilde{c} - \theta - c_i] > (P^0)^{-\gamma}w_y^0.$$

Noting that P^*/P^0 can be written as $1 + \tilde{c}a_y$ yields

$$1/a_y + (2\theta\bar{c})^{-0.5} - \theta - c_i > (1/a_y)[1 + a_y(2\theta\bar{c})^{-0.5}]^\gamma$$

which can be satisfied for many parameter values (e.g., $a_y = \theta = 1$, $\bar{c} = 2$, $\gamma = 0.5$).[13]

III Dynamic Considerations

The model discussed above establishes that certain reforms that would have been popular ex post may not muster support ex ante. So far, it does not establish a *bias* toward protection, however. As mentioned in Section I, it is possible to come up with instances in which reform is embraced initially, only to prove unpopular once the identities of winners and losers are revealed. In a static setting, the logic of uncertainty works symmetrically, making both cases "equally" likely.

There is good reason to suspect, however, that in practice there will exist an asymmetry in favor of the status quo (protection). The asymmetry arises from the fact that new information is revealed in the case in which a reform is initially embraced and instituted, while no such thing happens when the reform is rejected from the outset. Therefore, if given a second chance, the electorate may reverse a reform that has been "mistakenly" embraced. Moreover, when considering a set of reforms that may possess a short life span due to the fact that it will be overturned in the future, rational forward-looking individuals may vote against reforms that initially appear to benefit them. By contrast, if an electorate initially chooses to reject a reform, the electorate will not change its vote. Since no new information is revealed in the latter case, an electorate that has refused reform once will continue to do so no matter how many times it is given an opportunity to reconsider.[14] Thus, there is an important asymmetry between the time consistency of the status quo and the time consistency of certain reforms.

We will now show (i) that reforms, even if instituted with majority support, may be short-lived and (ii) that there is a tendency toward inertia (toward the maintenance of the status quo) in these economies. To introduce dynamic considerations into the framework, we turn to a two-period version of the model. Individuals are able to vote at the beginning of each period on whether to institute (or continue with) the reform during that period. A decision not to continue with a reform that was previously instituted is taken to imply a return to the original relative prices. In each period, after voting, individuals decide whether or not to incur the investment cost θ (paid up front in its entirety) and, as before, whether or not to switch sectors and incur the individual-specific cost. They then earn the corresponding wage in that period. The possible outcomes are exhibited in Figure 14.3.

There are four possibilities: (i) reform is first instituted and then reversed because it proves unpopular; (ii) reform is instituted and sustained because it proves popular; (iii) reform is always opposed; and (iv) reform is first rejected and then accepted. While (i)–(iii) are possible equilibrium outcomes, (iv) is not if, in this two-period model, the second period is not lengthier than the first.

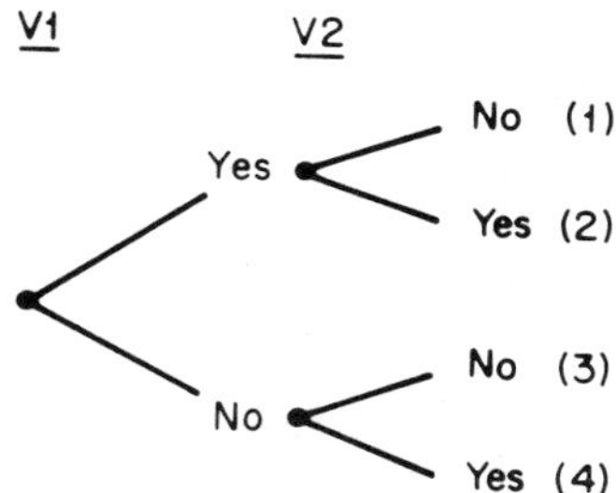

Figure 14.3
Possible outcomes when individuals vote in each of two periods

The problem posed by the existence of a period significantly lengthier than any other is that the possibility of strategic voting is introduced. In our two-period example this would entail all individuals voting against the reform in the first period and in favor of the reform in the second since, foreseeing that once uncertainty is resolved a majority will overturn the reform, as in case (i), individuals prefer to reject the reform in the first round in order to institute it in the second round, thereby preserving the reform for a greater length of time. In the more plausible case of periods of equal length, strategic voting of this sort will never occur. Case (iv) will never be an equilibrium, since if voters reject the reform no information is revealed and, consequently, there is no incentive to accept the reform in the following period. Since the existence of periods of uneven length is rather artificial, we henceforth rule it out, eliminating (iv) as a possible equilibrium outcome. Apart from this restriction, nothing qualitative in our results depends on the number of time periods or on the finiteness of individuals' horizons. Note, therefore, the bias toward the status quo: reforms that are initially rejected continue to be so, whereas some reforms that were previously accepted cannot be sustained.

To make the preceding discussion a bit more concrete, consider the same example as in the previous section, with identical parameters and with the same set of initial conditions. Suppose that the effect of the reform under consideration is to change relative prices from P^0 to $P' > P^* > P^0$. P' is such that sector-y (and, of course, then also sector-x) individuals would be willing to vote in favor of this reform if they thought that, once instituted, the reform would be permanent. Thus, P' must satisfy

$$v(P')\left\{[w'_x(1+\delta)-\theta]F(\tilde{c})-\int_0^{\tilde{c}} cf(c)\,dc+[w'_y(1+\delta)-\theta][1-F(\tilde{c})]\right\}$$
$$> v(P^0)w_y^0(1+\delta) \tag{5}$$

where w'_j is the equilibrium wage in sector j associated with P'. The terms in the braces constitute the expected income from the reform for an individual initially in sector y, and the expression on the right-hand side of the inequality is a sector-y individual's status quo utility. Note that the wage earnings of an individual are now multiplied by $1 + \delta$, which is the appropriate discounting of wages earned over two periods ($0 < \delta < 1$ is the individual's discount factor).[15] Letting P' be such that $\tilde{c} < \bar{c}$, expression (5) can be rewritten as

$$v(P')\left[\tilde{c}(1+\delta)F(\tilde{c})-\int_0^{\tilde{c}} cf(c)\,dc+w'_y(1+\delta)-\theta\right]>v(P^0)w_y^0(1+\delta)$$

and $\tilde{c}$ can be expressed as

$$\tilde{c}=\frac{a_yP'-a_x}{a_ya_x}.$$

Recalling that $w'_y = w_y^0 = a_y^{-1}$ and performing the appropriate substitutions yields

$$\left(\frac{(0.5+\delta)[a_yP'-a_x]^2}{[a_ya_x]^2\bar{c}}-\theta\right)a_y(1+\delta)^{-1}+1>\left(\frac{P'}{P^0}\right)^{\gamma}.$$

The above condition ensures that all y-sector individuals would vote in favor of a permanent trade reform that changes relative prices from P^0 to P', since their ex ante expected utility from this reform is greater than the level of utility enjoyed under the status quo. If, however, $F(\tilde{c})L_y^0 + L_x^0 < [1 - F(\tilde{c})]L_y^0$, then, since the individuals who have remained in sector y now enjoy a lower real wage than before, in the second period the majority of the population will vote against the reform and in favor of a return to the status quo.[16]

It should be noted that, although it may appear that reform would always be supported for a sufficiently large P, this is misleading. The size of the reform is constrained by the initial level of trade restrictions.

Will individuals still vote for the reform in period 1, knowing that there will be a return to the status quo following the second vote? Forward-looking individuals will realize that the first-period vote now presents a choice between the status quo and *temporary* reform. They will vote for the latter only if

$$v(P')\left[w_x' F(\tilde{c}) - \int_0^{\tilde{c}} cf(c)\,dc + w_y'[1 - F(\tilde{c})] - \theta\right] > v(P^0) w_y^0. \tag{6}$$

Notice that second-period wages are equal across sectors (given a return to the status quo).[17] Therefore, y-sector workers will vote for reform only if the expected first-period benefits exceed the costs. Since this condition is more restrictive than that of equation (5), as the differential between w_x and w_y now accrues for one period only, there will be cases in which a reform will be rejected even though it would have been embraced had it been perceived as permanent. Individuals will sometimes find it unprofitable to incur the investment costs for a transitory reform and, hence, will vote against the reform from the outset. However, the lower is δ (i.e., the more the future is discounted or the greater the interval between votes), the more likely it is that a reform that is accepted when permanent will still be accepted when temporary.

IV Concluding Remarks

Our framework has a number of interesting features. First, it shows how uncertainty regarding the identities of gainers and losers can prevent an efficiency-enhancing reform from being adopted, even in cases in which reform would prove quite popular after the fact. As the extended version of the model shows, there is a bias toward the status quo. Second, the model suggests that an appropriately large reform will be needed to get individuals to respond in the desired manner.[18] This is a conclusion shared with some other positive models of reform in which either hysteresis or asymmetric information plays a role (see Rodrik, 1989a, 1989b). Third, our model helps explain an apparent puzzle: in countries like Korea, Chile, and Turkey, radical trade reforms introduced by autocratic regimes have not collapsed (and indeed have turned out to be popular), even though they had little support prior to reform. Our framework makes clear why ex ante hostility to reform and ex post support are quite consistent with each other.

It should be clear that our argument does not rest on the assumption of a democratic voting mechanism. One could also, for example, obtain the same qualitative results if decisions were made according to the preferences of a median interest group. What is crucial to our results is that there be no mechanism that costlessly translates the intensity with which individuals favor a proposed reform into outcomes (e.g., frictionless lobbying). Such a mechanism would, of course, implement all reforms that increase efficiency.

The question may arise as to whether feasible transfer schemes exist to institute otherwise unpopular trade reforms by popular support. In most models, the answer would be trivially "yes." Here, there is an important consideration that constrains the use of such "bribing" mechanisms. Any such transfer scheme may be time-inconsistent, providing incentives to the ex post majority to renege on the agreement. Of course, such questions can be settled only by examining the equilibria of particular "bribing" games.

It should also be obvious that, while we have selected trade reform as an example, the logic applies to any reform that creates a distribution of gains and losses whose incidence is partially uncertain. Since this is a characteristic of any important policy change one can think of—whether it be macroeconomic stabilization in developing countries, welfare reform in advanced industrial countries, or transition to a market economy in socialist countries—the general principle established here with respect to the obstinacy of the status quo has wide relevance.

An interesting extension which we do not explore in this chapter would be to endogenize the set of reforms that are politically feasible and to allow individuals to choose not only between a specific reform and the status quo, but also among alternative reforms. A model with greater institutional structure would be needed to determine how these reforms are initially selected.

Notes

Raquel Fernandez's work was supported by NSF grant SES 89-08390 and by a Hoover Fellowship. Dani Rodrik's work was supported by the World Bank through a research project on Sustainability of Trade Reform (RPO 675-32) and by an NBER Olin Fellowship. We thank Loreto Lira for research assistance, the Japanese Corporate Associates Program of the Kennedy School for financial support, and Alberto Alesina, Guillermo Calvo, Avinash Dixit, Konstantine Gatsios, Larry Karp, Anne Krueger, Timur Kuran, Marc Lindenberg, Mike Mussa, three referees, and participants at the NBER Conference on Political Economics and at seminars at Boston University, Chicago Business School, Dartmouth College, the Federal Reserve Board, Harvard University, the International Monetary Fund, NBER Summer Institute, and Syracuse University for useful comments.

1. See Rodrik (1986) for another example.

2. We thank Jagdish Bhagwati for suggesting the formulation of our problem in terms of a "nonneutrality."

3. Anne O. Krueger (1989) coins the phrase "identity bias" to describe a somewhat related problem, one that arises from the possibility that the precise knowledge of the losers' identities evokes a more sympathetic response from the general population toward their plight than if their identities were unknown. This is a psychological Schellingesque distinction between statistical and individual-specific information which differs from ours (see Thomas C. Schelling, 1984, ch. 5). See also William Samuelson and Richard Zeckhauser (1988) for a broad discussion of the sources of status quo bias at the level of individual decision-making, and Timur Kuran (1988) for a review and critique of the related literature.

4. Even when the strictly economic case for free trade fails, economists are generally quick to embrace it for the same practical reason that Churchill embraced democracy, namely as the lesser evil among possible alternatives. See, for example, Paul Krugman (1987).

5. See Robert E. Baldwin (1985, ch. 1) and Bhagwati (1988) and the references therein. On median-voter models of trade policy, see in particular Wolfgang Mayer (1984) and Mayer and Raymond Riezman (1987).

6. For more detail on these cases, see our working paper (Fernandez and Rodrik, 1990).

7. Bhagwati (1981), for example, argues that elites in developing countries may sometimes support policy reforms which end up hurting them due to the policy-maker's occasional inability to establish the distributional impact of a reform.

8. For simplicity of exposition, we are assuming that the relocation cost is independent of the sector from which the individual is relocating.

9. However, individuals who desire to switch sectors are not free to do so without incurring both costs (i.e., were they to do so, it is assumed that their marginal product would be zero).

10. This zero–one behavior with respect to undertaking the general investment cost is a product of the linearity of technology. A decreasing marginal product of labor, as in the Ricardo-Viner model, would exhibit a continuously increasing proportion of individuals willing to incur the general investment cost as a function of relative prices.

11. We have confined our attention to a positive analysis of status quo bias. While the reforms that we consider are efficiency-enhancing, they are not Pareto-efficient, given the assumed absence of lump-sum transfers.

12. Throughout this discussion, in order to further simplify exposition, we assume that tariff revenue is distributed solely among those workers originally located in sector x.

13. Note that if $\gamma = 1$ (i.e., individuals only consume good X), then the above inequality can never be satisfied, since the wage increase in sector x would leave individuals with the same real wage as prior to the reform, and moreover, the individual would have paid the general and individual-specific investment cost.

14. This statement is subject to a caveat, as will be made clear in the exposition of the argument.

15. As expressed in (5), c_i is only incurred in the first period. We could have considered c_i to be incurred in each period without altering any of our conclusions.

16. A necessary condition for this phenomenon to occur is $\tilde{c} < \bar{c}/2$.

17. This allows us to bypass the question of whether sector-x individuals who have relocated in sector y must incur any costs if they wish to return to sector x.

18. However, this is no longer true if individuals are risk-averse; a large reform would magnify the uncertainty and could solidify the preference for the status quo on account of the greater risk.

References

Baldwin, Robert. 1985. *The political economy of U.S. import policy.* Cambridge, MA: MIT Press.

Bhagwati, Jagdish. 1981. Need for reforms in underdeveloped countries. In Sven Grassman and Erik Lundberg, eds., *The world economic order: Past and prospects,* 526–533. New York: St. Martin's.

Bhagwati, Jagdish. 1988. *Protectionism.* Cambridge, MA: MIT Press.

Fernandez, Raquel, and Rodrik, Dani. 1990. Why is trade reform so unpopular? On status quo bias in policy reforms. NBER working paper no. 3269.

Krueger, Anne. 1989. Asymmetries in policy between exportables and import-competing goods. NBER working paper no. 2904.

Krugman, Paul. 1987. Is free trade passé? *Journal of Economic Perspectives* 1:131–144.

Kuran, Timur. 1988. The tenacious past: Theories of personal and collective conservatism. *Journal of Economic Behavior and Organization* 10:143–171.

Mayer, Wolfgang. 1984. Endogenous tariff formation. *American Economic Review* 74:970–985.

Mayer, Wolfgang, and Riezman, Raymond. 1987. Endogenous choice of trade policy instruments. *Journal of International Economics* 23:377–381.

Rodrik, Dani. 1986. Tariffs, subsidies, and welfare with endogenous policy. *Journal of International Economics* 21:285–299.

Rodrik, Dani. 1989a. Promises, promises: Credible policy reform via signalling. *Economic Journal* 99:756–772.

Rodrik, Dani. 1989b. Policy uncertainty and private investment in developing countries. NBER working paper No. 2999. Forthcoming in *Journal of Development Economics.*

Samuelson, William, and Zeckhauser, Richard. 1988. Status quo bias in decision making. *Journal of Risk and Uncertainty* 1:7–59.

Schelling, Thomas. 1984. *Choice and consequence.* Cambridge, MA: Harvard University Press.

15 Why Are Stabilizations Delayed?

Alberto Alesina and Allan Drazen

Countries often follow policies which are recognized to be infeasible in the long run for extended periods of time. For instance, large deficits implying an explosive path of government debt are allowed to continue even though it is apparent that such deficits will have to be eliminated sooner or later. A puzzling question is why these countries do not stabilize immediately, once it becomes apparent that current policies are unsustainable and that a change in policy will have to be adopted eventually. Delays in stabilization are particularly inefficient if the longer a country waits the more costly is the policy adjustment needed to stabilize and if the period of instability before the policy change is characterized by economic inefficiencies. Fiscal imbalances are often associated with high and variable inflation; fiscal stabilization also stops inflation. This chapter studies the politico-economic determinants of delays in the adoption of fiscal adjustment programs.

The literature on the prestabilization dynamics implied by an anticipated future stabilization (e.g., Sargent and Wallace 1981; Drazen and Helpman 1987, 1990) assumes that the timing of the future policy change is exogenous.[1] Since in these models the long-run infeasibility of current policy is known from the beginning, what is missing is an explanation of why the infeasible policy is not abandoned immediately. Explanations of the timing of stabilization based on irrationality, such as waiting to stabilize until "things get really bad," are unconvincing: since the deterioration in the fiscal position can be foreseen, the argument depends on countries that delay stabilization being more irrational than others. Explanations that give a key role to exogenous shocks leave unexplained both why countries do not stabilize as soon as unfavorable shocks occur and why stabilizations that are undertaken often do not seem to coincide with significant observable changes in external circumstances.[2]

This chapter argues that the timing of stabilizations and, in particular, their postponement cannot be easily understood in terms of models in which the policymaker is viewed as a social planner maximizing the welfare of a representative individual. On the contrary, heterogeneity in the population is crucial in explaining these delays. In many cases, the process

Reprinted from *American Economic Review*, 81, (1991) 1170–1188, by permission of The American Economic Association.

leading to a stabilization can be described as a war of attrition between different socioeconomic groups with conflicting distributional objectives. Delays in stabilization arise due to a political stalemate over distribution; stabilizations occur when a political consolidation leads to a resolution of the distributional conflict.

More specifically, even though it is agreed that stabilization requires a change in fiscal policy to eliminate budget deficits, there may be disagreement about how the burden of the policy change is to be shared. When socioeconomic groups perceive the possibility of shifting this burden elsewhere, each group may attempt to wait the others out. This war of attrition ends, and a stabilization is enacted, when certain groups "concede" and allow their political opponents to decide on the allocation of the burden of the fiscal adjustment. Concession may occur via legislative agreement, electoral outcomes, or ceding power of decree to policymakers.

We present a simple model of delayed stabilization due to a war of attrition and derive the expected time of stabilization as a function of characteristics of the economy, including parameters meant to capture, in a rough way, the degree of political polarization. For example, the more uneven is the expected allocation of the costs of stabilization when it occurs, the later is the expected date of a stabilization. Hence, if unequal distribution of the burden of taxation is an indicator of political polarization, more politically polarized countries will experience longer periods of instability.[3] More institutional adaptation to the distortions associated with instability also implies later expected stabilization, while partial attempts to control the deficit prior to a full stabilization may make the expected time of full stabilization either earlier or later. We also show that, if it is the poor who suffer most in the prestabilization period, they bear the largest share of the costs of stabilization. The distribution of income is also related to the timing of stabilization. Conditions are derived under which a more unequal distribution of income implies either an earlier or later stabilization.

Our approach is related to the literature on dynamic games between a monetary and a fiscal authority with conflicting objectives (Sargent 1986; Tabellini 1986, 1987; Michael Loewy 1988). In that literature, a war of attrition is played between the fiscal and monetary authorities: an unsustainable combination of monetary and fiscal policies is in place until one side concedes.[4] Our shift in emphasis to a game between interest groups has several justifications. First, the assumption that the monetary authority is independent of the fiscal authority is unrealistic for most countries with serious problems of economic instability. Second, the difference in the objective functions of different branches of government may be related to their representing different constituencies; here, we tackle issues of heterogeneity directly.[5]

The chapter is organized as follows. Section I summarizes some regularities observed in a number of stabilizations which suggest using a war of attrition as a model. Section II presents a stylized model of stabilizations based on the empirical observations and shows how delays result from individually rational behavior. Section III presents comparative-static results on how the expected date of stabilization will differ in economies with different characteristics. The final section suggests extensions.

I Delayed Stabilization as a War of Attrition

No single model can explain every episode of delay in enacting a macroeconomic stabilization. Historical and current evidence suggests, however, that in many cases of instability due to severe fiscal imbalances, it was disagreement over the allocation of the burden of fiscal change that delayed the adoption of a new policy. We begin by noting common features of the stabilization process across several episodes, features which suggest modeling stabilization as a war of attrition.

1. There is agreement on the need for a fiscal change but a political stalemate over how the burden of higher taxes or expenditure cuts should be allocated. In the political debate over stabilization, this distributional question is central.

Sharp disagreements over allocating the burden of paying for the war were common in the belligerent countries after World War I (Alesina 1988; Eichengreen 1990). For example, in France, Germany, and Italy, the political struggle over fiscal policy was not about the need for reducing enormous budget deficits or the debt overhang, but over which groups should bear higher taxes to achieve that end. Parties of the right favored proportional income and indirect taxes; parties of the left proposed capital levies and more progressive income taxes (Haig 1929; Maier 1975).

In particular, France in the first half of the 1920's is a textbook example of a distributional war of attrition. The period 1919–1926 is marked by a high degree of polarization of the political debate and by large swings in the composition of the legislature. After it became clear, in the early 1920's, that the German war reparations would not have solved the French fiscal problem, the Chamber of Deputies was deadlocked for several years because of lack of agreement on feasible fiscal plans. For instance, in the fall of 1922 the centrist Minister of Finance proposed a 20-percent across-the-board increase in the income tax. The proposal was not approced in the Chamber, because of the opposition of both the Conservatives and the Socialists. The former proposed an increase in indirect taxes, which relied mostly on the poor (Maier 1975) and a reduction in the progressivity of the income tax. The latter proposed a capital levy, a more progressive income tax, and reduction in indirect taxation. The lack of a compromise led to an 18-month period of complete fiscal inaction, which implied a sharp rise in the inflation rate, capital flight, and speculative attacks against the franc. A conservative tax bill was not approved until March 1924. This attempted fiscal stabilization was, however, only temporary. The election of an internally divided "cartel des gauches" in the spring of 1924 initiated an additional period of fiscal instability. An endless debate within the leftist coalition on the imposition of a capital levy and the consequent fiscal inaction implied a further deterioration of the floating-debt problem.

Britain after the war also faced a large budget deficit; however, in contrast to the experience of France, Germany, and Italy, the dominant position of the Conservatives led to a rapid stabilization by means that favored the Conservatives' traditional constituencies.

Fiscal imbalances reappeared in the 1930's, as a result of the Great Depression. France, once again, provides an excellent example of a political stalemate due to distributional conflicts.[6] After a period of relative political and fiscal stability (1926–1932), the effects of the economic depression on fiscal revenues generated large budget deficits (after six years of surpluses) leading to the reappearance of a large stock of floating short-term debt (Jackson 1985); in contrast to the 1920's, budget deficits in the 1930's occurred in a deflationary situation. After six years of Conservative control of government, the left reported an electoral victory in 1932; however, the center-left radicals refused to form a coalition with the Socialists. From 1932 to 1936 a series of short-lived centrist (or center-left) governments failed to adopt a coherent fiscal policy because of the opposite political pressures from the Conservatives and the Socialists. The former were firmly committed to the gold standard and argued for a sharp deflation of nominal wages and prices with cuts in government spending and increases in indirect taxation to eliminate the deficit. The Socialists opposed wage cuts, argued in favor of public investment to sustain aggregate demand, and proposed, as in the 1920's, an increase in the level and progressivity of income taxation and various forms of capital taxation to eliminate the fiscal imbalance (Jackson 1985). The long debate over a proposal (opposed by the Socialists and favored by the Conservatives) for a cut of 20 percent of the salaries of public employees is emblematic of the political stalemate. In 1936, the Popular Front gained office, and a few months later the franc was devalued. Divisions within the coalition and lack of confidence in the business community led to a further economic deterioration and to the fall of the government, in 1938. A newly elected Conservative government attempted a fiscal stabilization; it is hard to say whether it would have succeeded or not because of the outbreak of the Second World War. Eichengreen and Sachs (1985) argue that, because of the delay in abandoning the gold standard and the incoherence and inaction of French economic policy in the 1930's, this country suffered particularly severe consequences of the Great Depression.

Current examples of delayed adjustments of fiscal imbalances due to political stalemate can be found in both OECD and LDC countries. Several authors have suggested that the recent increase in the debt/GNP ratios in several OECD economies is due to the failure of weak and divided coalition governments to agree on fiscal-adjustment programs.[7] The cases of Belgium, Ireland, and Italy, the three OECD countries currently with the highest debt/GNP ratio are good examples of this point of view. In several Latin American countries, and particularly in Argentina, the failure to stabilize in the face of endemic inflation has gone hand in hand with continued political polarization and instability and the failure of any group to consolidate its power effectively (Dornbusch and DePablo 1987). Similarly, in Israel in the 1980's, once the need for sharply restrictive aggregate demand policies to end the inflation was widely accepted, there was still disagreement over how the burden of restrictive policies would be distributed between labor and business.

2. When stabilization occurs, it coincides with a *political* consolidation. Often, one side becomes politically dominant. The burden of stabilization is sometimes quite unequal, with the politically weaker groups bearing a larger burden. Often this means the lower classes, with the burden of a successful stabilization being regressive.

The successful stabilizations in France (1926) and Italy (1922–1924) coincided with a clear consolidation of power by the right. In both cases, the burden fell disproportionately on the working class (Maier 1975). Poincaré's 1926 program included increases both of indirect taxes and of the income tax on the lower middle class. Except for a very mild "once and for all" tax on real estate, no capital levies were introduced. On the contrary, tax rates on the wealthiest fraction of taxpayers were substantially reduced, as documented by Haig (1929), who concluded that, when the fiscal crisis came to an end, "the remedy was sought in lightening the burden on rich taxpayers and by increasing the levy on those of moderate means" (p. 164).

The German stabilization of November 1923 followed a new Enabling Act giving the new Stresemann government power to cut through legislative deadlocks and quickly adopt fiscal measures by decree. Though the government that took power in August was a "Great Coalition" of the right and the left, by autumn "the far right was more dangerous and powerful than the socialist left," and government policy reflected the perceived need to appease conservative interest groups (Maier 1975, p. 384).

Giavazzi and Pagano (1990) document that the successful Danish fiscal adjustment, started in 1982, was made possible by the election of a conservative government with a solid majority. This ended a period marked by a series of minority coalition governments, unable to stop the growth of government debt.

3. Successful stabilizations are usually preceded by several failed attempts. Often a previous program appears to be similar to the successful one.

In a war of attrition, the cost of waiting means that the passage of time will imply concession on the same terms that a player earlier found "unacceptable." The components of the successful Poincaré stabilization of 1926 are quite similar to his program of 1924. Several unsuccessful atempts in Germany appear to be quite similar ex ante to the November 1923 program (Dornbusch 1988). Many aspects of the July 1985 stabilization in Israel had been previously proposed but rejected by the government.

In summary, the central role of conflict over how the burden of stabilization is to be shared, the importance of political consolidation in the adoption of a program, and the fact that programs that were previously rejected are agreed to after the passage of time, suggests modeling delayed stabilization as arising from a war of attrition between different socioeconomic groups.

In the basic war-of-attrition model from biology (Riley 1980), two animals are fighting over a prize. Fighting is costly, and the fight ends when one animal drops out, with the other gaining the prize. Suppose that the two contestants are not identical, either in the costs of remaining in the fight or in the utility they assign to the prize. Suppose further that each contestant's value of these is known only to himself, his opponent knowing only the distribution of these values. The individual's problem is then to choose a time of concession based on his type (i.e., the value of his costs and payoffs), on the distribution of his opponent's possible type, and on the knowledge that his opponent is solving the same problem. In equilibrium, the time of concession is determined by the condition that, at the optimal time, the cost of remaining in the fight another instant of time is just equal to the expected gain from remaining, namely the probability that the rival drops out at that instant multiplied by the gain if the rival concedes.

For a war of attrition between heterogeneous individuals to give expected finite delay in concession under incomplete information, two obvious features are important. First, there must be a cost to remaining in the fight, that is, to not conceding. Second, the payoff to the winner must exceed that to the loser. In the next section, we show how stabilizations may be modeled with these features in mind.

II The Model

We consider an economy as in Drazen and Helpman (1987, 1990) in which the government is running a positive deficit (inclusive of debt service) implying growing government debt.[8] Stabilization consists of an increase in taxes which brings the deficit to zero, so that government debt is constant. We assume that, prior to an agreement on how to share the burden of higher taxes, the government is limited to highly inefficient and distortionary methods of public finance. In particular, monetization of deficits, with the associated costs of high and variable inflation, is often a main source of government revenue prior to a fiscal stabilization. The level of distortionary financing and, hence, the welfare loss associated with it rise with the level of government debt, where welfare losses may differ across socioeconomic groups.[9]

A second type of cost to continuing in a war of attrition is political. For a group to prevent the burden of a stabilization being placed on it, it must mobilize and use resources for lobbying activities to influence the outcome of the legislative process. Different groups may differ in their political influence and therefore in the level of effort needed to continue fighting. In the development of the model, the first interpretation of prestabilization costs is stressed, but we will return to political interpretations in the concluding section.

The benefit of stabilization derives from the move away from highly distortionary methods of financing government expenditures. In this respect, stabilization benefits everybody. The differential benefits reflect the fact that the increase in nondistortionary taxes is unequally distributed.

Concession in our model is the agreement by one side to bear a disproportionate share of the tax increase necessary to effect a stabilization. As the examples in the previous section illustrate, effective concession may be reflected in a formal agreement between the various sides (as in the Israeli case), in the formation of a new government that is given extraordinary powers (as in the French or German cases), or in the outcome of elections in which one side gains a clear majority and opposing groups decide not to block their program any longer.[10]

More formally, consider a small open economy which issues external debt to cover any deficits not covered by revenues. The economy is composed of a number of heterogeneous interest groups which differ from one another in the welfare loss they suffer from the distortions associated with the prestabilization methods of government finance.

Until $t = 0$, the government budget is balanced, with external government debt constant at level $b_0 \geq 0$. At $t = 0$ a shock hits, reducing available tax revenues. From $t = 0$ until the date of stabilization, a fraction $(1 - \gamma)$ of government expenditure (inclusive of interest payments) is covered by issuing debt, and a fraction γ is covered by distortionary taxation. What is important is not that γ is fixed, but that it is positive. Calling g_0 the level of expenditures from $t = 0$ until a policy change, debt $b(t)$ evolves according to

$$\dot{b}(t) = (1 - \gamma)[rb(t) + g_0] \tag{1}$$

where r is the constant world interest rate. Taxes before the date of stabilization are thus

$$\tau(t) = \gamma[rb(t) + g_0]. \tag{2}$$

Equation (1) may be solved to yield

$$b(t) = b_0 e^{(1-\gamma)rt} + \frac{g_0}{r}(e^{(1-\gamma)rt} - 1). \tag{3}$$

This implies that (2) may be written as

$$\tau(t) = \gamma r \bar{b} e^{(1-\gamma)rt}. \tag{4}$$

where $b \equiv b_0 + g_0/r$, which can be shown to be the present discounted value of future tax payments for any nonzero values of γ before and after stabilization.

A stabilization consists of an increase in taxes sufficient to prevent further growth in the debt. Hence, taxes to be levied from the date of stabilization T onward are

$$\tau(T) = rb(T) + g_T \tag{2'}$$

where g_T is the level of expenditures after a stabilization. If we assume, for simplicity, that $g_T = g_0$, (2′) becomes

$$\tau(T) = r\bar{b}e^{(1-\gamma)rT}. \tag{4'}$$

Equations (3) and (4) imply that, before the stabilization, both the debt and the distortionary taxes grow exponentially. From the time of stabilization onward, the level of debt is constant. At time T, taxes jump upward to the level given in (4′) and remain constant afterward.

An agreement to stabilize is an agreement on how the taxes $\tau(T)$ are to be apportioned between different interest groups. For simplicity, assume that there are only two groups.[11] The "loser" assumes a fraction $\alpha > \frac{1}{2}$ of the tax burden at T, the "winner" a fraction $1 - \alpha$. The fraction itself is not bargained on: it is a given parameter meant to capture the degree of polarization in the society. A value of α close to 1 represents a high degree of polarization or a lack of political cohesiveness.

Taxes after an agreement on a stabilization are assumed to be nondistortionary. What is important is that they are *less* distortionary than taxes before a stabilization; otherwise, there would in general be no incentive to concede, that is, to stabilize.

Infinitely-lived groups differ from one another in the utility loss they suffer due to distortionary taxes. We will index group i's loss by θ_i, where θ is drawn from a distribution $F(\theta)$, with lower and upper bounds $\underline{\theta}$ and $\bar{\theta}$;

θ_i is known only to the group itself, other groups knowing only the distribution $F(\theta)$. For simplicity, we assume that the utility loss from distortionary taxes, K_i, is linear in the level of taxes, namely,[12]

$$K_i(t) = \theta_i \tau(t). \tag{5}$$

The prestabilization distortionary tax can be viewed as the inflation tax. Obviously, the treatment of inflation in this nonmonetary model is very stylized; what is crucial in this model is the problem of fiscal adjustment, not the monetary dynamics per se.[13]

Flow utility depends on consumption (c), government spending (g), and the cost (K). Though we leave the dependence of utility on government expenditure implicit (since g is constant over time), this dependence is important below in treating problems of feasibility. The level of income, y, is assumed for most of the chapter to be constant across individuals. The possible effects of distribution of income on the timing of a stabilization are considered below. The flow utility of group i is linear in consumption and of the form

$$u_i(t) = c_i(t) - y - K_i(t). \tag{6}$$

Subtracting y in the utility function is simply a normalization. The level of income is assumed to be high relative to the interest payments on the debt; the importance of this assumption will be made precise below. After a stabilization, $K_i = 0$, as taxes after a stabilization are nondistortionary. Henceforth, to simplify matters, the subscript on the function u_i is suppressed.

Each group maximizes expected present discounted utility by choice of a time path of consumption and a date to concede and agree to bear the share α of taxes if the other group has not already conceded. We denote flow utility before a stabilization by $u^{\mathrm{D}}(t)$ and the lifetime utility of the loser and the winner from the date of stabilization onward by $V^{\mathrm{L}}(T)$ and $V^{\mathrm{W}}(T)$, respectively. If stabilization occurs at time T, lifetime utility of the winner and of the loser may then be written as

$$U^j(T) = \int_0^T u^{\mathrm{D}}(x) e^{-rx}\,dx + e^{-rT} V^j(T) \quad j = W, L \tag{7}$$

where the discount rate equals the interest rate r. Expected utility as of time 0 as a function of one's chosen concession time T_i is the sum of $U^{\mathrm{W}}(X)$

multiplied by the probability of one's opponent conceding at X for all $X \leq T_i$ and $U^{\mathrm{L}}(T_i)$ multiplied by the probability of one's opponent not having conceded by T_i. If we denote by $H(T)$ the distribution of the opponent's optimal time of concession (this is, of course, endogenous and will be derived below) and by $h(T)$ the associated density function, expected utility as a function of T is

$$\begin{aligned}\mathrm{EU}(T_i) &= [1 - H(T_i)]U^{\mathrm{L}}(T_i) + \int_0^{T_i} U^{\mathrm{W}}(x)h(x)\,dx \\ &= [1 - H(T_i)]\left[\int_0^{T_i} u^{\mathrm{D}}(x)e^{-rx}\,dx + e^{-rT_i}V^{\mathrm{L}}(T_i)\right] \\ &\quad + \int_{x=0}^{x=T_i}\left[\int_0^x u^{\mathrm{D}}(z)e^{-rz}\,dz + e^{-rx}V^{\mathrm{W}}(x)\right]h(x)\,dx. \qquad (8)\end{aligned}$$

The time path of consumption and T_i are chosen to maximize (8).

With linear utility, any consumption path satisfying the intertemporal budget constraint with equality gives equal utility. Denote by c^{D}, c^{L}, and c^{W} consumption before a stabilization, after a stabilization for the loser, and after a stabilization for the winner, respectively. Assuming that each of the two groups pays one-half of taxes before a stabilization, we have the lifetime budget constraints:

$$\begin{aligned}&\int_0^T c^{\mathrm{D}}(x)e^{-rx}\,dx + \int_T^\infty c^{\mathrm{L}}(x)e^{-rx}\,dx \\ &\quad = \int_0^T (y - \tfrac{1}{2}\gamma r\bar{b}e^{(1-\gamma)rx})e^{-rx}\,dx + \int_T^\infty (y - \alpha r\bar{b}e^{(1-\gamma)rT})e^{-rx}\,dx \qquad (9)\end{aligned}$$

$$\begin{aligned}&\int_0^T c^{\mathrm{D}}(x)e^{-rx}\,dx + \int_T^\infty c^{\mathrm{W}}(x)e^{-rx}\,dx \\ &\quad = \int_0^T (y - \tfrac{1}{2}\gamma r\bar{b}e^{(1-\gamma)rx})e^{-rx}\,dx + \int_T^\infty (y - (1-\alpha)r\bar{b}e^{(1-\gamma)rT})e^{-rx}\,dx. \qquad (10)\end{aligned}$$

The following consumption path is then clearly feasible:[14]

$$c^{\mathrm{D}}(t) = y - \frac{\gamma}{2}r\bar{b}e^{(1-\gamma)rt} \qquad 0 \leq t < T \qquad (11a)$$

$$c^{\mathrm{L}}(t) = y - \alpha r\bar{b}e^{(1-\gamma)rT} \qquad t \geq T \tag{11b}$$

$$c^{\mathrm{W}}(t) = y - (1-\alpha)r\bar{b}e^{(1-\gamma)rT} \qquad t \geq T. \tag{11c}$$

Flow utility before a stabilization is the following:

$$\begin{aligned} u_i^{\mathrm{D}}(t) &= -\frac{\gamma}{2}r\bar{b}e^{(1-\gamma)rT} - K_i \\ &= -\gamma r(\tfrac{1}{2} + \theta_i)\bar{b}e^{(1-\gamma)rt} \end{aligned} \tag{12}$$

which is the income effect of taxes plus the welfare loss arising from taxes being distortionary.

With constant consumption after a stabilization, discounted utility V^j ($j = \mathrm{W}, \mathrm{L}$) is simply constant flow utility for each group divided by r. Using (11) and (6) (where $K_i = 0$ after a stabilization), one immediately obtains

$$V^{\mathrm{W}}(T) - V^{\mathrm{L}}(T) = (2\alpha - 1)\bar{b}e^{(1-\gamma)rT} \tag{13}$$

which is the present discounted value of the excess taxes that the loser must pay relative to the winner.

The optimal concession time for a group with cost θ_i, T_i, can now be determined.[15] We will first derive the solution for the case in which the problem of debt service exceeding income is ignored and then show how this solution is modified when the issue of feasibility is explicitly considered.

We further assume, for the time being, that $\underline{\theta} > \alpha - \frac{1}{2}$. We discuss the economic meaning of this assumption below. Since the distribution $H(T)$ is not known, equation (8) cannot be used directly. However, by showing that T_i is monotonic in θ_i, we can derive the relation between $H(T)$ and the known $F(\theta)$, namely, $1 - H(T(\theta)) = F(\theta)$.

LEMMA 1 $T_i'(\theta_i) < 0$.

(See Appendix for a proof.)

We now want to find a symmetric Nash equilibrium in which each group's concession behavior is described by the same function $T(\theta)$. In this equilibrium, if all other groups behave according to $T(\theta)$, group i finds it optimal to concede according to $T(\theta)$. Thus, the expected time of stabilization is the expected minimum T, with the expectation taken over $F(\theta)$. There may be asymmetric equilibria (i.e., where groups behave according to different $T(\theta)$) even though each group's θ is known to be drawn from the same distribution $F(\theta)$. For example, there are equilibria in which one group concedes immediately. We do not investigate such equilibria, since our interest is in demonstrating that this type of model can yield delay.[16]

PROPOSITION 1 There exists a symmetric Nash equilibrium with each group's optimal behavior described by a concession function $T(\theta)$, where $T(\theta)$ is implicitly defined by

$$\left[-\frac{f(\theta)}{F(\theta)}\frac{1}{T'(\theta)}\right]\frac{2\alpha-1}{r}=\gamma(\theta+\tfrac{1}{2}-\alpha) \tag{14}$$

and the initial boundary condition

$$T(\bar{\theta})=0. \tag{15}$$

(See Appendix for proof.)

The right-hand side of (14) is the cost of waiting another instant to concede. The left-hand side is the expected gain from waiting another instant to concede, which is the product of the conditional probability that one's opponent concedes (the hazard rate, in brackets) multiplied by the gain if the other group concedes. Concession occurs when the (group-specific) cost of waiting just equals the expected benefit from waiting.

The role of the assumption $\underline{\theta} > \alpha - \frac{1}{2}$ should now be clear. If a group has a cost θ such that $\theta + \frac{1}{2} < \alpha$, the group would always prefer to wait than to concede, since the cost of living in the unstabilized economy and bearing half the tax burden would be less than the cost associated with being the "loser." That is, the group's $T(\theta)$ would be infinite. The above assumption means that stabilization occurs in finite time with probability 1 (ignoring any feasibility issues, to be discussed below).

Equation (14) is also useful in understanding the evolution of the war of attrition from the viewpoint of one side. Consider a group with $\theta < \bar{\theta}$. At time 0, there is some probability that its opponent has $\theta = \bar{\theta}$ and will concede immediately. If no one concedes at time 0, both sides know that their opponent is not type $\bar{\theta}$. At the "next" instant the next-highest type concedes and so on, so as time elapses each side learns that its opponent does not have a cost above a certain level. When the conditional probability of an opponent's concession in the next instant (based on what the group has learned about his highest possible cost) is such that (14) just holds, it is time to "throw in the towel."

Let us now consider the issue of feasibility. From equation (11b), it follows that a stabilization in which one group pays a share α of taxes is not feasible after $T = [1/(1-\gamma)r]\ln(y/\alpha r\bar{b})$. Indicate this value with T^* and let θ^* be the associated cost defined by $T(\theta^*) = T^*$. Suppose, therefore, that if no concession has occurred by T^* the government closes the budget deficit by a combination of expenditure cuts and distortionary taxes which imply very large loss of utility. If the utility loss is sufficiently high, a group with $\theta < \theta^*$ would prefer to concede at T^* than to have the distortionary solution imposed. The government's threat thus implies that the distribution of concession times will have a mass point at T^*, with concession occurring at that point with probability 1 if it has not occurred before. If both groups concede at T^* a tie-breaking rule is used: a coin is flipped, with the loser bearing the share α of nondistortionary taxes.

To close the argument, the existence of a mass point at T^* means that groups with costs close to but above θ^* (i.e., groups that would have conceded *before* T^* under strategy $T(\theta)$ if there were no mass at T^*) will now find it preferable to wait until T to concede under the tie-breaking rule. Define $\tilde{\theta} > \theta^*$ as the cost when a group is indifferent between being the stabilizer at $\tilde{T} = T(\tilde{\theta})$ and waiting until T^* to be the stabilizer with probability $\frac{1}{2}$. The addition of the government's threat at T^* will therefore not affect optimal strategy for groups with $\theta \geq \tilde{\theta}$. Since T^* is increasing in y and $\tilde{T}$ is increasing in T^*, $\tilde{T}$ would be increasing in y. Thus, as y increases, the fraction of the distribution of groups whose behavior is described by $T(\theta)$ in Proposition 1 rises. Put another way, for fixed y arbitrarily high, the time until the solution in Proposition 1 holds can also be made arbitrarily long.

If we relax the assumption that $\underline{\theta} > \alpha - \frac{1}{2}$, it is possible that no group concedes, and stabilization takes place only due to intervention as above. This seems to be consistent with historical experience. Maier (1975) argues that inflation stabilization in Germany and France in the 1920's was possible only because the costs of living with inflation were perceived as too high by participants in the political process. In contrast, the budget imbalances in France in the 1930's, which were not accompanied by high inflation, were not resolved until the Second World War broke out. That is, the costs of the fiscal crisis may not have been perceived as sufficiently high to induce any group to "concede."

Given concession times as a function of θ, the expected date of stabilization is then the expected minimum T, the expectation taken over $F(\theta)$.

With n players the probability that a given θ is the maximum (so that $T(\theta)$ is the minimum) is its density $f(\theta)$ multiplied by the probability that no other θ is higher, namely $[F(\theta)]^{n-1}$, multiplied by n. With $n = 2$, the expected value of minimum T (i.e., the expected time of stabilization T^{SE}) is thus

$$T^{\mathrm{SE}} = 2\int_{\underline{\theta}}^{\bar{\theta}} T(x)F(x)f(x)\,dx. \tag{16}$$

As long as all participants in the process initially believe that someone else may have a higher θ, stabilization does not occur immediately. The cumulative distribution of stabilization times T is therefore 1 minus the probability that every group has an θ lower than the value consistent with stabilization at T. With two groups, this is

$$S(T) = 1 - [F(\theta(T))]^2 \tag{17}$$

where $\theta(T)$ is defined by $T(\theta) = T$.

Two observations are useful in helping to explain the key role of heterogeneity. Suppose, first, that all groups are identical, as in a representative-agent model. If we interpret this as there being a single agent, he knows with probability 1 that he will be the stabilizer. Since u^{D} is negative, equation (8) implies that expected utility is maximized by choosing T_i equal to 0, that is, by stabilizing immediately. Intuitively, if an individual knows that he will end up bearing the cost of a stabilization, a cost to waiting implies that it is optimal to act immediately.

Heterogeneity alone is not sufficient, however, to delay stabilizations. There must also be uncertainty about the cost to waiting of other groups. If it is known to all that a group has higher costs than anyone else, optimal behavior will imply that this group concedes immediately. Intuitively, stablization is postponed because each interest group believes the possibility that another group will give up first.

In addition, it is interesting to compare the sense in which stabilization becomes "inevitable" in this chapter with that used in Sargent and Wallace (1981) and Drazen and Helpman (1987, 1990). In those papers, a positive deficit (exclusive of debt service) implies that government debt is growing faster than the rate of interest, so that its present value is not converging to 0. The failure of this transversality condition to hold (and hence the long-run infeasibility of the path) is what makes the stabilization inevitable. Here, the war of attrition ends in finite time with a stabilization, even if debt grows more slowly than the rate of interest. Hence, our approach indicates why countries whose policies are technically feasible (in the sense that the present discounted value of the debt goes to zero) will eventually stabilize if current policies involve welfare loss.

III Why Do Some Countries Stabilize Sooner than Others?

We can now ask how different parameter values affect the expected time of a stabilization. Our goal is to see whether observable characteristics of economies explain why some countries stabilize sooner than others. These results are presented in several propositions and explained intuitively. The proofs are in the Appendix. We proceed under the assumption that $\underline{\theta} > \alpha - \frac{1}{2}$.

A Distortionary Taxes or Monetization

PROPOSITION 2 When the utility loss from distortionary taxation is proportional to the level of taxes, financing a greater fraction of the prestabilization deficit via distortionary taxation (a higher γ) implies an earlier date of stabilization.

This result may seem surprising, for it says that an attempt to control the growth of government indebtedness may actually hasten the date of stabilization. A higher γ on the one hand implies a greater distortion for a given deficit, inducing earlier concession. However, making more of an effort to reduce the deficit implies that government debt grows more slowly, and hence the distortions which induce stabilization also grow less fast. The first effect dominates because our proportional specification in (5) implies that both the gain from being the winner and the loss from no stabilization are proportional to the size of the debt, so that a slower growth of the debt does not in itself change their relative magnitudes.[17] Higher monetization has the effect of raising the cost of the distortions in the unstabilized economy relative to the gain from having another group stabilize *at each point in time.* This result is consistent with the idea that it is easier to stabilize hyperinflations than inflations that are "only" high.[18]

B Costs of Distortions

PROPOSITION 3 An increase in the costs associated with living in an unstable economy, for an unchanged distribution of θ, will move the expected date of a stabilization forward.

Countries with institutions that lessen the utility loss from distortionary financing of government expenditures (such as indexation) will, *other things equal*, be expected to postpone stabilization longer.[19] If the utility loss is an increasing (perhaps convex) function of inflation, a sharp acceleration of inflation will lead to a stabilization. This would explain the timing of the French and German stabilizations.

C Political Cohesion

PROPOSITION 4 If $\alpha = \frac{1}{2}$, stabilization occurs immediately; the larger is α above $\frac{1}{2}$, the later is the expected date of stabilization.

The difference in the shares of the burden of stabilization, α, could be interpreted as representing the degree of political cohesion in the society. Countries with α close to $\frac{1}{2}$ can be characterized as having high political cohesion, since the burden of stabilization is shared relatively equally, while those where the burden is very unequal, so that α is close to 1, are more polarized or less cohesive. When the relative burden of a stabilization is unequally distributed, the gain from waiting in the hope that one's opponent will concede is larger. Hence, each group holds out longer.

This intuitive result suggests a relationship between measures of political stability and macroeconomic outcomes. Roubini and Sachs (1989a, 1989b) argue that governments composed of large, short-lived, and uncohesive coalitions are associated with large budget deficits. They construct an index of political cohesion and stability in the government and show a strong correlation between that index and budget deficits after 1973 in several industrial countries. One explanation of this finding that is consistent with our model concerns the decision-making process within the coalition. Large coalitions of politically diverse parties find it particularly hard to reach agreements on how to allocate tax increases or expenditure cuts among the constituencies represented by coalition partners. In the absence of such an agreement, deficits grow. Cukierman, Edwards, and Tabellini (1990) argue that the level of inflation in a cross section of countries is inversely related to measures of political stability.

D Income Dispersion and Longer Delays in Stabilizing

Finally, we consider the implications of dropping the assumption that all groups have the same income. Greater dispersion in the distribution of income can affect the timing of stabilization if a group's cost is a function of its income. As emphasized above, delays can only occur if relative costs are unknown to each group. If relative costs depend upon relative income levels, this implies that delays are observed only when relative positions in income distribution are unknown.

An increase in income inequality may make relative income levels more apparent, leading to an immediate stabilization. Consider instead a mean-preserving spread in the distribution of income, maintaining the assumption of uncertainty about relative incomes. Intuitively, one may conclude that this should also lead to an earlier stabilization, since it means that some group will have a higher cost and thus concede earlier. Such reasoning is incomplete, for it ignores the change in behavior (i.e., in the function $T(\theta)$) induced by the change in the distribution of costs. The fatter upper tail for costs means that each group perceives a higher likelihood that its opponents' costs have increased. This perception would lead it to hold out longer.

PROPOSITION 5 If the utility loss due to distortionary taxes is a decreasing, convex function of income and if income is unobservable, a mean-preserving spread in the distribution of income $G(y)$ that keeps the expected minimum of the y's constant implies a later expected date of stabilization.

Note that if $\theta'(y) < 0$, it is the "poor" who lose the war of attrition, since the "rich" suffer less from the prestabilization distortions and can hold out longer.

The assumption of uncertainty about relative incomes is perhaps more realistic under the second interpretation of the costs provided in Section II, namely, as resources that must be devoted to the political process to avoid bearing a disproportionate share of the burden of stabilization. In this case, the level of group-i income, y_i, would then be interpreted as the resources available for political purposes. With uncertainty both about the relative political skills of groups and about what fraction of their total income they are willing to devote to the political struggle, assuming uncertainty about relative "income" is more realistic.

An empirical finding consistent with Proposition 5 is presented by Berg and Sachs (1988), who find a correlation between the degree of income inequality and the frequency of debt rescheduling: countries with a more unequal income distribution have experienced more difficulties in servicing their external debt. Although this evidence is not directly related to the timing of stabilizations, it is consistent with the idea that countries with more income inequality will, at a given level of debt, find it more difficult to adopt policies necessary to insure solvency.

IV Summary and Extensions

Delayed stabilizations can be explained in a model of rational heterogeneous agents. However, in contrast, the same model with a rational representative individual would yield immediate stabilization. Since many of the results are summarized in the introductory section, we conclude by discussing some generalizations and by touching on some issues that the model did not address but which are important in explaining stabilization.

First of all, even though we considered the example of a delayed budget adjustment, our argument is much more general. Any efficient policy change with significant distributional consequences can be delayed by a "war of attrition": trade and financial liberalizations are additional examples of this type of policy reform.[20]

Second, for simplicity, no changes in external circumstances following the original shock were considered. More generally, during a war of attrition, a change in the environment (including aid or foreign intervention) may lead to a change in agents' behavior and rapid concession by one side. Even (or especially) when this change is foreseen, the war of attrition is crucial in the delay of stabilization until the external change.

A third generalization involves a more precise formalization of the political process. In particular, this would lead to a more satisfactory characterization of the political costs involved in sheltering oneself from bearing the burden of stabilization. As in the model above, such costs may increase with the size of the outstanding debt: as the difference between payoffs of winners and losers rises, as a result of the growing level of the debt, each side should be willing to spend more time and resources in lobbying activities to induce its rivals to concede. Since different groups differ in their political influence or access to resources, such direct political costs will be central to the timing of concession.

A political model also suggests alternative interpretations of some of our results. For example, in Proposition 3, the effect of a shift in the distribution of θ could be interpreted as follows. Countries with political institutions that make it relatively more difficult for opposing groups to "veto" stabilization programs not to their liking will stabilize sooner. In addition, we have not explicitly considered important political events such as elections, the timing of which may be related to the timing of stabilizations. An electoral victory of one side may make it more difficult for the opponents to block its program and shelter themselves from the burden of stabilization. Thus, one might expect successful stabilizations following elections with a clear winner. In the terminology of our model, an electoral landslide may be an important signal of the distribution of the relative strength of different groups.

Finally, we note some issues that we did not discuss. The first is credibility. Delays in successfully stabilizing an economy are related to what determines the probability of success, where the "credibility" of a program has come to be seen as a crucial ingredient of success. One notion of credibility is simply whether or not the economics of a program "make sense." For example, the Brazilian Cruzado Plan of 1986 was not seen as credible. While technical feasibility is necessary for success, it is clearly not sufficient, as the failure of apparently well-designed programs indicates. This notion of credibility thus lacks predictive power, as Dornbusch (1988) argues, since successful and unsuccessful programs often appear to be quite similar ex ante. As an example, he refers to the great similarity between Poincaré's successful 1926 program and the failed 1924 attempt as well as several unsuccessful attempts in Germany prior to the November 1923 program.

A second notion of credibility concerns the degree of commitment of a policymaker to the plan, in that he is unlikely to give in to pressure to abandon fiscal responsibility and revert to inflationary finance.[21] This has been formalized in terms of "strong" and "weak" policymakers with different objective functions. A weak policymaker, after a period of mimicking the strong one, abandons policies of monetary restraint. If the public is uncertain about the degree of commitment of the policymaker to fiscal responsibility, success is less likely. In these models, the policymaker's "type," which is crucial, is both exogenous and unobservable. For this reason, credibility as commitment also lacks predictive power.

Our model suggests that successful stabilizations need not be associated with a sharp change in external circumstances, nor does the program being implemented need to look sharply different from what had previously been proposed. The credibility and success of a program reflects the political support it can muster. A main message is that necessary changes in the level of political support may simply result from the passage of time, so that a program that was unsuccessful at one point in time may later be successful. In the war of attrition, passage of time and the accumulation of costs lead one group to give in and make a previously rejected program economically and politically feasible. This may come via the political consolidation of one "group" which forces its opponent to "throw in the towel" in the war of attrition. The role of political consolidation as an element of "credibility" is also emphasized by Sargent in his discussion of hyperinflations and in his comparison of Poincaré and Thatcher (Sargent 1982, 1984).

Second, in reality, successful stabilizations are not one-shot affairs. One component of success is the design of how the adjustment process should be spread out over time. Our notion of timing emphasizes the beginning of a successful program, not the timing of its stages once it has begun. Theoretically, these different notions of timing can be separated, with this chapter addressing the question of why significant policy changes, multistage or otherwise, are delayed. In fact, since stabilization takes time, programs often appear to be successful for a period of time, only to fail subsequently. Hence, the issue of delayed stabilization should ideally be considered simultaneously with issues of both partial and multistage stabilizations.

Appendix

Proof of Lemma 1 Differentiating (8) with respect to T_i, one obtains

$$\frac{d\mathrm{EU}}{dT_i} = e^{-rT_i}\left\{h(T_i)[V^{\mathrm{W}}(T_i) - V^{\mathrm{L}}(T_i)] + [1 - H(T_i)]\left[u_i^{\mathrm{D}}(T_i) - rV^{\mathrm{L}}(T_i) + \frac{dV^{\mathrm{L}}(T_i)}{dT_i}\right]\right\}. \tag{A1}$$

Using the definitions of $V^{\mathrm{W}}(T)$, $V^{\mathrm{L}}(T)$, and $u_i^{\mathrm{D}}(t)$, (A1) becomes

$$\frac{d\mathrm{EU}}{dT_i} = e^{-rT_i}\left\{h(T_i)(2\alpha - 1)\bar{b}e^{(1-\gamma)rT_i} + [1 - H(T_i)]\left[\gamma r\left(\alpha - \frac{1}{2} - \theta_i\right)\bar{b}e^{(1-\gamma)rT_i}\right]\right\}. \tag{A2}$$

Differentiating with respect to θ_i, we obtain

$$\frac{d^2\text{EU}}{dT_i\,d\theta_i} = \{-[1 - H(T_i)]\gamma r\bar{b}e^{(1-\gamma)rT_i}\}e^{-rT_i} < 0. \tag{A3}$$

Equation (A3) means that, when others are acting optimally, $d\text{EU}/dT$ is decreasing in θ_i. Optimal concession time T_i is therefore monotonically decreasing in θ_i.

Proof of Proposition 1 Suppose that the other interest group is acting according to $T(\theta)$, the optimal concession time for a group with utility cost θ. Choosing a time T_i as above would be equivalent to choosing a value $\hat{\theta}_i$ and conceding at time $T_i = T(\hat{\theta}_i)$. After the change in variables, equation (8) becomes

$$\begin{aligned}\text{EU}(\hat{\theta}_i, \theta_i) = F(\hat{\theta}_i)\left[\int_{\hat{\theta}_i}^{\bar{\theta}} - u^{\text{D}}(x)e^{-rT(x)}T'(x)\,dx + e^{-rT(\hat{\theta}_i)}V^{\text{L}}(T(\theta_i))\right]\\ + \int_{x=\hat{\theta}_i}^{x=\bar{\theta}}\left[\int_{x}^{\bar{\theta}} - u^{\text{D}}(z)e^{-rT(z)}T'(z)\,dz + e^{-rT(x)}V^{\text{W}}(T(x))\right]f(x)\,dx.\end{aligned} \tag{A4}$$

Differentiating with respect to $\hat{\theta}_i$ and setting the resulting expression equal to zero, we obtain (dropping the i subscript)

$$\begin{aligned}\frac{d\text{EU}}{d\hat{\theta}} &= f(\hat{\theta})[V^{\text{W}}(T(\hat{\theta})) - V^{\text{L}}(T(\hat{\theta}))]\\ &\quad + F(\hat{\theta})\left[u^{\text{D}}(\theta, \hat{\theta}) - rV^{\text{L}} + \frac{dV^{\text{L}}}{dT}\right]T'(\hat{\theta}) = 0\end{aligned} \tag{A5}$$

which becomes, after substitutions,

$$\frac{d\text{EU}}{d\hat{\theta}} = -f(\hat{\theta})(2\alpha - 1) - F(\hat{\theta})\gamma r\left(\theta + \frac{1}{2} - \alpha\right)T'(\hat{\theta}) = 0. \tag{A6}$$

Now, by the definition of $T(\theta)$ as the optimal time of concession for a group with cost θ, $\hat{\theta} = \theta$ when $\hat{\theta}$ is chosen optimally. The first-order condition (A6) evaluated at $\hat{\theta} = \theta$ implies (14). (Substituting $T'(\theta)$ evaluated at $\hat{\theta}$ from (14) into (A6), one sees that the second-order condition is satisfied, since (A6) then implies that $\text{sign}(d\text{EU}/d\hat{\theta}) = \text{sign}(\theta - \hat{\theta})$.)

To derive the initial boundary condition, note first that, for any value of $\theta \leq \bar{\theta}$, the gain to having the opponent concede is positive. Therefore, as long as $f(\bar{\theta})$ is nonzero, groups with $\theta < \bar{\theta}$ will not concede immediately.

This in turn implies that a group with $\theta = \bar{\theta}$ (i.e., a group that knows it has the highest possible cost of waiting) will find it optimal to choose $T(\bar{\theta}) = 0$.

Proof of Proposition 2 A higher fraction of prestabilization deficits financed by taxation corresponds to a higher value of γ. Comparing the optimal time of concession as a function of θ for $\tilde{\gamma} > \gamma$, we have

$$T'(\theta) = \frac{f(\theta)}{F(\theta)} \frac{(2\alpha - 1)/r}{\gamma(\theta + \frac{1}{2} - \alpha)} \tag{A7}$$

$$\tilde{T}'(\theta) = -\frac{f(\theta)}{F(\theta)} \frac{(2\alpha - 1)/r}{\tilde{\gamma}(\theta + \frac{1}{2} - \alpha)}. \tag{A7$'$}$$

Since $V^{\mathrm{W}} - V^{\mathrm{L}}$ is the same in both cases, the initial boundary condition is the same for γ and $\tilde{\gamma}$, that is, $T(\bar{\theta}) = \tilde{T}(\bar{\theta}) = 0$. Inspection of (A7) and (A7′) indicates that $\tilde{T}'(\theta) > T'(\theta)$ for all values of θ. Combining these two results, we have that $T(\theta) > \tilde{T}(\theta)$ for $\theta < \bar{\theta}$. Equation (16) then implies that $\tilde{T}^{\mathrm{SE}} < T^{\mathrm{SE}}$.

Proof of Proposition 3 A multiplicative shift in θ has an identical effect to an increase in γ in Proposition 2. By an argument analogous to the one used in that proof, $T(\theta)$ will shift down, and hence T^{SE} will fall.

Proof of Proposition 4 When $\alpha = \frac{1}{2}$, $V^{\mathrm{W}} = V^{\mathrm{L}}$. Since there are costs to not conceding, it is optimal to concede immediately. To prove the second part of the proposition, the same argument as in Proposition 2 shows that $T(\bar{\theta}) = \tilde{T}(\bar{\theta}) = 0$ for $\tilde{\alpha} > \alpha$. Since the right-hand side of (14) decreases with an increase α, $\tilde{T}'(\theta) < T'(\theta)$ for all values of θ. Using the same reasoning as in Proposition 2, we have that $\tilde{T}(\theta) > T(\theta)$ for $\theta < \bar{\theta}$. Equation (16) implies $\tilde{T}^{\mathrm{SE}} > T^{\mathrm{SE}}$.

Proof of Proposition 5 Suppose $\theta_i = \theta(y_i)$ with $\theta' < 0$, where a group's income y_i is unobservable. Let $G(y, \sigma)$ be the distribution of income with bounds $\underline{y}$ and $\bar{y}$, where increases in σ correspond to a more dispersed income distribution. Increasing σ corresponds to a mean-preserving spread of income if for some $\tilde{y}$

$$G_\sigma(y, \sigma) \geq 0 \quad \text{for } y \leq \tilde{y}$$

$$G_\sigma(y, \sigma) \leq 0 \quad \text{for } y > \tilde{y}.$$

The expected minimum value of y can be written as

$$E(y_{\min}) = 2\int_{\underline{y}}^{\bar{y}} [1 - G(x,\sigma)]g(x,\sigma)x\,dx \tag{A8}$$

which by integration by parts equals $\int_{\underline{y}}^{\bar{y}} [1 - G(x,\sigma)]^2\,dx$. Constant expected $y_{\min}$ implies

$$\int_{\underline{y}}^{\bar{y}} [1 - G(x,\sigma)]G_\sigma(x,\sigma)\,dx = 0. \tag{A9}$$

Equations (A9) and (16) imply

$$T^{\mathrm{SE}}(\sigma) = 2\int_{\underline{y}}^{\bar{y}} T(x,\sigma)[1 - G(x,\sigma)]g(x,\sigma)\,dx. \tag{A10}$$

Repeated integration by parts implies that (A10) can be written as

$$T^{\mathrm{SE}}(\sigma) = \frac{2\alpha - 1}{r\gamma}\left\{\frac{-\frac{1}{2}}{\theta(\underline{y}) + \frac{1}{2} - \alpha} + \frac{1}{2}\int_{\underline{y}}^{\bar{y}} (1 - G(x,\sigma))^2\left[\frac{1}{\theta(x) + \frac{1}{2} - \alpha}\right]^2 \theta'(x)\,dx\right\} \tag{A11}$$

If the change in σ does not affect the lower bound $\underline{y}$ and if $(d^2\theta/dy^2) \geq 0$, we have

$$\begin{aligned}\frac{dT^{\mathrm{SE}}(\theta)}{d\sigma} &= -\frac{2\alpha - 1}{r\gamma}\int_{\underline{y}}^{\bar{y}} [1 - G(x,\sigma)]G_\sigma(x,\sigma)\left[\frac{1}{\theta(x) + \frac{1}{2} - \alpha}\right]^2 \theta'(x)\,dx \\ &\geq -\frac{2\alpha - 1}{r\gamma}\frac{\theta'(\tilde{y})}{[\theta(\tilde{y}) + \frac{1}{2} - \alpha]^2}\int_{\underline{y}}^{\bar{y}} [1 - G(x,\sigma)]G_\sigma(x,\sigma)\,dx = 0.\end{aligned} \tag{A12}$$

Notes

We thank Barry Eichengreen, Raquel Fernandez, Stephan Haggard, Elhanan Helpman, Peter Kennen, Barry Nalebuff, Dani Rodrik, Howard Rosenthal, Jeffrey Sachs, two referees, and participants of several seminars for very helpful comments. Substantial revisions of this work were performed while Alesina was an Olin Fellow at the NBER; he thanks the Olin and Sloan Foundations for financial support. Drazen's research was supported by National Science Foundation Grant No. SES-8706808.

1. In Sargent and Wallace (1981) and Drazen and Helpman (1987), the timing of stabilization is deterministic and exogenous; in Drazen and Helpman (1990), the timing is stochastic, but the distribution of the time of stabilization is exogenous.

2. See Athanasios Orphanides (1989) for a model in which a rational government delays a stabilization program to take advantage of more favorable exogenous circumstances.

3. The effects of political instability on the path of government debt is studied in a different framework by Alberto Alesina and Guido Tabellini (1989, 1990), Torsten Persson and Lars Svensson (1989), and Tabellini and Alesina (1990).

4. David Backus and John Driffill (1985a, 1985b) and Tabellini (1988) discuss a war of attrition between trade unions and a central bank, leading to periods of inefficient outcomes. An additional application of the war-of-attrition model is in the labor-strike literature; for a survey see John Kennan and Robert Wilson (1988).

5. Kenneth Rogoff (1985) suggests that it may be optimal to appoint a central banker with preferences that do not coincide with social preferences. In this case, however, the central bank's preferences are known by the public, while a war of attrition requires uncertainty about an opponent's characteristics.

6. We are grateful to Barry Eichengreen for pointing out to us this example.

7. See Nouriel Roubini and Jeffrey Sachs (1989a, 1989b) for statistical evidence on post-1973 OECD democracies, Francesco Giavazzi and Marco Pagano (1990) on Denmark and Ireland, and Giavazzi and Luigi Spaventa (1988) on Italy.

8. Since we are considering an economy with constant output, this is equivalent to a rising debt/GNP ratio.

9. The view that the utility loss from living in an unstabilized economy flows from the use of distortionary financing of part of the government deficit raises an obvious question: why not simply accumulate debt until an agreement can be reached on levying less distortionary taxes? We suggest that there may be constraints on the rate of growth of the debt, especially if it is external, but do not model this here.

10. Elections may also give one side a clear mandate not because its opponents have conceded on their distributional objectives, but because a majority of voters see that side as more *competent* to handle an economic crisis. The issue of competency is not considered here.

11. This may be generalized easily to more than two groups if we keep the assumption of exogenously fixed shares: if one group agrees to pay a share $\alpha > 1/n$, each other group pays $(1 - \alpha)/(n - 1)$ of the burden. A more general approach is that once one group concedes, the $n - 1$ groups remaining engage in a "second-round" war of attrition, and so on. This may lead to similar results, but it is a much more complex problem, which we have not explored.

12. We could adopt a more general specification for K_i, such as

$$K_i(t) = \theta_i[\tau(t)]^{1+m} \quad m > 0.$$

The qualitative features of our results do not change with this more general specification. The differences will be emphasized in what follows.

13. The technical difficulty in developing an explicitly monetary model in this framework is the following. Money demand should depend on expected inflation. The latter, in turn, is a function of the perceived probability that a stabilization program is adopted in each period. While in Drazen and Helpman (1990) this probability is exogenous, in this chapter it is endogenously determined and will depend on utility and, therefore, on expected inflation. Hence, equilibrium would mean a fixed point in this probability function. Thus, it appears to be technically infeasible to derive endogenously this probability distribution in a model in which the distribution itself affects utility via the decision aboout money-holding.

14. We impose a condition below which insures that consumption is not negative in every period.

15. This derivation follows Christopher Bliss and Barry Nalebuff (1984).

16. Of course, if different groups' endowments are perceived to be drawn from different distributions, each group will have a different $T_i(\theta)$. See, for example, Drew Fudenberg and Jean Tirole (1986).

17. When the utility loss from distortionary taxation rises more than proportionally with the level of taxes (as in note 11), the effect of slower growth of the deficit may dominate. It can be shown (details are available from the authors upon request) that low-θ groups will concede later, so that if it happens that both groups have low θ, increased γ will mean a later date of stabilization.

18. Drazen and Vittorio Grilli (1990) use a war-of-attrition model to investigate how an economic "crisis," defined as a period of high (and thus costly) inflation, actually raises total welfare by inducing agreement over a policy change.

19. The caveat here is that increased indexation may induce greater monetization or higher prices for a given level of monetization.

20. Raquel Fernandez and Dani Rodrik (1990) suggest a different explanation for the postponement of the adoption of trade reform, based on a bias in favor of the "status quo" with majority voting. Our approach and theirs are not inconsistent.

21. Rodrik (1989) studies trade reforms from this perspective. Backus and Driffill (1985a, 1989b), Robert Barro (1986), and Tabellini (1988) study monetary policy.

22. This proof closely follows Bliss and Nalebuff (1984).

References

Alesina, Alberto. 1988. The end of large public debts. In F. Giavazzi and L. Spaventa, eds., *High public debt: The Italian experience*, 34–79. Cambridge: Cambridge University Press.

Alesina, Alberto, and Tabellini, Guido. 1989. External debt, capital flight, and political risk. *Journal of International Economics* 27:199–220.

Alesina, Alberto, and Tabellini, Guido. 1990. A positive theory of fiscal deficits and government debt. *Review of Economic Studies* 57:403–414.

Backus, David, and Driffill, John. 1985a. Rational expectations and policy credibility after a change of regime. *Review of Economic Studies* 52:211–222.

Backus, David, and Driffill, John. 1985b. Inflation and reputation. *American Economic Review* 75:530–538.

Barro, Robert. 1986. Reputation in a model of monetary policy with incomplete information. *Journal of Monetary Economics* 17:1–20. Reprinted as chapter 5 in volume 1 of this work.

Berg, Andrew, and Sachs, Jeffrey. 1988. The debt crisis: Structural explanations of country performance. *Journal of Development Economics* 29:271–306.

Bliss, Christopher, and Nalebuff, Barry. 1984. Dragon-slaying and ballroom dancing: The private supply of a public good. *Journal of Public Economics* 25:1–12.

Cukierman, Alex, Edwards, Sebastian, and Tabellini, Guido. 1990. Seignorage and Political Instability. Centre for Economic Policy Research (CEPR) working paper no. 381.

Dornbusch, Rudiger. 1988. Notes on credibility and stabilization. NBER working paper no. 2790.

Dornbusch, Rudiger, and DePablo, Juan Carlos. 1987. Argentine debt and macroeconomic instability. NBER working paper no. 2378.

Drazen, Allan, and Helpman, Elhanan. 1987. Stabilization and exchange rate management. *Quarterly Journal of Economics* 52:835–855.

Drazen, Allan, and Helpman, Elhanan. 1990. Inflationary consequences of anticipated macroeconomic policies. *Review of Economic Studies* 57:147–167.

Drazen, Allan, and Grilli, Vittorio. 1990. The benefit of crises for economic reforms. NBER working paper no. 3527.

Eichengreen, Barry. 1990. The capital levy in theory and practice. In R. Dornbusch and M. Draghi, eds., *Public debt management: Theory and history*, 191–220. Cambridge: Cambridge University Press.

Eichengreen, Barry, and Sachs, Jeffrey. 1985. Exchange rates and economic recovery in the 1930s. *Journal of Economic History* 45:925–946.

Fernandez, Raquel, and Rodrik, Dani. 1990. Why is trade reform so unpopular? On status quo bias in policy reforms. NBER working paper no. 3269.

Fudenberg, Drew, and Tirole, Jean. 1986. A theory of exit in duopoly. *Econometrica* 54:943–960.

Giavazzi, Francesco, and Pagano, Marco. 1990. Can severe fiscal contractions be expansionary? Tales of two small European countries. In Olivier Blanchard and Stanley Fischer, eds., *NBER Macroeconomic Annual 1990*, 75–111. Cambridge, MA: MIT Press.

Giavazzi, Francesco, and Spaventa, Luigi. 1988. *High public debt: The Italian experience.* Cambridge: Cambridge University Press.

Haig, Robert. 1929. *The public finance of postwar France.* New York: Columbia University Press.

Jackson, Julian. 1985. *The politics of depression in France.* Cambridge: Cambridge University Press.

Kennan, John, and Wilson, Robert. 1988. Strategic bargaining methods and interpretation of strike data. Manuscript, New York University.

Loewy, Michael. 1988. Reaganomics and reputation revisited. *Economic Inquiry* 26:253–264.

Maier, Charles. 1975. *Recasting bourgeois Europe: Stabilization in France, Germany, and Italy in the decade after World War II.* Princeton: Princeton University Press.

Orphanides, Athanasios. 1989. The timing of stabilizations. Manuscript, Massachusetts Institute of Technology.

Persson, Torsten, and Svensson, Lars. 1989. Why a stubborn conservative would run a deficit: Policy with time-inconsistent preferences. *Quarterly Journal of Economics* 104:325–346. Reprinted as chapter 5 in the current volume of this work.

Riley, John. 1980. Strong evolutionary equilibrium and the war of attrition. *Journal of Theoretical Biology* 82:383–400.

Rodrik, Dani. 1989. Promises, promises: Credible policy reforms via signalling. *Economic Journal* 99:756–772.

Rogoff, Kenneth. 1985. The optimal degree of commitment to an intermediate monetary target. *Quarterly Journal of Economics* 100:1169–1190. Reprinted as chapter 9 in volume 1 of this work.

Roubini, Nouriel, and Sachs, Jeffrey. 1989a. Government spending and budget deficits in the industrial democracies. *Economic Policy* 8:100–132.

Roubini, Nouriel, and Sachs, Jeffrey, 1989b. Political and economic determinants of budget deficits in industrial democracies. *European Economic Review* 33:903–933.

Sargent, Thomas. 1982. The ends of four big inflations. In R. Hall, ed., *Inflation*, 41–98. Chicago: University of Chicago Press.

Sargent, Thomas. 1984. Stopping moderate inflations: The methods of Poincaré and Thatcher. In R. Dornbusch and H. Simonsen, eds., *Inflation, debt and indexation*, 54–96. Cambridge, MA: MIT Press.

Sargent, Thomas. 1986. Reaganomics and credibility. In T. Sargent, ed., *Rational expectations and inflation*, 19–39. New York: Harper and Row.

Sargent, Thomas, and Wallace, Neil. 1981. Some unpleasant monetarist arithmetic. *Federal Reserve Bank of Minneapolis Quarterly Review* 5:1–17.

Tabellini, Guido. 1986. Money, debt, and deficits in a dynamic game. *Journal of Economic Dynamics and Control* 8:427–442.

Tabellini, Guido. 1987. Central bank reputation and the monetization of deficits. *Economic Inquiry* 25:185–201.

Tabellini, Guido. 1988. Centralized wage setting and monetary policy in a reputational equilibrium. *Journal of Money, Credit, and Banking* 20:102–118.

Tabellini, Guido, and Alesina, Alberto. 1990. Voting on the budget deficit. *American Economic Review* 80:37–52. Reprinted as chapter 6 in the current volume of this work.

16 Economic Reform and Dynamic Political Constraints

Mathias Dewatripont and Gerard Roland

1 Introduction

Governments, and political decision-makers in general, always face political constraints when elaborating reform proposals. They know that the need to overcome potential opposition from various groups of the population constrains proposals for change. Political constraints vary, depending on the specific institutional structure of society, and are clearly different under a military dictatorship than under a parliamentary democracy. The role of political constraints seems particularly important in Eastern Europe today, where new democratic governments face the huge task of achieving the transition to a market economy. While the introduction of democracy may have removed some important obstacles to economic change (namely, the veto power of a powerful nomenclatura under communist one-party rule), fears are expressed that it could potentially jeopardize economic reforms which may, during the transition period, hurt a majority of the population.[1]

What can economic theory tell us about optimal economic reform under political constraints? This chapter starts addressing this ambitious question by looking at structural reform, focusing on a *restructuring* of economic sectors which requires massive redundancies and a significant rise in labour productivity. Our model illustrates the case of planning bureaucracies in the East, or old obsolescent industries faced with international competition both in the East and the West. When designing politically acceptable structural reforms, Governments are typically faced with a tradeoff between the *budgetary cost* of the reform and its degree of *allocative efficiency*: massive redundancies might yield rapid efficiency gains, but at a great budgetary cost, whereas gradual plans for restructuring involve less in terms of compensation payments, but imply a slower move towards allocative efficiency. When the workforce is heterogeneous, it is moreover optimal, from both points of view, to try to induce the exit of workers with the best relative outside opportunities: inducing them to leave will be both less expensive and more productive.

Reprinted from *Review of Economic Studies*, 59, (1991), 703–730, by permission of Review of Economic Studies Limited.

Section 2 presents our model, which uses the dynamic adverse selection paradigm (see, for example, Caillaud et al. 1988), to analyse the problem of a Government faced with this heterogeneous workforce. We model the Government as the *agenda-setter* (in the sense of Romer and Rosenthal, 1979) who holds the initiative for offering reform plans, possibly at several points in time. Any plan can be implemented provided it receives political approval. We distinguish two levels of political constraints: *unanimity* or *majority*, among workers inside the sector at the time the reform plan is proposed. Sections 3 to 6 examine these two rules in turn, first in a static, one-offer case and then in a dynamic, two-offer case.

Our first insight concerns *gradualism*. In a static problem, limiting redundancies in comparison to the allocative optimum may be profitable for the Government: exit fees can be lower, because only workers with the highest relative outside opportunities must be compensated. When such a "partial" reform is the static optimum, the dynamic case will exhibit gradualism, because it becomes sequentially optimal for the Government to keep shrinking the workforce, through a new reform plan, once the first reform has been enforced. While this insight is not theoretically new (see, for example, the literature on bargaining, ratcheting or contract renegotiation under adverse selection), it illustrates how dynamic adverse selection may yield gradualism as an optimal reform path.

Our main new theoretical insight concerns the role of dynamics under majority rule. We show that, in the absence of pre-commitment, the Government may end up with a *higher payoff* than by committing itself to a single offer. The possibility of proposing new reforms tomorrow allows the Government to "play the minority of tomorrow against the minority of today" and get a 66% approval for a reform lowering the payoff of 66% of the working population of the sector in comparison to the initial status quo. Indeed, workers who expect to be in the minority of losers in the future, when a reform will be proposed after a rejection of today's proposal, are prepared to make *concessions* from the initial status quo in order to avoid this outcome. These concessions can be used by the Government to put another group of workers in the minority and to lower the cost of reform even more. We therefore have a case where repeated offers can improve rent extraction, compared to the one-offer case.

It is interesting to compare this result with the traditional results of the literature on bargaining or contracting theory under adverse selection. From that literature, we know that, under a stationary environment, it is optimal for the uninformed party to *commit* to a *single take-it-or-leave-it offer* for the entire time-horizon. Not being able to commit to a single offer only lowers the payoff of this party (see for example Gul, Sonnenschein, and Wilson 1986 and Hart and Tirole 1988 for the case of a durable-good monopoly; Dewatripont 1989 for labour contract renegotiation; or Laffont and Tirole 1988, 1990 on ratcheting and renegotiation in procurement). The same effect is found in our model when the Government needs *unanimity* to implement its reform. Intuitively, under such a decision, the workers' expectations of future reforms only make it harder to convince them to vote for early reforms, because they know they can only gain from unanimously approved reforms in the future. Contrary to the above-mentioned bargaining and contracting literatures, a key ingredient for our result under majority rule is that participation or political approval constraints are *endogenously altered* over time, rather than being *exogenously given.*

The use of repeated proposals by the Government to improve its own payoff has been analysed in general voting problems with myopic voters by McKelvey (1976), and has been extended, in a more specific context, by Rosenthal (1989) to the case of rational voters facing a budget-maximizing Government. In this respect, our results complement Rosenthal's approach by allowing for *endogenous changes* in the voting population, since we assume that workers who leave today do not vote on tomorrow's proposals. Such endogenously shifting voting populations have been considered by Roberts (1989). He analyses, in an infinite-horizon framework, the problem of a union whose workers can vote to move along an exogenously given wage-employment schedule. His main focus however, is different from ours, since he concentrates on "unraveling" seniority-based layoff decisions and on hysteresis behaviour in the face of business cycle shocks.

From the point of view of economic reform, our approach illustrates how political constraints may be weakened through dynamic agenda control. The resulting lesson is that the explicit majority rule introduced in democratic reforms may in some cases allow a reform-minded Government to obtain a majority vote for measures hurting majority interests in comparison to the status quo, by credibly threatening to shift majorities in the future.

This chapter is only a first step in the analysis of the political economy of economic reform. After briefly summarizing our results, Section 7 discusses directions for research.

2 The Model

In this chapter, we present a simple model of structural adjustment in an economy in transition. We concentrate on the case of *a sector which must be made smaller*, either because of decreased protection from international competition or because the function fulfilled by this sector has become less important in the emerging economic system (e.g. the planning bureaucracy). Typically, such a structural adjustment requires (i) *raising productivity*, and (ii) retaining in the sector workers whose *comparative advantage* is not to leave. For example, workers may differ in their valuation of leisure, or in their desire to adapt to the new organizational mode implied by the higher productivity requirement. Such individual attributes are however private information, so that the reform-minded Government will have to induce workers to reveal them through monetary incentives.

For the sake of simplicity, we assume the initial working population in the sector to be composed of *three groups*, each of unit mass, of identical and infinitesimally small workers,[2] who will differ in their disutility of work. Three groups of workers is the smallest number allowing one to meaningfully talk about endogenous majorities in favour of or against reform plans.

Again for simplicity, we assume *productivity* to be *common* to all workers in the sector, and to be a *choice variable* for the Government. It is denoted by e and can take two values: $e = 1$ (low productivity), and $e = 2$ (high productivity). Specifically, prior to the reform, all three groups of workers are in the sector, each producing group output $q(1)$. It is an option for the Government to reorganize production so that each worker in the sector produces $q(2) > q(1)$. Such a reorganization is assumed to be technologically irreversible. Moreover, there is no shirking by workers in this model as productivity is fully determined by technology.

By normalization, each worker's outside opportunity is zero. When working in the sector, a worker's utility is his wage minus e times his unit disutility of effort if required productivity is $q(e)$. Workers are defined by unit disutilities of effort, which can take three values, $\underline{x} < x < \overline{x}$. We shall thus talk about the $\underline{x}$ group, the x group and the $\overline{x}$ group of workers, and we shall equivalently talk about the Government setting productivity or effort targets. The initial situation in the sector is thus one where all three groups work at $e = 1$, and for a wage $w > \overline{x}$. Respective utility levels are thus $(w - \overline{x})$, $(w - x)$ and $(w - \underline{x})$.

We assume the following *institutional rules*:

(a) The Government is the *agenda-setter*. It is thus free to make any reform proposals.

(b) Workers only have the right to give their opinion on reform proposals, but the Government needs the approval of an *exogenously given* percentage of workers to implement the reform.

(c) The objective of the Government is the same as in the *regulation framework*, that is, maximization of net allocative surplus (output minus disutility of effort) minus the distortionary cost of monetary payments to workers remaining or leaving the sector (since these are implicitly financed by taxation). We call λ this cost per unit of monetary payments.[3]

In the initial situation, the value of the Government's objective function is thus:

$$3q(1) - (\underline{x} + x + \overline{x}) - \lambda 3w.$$

In order to simplify the analysis, we do not take a general equilibrium viewpoint in which the Government is endogenous, or where individuals can vote on the agenda-setting procedure or the precise majority rule needed to implement reforms. This allows us to avoid the usual indeterminacies in voting problems. Moreover, it makes sense given that our focus is *sectoral* instead of *macroeconomic*, since the group of workers under analysis forms only a minority of the working population. It is thus reasonable to assume that these workers face a given set of institutional rules, even though they are strong enough for the Government to have to take their opinion into account. The necessity of approval of a given percentage of these workers could be seen either as an explicit institutional rule or as a way to model worker bargaining power. Finally, the Government's objective function is utilitarian, and thus takes into account distortions induced by taxation. When these distortions can be reduced, all individuals typically share the benefits. Since workers inside the sector under analysis make up only a small fraction of the population, they can reasonably ignore this feedback on their standard of living.

We can now define allocative efficiency. We assume:

$$(1 + \lambda)x \geqq q(1) \geqq q(2) - q(1) \geqq (1 + \lambda)\underline{x}. \qquad (1)$$

Under (1), allocative efficiency is achieved when only the $\underline{x}$ group remains in the sector and individuals are asked to produce $q(2)$. Indeed, consider for example raising productivity from $q(1)$ to $q(2)$ for the $\underline{x}$ group. In order to compensate them for the increased effort, their wage would have to rise by $\underline{x}$, with a distortionary cost of $\lambda\underline{x}$. This total cost of $(1 + \lambda)\,\underline{x}$ is however lower than the additional output $q(2) - q(1)$. By similar arguments, one can see that it is better for the x and $\overline{x}$ group to leave the sector rather than to produce $q(1)$ or $q(2)$.

In a static (one-period) framework, given informational constraints (the distribution of worker types is common knowledge, individual types are private information), a reform scheme is a triple (w_1, e_1, b_1) specifying a wage and a productivity level in the sector as well as an exit bonus. Workers choose between (w_1, e_1) and b_1 if this reform is accepted. Otherwise, they keep working at $e = 1$ and wage w, which is the status quo.[4] In a two-period framework, a reform scheme in the first period is a sextuple $(w_1, e_1, b_1, w_2, e_2, b_2)$, where b_t is the exit bonus received when leaving at t. Similarly, a second-period reform scheme is a triple (w_2', e_2', b_2'). In case of rejection at $t = 2$, (w_2, e_2, b_2) is executed if the initial reform was accepted, otherwise the initial status quo prevails.

As political constraints will oblige the Government to compensate potential losers, allocative efficiency may only be attainable at high costs. Moreover, as the three types of workers are indistinguishable, the compensation schemes offered must be incentive compatible. As a consequence, second-best solutions will not necessarily imply full reform, with groups x and $\overline{x}$ ousted from production. Other reform schemes may be, on the whole, more attractive.

We assume voting to be costless. Given that, under less-than-unanimity rule, an individual vote has no impact on the outcome, there are of course two equilibrium outcomes to each voting game: acceptance and rejection. We however disregard coordination failures, by assuming that voters play *weakly dominant strategies* when voting: even though individual voters are small, they are assumed to vote according to their best interest. We furthermore assume this to happen in a *time-consistent* way, that is individuals cannot "threaten" to deviate from weakly dominant strategies in the future in order to obtain better deals from the Government.

In the following sections, we analyse in turn the unanimity and majority cases, each time in a one-period and a two-period framework. Both unanimity and majority rules seem to be relevant ways of looking at political constraints, and the comparison of outcomes under the former and the latter allows to show the effect of the relaxation of political constraints on allocative outcomes. Unanimity might seem less relevant than majority for understanding the effects of political constraints. However, not only is unanimity required in many institutional contexts, but one might also view it as a way to model consensual decision-making, whereas majority rule can be seen as a way to examine more conflictual contexts. The degree of consensus or conflict in society, that is, the degree of polarization, plays an important part in recent advances in political economy, especially in a macroeconomic framework, in the context of public debt decisions (Alesina and Tabellini 1990) or delays in stabilization programmes (Alesina and Drazen 1991).

3 Static Framework, Unanimity Rule

In this one-period problem, the Government's reform proposal (w_1, e_1, b_1) must leave everybody as well off as in the status quo in order to be accepted. Under such a unanimity rule, two types of reforms could be optimal:

Full Reform (*F*):

$$w_1 = w + \underline{x}, \quad e_1 = 2, \quad b_1 = w - x.$$

Partial Reform (*P*): Two possible cases can be considered:

$$w_1 = w, \qquad e_1 = 1, \quad b_1 = w - \overline{x},$$

$$w_1 = w + x, \quad e_1 = 2, \quad b_1 = w - \overline{x}.$$

Note that these reforms involve wage and bonus payments which are minimized subject to the incentive and full compensation constraints. A *full reform* involves keeping only $\underline{x}$ in the sector. From (1), we know that raising their effort to 2 while raising their wage by $\underline{x}$ to compensate them is efficient. Inducing exit by x and $\overline{x}$ while compensating all of them requires $b_1 \geqq w - x$. This leaves x as well off as in the status quo, while giving $\overline{x}$ (which are indistinguishable from x) an extra rent of $(\overline{x} - x)$ in comparison to the status quo. One can check that all incentive constraints are strictly satisfied with this reform plan. The value of the Government's objective function, $V(F)$, will be:

$$V(F) = (q(2) - 2\underline{x}) - \lambda(w + \underline{x} + 2(w - x)).$$

A *partial reform* involves keeping $\underline{x}$ and x in the sector, in which case $e_1 = 1$ or $e_1 = 2$ can be optimal since, by (1), $(1 + \lambda)x > q(2) - q(1) > (1 + \lambda)\underline{x}$. A partial reform implies an allocative cost in comparison to a full reform, but allows b_1 to drop to $w - \bar{x}$, since only $\bar{x}$ must be compensated. The advantage of a partial reform is thus that no group of workers gains any rent in comparison to the status quo. Once again, all incentive constraints are satisfied, and the value of the Government's objective function, $V(P)$, is:

$$V(P) = \text{Max}\{2q(1) - \underline{x} - x - \lambda(3w - \bar{x});$$
$$2q(2) - 2\underline{x} - 2x - \lambda(3w - \bar{x} + 2x)\}.$$

Note that we concentrate here on reforms in which individuals make *deterministic* choices. More general reforms could involve individuals being offered *lotteries*. For example, under partial reform with $e_1 = 2$, there is too much inefficiency relative to what is required by incentive compatibility to have x stay: the x group could be offered a lottery of either $(e_1 = 2, w_1 = w + x)$ or $(e_1 = 0, b_1 = w - x)$ where, provided the probability of the first option is high enough, the $\bar{x}$ group will not be induced to prefer this lottery to a bonus of $w - \bar{x}$. Note also that under full reform and partial reform with $e_1 = 1$, there is no room for such an improvement, because the incentive compatibility (IC) and full compensation constraints are already binding.

Beyond the aspect of realism, our focus on deterministic reforms is made for simplicity, and is justified by the fact that the insights developed below are robust to generalizations to random reforms (see our discussion in Section 4 and note 13 in Section 6).

Reforms P and F are thus the optimal deterministic reforms. Note that one can check that P dominates the status quo (which yields a Government payoff of 3 $q(1) - (\underline{x} + x + \bar{x}) - 3\lambda w$): one does better than the status quo by inducing $\bar{x}$ to exit with a bonus of $w - \bar{x}$. Reforms P and F also dominate reforms where *identical* individuals make *different deterministic* choices in terms of exiting or not. Indeed, given the linearity of our technology, such reforms are not optimal.

Proposition 1 compares P and F:

PROPOSITION 1 Under (1), when x tends to $\underline{x}$, partial reform dominates full reform, and the opposite is true when x tends to $\bar{x}$.

Proof

$$V(P) - V(F) = \text{Max}\{(q(2) - 2(1 + \lambda)x) + \lambda(\bar{x} + \underline{x} - 2x);$$
$$(q(1) - (1 + \lambda)x) - (q(2) - q(1) - (1 + \lambda)\underline{x}) + \lambda(\bar{x} - x)\}.$$

In both expressions, the last term is the difference in rents conceded to the various groups, while the other terms reflect the allocative loss of P versus F (which is positive by (1), which implies $q(2) < 2(1 + \lambda)x$, $q(1) < (1 + \lambda)x$ and $q(2) - q(1) > (1 + \lambda)\underline{x}$). When x tends to $\bar{x}$, the difference in rents also becomes favourable to $F(\bar{x} + \underline{x} - 2x) < 0$ then, while $\bar{x} - x \to 0$), which dominates. When x tends to $\underline{x}$ instead, having $e_1 = 2$ for $\underline{x}$ and x is almost allocatively optimal ($q(2) \to 2(1 + \lambda)x$), and P dominates through better rent extraction ($\bar{x} + \underline{x} - 2x > 0$). ‖

The intuition underlying Proposition 1 follows standard adverse selection arguments (see Caillaud et al. 1988). The problem of full as well as partial reform here is that compensation of x allows $\bar{x}$ to grab extra rents. When x is induced to leave, it must receive $w - x$ as bonus, so that $\bar{x}$ gains $\bar{x} - x$ in comparison to the status quo. One way to reduce the rents enjoyed by $\bar{x}$ is to have allocative inefficiency for x; that is, keep them working. This involves an allocative cost which has to be balanced against the rents enjoyed by $\bar{x}$, which go to zero under partial reform. Partial reform tends to dominate when x tends to $\underline{x}$: the allocative cost becomes small, while the rent extraction gain ($\bar{x} - x$) becomes large. Otherwise, full reform will tend to dominate. For example, if one assumes

$$2(q(2) - q(1)) < \underline{x} + x + 2\lambda x, \tag{2}$$

then $e_1 = 1$ is optimal under partial reform. In this case, $V(P) - V(F) = 2q(1) - q(2) - (x - \underline{x}) + \lambda(\bar{x} + \underline{x} - 2x)$, so that P dominates iff

$$x < \tfrac{1}{2}(\underline{x} + \bar{x}) - \frac{1}{2\lambda}(q(2) - 2q(1) + (x - \underline{x})). \tag{3}$$

This condition reveals that partial reform is better than full reform if x is smaller than half the distance between $\underline{x}$ and $\bar{x}$ minus a fraction of the allocative surplus of having only $\underline{x}$ working at $e_1 = 2$ instead of having $\underline{x}$ and x working at $e_1 = 1$.

4 Unanimity Rule in a Two-Period Problem without Commitment

The previous section stressed the possibility of the optimality of a partial reform over a full reform when its ability to do better in terms of rent extraction more than compensates its poorer performance in terms of allocative efficiency. In a two-period problem without commitment, partial reforms will become *gradual reforms*: once the $\bar{x}$ group is induced to leave in period 1, it becomes optimal in period 2 to induce the x group to leave, with a bonus $b_2 = w - x$. Such gradualism will of course be anticipated by $\bar{x}$, who will exit in period 1 only if their bonus leaves them better off than by exiting in period 2.

The idea that, in a dynamic context without commitment, partial reforms will give way to gradual ones is a familiar idea from sequential bargaining under incomplete information (see for example Gul et al. 1986) or from contract theory, both in the case of short-term contracts and ratcheting (see Laffont and Tirole 1988) or long-term contracts with renegotiation (see Dewatripont 1989; Hart and Tirole 1988; and Laffont and Tirole 1990). In all these cases, information revealed in early stages of the game (acceptance of bargaining offers, or execution of contracts) reveals information about the type of the privately informed party, and opens the way for further moves toward allocative efficiency.

The same is true here, where decisions to remain in the sector in period 1 reveal information about worker types, and allow the Government to complete the initial partial reform. Having a unanimity rule means that the problem is similar to the two-party long-run contracting problem with voluntary renegotiation. This work is the first, to our knowledge, to apply these concepts to the study of problems of economic reform.[5]

We now want to characterize the optimal Perfect-Bayesian equilibrium (PBE) from the point of view of the Government. The Government will offer reform $(w_1, e_1, b_1, w_2, e_2, b_2)$ in period 1, and can offer reform (w_2', e_2', b_2') in period 2. Let us call $(\tilde{w}_2, \tilde{e}_2, \tilde{b}_2)$ the resulting period-2 outcome, which will be correctly anticipated in equilibrium. In case the initial plan is rejected, the status quo prevails in period 1, and it is in the interest of all workers to stay in the sector. In period 2, $(\tilde{w}_2, \tilde{e}_2, \tilde{b}_2)$ is then accepted as detailed in Proposition 1, since the environment is stationary. In order to have an initial proposal accepted, the Government must thus make an offer such that $(w_1, e_1, b_1, \tilde{w}_2, \tilde{e}_2, \tilde{b}_2)$ leaves all workers as well off as under rejection followed by the continuation equilibrium offer the Government will make in period 2.

For simplicity, let us assume condition (2) is satisfied, so that $e_1 = 1$ is optimal under partial reform. Let us consider the following gradual reform:

Gradual Reform (*G*):

$$w_1 = w, \qquad e_1 = 1, \quad b_1 = (w - \bar{x}) + (w - x);$$

$$w_2 = w + \underline{x}, \quad e_2 = 2, \quad b_2 = w - x.$$

In the first period, the $\bar{x}$ group will leave with bonus b_1. In the second period, the x group will leave with bonus b_2. The wage increases to $w + \underline{x}$ in order to keep the $\underline{x}$ group in the sector. For reasons of incentive compatibility, the first-period bonus must be at least $w - \bar{x} + b_2$. If this were not the case, group $\bar{x}$ would not separate from x in the first period. The objective function of the Government becomes:

$$V(G) = (2q(1) - (\underline{x} + x) - \lambda(2w + (w - \bar{x}) + (w - x))$$
$$+ (q(2) - 2\underline{x}) - \lambda((w + \underline{x}) + (w - x)).$$

Proposition 2 compares G with full and partial reforms, which simply repeat F and P of Section 3 twice (F becomes $w_1 = w_2 = w + \underline{x}$, $e_1 = e_2 = 2$ and $b_1 = 2(w - x)$, while P becomes $w_1 = w_2 = w$, $e_1 = e_2 = 1$ and $b_1 = 2(w - \bar{x})$).

Table 16.1 first summarizes workers' net gains from the various reforms over the two periods (with $e = 1$ until the x group has left):

PROPOSITION 2 (i) If, in the static problem, $V(F) > V(P)$, full reform is optimal and can be sustained as unique PBE in the two-period problem without commitment.

Table 16.1
Net gains in comparison to the status quo (maintained over two periods)

Reform	Gains of $\underline{x}$ group	Gains of x group	Gains of $\bar{x}$ group
F	0	0	$2(\bar{x} - x)$
P	0	0	0
G	0	0	$\bar{x} - x$

(ii) If, in the static problem, $V(P) > V(F)$, partial reform dominates gradual reform which, in turn, dominates full reform. While partial reform cannot be sustained as a PBE, gradual reform can be sustained as unique PBE.

Proof See Appendix.

The intuition underlying Proposition 2 can be described as follows. First, when full reform is optimal in the one-period problem, replicating it twice is the two-period optimum without commitment. It is also a PBE since, once allocative efficiency has been achieved, there is no additional possibility for a Pareto-improving reform. The second part of Proposition 2 concerns a case where the rent extraction problem is important enough for partial reform to dominate full reform in the static problem. In this case, gradual reform, which is an average of full and partial reforms realized over time, dominates a strategy of full reform imposed from the beginning. From the Government's point of view gradual reform is not as good as partial reform maintained over the two periods, but such a reform is not sustainable without exogenous commitment powers. The absence of commitment thus has the same adverse effect as in the voluntary ex-post renegotiation literature. In fact, under a stationary economic environment, it is well known that a multi-period optimum with commitment is simply the replication of the one-period optimum in each period (see for example Hart and Tirole 1988). Thus, if no random reform dominates P, replicating P twice would be the optimum with commitment in our problem. The optimum without commitment could still involve some randomness, so that G might not be the overall optimal reform. *Still, when $V(P) > V(F)$ in the static problem, the optimal reform has to be gradual*, in that some x workers do not exit with probability one at $t = 1$. The key to Proposition 2 is that repeating F twice, which is the optimal full reform, is not the best the Government can achieve when $V(P) > V(F)$.

The result of Proposition 2 could be extended to a stationary infinite-horizon problem to generate Coasian dynamics, since we are in the same framework as the durable-good monopoly problem (Gul et al. 1986; Hart and Tirole 1988[6]). This means that the extent of gradualism, that is, the length of time before allocative efficiency is attained, depends on the frequency with which reform plans can be offered by the Government. Typically, delay between offers will be non-trivial, and so will be the importance of gradualism.

5 Static Framework and Majority Rule

We now come back to a one-period problem and relax the Government's political acceptance constraint from unanimity to a majority rule where one group may be hurt. (This Section is in the same spirit as Lewis, Feenstra, and Ware 1990, which we discuss below). With only three groups of identical size, this means any majority rule between 50% and 66%. As mentioned in Section 2, workers are assumed to play weakly dominant strategies when voting (which breaks their indifference when they expect to have no decisive influence on the outcome of the vote).

Moving to majority rule expands the set of potentially optimal reforms as follows:

Full Reforms,

$F_{\underline{x}}$ (*$\underline{x}$ hurt*): $w_1 = w - x + 2\underline{x}$, $e_1 = 2$, $b_1 = w - x$,
F_x (*x hurt*): $w_1 = w + \underline{x}$, $e_1 = 2$, $b_1 = \max\{w - \bar{x}, w + \underline{x} - 2x\}$.

Partial Reforms,

P (*nobody hurt*): $w_1 = w$, $e_1 = 1$, $b_1 = w - \bar{x}$,
P_x (*x hurt*): $w_1 = \max\{w + \underline{x}, w - \bar{x} + 2x\}$, $e_1 = 2$, $b_1 = w - \bar{x}$,
$P_{\bar{x}}$ (*$\bar{x}$ hurt*): $w_1 = w + x$, $e_1 = 2$, $b_1 = w + x - 2\bar{x}$.

As before, these reforms already involve minimal wage and bonus payments subject to IC and political constraints. *Full reforms* involve keeping only the $\underline{x}$ group in the sector. It is then optimal (by (1)) to set $e_1 = 2$.[7] One option is to hurt this $\underline{x}$ group in comparison to the status quo. This means not hurting the others (and thus $b_1 \geqq w - x$) while setting w_1 just high enough not to induce $\underline{x}$ to exit (and thus $w_1 \geqq 2\underline{x} + b_1$), which yields $F_{\underline{x}}$. Another option is to hurt a group other than $\underline{x}$. Under full reform, it is not possible to hurt $\bar{x}$ without hurting x, so that the only other potential option is F_x. In that case, w_1 protects $\underline{x}$($w_1 \geqq w + \underline{x}$, to compensate them for their higher effort), while b_1 is set so as to protect $\bar{x}$($b_1 \geqq w - \bar{x}$) and to induce x to exit ($b_1 \geqq w_1 - 2x$).

Three types of *partial reforms* are possible. One possibility is to keep $\underline{x}$ and x working at $e_1 = 1$. In such a case, no group can be hurt in comparison with the status quo, since we must have $w_1 \geqq w$, and thus, by IC, $b_1 \geqq w - \bar{x}$. This yields P as the optimum, as in Section 3. On the other hand, no group strictly gains in comparison with the status quo, which is not the case under full reform if $b_1 > w - \bar{x}$, or below when $e_1 = 2$ and $w_1 > w + \underline{x}$. Indeed, another possibility is to have a partial reform with $e_1 = 2$. One option is to hurt $\bar{x}$ compared to the status quo. This means not hurting the others (so that $w_1 \geqq w + x$), while setting b_1 just high enough to induce $\bar{x}$ to exit ($b_1 \geqq w_1 - 2\bar{x}$), which yields $P_{\bar{x}}$. Another option is to hurt x or $\underline{x}$. Under partial reform, it is not possible to hurt $\underline{x}$ without hurting x, which leaves P_x as the final option: b_1 is set to compensate $\bar{x}$ ($b_1 \geqq w - \bar{x}$), while w_1 is set to compensate $\underline{x}$ ($w_1 \geqq w + \underline{x}$) and to induce x not to exit ($w_1 \geqq w - \bar{x} + 2x$).

These five reform schemes exhaust the potential *deterministic* optima.[8] Proposition 3 shows that each of them can indeed be the optimal deterministic reform. Define first $\hat{q} = q(1)/(1 + \lambda)$ and $\tilde{q} = (q(2) - q(1))/(1 + \lambda)$. Condition (1) tells us $\underline{x} < \tilde{q} < \hat{q} < x < \bar{x}$. Proposition 3 considers $\underline{x}$, $\tilde{q}$, $\hat{q}$ and $\bar{x}$ as given and shows the various configurations of optimal reforms when x moves from $\hat{q}$ to $\bar{x}$.

PROPOSITION 3 Under majority rule, depending on parameter values, the possible static optima are given by one of these five cases:

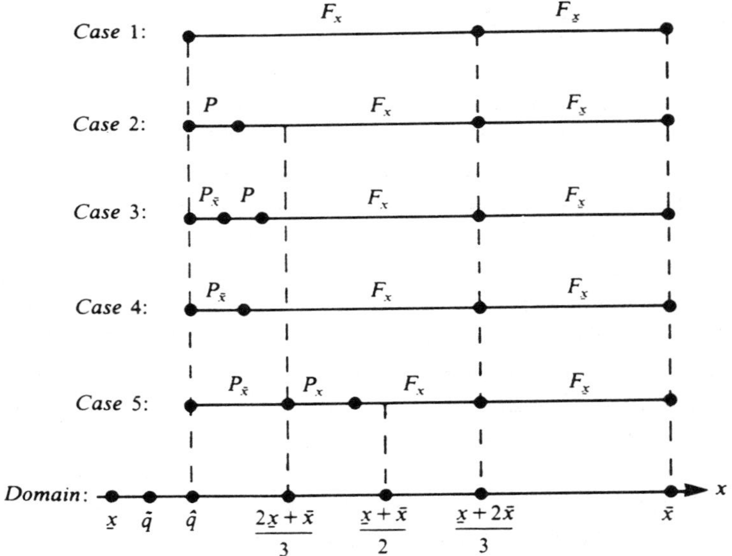

Proof See Appendix.

The Appendix provides a proof and an extensive discussion of Proposition 3. We concentrate here on the underlying intuition to highlight its main features:

(i) As in Proposition 1, partial reform dominates full reform only if x is close enough to $\underline{x}$ (so that the allocative cost of keeping x working is small) and if λ is not too small. Otherwise, the rent extraction motive becomes unimportant, and we are in fact in Case 1.

(ii) Depending on parameter values, *any two-group majority can emerge at the optimum.* From Proposition 3, it is clear that, for x close to $\underline{x}$, the Government seeks and obtains the approval of the two groups which are most *similar* in terms of disutility of effort. On the other hand, when x is close to $(\underline{x} + \bar{x})/2$, the Government seeks and obtains the approval of the two *extreme* groups, and the x group is hurt.

The intuition for full reforms (F_x versus $F\underline{x}$) and for partial reforms (P_x versus $P_{\bar{x}}$) is very similar. Consider full reforms first. $F_{\underline{x}}$ hurts $\underline{x}$ by setting $b_1 = w - x$ and $w_1 = w - x + 2\underline{x}$, so that x are as well off as in the status quo, $\bar{x}$ gain $(\bar{x} - x)$, and $\underline{x}$ lose $(x - \underline{x})$.[9] In contrast, F_x sets $w_1 = w + \underline{x}$ and $b_1 = w - \bar{x}$.[10] Now $\underline{x}$ and $\bar{x}$ are as well off as in the status quo, while x lose $(\bar{x} - x)$. Comparing with $F_{\underline{x}}$, the $\underline{x}$ group gains $(x - \underline{x})$, while the *two other groups* lose $(\bar{x} - x)$. Hurting x thus has the additional advantage for the Government to extract more rents from $\bar{x}$, since it involves lowering b_1 which two groups end up choosing. The two full reforms only differ in terms of rent extraction, by an amount equal to $(x - \underline{x}) - 2(\bar{x} - x)$, which means that they are equivalent at $3x = \underline{x} + 2\bar{x}$. For x larger than that

Table 16.2
Net gains in comparison to status quo payoffs

Reform	Restriction on parameters	Gains of $\underline{x}$ group	Gains of x group	Gains of $\bar{x}$ group
$F\underline{x}$	—	$-(x - \underline{x})$	0	$\bar{x} - x$
Fx	$2x > \underline{x} + \bar{x}$	0	$-(\bar{x} - x)$	0
Fx	$2x < \underline{x} + \bar{x}$	0	$-(x - \underline{x})$	$(\bar{x} + \underline{x} - 2x)$
P	—	0	0	0
Px	$2x > \underline{x} + \bar{x}$	$(2x - \underline{x} - \bar{x})$	$-(\bar{x} - x)$	0
Px	$2x < \underline{x} + \bar{x}$	0	$-(x - \underline{x})$	0
$P\bar{x}$	—	$x - \underline{x}$	0	$-(\bar{x} - x)$

value, taking away $(x - \underline{x})$ from $\underline{x}$ becomes so important that $F_{\underline{x}}$ dominates, while, in the opposite case, F_x dominates.[11]

The same argument is valid, mutatis mutandis, for partial reforms, where $P_{\bar{x}}$ sets $w_1 = w + x$ and $b_1 = w + x - 2\bar{x}$, while P_x sets $b_1 = w - \bar{x}$ and $w_1 = w + \underline{x}$[12] (which is lower by $(x - \underline{x})$ in comparison to $P_{\bar{x}}$: the x group is hurt but the extra rents enjoyed by $\underline{x}$ in comparison to the status quo have also disappeared). These two partial reforms only differ in terms of rent extraction, by an amount $(\bar{x} - x) - 2(x - \underline{x})$. For x lower than $(2\underline{x} + \bar{x})/3$, taking away $(\bar{x} - x)$ from $\bar{x}$ under $P_{\bar{x}}$ dominates, while in the opposite case P_x dominates.

(iii) Finally, the Government may find it optimal to propose a *partial reform which hurts no one* in comparison to the status quo (P). Indeed, the only way to hurt a single group under partial reform is to set $e_1 = 2$. Otherwise, if two groups keep working at $e_1 = 1$ and at least one must be compensated, one must have $w_1 \geqq w$. But this means that exiting workers cannot be hurt either. Such a partial reform P becomes attractive when setting $e_1 = 2$ under partial reform is too expensive (because $q(2) - q(1)$ is too low) and when x is not too high (then, full reform involves a limited allocative gain in comparison to P, and gives extra rents to $\bar{x}$ in comparison to P, because b_1 is then above $w - \bar{x}$).

While these are the three main insights of Proposition 3, the Appendix deatils the reasons for the exact configurations of possible optima. In our view, the most interesting results of Proposition 3 lie in (ii) above, which explains the tradeoffs behind the various majority choices by the Government. These results have a similar flavour as those of Lewis, Feenstra and Ware (1990), who consider a static problem of optimal agricultural reform starting from a status quo of output subsidization. Their framework is more complex than ours, with a uniform distribution of worker types and individualized output levels. They show that the type of majority the Government seeks depends on the nature of worker heterogeneity. When they differ mainly in productivity *within* the sector, the Government finds it profitable to seek the support of the less productive workers. Conversely, when they differ mainly in terms of *outside* opportunities, the more productive workers make up the majority. Finally, when both sources of heterogeneity are important, majorities of "extremes" may emerge. While various assumptions distinguish the two models, our simplified three-group framework makes the tradeoffs behind the various majority choices quite transparent. Moreover, it allows us to extend the analysis to a dynamic framework, which is the purpose of Section 6.

6 Majority Rule with Two Periods and No Commitment

As in Section 4, we now extend the static framework of the previous Section to a two-period problem without commitment. We keep the assumption of a majority rule between 50 and 66%. Under partial reform, with only two groups of identical size as the second-period voting population, we break potential ties by requiring a majority rule *strictly* above 50%. As in Section 4, workers compare the initial reform plan with the status quo followed by a second-period reform proposal, which is described in Section 5. As explained in Section 2, we assume that workers play time-consistent weakly dominant strategies when voting.

The main insight of this Section can be explained in relation to Section 4 which required unanimity for the implementation of a reform plan. In that case, having two proposals instead of one could only hurt the Government: it made it harder to convince voters to support the initial proposal, because they could only gain in comparison to the status quo in the case where initial rejection was followed by a new proposal. Under majority rule, this is no longer the case: some voters expect to lose in comparison to the status quo if the initial reform is rejected. It is then possible for the Government to include this second-period minority in its first-period majority, and use it to hurt another group of workers who become the first-period minority. This Section details the cases where such a strategy is profitable, and whether and when it allows the Government to achieve a payoff in the two-offer case without commitment which is higher than in the one-offer case.

As in Section 4, we seek to characterize the optimal PBE for the Government. We still denote by $(w_1, e_1, b_1, w_2, e_2, b_2)$ and (w_2', e_2', b_2') the period-one and period-two reform proposals, and $(\tilde{w}_2, \tilde{e}_2, \tilde{b}_2)$ the (correctly predicted) continuation equilibrium in period two. For simplicity, we assume parameter values which yield Case 4 of Proposition 3,[13] that is, $P_{\bar{x}}$, F_x and $F_{\underline{x}}$ are the only possible static optima. This leaves us with a set of reforms which is rich enough, both from the point of view of allocation of labour and of political majorities. We successively consider the cases where the static optimum involves full reform and partial reform.

Full Reform as Static Optimum

In this case, the static optimum is thus $F_{\underline{x}}$ if $3x > 2\bar{x} + \underline{x}$ and F_x if $3x < 2\bar{x} + \underline{x}$. We define F_{ij} as a cost-minimizing first-period reform proposal which (i) *is made under the threat of* F_j *in period two (with* $j \in \{\underline{x}, x\}$*) in case of rejection*; (ii) *hurts group* i *(with* $i \in \{\underline{x}, x, \bar{x}\}$*) in comparison to rejection followed by* F_j*; and* (iii) *seeks allocative efficiency from period one on.*

When F_x is the static optimum, we shall be particularly interested in comparing F_{xx} with $F_{\underline{x}x}$. Similarly, when $F_{\underline{x}}$ is the static optimum, we shall compare $F_{\underline{x}\underline{x}}$ with $F_{x\underline{x}}$. The reason for such comparisons is that the above reforms will turn out to include the optimal ones. All the above reforms involve the same allocation of labour ($e_1 = e_2 = 2$, with x and $\bar{x}$ exiting at $t = 1$). They thus differ only in terms of their total monetary payments to workers, which we call M_{ij} for reform F_{ij}.

First, concerning $F_{\underline{x}\underline{x}}$ and F_{xx}, the best one can hope for is to replicate $F_{\underline{x}}$ and F_x twice, that is:

$$M_{\underline{x}\underline{x}} = 4(w - x) + 2(w - x + 2\underline{x});$$

$$M_{xx} = 4(w - \bar{x}) + 2(w + \underline{x}) \quad \text{for } 2x \geqq \underline{x} + \bar{x},$$

or

$$= 4(w + \underline{x} - 2x) + 2(w + \underline{x}), \quad 2x \leqq \underline{x} + \bar{x}.$$

When the static optimum is F_i, then F_{ii} is politically viable, since it simply doubles the gains and losses of F_i. Since only one group loses, it will be the only one opposing F_{ii} in period one. And since only one group strictly gains in F_i in comparison to the status quo, replicating F_i twice is the best one can do in F_{ii} (IC and political constraints remain binding, as in F_i).

When the static optimum is $F_{\underline{x}}$, one can also compute $F_{x\underline{x}}$, which protects $\underline{x}$ and $\bar{x}$ in comparison to rejection followed by $F_{\underline{x}}$. In $F_{\underline{x}}$, the $\bar{x}$ group gains $(\bar{x} - x)$ and the $\underline{x}$ group loses $(x - \underline{x})$ in comparison to the status quo (since $b_1 = w - x$ and $w_1 = w - x + 2\underline{x}$). In $F_{x\underline{x}}$, we must thus have:

$$b_1 \geqq 2(w - \bar{x}) + (\bar{x} - x) = 2(w - x) - (\bar{x} - x),$$

$$w_1 + w_2 \geqq 2(w + \underline{x}) - (x - \underline{x}) = 2(w - x + 2\underline{x}) + (x - \underline{x});$$

so that:

$$M_{x\underline{x}} = 2b_1 + w_1 + w_2,$$

$$= 2(2(w - x) - (\bar{x} - x)) + 2(w - x + 2\underline{x}) + (x - \underline{x}).$$

One thus sees that b_1 gives the $\bar{x}$ group its status quo payoff plus $(\bar{x} - x)$, as in $F_{\underline{x}}$, and $w_1 + w_2$ gives the $\underline{x}$ group its status quo payoff minus $(x - \underline{x})$, as in $F_{\underline{x}}$ (the wage is raised to compensate for higher effort in both periods in comparison to the status quo). On the other hand, the overall loss of the x group is of $(\bar{x} - x)$ in comparison to the status quo, and thus also in comparison to $F_{\underline{x}}$.

Similarly, when F_x is the static optimum, $F_{\underline{x}x}$ only protects x and $\bar{x}$ in comparison to rejection followed by F_x. For $2x \geqq \underline{x} + \bar{x}$, we have an exit bonus of $w - \bar{x}$ and a wage of $w + \underline{x}$ in F_x. The x group thus loses $\bar{x} - x$ in comparison to the status quo, while the $\bar{x}$ group receives its status quo payoff. In $F_{\underline{x}x}$, we must thus have:

$$b_1 \geqq (w - x) + (w - \bar{x}).$$

On the other hand, since $F_{\underline{x}x}$ does not seek to gain the votes of the $\underline{x}$ group, $w_1 + w_2$ is simply set at the minimum level which keeps them from exiting:

$$w_1 + w_2 \geqq b_1 + 4\underline{x}.$$

This gives us:

$$\begin{aligned} M_{\underline{x}x} &= 2b_1 + w_1 + w_2, \\ &= 2(w - x + w - \bar{x}) + (w - x + w - \bar{x} + 4\underline{x}) \quad \text{for } 2x \geqq \underline{x} + \bar{x}. \end{aligned}$$

When $2w \leqq \underline{x} + \bar{x}$, the only change in F_x is that the exit bonus becomes $w + \underline{x} - 2x$, and one can derive:

$$M_{\underline{x}x} = 2(2(w - x) + (\underline{x} - x)) + (2(w - x) + (\underline{x} - x) + 4\underline{x}) \qquad \text{for } 2x \leqq \underline{x} + \bar{x}.$$

Table 16.3 summarizes workers' net gains of the various reforms *over the two periods.*

Proposition 4 now compares the four F_{ij}'s detailed above:

PROPOSITION 4 Assume that, in the one-offer case, full reform is optimal. Then, for $3x \geqq 2\bar{x} + \underline{x}$, $F_{\underline{x}\underline{x}}$ can be supported as a unique PBE and dominates $F_{x\underline{x}}$. But, for $3x \leqq 2\bar{x} + \underline{x}$, $F_{\underline{x}x}$ can be supported as a unique PBE and dominates F_{xx}.

Proof Let us first compare the various F_{ij}'s, i.e. the various M_{ij}'s, the only elements by which they differ. For $3x \geqq 2\bar{x} + \underline{x}$, the choice is between $F_{\underline{x}\underline{x}}$ and $F_{x\underline{x}}$, and one can check that $M_{\underline{x}\underline{x}} - M_{x\underline{x}} = 2(\bar{x} - x) - (x - \underline{x}) \leqq 0$.

Table 16.3
Net gains in comparison to the status quo (maintained over two periods)

Reform	Restriction on parameters	Gains of $\underline{x}$ group	Gains of x group	Gains of $\bar{x}$ group
$F\underline{x}\underline{x}$	$3x > \underline{x} + 2\bar{x}$	$-2(x - \underline{x})$	0	$2(\bar{x} - x)$
$Fx\underline{x}$	$3x > \underline{x} + 2\bar{x}$	$-(x - \underline{x})$	$-(\bar{x} - x)$	$(\bar{x} - x)$
Fxx	$\frac{\underline{x} + \bar{x}}{2} < x < \frac{\underline{x} + 2\bar{x}}{3}$	0	$-2(\bar{x} - x)$	0
$F\underline{x}x$	$\frac{\underline{x} + \bar{x}}{2} < x < \frac{\underline{x} + 2\bar{x}}{3}$	$-(\bar{x} + x - 2\underline{x})$	$-(\bar{x} - x)$	$(\bar{x} - x)$
Fxx	$2x < \underline{x} + \bar{x}$	0	$-2(x - \underline{x})$	$2(\bar{x} + \underline{x} - 2x)$
$F\underline{x}x$	$2x < \underline{x} + \bar{x}$	$-3(x - \underline{x})$	$-(x - \underline{x})$	$2\bar{x} + \underline{x} - 3x$

For $3x \leqq 2\bar{x} + \underline{x}$, the choice is between F_{xx} and $F_{\underline{x}x}$. When $2x \geqq \underline{x} + \bar{x}$, $M_{\underline{x}x} - M_{xx} = 2\underline{x} + \bar{x} - 3x < 0$, and, when $2x \leqq \underline{x} + \bar{x}$, $M_{\underline{x}x} - M_{xx} = \underline{x} - x < 0$. Thus, $F_{\underline{x}\underline{x}}$ dominates $F_{x\underline{x}}$ for $3x \geqq 2\bar{x} + \underline{x}$, and $F_{\underline{x}x}$ dominates F_{xx} for $3x \leqq 2\bar{x} + \underline{x}$.

Can $F_{\underline{x}\underline{x}}$ be supported as a PBE in the first case? The offer by the Government can for example involve $w_1 = w_2 = w - x + 2\underline{x}$, $b_1 = 2(w - x)$ and $b_2 = 0$. If only $\underline{x}$ remain in the sector, $\tilde{w}_2 = w_2$ (there is no way to offend anyone because everybody is identical; the efficient (e_2, w_2) will thus be executed as such), and an individual from group x or $\bar{x}$ cannot make any difference on the next-period vote by staying in the sector. Taking b_1 is thus better than (w_2, b_2) for x and $\bar{x}$. As for $F_{\underline{x}x}$, the same discussion remains valid, for example with $w_1 = w_2 = w - x + 2\underline{x} + (x - \underline{x})/2$.

It remains to establish that $F_{\underline{x}\underline{x}}$ and $F_{\underline{x}x}$ can be supported as *unique* PBE's. The above-mentioned arguments showed that no *single* individual found it in its interest to deviate. But could *groups* of individuals gain by coordinating on another behaviour after acceptance of the first-period reform? The answer is no, provided b_1 is raised by an arbitrarily small amount in $F_{\underline{x}\underline{x}}$ and $F_{\underline{x}x}$ to make it strictly optimal for x and $\bar{x}$ to leave at $t = 1$ instead of taking $w_1 + w_2$. In fact, for some x (or $\bar{x}$) to choose w_1 over b_1, they must expect $b_1 \leqq w_1 - 2x + \max\{\tilde{w}_2 - 2x, \tilde{b}_2\}$ (respectively, $b_1 \leqq w_1 - 2\bar{x} + \max\{\tilde{w}_2 - 2\bar{x}, \tilde{b}_2\}$). That is, each x (or $\bar{x}$) who deviates must expect, at $t = 2$, more than max $\{w_2 - 2x, b_2\}$ (respectively max $\{w_2 - 2\bar{x}, b_2\}$). But this cannot happen. Assume for example that b_2 has been chosen so that $b_2 < w_2 - 2\bar{x}$, that is, everybody prefers $(w_2, e_2 = 2)$

to b_2. Then, either the Government could push for a *partial reform* at $t = 2$, with $w_2' = \tilde{w}_2 = w_2$ at $b_2' = \tilde{b}_2 = w_2 - 2\bar{x}$ (there is no way to hurt a single group); or it could alternatively push for a *full reform* at $t = 2$, where either the $\underline{x}$ group is hurt (if they are a minority), at $b_2' = \tilde{b}_2 = w_2 - 2x$ and $w_2' = \tilde{w}_2 = w_2 - 2x + 2\underline{x}$, or where nobody is hurt (if the $\underline{x}$ group is the majority), at $b_2' = \tilde{b}_2 = w_2 - 2x$ and $w_2' = \tilde{w}_2 = w_2$. Note that, in none of these cases do we find the x group receiving more than $\max\{w_2 - 2x, b_2\}$ (in fact, in no reform considered in Proposition 3 do they strictly gain in comparison to the status quo). They will thus not find it in their interest to stay in the sector at $t = 1$. In such a case, it will be optimal for the Government to push for $w_2' = \tilde{w}_2 = w_2$ and $b_2' = \tilde{b}_2 = w_2 - 2\bar{x}$ in case some $\bar{x}$ have stayed in the sector at $t = 1$. But, then, they do not receive more than $\max\{w_2 - 2\bar{x}, b_2\}$, so that deviating is not optimal for them either. There is thus no PBE where some x or $\bar{x}$ remain in the sector at $t = 1$ after $F_{\underline{x}\underline{x}}$ and $F_{\underline{x}x}$ have been accepted. These are thus unique PBE's.

Proposition 4 tells us that, *whenever full reform is the static optimum, the initial plan will always be opposed by $\underline{x}$ (even when the static optimum is F_x).* Moreover, having two offers without commitment is either equivalent or strictly better than having only one offer. To understand this, remember that $b_1 = w - x$ and $w_1 = w - x + 2\underline{x}$ in $F_{\underline{x}}$ while, in F_x, $b_1 = w - \bar{x}$ and $w_1 = w + \underline{x}$.[14] The tradeoff is thus: does one lower b_1 by $(\bar{x} - x)$ (in F_x), or does one lower w_1 by $(x - \underline{x})$ (in $F_{\underline{x}}$)?

In $F_{\underline{x}}$, the winner is the $\bar{x}$ group, who gain $(\bar{x} - x)$, and the loser is the $\underline{x}$ group, who lose $(x - \underline{x})$. In $F_{\underline{x}\underline{x}}$, gains and losses are doubled. In $F_{x\underline{x}}$ instead, one hurts x in period 1, while protecting $\underline{x}$ and $\bar{x}$ in comparison to rejection plus $F_{\underline{x}}$. Protecting $\underline{x}$ and $\bar{x}$ means that, in comparison to the status quo, $\bar{x}$ have to gain $(\bar{x} - x)$, and $\underline{x}$ can lose at most $(x - \underline{x})$.[15] Thus, $F_{x\underline{x}}$ is really an average of $F_{\underline{x}}$ and F_x so that, by the linearity of our problem, it is dominated by $F_{\underline{x}\underline{x}}$.

This is not true when F_x is the static optimum, where one can hurt $\underline{x}$ much more. In F_x, there is no winner and one strict loser, the x group, who loses $(\bar{x} - x)$ (since $b_1 = w - \bar{x}$). While F_{xx} doubles x's loss, $F_{\underline{x}x}$ does better. On the one hand, it keeps x's loss at $(\bar{x} - x)$, thus raising b_1 by $(\bar{x} - x)$ for x and $\bar{x}$ in comparison to F_{xx}. On the other hand, the slightly higher rents conceded to x and $\bar{x}$ are more than compensated by the wage cut on $\underline{x}$ who lose $(\bar{x} - x) + 2(x - \underline{x})$ compared to F_{xx}. One can hurt $\underline{x}$ more than in $F_{\underline{x}\underline{x}}$: now $w_1 + w_2 = 2(w - x) - (\bar{x} - x) + 4\underline{x}$. This is possible because b_1 is lower by $(\bar{x} - x)$ than with $F_{\underline{x}\underline{x}}$ and the lower the bonus the lower the minimum incentive compatible wage for $\underline{x}$.

The idea of $F_{\underline{x}x}$ is thus to "buy cheaply" the votes of the x group, who know that, in case of rejection, they lose afterwards anyway. Being able to lower their payoff in comparison to the status quo has two advantages: it also lowers the rents to be conceded to $\bar{x}$, and it allows one to cut even further the wage bill of the $\underline{x}$ group. The same advantage does not exist when $F_{\underline{x}}$ is the static optimum, because, then, if one wishes to make x the initial losers (that is, choose $F_{x\underline{x}}$), having to protect $\underline{x}$ and $\bar{x}$ in period 1 effectively limits the amount of rents one can extract from x. Note also that another way to see the difference between $F_{\underline{x}\underline{x}}$ and $F_{\underline{x}x}$ is that, while in the first case, nobody votes for a plan that is worse for them than the status quo, in $F_{\underline{x}x}$ the group x ends up voting for a plan in which they concede $(\bar{x} - x)$.

Proposition 4 also establishes that $F_{\underline{x}\underline{x}}$ and $F_{\underline{x}x}$ can be sustained as unique PBE's. This is first because, once only the $\underline{x}$ group remains in the sector at $t = 2$, there is no way for the Government to play one group against another, because all voters are identical. Since the two reform plans are incentive compatible, each of them is a PBE, because an individual worker deviation has no consequence on future votes. For the reform plans to be *unique* PBE's, one must then check that *coordinated* deviations cannot be equilibria either. This is because one can prove that the x and $\bar{x}$ groups cannot hope to strictly improve their payoff by collectively staying in the sector in period one after the initial reform has passed and influencing the second-period vote.

Proposition 5 completes Proposition 4 by establishing the optimality of $F_{\underline{x}\underline{x}}$ and $F_{\underline{x}x}$. While it provides a significant characterization result, its proof is tedious and not very illuminating.

PROPOSITION 5 When $F_{\underline{x}}(F_x)$ is the static optimum, $F_{\underline{x}\underline{x}}(F_{\underline{x}x})$ is optimal in the two-offer case without commitment.

Proof See Appendix.

The insight of Propositions 4 and 5 that the Government can do better in some cases with two offers than with one take-it-or-leave-it offer contradicts the results which can be found in the bargaining or contracting literature. We stressed in Section 4 that this did not happen under unanimity, which is a case parallel to voluntary contract renegotiation. The case of majority rule is somehow in-between this case and that of ratchet models. In the latter, the Government is not committed to respecting any long-run contract while, here, it needs the approval of a majority of workers to implement any new reform plan. A key difference is however that, in ratchet models, a take-it-or-leave-it offer allows the Government to threaten the other party with the worst possible outcome, namely its exogenous individual-rationality payoff. This is not the case in a voting problem, since the status quo payoff is not the worst that can happen to workers: they can lose more, in terms of higher effort or lower wages and bonuses, in reform proposals where they are in the minority. This is why the expectation of future offers may induce concessions, in contrast to the bargaining or contract literature.

The driving force behind our result is the ability of the Government to credibly threaten to switch majorities. This ability depends on the time dependence of our problem, specifically, our finite-horizon assumption. Under a stationary infinite-horizon problem, majority switches could take place only in the presence of multiple equilibria. Otherwise, a rejection would be followed by the same equilibrium proposal by the Government. Only if the Government were *indifferent* between several reform proposals could it threaten to "break the tie" in the future in a way which would be contingent on previous votes.

In terms of economic reform, our finite-horizon assumption can be justified for example by the finiteness of Government terms or by the obsolescence of capital goods which end up not being replaced in the case of declining demand. One could even extend the analysis by modifying the exogenous environment parameters between the two periods.

Partial Reform as the Static Optimum

Let us end this section with the case where $P_{\bar{x}}$ is the static optimum. Here, we have the same problem as in the case of unanimity: replicating $P_{\bar{x}}$ twice (we shall call this solution $P_{\bar{x}\bar{x}}$) is not time-consistent, because once the $\bar{x}$ have left at $t = 1$, it becomes optimal to have x leave at $t = 2$. Under unanimity, we had two results: optimality of partial reform in the static case led to *gradualism* with two periods and no commitment, and to an outcome which was *strictly worse* than the replication of the optimal static partial reform. These two results are preserved under majority rule even though, as with $F_{\underline{x}x}$ above, the Government will end up lowering the payoff of *two-thirds* of the population in comparison to the status quo.

We will show that the optimal reform will be gradual and will hurt x in comparison to the status quo followed by $P_{\bar{x}}$. Remember that $P_{\bar{x}}$ can be optimal only for $3x \leqq 2\underline{x} + \bar{x}$, and involves an effort of 2, a wage of $w + x$ and a bonus of $w + x - 2\bar{x}$ so that, in comparison to the status quo, $\underline{x}$ gain $(x - \underline{x})$, $\bar{x}$ lose $(\bar{x} - x)$, and x do not gain or lose anything. We shall be interested in the following gradual reform plan:

$\bar{x}$ leave at $t = 1$, x leave at $t = 2$,

$$e_1 = e_2 = 2,$$

$$w_1 + w_2 = 2(w + \underline{x}) + (x - \underline{x}),$$

$$w_1 + b_2 = 2(w + \underline{x}) + (x - \underline{x}) - 2x,$$

$$b_1 = 2(w + \underline{x}) + (x - \underline{x}) - 2x - 2\bar{x}.$$

Let us call this plan $G_{x\bar{x}}$, since the plan is proposed under the threat of $P_{\bar{x}}$, and has the same "flavour" as P_x, since reform is partial at $t = 1$, and will then be opposed by x. Indeed, $w_1 + w_2$ gives $\underline{x}$ the status quo payoff plus what they gain under $P_{\bar{x}}$. Then, $w_1 + b_2$ and b_1 are computed to satisfy incentive compatibility. Under $w_1 + b_2$, x lose in comparison to the status quo (while $P_{\bar{x}}$ keeps their status quo payoff), since $w_1 + b_2 = 2w - (x - \underline{x}) < 2w$, while they work as much as under the status quo. Finally, b_1 is set at the minimum level that induces $\bar{x}$ to leave at $t = 1$, but this gives them extra rents in comparison to the status quo followed by $P_{\bar{x}}$ in which they lose $(\bar{x} - x)$ (their payoff would then be $(w - \bar{x}) + (w + x - 2\bar{x}) < b_1 = 2(w - \bar{x}) - (x - \underline{x})$, since $x - \underline{x} < \bar{x} - x$). Proposition 6 establishes the optimality of $G_{x\bar{x}}$.

PROPOSITION 6 Assume that $P_{\bar{x}}$ is the static optimum. Then, $G_{x\bar{x}}$ can be sustained as a unique PBE, and is optimal in the two-offer case without commitment. It is however worse than the time-inconsistent reform $P_{\bar{x}}$.

Proof See Appendix.

The arguments used to prove Proposition 6 are similar to the ones used in the proofs of Propositions 4 and 5. The main difference here in comparison to cases where full reform was optimal in the static case is the *cost* of having two offers without commitment. This cost is similar to the unanimity case: for x close to $\underline{x}$, a partial reform with $e_1 = e_2 = 2$ is optimal, in order to extract a lot of rents from $\bar{x}$. Lack of commitment however tends to bring the effort of the x group down to zero at $t = 2$, thus limiting rent extraction from $\bar{x}$.

In contrast to unanimity, there is an advantage to having two offers and that is hurting *two groups* in comparison to the status quo: here, the Government "buys cheaply" the votes of the $\bar{x}$ group, who are threatened by $P_{\bar{x}}$, in order to hurt x too. This stands in contrast with $P_{\bar{x}\bar{x}}$, where only the $\bar{x}$ group is hurt. This advantage of having two offers is however dominated by the cost of limited commitment.

The Proposition also tells us that gradualism is good, as under unanimity, when partial reform is optimal in the static case. Finally, it is shown that $G_{x\bar{x}}$ can be sustained as a unique PBE: under strict majority rule, the second-period outcome is stable (the Government cannot get away with hurting anybody more than it already does), and the $\bar{x}$ group would lose by staying at $t = 1$, either individually or collectively.[16]

7 Potential Applications of the Model

The model analysed in this chapter and the results derived from it can be used to try to shed light on some aspects of economic reforms and their policy implications.

One of the main results is that the presence of informational asymmetries provides reasons for gradualism in the shrinkage of outdated industries or sectors. Gradualism is desirable when significant worker heterogeneity makes rent extraction problems relevant. This can be the case when the Government has little knowledge about the degree of adaptability of individual workers to new production or organization methods, and has reasons to believe they differ strongly in these respects. Gradual policies have been used in Europe when shrinking obsolescent sectors such as coal mines or the steel industry.

This issue of gradualism is also highly relevant in Central and Eastern Europe, where the transition to market economies requires huge industrial restructuring and labour redeployment. Restructuring policies are clearly subject to political constraints as they will involve large parts of the population. Here too, gradualism can prove less costly since, under the central planning system, workers enjoyed numerous hidden rents. The tradeoff between rapid but costly restructuring and more gradual policies, cheaper in terms of exit bonuses and working in favour of balanced budget policies, is central in the policy debates in the former GDR where the transition process is the most advanced.[17] It will also be central to the future policy choices in the other post-socialist countries.

To avoid any confusion, the model developed in this chapter only encompasses one dimension of the transition process in Eastern Europe, that of restructuring, perhaps the most politically difficult phase of transition (Roland 1991). A multi-dimensional analysis of all important phases of transition, (including privatization, institutional and legal reform, price liberalization and stabilization, as well as restructuring) should capture the complementarity of reforms and the comprehensive nature of transition. (One could perhaps use the framework of Milgrom and Roberts, 1990.) Indeed, these ideas have often been emphasized by economists such as Kornai, Eastern reform economists or Western comparative economists, and have recently been very forcefully expressed by leading Western advisers to Eastern European governments (Sachs 1990). The issue of "big bang" versus "gradualism" is also different if one examines stabilization (van Wijnbergen 1991) instead of economic restructuring, as in this chapter.

The result on changing majorities and the possibility of damaging majority interests in a majority vote, though theoretically interesting and intriguing, may seem somewhat remote from the current policy debates around Eastern Europe. This is partly due to the abstract formulation of the model. Applying the model to the Eastern European context, in the case of full reforms, our result can roughly be translated as follows. At some point, a Government's push for restructuring implies massive redundancies. Only modest wage increases will be allowed to compensate for the higher productivity, and exit bonuses will be low. A majority will be less well off during the transition period, but these plans will still be accepted. Workers with only average outside opportunities who know they will have to leave their job may be resigned to accepting these plans, fearing that if they joined a coalition with those workers who demand higher wage increases, they would only end up with an even lower bonus.

The main objection one might raise against such a "divide and rule" scheme is that some Eastern European governments are too weak and lack the necessary legitimacy to implement such policies. But then, one of the main lessons of this chapter is to emphasize the value of legitimacy by showing how stable governments can, in a democratic setting, overcome the potentially massive opposition of vested interests in order to achieve allocative efficiency.

8 Concluding Remarks

This chapter has modelled structural reform processes using the tools of dynamic adverse selection models. It has generated several insights concerning the political economy of such reforms:

(i) It has shown how *gradualism* can emerge as a sequentially optimal reform path when the budgetary cost of reform is a significant determinant of optimality.

(ii) It has analysed the *majority choice* of reform-minded Governments in a simple three-group framework. We have seen that, when two groups of workers tend to be *similar* (x tending to $\underline{x}$, or to $\bar{x}$), the Government seeks to gain their votes and chooses to hurt the remaining group (when x tends to $\bar{x}$, both are compensated for leaving, and the wage for $\underline{x}$ grows less than their productivity; when x tends to $\underline{x}$, both are compensated for higher productivity, while the $\bar{x}$ group is induced to leave without full compensation). Instead, when the intermediate group is not similar to either of the two extremes (x tending to $(\underline{x} + \bar{x})/2$), the Government seeks the votes of these extremes and hurts the intermediate group. The advantage of doing so however is also to limit the payoff of one extreme group (through a lower exit fee if x leave with $\bar{x}$, or a lower wage if x stay with $\underline{x}$).

(iii) The dynamic majority rule case has turned out to be particularly interesting. We have seen in that case how the threat of future reforms can allow the Government to play the minority of tomorrow against another minority today, and to obtain a majority vote on measures hurting majority interests. From the point of view of economic reform in Eastern Europe, this means that democratic reforms are not necessarily a cause of inertia, provided the government is in firm control of the agenda.

These insights are only a first step in the analysis of economic reforms under dynamic political constraints, and further developments are necessary. It would be interesting to generalize our insights to more general worker heterogeneity and to a multi-period framework, to investigate general upper bounds on the proportion of people one can hurt in comparison to the status quo. Another interesting question is the effect of bundling or aggregating reform proposals for different sectors. If the distribution of worker types varies strongly across sectors, or across firms within individual sectors, then the government may prefer individualized proposals to a single reform proposal. But, just as the threat of future proposals allows one to extract concessions for current reforms, one might examine whether the bundling of proposals and the threat of reform in one sector might allow one to extract concessions in another sector in the case where there is interdependency between reform outcomes. More generally, one might examine if the bundling of different reform proposals, affecting individual welfare in different ways, could allow an increase in the government's payoff. Finally, the dynamic agenda-setting framework could be adopted to study large-scale reforms other than economic restructuring. This subject is very topical in light of current changes now occurring in Eastern Europe.

Appendix

Proof of Proposition 2 Let us start with part (ii). It is straightforward to check that $V(G)$ is the average of the full and partial reform Government payoffs. When, in the static problem, $V(P) > V(F)$, gradual reform is thus better than full reform but worse than partial reform in the two-period problem.

That partial reform cannot be sustained as an equilibrium is clear: once the $\bar{x}$ group has left, offering $(w_2', e_2', b_2') = (w + \underline{x}, 2, w - x)$, which induces x to leave, is better for the Government, and acceptable for all workers, than keeping $\underline{x}$ and x inside the sector with $w_2 = w$ and $e_1 = 1$.

Reform G is instead sustainable as a PBE, because:

• if G has been accepted and only the $\bar{x}$ group has left in period 1, the Government cannot offer a new plan which does better for everybody than the continuation of G in period 2, since this continuation is allocatively efficient.

• if G has been accepted, it is optimal to leave if and only if one is of type $\bar{x}$ in period 1, and of type x in period 2 (indeed, this is incentive compatible under G). Moreover, even if some $\bar{x}$ workers remain in the sector in period 1, the Government cannot improve its payoff by offering anything else than $w_2 = w + \underline{x}$ and $b_2 = w - x$ (which would be taken by any x or $\bar{x}$ worker left in the sector) which would be acceptable to all remaining workers. It is thus an equilibrium decision for $\bar{x}$ workers to leave at $t = 1$, and for other workers to stay at that time.

• finally, when G is proposed at $t = 1$, it is an optimal strategy for each worker not to veto it, because each gains the same amount in G and under the status quo followed by P in period 2. Indeed, under P, with $e_2 = 1$ (which, by assumption, is the static optimum), all workers are exactly as well off as in the status quo while, under G, two groups are as well off as in the status quo, and the $\bar{x}$ group even gains $(\bar{x} - x)$ in comparison to the status quo.

The above arguments even imply that G is sustainable as the *unique* PBE: since (w_2, e_2, b_2) is allocatively efficient, we shall have $(w_2', e_2', b_2') = (w_2, e_2, b_2)$ whatever the exit decisions at $t = 1$ if G has been accepted: there is thus no other continuation equilibrium, where *groups* of $\bar{x}$ workers would remain in the sector in the hope of a more favourable deal than (w_2, e_2, b_2) in period 2. This completes the proof of part (ii).

Concerning part (i), similar arguments as the ones developed above for G can be used to show that F repeated twice can be sustained as unique PBE. In particular, exiting at $t = 1$ once the plan has been accepted is a good idea for x and $\bar{x}$ workers, who cannot hope for $b_2 > w - x$ at $t = 2$. And voting for full reform is optimal at $t = 1$, since it doubles the gains of F for each worker; it is thus better than the status quo followed by F, which is what workers have to expect if the initial plan is voted down at $t = 1$.

Finally, when $V(F) > V(P)$ in the static problem, full reform dominates partial as well as gradual reforms. G is the average over time of P and F. It concedes no rents in comparison to the status quo to $\underline{x}$ and x, and concedes $(\bar{x} - x)$ to $\bar{x}$. This is just like having the status quo followed by F. There is thus no acceptable gradual reform which could extract more rents from any group of workers. Since we assumed (2) to be satisfied, G is thus the optimal gradual reform which, in turn, means that F, repeated twice, is the optimal deterministic reform when $V(F) > V(P)$ in the static problem. ||

We now provide a proof and an extensive discussion of Proposition 3, which corresponds to Propositions A1 to A4 below. First define $\tilde{S}^* = q(2) - 2(1 + \lambda)\underline{x}$ as the allocatively efficient surplus and $S^* = \tilde{S}^* - 3\lambda w$. This will allow us to write in an easily comparable fashion the Government objective function for the five possible reforms:

$$V(F_{\underline{x}}) = S^* + 3\lambda x.$$

$$V(F_x) = S^* + \lambda(\underline{x} + 2\overline{x}) \quad \text{if } 2x \geqq \underline{x} + \overline{x},$$

$$= S^* + \lambda(4x - \underline{x}) \quad \text{if } 2x \leqq \underline{x} + \overline{x}.$$

$$V(P) = S^* - ((q(2) - q(1)) - (1 + \lambda)\underline{x})$$

$$+ (q(1) - (1 + \lambda)x) + \lambda(x + \underline{x} + \overline{x}).$$

$$V(P_x) = S^* + (q(2) - 2(1 + \lambda)x) + \lambda(2x + \overline{x}) \quad \text{if } 2x \leqq \underline{x} + \overline{x},$$

$$= S^* + (q(2) - 2(1 + \lambda)x) + \lambda(2\underline{x} + 3\overline{x} - 2x) \quad \text{if } 2x \geqq \underline{x} + \overline{x}.$$

$$V(P_{\overline{x}}) = S^* + (q(2) - 2(1 + \lambda)x) + \lambda(2\underline{x} + 2\overline{x} - x).$$

We first compare the two pairs of reforms with identical allocation of labour: $F_{\underline{x}}$ and F_x, and P_x and $P_{\overline{x}}$ (with $e_1 = 2$, in contrast to P):

LEMMA 1 $V(F_x) \geqq V(F_{\underline{x}})$ iff $3x \leqq \underline{x} + 2\overline{x}$.

Proof If $2x \leqq \underline{x} + \overline{x}$, $V(F_x) - V(F_{\underline{x}}) = \lambda(x - \underline{x}) > 0$. If $2x \geqq \underline{x} + \overline{x}$, $V(F_x) - V(F_{\underline{x}}) = \lambda(\underline{x} + 2\overline{x} - 3x) \geqq 0$ iff $3x \leqq \underline{x} + 2\overline{x}$. ‖

When one hurts $\underline{x}$, the nearer x is to $\overline{x}$, the lower the exit bonus $(w - x)$ and the extra rent $(\overline{x} - x)$ accruing to $\overline{x}$, and the more one can hurt $\underline{x}$ and still give them the incentive to keep working. The lower the x, the lower these advantages. It then becomes interesting to hurt x instead of $\underline{x}$ in order to restrict the extra rent of $\overline{x}$ to zero. For $3x \leqq \underline{x} + 2\overline{x}$, rent payments become lower compared to $F_{\underline{x}}$.

LEMMA 2 $V(P_{\overline{x}}) \geqq V(P_x)$ iff $3x \leqq 2\underline{x} + \overline{x}$.

Proof If $2x \geqq \underline{x} + \overline{x}$, $V(P_x) - V(P_{\overline{x}}) = \lambda(\overline{x} - x) > 0$. If $2x \leqq \underline{x} + \overline{x}$, $V(P_x) - V(P_{\overline{x}}) = \lambda(3x - \overline{x} - 2\underline{x}) \geqq 0$ iff $3x \geqq \overline{x} + 2\underline{x}$. ‖

Under partial reform with $\overline{x}$ hurt, the nearer x is to $\underline{x}$, the lower the wage can be, and thus the bonus. Hurting x instead of $\overline{x}$ would mean giving excessively high compensation rents to $\overline{x}$. On the other hand, wages could not be lowered too much without hurting $\underline{x}$. This becomes less true when x is higher. P_x then becomes the best solution: paying lower wages to the two groups working at the cost of a higher rent to the third group is then better under partial reform.

LEMMA 3 $V(F_x) \geqq V(P)$ for $3x \geqq 2\underline{x} + \overline{x}$.

Proof If $2x \geqq \underline{x} + \bar{x}$, $V(F_x) - V(P) = (q(2) - q(1) - (1 + \lambda)\underline{x}) - (q(1) - (1 + \lambda)x) + \lambda(\bar{x} - x) > 0$. The first and third expressions between parentheses are positive and the second is negative. If $2x \leqq \underline{x} + \bar{x}$ but $3x \geqq 2\underline{x} + \bar{x}$, $V(F_x) - V(P) = (q(2) - q(1) - (1 + \lambda)\underline{x}) - (q(1) - (1 + \lambda)x) + \lambda(3x - 2\underline{x} - \bar{x}) \geqq 0$. Indeed, the first and third expressions are non-negative while the second is non-positive. ||

P can be inferior to F_x because of the allocative loss from keeping a low level of effort *and* from keeping x working. Moreover, nobody loses under P whereas under F_x, the x group loses (but $\bar{x}$ may strictly gain). However, for x sufficiently close to $\underline{x}$, P may be better than F_x: on the one hand, the two solutions are then almost equivalent from an allocative point of view and, on the other hand, F_x implies high bonus payments with extra rents to $\bar{x}$ in comparison to P (indeed, under F_x, $b_1 = \max\{w - \bar{x}, w + \underline{x} - 2x\} > w - \bar{x}$ for x close to $\underline{x}$).

In fact, $F_{\underline{x}}$ and F_x involve the optimal allocation of labour. Proposition A.1 tells us when they are optimal:

PROPOSITION A.1 For $\underline{x} + \bar{x} \leqq 2x$, full reform is optimal. For $3x \leqq \underline{x} + 2\bar{x}$, F_x is optimal. Otherwise $F_{\underline{x}}$ is optimal.

Proof Lemma 1 tells us which solution is better among $F_{\underline{x}}$ and F_x. The proposition will be proved if we show that, for $2x \geqq \underline{x} + \bar{x}$, F_x is better than P_x, other reform schemes being dominated in this region, as shown in Lemmas 1 to 3. For $\underline{x} + \bar{x} \leqq 2x$, $V(F_x) - V(P_x) = -(q(2) - 2(1 + \lambda)x) + \lambda(2x - \underline{x} - \bar{x}) > 0$, because the first expression between parentheses is negative and the second is non-negative. ||

The higher is x, the higher the allocative loss in keeping them working. More specifically, in the region $\underline{x} + \bar{x} \leqq 2x$, F_x dominates P by Lemma 3. Moreover, the exit bonus under the partial reform P_x (which dominates $P_{\bar{x}}$) is the same as under the full reform F_x and wages are even higher. The $\underline{x}$ are thus paid more than in F_x and the extra wages for keeping x working at a high effort level exceed the gain from a higher output level. Full reform is thus optimal.

For $2x \geqq \underline{x} - \bar{x}$, we see that the results are independent of λ or the values of $q(1)$ or $q(2) - q(1)$, provided they satisfy $(1 + \lambda)x \geqq q(1) \geqq q(2) - q(1) \geqq (1 + \lambda)\underline{x}$. The same is not true for $2x \leqq \underline{x} + \bar{x}$, as is shown in the next three propositions, where it may become better to distort the allocation of labour. In fact, we shall distinguish two cases, $3x \leqq 2\underline{x} + \bar{x}$ and $3x \geqq 2\underline{x} + \bar{x}$.

PROPOSITION A.2 For $\frac{1}{3}(\bar{x} + 2\underline{x}) \leqq x \leqq \frac{1}{2}(\bar{x} + \underline{x})$, the optimum will be P_x if $\varepsilon \equiv \lambda(\bar{x} + \underline{x} - 2x) + (q(2) - 2(1 + \lambda)x) \geqq 0$; otherwise, it will be F_x.

Proof By Lemmas 1 to 3, only P_x and F_x are left as possible optima on that region.

$V(P_x) - V(F_x) = \lambda(\bar{x} + \underline{x} - 2x) + (q(2) - 2(1 + \lambda)x)$. ||

Similarly, as in the result of Proposition A.1, the higher the x, the higher the allocative loss from keeping them working. However, if, for $2x < \underline{x} + \bar{x}$, wages under F_x and P_x are the same, the exit bonus is higher under F_x. Even though there is an allocative loss from keeping x working, when x comes closer to $\underline{x}$, this allocative loss becomes smaller whereas the gain in bonus payment over F_x becomes greater.

Recall however from Lemma 2 that $P_{\bar{x}}$ becomes better than P_x for x sufficiently close to $\underline{x}$. The general optimality of $P_{\bar{x}}$ in that region is now demonstrated.

PROPOSITION A.3 Taking $\underline{x}$ and $\bar{x}$ as given, and making sure we keep $(1 + \lambda)x \geqq q(1) \geqq q(2) - q(1) \geqq (1 + \lambda)\underline{x}$, $P_{\bar{x}}$ becomes optimal for x tending to $\underline{x}$.

Proof By Lemmas 1 to 3, only P, $P_{\bar{x}}$ and F_x are left as candidates (by Lemma 2, $P_{\bar{x}}$ dominates P_x for $3x \leqq 2\underline{x} + \bar{x}$). We have the following expressions:

$$V(P_{\bar{x}}) - V(P) = (q(2) - 2(1 + \lambda)x) + (q(2) - q(1) - (1 + \lambda)\underline{x})$$
$$-(q(1) - (1 + \lambda)x) + \lambda(\bar{x} + \underline{x} - 2x),$$

$$V(P_{\bar{x}}) - V(F_x) = (q(2) - 2(1 + \lambda)x) + \lambda(2\bar{x} + 3\underline{x} - 5x).$$

When $x \to \underline{x}$, we also have $q(1) \to (1 + \lambda)x$, $q(2) - q(1) \to (1 + \lambda)x$, $q(2) - q(1) \to (1 + \lambda)\underline{x}$, and $q(2) \to 2(1 + \lambda)x$, so that all brackets with $q(\cdot)$'s tend to zero, and $V(P_{\bar{x}}) - V(P) \to \lambda(\bar{x} - \underline{x}) > 0$ and $V(P_{\bar{x}}) - V(F_x) \to 2\lambda(\bar{x} - \underline{x}) > 0$. ||

When x is almost indistinguishable from $\underline{x}$, it is allocatively almost identical to having a partial reform with a low or high level of effort, or a full reform, along with the necessary wage adjustments. On the other hand, compared to P or F_x, $P_{\bar{x}}$ is the only reform scheme that hurts $\bar{x}$ and thus minimizes bonus payments.

LEMMA 4 For $3x < (\bar{x} + 2\underline{x})$, $V(P) \geqq V(P_{\bar{x}})$ iff $\varepsilon' \equiv \lambda(\bar{x} + \underline{x} - 2x) + (2(q(2) - q(1)) - (1 + \lambda)(\underline{x} + x)) \leqq 0$.

Proof $V(P_{\bar{x}}) - V(P) = \lambda(\bar{x} + \underline{x} - 2x)(2(q(2) - q(1)) - (1 + \lambda)(\underline{x} + x))$. ||

$P_{\bar{x}}$ has a lower exit bonus. Moreover, if the gain from increasing the effort for $\underline{x}$ more than compensates the loss from increasing the effort for x, $P_{\bar{x}}$ is better than P. On the contrary, the cost of increasing the effort for x may be so high as to make P a better solution. The extent of the decrease in marginal productivity is crucial here in discriminating between the two reform schemes.

LEMMA 5 Taking all parameters except x as given, either there is no x such that P_x is optimal, or there is no x such that P is optimal.

Proof One can check that ε and ε' are decreasing in x, so that, if P and P_x have to ever dominate $P_{\bar{x}}$ and F_x on their respective regions, they must dominate it at $3x = 2\underline{x} + \bar{x}$, that is, one must have $\varepsilon \geqq 0 \geqq \varepsilon'$ for that value of x. This is however impossible, because, for a given x,

$$\begin{aligned}\varepsilon - \varepsilon' &= q(2) - 2(1 + \lambda)x - 2(q(2) - q(1)) + (1 + \lambda)(\underline{x} + x)\\ &= [q(1) - (1 + \lambda)x] - [q(2) - q(1) - (1 + \lambda)\underline{x}] < 0. \quad ||\end{aligned}$$

From Lemma 4, marginal productivity of effort must be strongly decreasing for P to dominate $P_{\bar{x}}$. On the other hand, from Proposition A.2, for P_x to dominate F_x, marginal productivity must be almost non-decreasing and as high as possible, without however changing the conditions for allocative efficiency. The two requirements are contradictory.

PROPOSITION A.4 For $3x < (2\underline{x} + \bar{x})$, $P_{\bar{x}}$, P or F_x can be optimal.

Proof By Proposition A.3, $P_{\bar{x}}$ will be optimal if x tends to $\underline{x}$. On the other hand, for $3x$ close to $2\underline{x} + \bar{x}$ (value at which $V(P_{\bar{x}}) = V(P_x)$, F_x will dominate if $\varepsilon' > 0$ and $\varepsilon < 0$, since all these $V(\cdot)$'s are continuous. This can happen without problem, since we know, from the proof of Lemma 5, that $\varepsilon < \varepsilon'$.

Finally, P can dominate if $\varepsilon' < 0$, and $V(P) - V(F_x) = (q(1) - (1 + \lambda)x) - (q(2) - q(1) - (1 + \lambda)\underline{x}) + \lambda(\bar{x} + 2\underline{x} - 3x) \equiv \varepsilon'' > 0$. One can check that the best chance for $\varepsilon' < 0$ is for $q(2) - q(1) \to (1 + \lambda)\underline{x}$ and $q(1) \to (1 + \lambda)x$. When that happens, $\varepsilon'' \to \lambda(\bar{x} + 2\underline{x} - 3x) > 0$, and $\varepsilon' \to \lambda(\bar{x} + \underline{x} - 2x) + (1 + \lambda)(\underline{x} - x)$, which is negative when $\lambda(\bar{x} + 2\underline{x} - 3x) < (x - \underline{x})$, which can happen too. ||

Propositions A.1 to A.4 taken together are equivalent to Proposition 3 in Section 5, which contains the overall intuition for the possible configurations of optima as x goes from $\hat{q}$ to $\bar{x}$.

Proof of Proposition 5 For each case, we compare the allocatively efficient $F_{\underline{x}\underline{x}}$ or $F_{\underline{x}x}$ with the equilibrium $(w_1, e_1, b_1, \tilde{w}_2, \tilde{e}_2, \tilde{b}_2)$, which has to be incentive compatible (IC). Each time, we shall compare $M_{\underline{x}\underline{x}}$ or $M_{\underline{x}x}$ with the payments of the other solutions, and show that $M_{\underline{x}\underline{x}}$ or $M_{\underline{x}x}$ is lower, after adjusting for the difference in labour allocation.

Case A $3x \geqq \underline{x} + 2\bar{x}$, so the basis of comparison is $F_{\underline{x}\underline{x}}$, with $M_{\underline{x}\underline{x}} = 6w - 6x + 4\underline{x}$. We already know $F_{\underline{x}\underline{x}}$ dominates $F_{x\underline{x}}$. Moreover, a full reform at $t = 1$ hurting $\bar{x}$ through a low b_1 is infeasible because it would automatically hurt x even more. $F_{\underline{x}\underline{x}}$ is thus the optimal full reform (and of course dominates full reform with $e_1 = 1$ and/or $e_2 = 1$). Clearly, $F_{\underline{x}\underline{x}}$ is also better than keeping everybody at $t = 1$ (at $e_1 = 1$ or $e_1 = 2$), followed then by $F_{\underline{x}}$.

Two more possibilities have to be considered: partial reform, with $e_1 = 1$ or $e_1 = 2$. In both cases, the x group will leave at $t = 2$. Two groups will have to be protected, while the third payoff will be determined by IC. First, $e_1 = 2$:

(i) the x group is hurt at $t = 1$ in comparison to rejection plus $F_{\underline{x}}$. This implies:

$$w_1 + \tilde{w}_2 \geqq 2(w + \underline{x}) - (x - \underline{x}),$$

$$b_1 \geqq (w - x) + (w - \bar{x}),$$

and, by IC,

$$w_1 + \tilde{b}_2 \geqq (w - x) + (w - \bar{x}) + 2x \quad \text{(otherwise, } x \text{ take } b_1).$$

Total payments are thus $\geqq (6w - 6x + 4\underline{x}) + (3x - \underline{x} - 2\bar{x}) + 2x > M_{\underline{x}\underline{x}} + 2x$, so this reform is worse than $F_{\underline{x}\underline{x}}$ because $q(2) < 2(1 + \lambda)x$ (here the x group has $e_1 = 2$ instead of $e_1 = 0$ in $F_{\underline{x}\underline{x}}$).

(ii) the $\underline{x}$ group is hurt at $t = 1$ in comparison to rejection plus $F_{\underline{x}}$. This implies:

$$w_1 + \tilde{b}_2 \geqq 2w,$$

$$b_1 \geqq (w - \bar{x}) + (w - x),$$

and, by IC,

$w_1 + \tilde{w}_2 \geqq 2w + 2\underline{x}$ (otherwise, $\underline{x}$ take $w_1 + \tilde{b}_2$).

Total payments are thus $\geqq (6w - 6x + 4\underline{x}) + (3x - 2\underline{x} - \bar{x}) + 2x > M_{\underline{x}\underline{x}} + 2x$ as in (i).

(iii) the $\bar{x}$ group is hurt at $t = 1$ in comparison to rejection plus $F_{\underline{x}}$: the problem here is that it implies $w_1 + \tilde{b}_2 \geqq 2w$, so that $\bar{x}$ cannot lose here in comparison to (ii), which dominates (iii).

Under partial reform with $e_1 = 1$ and $F_{\underline{x}}$, only x can be hurt by proposing to them a wage and bonus just big enough to keep them working in period 1. We have:

$$w_1 + \tilde{w}_2 \geqq 2w + 2\underline{x} - (x - \underline{x}) - \underline{x},$$

$$b_1 \geqq (w - x) + (w - \bar{x}),$$

and, by IC,

$$w_1 + \tilde{b}_2 \geqq (w - x) + (w - \bar{x}) + 2x - x.$$

So the lower bound on payments is as in (i) above $-(x - \underline{x})$. This is worse than (i) above, by the assumption that $2(q(2) - q(1)) \geqq (1 + \lambda)(\underline{x} + x)$ made to rule out P as a static optimum (see note 13). Note that $\bar{x}$ cannot be hurt in period 1, since effort is low and they are already hurt in period 2. And $\underline{x}$ cannot be hurt because effort is low. Other solutions thus involve higher payments for the same allocative surplus.

We have considered all partial reforms, all dominated by $F_{\underline{x}\underline{x}}$, which is optimal.

For $3x \leqq \underline{x} + 2\bar{x}$, $F_{\underline{x}x}$ becomes the basis of comparison, and it is the optimal immediate full reform (it dominates F_{xx}, and hurting $\bar{x}$ would hurt x too, which is not politically feasible), and is also clearly better than keeping everybody at $t = 1$. Partial reforms remain to be considered, in a similar way as above.

Case B $\frac{1}{2}(\underline{x} + \bar{x}) \leqq x \leqq \frac{1}{3}(\underline{x} + 2\bar{x})$, so that $M_{\underline{x}\underline{x}} = 6w - 3\bar{x} - 3x + 4\underline{x} \leqq M_{xx} = 6w - 4\bar{x} + 2\underline{x}$.

First, consider partial reforms with $e_1 = 2$:

(i) the x group is hurt, so that:

$$w_1 + \tilde{w}_2 \geqq 2(w + \underline{x})$$

$$b_1 \geqq 2(w - \bar{x})$$

and, by IC,

$$w_1 + \tilde{b}_2 \geqq 2(w - \bar{x}) + 2x.$$

Total payments $\geqq 6w + 2\underline{x} - 4\bar{x} + 2x = M_{xx} + 2x$, which is even worse than M_{xx}, since $q(2) \leqq (1 + \lambda)2x$.

(ii) the $\underline{x}$ group is hurt, so that:

$$w_1 + \tilde{b}_2 \geqq 2w - (\bar{x} - x),$$

$$b_1 \geqq 2(w - \bar{x}),$$

and, by IC,

$$w_1 + \tilde{w}_2 \geqq 2w - (\bar{x} - x) + 2\underline{x}.$$

Total payments $\geqq 6w + 2\underline{x} - 4\bar{x} + 2x$, as in (i).

(iii) the $\bar{x}$ group is hurt, so that:

$$w_1 + \tilde{w}_2 \geqq 2(w + \underline{x}),$$

$$w_1 + \tilde{b}_2 \geqq 2w - (\bar{x} - x),$$

and, by IC,

$$b_1 \geqq 2w - (\bar{x} - x) - 2\bar{x}.$$

Total payments $\geqq 6w + 2\underline{x} - 4\bar{x} + 2x$, as in (i).

Then, consider partial reforms with $e_1 = 1$:

(i) the x group is hurt, so that:

$$w_1 + \tilde{w}_2 \geqq 2w + \underline{x},$$

$$b_1 \geqq 2w - 2\bar{x},$$

and, by IC,

$$w_1 + \tilde{b}_2 \geqq 2w - 2\bar{x} + x.$$

Total payments $\geqq 6w + 2\underline{x} - 4\bar{x} + 2x - (x + \underline{x})$. It is the same as in (i) above, minus $(x + \underline{x})$, and thus worse than (i) under the assumption that $2(q(2) - q(1)) \geqq (1 + \lambda)(x + \underline{x})$, made to rule out P as static optimum.

(ii) the $\underline{x}$ group is hurt, so that:

$b_1 \geqq 2(w - \bar{x})$,

$w_1 + \tilde{b}_2 \geqq 2w - (\bar{x} - x) - x$,

and, by IC,

$w_1 + \tilde{w}_2 \geqq 2w - (\bar{x} - x) - x + 2\underline{x}$.

Total payments $\geqq 6w - 4\bar{x} + 2\underline{x} = M_{xx}$, with an allocative surplus $2q(1) + q(2) - 3\underline{x} - x$.

$$\begin{aligned} V(F_{\underline{x}x}) &= (2q(2) - 4\underline{x}) - \lambda(6w - 3\bar{x} + 4\underline{x} - 3x) \\ &\geqq (2q(1) + q(2) - 3\underline{x} - x) - \lambda(6w - 4\bar{x} + 2\underline{x}) \\ &\Leftrightarrow [q(2) - q(1) - (1 + \lambda)\underline{x}] - [q(1) - (1 + \lambda)x] + \lambda(2x - \underline{x} - \bar{x}) \\ &\geqq 0, \end{aligned}$$

which is true.

(iii) the $\underline{x}$ group cannot be hurt because effort is low, so hurting x or $\bar{x}$ is strictly better. We have considered all partial reforms, all dominated by $F_{\underline{x}x}$, which is optimal for $\frac{1}{2}(\underline{x} + \bar{x}) \leqq x \leqq \frac{1}{3}(\underline{x} + 2\bar{x})$.

Case C F_x is optimal in the static case, but $2x \leqq \underline{x} + \bar{x}$, so that $M_{\underline{x}x} = 6w + 7\underline{x} - 9x$, and $M_{xx} = 6w + 6\underline{x} - 8x = M_{\underline{x}x} + (x - \underline{x})$.

First, consider partial reforms with $e_1 = 2$:

(i) the x group is hurt, so that:

$w_1 + \tilde{w}_2 \geqq 2(w + \underline{x})$,

$b_1 \geqq (w - \bar{x}) + (w + \underline{x} - 2x)$,

and, by IC,

$w_1 + \tilde{b}_2 \geqq 2(w + \underline{x}) - 2x$.

Total payments $\geqq 6w + 7\underline{x} - 9x - (2\underline{x} + \bar{x} - 3x) + 2x = M_{xx} - (\underline{x} + \bar{x} - 2x) + 2x$, with a gain of surplus of $q(2) - 2x$. The total gain over M_{xx} is $\lambda(\bar{x} +$

$\underline{x} - 2x) + (q(2) - 2(1 + \lambda)x)$, i.e. ε which is negative by the assumption made to exclude P_x as a static optimum (see note 13 and Proposition A.2).

(ii) the $\underline{x}$ group is hurt, so that:

$b_1 \geqq 2(w - x) + \underline{x} - \bar{x}$,

$w_1 + \tilde{b}_2 \geqq 2w - (x - \underline{x})$,

and, by IC,

$w_1 + \tilde{w}_2 \geqq 2w - (x - \underline{x}) + 2\underline{x}$.

Total payments $\geqq 6w - 4x + 5\underline{x} - \bar{x}$, as in (i) above.

(iii) the $\bar{x}$ group is hurt, so that:

$w_1 + \tilde{w}_2 \geqq 2(w + \underline{x})$,

$w_1 + \tilde{b}_2 \geqq 2w - (x - \underline{x})$,

and, by IC,

$b_1 \geqq 2w - (x - \underline{x}) - 2\bar{x}$.

Total payments $\geqq (6w + 7\underline{x} - 9x) + 2x + (5x - 3\underline{x} - 2\bar{x}) = M_{\underline{x}x} + 2x + (5x - 3\underline{x} - 2\bar{x})$, which is worse than $M_{\underline{x}x}$ for $V(P_{\bar{x}}) < V(F_x)$, which is true by assumption.

Finally, consider partial reforms with $e_1 = 1$:

(i) the x group is hurt, so that:

$w_1 + \tilde{w}_2 \geqq 2w + \underline{x}$,

$b_1 \geqq 2w + \underline{x} - 2x - \bar{x}$,

and, by IC,

$w_1 + \tilde{b}_2 \geqq 2w + \underline{x} - 2x$.

The lower bound on total payments differs from (i) above only by $2\underline{x}$, which is worse than (i) because of our assumption $2(q(2) - q(1)) \geqq (1 + \lambda)(x + \underline{x}) \geqq x + \underline{x} + 2\lambda\underline{x}$.

(ii) the $\underline{x}$ group is hurt, so that:

$b_1 \geqq 2w + \underline{x} - 2x - \overline{x}$,

$w_1 + \tilde{b}_2 \geqq 2w - x - (x - \underline{x})$,

and, by IC,

$w_1 + \tilde{w}_2 \geqq 2w - x - (x - \underline{x}) + 2\underline{x}$.

Total payments $\geqq 6w + 5\underline{x} - \overline{x} - 6x$, which is dominated by $F_{\underline{x}x}$ (given $2x \leqq \underline{x} + \overline{x}$): the objective function here is $[2q(1) + q(2) - x - 3\underline{x}] - \lambda[6w + 5\underline{x} - \overline{x} - 6x]$. This minus $V(F_{\underline{x}x})$ *equals* $(q(1) - (1 + \lambda)x) - (q(2) - q(1) - (1 + \lambda)\underline{x}) + \lambda(\underline{x} + \overline{x} - 2x) < 0$.

(iii) the $\overline{x}$ group cannot be hurt because effort is low, so (iii) is dominated by (ii) or (i).

We have considered all partial reforms, all dominated by $F_{\underline{x}x}$ when $2x \leqq \underline{x} + \overline{x}$ and when F_x is the static optimum. ||

Proof of Proposition 6 We proceed in three steps:

(a) we show that $V(P_{\overline{x}\overline{x}}) \geqq V(G_{x\overline{x}})$,

(b) we prove the optimality of $G_{x\overline{x}}$ in the absence of commitment,

(c) we establish that $G_{x\overline{x}}$ can be sustained as unique BPE.

(a) $V(G_{x\overline{x}}) = 3q(2) - 2x - 4\underline{x} - \lambda(6w + 3\underline{x} - x - 2\overline{x})$.
$V(P_{\overline{x}\overline{x}}) = 4q(2) - 4x - 4\underline{x} - \lambda(6w + 6x - 4\overline{x})$.
$V(P_{\overline{x}\overline{x}}) - V(G_{x\overline{x}}) = q(2) - 2(1 + \lambda)x + \lambda(3\underline{x} + 2\overline{x} - 5x)$,
which is >0 iff $V(P_{\overline{x}}) > V(F_x)$, which proves (a).

(b) We have to compare $G_{x\overline{x}}$ with other gradual reforms, full reforms, and delayed reforms (which keep everybody at $t = 1$, in order to apply $P_{\overline{x}}$ at $t = 2$).

(i) *Other gradual reforms:* Note that, in $G_{x\overline{x}}$, the x group is hurt and, by IC, it is already impossible to avoid giving $\overline{x}$ extra rents in comparison to the status quo plus $P_{\overline{x}}$. It is thus impossible to hurt $\overline{x}$ without hurting x. What is possible is to hurt solely $\underline{x}$ in comparison to the status quo plus $P_{\overline{x}}$. This would yield, with $e_1 = e_2 = 2$:

$w_1 + \tilde{b}_2 \geqq 2w$;

$b_1 \geqq 2(w - \overline{x})$, by IC;

$w_1 + \tilde{w}_2 \geqq 2(w + \underline{x})$, by IC.

The payoffs of $\bar{x}$ and $\underline{x}$ are determined by IC, and $\underline{x}$ will vote against the plan, because $P_{\bar{x}}$ would offer them *more* than the status quo, which is what they receive here. Total payments $\geqq 6w + 2\underline{x} - 2\bar{x}$, which is higher than in $G_{x\bar{x}}$, for the same allocative surplus, and thus worse. Having an effort of 1 at $t = 1$ or $t = 2$ would be even worse, both allocatively (by our assumptions) and in terms of rent extraction from $\bar{x}$ (they can be left worse off only if $e = 2$ for x at some period). $G_{x\bar{x}}$ is thus the optimal gradual reform.

(ii) *Full reforms:* If one does not want to hurt x, one cannot hurt $\bar{x}$ either. Hurting $\underline{x}$ then gives (with $e_1 = e_2 = 2$ being optimal):

$$b_1 \geqq 2(w - x),$$

$$w_1 + \tilde{w}_2 \geqq 2(w - x) + 4\underline{x}.$$

The total surplus is then $\leqq 2q(2) - 4\underline{x} - \lambda(6w - 6x + 4\underline{x})$, and one can check that it is lower than $V(G_{x\bar{x}})$ for $q(2) - 2(1+\lambda)x + \lambda(3\underline{x} + 2\bar{x} - 5x) > 0$.

The other full reform involves hurting $x(e_1 = e_2 = 2$ is still optimal):

$$w_1 + \tilde{w}_2 \geqq 2(w + \underline{x}) + (x - \underline{x}),$$

$$b_1 \geqq 2(w + \underline{x}) + (x - \underline{x}) - 4x \quad \text{by IC.}$$

In fact, $\bar{x}$ are strictly better off with b_1 than with the status quo plus $P_{\bar{x}}$ (where they get $2(w - \bar{x}) - (\bar{x} - x)$), since $4x < \underline{x} + 3\bar{x}$. This full reform involves total payments $\geqq 6w + 3\underline{x} - 5x$, and is thus more expensive than the above one. $G_{x\bar{x}}$ thus dominates full reforms.

(iii) *Delayed reforms:* In $G_{x\bar{x}}$, $\bar{x}$ receive extra rents in comparison to the status quo plus $P_{\bar{x}}$. The way to avoid that is to delay the reform, that is, keep everybody at $t = 1$, with $e_1 = 1$ (and $w_1 = w$) or $e_1 = 2$ (and $w_1 \geqq w + x$, to make $\underline{x}$ and x happy) and to implement $P_{\bar{x}}$ at $t = 2$. With $e_1 = 1$, we have:

$$w_1 + \tilde{w}_2 = 2w + x,$$

$$w_1 + \tilde{b}_2 = 2w + x - 2\bar{x}.$$

The total surplus is then $3q(1) + 2q(2) - \bar{x} - 3x - 3\underline{x} - \lambda(6w + 3x - 2\bar{x})$. When one subtracts $V(G_{x\bar{x}})$ from this expression, one gets $(2q(1) - x - \bar{x} - 2\lambda x) - (q(2) - q(1) - (1 + \lambda)\underline{x}) - 2\lambda(x - \underline{x}) < 0$, so that $G_{x\bar{x}}$ dominates this delayed reform.

With $e_1 = 2$, we have:

$$w_1 + \tilde{w}_2 = 2w + 2x,$$

$$w_1 + \tilde{b}_2 = 2w + 2x - 2\bar{x}.$$

The total surplus is then $5q(2) - 2x - 4x - 4x - \lambda(6w + 6x - 2x)$. When one subtracts $V(G_{xx})$ from this expression, one gets $(2q(2) - 2x - 2\bar{x} - 4\lambda x) - 3\lambda(x - \underline{x}) < 0$, so that $G_{x\bar{x}}$ dominates this other delayed reform too. This proves (b).

(c) Assume the Government offers a plan $e_1 = e_2 = 2$, $w_1 = w_2 = w + \underline{x} + (x - \underline{x})/2$, $b_2 = w + \underline{x} + (x - \underline{x})/2 - 2x + \eta$, and $b_1 = 2(w + \underline{x}) + (x - \underline{x}) - 2x - 2\bar{x} + 2\eta$, with η arbitrarily small but positive (to make all incentive constraints strictly satisfied). In this case, if the majority required to change the status quo is strictly above 50%, $(\tilde{w}_2, \tilde{b}_2) = (w_2, b_2)$ if only $\underline{x}$ and x stay at $t = 1$. Indeed, (w_2, b_2) leads to an efficient outcome, and there is no way for the Government to hurt anybody in comparison to this outcome. This plan can be sustained as a PBE, because no *individual* $\underline{x}$ can change (w_2, b_2) by staying at $t = 1$ instead of leaving, and because staying makes them worse off then.

This plan would not be sustainable as a unique PBE if a *group* of $\bar{x}$ workers could do better by staying at $t = 1$ instead of leaving. But this cannot happen, because they cannot hope for $\tilde{w}_2 > w_2$ or $\tilde{b}_2 > b_2$ at $t = 2$. Indeed, $e_2 = 2$ is already technologically given, and the Government would be interested only in lowering w_2 or b_2. Leaving at $t = 1$ is thus strictly optimal for $\bar{x}$. This proves (c) and completes the proof of Proposition 6. ||

Notes

We thank Patrick Bolton, Marjorie Gassner, Tracy Lewis, Marco Pagano, Howard Rosenthal, Jean Tirole and two anonymous referees for helpful suggestions.

1. See Roland (1991) on the role of numerous hidden rents enjoyed by large portions of the population, especially in industrial sectors, as a source of resistance to change, and on their implications for devising sequencing tactics during the transition process.

2. Assuming a continuum of workers simplifies the analysis because *individual* worker actions will not reveal any information to the Government.

3. One could also multiply output by $(1 + \lambda)$ if it saves taxes, but not if it is a non-marketable public good. This is simply a question of normalization in any case.

4. In the status quo, workers prefer $(w, e = 1)$ to leaving with a zero bonus.

5. See Dewatripont and Maskin (1990) for applications of contracting and renegotiation under adverse selection.

6. The unanimity case is equivalent to Hart and Tirole's "rental model with long-term contracts and voluntary renegotiation" which they prove to be equivalent to the usual "sale model" of durable goods.

7. This is not only allocatively efficient, but also relaxes IC constraints, since the x group has less incentive to remain in the sector.

8. One can check that keeping all workers in the sector is suboptimal: the two options are $w_1 = w$ and $e_1 = 1$, or $w_1 = w + x$ and $e_1 = 2$, respectively dominated by P and $P_{\bar{x}}$: one can do better than keeping everybody by having $\bar{x}$ leave with $b_1 = w - e_1\bar{x}$. Moreover, as in Section 3, reforms where identical individuals make different *deterministic* choices on exit are also suboptimal, given the linearity of our technology.

9. See Table 16.2 for a summary of the net gains of the various reforms for the three groups of workers.

10. For $2x > \underline{x} + \bar{x}$, the case on which we concentrate for the sake of intuition.

11. For $3x < \underline{x} + 2\bar{x}$, F_x dominates $F_{\underline{x}}$. Moreover, for $2x < \underline{x} + \bar{x}$, $b_1 > w - \bar{x}$ in F_x (otherwise, with $w_1 \geqq w + \underline{x}$, the x group would have no incentive to exit).

12. For $2x < \underline{x} + \bar{x}$, which is the relevant case of comparison, because only then can partial reforms dominate (see Proposition 3).

13. For example, we exclude P by assuming $2(q(2) - q(1)) \geqq (1 + \lambda)(\underline{x} + x)$ (see Lemma 4 in the Appendix) and P_x by assuming $\varepsilon < 0$ at $3x = 2\underline{x} + \bar{x}$ (see Proposition A.2 in the Appendix).

14. For $2x > \underline{x} + \bar{x}$, the case on which we focus here for the sake of intuition.

15. See Table 16.3 for a summary of the net gains of the various reforms for the three groups of workers.

16. Note that, as in Section 4, Propositions 4 to 6 restrict attention to deterministic reforms where identical individuals make identical choices about exiting or not. As in Section 4, the desirability of gradualism does not depend on such a restriction, because these reforms would involve some x or $\bar{x}$ workers staying at $t = 1$ (and possibly $t = 2$). Direct full reforms are certainly dominated when $P_{\bar{x}}$ is the optimal static reform, as proved in Proposition 6. Also unaffected by our restriction is the main result of this Section, namely the possibility to use the threat of future reforms to extract concessions in the initial reform. The only result which could be affected is the fact that, when $P_{\bar{x}}$ is the static optimum, the Government cannot do as well as $P_{\bar{x}\bar{x}}$ with two periods and no commitment, through the use of more sophisticated gradual reforms. Such a possibility only reinforces the main conclusion of this Section.

17. See also Dewatripont and Roland (1992).

References

Alesina, A., and Drazen, A. 1991. Why are stabilizations delayed? *American Economic Review* 81:1170–1188. Reprinted as chapter 15 in the current volume of this work.

Alesina, A., and Tabellini, G. 1990. A positive theory of fiscal deficits and government debt. *Review of Economic Studies* 57:199–220.

Caillaud, B., Guesnerie, R., Rey, P., and Tirole, J. 1988. Government intervention in production and incentives theory: A review of recent contributions. *Rand Journal of Economics* 19:1–26.

Dewatripont, M. 1989. Renegotiation and information revelation over time: The case of optimal labor contracts. *Quarterly Journal of Economics* 104:589–619.

Dewatripont, M., and Maskin, E. 1990. Contract renegotiation in models as asymmetric information. *European Economic Review* 34:311–321.

Dewatripont, M., and Roland, G. 1992. The virtues of gradualism and legitimacy in the transition to a market economy. *Economic Journal* 102:291–300.

Gul, F., Sonnenschein, H., and Wilson, R. 1986. Foundations of dynamic monopoly and the coase conjecture. *Journal of Economic Theory* 39:155–190.

Hart, O., and Tirole, J. 1988. Contract renegotiation and coasian dynamics. *Review of Economic Studies* 55:509–540.

Laffont, J., and Tirole, J. 1988. The dynamics of incentive contracts. *Econometrica* 51:1153–1175.

Laffont, J., and Tirole, J. 1990. Adverse selection and renegotiation in procurement. *Review of Economic Studies* 57:597–625.

Lewis, T., Feenstra, R., and Ware, R. 1990. Eliminating price supports: A political economy perspective. *Journal of Public Economics* 40:150–186.

McKelvey, R. D. 1976. Intransitivities in multidimensional voting models and some implications for agenda control. *Journal of Economic Theory* 12:472–482.

Milgrom, P., and Roberts, J. 1990. The economics of modern manufacturing: Technology, strategy and organization. *American Economic Review* 80:511–526.

Roberts, K. 1989. The theory of union behaviour: Labour hoarding and endogenous hysteresis. London School of Economics, STICERD discussion paper TE.89–209.

Roland, G. 1991. The political economy of sequencing tactics in the transition period. In L. Csaba, ed., *Systemic change and stabilization in Eastern Europe*. Aldershot, Eng.: Dartmouth.

Romer, T., and Rosenthal, H. 1979. Bureaucrats versus voters: On the political economy of resource allocation by direct democracy. *Quarterly Journal of Economics* 93:563–587.

Rosenthal, H. 1989. The setter model. In J. Enelow and M. Hinich, eds., *Readings in the spatial theory of elections*. Cambridge: Cambridge University Press.

Sachs, J. 1990. Eastern Europe's economies: What is to be done? *The Economist*. January 13:19–24.

Van Wijnbergen, S. 1991. Intertemporal speculation, shortages and the political economy of price reform: A case against gradualism. CEPR discussion paper no. 510.

Index